Arab
Women
Writers

Arab Women Writers

A Critical Reference Guide
1873–1999

Edited by
Radwa Ashour
Ferial J. Ghazoul
Hasna Reda-Mekdashi

Translated by Mandy McClure

The American University in Cairo Press
Cairo   New York

First published in Arabic in 2004 by Nour: Foundation for Research and Studies,
Cairo, and the Higher Council of Culture, Cairo as *Dhakira li-l-mustaqbal:
mawsu'at al-katiba al-'arabiya*. Copyright © 2004 by Nour: Foundation for
Research and Studies, Cairo.

Dar el Kutub No. 20264/07
ISBN 978 977 416 146 9

Dar el Kutub Cataloging-in-Publication Data

Ashour, Radwa
    Arab Women Writers: A Critical Reference Guide, 1873–1999 / edited
by Radwa Ashour, Ferial J. Ghazoul, Hasna Reda-Mekdashi; translated by
Mandy McClure—Cairo: The American University in Cairo Press, 2007
       p.   cm.
       ISBN 977 416 146 7
       1. Arabic literature—women authors I. Ashour, Radwa (ed.)
       II. Ghazoul, Ferial J. (jt. ed.) III. Reda-Mekdashi, Hasna (jt. ed.)
       IV. Title
       928.1

1 2 3 4 5 6 7 8 14 13 12 11 10 09 08

Printed in Egypt

In memory of Latifa al-Zayyat (1923–1996)

Contents

Contributors

Editorial Board
Radwa Ashour
Ferial J. Ghazoul
Amina Rachid
Mohammed Berrada
Hasna Reda-Mekdashi
Emad Abu Ghazi

Contributors
Emad Abu Ghazi
Egyptian university professor. He received his B.A. in history from Cairo University in 1976 and a Ph.D. in historical documents from Cairo University in 1995. He teaches in the libraries, documents, and information department at Cairo University. His works include *Tuman Bay al-sultan al-shahid*, *Tatawwur al-hiyaza al-zira'iya fi 'asr al-mamalik al-Jarakisa*, *al-Judhur al-tarikhiya li-azmat al-nahda fi Misr*, and *Masirat al-mar'a al-Misriya* (with Hoda Elsadda).

Radwa Ashour
Egyptian novelist and critic. She received a Ph.D. in African-American literature from the University of Massachusetts in 1975. She is a professor of English literature at Ain Shams University, Cairo. She has published six novels, two short-story collections, and four books of criticism. Her novels include *Thulathiyat Gharnata*. Her most recent works are a book of criticism *(Sayyadu al-dhakira)*, a collection of stories *(Taqarir al-sayyida*

Ra), and a novel *(Qit'a min Urubba)*. She was awarded the Constantine Cavafy International Award for Literature (2007).

Mohammed Berrada
Moroccan critic and novelist. He received a Ph.D. in literary criticism from the Sorbonne in 1973. He served as the head of the Moroccan Writers' Union for three sessions (1977–1983) and taught literature and criticism at Muhammad V University in Rabat until 1998. He has translated several works from French into Arabic, among them Roland Barthes's *Le degree zero de l'écriture*, Jean-Marie le Clézio's *Printemps et autres saisons*, and Paul Ricoeur's *Du texte à l'action* (with Hassan Bu Ruqaya). His works include the short-story collection, *Salkh al-jild*, and the novels *Lu'bat al-nisyan, al-Daw' al-harib, Mithl sayf la yatakarrir*, and *Imra'at al-nisyan*. He has written a book on criticism, *As'ilat al-riwaya: as'ilat al-naqd* (1996).

Hoda Elsadda
Egyptian critic. She received her Ph.D. in English literature from Cairo University in 1988. She was professor of English and comparative literature at Cairo University and a founding member of the Women and Memory Forum. She holds a chair in the study of the contemporary Arab world at Manchester University. She has published on comparative literature, cultural studies, feminist criticism, oral narrative, autobiography and history, and Arab women's issues. With Salwa Bakr, she issued the periodical, *Hajar*, on women's issues. She edited the collection, *Zaman al-nisa' wa-l-dhakira al-badila*, and redacted and edited Malak Hifni Nasif's *Nisa'iyat*. She was also the editor of *Min ra'idat al-qarn al-'ishrin: shakhsiyat wa qadaya*. She is associate editor of the online edition of the *Encyclopedia of Women in Muslim Cultures* published by E.J. Brill, and a member of the editorial board of the *International Journal of Middle Eastern Studies*.

Ferial J. Ghazoul
Iraqi critic. She received her Ph.D. in English and comparative literature from Columbia University in 1978. She is currently a professor of English and comparative literature at the American University in Cairo and the chief editor of *Alif: Journal of Comparative Poetics*. She has translated much Arabic poetry into English, including Muhammad 'Afifi Matar's *Ruba'iyat al-farah*. She has also translated works of criticism from English and French into Arabic. She has published studies on literary theory and Arab women's literature, as well as English, African, Indian, and South American literature. Her full-length works include *Nocturnal Poetics: The Arabian Nights in a Comparative Context* and *Sa'di Yusuf*.

Subhi Hadidi
Syrian critic, researcher, and translator who lives in Paris. He received his education from Damascus University and continued his studies in Britain and France. He has published critical studies, research, and translations in several Arabic periodicals, focusing on contemporary Arabic poetry. He has translated several literary and non-fiction works into Arabic, including Montgomery Watt's *Islamic Political Thought*, Ken Kesey's *One Flew over the Cuckoo's Nest*, Claude Lévi-Strauss's *Myth and Meaning*, and selected essays by Edward Said.

Haidar Ibrahim
Sudanese critic. He received a Ph.D. in sociology from Frankfurt University in 1978. He has taught in Sudan and worked in the National Council for Arab Culture in Rabat. He was the secretary-general of the Arab Sociology Association in 1998 and has published the journal, *Idafat*. He is currently the head of the Center for Sudanese Studies in Cairo and the editor of *Kitabat Sudaniya*. His works include *al-Tayyarat al-Islamiya wa qadiyat al-dimuqratiya*, *al-Dimuqratiya wa-l-mujtama' al-madani fi-l-Sudan*, *al-'Awlama wa jadal al-huwwiya*, *Mawaqif fikriya*, and *al-Din wa-l-thawra fi-l-'alam al-thalith*.

Yumna al-'Id
Lebanese critic and writer. She received a Ph.D. in literature and criticism from the Sorbonne in 1977. She was a professor of literary criticism at the Lebanese University and has been a visiting faculty member at several Arab and European universities. She is a member of the consulting board of the Book in Newspaper/Kitab fi Jarida project. Her works include *Qasim Amin: tahrir qiwamat al-mar'a* (1970), *Amin al-Rayhani rahhalat al-'Arab* (1970), *Fi ma'rifat al-nass* (1983), *al-Rawi: al-mawqa' wa-l-shakl: bahth fi-l-sard al-riwa'i* (1986), *Fi-l-qawl al-shi'ri* (1987), *Taqniyat al-sard al-riwa'i fi daw' al-manhaj al-bunyawi* (1990), *al-Kitaba: tahawwul fi-l-tahawwul: muqaraba li-l-kitaba fi zaman al-harb al-Lubnaniya* (1993), and *Fann al-riwaya al-'Arabiya bayn khususiyat al-hikaya wa tamayyuz al-khitab* (1998). She won the al-'Uways Cultural Prize in 1992/93 for criticism and literary research.

Su'ad al-Mana
Saudi critic. She received a Ph.D. in Arabic literature and criticism from the University of Michigan in 1986. She is currently a professor of classical Arabic literature and criticism at King Sa'ud University. Her research interests include feminist criticism and women's writing. Her published research articles include studies on Ibn Rushd, al-Siljamasi, Arabic criticism from the classical age, and women's writing in Saudi Arabia.

Iman al-Qadi

Syrian critic. She received a Ph.D. in modern Arabic literature from Damascus University in 1995. She is a faculty member at the Arabic department at Damascus University and has taught in the Arabic department at Zayid University in the United Arab Emirates since 1998. She has made contributions to several Arabic periodicals. Her books include *al-Riwaya al-nisawiya fi bilad al-Sham: al-simat al-nafsiya wa-l-fanniya 1950–1985*.

Amina Rachid

Egyptian critic. She received a Ph.D. in comparative literature from the Sorbonne in 1976. She was a researcher at the Centre National de la Recherche Scientifique in France from 1970 to 1987 and has been a professor of French literature and language at Cairo University since 1987. She is the chief editor of the journal *Nur*, a review of Arab women's literature. She has published essays and studies in literary criticism in periodicals in France and Egypt, and has translated Annie Ernaux's *La place* and Georges Perec's *Les choses* into Arabic (the latter with Sayyid Bahrawi). Her most important works include *Qissat al-adab al-Faransi* and *Tashazzi al-zaman fi-l-riwaya al-haditha*.

Hasna Reda-Mekdashi

Lebanese publisher. She received a B.A. in political science from the Beirut College for Women (now Lebanese American University) in 1969, and an M.A. in Middle East Area Studies from the School of Oriental and African Studies (SOAS), London University, in 1971. She is the former director of the prominent children's literature publishing house Dar al-Fata al-'Arabi, and founding member and managing director of Nour: Foundation for Arab Women's Research and Studies, Cairo. She initiated and co-edited the *Nour Quarterly Journal* for reviews of Arab women's books, and initiated and co-directed the First Arab Women's Book Fair in Cairo in 1995.

Hatem M. al-Sager

Iraqi critic. He received his Ph.D. in modern Arabic literature and criticism and has been a professor of literature and criticism at Sana'a University since 1995. He was the chief editor of the monthly cultural periodical, *al-Aqlam*, for several years. He is a founding member of the Book in Newspaper/Kitab fi Jarida project, inaugurated in 1996. His works include *al-Asabi' fi mawqid al-shi'r*, *Ma la tu'addihi al-sifa*, *Kitabat al-dhat*, *Tarwid al-nass*, and *Maraya Narsis*.

Researchers who contributed to the bibliographies

Hasna Reda-Mekdashi, Lebanon

Afaf Abdel-Moati, Amani Abu Zayd, Daliya Mustafa, Munira Sulayman, and Hoda Elsadda (supervisor), Egypt

Haidar Ibrahim, Sudan

Ferial J. Ghazoul, Iraq

Radwa Ashour, Palestine and Jordan

'Abd al-Hamid al-'Aqqar and 'Abd al-Rahim al-'Allam, North Africa

Manal 'Isa, the Gulf and Arabian Peninsula

Intilaq al-Mutawakkil, Yemen

'Abd al-Hamid al-'Aqqar, 'Abd al-Rahim al-'Allam, and Layla al-Khatib, Bibliography of Works in French

Emad Abu Ghazi, supervisor, Bibliography of Works in Arabic

Introduction

Radwa Ashour, Mohammed Berrada, Ferial J. Ghazoul, and Amina Rachid

Unlike many other women writers, Arab women writers draw on a rich, ancient heritage, which stretches back to civilizations that flourished in the region before the Islamic conquest. As for the Arabic heritage, it takes us back to a venerable ancestor, al-Khansa', whose poems and recorded exploits give her a secure position in the canon. Among the anecdotes related about her is this enlightening story: it is said that al-Khansa' went to al-Nabigha while he was sitting in 'Ukaz and recited her famous ra'iya poem to him.[1] Al-Nabigha told her, "If Abu Basir [al-A'sha] had not already recited to me, I would have said that you are the greatest poet of the Arabs. Go, for you are the greatest poet among those with breasts." Al-Khansa' replied, "I'm the greatest poet among those with testicles, too."

There is no need to comment here on the verbal pluckiness of al-Khansa', which many European and feminist critics might well envy.

Al-Khansa' emerges positively in the culture; others were ostracized and held up as the epitome of wickedness and depravity. In later periods—the 'Abbasid, Umayyad, and Andalusian eras—biographical dictionaries and literary encyclopedias are filled with the names of hundreds of women, including female poets. One researcher counted 242 female poets, from al-Khansa' to Wallada Bint al-Mustakfi, and in her study of women in the 'Abbasid period, Wajda al-Atraqji counts forty-five female poets in the first hundred years of the 'Abbasid period.[2] Some of these women, like Wallada Bint al-Mustakfi,[3] belonged to the ruling elite. Two lines of poetry attributed to her were said to have been embroidered on her clothing in gold:

1

I was made for the high things in life, by God
When I walk, I swagger with pride.
I give my cheek to my lover
And my kiss to the one who craves it.

The names also included devout believers who composed Sufi poetry, most prominently Rabi'a al-'Adawiya,[4] as well as singing slave girls who were poets. The tenth-century scholar Abu-l-Faraj al-Isfahani composed a book entitled *Rayy al-zama fi man qal al-shi'r min al-ima* (Thirst-quenching Excerpts from Lives of Slave Girl Poets) which contains the biographies of thirty-one slave girls and excerpts from their poetry.[5] Perhaps some women researchers will examine the lives of this third group of poets, reading their poetry and analyzing their portrayal in the medieval biographical dictionaries, truncated or imprisoned as they are under the rubric of "slave girl." So far no researchers have looked closely at these talented poets, caught in their existential dilemma as owned women, yet whose pre-established role required a perpetual exploitation of wit, cunning, and deception. These were women who combined two odd functions: they were to serve, submit, and pleasure, but at the same time, they were peers and rivals in poetry, who might win the upper hand with a unique thought or an eloquent turn of phrase.

Contemporary Arab women writers draw on a rich, complex tradition that encompasses the believer who recites poetry about divine love; the princess who possesses knowledge, power, and standing; the slave girl trained in the lute and pleasuring her master; the strong, free woman capable of public, eloquent speech, at times bold or even obscene; and the shy woman who speaks in a low voice from behind the curtain. The mother of them all is, of course, Sheherazade, the mistress of speech, who tells stories upon stories. Her tales go beyond time and place, and through them, she takes leave of the king's bedchamber and steps into the wider world.

The purpose of this reference guide to Arab women writers in the twentieth century is not to extol women or their texts. It is rather to document a phenomenon and present it to readers, allowing them to gain a better knowledge of this influential cultural presence in Arab societies. Perhaps it can be a mirror to women writers themselves, allowing them a space for self-reflection as they view the sum total of their efforts, accomplished in a little over one hundred years. Certainly, no matter what our evaluation of the corpus of contemporary Arab women writers, their texts—the entirety of the texts they have produced—have added something, be it a different perspective, a new tone of voice, or a distinct sensibility formed over centuries of silence and oppression in a world long ruled by patriarchy. This sensibility has also been shaped by the multiplicity of roles that women play and perform, even after they were sufficiently emancipated to go out and work as writers.

*

The French historian Clot Bey says that Napoleon spoke to him of General Menou's treatment of his Egyptian wife and how it influenced Egyptian women's ambitions to change their circumstances. General Menou, a leader of the French expedition in Egypt (1798–1801), married a woman from Rosetta and, so the story goes, treated her like Frenchmen treated their women (that is, Frenchmen of the aristocracy and middle class). Clot Bey relates a story told by Napoleon, that General Menou took his wife with him to various functions, walking next to her and offering his arm to her. He would choose a seat for her at the head of the dinner table and bring her whatever food she desired. When she told this to the women at the public bath, their faces are said to have filled with hope, and they thought it a sign that their circumstances would change. They sent a letter to "Sultan" Bonaparte asking him to force their husbands to treat them the way Menou treated his wife.[6]

Despite its peculiarity, the anecdote is significant. It is difficult to ignore the proposed source of change (France/Europe, represented by General Menou and Bonaparte). We are adding nothing new if we note that women's liberation, like other aspects of the renaissance in the Arab world, raised a problematic contradiction between a liberation enterprise motivated by a desire for modernization and advancement and a viewpoint that saw the colonizer as the primary source of this modernization. Napoleon's story about the woman of Rosetta and her French husband is highly suggestive. The Frenchman is a general who came by force of arms to execute his mission of plunder and control; the woman was from Rosetta, the site of one of the most prominent chapters of the popular resistance to the French campaign. The men of Rosetta, none of whom took their wives to public functions—indeed, they would not condemn one of their own for beating his wife—stood up to face the invasion and gave their lives in the process.

The dilemma encapsulated so simply and clearly by the anecdote would set the issue of women's liberation on two divergent paths: the first would follow the road laid out by the story of General Menou highlighting the part while ignoring the whole. The second would be aware of its link to national and social liberation movements. This latent contradiction may explain why Lord Cromer—the most prominent figure in the history of the British occupation of Egypt—and pro-occupation Egyptian newspapers, such as *al-Nil* and *al-Muqattam*, were so enthusiastic about women's liberation, and also why women and men who took up the call of women's emancipation also contributed to the nationalist movement and why their names are linked with the opposition to colonialism.

This reference guide is not about the history of the Arab women's movement and women's liberation. It is rather an effort to delineate the literary output of Arab women in the modern period, from the last two decades of the nineteenth century to the end of the twentieth century. But needless to say, Arab women would not have contributed to literature without the call to escape the bonds of the enclosed home and enter the public sphere, even shape it to a certain degree. The beginning of women's education in schools, and later in universities, was a basic step on this road, and it could not have continued without the efforts of pioneering women in Egypt, Syria, and Lebanon, followed by Iraq and Palestine, and later Jordan, Arab North Africa, Sudan, and the Arabian Peninsula.

These efforts began in the last two decades of the nineteenth century in Syria, Lebanon, and Egypt, and they continued until the First World War. Women's associations were founded, starting with Bakurat Suriya (Syrian Dawn), founded by Maryam Nimr Makariyus in Beirut in 1880, and Zahrat al-Ihsan (Flower of Charity), established the same year. The tradition of literary salons began with the salon of Maryana Marrash in Aleppo, Princess Nazli Fadil's salon in Cairo,[7] and Alexandra Khuri Averino's salon in Alexandria. This was followed by the emergence of newspapers and magazines: in 1892, Hind Nawfal's *al-Fatah* appeared in Alexandria, the same year that Jurji Zaydan started *al-Hilal*. The next year, a monthly women's magazine appeared in Aleppo, *al-Mar'a*, published by Madiha al-Sabuni. In the four decades from 1892 to 1939, the eve of the Second World War, twenty-four women's periodicals were published and circulated in the cities of the Arab East. In addition to Cairo, Damascus, Beirut, and Baghdad, periodicals founded by women were published in Alexandria, Mansura, and Fayyum in Egypt; Tripoli in Lebanon; and Hums, Hama, and Aleppo in Syria.[8] Lebanese Maronite women, many of whom settled in Egypt, played a prominent role in establishing most of these journals. They in turn helped lay the groundwork for the publication of Qasim Amin's *Tahrir al-mar'a* (The Liberation of Women).[9] This period also saw the publication of encyclopedias about the lives of famous women, the most well-known being Zaynab Fawwaz's *al-Durr al-manthur fi-l-tabaqat rabbat al-khudur* (Scattered Pearls in the Lives of the Harem Dwellers), published in 1894. Fifteen years earlier, in 1879, *Ma'rid al-hasna' fi tarajim mashahir al-nisa'* (An Excellent Exposition on the Biographies of Famous Women), by Maryam Nasr Allah al-Nahhas, a Syrian from Tripoli, was printed at al-Misr newspaper press in Alexandria. From 1892 to 1939, Egypt alone saw the publication of 571 biographies of women (written by both men and women) in eighteen periodicals.[10] These biographies were the product of a fruitful conjunction of two traditions: the rich Arabic tradition of biography and biographical dictionaries, and the European tradition of writing about famous women.[11]

With only two female voices—Warda al-Yaziji (1838–1924) in Lebanon and 'A'isha al-Taymuriya (1840–1902) in Egypt—the 1880s gave no hint that a multitude of women writers were preparing to emerge into the public eye. These writers boldly chose two outlets: journalism, which gave immediate access to the reading public and allowed them to shape public opinion, and the novel, the most malleable literary genre and the newcomer to Arabic culture. In journalism, women did not limit their articles to women's magazines, and they did not write only about the status of women and their demands. Some wrote under their own names (Warda al-Yaziji and 'A'isha al-Taymuriya, the most prominent examples), and some wrote under a pseudonym. Zaynab Fawwaz (1846–1914) published her first novel under the soubriquet "an Egyptian woman," although the second edition was printed under her name. Malak Hifni Nasif (1886–1918) published all her articles under the name Bahithat al-Badiya (Seeker in the Desert). Her book *Nisa'iyat* (Women's Things), 1910, was published using the same name. The use of pseudonyms was so widespread that in 1908 the Association for the Advancement of Women in Egypt launched a campaign to defend the right of women to use their names, arguing that Islamic law allowed, and even enjoined, it. Although the head of the association, Fatima Rashid, declared a year later that in response to the association's campaign women had started to publish under their own names in newspapers and magazines, it was not so simple.[12] The custom of women using pseudonyms or signing their works with initials—or not at all—has remained widespread in many Arab countries until recently.

As for the second outlet, novels by women were issued at a brisk, indeed astonishing pace, given women's recent return to writing after such a long hiatus, and the novelty of the literary form itself. Alice Butrus al-Bustani published the novel *Sa'iba* (Correct) in 1891. Zaynab Fawwaz published *Husn al-'awaqib aw Ghada al-zahira* (Fine Consequences, or Radiant Ghada) in 1899 and *al-Malik Qurush aw malik al-Furs* (King Cyrus or the King of the Persians) in 1905 (she published a play, *al-Hawa wa-l-wafa'* [Love and Fidelity] in 1893). Next came 'Afifa Karam's novel *Badi'a wa Fu'ad* (Badi'a and Fu'ad) in 1906, followed by *Fatima al-badawiya* (Bedouin Fatima) and *Ghadat 'Amshit* (The Beauty of 'Amshit) in 1914. In 1904, Labiba Hashim wrote a novel, *Qalb al-rajul* (A Man's Heart), followed by Labiba Mikha'il Sawaya's novel *Hasna' Salunik* (The Beauty of Salonica) in 1909 and Farida Yusuf 'Atiya's *Bayn al-'arshayn* (Between the Two Thrones) in 1912. These novelists were all from Lebanon; some of them, like Zaynab Fawwaz and Labiba Hashim, settled in Egypt while others, like 'Afifa Karam, settled in the United States.

The intensive presence of women constituted a native incubator for ideas about women's liberation, pushing the issue into the public sphere, where it became a topic of debate among the greatest writers of the nation. Butrus al-Bustani (1819–1883) in Lebanon was the first to talk about women's right to education, advocating the idea in 1847. Rifa'a al-Tahtawi (1801–1878) in Egypt wrote *al-Murshid al-amin li-l-banat wa-l-banin* (The Faithful Guide for Girls and Boys) in response to a request from the Egyptian Ministry of Education to "compose a book on the humanities and pedagogy that can be used for the education of both boys and girls."[13] In his introduction, al-Tahtawi praises Khedive Isma'il for opening up education so that "girls, like boys, can compete to come up with the most novel ideas. He made the acquisition of knowledge the same for both groups; he did not make knowledge like inheritance, in which men enjoy double the share of women."[14] In 1895, Muhammad ibn Mustafa ibn Khuja al-Jaza'iri published his book, *al-Iktirath fi huquq al-inath* (On the Rights of Women), followed by Qasim Amin's *Tahrir al-mar'a* (The Liberation of Women) in 1899 and *al-Mar'a al-jadida* (The New Woman) in 1901.[15] Next came *Imra'atuna fi-l-shari'a wa-l-mujtama'* (Our Women in Law and Society) in 1929, by Tahir Haddad al-Tunsi, who a year earlier had released a book about Tunisian workers and the rise of the trade union movement. Prominent writers took a position on the women's issue and stepped up to defend their rights, most prominently Ahmad Lutfi al-Sayyid in Egypt, Amin al-Rayhani in Lebanon, and the poets Jamil Sidqi al-Zahawi and Ma'ruf al-Rasafi in Iraq.

These were the beginnings of Arab women's writings in the modern period. The writing styles and genres chosen by women showed that they drew on the classical Arabic heritage while at the same time they benefited from and imitated available European writings. Significantly, women writers ignored the popular, folkloric tradition, seeing what they wrote as part of "high" culture that had no relation to the songs and popular stories of oral tradition produced by women in the vernaculars.[16] Why? The writers' social status might not offer a full explanation. There is another element that cannot be denied: their rebellion against traditional women's roles and their desire to prove their ability to write, an activity linked with the educated elite, particularly since many men belittled their intellectual capacities. Whether this explanation is sound or not, the fact remains that the pioneering generation and the generations that followed ignored women's oral tradition, thus neglecting a rich cultural vein. Arab women as creators of oral text have a continuous, rich, and varied story that stretches over hundreds of years of history and culture.

At the end of the nineteenth century, women—both as writers and critics—helped to disseminate women's achievements. Mayy Ziyada (1886–1941) continued this tradition in the first half of the next century, writing biographies of three women writers: Warda al-Yaziji, 'A'isha al-Taymuriya, and Malak Hifni Nasif. In doing so, she bequeathed to herself and later generations of writers a legacy of modern Arab women's writing. Ziyada wrote and a later generation of women writers read and drew inspiration—and not only in Syria, Lebanon, and Egypt, for the circle widened beyond these three countries. In the 1930s and 1940s, women writers from Iraq and Palestine emerged, in addition to Egypt, Syria, and Lebanon. They wrote articles for the press and radio, short stories, and poetry. The 1950s witnessed the start of a creative surge of female writers in all types of literary genres. The decade opened with the publication of the novel *al-Jamiha* (The Defiant Woman) by Amina al-Sa'id in Egypt and *Arwa bint al-khutub* (Arwa, Daughter of Woe) by Widad Sakakini from Syria; it closed with three novels, considered even then significant milestones in the evolution of Arab women's writing. In 1958, Layla Ba'labakki published *Ana ahya* (I Live), followed a year later by Collette Khuri's *Ayyam ma'ah* (Days with Him). The next year, Latifa al-Zayyat in Egypt published *al-Bab al-maftuh (The Open Door)*. Two years later, Layla 'Ussayran released *Lan namut ghadan* (We Will Not Die Tomorrow), followed by Emily Nasrallah's *Tuyur Aylul* (The Birds of September). Despite their differences, these novels presented a new voice that explored women's relations with themselves and with men, with fathers and mothers, and with the surrounding political and social environment. In the same decade, Palestine offered one of the most mature experiments in the short story, in the writings of Samira 'Azzam. In poetry, there was Nazik al-Mala'ika in Iraq, whose poem "al-Kulira" (Cholera), published in 1947, was a pioneering work in modern free verse, as well as Fadwa Tuqan and Salma Khadra Jayyusi in Palestine, the first of whom started with the classical Arabic ode, or *qasida*, before moving to free verse and the second of whom chose the new form for her poems from the beginning.

The texts produced from the end of the 1940s through the early 1960s are the link between the old and new generations across the Arab world, from Mauritania, Morocco, Algeria, and Tunisia in the west, to the Gulf countries in the east, from Sudan and Yemen in the south, to Iraq and the Levant in the north.

Nawal al-Sa'dawi was another pioneer who raised several issues related to women's freedom and drew attention to the possibilities offered by the methodologies of the feminist movement in Europe and the U.S. in the early 1960s. In many books—including sociological studies, stories, novels, and journal articles—Nawal al-Sa'dawi put forth a new, bold, influential discourse picked up by later generations of women writers, who reproduced it, developed it, and used it as a starting point for a path that sometimes converged with that discourse and sometimes parted ways with it.

In the last third of the twentieth century, Arab women's writing evolved along divergent paths. While women from older generations continued to write, new generations worked to steep themselves in their own time, place, and experience, and to develop the craft of writing. In poetry, women went beyond the classical *qasida* form to free verse and prose poetry, at times managing to overcome sentimentality and the tropes of romantic expression. In contrast to the first half of the twentieth century, the short story and the novel received the largest share of women's creative attention. Women wrote texts trying to capture a complex, complicated reality burdened by contradictions and anxieties. Women wrote about national struggle, civil war, political and social oppression, and corruption as much as they wrote about relations with men and their status in a male-dominated society, trying to express themselves as both women and citizens. In their attempts to capture their own experience, women chose various forms of writing. They produced realistic novels with a clear chronological order and an omniscient narrator, depicting some aspect of Arab life in Beirut, Cairo, Tunis, or Baghdad, or they turned to a small town or far-flung village to depict the lives of its inhabitants. They produced modernist texts in which the collapse of all assumptions, the fragmentation of time, and the isolation of the individual come together to impose a different novelistic form. They wrote historical novels in which they address their own reality through writing about former ages. In autobiographies, women documented their life stories or some part of their lives, such as the experience of childhood or political detention, or the story of a trip to the West. At times, they speak directly in the first person, relating events in chronological order; other times, they invent styles to meet their needs. In contrast, women's creative efforts were directed less at drama, and there are relatively few women playwrights compared to other types of writers. Is this because playwrights need an active theater movement in which they can take part, which exists in only a very few Arab countries? Or did talented women playwrights turn to writing for television?

Arab women's writing has dealt with a diversity of themes addressed in various styles, although historical concerns and an awareness of a double burden remains a basic theme in their writing. With the exception of Palestine, all Arab countries won national independence, but they did not find freedom, justice, or prosperity, and the problems and contradictions grew. The Zionist state has grown more violent, American hegemony fiercer, and national governments have contributed to the internal fractures with their repressive practices and their immobility in the face of fundamental change. Class gaps have widened, and the rift between men and women has deepened. There is an increasing contradiction between appearance and truth, word and deed, hope and illusion. This confused, often chaotic social reality is reflected in both men and women and their relationships with the self, others, and the surrounding environment.

Since the 1970s, Arabic literature has entered the age of doubt, and the question mark has replaced certainty. Arab women novelists have written about war, frustration, the erosion of all preconceptions, and a reality even stranger than fiction. More and more women writers have turned to the literature of exile and marginalization.

Today, the situation is fraught with ambiguity. Women are open to global issues, and they have a keen awareness of their location vis-à-vis language and discourse, and culture and ideology. At the same time, they are being reimprisoned by ideas about particularity and the body disseminated by certain feminist circles. The public and private spheres are increasingly intertwined, and a significant segment of women have learned their rights and duties. They have learned the importance of writing, thought, theory, and practice, which qualifies them to occupy a place in Arab culture distinguished by intense questioning and animated rebellion. Now they must face the challenge of social and intellectual forces that want to return them to their seclusion with weapons that are much more dangerous and deceptive because they replace violence, tyranny, and ideology with reason, praise, and compliment. We will not fall in the trap of praising women's writing *a priori* or sentencing them to the prison of "women's writing" with its predetermined subjects. It is a field open to all experiments and the future.

*

The reader will notice in the essays about the literature of each country, or set of countries, that the social and historical context which shaped women's experience has gradually led them away from cautious, direct, and sentimental writing—and occasionally simplistic moralizing—to more complex texts that convey a desire to capture women's experience. This is a writing that allows political and social questions to be raised and can be either revelatory or reticent. In both cases, there is a space for imagination, experimentation, artistic play; and a sounding of voices absent from the prevailing discourse. As women's writing evolved, women pioneered new creative horizons that met their need to depict their experiences and knowledge.

In our attempt to understand and inform others about Arab women's writing in the modern age, we have tried to consider the historical context, which has seen transformations in ideas about literature and writing. Naturally, the historical differences between one Arab country and another will be reflected in the status of women and their writings, which will in turn help to shape those writings. If this is true for previous decades, we cannot ignore the fact that the current scene is giving us mature, distinguished literature, both from pioneering countries and from those that followed later; there is no difference between the center and the margins. Writing women from various Arab countries are growing daily more aware of the exigencies of thoughtful, artistic writing, going beyond pure ideological criteria and fragile, direct moralizing or didacticism. The role of the pioneers was important and necessary, and for this reason we have at times focused on them in the analyses, but this does not mean we deny the great strides that Arab women writers have made in quality and quantity, depth and portrayal, structure and texture, playfulness, imagination, technical experimentation, and adventurousness. Every essay on each country or group of countries deals with this in more detail.

In a world in which gains are being eroded and frustrations are mounting, and the crisis of the marginalized—both men and women— deepens, knowledge becomes even more vital, as does the need to reconstruct meaning and value. This reference guide is not part of the fashionable interest in women's literature, but grew out of a concern to increase awareness of women's issues in our societies and provide information about women's literary achievements. This work hopes to add to the creative efforts of Arab intellectuals, both men and women; if it achieves even part of this, it will have attained its objective.

*

This project began as an idea proposed by the Nour Foundation to Dr. Latifa al-Zayyat, who greeted it with enthusiasm, helped draft the preliminary outlines of the project, and proposed the names of researchers. Detailed discussions about the guide began in the early meetings in the home of Latifa al-Zayyat. In later meetings at the Nour Foundation, the idea evolved with the participation of other women and men. We agreed that Latifa al-Zayyat would be the editor in chief and write the introduction, but on September 10, 1996, Latifa al-Zayyat passed away. Work continued on the guide and went through several phases before reaching this draft, which we hope meets both our objectives and the expectations of researchers and readers. The work was collective. All materials, both bibliographical and analytical, were put up for discussion and review, as was the arrangement of the materials. However, each researcher reserved the right to address the materials in accordance with his or her own viewpoint and critical approach.

Initially, we thought that Syria and Lebanon should logically be covered by one essay, since Lebanon was part of Syria until 1923. We also thought Jordan and Palestine should be covered by one essay due to their intertwined nature. Similarly, we thought it appropriate and useful to have one study cover all of Arab North Africa, and another cover the countries of the Arabian Peninsula and Gulf area. We were able to follow through on these decisions with the exception of the essay on Syria and Lebanon. There we were forced to distribute responsibility to three critics. It took more time than we expected. Some did the job and others withdrew due to previous obligations. We had to redistribute responsibility, in some cases more than once.

The bibliography includes the creative writings of twelve hundred women writers from the last third of the nineteenth century through 1999. This task was made more difficult after we discovered that many libraries had huge gaps, and many books had neither date of publication nor names of publishers. In some cases, documentation was inaccurate, and there are few serious studies in the field.

Such is the guide between your hands. Ten critics and several assistant researchers worked on it. It is both a significant and modest effort. Gaps and shortcomings are difficult to avoid completely in a work of this size with these limited capabilities. Nevertheless, we have tried to provide a comprehensive source covering what women from the Arab world have written over 120 years. In the essays, we sought to describe the evolution of Arab women's writing in that geographical area. In the Arabic version of the reference guide, we provided excerpts from women's creative writing from various regions, in addition to bibliographic materials and essays. We hope that this translation of the essays and bibliographies will be followed by another translated volume of selected texts that represent women's literature from the Arab world.

Notes

1 Al-Khansa' (ca. 575–664). Her given name was Tumadir. She was born in the pre-Islamic period and lived to see the arrival of Islam. Her brothers Mu'awiya and Sakhr were killed early, and later her four children died at the battle of al-Qadisiya. She was renowned for her elegies.

2 See Fatma Moussa-Mahmoud, "Turkey and the Arab Middle East," in Claire Buck, ed., *The Bloomsbury Guide to Women's Literature* (London: Bloomsbury, 1992), p. 211.

3 Wallada Bint al-Mustakfi (d. 1091) was an Andalusian poet from Cordoba, the seat of literature. She was involved in a fabled romance with the poet and minister Ibn Zaydun.

4 Rabi'a al-'Adawiya (d. 752) was a woman from Basra who started out her life as a singer and musician in pleasure houses and later became a Sufi ascetic. Some say she died in Jerusalem, while others say it was Basra.

5 Abu-l-Faraj al-Isfahani, *al-Ima' al-shawa'ir*, edited by Nuri Hammudi al-Qaysi and Yunus Ahmad al-Samirra'i (Beirut: Dar al-Kutub and Maktabat al-Nahda al-'Arabiya, 1984).

6 Joseph Zeidan, *Arab Women Novelists: The Formative Years and Beyond* (New York: State University of New York, 1995).

7 Nazli Fadil was the daughter of Mustafa Fadil, the half brother of Khedive Isma'il. Her salon was frequented by men of state, prominent journalists, and foreign and Egyptian writers, but no women attended this salon. She maintained close relations with British occupation officials in Egypt and was a friend of Lord Kitchener.

8 See the appendices in Joseph Zeidan, *Arab Women Novelists*.

9 Nahawand al-Qadiri 'Isa, "Tahrir al-mar'a ma bayn al-sahafa al-nisa'iya al-Lubnaniya wa Qasim Amin: intilaq al-da'wa wa hudud al-waqi'," in *Mi'at 'am 'ala tahrir al-mar'a* (Cairo: Supreme Council for Culture, 2001), part 1, pp. 514–15.

10 Marilyn Booth, *May Her Likes Be Multiplied: Biography and Gender Politics in Egypt* (Berkeley and Los Angeles: University of California, 2001).

11 Ibid.

12 Beth Baron, *al-Thaqafa wa-l-mujtama' wa-l-sahafa*, trans. by Lamis al-Naqqash (Cairo: Supreme Council for Culture, 1999), p. 50.

13 Rifa'a al-Tahtawi, *al-Murshid al-amin li-l-banat wa-l-banin*, in Muhammad 'Emara, ed., *al-A'mal al-kamila* (Beirut: Arab Institute for Research and Publishing, 1973), part 2, p. 273.

14 Rifa'a al-Tahtawi, *al-Murshid al-amin*, p. 273.

15 Amin's two books were translated into English and published as a single volume, *The Liberation of Women and The New Woman*, trans. by Samiha Sidhom Peterson (Cairo: American University in Cairo Press, 1992).

16 Beth Baron, *al-Thaqafa wa-l-mujtama'*, p. 24.

1   Lebanon

Yumna al-'Id

Introduction

As a poet, al-Khansa' was held in high esteem. She had her own place in the 'Ukaz market next to the equally renowned poet al-Nabigha, and the Prophet attested to her poetic superiority by dubbing her "the best poet" (notably, not the best *female* poet). Critic and grammarian al-Mufaddal al-Dabbi (d. 786) was of the opinion that among all the Arabs, al-Khansa' had composed the best line of auto-panegyric, while in his *Kitab al-Aghani* (Book of Songs) tenth-century scholar Abu-l-Faraj al-Isfahani includes her among those poets whose verses were chosen for the one hundred songs sung in the days of Harun al-Rashid. But when the Umayyad poet Jarir was asked who the best poet was, he responded, "Me, were it not for that devious woman."[1] Jarir's description of al-Khansa' as "devious" implicitly attests to her superiority even as he rejects it. Women were not usually superior; therefore, al-Khansa' is devious, or somehow underhanded.

Fuhula, or poetic virility, was a value that inhabited the popular consciousness, referring to that which ensured the continuity and sovereignty of the tribe. Poets who composed satirical lampoons or panegyric, for themselves or others, were valued over those who composed elegiac or lyric poetry, just as those who waged war and fought were held in more esteem than those who lovingly and with a willing spirit produced with their hands, served, educated, and raised children. Such values, grounded in social or historical conditions, sanctify the continuity of power and justify its authority, despite changing conditions and historical developments. The injustice they entail is great for the ruled, and even greater for women, who are twice burdened, once by their sex and again by their social status as part of the ruled.

Realizing the strong links between the political, the literary-cultural, and the social, women at the beginning of the Arab renaissance understood that their own liberation was dependent on liberating the collective consciousness from traditional values that sanctified their inferiority and made them, according to 'Anbara Salam al-Khalidi (1898–1986) in her memoirs, hostages to "imprisoning walls" and "draping curtains."[2] For the same reason, men of the renaissance also realized that national liberation and societal development were vitally dependent on women's emancipation, which would bring them out of a seclusion that strangled their abilities to a world which they could take part in shaping. In both cases—women's desire for their own liberation and men's desire for national liberation—women were seen as the cornerstone of the construction and advancement of society. The school, as a means of instilling and disseminating knowledge, was thus the starting point of the renaissance in the Arab East. In Lebanon, foreign missions were active in establishing schools early on. The first was the Anglican mission, which established what later became known as the American University in 1820. More schools followed, and by 1860 there were thirty-three, most of them in Beirut.

Beirut was well situated to be the link between East and West, a free space for cultural dialogue, open to the West and its rationalist civilization. With the escalating Druze-Christian sectarian conflict in Mount Lebanon from 1840 and the 1860 massacres, there was a marked increase of foreign communities in Beirut, and Western consulates and the main mission schools relocated there.[3] It was in these foreign, religious schools that most female pioneers were educated. They were Christians, and they represented the minority that came from educated, well-off, enlightened households. Initially, education was not within the reach of the poor and it was not for girls. The few national schools that existed were established for boys, and people saw no good in sending their girls to school.

The first pioneer, Zaynab Fawwaz (1846–1914), did not go to school. Chance alone gave the child—born into a modest, rural home—the opportunity to learn to read and write. Fatima Khalil, the wife of 'Ali Bey al-As'ad, then the feudal lord of Mount 'Amil, taught the young Zaynab. With her intelligence and zeal, Zaynab read voraciously and eventually stepped into the spacious world of knowledge in Egypt.

The Christian nature of education at the foreign missions meant that enlightened Muslims who were willing and able to educate their girls refrained from sending them to the foreign schools, fearing that the wider public would accuse them of blasphemy and that their daughters would be harmed or humiliated as a result. Thus, while Warda al-Yaziji (1838–1924), Labiba Mikha'il Sawaya (1876–1916), and Labiba Hashim, for example, went to American missionary schools, 'Ali Salam, a prominent and enlightened Muslim of Beirut, sent his daughter 'Anbara to a *shaykha* (learned woman) who taught girls basic reading skills. The writer 'Anbara Salam al-Khalidi related later how, when she was ten years old, people would shout at her, "Go home!" as she was on her way to her lessons. She spoke of how Professor 'Abd Allah al-Bustani was persuaded by her father to teach her the principles of Arabic at home and how prominent Muslims convinced one another that "the advancement of the community starts with the education of girls,"[4] which prompted them to establish a girls' school in Beirut.

It was forbidden for a girl to appear in a public place, and her voice was taboo. The day that 'Anbara Salam stood on the podium to speak, wearing her full veil, one of the men spoke up, "What an inauspicious disgrace! How can her father allow his daughter to speak before a gathering of men? By God, by God, I'd like to shoot her and spare the world from her."[5] The young 'Anbara had to wait until 1928 to remove her face veil, while Warda al-Yaziji, older than her, had left hers behind decades earlier.

There was thus a vital need to establish national schools for girls and awaken public opinion as to the importance of girls' education. Both Christian and Muslim women pioneers in Lebanon stepped up to the task. In 1881, Emily Sursuq and Labiba Jahshan jointly founded the first institute for girls' education. It was, as Salma al-Sa'igh said, a model for the establishment of institutes in the East and in "preserving the national language most perfectly."[6] In addition to schools, pioneering women founded women's associations and salons to support the women's awakening, give them a space in society, and contribute to their advancement. In 1914, women in Beirut established a women's association called the Vigilance of the Arab Woman. In 1917, a girls' club was opened which soon became a literary and social salon that received distinguished writers, poets, and doctors passing through Beirut. The women were not intimidated by rumors at the time that "mixed dances were constantly held [in the club]."[7] After the First World War, Julia Tu'ma Dimashqiya, a Christian married to a Muslim, established a women's association for women of both confessions whose objective was "elevating women's cultural level."[8]

Women pioneers of the renaissance in Lebanon were mindful of discrimination between Christians and Muslims, sought to strengthen the Arabic language as part of the liberation project from Ottoman tyranny and Turkization, and took Arab nationalism as their national identity.

In 1928, a number of women's associations from Syrian and Lebanese cities met to form the Women's Union, and the union's first conference was held the same year, achieving its aspirations for religious and national inclusiveness. The conference cemented the literary status of women, embodied in the first female pioneer to revive Arabic poetry, Warda al-Yaziji: to mark the occasion, a commemorative portrait of her was unveiled on a wall in Beirut's National Library next to other prominent Lebanese writers. 'Anbara Salam was named the representative of women at the conference as an expression of the Muslim-Christian concord: Salma al-Sa'igh commented, "She's a Muslim and al-Yazijiya is a Christian! Literary ties are the strongest bonds, and devotion to knowledge is like devotion to religion. God created people of knowledge, like people of religion, to serve the truth."[9]

Lebanese women also played a notable role in establishing and writing for newspapers and magazines. Alexandra Khuri Averino founded *Anis al-jalis* in 1898, followed by Labiba Hashim's *Fatat al-sharq* in 1906 and 'Afifa Karam's *al-Mar'a al-Suriya* in 1911. Most of them settled in Egypt or the Americas, like many male Lebanese writers and intellectuals, searching for spaces of freedom, and this was a decisive factor in establishing their presence as writing women.

Zaynab Fawwaz, the first to write of women's issues in the Egyptian press, first and foremost in *al-Nil*, considered girls' education "the primary foundation" for the improvement of young people. According to Fawwaz, a child raised by an ignorant mother learns all the faults that stem from this ignorance, and no teacher or school can correct them, just as one cannot shore up an unstable building. Fawwaz concluded that the benefit of educating women accrues to men in particular in "childrearing, housekeeping, and companionship to the husband."[10] In highlighting women's role in social improvement, Zaynab Fawwaz reconsidered the work that women do in the home—work that is deemed worthless and insignificant by men. In her newspaper articles, Fawwaz was keen to stress equality between men and women: "Know that the spirit is an abstract essence, neither male nor female, but it is influenced by the physical form, and thus the capacities of men and women differ. Each one is half the world, and the importance of their positions derives from this equal proportion."[11]

Mayy Ziyada (1886–1941) also made substantial contributions to newspaper writing. Ziyada came to Egypt from a convent school in Nazareth. Since her father was an editor for the Cairo-based *al-Mahrusa*, she met many writers and journalists. After studying Arabic and the Arabic literary tradition, she gave lectures and speeches, and her literary salon attracted intellectuals, writers, and poets. Most of her lectures were published as articles in the press. In her articles and talks, Mayy Ziyada evinced a deep awareness of the right of human beings, particularly women, to freedom and justice. She went beyond the liberation of Arab or Eastern women in her writings to address the institution of human slavery in history, linking it to systems of human governance. She believed that in liberational revolutions, like the French revolution, women found the opportunity to rise "from under the feet of the crushing master."[12] In the family, she maintained, the master is the father; he rules over the members of the family much as his leader rules over him.[13] Ziyada defined nationalism as a human concept that went beyond religious identity and social and religious differences and gave everyone his or her due.[14] On the basis of this definition, Ziyada engaged those who disregarded the Arabs' rights and saw them only as desert-dwellers who are good at nothing "save plundering, theft, and destruction."[15] She highlighted the value of Arab civilization and its contributions to the world and discussed the importance of Arabic, seeing in its emergence "a link of goodness and light between the empty ages and the modern centuries."[16]

Like other writers of her era, Mayy Ziyada addressed two major issues in her writings: religious identity, and language and national identity. As we shall see, in Lebanon these two issues had a profound impact on literary production.

The novel
The beginnings
It was in the flourishing press of Egypt and the Levant during the last three decades of the nineteenth and the early twentieth centuries that Arabic fiction saw its renaissance. The Lebanese were active in both writing and translating Western stories, particularly from French. In the Arabic press, several newspapers published original and translated stories including: *al-Janan*, established by Butrus al-Bustani in Beirut in 1870; *al-Mashriq*, established by the Jesuits in Beirut in 1898; *al-Diya'*, established by Ibrahim al-Yaziji in 1898; and *Fatat al-sharq*, established by Labiba Hashim in 1906.

In his history of this period, Dr. Muhammad Yusuf Najm notes that Lebanese writers neglected to mine the folkloric tradition, a copious, varied oral heritage that related "the stories of local heroes and the deeds of the princes and shaykhs who successively ruled the mountain."[17]

Husn al-'awaqib
A reading of the works of women pioneers in fiction reveals that they are characterized by a focus on the local Lebanese context. Zaynab Fawwaz's *Husn al-'awaqib* (Fine Consequences) 1899, for example, tells the story of feudal princes in southern Lebanon and their struggle for power. The conflict is between cousins: Shakib, an orphan raised by his uncle, and Tamir, the son of the same uncle. It is a struggle within the family, not between rulers and the ruled. The ruled have no interest in it; on the contrary, the fighting between local feudal lords will only bring tragedy and loss to the workers, loss of both their livelihoods and children. The values of love and goodness, and a faith that God will punish evil and evildoers, govern the conflict in the novel and emerge as the cause of the victory of the workers on the local prince's lands and in his manor. The

victory of good in the novel seems to illustrate a longing for the peace and stability experienced by the author in the days when her father worked in the local lord's manor and she was blessed with the lady's charity.

The novel combines the social and political. The struggle between Shakib and Tamir over the feudal principality is, at the same time, a struggle for the love and hand of Fari'a. Shakib's goodness is reinforced by his sincere love for Fari'a. The novel is built around these two political-moral values, but it comes out against the tradition that gives the principality to the eldest son. The evil Tamir is older than the good Shakib, and Fari'a, whose love is the object of the struggle, would traditionally go to the lord of the principality. This story, however, breaks with tradition, and the victory of good thus goes hand in hand with the victory of love: Shakib, whose victory represents the victory of goodness, also wins the love of his uncle, Tamir's father, who will leave him the principality and marry him to his beloved Fari'a, who loves him as well. At the end of the novel, positions are handed out to the supporters of the good prince, Shakib. Seen from the perspective of the time in which it was written, the reader, like the peasants and hired hands at the manor, feels reassured about life under the prince: he is good, even if he is a feudalist.

Husn al-'awaqib is grounded in the historical period in which it appeared, describing people's conduct and customs, as well as places and contexts that take the reader to the Lebanese countryside. Stylistically, the novel contains certain aspects of traditional, popular narrative and oral lore. For example, each chapter begins with a note reminding the reader of where the last chapter ended, much like the custom in oral tradition. Like Sheherazade, Fawwaz links her beginnings with where she left off, as if the blank whiteness of the paper between chapters is the white brightness of day between one night and the next. In both white spaces, there is silence and an absence: the absence of women until they resume speaking. Perhaps Zaynab Fawwaz's reminders to the reader, like Sheherazade in her nightly stories, are written to reaffirm her existence and the possibility of life. We have no evidence that Fawwaz read *The Thousand and One Nights* and therefore cannot document the influence of Sheherazade's oral-based narrative; we can conclude, however, that women seem to have a knack for storytelling and that this orality is a vestige of this ancient mode.

Qalb al-rajul
Like *Husn al-'awaqib*, Labiba Hashim's *Qalb al-rajul* (A Man's Heart) 1904, references a local context and events lived by the Lebanese. The author begins her novel like this: "We might not add to the reader's knowledge of the sectarian strife that occurred in Mount Lebanon in 1860, or of the ghastly massacres and the shedding of innocent blood that forced most

Christians to flee from the sword and disperse to the ends of the earth."[18] That is, the author sets her novel in this period not to relate history, but to talk about the fate of the displaced and the tragedy that grew out of the strife. More particularly, the novel is the story of Christians displaced from their villages and towns, and the mountainous areas of Dayr al-Qamar and Bayt al-Din. It is also the story of the places in which they searched for a livelihood: Beirut, the city of trade and hotels, and Egypt, "where business is about advancement and the opportunities in government offices belong to the capable," as Rosa says to 'Aziz.[19]

The novel is not the story of a hero, but the story of people who meet as anyone in Egypt and the Levant might have met at the time. They move, separate, and meet up again, brought together by the circumstances of work, and in the meantime love and friendships develop, along with contradictions. The novel is not, as Dr. Muhammad Yusuf Najm argues, "a defense of women from beginning to end."[20] The love story between 'Aziz and Rosa is, first and foremost, a story of exile and alienation, from oneself and one's country, after events in Mount Lebanon separate 'Aziz from his father and death deprives him of his mother. The tragedies that befall Rosa do not happen because she is a woman, nor are 'Aziz's sufferings specific to his being a man. Rather, they grow out of this beginning, from what happened to 'Aziz's father Habib Nasr Allah and his mother Fatina. In other words, they are linked to conditions in Lebanon, which are represented in relationships between individuals and their conduct, and in the dissolution of these relationships and departures. More than one thread comes together to weave the love story between 'Aziz and Rosa, and later between 'Aziz and Mary, and the fabric of this story is stretched over the novel's deeper, more indirect story of the sectarian strife and what happened to Christians.

The novel begins with the story of Habib Nasr Allah, 'Aziz's father, and how he met Fatina, whom he fell in love with and married. It puts us in the heart of the sectarian strife and sets the love story in that time, making the action between characters a way of explaining the strife even as the developing plot fleshes out the events. The novel's beginning highlights the chaos in Mount Lebanon: armed men attack Habib and Fatina and the two are separated. The beginning refers to events as "strife," but does not attribute them to religious bigotry. Indeed, the novel relates the Druze Junblat family's kind treatment of the Christian Fatina. Sayyid al-Mukhtara takes in Fatina's mother after the death of her husband in Dayr al-Qamar in 1841. When her mother dies, the local lord's family cares for Fatina as their own daughter. Habib, a Christian, falls in love with Fatina as a Druze before he learns that she is, in fact, a Christian.

The love stories in *Qalb al-rajul* use love to construct a story of non-sectarianism. Lovers do not meet by coincidence, as is the case in most novels of the period, and this marks the text as a pioneer in the history of the Arabic novel. The initial meeting between 'Aziz and Rosa, for example, is largely a product of business meetings between merchants from Egypt and Beirut, who go to France and England to buy goods and fabrics. 'Aziz meets Yusuf Rafa'il on the train between Paris and Marseille; Rosa is returning with her father from Paris, where she studies. The love that is born on the train and grows on the steamship between Marseille and Alexandria is a love marked by diaspora and doomed to separation. The events in the novel intertwine to weave spaces, the characters' identities, and their fates, which are determined by historical circumstances. In this way the narrative exposes the wound in the heart of a man, 'Aziz, who has experienced the loss of his family and his country and gone in search of the self.

Labiba Hashim was a modernist pioneer. She possessed a marked ability to construct a plot, create living characters, and bring together the threads that connect them. At the same time she was keen to highlight the local context and strove to bring it to life in a novel that uses prose grounded in everyday speech.

Badi'a wa Fu'ad

Two years after *Qalb al-rajul* was published, 'Afifa Karam's (1883–1924) *Badi'a wa Fu'ad* (Badi'a and Fu'ad) appeared in 1906. By this point the contributions of pioneering women writers began to become a phenomenon in their own right: their works had proved able to create readable fictional worlds, enjoyable for their local, living characters who evoke a real world and issues of concern.

Badi'a wa Fu'ad does not mimic reality; it is not a piece of didactic literature, and it does not use history to talk about history, like most novels of the period, for example, *Dhat al-khidr* (Lady of the Harem) 1884, by Sa'id al-Bustani, filled, according to Dr. Muhammad Yusuf Najm, with "sermons";[21] *al-Din wa-l-'ilm wa-l-mal* (Religion, Knowledge, and Money) 1903, by Farah Antun, which is, by the author's own admission, "a social, philosophical discourse on the nature of money, knowledge, and religion";[22] and *al-'Ayn bi-l-'ayn* (An Eye for an Eye) 1904, by Niqula Haddad, which is dominated by its didacticism. *Badi'a wa Fu'ad* takes up three themes that stand, even today, at the forefront of Arab culture: class differences, the relationship between East and West or the issue of cultural dialogue, and women's liberation. The novel addresses these themes through the behavior of its characters, their feelings, their words, and their historically conditioned relations to the places where they live.

Badi'a is the protagonist, and it is in her that the themes of the narrative meet. As a woman, she embodies a critical perspective that sees women as concerned with social issues and as active agents in the process of reform and change. Badi'a is a poor girl who works as a servant in the home of Fu'ad's wealthy family. Fu'ad's love for her casts a critical, scrutinizing light on relations between two different social classes. It is the human qualities that Badi'a possesses, rather than money, that make her Fu'ad's equal. Badi'a is simple, faithful, and has a sound view of the state of her society. In the novel, she takes issue with her friend, Lucia, who has fallen under the spell of the West. While Badi'a is not anti-West, she opposes blind imitation and the adoption of harmful Western customs such as gambling. The novel's treatment of East-West relations is remarkable for the author's ability to divide the setting of the novel between Lebanon and the U.S. This is accompanied by a portrayal of the customs and traditions of each country, as well as the misery of Syrian and Lebanese immigrants in the U.S.

The relationship between Badi'a and Lucia unfolds around the issue of East–West relations and the meaning of freedom. Badi'a tells her friend, who is enchanted by Western civilization, that contrary to Lucia's beliefs, freedom does not mean sexual freedom, but a woman's freedom to work, participate, and assume responsibility. With her character, conduct, and opinions, Badi'a leads the debate among women, ultimately imbuing them with an awareness that they are distinct individuals, rather than people united by their common femaleness.

The narrative leads the reader to a perspective that holds that good, like evil, is not the particular province of one country or sex. They exist both here and there, and in both women and men. This perspective opens up the possibility of real change. The novel ends with Fu'ad's father blessing his son's marriage to Badi'a after having first rejected her and incited his son against her. Love's triumph at the end of the narrative is thus a victory for the humanity of people and an embrace of justice and equality.

After the beginnings

Despite the significant contribution of the renaissance pioneers, literary production in Lebanon declined after the First World War until the early 1950s. For women the decline was, in fact, a complete hiatus. The retreat may be attributable to geopolitical disturbances that affected the Levant and their implications for religious identity in Lebanon.

In 1920, the state of greater Lebanon was established under French mandate after the Syrian provinces of Sidon and Tripoli were annexed to Mount Lebanon. At the same time, Beirut was cut off from Acre, Haifa, and Nablus—cities that had formerly been part of the province—to become the capital of the new Lebanon. The country's identity and structure were redrawn along with its borders. Whereas the name Lebanon had referred to the Druze-Christian mountain area, it now referred as well to former areas of Syria with a majority Muslim population. The change was not only cartographical, but affected the country's religious and sectarian identity. Although the populations of the annexed or separated territories all demanded independence from the French mandate, the issue of national identity remained contested. The conflict was dormant until after independence in 1943 when the issue of the constitution and the confessional nature of the newly formed nation state came to the fore.

Lebanon, with its new borders and system of governance, required a character. During the battle for independence and the end of the mandate, it seemed to be taking shape by consensus, but this soon gave way to an internal identity conflict that involved both the larger Arab identity and the local national identity, constrained as it was by confessionalism. The conflict would recede momentarily only to come to the surface again every time an Arab country experienced a revolution (the Nasserist revolution, the Algerian revolution) or every time Lebanon entered, or tried to enter, an alliance with the West (the Eisenhower Pact in 1958).

The novel in Lebanon in this fragile period suffered an existential crisis. Only a few novels even by male authors appeared in this period, the most prominent being *al-Raghif* (Loaf of Bread) 1939, by Tawfiq Yusuf 'Awwad. The novel is set in the past, during the First World War, and it tells the story of the resistance of the hero, Sami, to Ottoman rule. With the exception of *Arwa bint al-khutub* (Arwa, Daughter of Woe), 1949, by Widad Sakakini, our research has unearthed no other novel written by a woman in this period. At the time Sakakini was living in Syria, which no longer included Lebanon. With its perspective and general atmosphere, her work marks the end of the didactic novel. As such, it belongs to the previous, early novelistic period and does not reflect the contemporary reality of women and their struggle.

Arwa bint al-khutub addresses one type of oppression: men's view of women as sexual objects. Arwa, the novel's heroine, is falsely accused of adultery after rejecting the advances of her husband's brother, 'Abid. Arwa is a victim, and her beauty and femininity are the sources of her suffering. She wishes that God had created her "a misshapen, ugly thing that repels the eyes and repulses the heart."[23] To save herself, she turns to God's service and becomes a saint, sought out for her blessings and intercessions, even by those who have wronged her. The novel stands in stark contrast to women's struggle in Lebanon to change the predominantly masculine collective consciousness.

Although women did not write novels at this time, they were active in social and national work. After the First World War, Salma al-Sa'igh says they worked "to create national industries to prevent people from emigrating in search of a livelihood, to improve the status of the working classes, to raise literary standards, and revise educational systems to suit the dignity of the nation and the needs of the age."[24] In addition, many took part in the resistance to the mandate and demonstrations for independence. Some women were shot by occupation soldiers. Women boldly confronted sectarianism and took off their veils; after the massacres of 1948 in Palestine, they took a stance against the Balfour Declaration, which gave the Jewish people a national homeland in Palestine; and they took part in several women's conferences and joined other Arab women in the international peace and disarmament movement.

The true beginnings of the novel in Lebanon

Women returned to the novel in the 1950s, which can be considered the true beginning of the Arabic novel in Lebanon—that is, a novel about a particular context that seeks out forms and styles to elevate the particular to the universal.

The burst of novelistic writing in Lebanon, by both sexes, coincided with several factors: the spread of state-run education along with the establishment of secondary schools and the University of Lebanon in 1952. More girls went to school and enrolled in institutions of higher learning. In 1948, Lebanon signed the Convention on Human Rights, which upheld gender equality. In 1951, the Lebanese government approved a law enshrining full equality between the sexes in elections and representation. Finally, several literary journals were founded in Beirut, which occupied a prominent cultural place among countries in the region. These publications included, for example, *al-Adib* (The Author) 1942, *al-Thaqafa al-wataniya* (National Culture) 1952, *al-Adab* (Belles Lettres) 1953, and *Sh'ir* (Poetry) 1957. These publications were known for their interest in modern culture and literature, and their establishment was accompanied by the founding of publication and printing houses that disseminated Arabic literature and invigorated literary production.

Ana ahya

It was in this climate that Layla Ba'labakki published her first novel, *Ana ahya* (I Live), in 1958.[25] It was a milestone in the development of the Arabic novel in Lebanon, while at the same time it expressed a sophisticated view of the relationship of writing women to what they write about.

Like Sheherazade, the novel's feminine first person possesses the authority of speech, but the first person here does not use an oral storytelling mode or relate the tales of others, but writes and talks about the self, making the act of writing the female equivalent of life: I write, therefore I live. Ba'labakki pulls off the narrator's mask, narrowing the distance between the storyteller and the woman whose story is told. The narrator is the protagonist and the feminine first person. She puts herself in the position of someone speaking about herself, as if she is telling her own story, giving it a sense of truth and realism. The female writer thus bears responsibility for the possible flaws in her character that might result from the conduct of the female narrator, who merges with the author, her speech, and her bold, critical stance.

Lina Fayyad, the novel's protagonist and narrator, is a bold woman: she chooses, desires, speaks, and acts. She is a character from the modern Beirut that emerged following the Second World War. Lina engages her reality in all its interrelated levels, offering a portrait of what happens— or what might happen—when a woman is possessed of self-awareness. She dreams of a future in which a person's individuality is the symbol of her liberty and the individual's awareness of her right to exercise her will and assume responsibility creates the collective consciousness.

Lina rebels against several male-dominated institutions on the domestic, social, economic, political, and cultural level. In so doing, she wages her two-pronged battle for liberation, as a woman and as an individual in society. Lina rejects society's image of her. The link she makes between free choice, will, and responsibility for one's actions is informed by Sartre's existentialism and springs from a Beirut culture fostered by periodicals and translations. Lina's character is marked by Western culture, but in the novel it is reformulated in relation to her reality from a social, nationalist, liberational perspective. Lina rejects patriarchy and rebels against herself, taking the principles of free choice, will, and responsibility, but she also rebels against the bourgeois class of Beirut that emerged after the Second World War. That is, she rejects an economy that, in Lebanon, did not rely on production, but on exploitation and transit trade. Lina's father, a prominent figure in the city who functions as a middleman and betrays his country, embodies this economy.

Layla Ba'labakki's discourse in the novel is based on a critical, liberational, national, subjective stance, not on a masculine dichotomy. Lina falls in love with Baha', who, as a member of the Communist party, is not an independent individual, but subservient, intellectually at least, to the party. When they disagree on the concept of liberty and revolution, it has an effect on how Baha' views Lina; for him, Lina becomes just a woman he desires, a wrapper he can throw away at will or "an insect on a chair, dead."[26]

The attempts by the protagonist of *Ana ahya* to eradicate gender differences as a value judgment fail, and her hope that women will be seen as individuals who possess a will and freedom is frustrated. The male figure, whether father, the head of an institution, a university professor, or a person who holds power in the social structure, oppresses and obstructs the liberation process; in the novel, he is the cause. It is this complex construct, rather than a simple masculine-feminine dichotomy, on which Layla Ba'labakki's novel is built. The novel ends as Lina's dream is shattered and she is forced to return to her home, the symbol of closed space and patriarchal authority. Perhaps this is why Mira, the heroine of Ba'labakki's second novel, *al-Aliha al-mamsukha* (The Deformed Gods) 1960, screams, "I've had it up to here with fathers. If he weren't dead, I'd wish he was."[27] It is as if the only way out of the falsity of this collective consciousness is by crushing the image of the father. In this instance, the father is crushed through the use of a bold language that breaks the taboo of the relationship with the father, a powerful symbol of more than one type of authority.

The importance of *Ana ahya* lies in its discourse; language is not used as a container to hold new, alien ideas. Rather, Ba'labakki's language seeks to demolish an authoritarian discourse that reinforces the sanctity of masculine rhetoric. The novel's language seeks a reality that is rejected by the prevailing culture. It gives voice to feminine whispers and repressed thoughts to ask questions. Using brief expressions and truncated, anxious dialogues, it tries to create a language capable of expressing new meanings and produce a discourse with a new rhetoric and aesthetic.

Fatah tafiha

Muna Jabbur's first novel, *Fatah tafiha* (Silly Girl) 1962 sets out from the language forged by Layla Ba'labakki and builds on it aesthetically.[28] In so doing, she sets the Arabic novel written by women in Lebanon on a new path, breaking down the walls of the female subject to reveal its repressed, inner kernel. In modern Beirut, at the time of the arrival and advancement of knowledge and the mixing of men and women, female repression comes out into the light of writing. The discourse points to the subject's capacity for self-awareness and the courage to strip it bare.

Muna Jabbur does not blindly imitate Layla Ba'labakki, but walks in her path to differ from her. Nada, the protagonist of *Fatah tafiha*, uses the language of *Ana ahya*'s Lina to speak, but Nada, the character who endows the novel with its deeper significance, differs. Nada hates men, not as a symbol of authority like Lina, but as men. At the same time, she hates herself as a woman. Nada's complex in the novel is sex, while Lina's is male authority and the structure of society. Thus do the two novels part ways on the new path. The heroine of *Fatah tafiha* has developed a pathological complex because she is deprived of paternal love and her mother's embrace. She emerges in the novel as a seeker, not for work or an external space, but for a non-masculine man who can compensate her for the loss and rescue her from her nightmares and loneliness.

Jabbur's language in her second novel, *al-Ghirban wa-l-musuh al-bayda'* (The Ravens and the White Gowns) 1966, approaches a confessional mode,[29] seeming to confirm the autobiographical elements suggested by the language of the first novel. Explicitly and clearly, Kawthar expresses her need for her father's love. She leaves aside the language of the objective narrator to adopt a mode of direct address, opening a large parenthetical aside addressed not to us, but directly to her father and her deprivation of his love. She then confesses the truth to herself and to us: "I need love." As if recognizing her neglect of her mother in the first novel, in the same style she says, "How I long to know you, mother." Then she tells us, "How I revere her and to revere her I challenge the nothingness that crushed her and raised me." This deprivation leads her to a lesbian relationship and she confesses, "Paula . . . for the first time in my life, I've known with her that a woman's relationship with a woman can be much more violent and profound than a man's relationship with a man."[30]

Jabbur's novelistic discourse seems constrained and shaped by the gendered body of the female narrator. Talk about the relationship both of Jabbur's protagonists have to their bodies is intimate, interior, and almost confessional, tantamount to a denuding on the level of language. Jabbur's significance lies in the way her narrative is employed to develop the self-consciousness of the protagonist in both novels, using a conversational language that in the first novel finally leads Nada to distinguish between one man and another and one woman and another, and in the second novel leads Kawthar to expose the real cause of her psychological trauma. "I'm a child, a child, a child. Carry me," she tells Hisham. It is as if writing here is a laboratory in which to read one's inner self. It leads Jabbur's heroine, Kawthar, to knowledge and the ability to continue living in the imaginary world of the novel within the bounds of its social logic.

But writing was not able to save the author herself. Muna Jabbur committed suicide even before her second novel was published. It seems that reality was stronger than fiction, which managed to expose the truth but failed to take time backward. Jabbur killed herself after leading her protagonist to the realization of her innocence and the recognition of her incapacity: "I understand how innocent and incapable I am," Kawthar tells Hisham.[31]

Muna Jabbur fell silent—"silence is a god among gods," as Kawthar says[32]—leaving the language of the female body to future generations. There is a lesson here, embodied by the character of Kawthar and her tortured life, that encourages a concern with women's sexual education. Kawthar trembles as she reads about the secrets of sex, after which she dreams that a naked man is chasing her. She cannot run; she screams, but no sound emerges. Her eyes remain fixed on his lower abdomen as he pants. The man becomes every man, the male a nightmare. He runs after her and yells at her to look at his body, but she can only hate him and herself.

Tuyur Aylul

Emily Nasrallah's first novel, *Tuyur Aylul* (The Birds of September) 1962,[33] differs from the novelistic discourse of Layla Ba'labakki and Muna Jabbur. The variation enriches the Arabic novel in Lebanon and reinforces women's presence and their contributions to the novel. *Tuyur Aylul* tells the story of two times: village time, where the present corresponds to the past, and city time, where the present exposes the alienation of its dwellers. Between the two times, writing gives birth to a nostalgic memory, and Emily Nasrallah carves out a space of action and presence in this memory.

Yet the novel's nostalgia is not naive. The novel writes about the past to revive the time of the Lebanese village and hold it up as a mirror to the present. In so doing, Nasrallah posits a cultural consciousness that sees identity as residing in a belonging to the land, and views urbanity as a city that becomes a whale, swallowing everything in its path. Meanwhile the village, as Raji says in the novel, remains "a forgotten point in the world of existence."[34] Within the constraints of this contradiction, Emily Nasrallah creates the village world of her novel, beautiful despite its bitterness.

It is largely women who suffer because of the contradiction. The time of the village has left them prisoner to its traditions and beliefs: they live in the village and the village lives in the past. The novel talks about traditions and beliefs, which, like high walls, prevent girls from learning about love, which the villagers see as "a mortal sin." It speaks about women whose sole value lies in the number of male children they bear, and about love and its victims. Maryam dies a victim of the social difference between her family and her lover's family; Najla is a victim of what the villagers consider "the most distasteful of taboos," a marriage to someone from a different sect. The novel speaks of the migration of young people who are stripped of their land, tortured, leaving behind the village girls they love. For Emily Nasrallah, emigration strips one of memory and threatens one's identity. Ties to the land lie at the root of this Lebanese identity.

Identity and land remain important issues in most of Nasrallah's later novels as well. In *al-Iqla' 'aks al-zaman (Flight Against Time)* 1981, for example, she gives us the village character of Radwan, who clings to his land and to rural Lebanese values. Radwan leaves America, his children, and his grandchildren and flies against time to his village in southern Lebanon, which he hears has been invaded by Israel. He flies toward death, in the face of all those Lebanese who leave their country seeking safety.

Issues of belonging and identity are not merely situations in Nasrallah's novels, but a discourse through which the author creates her own novelistic language. The language is woven from the lexicon of the Lebanese village, from the villagers' modes of speech, the chatter of women, the proverbs of the elders, and the oral tales preserved in the collective memory. It pulses with the heart of these simple people and the sun's rays over the village plains and mountain peaks. With its poetic, lyrical rhythms, Nasrallah's language creates a framework for Lebanese identity and determines its linguistic features. In this she is drawing on a prose that has distinguished other Lebanese writers, such as Amin Nakhla in *al-Mufakkira al-rifiya* (The Country Notebook) 1945 and Fu'ad Sulayman in *Tammuziyat* (Things of July) 1953. Like them, she gives Lebanon—with its new borders, no longer administratively attached to Greater Syria—a meaning and a shape.

Within this language, novels written by women developed several distinctive characteristics in discourse and characters' diction that enriched Arabic narrative. These staked out the local particularity of the novel while at the same time illustrating Arabic's ability to live and speak in the tongue of more than just one social class.

Lan namut ghadan
Layla 'Ussayran for example, in her novel *Lan namut ghadan* (We Will Not Die Tomorrow) 1962,[35] chooses a narrative mode that reflects the Beirut aristocracy, creating for her characters a language that expresses the emptiness of their lives and the triviality of their conversations. She then uses this to tell us about the sufferings of the novel's heroine, 'A'isha, who travels to Egypt and discovers, in the Dar al-Nahda Press, people with different behavior and ways of life, thought, and conversation, evoking socialist Nasserist Egypt. By identifying with this pan-Arab consciousness and through her love for Ahmad, an Egyptian, 'A'isha finds a way to realize and liberate herself from the trivial life of her own capitalist class.[36]

Arab national identity as a perspective appears in more than one of 'Ussayran's novel. *'Asafir al-fajr* (Dawn Sparrows) 1968 identifies with the Palestinian cause, embodied in the struggle of Maryam and Suhayr, as well as Khalid's death. In these novels, Arab nationalism represents a way to bring the female subject and the city of Beirut out of its vacuum. In tandem with this, the novel rejects a class discourse because this class in 'Ussayran's novels—the capitalist aristocracy—rules the destiny of Lebanon and leads it to emptiness, diverting it from the novel's message of struggle-oriented Arab nationalism.

Hayy al-Lija
Unlike Layla 'Ussayran, Bilqis Humani, in her novel *Hayy al-Lija* (The Lija Quarter) 1967, uses the language of ordinary people and their colloquial speech to reveal a world of the marginalized poor who, because of their language, are absent from literature. At the same time, she reconsiders the logic of male-female relations in this world.

The Lija Quarter is an area of Beirut whose residents emigrated from the southern countryside, not to America, but to poor areas of the capital, created sociologically by an economy based on tourism, services, finance, and agricultural decline, which in the south, unlike Mount Lebanon, has not been compensated for by tourism—since the villages are located near Israel—or by trade, which was disrupted after the occupation of Palestine in 1948.

Fatum, aged fourteen, marries her cousin 'Abduh. 'Abduh escapes from his large family, all crowded into one room, to lose himself in gambling, drinking, and whoring. He looks for compensation and makes up for his failure by exercising his male authority over Fatum, mother of his many children. Because of his conduct, he falls ill, and because of poverty and the lack of education, the logic of action-reaction governs Fatum's relationship with her husband. The balance of power shifts, Fatum and 'Abduh trade places, and she begins to exercise her authority over her sick husband; she is now the stronger partner. Authoritarianism is reproduced even when the roles are reversed. Here, authoritarianism is not a male characteristic, but is related to poverty and people who lack the consciousness to rebel against it. *Hayy al-Lija* is a novel about the misery of migrants from the villages of the Shiite south in a city that is indifferent to the poor, and this misery leads us to reconsider the logic governing the male-female conflict.

Hayy al-Lija was an early, although indirect, allusion to a Lebanese problem that was greatly exacerbated with time: the intersection of social class, sect, and demography. The residents of the Lija Quarter are poor Shiites, and their neighborhood, like the belts of desperation surrounding the capital, is cut off from the body of the city while still part of it. Tawfiq Yusuf 'Awwad later dealt with the subject of *Hayy al-Lija* in his novel *Tawahin Bayrut (Death in Beirut: a Novel)* 1969. The heroine of his novel, Tamima, a Shiite from the south, engages in a relationship with the city and knowledge through her relationship with Hani, a Christian university student. 'Awwad thus links the characters' sect and their social and cultural identities. In the novel *Faras al-shaytan* (The Devil's Coach Horse) 1975, Hanan al-Shaykh offers another example of this complex relationship in the form of a conflict experienced by the novel's protagonist, Sara, due to the contradictions between her conservative Shiite environment and the modernity she experiences in school, and the contrast between the city's other quarters and her own neighborhood.

Qualitative leap during the Lebanese civil war

Lebanese writers were always called poets rather than novelists because of the paucity of novels that appeared in the decades after the First World War and before the 1960s, and the flourishing of poetry in the same period. But in the late 1960s and early 1970s, there was a qualitative leap in the novel.

Writers explored the contradictions and complexities of reality and its possible ramifications, and they worked on creating a multi-pronged discourse whose language expressed multiple viewpoints and nuances in diction, mindful of speech variations in a society that was becoming more sharply divided and on the verge of civil war. In this endeavor, they were part of the overall development of the Arabic novel across the Arab world, but they were striving to develop a distinctive style of their own.

Women writers made prominent contributions to what we could call the revival of the Arabic novel in Lebanon, which flourished during the Lebanese civil war. While the beginnings of this leap can be seen in the 1970s, in writers such as Hanan al-Shaykh and her novels *Intihar rajul mayyit* (Suicide of a Dead Man) 1970 and *Faras al-shaytan*, it crystallized in the early 1980s during the peak of the war, in tandem with the creative resurgence embodied by Lebanese male writers such as Elias Khoury, Hasan Dawud, Ahmad al-Zayn, and Rashid al-Da'if.

Hikayat Zahra

Hanan al-Shaykh's *Hikayat Zahra (The Story of Zahra)* 1980 appeared to offer a rich world in which the fate of an oppressed woman merges with the fate of a society built on contradictions;[37] Zahra's pathology becomes sharper as the contradictions between segments of society are exacerbated, finally reaching an explosive climax: the explosion of Zahra's body and the implosion of civil society. Zahra's trauma is rooted in her childhood, in the time before the war, when she internalized all forms of social authority and patriarchal oppression. As she ages, Zahra absorbs external conflicts into the depths of her self; her suffering mirrors the collective suffering of women and refers to the strong link between women's suffering and war.

Within her small family, Zahra is aware of the gender discrimination that separates her from her brother. She later experiences more heightened forms of discrimination in the larger society in the form of several male types, such as Malik, a friend of her brother Ahmad, to whom Zahra loses her virginity, feeling nothing "but fear."[38] Zahra continues to have sex with Malik, although she is not aroused when he kisses her or flings himself on top of her. He does not mind, and she does not understand why she does not stop herself from going to him. Through this experience, Zahra is a witness to her repeated rape because of the fear ingrained in her since childhood, and this relationship scars all her future relationships with men. Zahra's pathology takes hold of her and leads her to see every man as a rapist, including even those closest to her, in the form of her emigrant uncle in Africa. As soon as the war erupts, Zahra is comforted by the fact that the war has crushed patriarchal authority in the family and exposed society's ills, long hidden under Lebanon's brilliant and beautiful, but deceptive, face.

During the war, Zahra undergoes an internal rebirth, ridding herself of fear and terror, but the irony is that she is engaged in a sexual relationship with a sniper, the god and symbol of the war. This paradox is a condition for Zahra's rebirth and the shattering of the father/authority figure, the symbol of the pre-war era, along with other now obsolete symbols: the treacherous mother, the spoiled brother, and other male figures. Using this paradox, Hanan al-Shaykh articulates a discourse based on an intersection of time: the pre-war and post-war era intersect in Zahra.

Hajar al-dahk

In addition to Hanan al-Shaykh, the works of Hoda Barakat constitute a fine example of the Lebanese novelistic discourse that takes shape after the civil war. The intersection of issues of masculinity and femininity with war, started by Hanan al-Shaykh, comes to the fore, expressed in a cohesive, well-crafted structure that heralds a new form of the novel.

Khalil, the hero of Hoda Barakat's *Hajar al-dahk (The Stone of Laughter)* 1990,[39] has an identity crisis. Khalil is attractive and handsome in a feminine way; he does not desire women, but has repressed homosexual tendencies that emerge subconsciously in sexual dreams. The author makes him different from the other men around him. He is cowardly and inclined to "peace, to safety," and an "inability to stand the sight of blood." For that reason he has never concerned himself with politics although he feels "deeply ashamed of his friends who were rowdy at demonstrations and speeches." When the war breaks out, the hero stakes out a middle ground among his companions, composed of two groups: those younger than him who start managing "people's public and private lives" and are concerned "even with water, with bread, with dreams, with emigration," and men of his own age, who grip "the important things in life . . . holding the tools of understanding, awareness and close attention to theory."[40]

At various intervals the narrator's voice intersects with Khalil's voice, creating a sort of alliance between the two whose objective is to critique the thinkers, politicians, journalists, leaders, and party figures responsible for the war. The novel suggests that all of these intellectuals are opportunistic and questions the integrity of the parties to which they belong. But the transformations experienced by the protagonist during the war—changes in his character and his relationships—embody the symbolic dimensions of the novel's discourse. Khalil, whose femininity stands at odds with the masculinity of war, gradually acquires masculine characteristics, seemingly when the narrator/author is not looking, as if the pacifist hero betrays his authorial creator. Using a sudden narrative device, the narrator moves from outside the text, where she was using the third-person voice, to inside the text, taking up the first person and mirroring the sudden transformation of Khalil, who becomes a perfect embodiment of the masculine dimension of war. The narrator/author inserts herself into the text directly, commenting, "Khalil is gone, he has become a man who laughs. And I remain a woman who writes."[41]

Hoda Barakat's innovation is that she is able to embody the intersection of masculinity and femininity with war in a male protagonist whose feminine side merges with the author/narrator, suggesting that the integration of these two sides makes a complete human being and that their complete separation leads to gender stratification and, in turn, a society of violence. Before the hero's transformation, Khalil and the author/narrator concur in their opposition to the masculinity of war, which, according to the logic of the text, is a war that has no place for pacifists or innocents and has given rise to sloganeering and false claims about nationalism, patriotism, democracy, and love of one's country. The hero's transformation into the epitome of masculinity, violence, and bloodlust not only signifies his estrangement from the female author/narrator, but also testifies to the truth of the ideological perspective on which the narrator's anti-war stance is based.

Ahl al-hawa

Starting out from the gender dualities contained by one sex, in her second novel, *Ahl al-hawa (Disciples of Passion)* 1993, Barakat sets up a male narrator who knows that his masculinity is also informed by femininity. He is a man who kills the wife he loved—or so he imagines. The novel presents him in a long monologue, reflective and confused, torn between illuminations that give us, the readers, hope and make us reconsider the meaning of madness, sanity, masculinity, and its relationship to femininity, and between ruminations on the relationship between masculine violence and war, and the relationship of the self to others, whether the same or different.

In a crime of passion, the man kills someone who differs from him (a woman) just as in the Lebanese war men killed others who differed from them religiously or ideologically. But in the novel, from the perspective of an implied author, the man who does this sees another man, a person like him, dead, and he can no longer exist but outside himself. This wholly external existence is represented by madness in the novel, and this madness, a reflection of his relationship with a different Other, makes the man exceptional. He sees woman as difference, but he is part of the same difference and thus sees some human resemblance. Femininity is set up as the soul of the madman, existing outside his act of murder. The novel asks a question: does the man realize the meaning of his search for similarity in the difference of the Other? Does he realize the meaning of his exceptionalism and his acceptance of difference?

Ahl al-hawa is a novel about the intertwined relationship of masculinity and femininity, the murder of the Other and the need for it, and a self-absorption that recognizes only the similar and simultaneously rejects and loves the Other. Using the intricate relationship of femininity and masculinity, Hoda Barakat takes the novel to a high aesthetic plane, blazing an important trail for the Lebanese novel, one that firmly grounds women's novels in the larger literary context while creating a distinctive Arabic novelistic discourse. This distinctiveness stems primarily from the creation of a complex, ambiguous character, seemingly insane, whose rich language captures the madness of the man's actions. Madness here is used to create an aesthetic capable of generating a deep sense of the tragedy and oppressive weight of reality.

Hayat wa alam Hamad ibn Silana

With Najwa Barakat, war as death fuses with the contours of a new novelistic language that reflects a trend in fiction that novelist Edwar al-Kharrat called "contemporary myth." "The style turns to legend, myth, and popular traditions while also addressing issues of everyday life, with its cast of characters and scenes, whether set in the past or the present."[42]

In her novel *Hayat wa alam Hamad ibn Silana* (The Life and Pains of Hamad ibn Silana) 1995, Najwa Barakat shows death to be the one true fact of existence. But the fact is not set in a context of pessimism, nihilism, or alienation, but in an unfamiliar novelistic atmosphere that blends fantasy, myth, and realism and uses both poetic language and novelistic narrative.

In this novel, alternately realistic and fantastical, the masculine and the feminine merge completely and the differences between them become negligible. The protagonist, Hamad, is both masculine and feminine. He is the only son among seven daughters, who were raised by their father 'Aql "as if they were males."[43] Hamad is breathtakingly handsome: "troubling and frightening, like the Virgin."[44] His sexual identity crisis is linked to his status as the sole boy among seven girls and his resemblance to his mother, Silana. As a result of their intimacy, everyone calls him "Hamad, the son of his mother,"[45] as if he has no relation at all to his father 'Aql. But ironically, Hamad is not saddened by his mother's sudden death as one would expect—particularly since he grew into adolescence without ever cutting the umbilical cord that bound him to her. After Silana's death, Hamad sets out through three different stories—the stories of Ri'bal, Francis, and Qays—that follow the tale of Silana on a long journey of searching, which symbolizes the development of his consciousness. After the journey is over and he returns to the home he left after his mother's death, death is revealed as a painful existential fact that is finally recognized by Hamad, who had denied and rejected it. Yet this recognition of death would not have been possible if Hamad's consciousness had not evolved and freed itself from his crisis of identity, which sprang from his childish connection to his mother's womb.

As a representative of the young generation of novelists whose consciousness was formed in the midst of civil war, it is difficult for Najwa Barakat not to bring death into her novels, even if they do not directly address the war. Najwa Barakat pauses at the fact of death for every person, man or woman, a fact that touched the consciousness of her generation as an inevitability that takes precedence over all else. Perhaps for this reason, her second novel, *Bas al-awadim* (A Busload of Folks) 1996, which sets up a distinctly Arab space (the bus) filled with characters with various objectives and proclivities, dramatizes the common characteristics of the passengers on the bus, whose journey symbolizes life itself and how individuals deal with it. In terms of language, *Bas al-awadim* draws on and imitates the narrative style of medieval histories as well as the Sufi tendencies rooted in the Arabic literary tradition, and this style embodies a modern way of reading the individual. The human being in Barakat's text is always complicit; his innocence is the big lie. The novel's technical elements are brought together to serve the tragic end of the passenger characters, signifying one form of collective death.

The novel in the last decade of the twentieth century
Women writers continued to produce novels in the 1990s after the civil war. In some of these novels, female characters are already liberated from oppressive male authority. Women impose their bodies as a fact and live in them heedless of the guilt complex sanctified by male values and far removed from the pathological trauma of the heroines of *Fatah tafiha* or *Hikayat Zahra* or the rebellious conduct of the heroine of *Ana ahya*.

In *Hiba fi rihlat al-jasad: sira thaniya* (Hiba on a Journey of the Body: A Second Story) 1994, Ilham Mansur continues Hiba's journey that she began with *Ila Hiba (sira ula)* (To Hiba: A First Story) 1991. The novel observes the submission of the self to the rhythms of the body and its sensual needs. For Hiba, sex is a need, not a sin or a desecration; it is as if the war, which forms the background of Mansur's two novels, destroyed all sexual taboos along with traditions.

In Raja' Ni'ma's *Maryam al-nur* (Maryam of Light) 1995, the novel leaves behind everything outside of love and human relationships, as if love is the only thing that should be plumbed to the depths. The novel ponders the reality of war and poses an intimate relationship between it and the pathologies of the characters, positing the victory of love as the sole value capable of soothing wounds in the psyche, regardless of gender.

In *Rihlat al-tifla* (The Child's Journey) 1991, by Nadiya Zafir Sha'ban, the reader is struck by the powerful humanism of the text and its elevation of love. The novel tells the story of a Spanish doctor and a Lebanese student living in Spain who are bound by the heavy memory of the violence of history: his desperate childhood memories of the Spanish civil war and her living, daily memory of the wounds inflicted on her country, which is drowning in a civil war. In love, the doctor finds his lost childhood and the warmth he was deprived of by the icy past; the student finds a well of love and security and a person who teaches her the meaning of joy. The lovers cross civilizations and cultural divides, and love gives them the sense of belonging they have both lost. Both were strangers in their own countries, but love teaches them that exile and alienation are inscribed, first and foremost, in the self and thus much crueler than physical exile from one's homeland. Love in Sha'ban's novel is a human characteristic that rises above social violence and scenes of war that burden memory.

In Iman Hamidan Yunus's *Ba' mithl bayt . . . mithl Bayrut (B as in Beirut)* 1997, the war destroys love: women live the daily grind of war and lose the intimate ties that were all that remained to them after the death and destruction. Talal is injured and loses his arm; as a result he withdraws into himself and he and his wife are estranged. Alienation enters their home and takes up residence in their bed. Forced displacement and migration leave neighbors homeless, windows and balconies lose their function as rooms close in on themselves, shelters are dark and menacing. The author uses a language similar to the daily speech of women, the language of private concerns that is nevertheless rooted in nobility of feeling and the anxiety of women as they take in the world around them.

Shita' mahjur (A Forsaken Winter) 1996, by Renée al-Hayik, creates a different world of war, but it reflects the grief and loneliness of the protagonist, Muna, a forty-something mother, after the marriage of her only daughter. Muna's sense of loneliness is translated into silence and calm. In addition to her daughter, she misses a man as she endures the daily routine of home and work. The novel is about Muna's experience of loss as a woman: she is a mother who represses her sense of motherhood, and a still-young woman living alone. The language in *Shita' mahjur* captures the sense of loneliness in its descriptions of the cold and ice that penetrate the body's extremities. The novel's language reaches an aesthetic level that deepens the meaning of loneliness, which becomes not merely the loneliness of a particular woman, but the loneliness of a human being in a country that is just emerging from the heat of war. It seems that the fighting has created a type of interior estrangement in which questions about the future are even more difficult to face than war itself.

Several general conclusions can be drawn from the foregoing survey. Firstly, in the pioneering period, writing women made valuable contributions to the evolving Arabic novel. Labiba Hashim's *Qalb al-rajul* was published even before Muhammad Hasanayn Haykal's *Zaynab* (Zaynab), issued in Egypt in 1914 and held by some to be the first Arabic novel. Its literary significance is thus equivalent to that of *Zaynab* and may even surpass it somewhat in the sophistication of its plot, the variety of its settings, and the diversity of characters and their fates. The refusal to recognize the value of women's writings raises questions about literary criticism and history, not about women's writing itself. Women's novelistic production in Lebanon evolved in tandem with the Lebanese novel, helping to articulate it, making qualitative contributions that have distinguished the Arabic novel in general, and giving the Lebanese novel a local flavor. The discourse of women's novels does not address the relationship of masculinity-femininity from a negative stance only, but from the perspective of emancipation of the self and the collective consciousness. In turn, the discourse of women novelists is not an feminist counter-discourse, but one that strives to reach a literary, aesthetic level that can speak about the right of human beings to life and liberty.

The short story
Introduction
The beginnings of the short story written by women are still obscure for several reasons. Most importantly, the word "story" was not used as a precise term, but was applied to all sorts of narrative texts, including long texts that today would be identified as novels.[46] Short texts were closer to tales and were published in newspapers, and most of them were imitations of Western stories.

Collections by authors who are considered pioneers of the short story in Lebanon include Gibran's *al-Arwah al-mutamarrida (Spirits Rebellious)* 1908 and Mikha'il Na'ima's *Kan ma kan* (Once Upon a Time) 1927, both representatives of the Exile School of Arabic literature, and Khalil Taqi al-Din's *'Ashar qisas* (Ten Stories) 1927 and Tawfiq Yusuf 'Awwad's *al-Sabi al-a'raj* (The Lame Boy) 1933. Although we have found no similar collections by women writers, it should be noted that the publication of short-story collections is not the same thing as the actual writing of stories or their publication individually.

The beginning
Some of the stories in the collection *Kan ma kan*, for example, published in 1927, were written during the First World War, which raises questions about the true beginnings of the short story written by women.[47] The first identified collection by a woman dates to 1945, Widad Sakakini's *Maraya al-nas* (People's Mirrors). If the short story began to take shape in Lebanon after the Second World War, after an interruption of some seven years

because of the war, according to novelist Suhayl Idris,[48] Widad Sakakini can be considered a milestone in women's attempts to make short-story writing a craft based on capturing snatches of life and to minimize the didacticism that characterized the early stories from the late nineteenth and early twentieth centuries.

In her first collection, *Maraya al-nas* (People's Mirrors) 1945, Widad Sakakini employs a descriptive, analytical language that helps her pierce the various psychological levels of her characters. One story in the collection, "Hajir al-'anis" (Hajir the Spinster), is particularly striking in that the author is able to expose Hajir's interior world by following her behavioral transformations, which result not from her nature, but from her family and social surroundings. Hajir does not marry and is thus labeled a spinster, a value-laden term that gives the unmarried woman a lower status than the married one. As a result, despite her education, the people around her view her either with pity or with condescension, which only heightens her sense of inferiority. Hajir despises her father and mother, holding them both responsible for her condition and the fact that they both see her as a spinster. Hajir acts like a child and feels increasingly bitter with the passing of the years; she worries about finding a husband, grieves, and finally loses hope, falling prey to feelings of envy and bitterness. The author captures Hajir's feelings in her negative transformations, portrayed as reactions to an oppressive, male-dominated society. Her description is accompanied by a sophisticated depiction of the physiological changes that Hajir undergoes, a reflection of the impact on her of the value system that surrounds her.

The subjects of Widad Sakakini's stories vary, as do their quality, but they remain, to use her words, "what life dictated and events foreordained."[49] Sakakini's virtue lies in her ability to make the language of the story supple enough to suit real life and her minimal use of heavy, decorative oratorical and rhetorical devices.

After the beginning

During the 1950s and 1960s, several short-story collections written by women appeared, evincing various styles and a distinct expressive language. In *Ma' al-hayah* (With Life) 1956, for example, Salwa Mahmasani Mu'mina uses realism, like Marun 'Abbud, to portray village characters and their lives. In the same period, Rose Ghurayyib published *Khutut wa zilal* (Lines and Shadows) 1958, with women as protagonists. The narrative uses a female first-person narrator, and the narrating subject spans the old and the new. The narrator's question is placed in a transitional period and contains an invitation to absorb the exigencies of contemporary life. We should not simply stand in wonder before the Other (the woman) or the Western culture that brought us this modernity, but face the necessary challenges to move from the old to the new. The narrator seems to be a mask for the author, who was born in the early part of the century and witnessed a changing reality. She writes about it, registering a stance toward modernity that has few peers among women of her generation, or even among men.

Salwa Safi makes intelligent, fascinating use of a diary-type format in some of her realistic stories, creating short intervals of time similar to diary entries and using a narrative that evokes lived experience. A good example is "al-Qist al-akhir" (The Final Installment), in the collection *Hadiqat al-sukhur* (Rock Garden) 1969.

In her collection *Yabqa al-bahr wa-l-sama'* (The Sea and Sky Remain) 1966, Nur Salman forgoes realism and narrative for a lyrical, poetic language based on confessional, confidential tones, bringing her stories closer to poetic reflections. In some stories, such as "al-Sa'a al-sabi'a" (Seven o'Clock), a celebratory tone gradually recedes to allow the female voice to express its rebellion against man's exploitation of woman.

Modernism and its exceptions

With the appearance of Layla Ba'labakki's collection, *Safinat hanan ila al-qamar* (A Spaceship of Tenderness to the Moon) 1963, the plot disappears and, with it, psychological judgment. The author distills time into moments of women's interior conversations with the self. In all the stories, a woman divulges her feelings, ideas, and opinions about a man bound to her in a relationship of love, friendship, or marriage.

Layla Ba'labakki's innovation in the collection is not only her creation of a modern form of women's narrative, but her modernization of male-female relationships. In the story, "Hadiqa saghira" (A Small Garden), the reader examines a woman's love for her husband—not because he is a husband, but because the woman/wife loves what is between them, which is informed or enlightened by another, more ambiguous relationship between the woman and another man. The woman does not express her love for the second man, but remembers him with fondness and longing. This second relationship allows for no hatred or jealousy, or anything that may intrude on the first relationship. The story suggests the possibility of a special, triangular relationship: a woman and two men, each of whom has a different kind of relationship to the woman. It presents love as rich and varied—a concept which the woman in the story seems to need. The ambiguity has several functions; most importantly, it puts the reader on the thin line separating pure sex from a relationship in which feelings swing between friendship and the intimacy of love.

As the modern structure of the Arabic short story took shape between the 1970s and 2000, women also gained a firmer foothold in the field. Lebanese women writers, like male writers and women writers from other

Arab countries, rebelled against the traditional story structure, trying to loosen it up by foregoing external psychological characterizations and letting characters express themselves freely, and by moving at will between the narrative past, present, and future, such that they collapsed into one and the time-honored chronology was broken. Time is distilled into the moment, which becomes the alchemy of life, as we shall see.

It should be noted that these modernist tendencies were not universal; not all women writers joined the trend, though most of them skillfully created rich, serious themes. Emily Nasrallah, for example, a novelist first and foremost, did not base her short stories in the immediate moment, but continued to stretch time out much as in her novels. However, she did bring something new to the short story in her collection, *al-Mar'a fi 17 qissa* (Women in 17 Stories) 1984.[50] Though dissimilar, the stories are tangentially related by a common mood. The collection tells the stories of seventeen women of various statuses and personalities, with different reactions and ways of handling the violence of male society. Even so, they form an integrated world that consecrates a particular image and a particular language that reveals something profound about women's status. At the same time, this fictional world aspires to its own aesthetic value, different from the prevailing values by which society continues to subjugate women.

In her collection, *Hibal al-hawa'* (Ropes of Air) 1991, Sunya Bayruti closely follows Nasrallah, addressing various aspects of women's reality in twenty-four stories. Women are mothers, but tradition and custom impose duties on them that exceed their energies; they are wives, and because of marriage, they squander their private lives; they are widows who mourn their widowhood and the lives they spent as anonymous beings next to their late husbands. Bayruti tends to compact narrative time with great craft in her last collection, *Madar al-lahza* (Circuit of the Moment) 1994. But in several stories in the collection, this tendency remains simply a technique that is not fully exploited to intensify time and enrich the discourse.

Rafif Fattuh is striking in her remarkable treatment of male-female relationships and her ability to make them signify on the structural level of the story itself. In her collection, *Tafasil saghira* (Little Details) 1980, she writes about men, making them the subjects of the story, but she is careful not to appear to be writing against them. Although she allows the feminine first person to speak, she does not let that voice appropriate them. Instead, narration shifts from the feminine first person to the third-person masculine to the first-person plural. This movement is matched by the sectional structure of the stories. A perfect example is in the story, "Chez Temporel," in which the author breaks down the boundaries between statements, casting doubt on their provenance. The author, the female, stands behind what the text says about the man, but the feminine first person declares, almost as a reflex, that she has no knowledge of the cause of the man's misery and, as such, is not responsible for his suicide.[51] The story refers to something beyond the relationship between a man and a woman, to a world in which things between men and women become merely small details and their common suffering refers to what is outside them, namely the war in Lebanon.

In the collection *Bayrut: al-aziqqa wa-l-matar* (Beirut: Alleys and Rain) 1979, written shortly before the war, Fattuh casts her critical eye on local and Arab reality. In the story, "al-'Ubur" (The Crossing) 1973, for example, she takes up the contradiction between Arab liberation and an oblivious Beirut society. In "al-Ghuraba' yabtasimun" (Strangers Smile) 1974 and "Mashhadan wa muhakama" (Two Scenes and a Trial) 1974, she observes national discord. In stories about women's emotions and loss, she links these sentiments with Lebanon's imbalances, as exemplified by the capital, Beirut. What appears clearly in this collection, the author cleverly tries to push into the background without totally eliding it in *Tafasil saghira*; instead of clarity and unambiguous meaning, she seeks to create a structure that uses brevity and absence to allude to more than one meaning.

More than one woman writer turned to public issues in this stage of the short story, and most were led to look for methods and languages that go beyond direct narrative. They were not all equally successful, and some of their stories remain simply attempts. Wisal Khalid, in her collection *Tadhkara li-matahat al-qarya* (A Ticket to the Village Maze) 1973, gives voice to nationalist concerns and rejects Western practices and our corresponding sense of inferiority, experimenting with an ironic, symbolic language. In the collection *Raqiq al-qarn al-'ishrin* (Twentieth-Century Slave) 1979, Najwa Qal'aji rails against the manifestations of a century whose achievements have harmed mankind, using symbolism and fantasy and drawing on religious stories and popular traditions. Su'ad al-As'ad wrote stories about poverty and racial discrimination, collected in *Ghadan sa'a'ud* (Tomorrow I Shall Return) 1983, using a reflective poetic language.

All of these attempts adopted an experimentalism that appeared in Raja' Ni'ma's collection, *al-Sura fi-l-hulm* (The Image in the Dream) 1979. In the story "al-Dukhul fi-l-sura" (Entering the Image) 1974, the author uses mythical allegory, making the sea a symbol of marriage and the whale a boat that carries a girl to her husband. In "Layla wa-l-dhi'b" (Layla and the Wolf) 1977, she attempts a multilayered story that allows her to use material from folktales, such as the story of the wolf and the three goats, to evoke an extensive historical memory in which women are the victims. Giving a twist to the fabled ancient romance of Layla and Qays, she writes a story in which Layla loves Qays, but Qays is busy managing tribal affairs and solving the tribe's problems.[52] In "al-Mutarada" (The Pursuit) 1972, an external monologue attributed to a brother who kills his sister intersects with a narrative of indirect discourse distinguished by its fast-paced rhythm, which mimics the brother's pursuit of his sister and the movement of flitting images that cross the girl's mind as she alternately waits for death and hopes for life.

Mature modernism

Hadiya Sa'id stands out here, occupying an important place among Arab short-story writers, both male and female, in Lebanon and the wider Arab world. In his analysis of her collection *Rahil* (Departure) 1989,[53] Edwar al-Kharrat considers her a writer who "tightly grips the reins of storytelling experience." He sees her maturity "represented in her treatment of modernist storytelling techniques," noting that signs of this maturity include "the variety of characters who quickly pass after a brief, illuminating light is shined on them" and her use of "minute details to bring a scene to life and her brief character outlines."[54] From 1981 to 1989, Hadiya Sa'id published four collections of short stories, all of which were written during the war, which explains the drama and pain of her worlds—the pain of the author, looking for a language, structures, and technical possibilities that can evoke the drama of reality and push perspectives, feelings, and endurances of the spirit into the world of writing.

In the story, "Laylatan" (Two Nights) from the collection *Rahil*, against the rhythms of a seemingly simplistic language, the reader discovers a world brimming with all the possible trauma and scars that the war of Beirut could possibly inflict on anyone who lived it. To achieve this, the author dexterously focuses on schizophrenia, pairing the narrator's suffering with the structure of the story. On the first night, the female narrator meets Mahmud, thinking he is Hazim. Rapidly, and with understated significance, the narrator presents a card containing an autobiographical snippet. It is only a few lines, but it alludes to her arrival from Tunisia, her job, and her meeting with Mahmud in the hotel lobby. It is enough to indicate her wretched condition upon her arrival to Beirut and her tremulous memory. On the second night when the man comes, she calls him Mahmud, while "Mahmud" tries to prove that he is Hazim. The confusion between Hazim and Mahmud deepens in the following scenes, not only for the narrator, but for the reader as well, because of the contradictory assertions in the dialogue. The mystery man hits the narrator, and the violence of the scene escalates, rendered in almost cinematic or dramatic form.[55] The man wants to prove the truth of his identity and she experiences bitterness, splintering, and dissonance. The fissure mirrors contradictions in the national identity, represented by the two faces of Hazim/Mahmud, a Palestinian, and the dissonance is embodied in the

Lebanese narrator's schizophrenia. Cracks appear between the self, the private, and the Lebanese on one hand and between the larger Arab polity on the other, an issue raised by the Palestinian presence in Lebanon and the relationship between this presence and the war.

Although Hadiya Sa'id focuses on public concerns and anxieties, they only appear in her stories through their particular effect on the human being. In the introduction he wrote to Sa'id's collection *Ya layl* (O Night) 1987, Ghalib Halasa remarks on this relationship between the public and private and how the author addresses it. In some stories in the collection, Halasa notes how Sa'id's ability to make references to the public reveals "a human condition: the human condition in the heart of oppression."[56] For example, in the story, "Lan ya'ti" (He Won't Come), a visitor expresses his sense of comfort in the narrator's dark, warm room, remarking, "This place is so intimate it takes me back to my childhood."[57] Halasa sees the room as the womb, and the visitor's sense of comfort alludes to the public violence waiting for him outside:

> The narrator, in her exhaustive quest to reconnect what was severed in exile, ultimately turns to myth, but in a spirit of hopelessness and futility. She does not believe in it, but she practices it just in case. The author manages to make familiar a ritual that is far removed from us and her and to communicate a profound religious sensibility through the use of an unfamiliar language.[58]

Hadiya Sa'id is a modernist pioneer. She is bold enough to combine seemingly incongruous techniques, which in her hands become original and inventive. In the story "Hal ra'ayt ma ra'ayt?" (Did You See What I Saw?), also in *Rahil*, fantasy is used to refer to the public sphere. The female narrator sees ghosts of a corpse she saw in a swimming pool, and she asks others if they saw what she did, as if what she sees is not the truth, but merely an image from the labyrinth of memory. But the narrator, and behind her the author, is not afraid of interrupting the course of the story and the present tense to drag in parts of her own autobiography. She puts them in brackets, as quick notations in a fantastic context. They do not explain the narrator's visions, but only accompany them, raising questions that the story does not presume to answer.

Like Hadiya Sa'id, the stories of Hoda Barakat also helped to further entrench modernism in the short story, but hers is modernism of a different kind, distinguished by an abundance of details and black, satirical language. Hoda Barakat began her literary life as a writer of short stories; her first published work was the collection *Za'irat* (Visitors) 1985, after which she began writing the novels for which she became justly renowned.

In *Za'irat*, Barakat groups her stories into small blocs which, despite the variety of subjects, are all dominated by a particularly female rhythm which makes them seem more like a panoramic view of women's daily, unchanging lives. The stories speak about the lives of women as if they are one life, one album with many photographs; they do not reveal different lives, but rather expose the tasks and concerns that become burdensome and repetitive with the daily passage of time. The title of one story, "Salwa fi tamrin wahid aw Salwa fi baytiha" (Salwa in One Drill, or Salwa at Home), is enough to lay Salwa's life bare: it is one routine inside the home. Its effect on Salwa is to make her obsessed with cleanliness: "She shuts the door on the emptiness of the apartment and feels enormously self-confident; she is the lone knight on a field of chaos, which looms like an unshakeable fate."[59]

The reader can easily discern the author's critical view of Salwa's self-confidence. It is a critique accompanied by satire, even black humor. Salwa "has nightmares in which she sees only filth, very many types of very terrible filth, that leave her, even after she wakes, filled with a panic that grips the bottom of her stomach and pulls up."[60] It is as if Salwa's femininity is being stripped from her, like the life that has been stripped from her. The equation frightens Salwa because she wants her femininity, but not at the expense of her life.

After the Lebanese civil war, Hanan al-Shaykh, known first and foremost as a novelist, published her second collection of short stories, *Aknus al-shams 'an al-sutuh (I Sweep the Sun off Rooftops)* 1994.[61] The world of the stories is largely a woman's world. In some of them time stretches out, as if in a novel, to encompass women in more than one guise. For example, the stories speak of 'A'isha, a Moroccan in London; Aunt Samiya, an Egyptian; Ingrid, a Dane in Sana'a; and the Yemeni woman Qut al-Qulub, who other women believe has turned a man into a billy goat. The stories talk about the magic potions the women give her and the written amulets they pass to her "under cover of darkness"; about a woman whose husband betrays her, but who tells him, "My misery led me to you"; about women's fear of what they read about in the afterlife, ". . . women who were burned, whose tongues dangled down to their breasts, because they said to their husbands, Divorce me, without cause." The author indicates that the latter quote was taken from *al-Isra' wa-l-mi'raj*, the story of Muhammad's ascent to the seven heavens.[62]

Hanan al-Shaykh skillfully binds the psychological interior to the social exterior, giving rise to paradoxes in the process. 'A'isha the Moroccan, for example, is said by all to have been Anglicized, but her home in London remains Moroccan in its furnishings and scents ("Aknus al-shams 'an al-sutuh"). Ingrid the Dane, who represents Western civilization and is a product of its modernity, says about Yemen: "This was paradise."[63] The same backwardness of which Mahyub, a Yemeni, complains reassures Ingrid. These paradoxes in behavior, civilization, and social surroundings allude to acculturation and its relation to identity; they speak of a world of women with rich, diverse relationships to men and the world.

In addition to Hanan al-Shaykh, Renée al-Hayik's collection, *Burtrayh li-l-nisyan* (A Portrait of Forgetting) 1994, is also noteworthy. The stories give voice to an anxiety that does not spring directly from the war, but from existence itself, as if the war has turned existence into a state of hopelessness and loneliness or as if the lives people lived during the war were not their lives, but merely a trick of time. In "Yaqzatan" (Two Awakenings), a man thinks, "He didn't know how he had passed forty without noticing. He hadn't been conscious of it, as if he were in a long coma."[64] He sees a youthful girl who makes him realize—he, the forty-year-old man—the meaning of time and the truth of death.

Several general remarks can be made about the foregoing survey of the short story. Firstly, short-story writing has been characterized by a diversity of styles and an attempt to shake loose familiar forms. Secondly, women writers in Lebanon, particularly during and after the war, preferred the novel over the short story, and many short-story writers, despite their success, began to turn to novels. Although we cannot claim to know the reason, we can surmise that a person writing in a time of war and from the experience of having lived the war might find in the novel the kind of imaginative space that is unavailable in the short story, given the constraints of concentration, brevity, and immediacy. Thirdly, the desire of male Lebanese novelists to escape the bonds of the traditional novel are matched by the desire of some women writers during and after the war, when they wrote texts that defy generic classification. These are texts of artifice, sometimes beautiful in their deceptiveness. I would mention, for example, 'Alawiya Subh's *Nawm al-ayyam* (The Sleep of Days) 1986 and Sabah Zouein's *al-Bayt al-ma'il wa-l-waqt wa-l-judran* (The Slanting House and Time and the Walls) 1995. I believe the desire to escape restrictions is one factor among several that explains women writers' remarkable engagement with prose poetry in the 1980s and even more so in the 1990s, as we shall see in the third and final section of this survey.

Poetry
Introduction
Despite their small number, the women pioneers who helped to establish the Arabic novel also contributed to the revival of Arabic poetry. These include Egyptian poet 'A'isha Taymur (1840–1902) and Lebanese poet Warda al-Yaziji (1838–1924). The return to this poetic heritage marked the beginning of its renaissance and a means to modernize it. The Arabic poetic tradition represents the home of the language itself and the Arabs'

creative wealth. Those who stammered out poetry in their breasts had to return to it and study its rules of prosody, its rhetorical language, and its formal poetic structure. Such study was not available to women, imprisoned in the home and deprived of education, and when the doors of education were opened to them, it was initially in foreign mission schools that were uninterested in the Arabic poetic tradition and its fundamentals.

The pioneers

Warda al-Yaziji had advantages not given to others. She grew up in a house of learning and literature, and her father, Shaykh Nasif al-Yaziji, fostered her talents, teaching her the basics of language and instructing her in poetry and its various forms. The day she recited poetry, her male contemporaries were shocked and awed that this poetry, which constituted a light in the midst of the age's widespread ignorance, came from a girl. It was widely assumed that poetry was not in the nature or competence of women.

Warda al-Yaziji's poetry revived the traditions and aesthetics of Arabic poetry in its golden age. This was characteristic of the era as a whole and, indeed, a prerequisite for the renaissance of Arabic poetry. Literary history, however, makes note of the poet Mahmud Sami al-Barudi (1838–1904), but neglects al-Yaziji, who was his contemporary.

Warda al-Yaziji wrote in the classical *qasida* form and composed her poetic images in accordance with the classical aesthetic that paired verbal similarity with striking differences in meaning.[65] She composed panegyric and elegiac poems, as well as encomiums, greetings, and epistolary poems addressed to writers of the age.[66] Her love poetry is disguised, and instead of a lover, she addresses a woman friend. In a lecture on Warda al-Yaziji and her poetry, Mayy Ziyada noted:

> If she informs us that the lines are composed about a female friend, we realize that they contain things addressed to a male friend, but she has hidden them behind the veil of the feminine pronoun to conform to social rules that require a woman to conceal her emotions, even in poetry.[67]

Most of al-Yaziji's poems are elegiac. Modern critics have found fault with this and considered it a weakness. Perhaps the best response is that of Mayy Ziyada, who, following Edgar Allen Poe, notes, "The poetic genius is, at heart, melancholic. The dispositions that realize and embrace this, approach this genius with their sympathy for grief and sorrow."[68] With this, Mayy Ziyada reassessed not only women's poetry, but elegiac poetry in general, which traditional Arabic criticism did, and still does, value less than other forms of poetry due to its association with women and their feminine sensibilities, which stands at odds with *fuhula*, or poetic virility. Although most of Warda al-Yaziji's poetry is elegiac, I believe it constitutes the best poetry of the age. Free of mannerism or affectation, it flows with captivating images whose meanings stir the depths of the human heart, universal and timeless.

After the pioneers

After the pioneering age in Lebanon, women contributed little to the poetic renaissance for the next half-century, from the early 1900s to the early 1960s. Their absence is particularly remarkable considering the emergence of several prominent Lebanese male poets, both inside the country and abroad, including Rashid Salim al-Khuri, known as "the village poet" (1887–1984), Rashid Ayyub (1872–1941), Bishara al-Khuri (1885–1968), Fawzi al-Ma'luf (1899–1930), Salah Labki (1906–1955), Khalil Mutran (1872–1949), Iliya Abu Madi (1890–1957), Ilyas Abu Shabaka (1903–1947), Mikha'il Na'ima (1889–1988), and Gibran Kahlil Gibran (1883–1931).

I do not believe the reason for women's absence is to be found in women themselves, but in the cultural and experiential barriers that prevented them from opening the door to poetic experimentation. Perhaps the most important of these barriers is the fact that Arabic poetry, as noted above, has strong ties to the Arabic classical tradition, with its rules and structural and aesthetic requirements. Until the appearance of the prose poem, poetry of the twentieth-century renaissance complied with these rules and all the poetic traditions, which required a thorough knowledge of ancient prosody and a close familiarity with the culture of poetic language, which was completely divorced from everyday verbal expression. Poetry was entirely distinct from the narrative prose that nourished the short story and the novel and produced this new culture. Arabic poetry's grounding in the classical poetic tradition, with its strict rules and forms, is expressive of a link to a culture that women could not acquire, neither in school, nor in their social world. Initially, girls' schools in Lebanon were foreign schools, and these remained, without any real competition until the 1960s, the preferred place for the education of girls. These schools did not teach Arabic poetry and prosody. When national girls' schools later opened, they too did not include poetry and prosody in the curriculum, in contrast to boys' schools. Thus, we should not be surprised by the scarcity of female poets, or by the fact that the few who did emerge came out of homes with a culture of learning and poetry that nurtured their talents and compensated them for the deprivations of society.

Like Warda al-Yaziji, Lebanese poet Zahra al-Hurr (1917–2004) grew up in a home that fostered learning and poetry, as did other contemporary female poets like the Iraqi Nazik al-Mala'ika (1923–2007) and the Palestinian Fadwa Tuqan (1917–2003). Zahra al-Hurr once said in an interview, "I'm a poet by birth," alluding to the fact that the southern al-Hurr family produced many poets; its homes were filled with books, and cultural salons and poetry gatherings were popular. This environment gave her the basic knowledge on which her talent fed, while other women's talents went unnurtured. Nevertheless, Zahra al-Hurr, who wrote much of her poetry in the 1930s and the next four decades, had to wait until 1970 to find someone to help collect her poems and publish them in book form, in a collection significantly entitled *Qasa'id mansiya* (Forgotten Poems).[69]

The sense of confusion and anxiety that marks al-Hurr's romantic poetry does not mean she had no interest in the public social reality. She wrote more than one poem to commemorate national occasions, for example, expressing a revolutionary, anti-defeatist stance after the 1967 war and upholding Arab unity or decrying the communal bigotry of the Lebanese civil war. These poems posit peace as the equivalent of life, and love as poetry's gift to the homeland. Zahra al-Hurr also addressed the social condition of women and the cruelty of tradition and moral judgments. She sympathized with the prostitute and she critiqued divorce as a right given solely to men that left women and their children to an unknown, desperate fate. Her poetry was inspired by both Phoenician and Arab history. She revived major symbolic figures such as Cadmus, Adonis, Ashteroth, Abu Dharr al-Ghaffari, and al-Husayn ibn 'Ali, using a poetic, storytelling style. She was proud of her links to the south and the cultural and historical richness of Tyre, its major city.

In her conversation with nature, her language sheds the weight of traditional rhetoric that characterizes her occasional poetry. In poems about motherhood and love, her language approaches the freshness of speech, and her images are simpler and more transparent. Despite her observance of traditional prosody, she experimented with free verse, investing it with lighter rhythms that sent its images soaring.

Zahra al-Hurr was part of the same generation as Lebanese poets Fatima Rida (1903–1978) and Mayy Sa'ada (b. 1916), but she had the greatest presence and was most able to experiment and wander in the rich worlds of poetry.

More poetry by women

Starting in the 1960s, women began to engage in poetic experimentation, increasingly so in the late 1980s and particularly the 1990s. The relative explosion in women's poetry is attributable to the gains made by women in the preceding decades in education, culture, and social presence, as well as the heightened motivation to expression prompted by the Lebanese civil war. It is notable that women poets in these decades focused particularly on prose poetry.

The prose poem in Lebanon held out the possibility of renewing language and connecting it to a vernacular whose frame of reference—local, daily, lived experience—reinforced the independence of Lebanese identity, in a process known as the "Lebanonization" of language. In addition, women found prose poetry more suited to their historical relationship to speech, and at the same time, it compensated for the knowledge of prosody that was missing from their education.

Insaf al-A'war Mi'dad stands out among poets of the 1960s and 1970s for the distinctiveness of her poetic images, characterized by an aesthetic marked by profound, rich dimensions of meaning. At the forefront of these images are those expressing the current and historical condition of women. In one poem, woman has been cast out of the kingdom of time, ruled by the alpha, man. But women stand in the interstices to question the truth of this primacy and contemplate the slain female body, which shapes a question mark.[70] Women in Mi'dad's poetry destroy the prisons, and the wind and springs understand the banner of freedom they bear, suggesting that freedom has a strong link to nature:

Her scattered clothes,
Like dried out grass,
Cry above the rain,
Their tears evaporated by the sun.[71]

The discourse of most of her prose poems has feminine features whose meaning overcomes the familiar through their connotative potential and their associations with the universe and nature: "The sea strolls over my face."[72] "My blood is a festival for the sun."[73] For Mi'dad, this fusing of the feminine with nature is grounded in, firstly, women's unique experience of labor pains, which in her poetry become the "pain of roots." Woman, as the basis of existence and a condition for the continuity and renewal of life, is the root. Secondly, it is grounded in love, which in Mi'dad's poetry is a celebration of life in a moment of women's giving and tenderness. It is a naked moment shared by the trinity of woman, child, and man, but this trinity does not refer to the family, but to a sacred trinity found in the movement of the universe whose elements, according to the Druze faith, become one and give birth to the immortality of time.

Insaf al-A'war Mi'dad was able to invest her poetry with certain structural characteristics of the prose poem, most importantly organic unity, which, despite the poem's surface spontaneity, is the product of a conscious act to create an ordered structure for the poem. In the excerpt quoted above, the poem's rhythm is created internally by the parallel meanings more than by external verbal similarity, as in poetic prose.

We must note here that Lebanese women used poetic prose before the emergence of the prose poem.[74] In 1954, Idvik Juraydini Shaybub published her collection *Bawh* (Confession), followed in 1962 by a second collection. Rose Ghurayyib called the writing "poetic prose," remarking that the style was similar to "the style of the Gibranists and other masters of poetic prose."[75] What is remarkable in the poetic prose of Idvik Shaybub is her revelation of feelings of loss and loyalty for her beloved husband, whose memory she keeps alive by commemorating their own special places. Overall, the mode of expression used in the text is close to speech or storytelling; as such the texts are prose, but they derive their poeticity from the intensity of expression.

Poetic prose, whose ambiguity created poems that were neither classical odes nor free verse, was monopolized by several Lebanese women writers, particularly those with a grounding in Western culture. These include Hoda Adib, who was influenced by surrealist poetry. Her texts are awash with an ambiguity which Rose Ghurayyib considered evidence of "haphazardness and an extreme slide toward the chasms of surrealism."[76] Her poetry stands apart from the aesthetics of classical Arabic poetry, composed of musical linguistic constructions and meanings that stand in opposition to arbitrary ambiguity.

There is also Thérèse Aouad-Basbous,[77] whose language approaches a frenzy when she tries to create ambiguous, unfamiliar relationships between elements of existence, which she uses to express the sense of being under a heavy stone, a symbol of time. Finally, Mayy al-Rayhani's texts are also characterized by surrealist ambiguity based on futility and rejection. In her own words, she says she wants "existence as it is in a dream, in the imagination, at the height of irrationality."[78] In her second collection of poems, *Ismi siwaya* (My Name: Someone Else) 1974, the futility and rejection of reality become a wish for another world, a world whose freshness and newness create an equivalent of the feminine "I" and whose language is one that can express that "I." In destabilizing the language and breaking its rules, al-Rayhani tries to open the world of language onto something other than itself.

In the 1950s and 1960s, this destabilization of Arabic in Lebanese poetry sparked serious controversy and debate between those who clung to the essential Arab-ness of the language and those who worked to "Lebanonize" it. Some Lebanese female poets' attempts to break down the language intersect with their attempts to find a new language, liberated from traditional male rhetoric, as we will see when we discuss Sabah Zouein.

Only Sikna al-'Abd Allah, who, like Zahra al-Hurr, came from a family in the south that produced several poets, tried to innovate within the bounds of the inherited poetic tradition, writing free verse of the type pioneered by Nazik al-Mala'ika and Badr Shakir al-Sayyab. She published her first collection of poetry, *Mudhakkirat laji'a* (Memoirs of a Refugee), in 1969, but she only began to be noticed with the publication of her second collection, *Nihayat al-sada* (End of the Echo), in 1974. Sa'id 'Aql praised her skill and ambition and regretted the delay in publishing her poetry.[79] Noteworthy among Sikna al-'Abd Allah's poems are those that speak of a love, not for a husband, but for a lover who has left without excuse.

During the same phase, Basima Batuli published poems written in the classical mode in the collection, *Ma' al-hubb hatta al-mawt* (With Love until Death) 1978, as if she, too, was calling attention to the traditions of Arabic poetry and women's ability to appropriate its prosody. Basima Batuli continued to write classical poems even as prose poetry became the favorite form of Lebanese female poets. She published her second collection, *Mukallala bi-l-shawq* (Crowned with Desire), in 1996.[80] Her poems revolve around love as "the spark of existence," without which we cease to exist. For her, love is a companion of life, a condition and a passion that is difficult to tie down and eludes certainty. The poet refers to a mythical history in which the female was the sacred sex and a symbol of fertility.

In the mid-1980s, Huda Miqati published her first collection, *'Aba'at al-muslin* (Cloak of Muslin) 1985, in which love is manifested as a female trait that can reinvest relationships with men with a new beauty. Reminiscent of the *muwashshah* (Andalusian lyric poem) poets, most of Huda Miqati's poetry leans toward a sweet lyricism tinged with yearning and a longing to meet. The poems' meanings are for the most part familiar, but they derive their beauty from the quiet music of the rhythm and from the innocence and loftiness of love that infuse the images.[81]

Alice Sallum also sided with love in her poetry, equating it with peace. Her age—the time of the Lebanese civil war—needed, as she said, "poetry to prepare us for love."[82] Most of her poems, which observe the constraints of meter while varying the rhyme, deal with the suffering women endure from male violence and the prevailing moral system. Like the Romantic poets, Alice Sallum's poetry gives voice to loneliness, frustration, and a yearning for the unknown. Realizing the illusory nature of life, it tends toward dreams, the contemplation of time, and melancholy.[83]

In the 1990s, 'Inaya Jabir stands out. The prose poem in Jabir's hands is remarkable for its ability to express the female subject's difficult experience of love, in its deepest, richest sense. 'Inaya Jabir's short poems, their densely expressive images, and their occasional abrupt beauty seem cryptic, but to those who listen while freeing themselves from the din of the mundane and the clarity of similarity, they reveal the interior spaces of their worlds. Such a reading unearths an anxiety that captures a history of the hardship that love creates for women, and contains fates folded into a time that does not heed women's lamentations.

In 'Inaya Jabir's poems, the moment is emblematic of a feminine way of approaching time; time is concentrated, creating a moment heavy with angst:

Onward to midnight, I say.
We cleave to the midpoint, not after, not before.[84]

This angst is embodied in poetic images whose meanings coincide and intertwine, as if they are a history in which the female subject implodes from the intensity of the invisible. Taking her poetry over several collections as a whole, this angst appears to be two-pronged: it is the torment of time as a fleeting moment and the torment of a lover's departure. For 'Inaya Jabir, love is a troubling existential state ultimately related to a profound sense of time: a love that ends with the inevitable departure.[85] She scatters her interior self as poetry as a declaration of her feminine difference.

Love seen from a different perspective is also a theme in most of Maryam Shuqayr Abu Jawda's poems. In these poems, a highly musical rhythm combines with a tone of strength to defend women and their right to love. The poet praises love and considers it her hostage. As such, she addresses the one she loves with self-confidence. She is not a woman whose beauty lies in her frailty, but "a woman of the age," a new woman whose glory is "my strength and my inkwell."[86]

Unlike these other poets of love, Maggie 'Awn limits her poems to love without addressing the suffering latent in the male view of the female. Her snippets of prose derive their poeticity from multivalent images in which love intersects with elements in the universe such as time, rain, and earth. The bold confessional tone of Maggie 'Awn's texts reaches a level of rapturous passion never seen before except in Idvik Shaybub's poems for her late husband.

Maha Sultan's poems are also limited to love, but it is a love based on the contemplation of the movement of the universe and the relationship among its various elements: shadows draw the images of concrete things, silence is their language, and emptiness is their space for movement. It is the poetry of a fine-tuned sense of existence. The Beirut of the war also figures in Sultan's poems, and it is on the city and children that her poetry's melancholy hinges. Her poetry seems to takes refuge in a shadow that might evaporate into thin air.

In the same period, Sabah Zouein is also noteworthy. Like 'Inaya Jabir, she is preoccupied with making the female subject present through writing, but from a different perspective: the pursuit of a renewal of language. For Sabah Zouein, this search for renewal is focused on finding a form outside the perfect or complete form since, for her, perfection represents the death of speech. An incomplete form, or what she calls an imperfect form, is what allows women a different presence. The imperfection or flaw is her own choice because it is the inevitable result of writing outside the form. But the poet realizes that writing outside form does not exist; she thus alludes to the dilemma of writing both inside and outside form: "In the past I tried to attend to form; it was imperfection. This time, too, I tried to find form, but form killed me. So how does one write? How, outside the form, since outside of it does not exist?"[87]

In trying to break the constraints of form, Sabah Zouein writes poetry consisting of ruptured lines suggesting incomplete thoughts or meanings, which, on closer examination, seem to reverberate in an empty space, where poetic speech comes in the form of "blue ropes" that evoke ethereal distances. The lines are torn into bits, as if collecting them is impossible or as if they are merely signs of a life whose act of rebellion against gender constitutes its own dismemberment. Imperfection, or writing outside the perfect form, is a way of going beyond gender and all already-signified meanings. For the poet, it is neatness or emancipation from what the form signifies in its language. Imperfection in this sense is also the torment of a woman's existence in a world that denies her. This torment is a search that rejects a reversal of two sides of one equation or any form that is perfected with the addition of the feminine. To rebel against form, Sabah Zouein in some texts writes in free-standing, short, amputated lines without context:

Will I be able in the midst of destruction, and disappearance
like ashes in the skies?
It is necessary to step back a little.[88]

We must also take pause at Zouein's desire to escape "the treachery of the utterance" to realize that imperfection is not a search for a distinctly feminine form to counter the male form,[89] for such an opposition does not break the equation but simply changes the parties' location in it, and this role reversal does not go beyond gender to reach the human. It is a solution, but comes at the expense of one party to the equation.

Sabah Zouein wants writing to go beyond the gendered self by going beyond the form that produces it. Women leave the subjective for the act of writing itself, an act achieved by continuously rebelling against form. As such, writing for her is not "merely entering forms" but "entering a perpetual questioning."[90] For Zouein, woman rebels against descriptions that inscribe her in a gender by rebelling against form in her writing.

"She writes now," she says, as if she was not writing before, or as if she is "writing against writing,"[91] as Lina al-Tibi says. As the poet 'Abduh Wazin notes, "Sabah Zouein writes in an unstylistic style. Zouein has chosen a serious, bold game."[92]

What 'Abduh Wazin calls a "serious game" in fact refers to a school of poetry that aspires to renew the language, starting with the poet Unsi al-Hajj and including Shawqi Abu Shaqra. Sabah Zouein, whose poetry belongs to this school, has used the renewal of language to explore the issue of the feminine, but in her attempt to go beyond gender, she suggests an identity that goes beyond her starting point, the Lebanonization of language, to a more general human level. Yet, if Zouein aspires to a world based upon a particularity that denies itself—that is, on a linguistic particularity (Lebanese) that denies being Arabic—she actually aspires to a world that carries a paradox in itself. The paradox is found in the simultaneous renewal and denial of the language—that is, between the renewal of Arabic as a language and the denial of it for the sake of an impossibility: that of the Lebanese dialect as a language.

Nada al-Hajj creates a poetic language characterized by a prose-like simplicity and spiritual gentleness that give her texts a special flavor. With their prose-like nature, the texts constitute a moving recital or hymn to feelings of divine, sacred love whose language is poetry and whose spaces are wide open country. The poet's voice trembles with this love, expressing its ability, like Christ, to suffice with less.[93] In her second collection, *Anamil al-ruh* (Fingertips of the Spirit) 1994, the tone of her poetic voice is raised a register, as if the addressee has become a human being and she no longer needs him. But the poet soon gives voice to the suffering of an imposed, unchosen loneliness:

> A loneliness without choice,
> A loneliness of death, a loneliness of self-realization.[94]

Though she realizes that "the entire world is alone" and that loneliness is "the loneliness of faith in God, which suffices in its own sad self,"[95] in her last collection, *Rihlat al-zill* (Journey of the Shadow) 1999, Nada al-Hajj returns to the celebration of love, giving, and the word. She again turns to prayer "in the space of poetry."[96] Her poetry evokes that of her father, Unsi al-Hajj, and she manages to endow it with a distinctly Christian identity.

Rima Rahbani writes poetry in the Lebanese dialect that touches the depths of the human self, connecting the difficulty of one's relationship to the self with this earthly world. She writes about grief, fear, and loss, about ideas that resemble clouds, but not one another, about the truth that we hear in the darkness, about the passage of time in life, about the draining of color from all things and the way they fall into similarity, about places and life that goes on, and about faces that suddenly appear and are no more: the face of her father, 'Asi, whom she does not call by name. She is afraid that his scent will flee from the room as she tires of waiting for him for so long. Her poetry is written in a conversational style that is eminently readable. She expresses her feelings on life, people, and time, and when she talks about the particular and the subjective, it reaches the level of the universal. When reading her works, the Lebanese dialect is no longer an obstacle.

Some of the poetry written by women in the last two decades of the twentieth century deals with the war in Lebanon and the ensuing hardships. Notable among this poetry is that by painter Layla 'Assaf, distinguished by the poet's delicate, soft voice and a visual language based on the scene. A good example is her poem "Dajjat anfasihim" (The Clamor of their Breaths). As in a painting, the poem is built on a tableau taken from daily life, in all its innocence and ordinariness, of young men in a café.[97] The aesthetics of the poem are not based on figurative language, as is usually the case in Arabic poetry, but on the composition of the scene, which in its simplicity manages to convey the depth of the tragedy—the tragedy of innocent deaths in war time.

Miray Saba has also written noteworthy poetry about the tragedy of the Lebanese war: short passages that come together to weave, simply and subtly, the suffering of the self suspended between two places. Poet Wadi' Sa'ada calls her "the poet of the two horizons," referring to the horizon of the setting sun in Australia, where Saba lives, and the horizon of the rising sun in Lebanon. In both, he says, "the same torturous dance of the dust of the two places is played out: the dust of the ruined city (Beirut) and the dust of the other city (Sydney)."[98] Both places are lost—Beirut in death and Sydney in its formlessness. The poet feels for the loss of Beirut, expressed as a black cloud of dust that dances in front of those who once had dreams, but whose eyes now hold only "the remnants of a life that died there."[99]

Several general remarks can be made based on the foregoing survey of poetry. To begin, Lebanese women's turn to poetry is linked to two factors: the difficulty of learning the rules of classical Arabic prosody and the emergence of the prose poem in the 1950s. These two factors help explain women's preference for prose poetry and their relative latecomer status to the poetic experience. Love is an overwhelming theme in women's poetry. Although it may be a broad theme of poetry in general, women poets' preoccupation with love is characterized by loyalty and sincerity to the lover. It approaches love from a humanist perspective that rejects the master-slave relationship and refuses to accept traditional moral systems that make a woman—simply because she is a woman—less valuable than a man and deprive her of the right to a free existence and just life. Women are striving for a distinctive poetic discourse that breaks the masculinity of form and language without falling into masculine oppositions and dichotomies.

These remarks are particular to poetry, but more general observations can be made about women's writing as a whole. Overall, women writers favor prose, which is clearly related to the relatively recent advent of women's writing and their experience in real life. This partially explains why, particularly in the early stages, women were more receptive to the short story and the novel than to poetry with its traditional rhetoric. For the most part, women have limited themselves to familiar literary genres, or at least those most prominent in Arabic literature: the novel, the short story, and poetry. Experiments in playwriting are rare, even extremely so, seen only in Zaynab Fawwaz's *al-Hawa wa-l-wafa'* (Love and Fidelity) 1893, Dunya Muruwwa's *al-Zawja al-ghaniya* (The Rich Wife) 1967, and Thérèse Aouad-Basbous's *al-Bakara* (The Pulley) 1973. Even considering the relative neglect of drama in Arabic literature as a whole, women's contributions have not carved out a special space.

The same can be said of Lebanese women's autobiography. The small corpus that exists more closely resembles writing about reality and its manifestations than expressions of the female interior self in its particularity and its stifled intimacy. Thus did 'Anbara Salam al-Khalidi write about Beirut and its condition, while Salma al-Sa'igh wrote about the social condition of women and their activities to liberate themselves and their country in the first half of the twentieth century. The memoirs of Widad al-Maqdisi Qurtas are closer to travel literature, although they go beyond the genre and the travel narrative to touch on the larger issue of Palestine. In her literary treatment of the issue, Qurtas, according to poet Etel Adnan, emerges as "a novelistic character from Greek tragedy."

In a later period Emily Nasrallah turned to autobiography in *Fi-l-bal* (On the Mind) 2000, which has the particularity and subjectivity of autobiography; similarly, Layla 'Ussayran in *Shara'it mulawwana min hayati* (Colored Ribbons from My Life) 1994 focuses on her personal hardships, starting with being orphaned as a child and her self-alienation. Nevertheless, the corpus of Lebanese women's autobiographical writing remains small, which is why I did not devote a particular section to it, but simply allude here to those texts that shed light on issues and circumstances discussed by the pioneers: the condition of society and women in it. Because of their efforts, these images and concerns have been preserved in our literary memory.

It must be noted that women's experience with autobiography does not differ from men's. Arabic literature in general has eschewed this type of writing, compensating with what we might call autobiographical novels.

The reason can be found in the boldness and naked emotion demanded by autobiography in speaking about the self,[100] for such boldness brings with it a responsibility that is not admitted by family bonds or traditional Arab social custom.[101] In other words, the reason can be found in social ethics and systems which stand in the way of free expression, repress the self, and make talk about the body taboo.

Notes

1 See Bint al-Shati' ['A'isha 'Abd al-Rahman], "al-Khansa'" in *Nawabigh al-fikr al-'Arabi* (Beirut: Dar al-Ma'arif, 1957), pp. 51–52.

2 'Anbara Salam al-Khalidi, *Jawla fi-l-dhikrayat bayn Lubnan wa Filistin* (Beirut: Dar al-Nahar, 1997, second edition), p. 9.

3 Mas'ud Dahir, "Bayrut wa tahaddiyat al-thaqafa al-'Arabiya al-tali'iya 'ala masharif al-qarn al-hadi wa-l-'ishrin," *al-Mada*, 28, 2, 2000, particularly p. 6.

4 'Anbara Salam al-Khalidi, p. 27.

5 Ibid., p. 117.

6 Salma al-Sa'igh, *Suwar wa dhikrayat* (Dar al-Hadara, 1964, second edition), p. 86. According to the author, this institute was later known as the Zahrat al-Ihsan school, p. 89.

7 'Anbara Salam al-Khalidi, p. 114.

8 Salma al-Sa'igh, *Suwar wa dhikrayat*, p. 150.

9 Ibid., pp. 126–27.

10 Zaynab Fawwaz, *Husn al-'awaqib*, edited by Fawziya Fawwaz (Beirut: Cultural Council for Southern Lebanon, 1984), p. 18, note 38, which refers to *al-Rasa'il al-Zaynabiya*, p. 193, under the title, "Men of the Future and Girls' Education."

11 Ibid., p. 17, note 38, which refers to *al-Rasa'il al-Zaynabiya*, p. 191, under the title, "A Synopsis of Women's Lives."

12 Mayy Ziyada, *al-Mu'allafat al-kamila*, collected and edited by Salma al-Haffar al-Kuzbari (Beirut: Nawfal Foundation, 1982), vol. 1 (*Kitab al-musawab*), p. 537.

13 Ibid., p. 543.

14 Ibid., *Kitab al-madd wa-l-jazr*, p. 404.

15 Ibid., p. 422.

16 Ibid., pp. 424–25.

17 Muhammad Yusuf Najm, *al-Qissa fi-l-adab al-'Arabi al-hadith 1870–1914* (Beirut: Dar al-Thaqafa, n.d., introduction dated 1966), pp. 9–10.

18 Labiba Hashim, *Qalb al-rajul* (Egypt: al-Ma'arif Press, n.d.), p. 1.

19 Ibid., p. 39.

20 Muhammad Yusuf Najm, *al-Qissa fi-l-adab*, p. 131.

21 Ibid., p. 80.

22 Ibid., p. 95.
23 Widad Sakakini, *Arwa bint al-khutub* (Cairo: Dar al-Fikr al-'Arabi, 1949), p. 51.
24 Salma al-Sa'igh, *Suwar wa dhikrayat*, pp. 77–78.
25 Layla Ba'labakki, *Ana ahya*. I am referring to the edition published by Dar Majallat Shi'r in 1963.
26 Layla Ba'labakki, *Ana ahya*, p. 312.
27 Layla Ba'labakki, *al-Aliha al-mamsukha* (Beirut: Dar Majallat Shi'r, 1960), p. 126.
28 Muna Jabbur, *Fatah tafiha* (Beirut: Maktabat al-Hayat, 1962).
29 Muna Jabbur, *al-Ghirban wa-l-musuh al-bayda'* (Beirut: Maktabat al-Hayat, 1966).
30 Ibid., pp. 11, 26, and 162.
31 Ibid., p. 336.
32 Ibid., p. 292.
33 Emily Nasrallah, *Tuyur Aylul* (Beirut: Nawfal Foundation, 1986, sixth edition).
34 Ibid., p. 92.
35 Layla 'Ussayran, *Lan namut ghadan*. I am referring to the edition published by Dar al-Nahda, 1991.
36 Layla 'Ussayran, *Lan namut ghadan*, p. 163.
37 Hanan al-Shaykh, *Hikayat Zahra* (Beirut: Dar al-Adab, 1989, second edition); translated into English as *The Story of Zahra*, trans. by Peter Ford (London: Quartet Books, 1991).
38 Hanan al-Shaykh, *Hikayat Zahra*, p. 59.
39 Hoda Barakat, *Hajar al-dahk* (Beirut: Dar Riyad al-Rayyis, 1990); translated into English as *The Stone of Laughter*, trans. by Sophie Bennett (Reading: Garnet Publishing, 1994).
40 Hoda Barakat, *Hajar al-dahk*, pp. 17, 18, 39, and *Stone of Laughter*, pp. 14, 38.
41 Hoda Barakat, *Hajar al-dahk*, p. 250, and *Stone of Laughter*, p. 231.
42 Edwar al-Kharrat, *Aswat al-hadatha* (Beirut: Dar al-Adab, 1999), p. 35.
43 Najwa Barakat, *Hayat wa alam Hamad ibn Silana* (Beirut: Dar al-Adab, 1995), p. 14.
44 Ibid., p. 122.
45 Ibid., p. 71.
46 Muhammad Yusuf Najm considers the novels written by the pioneers to be stories, including the historical novels of Jurji Zaydan. See *al-Qissa fi-l-adab al-'Arabi al-hadith*.
47 An example is the story, "Sunnatuha al-jadida," written in 1914. See *Mikha'il Na'ima: al-majmu'a al-kamila* (Beirut: Dar al-'Ilm li-l-Malayin, 1970), vol. 2, p. 323.
48 Suhayl Idris, *al-Qissa fi Lubnan* (Institute for International Arab Studies, Arab League, 1957), p. 41.
49 Widad Sakakini, *Bayn al-Nil wa-l-nakhil* (Cairo: Dar al-Fikr al-'Arabi, 1947), introduction.
50 Some of the stories in the collection were written in 1979.

51 Rafif Fattuh, *Tafasil saghira* (Beirut: Arab Institute for Research and Publishing, 1980), p. 7.

52 Raja' Ni'ma, *al-Sura fi-l-hulm* (Beirut: Dar al-Afaq al-Jadida, 1979).

53 Hadiya Sa'id, *Rahil* (Rabat: African Arab Publishers, 1989).

54 Edwar al-Kharrat, in Hadiya Sa'id, *Rahil* (Rabat: African Arab Publishers), pp. 12–13.

55 In 1979, Hadiya Sa'id received first prize in the Gulf Television Festival for a dramatized documentary screenplay, "Tahqiq 'an Umm Hamid."

56 Hadiya Sa'id, *Ya layl* (Beirut: Dar al-Sadaqa Printing and Publishing, 1987), introduction, p. 11.

57 Ibid., p. 11.

58 Ibid., pp. 11–12.

59 Hoda Barakat, *Za'irat* (Beirut: Dar al-Matbu'at al-Sharqiya, 1985), p. 9.

60 Ibid., p. 12.

61 *Aknus al-shams 'an al-sutuh* was published in Beirut by Dar al-Adab, 1994 and translated into English as *I Sweep the Sun off Rooftops*, trans. by Catherine Cobham (London: Bloomsbury Publishing, 2002).

62 Hanan al-Shaykh, "Qut al-Qulub," in *Aknus al-shams*, p. 132, and "Qut al-Qulub," in *I Sweep the Sun*, p. 210. Hanan al-Shaykh, "Sahat al-katastruf," in *Aknus al-shams*, p. 60, and "Place de la Catastrophe," in *I Sweep the Sun*, p. 89. Hanan al-Shaykh, "Sarif aqlam al-mala'ika," in *Aknus al-shams*, p. 162, and "The Scratching of Angels' Pens," in *I Sweep the Sun*, p. 193.

63 Hanan al-Shaykh, "La budd min San'a'," in *Aknus al-shams*, p. 71, and "The Land of Dreams" in *I Sweep the Sun*, p. 55.

64 Renée al-Hayik, *Burtrayh li-l-nisyan* (Beirut: Arab Cultural Center, 1994), p. 99.

65 See her collection, p. 37.

66 Mayy Ziyada, *al-Mu'allafat al-kamila*, p. 203.

67 Ibid., p. 211.

68 Ibid., p. 223.

69 *Qasa'id mansiya* (Beirut: private publishing distributed by Dar al-Tali'a, 1970), p. 20.

70 Ihsaf al-A'war Widad, "Fi mamlakat al-zaman," *Hiya al-ula huwwa al-awwal* (Beirut: Dar al-'Awda, 1972).

71 Ibid., "Insan yajtarr nafsah," pp. 44–45.

72 Ibid., "Wajh," p. 63.

73 Ibid., "al-Iqa' al-surakhi."

74 The emergence of the prose poem in Lebanon is linked to the publication of a poem by Syrian poet Muhammad al-Maghut in no. 5 of the journal, *Shi'r*, in the winter of 1958; the journal put out its first issue in the winter of 1957. The first serious theoretical underpinnings of the prose poem were laid out by the poet Adonis in an article published in *Shi'r*, no. 14, in the spring of 1960. This poetic form became entrenched only in later decades.

75 Rose Ghurayyib, *Nasamat wa a'asir fi-l-shi'r al-nisa'i al-'Arabi al-mu'asir* (Beirut: Arab Institute for Research and Publishing, 1980), p. 398.

76 Ibid., p. 260.

77 Her collection, *Ana wa-l-hajar*, was published in 1993, but the texts were written from 1974 to 1980, which led us to include them in this period.
78 *Hafr 'ala-l-ayyam* (Beirut: Dar al-Rayhani, 1969), p. 56.
79 In the introduction to *Nihayat al-sada* (Beirut: Dar al-Kitab al-Lubnani, 1974), p. 9.
80 *Mukallala bi-l-shawq* (Beirut: privately published, 1996), p. 12.
81 *'Aba'at al-muslin* (Beirut: Dar al-Nahda, 1985), p. 10.
82 In the introduction to her collection, *La li-l-harb na'm li-l-hubb* (Beirut: Arab Institute for Research and Publishing, 1985), p. 7.
83 Alice Sallum, *Arhal ma'a al-zaman* (Beirut: Arab Institute for Research and Publishing, 1987), p. 133.
84 'Inaya Jabir, *Taqs al-zalam* (Beirut: Maryam Publications, 1994), p. 46.
85 Ibid., p. 111.
86 *Hadiqat Maryam* (Beirut: Maryam Publications, 1998), pp. 30, 21.
87 *Ma zal al-waqt da'i'an* (Cologne: al-Jamal Publications, 1993), p. 6, "Ila Khalid."
88 Sabah Zouein, *Ma zal al-waqt da'i'an*, p. 16.
89 Ibid., p. 16.
90 *Kama law anna khalalan, aw fi khalal al-makan* (Harisa, Lebanon: Antun Ilyas al-Shamali Press, 1988), p. 10.
91 Sabah Zouein, *Ma zal al-waqt da'i'an*, p. 13.
92 Sabah Zouein, *Bad'an min aw rubbama* (Beirut: Dar Amwaj, 1998), back cover.
93 Nada al-Hajj, *Salah fi-l-rih* (Beirut: Dar al-Nahar, 1988), p. 24.
94 Nada al-Hajj, *Anamil al-ruh* (Beirut: Dar al-Nahar, 1994), p. 60.
95 Ibid., p. 60.
96 Nada al-Hajj, *Rihlat al-zill* (Beirut: Dar al-Nahar, 1999), p. 14.
97 Layla 'Assaf, *Zill la yadhub* (Beirut: Dar al-Hamra', 1991), p. 79.
98 Miray Saba, *Raqsat al-ghubar* (Lebanon/Australia: al-Mukhtarat Publications, 1995), introduction.
99 Ibid., p. 11.
100 Yahya Ibrahim, *al-Sira al-dhatiya fi-l-adab al-'Arabi* (Beirut: Dar al-Nahda al-'Arabiya, 1974), pp. 11–12, where he discusses this lack of boldness: "Throughout the ages and up to the modern age, whatever they revealed about themselves, writers of autobiography in our Arabic literature did not reach the point at which they totally denuded the soul to disclose or confess something beyond the familiar."
101 For example, Hanna Mina talks of his sister's anger and rebuke of his novelistic autobiography, *Baqaya suwar*, because he spoke frankly about his father's drinking and the suffering it caused his mother and siblings. See Hanna Mina, *Hawajis fi-l-tajriba al-riwa'iya* (Beirut: Dar al-Adab, 1988), p. 103. Adonis has said that memoir "brings a responsibility to the author that he does not carry alone, and this is the problem; it is also borne by his family, his siblings, his relatives." See the interview with him in *al-Wasat*, no. 405, November 1, 1999.

2 Syria

Subhi Hadidi
Iman al-Qadi

The short story and poetry
Subhi Hadidi

Female literary pioneers in Syria, like Mary 'Ajami (1888–1965), Maryana Marrash (1848–1919), and Nazik al-'Abid Bayhum (1887– 1959) played an extremely important role in the struggle for women's emancipation in Syria and a no less significant role in the emancipation of men as well.[1] 'Ajami founded the magazine *al-'Arus* in 1910; the women's publication, the first of its kind, continued to appear despite Ottoman repression, which stood in stark contrast to the relative freedom of Egypt, for example. Her struggle for women was linked to the defense of Syrian men demanding their independence. Indeed, 'Ajami's stance on the martyrs of May 1916 was unique for a woman of that time. 'Ajami also adopted the cause of political prisoners much like contemporary human rights organizations, visiting prisons and publishing detailed exposés in the magazine about the desperate circumstances in detention centers and the mistreatment of detainees.[2] It is said that she demanded an interview with Jamal Pasha, the Ottoman tyrant who ruled Syria with iron, fire, and gallows, to ask for amnesty for detained nationalists. When he refused to meet her, she launched a vicious campaign in her magazine and so attacked him in poetry and prose articles, directly and indirectly, that people began to wonder how it was that the tyrant did not include her among the martyrs of al-Marja Square.

In Aleppo, Maryana Marrash established what would become one of the most important pulpits for women's voices: the literary club. She was the first Syrian female poet to take the decisive step of publishing a collection of poetry, having published several poems in the press. Most likely under the influence of her trip to France, where literary salons were widespread, Marrash in Aleppo inaugurated her literary salon, which was frequented by many male literary figures during the Ottoman period. The city's literary movement was invigorated as never before; here, too, Marrash was like Mayy Ziyada, indeed hers preceded Mayy's renowned salon in Cairo. 'Isa Fatuh relates the remarks of the prominent author Sami Kayyali about Marrash:

> The emergence of a woman writing in the press and composing poetry in this dark era was a significant event. Our recent history shows that it was rare for even men to read and write; her appearance in these dark nights was thus like a bright star in the center of the heavens.[3]

It is also significant that Marrash's collection of poetry, which contained elegiac and love poems, as well as ascetic and occasional verse, bore a title indicating full engagement with women's issues: *Bint fikr* (A Girl of Thought) 1893.

For her part, Nazik al-'Abid Bayhum did not only work against Turkish and French colonialism and establish the Red Star association, the predecessor of the Red Crescent, but went so far as to be directly involved in the Syrian Arab army. She took part in the famous battle of Maysalun, joined by the nationalist minister of defense, Yusuf al-'Azma, who died during the battle, allegedly in al-'Abid Bayhum's arms. It was no surprise, therefore (although it was unprecedented), that King Faysal I gave her the honorary rank of captain in the army.

Widad Sakakini (1913–1991), the fourth pioneer, is the author of the first narrative literary work by a woman that can truly be called a novel. Her *Arwa bint al-khutub* (Arwa, Daughter of Woe), published in 1949, was based on one pivotal issue—the social injustice experienced by a virtuous woman—and addressed several secondary issues as well. The novel takes the form of stories wandering between time and place. Arwa is a virtuous, submissive married woman satisfied with her life; her husband's brother makes advances to her while her husband is on a business trip. She rejects him and he accuses her of adultery. The judge passes on her the sentence of adultery: she is stoned and thrown out of Damascus. The rest of the novel's action progresses according to a traditional, set plot, which in scene after scene relates the persecution of Arwa until she obtains her final vengeance on this type of man, or perhaps all men. In fact, Sakakini did not flinch from her stance and even unapologetically justified it:

It pains me that in the 1940s, even as Arab women are shaking off their lethargy, learning and advancing, entering universities, and contributing to society, they are still accused of inadequacy and backwardness. Our most prominent writers blame them for every fault . . . So I took it upon myself to write a novel that would show women's ability to bear pain, which [these male writers] unjustly and falsely claim is antithetical to them. *Arwa bint al-khutub* is a portrait of the slander and abasement that women have endured. In it I gave expression to how women have suffered from the curse of men and how their dignity survives in their adherence to piety.[4]

Sakakini published five collections of short stories, the most prominent being *Maraya al-nas* (People's Mirrors) in 1945, a pioneering work in the history of Syrian women's short-story writing. In 1947, she published a second novel, *al-Hubb al-muharram* (Forbidden Love), as well as many articles and essays addressing various issues, from women's causes to literary criticism to translation.

Sociologically, the rise of narrative prose in the novel and the short story was indicative of the rise of a new middle class and the appropriation of many Western cultural values. Shakib al-Jabiri's *Naham* (Greed) 1937, for example, considered the first Syrian novel, observes a series of purely Western milieus and could have been written in France. The new middle class tried to reconcile local, feudal values with semi-liberal values (Sakakini's *Arwa bint al-khutub* is the best example). Discussing this imitation or reconciliation, Shakir Mustafa says:

> The modern story was born with modern Syrian society and was similarly influenced by Western civilization and its intellectual and social values. Its form, content, and social significance were all new. The ancient tradition, despite its charm, originality, and authenticity, could not meet the needs of the developing bourgeoisie and was unsuited to them. It gave expression to a medieval society, a life grounded in types of governance and economic and social relations that had begun to disappear. Social evolution was leading elsewhere.[5]

But poetry continued to be present during the period of the national liberation struggle against French colonialism, which eventually led to the evacuation of the French and the declaration of independence in 1946. It continued to be felt in later periods as well, after the Second World War, although the number of women poets, compared to male poets or even women prose and journalistic writers, was very small, for reasons that are still not sufficiently explained. As one might expect, women's poetry was dominated by burning issues of the day and the traditional poetic form, as is the case with the poems of Tal'at al-Rifa'i, for example.

While romantic and sentimental subjects were not completely absent, it is perhaps Nadiya Nassar (1938–1994) who leads the small group of female poets who distanced themselves somewhat from the grandstanding of those days—filled, in fact, with events that encouraged such grandstanding—and turned to matters of the heart and started writing love poetry. Following Nassar, Nabiha Haddad (1920–1977) chose sentimental and love poetry. She was the fifth of five prominent women poets from the province of Latakia that included 'Aziza Harun, Hind Harun, Fatima Haddad, and Maha Gharib. Her first collection, *Azhar laylak* (Lilacs) 1970, reflects, in addition to the themes of traditional love poetry, a keen sensitivity in its ability to touch the feelings of women and their longing for a conversational, healthy relationship with, first of all, the self and secondly with the Other, men. Hiyam Nuwaylati (1932–1977) combined the sentimental and the national. Over her nine collections of poetry, the concerns of women merge with national concerns. In *Zawabi' al-ashwaq* (Cyclones of Passion) 1974, *Washm 'ala-l-hawa'* (Love Tattoo) 1974, and *Kayf tammahi al-ab'ad* (How Distances Are Erased) 1974, she gives expression to local nationalism as well as wider Arab nationalism. Nuwaylati is distinctive among other Syrian women poets in her special sense of the meaning of life, which is light, sweet, elegant, sensitive, and occasionally ironic.

In this period, Syrian literature, both prose and poetry, was shaped by sociopolitical conditions, which had a profound impact on literary genres and forms (the novel, the short story, the traditional ode, free verse, and the prose poem), as well as their themes (national, social, psychological, the existential, alienation, and freedom) and certain intellectual and artistic trends (realism, expressionism, naturalism, existentialism, *littérature engagée*, and art for art's sake). On the political front, after the evacuation of the French, Syria fell into a complex web of external political pressures seeking to draw the country into the alliances of the time (the Common Defense, the Baghdad Pact, the Dulles Doctrine, the Eisenhower Doctrine). After the Palestinian *nakba* of 1948, the Arab–Israeli conflict also exercised a pull on political life, and several political parties emerged that represented various segments of Syrian society (the People's Party, the National Party, the Communist Party, the Ba'th Party). Parliamentary life flourished for three years after independence, followed by Husni al-Za'im's coup in 1949 and four later coups, which destabilized Syria. Nevertheless, we should note that from 1954 until the union with Egypt in 1958, Syria was blessed with an advanced, parliamentary democracy unlike any in the Arab world. Indeed, Syria was the first Arab country to apply real democracy with the rotation of power through free elections that allowed the representatives of various parties to reach the legislature. On the cultural front, Syria was home to a plethora of newspapers and magazines, political, cultural, and social, issued daily, weekly, and monthly. Twenty-five dailies were published in Syria in 1949, along with twelve bimonthlies, and three monthlies.[6] During this time, there was greater literary cross-fertilization between Syria and Egypt, Iraq, and the Levant, as well as a flourishing translation movement into Arabic. In addition, we witness the formation of literary and cultural salons and associations, particularly the League of Syrian Writers, which firmly established progressive and engaged literature and instituted a Marxist front in Syrian literature, which was needed to complete its aesthetic and intellectual heterogeneity.

Given these conditions, it is no wonder that the 1950s witnessed a qualitative leap in Syrian literature. Many Syrian women writers contributed to this vital development: Ulfat Idilbi, Salma al-Haffar al-Kuzbari, In'am Musalima, Mallaha al-Khani, Khadija al-Jarrah al-Nashawati (Umm 'Isam), and Munawwar Fawwal in narrative prose, and 'Afifa al-Hisni, Fatima Bidaywi, and Mahat Farah al-Khuri in poetry. It was not long before the appearance of major works in Syrian women's literature by Collette Khuri, Nadiya Khust, Ghada Samman, and Hamidah Nana in the novel and the short story, and Saniya Salih, Huda Numani, 'A'isha al-Arna'ut, and Da'd Haddad in poetry.

Today the student of contemporary Syrian literature can count hundreds of Syrian women writing novels, short stories, and poetry, who, with varying degrees of skill, produce texts that put Syrian literature on par with other Arabic literatures. They continue to write thanks to individual talent, hard work, practice, and polishing, but none of them, particularly the later generation of poets (the likes of Marah Biqa'i, Layla Maqdisi, Rula Hasan, Randa Qawshaha, and Fadiya Ghaybur) or novelists and short-story writers (Diya' al-Qasabji, Hayfa' Bitar, Wisal Samir, Umayma al-Khush, Jumana Taha, Hanan Darwish, and Rabab Hilal), can forget that they write mature, well-crafted texts thanks to the decades-long achievements of the pioneers: Mary 'Ajami, Maryana Marrash, and Nazik al-'Abid Bayhum.

*

Short-story writers can be divided into four generations: the generation of the 1950s (Ulfat Idilbi and Salma al-Haffar al-Kuzbari), the generation of the 1960s and 1970s (Qamar Kilani, Collette Khuri, Nadiya Khust, Dalal Hatim, Layla Saya Salim, and Ghada Samman), the mid-1970s and early 1980s generation (Mary Rashu, Malak Hajj 'Ubayd, and Nahla al-Susu), and the 1990s generation (Mayya al-Rahbi, Anisa 'Abbud, and Sahar Sulayman).

Although the logic of this division is based on several common characteristics, stylistic and historical, that do allow us to speak of 'generations' of writers, by the same logic, we must preserve some degree of relativity with these categories, and perhaps any type of categorization into generations, styles, or trends. The advantage of the division is that it allows the student a better analytical perspective, despite the methodological constraints it might involve. Nevertheless, it is safe to say that these categories are not merely chronological, but correspond to differences in form and content as well. Indeed, behind the chronological division, we can discern four major artistic categories.

The first generation represents the formative, pioneering years in which a woman merely signing a short story was enough, in and of itself, to indicate that she had conquered a field that was for so long a male monopoly. In the hands of women, the short story began to take on special characteristics—"pioneering" is simply the clearest and most obvious term to encompass it. This period also saw the establishment of form and the development of tools and themes, particularly in Idilbi's first collection, *Qisas Shamiya* (Damascene Stories) 1954, which is the clearest example of experimentation with language and artistic techniques.

The story, "Ya nayim wahhid Allah" (O Sleeper, Say That God Is One),[7] is not only one of the best short stories by Ulfat Idilbi, but is a pioneering example of women's short stories in Syria and in the wider Arab world. In fact, it is difficult when reading the story not to be reminded of the extraordinary *Qandil Umm Hashim (The Lamp of Umm Hashim)* 1944, by the prominent Egyptian author, Yahya Haqqi, with its focus on East and West. From its first lines, Idilbi confronts the reader with this paradox:

> He was from the heart of the East, from one of the oldest cities in the world, from the immortal Damascus. She was from the new world, from the country of skyscrapers and mechanical men. When they married, each carried inside a wish at odds with the other.

She wants to visit the East, "the land of the prophets," "the cradle of revelation," and "the wellspring of myths." He is dazzled by her country's civilization and wants to stay there.

When the Eastern man tells his Western wife about the traditions of Ramadan—the physical and spiritual fast, the ritual of the dawn crier with his drum and well-known call "O sleeper, remember God, O sleeper, say that God is One," the assembly of the family in the ancient Levantine home before the cannon that announces the breaking of the fast, Laylat al-Qadr "better than a thousand months," the religious dance of the Mehlevi Sufi order—she falls in love with these seductive Eastern charms and prods her husband to take her to Damascus. Pleased at the news that their son and his wife will soon be visiting Damascus, his family, to celebrate the visit and give the foreign wife a warm welcome, demolishes the old house to make way for another "in the modern style." Idilbi only reveals this violent, totally surprising dramatic climax in the last few lines of the story, building the narrative tension. She constructs the elements of the story slowly, with skillful deliberation and astonishing patience, without hinting at the final shock, laden with cultural and emotional significance.

Idilbi is a pioneer in form, language, and narrative technique, even when the subject of the story is traditional and romantic and despite what some call the "photographic realism" of her style. Her pioneering efforts should be better appreciated in comparison with what Salma al-Haffar al-Kuzbari does in her stories. Al-Kuzbari is more concerned with simile, metaphor, allusion, and various types of figurative language than she is with the technique of crafting the story and its artistic components. Her stories are drawn from the tales of grandmothers, from those simple plots that tell a moral lesson or strange tale, or depict traditional lives and social settings. The usually simple story structure starts with the introduction and development of the characters, then begins to spin the story in a direct, linear narrative thread. In "Umm al-banat" (The Mother of Girls), we hear the story of Fathiya, who has spent twelve years of her married life "never having lived a day but that she was pregnant or nursing." But in the hope of a boy she continues to give birth, until her body is debilitated and her heart weakens. She dies giving birth to her eighth child: a boy, Yasin. Then we move to another story about another woman who only bears girls, although this woman is smarter than Fathiya. She does not bear the burden herself, but lays it at the feet of her husband and decides to leave him. "You're a man who only has girls, while your sisters give birth to boys," she tells him.

Linking the two stories requires no special technique from al-Kuzbari. She leaves it to the grandmother to narrate the second story, after Hajja Wahiba narrated the first. She also lets the grandmother make the moral commentary on the two stories: "How great is the difference between these two women, Hajja. I wish Fathiya, your neighbor, would have possessed a small bit of the cunning and cleverness of this woman."

For women authors of the second generation, life was not so simple, neither in its external, social contexts, nor in its internal emotional and psychological dimensions, which are more complex and ambiguous. This, in turn, explains the great multiplicity of styles of women writers of this generation; indeed, it can seem that each writer, with her variations on subject matter, form, and technique, represents an independent school.

In the story, "al-Sarab" (The Mirage),[8] Qamar Kilani takes as her subject a unique, strange moment in which a woman dies after drinking a glass of water. "My death was haphazard, absurd, and almost ridiculously artless," the character says. "I drank a glass of water . . . It was as transparent and brilliant as a tear . . . It was so clean and limpid that it looked as if it had just fallen from the sky, but I died because I drank it." It is an absurd moment not only because Kilani is wholly unconcerned with explaining death by a glass of water, but also because the long recollection that ensues has nothing to do with the glass of water or the death. It follows no dramatic thread and develops only disparate bits and pieces of events from a long, disorderly past.

The story constitutes a leap in the stylistics of the Syrian short story. This is not one of Ulfat Idilbi's symbolic, realistic tales or a didactic story by al-Kuzbari. Rather, here the reader stands before the non-story and a stream-of-consciousness narrative borrowed from the novel. The narrative is broken, interrupted, and mostly interior; it is rare that external events intervene to shape it or direct its course. "Am I really dead?" asks the narrator, right before closing the long, meandering flow of remembrance with this heavy existential conclusion:

> The smoke is like thick black dust . . . the rain, sticky dark blood . . . The face becomes disfigured shards. I hear my last yelp . . . I hear it . . . clearly . . . I fall into a teardrop, a big teardrop and everything fades from my eyes . . . even the mirage. Life in its entirety seems a mirage in a mirage."

In contrast, Collette Khuri does tell a story, but in the end it is only an intense symbolic confrontation between Lina, who assumes the guise of a weak, ignoble mouse, and the black, green-eyed, glass cat she bought for her home. In this form, she wages her final battle with Tarif, the man she loved and lost to another woman. "I plucked your flower," he says. "I inhaled your essence and so you expired . . . Spring doesn't remember the withered flowers." "Dabab akhdar" (Green Fog),[9] like other stories by Collette Khuri, is an example of that type of women's literature that is immersed in the female psyche, defending women's right to love, life, and dignity, and occasionally excessive in its protest and in its elevation of the female narcissistic wound to the level of the general and universal. Khuri once said, "Since I always felt the need to express what was welling up inside me . . . the need to protest, the need to scream . . . and since I didn't want to scream with a knife, I screamed with my fingers and became a writer!!!"[10] (The exclamation marks are in the original.)

In "al-Wahida" (Alone),[11] Nadiya Khust also turns to the female, assigning her the task of first-person narration. In captivating, poetic language, she describes the landscape of changing seasons and the passage of time, alternating lushness with stark bareness, speaking about the imminence of death, the power of fate, and the need to survive and withstand:

> She pulled herself up straight, to stand like the names of alleys and the names of cities, in the name of memory, to stand in the name of coming eras. There is no one to hear her today, but she waits for the patient ones who have not yet appeared. She will wait for them like the ascetics who fled to the desert, the prophets who hid in the caves, the rebels who crossed the wasteland.

Nadiya Khust's female is not like that of Collette Khuri. They have wholly different concerns, and their perspectives on women's place in the universe are not only different, but contradictory. The reader of "al-Wahida" is convinced that Khust is talking about a woman of flesh and blood until the last few lines, when it turns out that she is speaking of a woman-tree. The tree decides to wage a battle for survival against the woodcutter, the axe, and the saw, responding to a call summoning her to survive in her place: "You still have a memory! Take refuge in it! Stay where you are."

This is not the traditional symbolic game in which a human being is portrayed as an animal, plant, or inanimate object in order to convey some moral lesson. Nor is it an attempt to flee from the direct, obvious symbol to a more ambiguous one. Rather it is an intelligent attempt to expand the concept of the feminine in a way that highlights its universality and so makes it represent questions of existence and non-existence, in addition to the feminine's well-known significations of fertility, growth, and giving. Khust's lone female figure, a testament to the right to survival, seems stronger and more human than Khuri's woman, who willingly goes to the man in her game of cat and mouse. It matters not that the first is a tree and the second is a real, flesh-and-blood woman. Indeed, Khust's achievement lies precisely in this substitution: she makes the feminine the locus of the universal, which encompasses both humans and trees.

Dalal Hatim, probably influenced by her long involvement in children's literature, writes a story of the dialogic relationship between a woman and her sparrow, locked up in a cage, and how the sparrow refuses the woman's offer of freedom, which only confirms what the woman has grasped that very instant: "It's no use . . . I was drawing from you the courage to flee from my cage as well . . . It seems we've made our own bars. We've grown accustomed to them and cannot live outside of them." "Zaynab wa-l-layl" (Zaynab and the Night) is not a parable or a throwback to the tradition of making a point using the logic of the bird or man's relationship to other beings.[12] Dalal Hatim does not draw a parable or a lesson, but attempts to represent the other side of women's relationships with an impossible kind of freedom. It represents that type of temporary escape that ultimately leads to further enslavement, if not to death. Zaynab wants to be like the bird which frees itself from the cage, but she quickly realizes that she is, in fact, already like the bird, for whom freedom is useless because its wings can no longer be used to fly. As the bird climbs the steps to its cage, Zaynab turns out the light and again drowns in the details of her home: her cage.

The bird in Layla Saya Salim's story performs the opposite function. It pecks on a lonely woman's window, singing heavy songs of bitterness, grief, submission, and longing, but ultimately, it brings the woman back to life, to "the heart of the world." This is the eponymous return of the story's title "al-Isti'ada" (The Return).[13] It is the return of the life force after a long hiatus in "a slippery, shaky world" that has no features save "the clouds of the old world and its silence." This is the return of a woman whom "distant ages have made a primitive woman who speaks of her sadness in tears." But she has not lost the sense and sensibility of interacting with "the scent of the wet earth, intoxicated by water, flashing with the joy of new life."

Salim also has extensive experience in children's literature. In "al-Isti'ada" she treats the adult reader like a child reader, presenting the miracle of the bird who creates life in the breast of the woman without being forced to convince the adult reader of the logic of this turn from desperation to hope. She does not wholly ignore the adult reader, but gives her a warm, densely poetic language and divides the already short story into independent passages that are nevertheless cohesive. It is perhaps one of the greatest losses to the Syrian short story that Layla Saya Salim has written very little for adults compared to her more than ten collections of works in children's literature.

In her early stories, Ghada Samman plumbed the depths of the female psyche, observing its most minute emotions and senses, through a dialogue with the self that also weaves in elements from the outside world, for example in "Magharat al-nusur" (The Eagles' Caves),[14] always with a strong desire to efface the distinctions between the female interior world and the objective outside world, which is often characterized by male hegemony, sometimes positive and at others negative. Samman's early style relies on interior monologues, intense emotional description, and the division of the scene into successive fast-paced segments. This style later changed, as did the subjects of Samman's stories and the poeticity of her narrative language.

The writers of the third generation—Mary Rashu, Malak Hajj 'Ubayd, and Nahla al-Susu—follow the traditions of the second generation to varying degrees. There is no clearly identifiable stylistic break. Mindful of the aforementioned reservations about the strategy of generational categories, we find many similarities in the writings of the 1970s and 1980s, a result of the prevalence of the same sensibility, similar social conditions, and the fact that writers of the second generation continued to produce short stories in this period as well.

In "Qawanin rahn al-qana'at" (Rules Bound by Convictions),[15] Mary Rashu observes the evolution of a female attorney, first through the cases she defends and secondly through the social significance of these individual cases. Nor does she neglect the woman's interior self between one case and the next. Nothing really happens in the story, for Rashu is not interested in building an event; rather her artistic concern centers on a fast-paced, flowing language and in arranging a large number of actions all narrated in the present tense, as if everything in the past and perhaps the future has been suspended and collapsed into one form: the present. There is a special charm in her subtle ability to simultaneously diffuse and intensify the emotional crux, then release it in bursts of multivalent meanings without taking time to catch her breath or even separate one sentence from another.

A social critique is also apparent in "Habibati Luma" (My Love Luma),[16] with the difference that Malak Hajj 'Ubayd does not manage the conflict of the story on both the emotional and social level, but on a much simpler and more powerful level. Young Luma fails to take first place in a music competition, not because her violin performance does not deserve it, but because the winner had to be Usama, the son of an official who "has a bodyguard and a car, and whose son Usama can win despite his poor playing." This sentence is put on the tongue of Luma, while her mother, the narrator, is stunned by this show of stinging critical consciousness. At the end of the story, the reader is not much surprised to find that Luma has given up music for good and has not touched a violin since that day. We are a bit surprised, however, when Malak Hajj 'Ubayd tries to save the situation at the end, noting that Usama failed at the final qualifying rounds in the capital and so will not represent his country at the world festival. In fact, these correctives are present in many of Hajj 'Ubayd's short stories, but they do not weaken the moral and critical force of each story.

Nahla al-Susu was one of the most promising names in the Syrian short story, and it is unfortunate that she stopped writing stories to take up writing for television and radio serials. "Araq sabahi" (My Sleepless Morning) is a fine example that reflects many of al-Susu's stylistic achievements in the short story:[17] a partial or complete absence of direct action, a plethora of consequences, an intense emotional recollection, an immersion in transient details, subjective dialogue, a thin dramatic thread that is usually pursued through the relationship with an ambiguous Other, and a great degree of poetry in language and scene. Usually these elements come together in her stories to craft one concrete moment, often nightmarish, always momentous, and alternately absurd, tangibly realistic, or abstract and figurative.

It should go without saying that the representatives chosen here for the current generation of women short-story writers—Mayya al-Rahbi, Anisa 'Abbud, and Sahar Sulayman—do not at all encapsulate the great variety of styles and subjects in the contemporary short story. There are dozens of other names that represent the mid- and late 1990s. I have chosen three stories because, in some form or another, they portray women in three guises: the real woman, the allegorical woman, and the archetypal woman.

In "Yawm fi hayat ustadha jami'iya" (A Day in the Life of a University Professor),[18] Mayya al-Rahbi compares the public life of a female university professor (with her students and colleagues she is severe, formal, and respectable) with her behavior when she goes home and closes the door on herself (where her daytime respectability is totally overturned, as she dances, guffaws, dresses up, and reads cheap gossip magazines). Al-Rahbi does this only to lead the reader to a final conclusion, totally human at heart, although it does not follow the classic feminist line that upholds a woman's strength no matter what the conditions. The conclusion is that the woman who is strong by day may be lonely, weak, and afraid at night. The professor's day ends like this:

> From the dark balcony off the kitchen, it looked to her like dancing ghosts wanted to leap inside. She rushed headlong into her bed, almost wanting to die of fright. She plunged into bed, enveloping herself and curling up. She covered her head with the blanket, curled up more tightly, calmed down and slept.

Anisa 'Abbud gives the reader an allegorical woman, using, like Nadiya Khust, the symbol of the tree. "Shajarat al-shatt" (The Tree on the Beach) is the neighbor of the proud sea,[19] the refuge of lovers, the hope of those who dream of a cure for rheumatism, the envy of those disappointed with life. Mahmud belongs to the third group; at the encouragement of the pasha, he volunteers to cut down the tree for its precious wood, which can be used to make a throne and a royal assembly table. With a zealous hysteria, he takes part in cutting the tree's blessed limbs after the pasha's saws prove incapable of the job. The tree finally falls, but on the head of Mahmud, the tree's old friend, who is now greedy for the pasha's reward.

Anisa 'Abbud's parable is straightforward, its symbolism not at all complex; one might even see it as naive. But the parable is not excessively symbolic or melodramatic. The balance between the natural and the figurative symbol ultimately serves the story, giving it a pliability of meaning and a peculiar poetic quality, which is further shored up by the nature of the symbols used (the tree, the sea, the interrelation of man and plant) and language brimming with figurative tropes and imagination:

> The tears flowed down its broken limbs as they tried to cut the trunk . . . They could not. The tree's hip was wounded and broke into small pieces. The tree wept and the sea was silent. The waves moved slowly. They heard the tree's moans, its wails that filled the vast expanse like strong gusts of wind.

Sahar Sulayman chooses the prototypical woman, or what anthropological criticism calls the "archetype," when, in the present, and on the tongue of a contemporary woman, she recalls a relationship between Harun al-Rashid and one of his slave girls. "Qa' al-bi'r" (The Bottom of the Well),[20] seeks to set loose the archetypal woman who spans time and place using the bold hypothesis that the immortal link between man and woman is a state of constant, eternal search for one another, whatever the circumstances of their original meeting, even a meeting between a sultan and a slave. Sulayman cannot avoid a slight bias to the woman, especially since privileging the slave girl's subjection over the sultan's tyranny is morally justified. But her sympathy is subtle and intelligent, and she constantly reminds the reader of the ephemeral nature of power and insists that the real eternal is what brought the sultan and the slave girl together in a primitive, raw relationship between man and woman. The ancient-contemporary slave girl says,

> I moved from city to city and palace to palace. The years passed and you, Harun al-Rashid, were with me. I slept with you, dreamed between your arms, and when my volcanoes erupted, I looked for your ringless fingers to pick up my cinders and rain down ice on my contours. Then I would cool off and give in to sleep . . .

*

Compared to women's short stories, poetry by Syrian women is much less complicated in terms of topics addressed, styles, and forms, and much easier to categorize generationally. With the exception of 'Aziza Harun, 'Afifa al-Hisni, and Ibtisam al-Samadi (all of whom write free verse), prose poetry is dominant in the works of Saniya Salih, Huda Numani, Da'd Haddad, 'A'isha al-Arna'ut, Lina al-Tibi, Salwa al-Na'imi, Maram al-Misri, and Hala Muhammad. In fact, Syrian women poets are no different from the overwhelming majority of Arab women poets in their preference for the prose poem, for various reasons, aesthetic, social, and intellectual.

Syrian women's poetry is directly linked to the act of emancipation—an act which I am convinced is linked to all women's literature, whether in countries dominated by traditional, conventional cultures or in those whose culture operates in a more open, liberal space. Without going into the details of the various schools of feminist criticism, this is a result of women's social status relative to men and uneven power relations in various fields, be they political, cultural, economic, social, or legal. Lines written by a female poet in the United States are no less emancipatory than lines written by an Arab woman poet, although the special merit of the latter must be recognized because she wages the battle for liberation in much more difficult circumstances that require greater determination, perseverance, and resistance.

Perhaps an examination of the most common themes in the poems of Syrian women poets—and, in fact, most Arab women poets—is the best way to get a sense of this act of liberation in its various guises and forms, which seem to correspond, intersect, and meet randomly only to ultimately create a harmonious landscape, one that is dialectical in the differences and similarities among poets and pulsing in its expression of the complex emotional structures of the woman poet. Briefly put, and given the limits of this analysis, there are three broad, universal concepts that constitute the major existential concerns in Syrian women's poetry: the body, language, and place.

As women poets throw off their bonds in pursuit of emancipation, the body is not the locus or object of sensual or material desire; that is, it is not the body in the sexual or bestial sense. It is simultaneously the locus of the self and its place of exile. As such, the self cannot be liberated and escape its exile unless the body is transformed into a speaking text instead of remaining simply a mass of flesh and organs. The woman poet's liberation from the body as a thing subjugated to fulfill animal desires is, at the same time, a liberation of the self from a series of psychological, social, cultural, and aesthetic conditions.

But the body is language, and the language of the female poet is not simply about using different words in the dictionary, which may accurately be said to have been masculine for a long period. Rather, language for the female poet is participating in the creation of meaning, carving out what might be seen as the woman's share of meaning in words, terms, and concepts. Language here is a demand for a wholesale reformulation of women's human experience—this time, from the female perspective—and a demand to make this new formulation a tool for a dialogue with men and perhaps with the entire outside world. This is because the other language—in some sense, the male language—is the primary language of the system from which the female poet seeks to free herself through the act of writing poetry. It is also a tool of oppression and its universalization, perhaps the most able to penetrate the depths of the self and fetter one's senses, perspectives, and dreams. This dominant language can become a heavy restraint that not only obstructs liberation, but transforms meaning into a linguistic prison and speech into silence.

Language is also a way for the woman poet to open up to her self, with the language of the self, instead of contending with the outside world in languages that cannot be separated from the dominant systems of oppression. The poem may be one of the most exalted forms of conversation between the female poet and her self, taking place far from restraints, prohibitions, and taboos, be they tangible or abstract. Finally, language is a means by which the female poet transforms her opening on to the self into a collective voice that speaks beyond simply personal concerns. It may be able to reconcile the self with the outside world, such that the self becomes—or aspires to become—the voice of others. Lina al-Tibi writes:

> I am my life's hoe.
> Like a lone gardener, I tend a forsaken land, my land.
> I spring up like thoughtless grass,
> And again I weed myself out.
> I carry my hoe, my heavy life.
> I go where I do not wish
> To plow another land, gardens that are not mine[21]

The body, whether as the essence of the self or transformed into language, cannot exist except in a place and as part of a place. I do not believe that most poems reflect a certain place as much as they lean toward the 'non-place' or the 'absolute place.' It is a figurative, imaginary space, a hypothetical site that witnesses the give-and-take dialectic between the body and language. In turn, it is a third material for the act of writing and the act of emancipation. It is not a physical landscape or a natural topography, but a complex web of the interactions of the self, history, and language. It is more like a lost paradise, seen as the incubator of the sense of alienation, oppression, or loss. In turn, it is an inseparable part of the profound motivation for liberation. Happily, Syrian women poets have evinced a subtle maturity in their treatment of place in the context of emancipation. They have not given in to the temptation to stigmatize it or see it as a prison, a wasteland, or a labyrinth, nor have they fallen prey to Orientalist generalizations that portray it as a veil that hides women or a tent that conceals romantic rendezvous.

Since our space here does not allow a more detailed treatment of the experience of each poet in this reference guide, it must suffice if I can only allude to several other general characteristics of contemporary poetry written by Syrian women. First of all, these poems are not forced to use masks. In general, the poet is the speaking voice in the poem, who appears as she is, unmasked. Or perhaps it can be said that she clings to one, universal mask, which might be the other face of woman aware of her unique place in the universe and in her relationship with man. As Salwa al-Naʿimi says:

> How can you want me to take off the mask of eternity,
> Though it is I
> Who have seen
> All roads, prostrated to me
> And the sun and the moon, to me?[22]

Women's poetry rarely takes refuge in myth and symbolism, as if the poet is saying that her subjects are innately symbolic or perhaps that she is in no need of symbolism. The poems of ʿAʾisha al-Arnaʾut, for example, are brimming with symbolic language and with elements that evoke myth, but the poems achieve their balance on other levels that are more seductive and magical than simply straightforward myth.

Syrian women poets do not play the role of the victim, nor do they rebel just for the sake of rebellion. They rarely take a nihilistic attitude to life and existence. This observation pertains even in those poems in which romanticism is dominant, like the poems of ʿAziza Harun and ʿAfifa al-Hisni.

Women in women's poetry are not the object of existential pain, moralizing, or love, whether Platonic or sensual. Usually the subject of love privileges an emotional balance between man and woman. This is especially true in the poetry of Maram al-Misri (despite her sensual bent) and Hala Muhammad (regardless of the prevalence of self-revelation).

Oftentimes Syrian women poets obscure their personal voice through the use of the masculine second-person singular. This achieves two goals at once: it establishes a dialogue with the male, as the interlocutor or Other, and it establishes a dialogue with the female subject as the first party of the conversation, or the 'other's other' so to speak. This is true for Huda Numani and Saniya Salih, for example.

In general the form of Syrian women's poetry is relatively stable, and it is rare for the reader to find sudden stylistic or experimental turns. The traditional *qasida* form has almost entirely disappeared, free verse has declined, and the prose poem has spread like fire in a haystack. However, this stability conceals a certain stagnation of expression that may quickly become a comfortable rigidity, especially when one recognizes that formally the Arabic prose poem has started to suffer from repetition and similarity. Its inner workings have been gradually exposed and some of its conventions have become purely linguistic exercises that any novice can effectively master. As such, women poets must be especially keen to develop forms, tools, and means of expression; otherwise the gulf will grow dangerously deeper between content and form, and meaning and structure.

The novel
Iman al-Qadi

In 1949, thirteen years after the first Syrian novel appeared, Widad Sakakini's *Arwa bint al-khutub* was published. It was followed by Salma al-Haffar al-Kuzbari's *Yawmiyat Hala* (Hala's Diary) 1950. Syrian women published five novels in the 1950s and sixteen in the 1960s; the numbers fell slightly, to thirteen, in the 1970s, while in the 1980s, twenty novels written by women appeared. The 1990s witnessed a leap in women's novelistic production to more than forty novels. This quantitative development is undoubtedly indicative of an evolution of Syrian society's view of women, as well as women's view of themselves and their role in society. At the same time, it is evidence that the social fears that prevent women from giving voice to their ideas and personal experiences have begun to crack.

But has the quantitative development of women's novels been accompanied by a concomitant artistic maturity? Can we say that women's novels now stand on firm ground? Have women writers become true partners in the novel, equal to their male counterparts in Syria and the wider Arab world? We will attempt to answer this question in the following pages through an analysis of the worlds of women novelists and how women approach the novel. We shall look closely at the psychological and intellectual characteristics of the female types that are usually the heroines of these novels and which give us a window on the writer's view of the self and the Other, whether that Other is men or society.

Women novelists have been divided into two generations for the purposes of this study: the founding generation of the 1950s and 1960s and the second generation of the following three decades.

The founding generation
The novels of all female writers of the first generation revolve around women as an issue and seek to portray women's reality in this period, but writers had different reasons for choosing the private female world, which was virtually cut off from the larger outside world. Some chose to write about women's lives simply because they wanted to write a novel in which

the protagonist was a woman, since they were more capable of representing the world of women given their own upbringing and experiences. These novels contain no special perspective on women's reality, but simply depict a series of events in which a woman is the main character. Their authors seem satisfied with the situation of women or, at least, they do not reject it entirely. This is the case for both of Salma al-Haffar al-Kuzbari's novels—*Yawmiyat Hala* and *'Aynan min Ishbiliya* (Eyes from Seville) 1965—and the two novels written by Amira al-Husni, *al-Azahir al-humr* (The Red Flowers) 1961 and *al-Qalb al-dhahabi* (The Golden Heart) 1963.

In contrast, the novels of other writers of this generation make central their rejection of women's reality and male traditions that elevate men's status and make women secondary, thus preventing them from exercising their human rights. Of course, the authors' stance and the way they approach this rejection differ. In *al-Hubb wa-l-wahl* (Love and Mud) 1963, In'am Musalima rejects the assumption that men should come first in women's lives by severing women's relationship with the Other and despising him. In contrast, in *Arwa bint al-khutub*, Widad Sakakini bitterly mocks men, portraying them as a mass of contradictions, treachery, and contempt who wallow in the desires of the flesh, while women become saints who flee from the body. The novels of Collette Khuri and Georgette Hannush condemn social traditions that limit women's freedom as individuals, demanding sexual freedom and the freedom to love.

Most women novelists of this period rebel against men's and society's erroneous conceptions of women, attributing them to men's arbitrary natures and the injustice of inhumane social relations. Widad Sakakini did not hide her objective in writing *Arwa bint al-khutub*, as noted in the excerpt quoted above in which she explains why she wrote the novel.[23]

The novel's protagonist, Arwa, is portrayed as a victim of men; her life is a series of male assaults, which she resists to preserve her chastity and her fidelity to her husband. The plot of the novel—which is melodramatic, contrived, and filled with fantastic coincidences—is constructed solely to condemn men and illustrate their cunning and treachery. The novel denies men the simplest virtues of religion and probity. They are led by their instincts, and because of this they do not fear committing the worst sins; they betray their brothers, deny goodness, exploit women and their loneliness, and deceive and betray them. After all the heroine's tribulations, the author highlights her innocence. Everyone who wronged her and mistreated her admits his error, and because she is pure and saintly, she forgives them, helps them, and heals them all of the illnesses that have afflicted them as a result of their injustices to her. Her husband, al-Nu'man, realizes his wife's chastity and purity and wants her to come back to him, but she asks the Lord to accept her soul because her sainthood refuses to repair the severed relationship between her and her husband. God answers her prayers and her spirit returns to its Maker while she is bowed in prayer, God having chosen her as pure and clean.

Sakakini's novel embodies a problematic stance toward men; it is a violent reaction growing out of the author's deep-seated sense of men's injustice and contempt for women. We rarely run up against this apoplectic attitude in the novels of other Syrian women. Georgette Hannush and Collette Khuri, for example, give the reader heroines who rebel against society's traditions, but they do not condemn men as individuals so explicitly and emotionally, although they do offer a critique of male treachery and disloyalty. Nevertheless, for their novels' female protagonists, men remain a goal, a refuge, and, given their superior strength, a support.

In *Dhahab ba'idan* (He Went Away) 1961 and *'Ashiqat habibi* (My Beloved's Lover) 1964, Georgette Hannush condemns social customs that prevent women from acting freely and honestly. The heroines of her two novels challenge tradition and seek to destroy it; their objective is individual happiness and enjoyment of life. Nawal is "a liberated girl who hates traditions . . . She wants to crush these traditions, even if she herself is crushed with them and her body parts scattered."[24] Layla wants to live as she pleases, and she cares nothing for people's opinions. When she falls in love, she is open about her relationship with her lover and sees nothing wrong with it. In her relationship, she makes no distinction between the heart and the body.

Rim, the protagonist of Collette Khuri's *Ayyam ma'ah* (Days with Him) 1959,[25] stands courageously against social tradition and customs to defend her convictions and what she believes is right. She rebels against her family's bourgeois traditions and seeks to prove herself as an individual. She wants to live a life freely chosen, not a life imposed on her. But this freedom, for her, is linked to a particular man, a lover who justifies her existence, consumes her, and encourages her to achieve her literary ambitions. Yet Rim has no problem with postponing these ambitions as long as she has a guiding, mentoring man. Indeed, she is willing to bury them and also renounce her freedom for the sake of her lover, without feeling cheated by denying her individual self and the ambitions she so ardently demands at the beginning of the novel: "My freedom does me no good. I would tear it apart and scatter it like feathers under the feet of a man I loved who felt affection for me."[26] The cornerstone of the rebellious Rim's life is a man, and her life is bound to him. When she finds him, she forgets poetry, art, and all her ambitions, and when she loses him, she remembers her literary talent and her desire to be different, as if her literary ambitions are held in reserve to compensate her for lost love.

Collette Khuri tries to offer the particular experience of a rebellious, ambitious girl who rejects the status quo. The protagonist has the potential to be a rich, complex fictional character who embodies the conflict between the past and the present, the individual and the collective, and reality and the possible, but the author imprisons the character in her relationship with Ziyad, a musician. For many, many pages, the reader encounters only Rim and Ziyad, and meetings and conversations with other characters all revolve around the relationship between the two. The author treats the relationship as an independent experience, divorced from other experiences and other dimensions in the two characters' lives. It thus seems isolated from its social surroundings, and the reader barely glimpses the social context, except through what other characters say about Rim and her courageousness.

In her later works, Collette Khuri continued to advocate individual freedom and to depict women's need for strong men, particularly in *Layla wahida* (One Night) 1961. In her most recent novel, however, *Ayyam ma'a al-ayyam* (Days with Days) 1979, she added another dimension to the concept of women's liberation.

Collette Khuri realized the value of work and independence in a woman's life, but she only reached this point in the 1980s. The heroine of her first novel, *Ayyam ma'ah*, works only to dispel the emptiness of her days and break the monotony of her life, like the heroines of many novels of the first generation. Rim's attitude is not substantially different from that of Nadida, the heroine of Widad Sakakini's *al-Hubb al-muharram*,[27] who does not see work as a means to complete her humanity and build an independent self, but only as a means to feed herself. If she finds a husband to care for her, there will no longer be any need to work: "If I married, I could do without this tiresome job."[28] For her, a husband is not merely the breadwinner, but the pillar of her life. If she loses him, she loses her inner calm and her spiritual balance. She forgets her education, and even despises it, because education has ruined her life by deflecting her from the normal path of women who only aspire to marriage and an indolent, monotonous life.

Clearly, the protagonist's confused, contradictory ideas about women and her submission to the status quo indicate that a new attitude about women has not yet taken root in the consciousness of the author—who, like most novelists of this period, speaks through her heroine—although in the early 1950s she sought to dispel false notions about women. In this novel, it is as if Sakakini is confirming the very accusations against women she earlier sought to refute.

Women novelists of the first generation proceed from a traditional view of women: they are weak and men are strong, the center of women's concerns and their lives. If women rebel, they rebel against the customs and traditions that prevent them from finding and meeting the great love. Even if a woman rebels against her man, she does not escape his closed circle, and if she educates herself or has literary ambitions, she keeps her distance from public or national concerns. She seems wholly isolated from the larger society's problems. Indeed public issues did not interest women novelists for more than two decades, for several reasons. First of all, writing women did not possess the necessary life experience to construct a good novel that could extract women from the realm of the self and enable them to create mature fictional worlds with a real social dimension. They were governed by traditions that deprived them of this experience: indeed, they measured their purity and probity by their distance from it. It was natural, then, for women writers to begin with the world they knew best: the world of the self, or a similar female world that they had no difficulty imagining and representing. When first embarking on a literary journey, any writer starts by talking about the most painful parts of the self, initially approaching the most problematic aspects of his or her private life and personal experience. In this period, the issue that most concerned women was women's personal deprivations in a society that did not recognize the most basic of their human rights. It is thus understandable that women writers sharpened their pencils to express this particular female concern.

The general political and intellectual climate in Syria encouraged an engagement with the individual problems of women and their demands for individual liberty, particularly the freedom to love. Syria in the 1950s had just obtained its independence, which fostered a turn to individual concerns after the primary public demand had been met. Syria opened up to both East and West, and its intellectuals became familiar with contemporary intellectual trends. Some were influenced by existentialism, which spread in France after the Second World War. The echoes of existentialism are clearly heard in the rebellion of the heroines of Georgette Hannush and Collette Khuri, who reject the authority of the father, the family, and society, upholding sexual freedom and the freedom of love.

Writers of the second generation
The social and political climate of the 1950s and most of the 1960s encouraged the dominance of women's concerns in the consciousness of Syrian women novelists. But the tragedy of the 1967 defeat, which created a new Arab reality and left deep fissures in the Arab intellect and psyche, prompted Syrian women novelists to change course. Novels of this period are no longer closed in on particularly women's concerns, but begin to marry women's issues to various topics of general concern. Women writers began to realize, to varying degrees, that the private could not be

separated from the public and that women could not stand at arm's length from the changes sweeping their country. National independence, still relatively young, was disrupted: Syrians lost the 1967 war and Israel occupied the Syrian Golan Heights (along with the Egyptian Sinai, the West Bank, and Gaza), without any real combat. The germ of fear, weakness, and defeat set in. As is normal in times of national crisis, the voice of the individual receded as the voice of the collective rose, with the larger collective pain taking precedence over individual pains. This does not mean that Syrian women novelists began to write about public issues directly after the 1967 defeat; several years passed before their perspectives matured. Certain events on the Syrian and Arab stage encouraged women to come out of their private, personal shells, most prominently the armed Palestinian resistance that emerged in 1968 and 1969; the October 1973 war, which instilled in the Arab psyche some of its lost confidence; and the Lebanese civil war, which had a notable impact on many Syrian women writers. Finally, there was the collapse of the Soviet Union—the Arabs' support in their conflict with Israel—and the signing of various unilateral peace treaties.

These political events were accompanied by social and economic change. Women were educated in increasing numbers, literacy efforts broadened, and an increasing awareness took root of the need for women to be educated and to work. The idea of women working was no longer rejected or held in contempt, but became a vital necessity dictated by the difficult economic conditions of the poor and middle classes. As women went out to work, new horizons opened in their relationships with men, including the new experience of male-female collegial relations. As a result, from the 1970s, female writers started offering some positive examples of the male character who supports women and recognizes their humanity and their important roles in life. These characters became slightly more common in the 1980s and 1990s, and the tone of recrimination receded. Women seemed more conscious of the movement of history and reality that shapes both women and men. This is an indication of an evolving awareness among both sexes, and it indicates that social and educational developments were narrowing the distance between the sexes and demolishing the artificial, historically determined distance between their worlds.

As a result of these factors, in the last three decades of the twentieth century the women's novel broke out of the shell of purely women's issues to engage public concerns and offer its own perspective on them. This does not mean, however, that it stopped addressing women's issues. Instead, it took both paths: the path of the individual, female subject and the path of the collective subject. Some women writers continued to focus on specifically women's issues, while others made connections between various aspects of society's pains and women's pain. Even those writers who most closely identified with the public did not stop giving voice to women's reality and their private, particular sufferings. However, these issues receded compared to others that were even more urgent; they were no longer the priority, and they were no longer addressed in complete isolation from other aspects of reality.

The image of women in novels of the second generation

In the novels of the second generation of writers, the reader notices the dominant presence of female characters. Women are usually the protagonists of the story while male characters often exist to complete the portrayal of the woman's world, shedding light on the writer's view of male-female relationships. Despite female characters' intellectual and ideological differences, and their varied class backgrounds and social experiences, we can identify three major female types in these novels: the stereotypical woman, the rebellious woman, and the new woman.

The stereotypical woman

The stereotypical woman of second-generation novels resembles the women of first-generation novels: she is subservient to a man and his will, whether she is highly educated, an intellectual, or a worker. For these female characters, men are their destiny and the center of their lives, and men are stronger, more aware, and more mature. If the man is unjust, persecutes, betrays, or abandons, the woman only issues defeated complaints, followed by forgiveness and, if he wishes, a humble return to him. If the female character has a job, it is conditional on his blessing and only within a strict framework that he defines. If she wants to work, it is not to achieve some human value, but to make money or fill the empty hours in which her husband is away. She adjusts to the whims of the man and sees her entire existence as dependent on him. The heroine of Ulfat Idilbi's *Dimashq ya basmat al-huzn (Damascus Bitter Sweet)* 1980, for example, is a smart, ambitious woman who, in response to the wishes of her revolutionary lover, takes part in the first demonstration to decry French colonialism in which Syrian women took part. She then abandons the national struggle, turns in on herself, refuses to return to school, and announces her withdrawal from social life. She decides to commit suicide when her parents die; her lover is already dead: her brother had him murdered to prevent his sister from breaking with the family's bourgeois traditions by marrying the son of a baker. The protagonist sees her continued existence as a betrayal of her lover; with him gone, so is her reason to live.

If an educated, cultured character sees her life as dependent on that of a man and makes her life revolve around him, it is no wonder we find illiterate or semi-literate characters clinging to the virtue of spousal obedience that verges on saintly veneration. The mother of the heroine in *Zayna* (Zayna) 1990, by Wisal Samir, gives her daughter advice that has been passed down to traditional women throughout the ages: "We learned in our lives not to resist the husband, not to wrong him even if he wrongs us. The husband, Wafa', is a little god."[29]

The rebellious woman
In novels of the last three decades of the twentieth century, the rebellious female character continued to appear, rejecting everything imposed on her and rising up against social conventions that restrict women, confine them to second-class status, deprive them of freedom, and allow men to impose their authority, persecute, or exploit them. The forms of women's rejection vary. Some of them impetuously and fruitlessly rebel against the authority of the father and class tradition, while others rebel against the authority of the husband and still others reject all institutions of authority, whether social, political, or revolutionary. While the demands of many of these characters are limited to individual and sexual freedom, and freedom from any social coercion, life experiences enrich others, putting them on the path to full independence based on economic independence. They begin aspiring to play an effective role outside the confines of a relationship with a man. In turn, the male-female relationship is non-hostile, mature, and balanced, although the characters reject most male practices and double standards.

Most rebellious characters are from the bourgeoisie; they are productive, highly educated, cultured, out of the ordinary, and may have some literary talent. Most combine these features with remarkable beauty. They strongly condemn the authority and injustice of men, despite their need for them and their desire to have an intimate experience with men that is unrestrained by customs or tradition. Khulud, the heroine of Hayfa' Bitar's *Qabw al-'Abbasiyin* (The Cellar of the 'Abbasids) 1995, holds all men in contempt, especially her father. She seeks revenge on men, but at the same time feels drawn to them, provoking a severe conflict arising from her contradictory impulses.

The father of the protagonist—an outstanding university student, from the Damascus bourgeoisie—persecutes her mother, turning the heroine into a sadist who seeks revenge on men, though not necessarily any particular man. She makes 'Aqil, a poor medical student, think she loves him, and she embarks on a physical relationship with him. She finds that sexual freedom gives her a psychological balance and mental clarity. Because she deals with 'Aqil as a victim, not a lover, she also engages in a physical relationship with a young German, even while she visits 'Aqil in his home, without any feelings of guilt. When the son of a wealthy

Damascus family who has just returned from America asks for her hand in marriage, she agrees immediately and confronts 'Aqil with the truth that she was not forced into the engagement. At this point, her revenge is achieved, with 'Aqil as the primary victim. He realizes that he has lived a huge lie, despite his love for her, and in a moment of desperation, he takes his own life. When 'Aqil's friends hold her responsible for his suicide and she realizes that her revenge has ended in a death, she has a nervous breakdown.

With this turn of events, the author holds women's distorted reality responsible for the destruction of both 'Aqil and Khulud. If Khulud had lived a normal, healthy life, she would have had healthy relationships with men and society, and neither she nor 'Aqil would have come to such a tragic end. Hayfa' Bitar manages to give the reader a problematic, torn character who seems the natural product of a deceptive, disturbed, conflicted social milieu that accepts in private what it publicly condemns.

If Hayfa' Bitar gives the reader a broken woman who rejects and simultaneously engages in social hypocrisy, Samar Attar, in *Lina: lawhat fatah Dimashqiya* (*Lina: A Portrait of a Damascene Girl*) 1982, portrays a girl who belongs to the Damascus bourgeoisie of the 1950s, but rejects its morals as she rejects everything in her country: men, Eastern traditions, religion, political parties, the military, university, family restrictions, friendship, and the nation. She also rejects violence of all types, particularly emotional violence, which wears many different disguises and which she doubts will disappear. As a result, she leaves for the West, to be able to express herself with the freedom she desires, without coercion or restrictions. Following James Joyce, she says, "I refuse to serve that which I don't believe in, whether it is my family, my friends, my country. I'll try the impossible to express myself the way I want, with the freedom I see fit."[30] The heroine refuses to bow her head like other girls and submit to majority opinion, no matter what it is, if it is not compatible with her own free thought.

Lina is almost unique in the Syrian women's novel. She does not reject part of the nation, but all of it, dreaming of a Utopian city that can realize the spiritual and mental advancement of the individual. It remains a dream, however, because she does not move toward it, but away from it when she decides to leave and stop taking action, choosing instead to wait passively for the future. Unlike other heroines, Lina does not see herself as uniquely beautiful, intelligent, or talented; she sees herself as unique because she was created in a time and place that are not her own. Those like her, who are capable of change, have not yet been born, and so she is angry at everything in the city that is not like her.

If Lina rejects her class and flees from it and her country to Paris, Sunya, the heroine of Qamar Kilani's *Bustan al-karaz* (The Cherry

Orchard) 1977, rejects the beliefs and morals of her class to become a leftist. She joins a leftist Palestinian organization active in Lebanon before the civil war, but her affiliation remains fragile and is easily broken: she does not choose it out of firm conviction, but because she is in love with a leftist Palestinian fighter. Since ideological convictions do not arise from a conscious decision, but out of deep-seated certainty, Sunya begins to chafe under party and revolutionary discipline after a few weeks in the resistance. She longs for freedom, finding various excuses. She "can't work alone . . . or without Sami,"[31] the young man she loves. She decides to flee further into the countryside. She takes refuge in her family's mountain retreat in Lebanon and is accidentally killed by a sniper's bullet.

Love temporarily strips Sunya of her class; she is, as she says, "a weak woman before love."[32] For a short time, under the influence of her sister Rim and her friends, Lina had joined the communist party, but in both novels Sunya and Lina quickly return to the choice that is closest to their social upbringing and character. They prefer to act as individuals, allowing a broad margin for personal freedom and greater situational flexibility. In both novels the choice seems futile: Sunya is killed and Lina runs away, her flight a declaration of defeat.

Lina rebels against everything, and Sunya rebels against her class; other heroines rebel against their husbands, rejecting their power and authority and the way they confine them in subjective and social frameworks that are incompatible with their humanity and their aspirations to live a healthy, dignified life. These female characters reject the two-faced nature of the intellectual and the inauthenticity of his culture and education, which is portrayed as a thin skin, liable to be shed at any social or personal provocation. In *Afrah saghira . . . afrah akhira* (Small Joys . . . Final Joys) 1996, by Hayfa' Bitar and *Shajarat al-hubb ghabat al-ahzan* (Tree of Love, Forest of Sorrow) 2000, by Usayma Darwish, the reader encounters two husbands, both with higher degrees from European universities. One is Syrian, the other from the Gulf. They love their wives—who also have university educations—and, while in European capitals, treat them as total equals, recognizing their humanity and their capacity to enjoy their freedom and live the lives they choose. But when they return home, they give in to the powerful influence of conservative Arab traditions. Each man becomes the instrument of his wife's oppression, thus embodying behavioral double standards. Their wives rebel and obtain divorce.

In these two novels, the voice of respect and loyalty to the self is heard clearly. Men are an important part of women's lives, but not the only part. Women do not sacrifice their independence to keep men. Rather they cling to their freedom and choice, and are capable of severing their relationships, despite the pain, blood, and angst of the amputation.

This type of female protagonist, whose pain transforms her into a healthy character who achieves her freedom and clings to it, is still not often found in Syrian novels written by women, although it is more common in novels of the 1980s and 1990s. Perhaps the best example of this type of character is the eponymous protagonist of *Furat* (Furat) 1998, by Mayya al-Rahbi. The heroine is baptized in the great Euphrates and shares some of its strength and purity. She stands in contrast to most heroines of other novels by Syrian women: she is not educated, elegant, or unique, and she is not the center of attention. She is a poor, rural woman who comes to the Syrian capital from a village around Dayr al-Zur. She does not finish primary school, she is wrapped from head to toe in a black cloak, and she gives herself in marriage to a man she had never laid eyes on before the wedding.

Furat is unconvinced by her village's laws and rejects them; she tries to resist, but fails and ultimately submits to her fate. She is forced into a marriage she does not want to a person whose face she does not know. Initially, she accepts her husband's crudeness, his cruelty, and his beatings, but her character, which naturally rejects and resists injustice, refuses to submit. She tries to defend herself: she openly resists her husband, returning his blows, whereupon he begins to fear her and stops beating her, leaving her the management of the house and the care of the children. When he dies of a disease, she refuses to return to her village as custom dictates, but insists on staying in Damascus and looking for work to preserve her children's dignity and save them the humiliation of begging in their uncles' homes. When her brother calls her a harlot and tries to beat her for rejecting the tribe's decree, she says, "Don't you dare come near me. The hand that is raised against me will be broken."[33]

Al-Rahbi manages to create a vivid character whose humane consciousness is shaped by her lived experience. The character comes alive and is fully grounded in reality. Both her words and actions are consistent with a strong, clear-sighted woman from the poorer class, despite the enormous evolution undergone by her understanding and her psyche. Mayya al-Rahbi establishes the authenticity of her character and makes her credible, not neglecting to show the reader the moments of human weakness that plague her. In one such moment, Furat thinks of her young neighbor and smiles at him at a time when her husband is neglecting her. The author portrays Furat's happiness when Abu Zaki comes to ask for her hand in marriage, despite her ultimate rejection of him. It is natural, after all, for a woman to take pleasure in the sense that she is still young and desirable, even though Furat does not consider marrying again but chooses to focus on raising her children, which she believes to be her primary task.

The new woman

The new woman is a type of female character almost wholly absent in previous periods; she starts to appear in the novels of the 1970s, which opened up to collective concerns and constructed fictional worlds based on the political and social reality in Syria and the Arab world. This character is a free, strong woman, keen to preserve her human dignity and her economic independence. She is engaged with public issues and concerns and believes that her personal fate and individual freedom are linked to the fate and freedom of her nation. She is a thinking, mature woman who constantly strives to enrich her interior world and has a balanced, flexible view of men—not at all impetuous or rash—although often she does not condone their behavior and their unhealthy view of women. This is a female character who refuses to waste her energies on fruitless, marginal conflicts, focusing instead on her work, which is the cornerstone of her life. For such characters, men are comrades and life partners with whom they must work to create a better life, both public and private. Since these women see men as partners, not as the foundation of their lives or as breadwinners, they are willing to totally renounce men without regrets if the relationship diverges from the correct path or men impinge on women's personal independence. For example, Nadiya, the heroine of Malak Hajj 'Ubayd's *al-Khuruj min da'irat al-intizar* (Escape from the Circle of Waiting) 1983, breaks off her relationship with Tariq because "one does not live by love alone."[34] She rejects a well-known, wealthy attorney even though she is over thirty because he has a conservative view of women and does not engage with national issues. On the other hand, she insists on fighting the crookedness and corruption in her workplace; as a result, she is punished, transferred to another position, and accused of moral depravity, the most painful accusation for women living in a system that valorizes women's honor while ignoring national honor. Nevertheless, Nadiya does not weaken or stand down, but continues to cling to her right to defend the national interest.

The new, engaged woman's defense of the nation does not stop with voicing her opinion; she may also take up arms, like Nadiya, the heroine of *al-Watan fi-l-'aynayn* (The Homeland) 1979, by Hamidah Nana. Nadiya believes that armed struggle is the only way to regain occupied territory, having lost faith in nationalist and Marxist political parties and in intellectuals, who seek solace in alcohol and sex after the 1967 defeat. Despite the crises experienced by the Palestinian resistance and Nadiya's disagreements with the armed Marxist organization she joins and then withdraws from—she is no longer convinced of the utility of operations outside the occupied territory, which obscure the internal struggle—her revolutionary nature continues to pull her toward her past. Having taken refuge in Paris, where she has a spiritual and ideological crisis of separation from her revolutionary past and her inability to live like millions of other women, she leaves France four years later and returns to a Beirut inflamed by civil war, to rejoin her old comrades. She works with them to find new alternatives after revolutionary dreams have killed ambition. Nadiya, a Syrian, has a heavy influence on Franc, a French leftist. Nadiya is the stronger party in the relationship, much like the heroine of Usayma Darwish's *Shajarat al-hubb ghabat al-ahzan*, who is the stronger partner in her relationship with the renowned English doctor, Colin. The new woman refuses to obey or emulate men, Eastern or Western.

Like these two characters, 'Alya, the protagonist of Anisa 'Abbud's *al-Na'na' al-barri* (Wild Mint) 1997, is stronger than the poet who loves her with all his heart and sees in her a rare woman. Everyone who loves 'Alya shares her opinions and sees her as unique. She is the example par excellence of the new woman, packing worthwhile action into each moment of her life. She teaches at a university in a coastal city and gives lectures on culture. She despises political mercenaries, condemning the revolutionaries' transformation into merchants and refusing to see a free voice become the mouthpiece of authority. She hates it when Randa, the wife of a businessman and contractor—a thief—becomes an influential patron of writers. 'Alya refuses to sell her professional conscience or bow her head. She is not cowed by fear when she decides to expel the granddaughter of an influential man from an exam for cheating; as a result, she is fired from the university and becomes just a body filling an empty chair in a state institution. When she learns that 'Ali, the poet she deeply loved who refused to sell his free voice, has joined the chorus of mercenaries, she feels that "life is a series of losses" and undergoes a severe crisis.[35]

'Alya's crisis stands apart from the crises of other heroines in Syrian women's novels: it is not a personal crisis, but a crisis of the nation. Although she is hurt that society continues to judge her like any traditional woman, and despite her rejection of the dominant attitudes to women in her society, she sees all this as only one aspect of her society's problems. What provokes her crisis and leads her to edge of a breakdown is 'Ali's fall; 'Ali was not merely a lover and potential husband, but represented the hope for an unsullied future.

With her impressive blend of fact and fiction, history and myth, Anisa 'Abbud gives the reader not only the story of a Syrian woman's life over three decades, but also the story of Syria from independence through the mid-1970s. The author ranges far and wide, tracing the winding paths of history to recall the ancient coastal kingdoms. She takes the reader through one thousand years of history to create a changing, yet stable world. The faces change, the bodies come and go, but the spirit is the same. 'Alya could be Anat or 'Ishtar or Mary. She changes guises in every age and takes on a new form, but she is one and the same: the original woman.

In *al-Na'na' al-barri*, the reader is offered a world filled with sorrow, pain, fragmentation, humiliation, and defeat. What is clean is soiled and tossed into the pit of nightmares. That which has been sullied rises on the corpses of others to acquire prominence and wealth. The wolf becomes a symbol, and the thief becomes a saint who performs miracles, his tomb a site of pilgrimage. A former traitor is blessed with influence and wealth to brandish his club against the honorable. Intellectuals become mouthpieces, the general public a herd of beasts, and the children of pre-revolutionary, traditional leaders inherit their fathers' positions and prominence. Honorable families are not "those who gave martyrs or fought or gave food to the hungry and deprived, or gave us learned men . . . They are not those whose women were widowed in the latest wars."[36] The honorable families are those that rest on piles of money.

Anisa 'Abbud portrays a contemporary, living female character, and through her, Syrian history in the second half of the twentieth century. In contrast, in *Hubb fi bilad al-Sham* (Love in the Levant) 1996, Nadiya Khust takes us back to the early twentieth century, giving us a glimpse of an important point in time in Syrian and Levantine life before the Sykes-Picot agreement tore Greater Syria into four countries. Khust takes up the social, political, and economic reality of the Levant between 1908 and 1913, from the fall of Sultan 'Abd al-Hamid right up to the First World War. Her objective here is to preserve the contours of an important point in contemporary Arab history, fearing it may be lost. This novel, like her other novel, *A'asir fi bilad al-Sham* (Cyclones in the Levant) 1998, is imbued with a sense of history, which leads her straight into the heart of politics. The novel is laden with sometimes repetitive historical information and details that impede the flow of the plot, but the reader can traverse many pages without losing the organizing thread of the narrative and without feeling that she has missed something the novel wants to say. The novel is a social document of this period in contemporary history, particularly in Damascus and Haifa. It shows the Zionist control over key positions in the Ottoman state and gives us dazzling female characters, the likes of which in this period surprise the reader.

The reader encounters three female characters in the novel who possess the characteristics of the new woman: Nafisa, Wajna Khatun, and Fatima. Perhaps the most distinguished is Nafisa, an educated woman who works in trade and agriculture, who is always occupied with things that set her apart from the traditional world of women. She rides horses, bears arms, and does not cover her face; merchants and farmers treat her with a great deal of respect and appreciation. She refuses to submit to her husband and believes that women are like men. She demands a divorce from her first husband because she refuses to live with his second wife; she gets a divorce from her second husband because, despite his great respect for her, he can no longer treat her like a wife, but only a dear friend. After the divorce, she continues to treat him like a friend, receiving him in her home and giving him business advice.

Nafisa rejects women's traditional role and contributes to public life. She earns the confidence of all those who know her. She seems ahead of her time, as does Wajna Khatun, a rich, beautiful widow who manages her own property, is interested in religious sciences, and debates with religious scholars during her pilgrimage to Mecca. Fatima, the third protagonist, is educated and self-reliant. She travels unaccompanied between Damascus, Haifa, and Egypt, and occasionally treats her husband as a companion, rather than a master who has rights that she does not.

A final example of the new woman can also be found in Ghada Samman's *Kawabis Bayrut (Beirut Nightmares)*. Samman lays bare the madness and irrationality of the Lebanese civil war and its pretense of defending religion. In more than one story/nightmare, the author shows that it is the rich, whatever their confession or religion, who are responsible for igniting the war. They are also the sole beneficiaries, while the poor of all religions are merely fuel for the war. The author condemns the sectarian war and exposes its causes, depicting its destructive consequences for Lebanon and the Lebanon-based Palestinian resistance. Like every new woman, Ghada Samman sees her personal destiny as tied up with that of the nation. She refuses to flee from the hell of war; after a ten-day experience of snipers, mortars, and sadistic nightmares, she reaches the conclusion that it is necessary to belong and take an active part: "Here . . . or nothing . . . Action, not escape and waiting."[37] This active participation may involve taking up arms when others leave one with no choice.

Like all new women, the author is a tough woman who makes her own personal choices. She lives her life like any young man, without fear or dread. She is freer, stronger, wiser, and more right-acting than her young neighbor, Amin, who despises her because, like most members of her family, he feels that she is "the man of the family":

[he] was shocked to discover that physiological differences between men and women were no longer of such great importance. He'd also been faced with the fact that inner strength and endurance don't necessarily reside in a neatly groomed moustache. In fact, they might even be found crouching beneath the soft exterior of a fragile-looking woman. My manliness seemed to awaken the womanliness in him, while my freedom was a challenge to his mental lassitude.[38]

Ghada Samman's persistent comparisons of men and women in this as well as her most recent novel, *al-Riwaya al-mustahila* (The Impossible Novel) 1997, and her keenness to highlight women's social oppression, show that Syrian women novelists, even as they were deeply involved with other public issues, did not ignore women's still problematic status in Arab societies. Samman approaches the condition of women as an important, complementary component of reality, as do all the novelists who give the reader examples of the new woman, open to all aspects of life in her society. When these writers give the reader new women they are not seeking to draw perfect female characters as much as trying to portray the larger society in which they live. In *al-Riwaya al-mustahila*, Ghada Samman tells the reader her life story, from childhood to early youth, but in the same context, with incredible skill and her remarkably distinctive style and language, she depicts social and political life in Damascus in the 1940s and 1950s. I do not believe that anyone has equaled Ghada Samman in laying bare this period with such depth, captivating transparency, or striking language.

In the novel, Ghada Samman not only recreates seventeen years of her life, but seventeen years in the rich life of Damascus, with its cosmopolitanism, social energy, human mosaic, popular proverbs, and politics. She distills an important moment in modern Syrian history, also giving the reader the unique example of a girl shaped by her special upbringing and personal qualities, a unique girl who is superior to her peers, both male and female, and yet stands apart from most heroines of Syrian women's novels in her lack of striking beauty. On the contrary, as her father says, "she looks like millions of other girls."[39]

Men and their relationship with women

I noted earlier that female characters heavily outweigh male characters in Syrian women's novels; only rarely are men the protagonists of the story. This is partly because women authors sought to highlight the hardships particular to women and partly because they knew the world of women much better than that of men. Familiarity with the world of men required a rich life experience that was not accessible to many of these female authors. I believe women novelists favored portrayals of educated male characters because they were much more familiar with them through their studies, work, and literary experience and also because they were keen to show up the false consciousness of the male intellectual, his double standards, and the negative impact these had on women. Male intellectual characters were followed by businessmen, workers, and farmers, but it is businessmen and merchants who appear as women's greatest persecutors.

Women's novels have given us men in various forms, closely observing men's relationships with women, which, in many cases, are based on oppression, although male characters are sometimes 'new' men who support women. Male characters may embody both of these attitudes, uncomfortable with wholeheartedly embracing one or the other. In novels that give us stereotypical or rebellious female characters, men are usually oppressors who do not recognize women's equality, even if they are educated or belong to a leftist party, like the hero of Khadija al-Jarrah Nashawati's *Arsifat al-sa'm* (Sidewalks of Tedium) 1973, a former communist who is openly derisive of women. This type of male character remained prominent until the mid-1970s when we begin to encounter, in novels that focus on public issues, some male characters who are supportive of women and have managed to overcome centuries of inherited contempt for and enslavement of women. For the most part, these male characters are educated or cultured, and involved in politics, as in Ulfat Idilbi's *Dimashq ya basmat al-huzn*, Umayma al-Khush's *al-Tawq* (Yearning) 1997, Mayya al-Rahbi's *Furat*, and Nadiya Khust's *Hubb fi bilad al-Sham*, most of whose male characters respect and appreciate women.

In addition to the oppressive intellectual and the open-minded intellectual, there also emerged the torn, conflicted intellectual, who vacillates between his rejection and acceptance of mistaken, antiquated concepts and is unable to totally free himself of them. The literary example of the open-minded man, who appeared with increasing frequency as women novelists turned to public concerns, remained, like the new woman, relatively rare. Indeed, he emerged in literature later than in reality. I believe this is partly because women writers often did not seriously engage with the difficult art of the novel. They did not look closely at reality in all its dimensions, and hence they did not observe transformations in people's consciousness. Not possessed of a clear intellectual perspective or overriding political and social concerns, they narrated scenes from their own lives or the life of a woman they knew or had heard of. I also believe that women writers wanted to portray women's suffering under the tyranny of men and the control that tradition exercised over them; thus they chose oppressive male characters or male characters torn between liberal and conservative thought, while female characters were chosen to illustrate the imbalances in male-female relationships.

The craft of the novel: reality and ambition
More than fifty years have passed since the birth of the Syrian woman-authored novel, and more than one hundred since the birth of the Arabic novel. As such, the observer might expect women's novelistic writing to have matured and moved on to the stage of experiment and innovation. In fact, however, this expectation is met in only a few novels. The pace of artistic development, along with intellectual evolution and maturity of approach, is still slow and is inconsistent with the accumulation of

novelistic experience, the intensive creativity of the novel in the Arab world, Syrian women's increasing turn to novelistic writing, and the burst of novels written by women. I believe the reason is that, for many women authors, the craft or artistry of the novel is not a major concern. Some novels are closer to a narrated tale, often unreadable, as is the case in works by Majida Buzu or Wafa' Hamarna, who summarizes the events of her novel, *Mamlakat al-hubb al-damiya* (The Bloody Kingdom of Love) 1990, in what she calls "an epilogue," as if summarizing a story she has read. Some novels are simply a superficial narrative about an ordinary woman's life; they often fail to produce lively fictional characters. Such is the case with *Harwala fawq saqi' Tulidu* (Clamor above the Toledo Frost) 1993, by Mary Rashu; *al-Saqi' yahriq al-bara'im* (The Frost Burns the Blossoms) 1996, by Fatima Mawardi; and *Zayna* by Wisal Samir. A novel that does not give us a unique human experience that moves our emotions, arouses our wonder, and disrupts our ease, forcibly transporting us to its own special world and giving us a new perspective on something we may or may not already know, is not a successful novel.

The production of fifty years has not prevented the publication of many novels that lack a creative spark; the reader still encounters in novels of the second generation the same weak points that marked novels of the first. Coincidence, for example, which plays such a great role in Widad Sakakini's *Arwa bint al-khutub*, Bint Barada's *al-Qalb al-dhahabi*, and In'am Musalima's *al-Hubb wa-l-wahl*, all published in the 1950s and early 1960s, continues to play the same role in shaping the plot in Qamar Kilani's *Ta'ir al-nar* (Bird of Fire) and Jamila al-Faqih's *Wa yabqa khayt min al-amal* (A Thread of Hope Remains), both published in 1981. The one-dimensional character who is either outrageously good or perfidiously evil, like those encountered in *'Aynan min Ishbiliya* (Two Eyes from Seville), published in 1965, is still found in some novels from the 1990s, such as *Zayna*. In contrast, a mature writer recognizes that a truly human character is complex and multidimensional, unevenly developed, and may have an overwhelmingly contradictory nature. The hastily drawn, sentimental characters and events of the 1960s novels of Salwa Harmaz al-Malluhi—*al-Mutamarrida* (The Rebel) 1966, *Da'i'a fi-l-madina* (Lost in the City) 1967, and *Maryam* (Maryam) 1968—also appear in *al-Ghurub al-akhir* (The Final Sunset), published in the mid-1980s, and *al-Tawq*, released in 1997. The only value of the latter is that it relates experiences from Syrian political prisons, devoting many pages to discussions of the torture of political prisoners and the psychological and physical pressures they endure. A reportage style and the intrusion of the authorial voice still characterize a not insignificant number of novels. In some novels, the reader can still find long, heavy, intellectual conversations that do not serve the novel, but simply illustrate the writer's own views, as in Umayma al-Khush's *al-Tawq*.

In terms of language, it is for the most part realistic narrative writing that occasionally tends toward expository prose. It often lacks any distinctiveness and is marred by repetitive similes. Remarkably, writers of the first generation, some of whom continued to write into the second generation, often show a greater concern for language, its structure, elegance, and correctness, than many novelists of the second generation. The language of first-generation novelists is usually carefully chosen, coherent, and rich, illustrating their mastery of the language; they use it flexibly and skillfully to avoid the monotony of simple informative prose. This is true for Widad Sakakini—who sometimes slips into rhymed prose—Salma al-Haffar al-Kuzbari, Hiyam Nuwaylati, and Collette Khuri. In fact, in many recent novels, the language is closer to a kind of hasty journalistic style, as in Wisal Samir's *Zayna*, which is full of grammatical and spelling errors.

Does the continued artistic weakness in second-generation novels— particularly those published in the 1990s, which should presumably have overcome the early rough patches and matured artistically—mean that Syrian women's experiment with the novel has been an artistic failure? The weaknesses in quite a few of these novels does not negate the successful contributions of many novelists of the first generation, such as Collette Khuri, Salma al-Haffar al-Kuzbari, and Ulfat Idilbi, or second-generation writers such as Nadiya Khust, Mayya al-Rahbi, Hamidah Nana, and Samar Attar, and it certainly does not outweigh the outstanding contributions of veteran writer Ghada Samman, or Anisa 'Abbud, whose first novel, published in 1997, secured her place as an important novelist, or Usayma Darwish, who, in her recently published first novel, revealed a remarkable talent and an astounding ability to handle the craft.

The contributions of these novelists, and others who are equally important, still do not constitute a large school of women writers who fulfill our ambitions and stake out a significant space for Syrian women's novels in the larger Arabic scene. This distinction is still limited to a few names, but it is hoped that it will extend to others. It is hoped that female novelists will approach the craft of the novel with a seriousness that will lead it away from superficial narrative of commonplace stories or hasty work to convey a political or social message. It is hoped that novelists, particularly young novelists, will take care to construct the worlds of their novels and leave behind the traditional framework of the nineteenth-century novel that characterizes many of them. Perhaps they will use the achievements of the modern novel to reveal authentic fictional worlds, not out of a desire simply to keep pace with modern techniques, as is the case with Mary Rashu in *al-Hubb fi sa'at ghadab* (Love in a Moment of Anger) 1998. In that novel, Rashu attempts to use the absurd and the world of nightmares to depict the heroine's psychological crisis, but she fails.

Similarly, Qamar Kilani uses symbolism in *Hubb wa harb* (Love and War) 1982 to create two worlds, one realistic and one symbolic, but she is unable to bring them together and make the symbol stand for the signified without making them correspond completely. The author speaks of the character of Falla, a symbol of Palestine, as if she is an appropriated country, not a human character of flesh and blood.

It is hoped that intellectual discourse can be kneaded into a mature craft and that political discourse can be woven into an artistic fabric, as we see in the works of Ghada Samman, Anisa 'Abbud, and Usayma Darwish, who use modern techniques not to make novelistic conquests, but to lay bare their novels' worlds and human characters who bear the cross of their pains and the fragments of their souls. These authors have managed to give the reader novelistic worlds that combine the realistic with the mythical and enchanted, and dreams with nightmares. The world of human beings in their novels coexists with the world of ghosts and the unseen. Times intersect, and voices and places—far and near, present or residing in the depths of memory—intertwine and merge. Childhood declares the power of its presence, the subconscious conjures up the wounds of a soul burdened by its baggage, and language exercises a violent, obvious presence.

Despite their weaknesses, novels by Syrian women have achieved much in terms of form and content. Their worlds are no longer closed in on the traditional world of women, and their primary issue is no longer the centrality of men and their relationship to women. Perspectives have expanded and broadened, and some female novelists have given us a mature reading of Syrian and Arab reality in works that have achieved a great degree of literary richness. The social developments in Syrian society, particularly its views of women, have created a climate that has encouraged women to express themselves and enrich their literary talents with knowledge and life experience, without which no real literature is possible.

Notes

1 Here I disagree with Joseph Zeidan, who notes in his *Arab Women Novelists: the Formative Years* (Albany: SUNY Press, 1995) that at the outset of the twentieth century Syria lacked the likes of Qasim Amin or Malak Hifni Nasif in Egypt or Muhammad Jamil Bayham and Nazira Zayn al-Din in Lebanon.

2 'Isa Fatuh, "Nahdat al-mar'a al-'Arabiya al-Suriya hatta muntasaf al-qarn al-'ishrin," *al-Ma'rifa*, no. 364, January 1994.

3 'Isa Fatuh, *Adibat 'Arabiyat: siyar wa dirasat* (Damascus: Cultural Seminar Association Publications, 1984).

4 Widad Sakakini, *Shawk fi-l-hasid fi-l-naqd wa-l-adab* (Damascus: Arab Writers' Union, 1981), p. 209.

5 Shakir Mustafa, *al-Qissa fi Suriya hatta al-harb al-'alamiya al-thaniya* (Cairo: 1957), p. 56, and Sayyid Hamid al-Nassaj, *Banurama al-riwaya al-'Arabiya al-haditha* (Cairo: Maktabat Gharib, n.d.).

6 Sayf al-Din al-Qintar, *al-Adab al-'Arabi al-Suri ba'd al-istiqlal* (Damascus: Ministry of Culture Publications, 1997).

7 Ulfat Idilbi, *Yadhak al-shaytan* (Damascus: Maktabat Atlas, 1970).

8 Qamar Kilani, *al-Mahatta* (Damascus: Arab Writers' Union, 1987).

9 Collette Khuri, *Ana wa-l-mada* (Beirut: al-Maktab al-Tijari, 1962).

10 Ibid., p. 113.

11 Nadiya Khust, *La makan li-l-gharib* (Damascus: Arab Writers' Union, 1990).

12 Dalal Hatim, *Imra'a faqadat ismaha* (Damascus: Arab Writers' Union, 1997).

13 Layla Saya Salim, "al-Isti'ada," *al-Mawqif al-adabi*, September–October 1987.

14 Ghada Samman, *'Aynak qadari* (Beirut: Ghada al-Samman Publications, 1979, fifth edition).

15 Mary Rashu, *Qawanin rahn al-qana'at* (Damascus: Arab Writers' Union, 1991).

16 Malak Hajj 'Ubayd, *al-Ghuraba'* (Latakia: Dar al-Hiwar, 1992).

17 Nahla al-Susu, "Araq sabahi," *al-Mawqif al-adabi*, March-April 1996.

18 Mayya al-Rahbi, *Imra'a mutaharrira li-l-'ard* (Damascus: Dar al-Ahali, 1995).

19 Anisa 'Abbud, *Ghasaq al-akasya* (Damascus: Arab Writers' Union, 1996).

20 Sahar Sulayman, "Qa' al-bi'r," *al-Mawqif al-adabi*, September–October 1997.

21 From the collection, *Huna ta'ish* (Beirut: Arab Institute for Research and Publishing, 1996), p. 34.

22 From the collection, *Ghiwayat mawti* (Cairo: Dar Sharqiyat, 1996), p. 99.

23 See 'Isa Fatuh, "Nahdat al-mar'a al-'Arabiya al-Suriya hatta muntasaf al-qarn al-'ishrin," *al-Ma'rifa*, no. 364, January 1994, and Iman al-Qadi, *al-Riwaya al-nisawiya fi bilad al-Sham: al-simat al-nafsiya wa-l-fanniya 1950–1985* (Damascus: al-Ahali, 1992).

24 Georgette Hannush, *'Ashiqat habibi* (Beirut: al-Maktab al-Tijari, 1964), p. 15.

25 Collette Khuri, *Ayyam ma'ah* (Damascus: Dar al-Anwar Press, 1980, second edition).

26 Ibid., p. 26.

27 2nd edition, 1952.

28 Ibid.

29 Wisal Samir, *Zayna* (Damascus: Dar al-Ahali, 1990), p. 221.

30 Samar Attar, *Lina lawhat fatah Dimashqiya* (Beirut: Dar al-Afaq al-Jadida, 1982), p. 364; translated into English as *Lina: A Portrait of A Damascene Girl* (Colorado Springs: Three Continents Press, 1994), p. 212.

31 Qamar Kilani, *Bustan al-karaz* (Damascus: Arab Writers' Union, 1977), p. 61.

32 Ibid., p. 255.

33 Mayya al-Rahbi, *Furat* (Damascus: Dar al-Ahali, 1998), p. 142.

34 Malak Hajj 'Ubayd, *al-Khuruj min da'irat al-intizar* (Damascus: Arab Writers' Union, 1983), p. 16.

35 Anisa 'Abbud, *al-Na'na' al-barri* (Latakia: Dar al-Hiwar Publishers and Distributors, 1997), p. 355.
36 Ibid., p. 282.
37 Ghada Samman, *Kawabis Bayrut* (Beirut: Ghada al-Samman Publications, 1981, fourth edition), p. 331; translated into English as *Beirut Nightmares*, trans. by Nancy N. Roberts (London: Quartet Books, 1997), although this particular quote is from a nightmare (no. 197) not included in the published translation.
38 Ghada Samman, *Kawabis Bayrut*, p. 63, and *Beirut Nightmares*, p. 76.
39 Ghada Samman, *al-Riwaya al-mustahila: fusayfisa' Dimashqiya* (Beirut: Ghada al-Samman Publications, 1997), p. 45.

3   Egypt

Hoda Elsadda

The inception of modern Arabic literature

The beginnings of modern Arabic literature in Egypt can be traced back to the era of Muhammad 'Ali (1805–1848), who took several measures to establish the foundations of the modern state.[1] Muhammad 'Ali sent his famed educational missions to France and Italy to equip Egyptian students with Western sciences,[2] and he founded a modern educational system based on the Western model that operated parallel to the traditional educational system headed by al-Azhar.[3] He set up the Bulaq Press in 1820, which printed both translations of Western works and Arabic works; private presses began to spread in 1860 and by the turn of the century there were 130. The year 1826 saw the first issue of *al-Waqa'i' al-Misriya*, heralding the arrival of modern journalism.[4]

Historians often point to the role played by Shaykh Rifa'a al-Tahtawi (1801–1873) in fostering modern writing. Sent by Muhammad 'Ali to Paris, upon his return he published his *Takhlis al-ibriz fi talkhis Bariz 1826–1831 (An Imam in Paris: al-Tahtawi's Visit to France 1826–1831)*, a record of impressions and observations of French society as seen through Eastern eyes. The work is a milestone in the evolution of modern writing, and many critics take it as the starting point for the classical era in modern Arabic literature in Egypt.[5] Rifa'a al-Tahtawi supervised an enormous translation enterprise, which had a clear impact on the development of Arabic writing, in both language and style, in addition to the role it played in familiarizing Arab society with Western classics. The classical era in modern Arabic literature lasted until 1914, the publication date of Muhammad Husayn Haykal's *Zaynab* (Zaynab), considered by some critics as the first Arabic

98

novel. The period from 1834 to 1914 saw several experiments in novelistic writing and translations of novels from European languages, which established the foundations for the flourishing and growth of various literary forms.⁶

The development and spread of the press played an important role in disseminating and fostering creative writing. From 1870, political conditions further created a climate that encouraged cultural production for a broad public of readers. As a result, Egypt became the center of enlightenment and culture in the Arab world, attracting intellectuals from various Arab countries who were fleeing the tyranny of rulers and searching for freedom. Ya'qub Sarruf, Faris Nimr, Bishara and Salim Taqla, Zaynab Fawwaz, Labiba Hashim, Mayy Ziyada, and others who contributed to newspapers and magazines all came to Egypt. *Al-Muqtataf* appeared in Cairo in 1885 (it was first published in Beirut in 1876, by owners Ya'qub Sarruf and Faris Nimr), followed by *al-Hilal* in 1892, and then a flood of newspapers and cultural magazines. Both men and women contributed to these papers, among them Muhja Bulus, Olga Dimitri, and Labiba Hashim, who wrote articles and engaged in dialogues and disputes with male writers. In 1892, the first women's magazine appeared, *al-Fatah*, published in Alexandria by Hind Nawfal. It was followed by many more—more than thirty by the early twentieth century.⁷

Women's writing evolved in tandem with modern writing in Egypt. Despite the special status of women at the time and the general absence of middle- and upper-class women in public life, a female presence was felt since the nineteenth century. Some women from the upper classes who were raised in tolerant environments managed to receive some education and contributed to social movements and the relevant cultural issues of the day. I therefore find it remarkable that Arabic criticism and literary history make no reference to early women's literature side by side with early literature written by men, although the cause of women was one of the most prominent social issues of the day. Indeed, it received such broad attention that almost all of those who were concerned with public issues addressed the issue of women in their writings in some form or another. Women's voices in this transitional period were also heard and were active on many levels. Given this, we must note the contradictions and obstacles that prevented the cultural elite from recognizing women's contributions. Just as the translation movement, the spread of education, and the press had an important impact on the beginnings of modern writing, the focus on the issue of women in the literature of the *nahda*, or renaissance, also had a significant influence on the beginning of women's writing and its development.

The woman question—women's role in society and the relationship between the sexes—occupied a prominent place in the concerns of pioneers of the renaissance, both men and women. For Rifaʻa al-Tahtawi, one of the most remarkable aspects of life in Paris was the status of French women and the respect shown them by society and men, as recorded in *Takhlis al-ibriz fi talkhis Bariz*. He later raised the issue of women's education in Egypt, seeing it as the basic means for the advancement of women in his own country, and he wrote *al-Murshid al-amin li-l-banat wa-l-banin* (The Faithful Guide for Girls and Boys). Women's education, linked with improving the general condition of women, thus became an issue of national concern. Qasim Amin, for example, believed that the backwardness of Egyptian society was bound up with the backwardness of its women, and he linked the improvement of women's status with social advancement, and women's liberation with national liberation from colonialism. Just as the emergence of modern literature is tied up with the beginning of the modern state, the cause of women was closely linked to the modernization of Arab societies, its problems, and their consequences.

Enlightenment thinkers focused on the status of women and addressed various related issues, such as education, work, childrearing, external appearance, and the relationship of all this to national development. Indeed, there is virtually no newspaper or magazine that does not contain some article on the woman question.[8] This interest in the cause of women had a significant, positive impact on women's general status, although there is a clear tendency to blame women and hold them responsible for society's backwardness and, thus, the burden of its advancement.[9]

The first reformers, who belonged to both Islamist and liberal schools of thought, adopted the basic assumptions of modernity,[10] absorbing the idea of Western cultural superiority and adopting a concept of development that saw progress in linear terms, with the West at the highest level and other societies seeking to catch up. They accepted the dichotomy of modernity versus tradition. As such, the writings of the pioneers contain innumerable representations of what they considered to be the status of contemporary Egyptian women, perpetually comparing this to what their status should be in the modern state. In this conceptual framework of the renaissance discourse, the example of the Western woman was posed as a symbol of modern society, which was compared to the customs, behavior, and appearance of Egyptian women, the symbol of traditional society.[11] Usually, the Western woman emerged more favorably than the Egyptian woman, and the latter was urged to follow in the path of her Western sisters in dress, behavior, education, and more. The newspapers and magazines of the period played an important role in establishing and disseminating such comparative representations of Western and Egyptian women.

The foregoing illustrates the roots of the connection between women and the issue of tradition versus contemporary life, and authenticity versus modernity. The pioneers linked the status and appearance of women to the development of a modern society, in the process planting the seeds of a problem that still hinders the discussion of many women's issues, particularly women's writing. Representations of women became a locus for conflicts on other issues which occupied thinkers of that century and still do. Society was increasingly modernized while still preserving some of its cultural particularity. In turn, women became the symbol of this authentic, particular identity and were thus burdened with the extremely difficult task of being simultaneously modern and traditional. Perusing the literature that presents images of the "contemporary" woman, one finds exhaustive attempts to reconcile Western modernity with the customs and traditions that women were charged with maintaining in Eastern societies, part of an intellectual construct that entailed an inevitable contradiction between the two sides of the equation.

The various dimensions of the relationship between women and modern society (in expectations, the concept and exercise of freedom, and conceptions of the self, the Other, and men) manifested themselves in different ways: in the way literary works were received, in the formation of the canon, in the recognition of some women writers and the exclusion of others, and in the criteria used to evaluate literary works. Indeed, we can use this relationship to explain the particularity of women's creative writing. This difference is not biological, but positional—that is, it is contextual, not innate, determined by women's locus in the symbolic cultural order and their relationship with it. Bearing in mind the modernizing context in which modern Arabic literature evolved, we would expect to find differences between the writings of men and women, shaped and determined by their different relationships with modern society and the different expectations about their roles in it. This context produced much writing that addresses the status of women in society, linking women's 'backwardness' with social backwardness and blaming women for their inferior status. In contrast, we do not find the same amount of writing about men's backwardness, and no connections are made between the backwardness of society and specific elements of the male character or men's lives. As such, women became the Other, inscribed and invested with all the latent problems and taboos; they were the mirror in which men looked to avoid facing the self. If we assume that writing is the site at which new identities are forged and old ones reformulated, we would expect women to express a different perspective, one determined by their different position in the symbolic order. Indeed, women's position is often close to that of other marginalized social groups, or those denied access to the discourse of the ruling cultural elite in a particular historical period.

When women entered the world of contemporary writing, they were acutely aware of the fraught nature of women's writing and the importance of women's self-expression. That is, women did not enter the field in a fit of imitation, blithely unaware of the challenges they faced. Like Virginia Woolf, 'A'isha Taymur (also known as al-Taymuriya) and Labiba Hashim gave voice to this sense of the expected difference between writing by men and writing by women and opined as to the reasons for the difference. We may agree or disagree with their opinions, but when women speak, we can expect them to blaze new trails or explore unknown regions of the human experience. In 1906, Labiba Hashim said:

> Men write about women the way they know and think; women write about themselves the way they believe and feel . . . [Women] are more cognizant of the condition of women, their weak points and how to win over . . . generations of women and take them to what is best for the country and of benefit to themselves.[12]

Hashim explained the difference by referencing the prevalent discourse of the time about the "natural" differences between men and women—how men possess the power of reason and women are moved by emotion and sentiment. 'A'isha Taymur, on the other hand, worked hard to make a place for herself in the cultural milieu of the nineteenth century and justify the importance of her literary contributions. She stressed the value of her writing to other women who were deprived of knowledge and the company of learned men—a condition she knew well by dint of her isolation, as a woman from the upper class who was deprived of the life experiences to which men had sole access. She opened her book, *Nata'ij al-ahwal fi-l-aqwal wa-l-af'al* (The Consequences of Circumstances in Words and Deeds) 1887, by discussing her status in the family, drawing attention to the importance of her book:

> Compassion for all those wronged parties who experienced what I experienced, and suffered what I suffered, led me to invent a story for them, to distract them from their troubles when thoughts close in and to divert them from their sorrows in the exile of loneliness, which is so much worse than exile from one's home.[13]

In *Mir'at al-ta'ammul fi-l-umur* (The Mirror of Contemplation) 1892, Taymur discussed women's different status in society through her critique of the conduct of husbands and wives in light of changing circumstances and the attendant, inevitable changes in the division of men's and women's social roles. She writes about a lion who is too lazy to hunt; his mate takes over the job until she becomes wholly responsible for feeding them. When the lion tries to impose his authority, the lioness laughs saying, "That was when you were you and I was I. Now the situation is reversed and I have become you and you me. I now owe you what you owed me, and you owe me what I owed you."[14]

Pioneering women writers in Egypt

'A'isha Taymur (1840–1902), an aristocratic young woman, composed poetry in Arabic, Persian, and Turkish and wrote prose works that are considered the precursor of modern fiction. Her father was of Turkish-Kurdish origin and her mother a manumitted slave of Circassian origin. Her family brought teachers to the house to instruct her in the Quran and Islamic jurisprudence. She tells her story with poetry and writing in the introduction to *Nata'ij al-ahwal fi-l-aqwal wa-l-af'al*, saying that she refused to learn the arts of drawing and embroidery and asked to attend the salons of learned men. Her father gave his consent and even encouraged her, but her mother was afraid of the woes and sorrow such a path might entail. Taymur wrote poetry, but stopped after her marriage and her absorption in domestic duties. In 1882, her father died, and she married three years later. As Zaynab Fawwaz says,

> She became her own master, so she brought in two women with knowledge of grammar and prosody, one called Fatima the Azharite and the other Stayta al-Tablawiya. She began to study grammar and prosody with them until she excelled and perfected them. She wrote fine poetry and began reciting long *qasida* poems and shorter *zajal* poetry.[15]

'A'isha Taymur devoted herself to prose and poetry and worked as a translator for the Khedival court. When her only daughter fell ill and died, she blamed herself. She mourned for seven years and burned all the poetry she had composed in this period. Taymur left one collection of poetry in Arabic, *Hilyat al-tiraz* (Decorative Embroidery) 1884, which contains love poetry, elegiac poetry, and panegyric, and was lauded by her contemporaries, both men and women. She left another collection of poetry in Persian, *Ashkufa*, as well as the prose works *Nata'ij al-ahwal fi-l-aqwal wa-l-af'al, Mir'at al-ta'ammul fi-l-umur, al-Liqa' ba'd al-shatat* (Meeting after Separation), and an incomplete manuscript for a novel.[16]

'A'isha Taymur's works are the first written works, in prose or poetry, by an Arab woman in the modern period. She opened a door that allowed more women to express themselves, and many women writers were inspired by her perseverance and aspirations.[17] In 1922, Mayy Ziyada wrote a biography of Taymur, which was at the same time a literary study from the point of view of a woman writer establishing the status of women's writing in the modern age. Ziyada sees Taymur as "a vanguard of women in the new age, who know their rights to freedom of emotion and their legitimacy within their natural limits. She was in the vanguard not only in the East but in the entire civilized world."[18] Ziyada considered *Nata'ij al-ahwal* "the spark of modern fiction,"[19] or, in other words, the first experiment with the art of the novel.

'A'isha Taymur addressed women's status in society, expressing her opinion in a long essay, *Mir'at al-ta'ammul fi-l-umur*. In it she contemplates relations between men and women in light of the changing gender roles she had experienced. With the document, she became one of the first people to take up the cause of women in the nineteenth century. In addition, she wrote a social essay, "La tasluh al-'a'ilat illa bi-tarbiyat al-banat" (Families Will Not Be Rectified But by the Education of Girls),[20] published in *al-Adab*. Some of her love poetry evinces a depth of feeling and a maturity of craft, and her elegies for her daughter deserve thoughtful regard.

Mayy Ziyada lauded Taymur for her sincerity of emotion,[21] the beauty of her poetic language, the power of her representation, and the beauty of her tone; she took her to task for her tendency to imitate, as a consequence of which she often "speaks in the language of men."[22] Ziyada attributed this to the fact that men held the reins of the poetic tradition, which encouraged Taymur and others like her to imitate their style to achieve recognition and appreciation. 'Abbas Mahmud al-'Aqqad thought her poetry "rose to the highest levels of poetry reached by writers in Egypt from the mid-nineteenth century up until the 'Urabi revolt." He considered it an exception to the rule, for women, he thought, were no good at poetry "because femininity in and of itself does not express its emotions . . . Indeed, it is more suited to concealing and suppressing emotion." He also thought that Taymur excelled only in elegiac poetry, "and this is why the greatest female poet to distinguish herself in Arabic—al-Khansa'—composed dirges and elegies." Al-'Aqqad opined that Taymur's best poems were the elegies: "as for the love poetry, it was merely a way to exercise her tongue, as she said more than once."[23] In contrast, 'A'isha 'Abd al-Rahman (known as Bint al-Shati') thought highly of Taymur's love poetry and was even of the opinion that her best lines of poetry were love poetry, not elegiac. She believed that 'A'isha Taymur was able to express, with unprecedented boldness, feelings of love and passion, devoting one third of her poetic collection to love poetry. 'A'isha 'Abd al-Rahman stressed her pioneering role in poetry, which opened broad horizons to women poets of the modern age: "Taymur's poetry marks a liberation from emotional asphyxiation, and it encouraged those women who came after her to express themselves freely and openly."[24]

Taymur introduced her own love poetry, as al-'Aqqad noted, by insisting that it was "courting no one, with the sole intention of exercising the tongue."[25] If al-'Aqqad took the expression literally to support his notion that women were not skilled at poetry and that elegiac poetry was the closest to a woman's nature, Mayy Ziyada and 'A'isha 'Abd al-Rahman interpreted the statement from a different perspective, mindful of the social pressures that prohibited women from confessing feelings of desire and love. 'A'isha 'Abd al-Rahman decided that Taymur's statement was essentially a clever ruse played upon her conservative environment.[26]

Speaking of *Nata'ij al-ahwal*, Mayy Ziyada said, "Like any respectable traditional story, this one has a king, a prince, a vizier, and a boon companion."[27] This was the model of the early experiments with the Arabic novel, which were melodramatic and sought both to entertain and convey a moral point.[28] In the novel Taymur uses the language of the *maqamat*, the picaresque Arabic genre that originated in the tenth century, consisting of a short narrative, usually one of a string of narratives, each of which is related by the same narrator about the same fictitious hero, with its traditional aesthetics that revolved around rhymed prose and allusion. Since modern Arabic literature diverged from this aesthetic, Mayy Ziyada considered the traditionalism in Taymur's writing to be a flaw, attributing it to imitativeness and imperfect poetic vision. Most literary historians have followed her, ignoring this important beginning that combined the old and the new.[29] 'A'isha Taymur belonged to the transitional generation of writers who had received an Arabic, Islamic education, grown up on the traditions of classical Arabic poetry, and absorbed the music of its rhetorical language. They were using these techniques even as the winds of change were bringing important transformations to Arabic literature and society as a whole. When these winds gathered momentum, they blew away the important history of the beginning of women's writing in the modern age.[30]

*

After 'A'isha Taymur, literary and cultural writing was taken up by many Arab women who came to Egypt looking for a favorable climate for self-expression and creative writing.[31] These included Zaynab Fawwaz, Labiba Hashim, Mayy Ziyada, and others, who made valuable contributions to the newspapers and journals that shaped cultural life in Egypt and the Arab world. Their literary works are important milestones in the birth and development of modern Arabic literature. Like 'A'isha Taymur, Zaynab Fawwaz (1846–1914) received a traditional religious education, reaching a high degree of specialization.[32] She made significant contributions to the social essay, defending women's cause and addressing various political, religious, and cultural topics. In 1904, she collected the articles into a book published at her own expense, *al-Rasa'il al-Zaynabiya* (The Zaynab Epistles). Zaynab Fawwaz played an important role in the late nineteenth century, when her articles and interests represented a transitional phase in Arab history. She had absorbed the Arabic cultural heritage and was inspired by its subjects and styles, which she then mixed with new literary trends coming from the West. She borrowed the medieval form and style of Arabic biography to write her most famous book, *al-Durr al-manthur fi tabaqat rabbat al-khudur* (Scattered Pearls in the Lives of the Harem Dwellers), which she started writing in 1891 and printed at the Bulaq Press in 1895. In it, Zaynab Fawwaz wrote biographies of 'A'isha Taymur and other contemporary writers, establishing a tradition followed by Mayy Ziyada of women writing about women—that is, their own histories of women's contributions within the dominant culture. Fawwaz also wrote *al-Hawa wa-l-wafa* (Love and Fidelity) 1893, a four-act play about a love story based in Iraq; *Husn al-'awaqib aw Ghada al-zahira* (Fine Consequences, or Radiant Ghada) 1899, a historical, didactic novel; and *al-Malik Qurush* (King Cyrus) 1905, a historical romance shot through with intrigue and adventure.

Zaynab Fawwaz's writings had an enormous impact on the newspapers and magazines of the time. In addition to her articles, which touched on various social and political issues, in *al-Durr al-manthur fi tabaqat rabbat al-khudur* she documented the legacy of women from various ages and countries, and the work became an authoritative source for many women writers, such as Malak Hifni Nasif, and especially the owners of and contributors to women's journals, who drew inspiration from it or reprinted large segments about women's achievements throughout the ages for their readers. Like 'A'isha Taymur and Muhammad al-Muwaylihi, Zaynab Fawwaz was a link between the Arab-Islamic culture on which she was raised and new literary forms inspired by the West, which the pioneers transmitted or adapted to express their social and cultural concerns. Fawwaz took an important Arabic literary form, the biographical dictionary, and introduced new material about her contemporaries and foreign women throughout the ages, using it to serve the cause of women by highlighting the achievements of women in various fields, thereby providing women writers with a huge amount of material in support of their efforts to bring women's voices to the reading public.

We should pause for a moment at the role played by these newspapers and magazines in fostering women's writing. As male pioneers transmitted or Arabized European works at the beginning of their creative lives, so did many women writers also translate Western novels and stories for publication in the Egyptian press, looking for special material in Western journals.

In addition, the owners of these magazines, mostly women, played a positive role in encouraging women to contribute to them by elevating writing to a noble pursuit. Alexandra Khuri Averino said in the first issue of *Anis al-jalis* in 1898,

> I solicit female champions of knowledge and distinguished writers who wish to elevate the members of their sex who have thus far lagged behind in the sources of knowledge to please send me their splendid epistles and brilliant gems, so that my magazine can publish their glories and preserve their works and exploits.[33]

In another text, Labiba Hashim called on women to "establish literary societies for mutual understanding, unity, and the exchange of ideas,"[34] in order to advance the condition of women and improve their status. At the same time, the press played an instructive role, going a long way toward demolishing widespread misconceptions about the weaker abilities of women by publishing sophisticated articles by women writers. Most of the women's press also devoted space to biographies of women, from the Arab world and elsewhere, and their documented achievements. "Famous Women" in Labiba Hashim's *Fatat al-sharq* was the most well-known of such columns. Moreover, these magazines raised a discussion about the concerns of Eastern women, starting with their perceptions of their relationship with the outside world and including conceptions about the self and how these diverged from or coincided with society's expectations. For example, there were discussions of women's freedom and their role in building the country, the importance of education, women's relationship with the family and their role in it, whether to wear the *hijab* or not, the difference between Western and Eastern women, and colonialism's role in curbing the freedoms of all members of society.[35]

Also discussed in women's magazines was the issue of whether women should sign their articles and stories, since it was widespread practice for women to use pseudonyms to conceal their identities. The debate on the topic was so fierce that in 1908 the Association for the Advancement of Women took up the cause to encourage women to sign with their real names.[36] A close reading of this issue sheds light on other issues related to society's view of writing women, its tolerance of their opinions, and the degree of freedom of expression and contribution they were allowed. First and foremost, the use of pseudonyms is connected to society's attitude toward the presence (or absence) of women in public life. Women concealed their identities to protect themselves and their families from society's distaste for the visibility of women. The anonymity of women's writing was also related to the veil, of the type then widespread that hid women's faces and concealed their identities. In addition, writing in the press had not yet been accepted as a profession in Arab society, nor were novelists and short-story writers accorded automatic respect. Journalism and writing in Egyptian society had not yet obtained the legitimacy of medicine or teaching, for example, particularly for women. When Haykal published his novel, *Zaynab* in 1914, he took the name "an Egyptian peasant" to conceal his true identity and protect his reputation as an attorney. There was also a tendency to adopt a pseudonym that revealed one's political or ideological leanings; thus, we find pseudonyms like "For Unveiling," "For Veiling," or "Rural." To make matters even more complicated, male authors sometimes adopted female pseudonyms either for political reasons[37] or to legitimize their speaking about women's issues.

The use of pseudonyms fostered a tendency to doubt women's abilities to express their opinions about and take part in social issues. The issue of women's writing was not yet settled, but stoked a debate in which both men and women participated.[38]

*

Women first contributed to the movement to translate and Arabize European stories and novels, after which they started writing historical novels following the model of their famous contemporaries.[39] Zaynab Fawwaz wrote novels at the end of the nineteenth century, and Labiba Hashim published "Hasanat al-hubb" (The Merits of Love) in 1898,[40] which she described as "a literary tale and an economic exhortation," in addition to a great many translated stories and novels published in *Fatat al-sharq*, which she founded and headed as editor in chief. These early novels were a blend of history and romance; they were presented to readers both as entertainment and as a source of information about the history of other peoples and countries. Initially, these novels eschewed the representation of contemporary events and figures, for the value of fiction was still not established, and women writers, like their male counterparts, did not feel they possessed the tools of creative expression that would allow them to represent reality in all its manifestations.

In 1904, Labiba Hashim published her novel *Qalb al-rajul* (A Man's Heart), a contemporary love story between Rosa, an Egyptian girl of Syrian origin, and 'Aziz. The novel traces the birth and development of their love, followed by their separation after 'Aziz betrays Rosa and fails to keep his word. The novel gives the reader the example of a woman who clings to her love despite the circumstances, in contrast to a man whose emotions are fickle and whose word is not sacred. (The title of the novel suggests that Hashim, wittingly or unwittingly, tried to deconstruct stereotypical representations of manhood and womanhood.) This was a point of controversy and a topic of debate in the writings of many of the pioneers, such as al-'Aqqad.

The issue attracted the attention of a writer at the turn of the century, who wrote an article celebrating Labiba Hashim's novel and encouraging men to write about "a woman's heart, and then we shall see which of the two hearts is more inconstant." He then questioned Hashim's conclusions in the novel: "A man, even if his character be mean and his heart base, will be dignified by his soul, which will elevate him beyond the depths of reproach. As for a woman, she does not have the same morality of soul, but is swayed by factors of contempt and revenge." He then discussed the loyalty of Rosa, the novel's heroine, holding her out as an exception that proves the rule.[41] A critical debate still rages as to whether Hashim's novel is the first in modern Arabic literature.

Other novels and stories by women followed, published in magazines either complete or in serialized form. Like male writers, female writers began to explore the depths of modern fiction, first following the path of imitation and Arabization before starting to write romantic novels and stories with Arab characters set in familiar places. Some critics describe the early efforts of writers, both men and women, as wholly divorced from the pressing issues of the day.[42] But we can glimpse a great interest in the issue of fiction writing itself and the development of the craft, particularly issues of writing and expression for women writers.

1914 and the rise of nationalism, contemporary issues, and romantic tendencies

In 1914, Egypt became a British protectorate and the First World War began. This was followed by the popular revolution of 1919, which gave voice to feelings of anger and desire for independence. The 1923 constitution disappointed Egyptians, who soon realized that the ruling monarchy was conspiring with the British colonizer. By the time Egypt obtained a conditional independence in 1936 that legitimized the colonial presence, the major question was no longer how to learn from the West and advance or how to use the tools of modern expression to create a new reality more suited to local needs, but how to reconcile borrowing from the West with its ugly colonial face. How do we stand up to it attempts to quash our particularity? How can we borrow from the West and fight it at the same time, and what is the correct path to progress?

Albert Hourani distinguishes later generations of reformers from the first reformers like 'Ali Mubarak and Rifa'a al-Tahtawi. The major concern of the last two figures was how to take from Western civilization and benefit from it to advance the Arab nation. They launched a major enterprise to modernize Egyptian society, which included a translation project at the Language School (under which more than two thousand books were translated), the establishment of modern schools, the founding of a printing house, and more. Later generations, however, had to confront Europe's other face: colonial Europe with its barbaric practices in colonial territories, which raised doubts that it possessed the keys to civilization and the means to elevate all of humanity.[43] The eruption of the Second World War and its tragedies further shook the image of the West and stripped it of its claims of enlightenment. During this period, writers were clearly interested in analyzing events in society, such as the relationship between East and West, with a focus on the element of conflict—whether explicit or implicit—and the divide between the two civilizations. The question of the nineteenth century—what do we take and what do we leave?—assumed a tragic significance. Whereas the first pioneers had raised the question to encourage the nation to take rapid advantage of the achievements of Western civilization—not plagued by a sense of threat or the feeling that this tyrannical, unjust Other would inevitably have to be resisted—the context of the question later changed, thus changing its meaning and significance. For the later generation, the question betrays contradictory desires and a simultaneous sense of attraction/revulsion, as well as a fear of the loss of identity and a desire to maintain it.

In creative writing, these altered concerns and hopes led to attempts to draw and describe the Egyptian character or, in contemporary parlance, Egyptian identity. This character was savagely attacked by colonial representatives, perhaps the best example being *L'Égypte et les égyptiens* (1893), a book by the Duke of Harcourt. In his own book, Qasim Amin responded to the allegations of the Duke and defended Egyptian peasants, soldiers, and the educated classes.[44] Attempts to define the features of Egyptian identity also led to an interest in particular topics, such as the perpetual comparisons between the Egyptian and the westerner, and writings about the countryside and peasants, the relationship between the intellectual and society, the role of women in modern society, and male-female relationships. All writers, whether men or women, addressed these subjects. With rising nationalism and the crystallization of the Egyptian character came an increasing sense of the self and its uniqueness, and a probing of its depths. Writers began to explore reality by conjuring up certain aspects of themselves, and we find a very intimate relationship between the protagonists of stories and novels and their authors, particularly in the early works.[45]

These political and cultural developments were accompanied by other important developments in women's status. In 1909, the women's branch of the Egyptian University opened its doors to receive women in the lecture halls, for women were not allowed to register at the colleges.[46] The lectures, given on Fridays, were attended by both foreign and Arab women of the likes of Labiba Hashim, Nabawiya Musa, and Malak Hifni Nasif. Lectures for the female public became widespread and were given at the offices of *al-Jarida*, the organ of the Umma party. Women took part in the 1919 revolution and were subjected to various forms of harassment and repression because they were women. In 1923, Huda Sha'rawi established the Egyptian Women's Union after the leaders of the Wafd party failed to give women the franchise as they had promised. The union issued the French-language magazine, *L'Egyptienne*, which became a pulpit for the writings of women like Sayza Nabrawi, Hawwa Idris, and others. The union also engaged in various other activities.

Prominent women writers at the time included Malak Hifni Nasif (Bahithat al-Badiya or Seeker in the Desert), Mayy Ziyada, Nabawiya Musa, Munira Thabit, Sayza Nabrawi, Hawwa Idris, and Huda Sha'rawi.

Their names are associated with social or political writing, though some also made considerable contributions to prose and poetry. Their writings were a starting point for all writing women. This period witnessed the spread of a type of literary writing, the narrative essay, which critics consider the first experiment with the short story. The form paved the way for other types of writing and ushered in a treatment of contemporary political and social issues in fiction. Malak Hifni Nasif (1886–1918) wrote many articles on important social and political issues of the hour, focusing on issues that touched on women's status in society. She addressed polygamy and divorce and stressed the importance of education for girls. She was quite formidable in the latter respect, since she herself was one of the first graduates of al-Saniya School in 1900, and she convinced the families of her friends and relatives to send their daughters to school. Perhaps one of her most important contributions was her critique of what she saw as the renaissance pioneers' eagerness to adopt the accouterments of Western modernity. She is significant because she represents an important trend in the writings of many women of the period.[47] We also cannot ignore the contributions of women who wrote in French; their writings had an impact on members of the upper class and some of the middle class as well, although they remained isolated from the more general cultural context. Journals of this period contain many examples of the narrative essay that address political and social issues of the day.

Another important step was first taken by Zaynab Fawwaz then followed by other women writers of later generations: the writing of stories with a personal dimension, inspired by some aspect of the writer's experience, a form close to biography and autobiography. Zaynab Fawwaz wrote about the lives of women; Mayy Ziyada later wrote biographies that contained some aspects of autobiography. They were followed in the early twentieth century by Nabawiya Musa, Munira Thabit, and Huda Sha'rawi. Ziyada wrote the biographies of three women: Malak Hifni Nasif, 'A'isha Taymur, and Warda al-Yaziji. Her book on Bahithat al-Badiya (the *nom-de-plume* of Malak Hifni Nasif), published in 1920 and considered the first of its kind, contained Nasif's Arabic writings and an analysis of her character in its cultural and social context. At the same time, it shed light on important dimensions of Ziyada's character and thought.[48] The book is difficult to pigeonhole, for it is both biography and autobiography. It is a descriptive, analytical narrative about a remarkable woman who lived in the late nineteenth and early twentieth centuries, but it also records important events in modern Egyptian history. Finally, it is about a unique relationship between two women, their interaction, and the historico-cultural context in which they lived. Looking at the book with a quantitative eye, we find that half of it is about Bahithat al-Badiya and the other half is about Mayy Ziyada. As will become clear in this brief review of women's writings in Egypt, women writers played a vanguard role in developing and expanding this literary genre, and Mayy Ziyada's work on Malak Hifni Nasif is a pioneering example of biography, in both form and content.

*

Nabawiya Musa (1886–1951) belonged to the pioneering generation that received a modern education and graduated from al-Saniya School. Like others of this generation, she worked as a teacher, then she became the first female Egyptian school principal. Musa wrote many articles in the journals of her day, such as *al-Balagh al-usbu'i, al-Siyasa*, and *al-Jarida*, before establishing *al-Fatah* in 1937, which was issued for several years. She was a pioneer of education in Egypt who stressed the importance of education in general, particularly for girls. She also addressed other social and political issues, motivated by her concern for education, which she considered the most pressing national issue.

In her forty-year battle to spread education, Nabawiya Musa wrote articles in newspapers and magazines that expressed her concerns, her objectives, and her affiliations. She then turned to literary forms, like poetry and memoir, which she used to convey her social message. Musa composed poems and published them in a collection; all of them are occasional poems written for a specific, practical purpose, as was the prevalent trend then. The poems celebrate a particular event or person, either a national occasion for which Musa declares her support or defines her stance on, or a figure who has special significance for her. For example, she wrote a poem for the funeral of Malak Hifni Nasif, celebrating her pioneering role and using her memory to raise the issue of women and education.

Nabawiya Musa also wrote a panegyric for the Khedive to win him over to her side against the machinations of certain officials in the Ministry of Education. Speaking about her objective in composing poetry, Musa affirmed that she had no ambition to devote herself to it. For her, poetry was a means of achieving her primary objective: the dissemination of education in Egypt. As such, her collection of poetry is "a comprehensive history of the Egyptian national movement and the women's renaissance in Egypt."[49]

Also significant is that she integrated personal experience into her social and political writings. Nabawiya Musa used stories from her life, her battles with the English education inspectors who looked down on Egyptian teachers, and her stand-offs with ministry officials and foreign principals, turning them into gripping story material and often using them to explain her ideas on the importance of liberating education from colonial control, improving the status of teachers and preserving their dignity, developing curricula to suit Egyptian students, and unifying curricula for boys and girls. Musa began writing these articles that blended her personal life and public issues for *al-Balagh al-usbu'i* and later continued in her own magazine, *al-Fatah*.[50] She first began to write her memoirs in serialized form, and only later collected them into a book, *Tarikhi bi-qalami* (My History by My Pen).[51]

If we compare female writers' early modes of self-expression with those of Haykal, Ibrahim al-Mazini, and al-'Aqqad, for example, we find that male writers put themselves in the center of events and focused on observing their interactions with reality and other figures. They followed the Romantic school in their analysis of the feelings and emotions of the hero/writer, highlighting his individuality and uniqueness and occasionally even celebrating his isolation from his environment and society. In contrast, women writers put themselves at the center of events, but did so in order highlight the external reality: their ideas and the public events that surrounded them. When Nabawiya Musa wrote her memoirs, she titled them "My History by My Pen" to place them in the broader public context. She is writing a history; although it is personal, the use of the term "history" connotes a rebellion against the idea of memoir as the story of an individual. History here is collective and central. Indeed, Nabawiya Musa chose to write only about her experience in education and her conflicts with the British colonial administration, remaining silent on many aspects of her life.

Munira Thabit did much the same thing in her memoirs, *Thawra fi-l-burj al-'aji: mudhakkirati fi 'ishrin 'aman 'an ma'rakat huquq al-mar'a al-siyasiya* (A Revolution in the Ivory Tower: My Memoirs of Twenty Years of Struggle for Women's Political Rights) 1946, when she declared that she would intentionally eschew personal issues and focus on the public and the political, to frustrate the expectations of men who always expect women to tell personal stories. If we agree that a text about one's life experience does not entail a realistic report about which events happened on which day, and that the line between autobiography and the novel is very thin, we must conclude that we are, in effect, always reading about how the self absorbs experience and about the birth of a consciousness that expresses some aspect of identity. If we wonder why Nabawiya Musa or Munira Thabit chose a more inclusive experience in their memoirs, we can find the answer in a modernity that accepted women's emergence in the public, cultural sphere combined with a keenness on the part of women to conceal their gendered identity, either by assuming male stances, opinions, and even appearances, or by remaining silent about their particular experiences as women. Nabawiya Musa chose the perspective of the teacher and school principal; that is, she focused on public and national issues that society believed were important and worthy of being inscribed in history. At the same time, she avoided personal, marginal issues that are not usually found in the official historical narrative. Mayy Ziyada chose to write her life story through her connection to other women. That is, she chose a method that highlights what we might call the collective self. As is clear, biography was one literary form explored by women early in their creative endeavors, and they continued to master and develop it.

*

In 1935, Suhayr al-Qalamawi published a collection of stories entitled *Ahadith jaddati* (My Grandmother's Stories). The introduction was written by Taha Hussein and it received a warm literary and critical reception. Al-Qalamawi was inspired by the form of traditional stories. The reader meets a grandmother and granddaughter bound by a bond of friendship and love, illustrated in the granddaughter's desire to listen to and enjoy her grandmother's tales, which are set within a larger frame story. Al-Qalamawi thus used the form of *The Thousand and One Nights* and introduced contemporary material into it, producing a text new in both form and content. Speaking about the past, the grandmother extracts moral lessons and maxims from her recollection of events. She draws comparisons between the past and the present while always favoring the past, although at times she does recognize the virtues of the present. For example, she tells the tale about how she wrongly imposed a severe punishment on her son, saying that in her day they did not understand the theories and rules of modern childrearing. The stories are punctuated by discussions between the grandmother and granddaughter about the differences between women in the past and the modern, educated woman. The grandmother criticizes the modern liberated woman, seeing this liberation as an erosion of her dignity, chastity, and good morals. In contrast, the granddaughter defends the girls of her generation from accusations of moral decay and sees those who do fall prey to moral laxity as victims. The grandmother also discusses the 'Urabi revolt and the impact of the defeat on the popular psyche, revealing a nationalist, political consciousness. Suhayr al-Qalamawi addresses the confrontation between past and present, old and new, in a relationship not of inevitable conflict, but of love and understanding. The grandmother and her granddaughter have different perspectives on an issue that will not be resolved even in the twentieth century, although the author suggests that time will resolve the conflict in favor of the new generation, which represents the modern view. Suhayr al-Qalamawi may have been convinced of the incompatibility of the two ages and may gradually have leaned toward the idea of a clean break, but literarily speaking, she did not practice this break in her early writings, but in form and content tried to represent reconciliation instead of conflict.

*

In the 1930s, novels and short stories began to appear that addressed aspects of the lives of modern women and the difficulties and problems they faced because of social changes, particularly in women's status and social roles. The authors of these stories and novels were largely women who had received some formal education and worked in teaching or journalism. They experimented with various forms of writing: creative, social, and political. For example, Munira Tal'at described her novel *al-Ba'isa* (The Wretched Woman) 1931 as "an Egyptian social, literary novel, realistic and representative."[52] Malak Surur wrote *Sabiha* (Fresh Young Woman) 1948 about a girl who lives in a fishing village, exploring her feelings toward the boy she raises. Also, in the 1930s the first generations of women began graduating from King Fu'ad University; many of them obtained public positions as teachers and journalists and many women started recording their experiences and expressing themselves in writing.

It was at this point that 'A'isha 'Abd al-Rahman (Bint al-Shati') began her academic and literary life. The Arabic canon is enriched by her literary works, as well as her fundamental contributions as a professor of Islamic studies, a field to which she devoted herself and in which she became by the end of the century a prominent specialist, known both locally and regionally. 'A'isha 'Abd al-Rahman began writing stories and articles in the 1930s for papers such as *al-Ahram, al-Balagh, al-Hilal, al-Nahda,* and *al-Nisa'iya*. She gained renown for her interest in the peasant, and her book *al-Rif al-Misri* (The Egyptian Countryside) 1936, was awarded a prize in an official competition on reforming the countryside and advancing the peasant. In the 1930s, she began to receive invitations to speak in public forums. Her novels include *Sayyid al-'izba: qissat imra'a khati'a* (Lord of the Manor: The Story of a Fallen Woman) 1944,[53] which tells the story of a poor girl who lives in the country. Her family is cruel to her and casts her out, and she is forced to work as a servant; she is seduced by her lord and becomes a fallen woman, considered a pariah by the villagers. The female narrator is sympathetic to Samira, the fallen woman, and tries to extend a hand to her, but fails to protect her. Rumors about Samira spread and her story is transmitted among the people, until she becomes, for the Bedouin who are ignorant of the origin of the story, "a blessed saint," for they "see the light of the saints on her face."[54] In this early story, 'A'isha 'Abd al-Rahman questioned the dichotomy of fallen woman/saint, wondering, with the reader, about the moral system that is applied arbitrarily to women and not men. As such, she contributed to the debate about masculinity and femininity.

Like many women of her generation, 'A'isha 'Abd al-Rahman wrote stories about types of women she had seen in real life, and she decided to record her observations about the fate of these women by deriving lessons from their experiences. Her stories bear names like "al-Maqhura" (The Downtrodden Woman), "al-Makhdu'a" (The Deceived Woman), "al-Mutanakkira" (The Disguised Woman), "al-Mughtasaba" (The Violated Woman), "al-Muhtala" (The Deceptive Woman), and "al-Rahiba" (The Nun). She first published these stories in *al-Hilal* then collected them in a book that was awarded a prize by the Arabic Language Academy in Cairo in 1953.[55]

One of the most important novels to cap this type of story, based on an analysis of various types of women in the modern era, was *al-Jamiha* (The Defiant Woman) 1950, by Amina al-Sa'id. The novel is about Amira, a girl who combines strength with emotion and whose life ends tragically. The author gives us a psychological portrayal of the protagonist and charts the course of her life, focusing on the circumstances in which the heroine was raised and thereby shedding light on the role of the father, for example, and his relationship with his daughter. Al-Sa'id records and observes in the novel by offering descriptive or expository statements about certain events and behaviors, rather than integrating her ideas into the folds of the plot, character development, and the novel's language. As such, the novel is not artistically mature, but it does represent a milestone in the development of realism.

1946: The student uprising

The 1940s and 1950s witnessed rapid cultural and political developments: the end of the Second World War, the defeat of 1948 and the establishment of Israel, the Cairo fire of 1952, the Egyptian street's rising anger against the British and the palace, the revolution of July 23, 1952, increased expectations of more freedoms, the agricultural reforms of September 1952, the evacuation of the British, the emergence of the non-aligned movement, the nationalization of the Suez Canal in 1956 as a response to the World Bank's refusal to fund the construction of the High Dam, the failure of the Tripartite Aggression against Egypt in 1956, and a rising sense of patriotism. The air was filled with a sense of liberation and hope, and Nasser became a national hero and a symbol of the revolution against imperialist forces and corruption. Influenced by Sartre's *What is Literature* (1947), a strong trend emerged in Arabic culture that encouraged a literature of engagement and highlighted the role of writers in giving voice to national issues. The journal *al-Adab* appeared in Beirut in 1953 and adopted Sartre's concept of *littérature engagée*, or committed literature, as a "nationalist" enterprise, seeking to marry political Arab nationalism with responsible freedom in literature and philosophy.[56] In short, there was movement and a sense of imminent change.

For women, these changes brought more liberties and encouraged them to enter the public sphere, and successive generations of female students graduated from various colleges. Women took part in national activities and the resistance. In 1945, Inji Aflatun established the League of Women University and College Students, in which Latifa al-Zayyat participated, followed by the Ad Hoc Women's Association. Inji Aflatun published two books, *Thamanun milyun imra'a ma'ana* (Eighty Million Women with Us) 1948 and *Nahnu al-nisa' al-Misriyat* (We Egyptian Women) 1949. In 1942, Fatima Rashid formed the Women's Party, and in 1951, Doria Shafik led some 1,500 women on a march to the parliament to demand women's rights. In 1952, the Women's Committee for Popular Resistance was founded and included members such as Inji Aflatun, Zaynab al-Ghazali, and Hawwa Idris. In 1954, Amina al-Sa'id brought out the journal *Hawwa'*, published by Dar al-Hilal; the magazine became a forum for addressing issues concerning women's status in society.

The fiction of this period paves the way for the more mature works of later generations. Romantic tendencies continued with stories about love, fidelity, and betrayal, and women writers developed the tools to express women's emotions and their feelings about men. As a whole, these stories and novels are characterized by their emotional, confessional style, and they often lack a dramatic plot or a profound analytical perspective that would endow the work with a psychological, social, or political dimension. In terms of content and objectives, these texts—whether matter-of-fact reportage style or romances—are an expression of different directions in writing, but both styles embody a particular phase in the development of women's consciousness. This was a period in which the female writer tried to rebel against the cultural system that oppressed her, though she adopted this same cultural system's masculine-feminine dichotomy. Women writers promoted stereotypes of women as the weaker and gentler sex, more emotional than rational. Not seeking to destabilize existing social values and constructs, they were content to stake a small claim that allowed them some measure of freedom of movement and expression. This is a perspective that does not seek to dismantle prevailing binary constructs, but rather works within them and accepts their basic assumptions. The majority of these writers did not produce exceptional or great literary works, but they remain important because they had an impact on the wider reading public. These stories dealing with scenes from women's lives, usually published in newspapers and magazines, ultimately gave voice to a point of view that had long been ignored. This type of writing persists to the present day, and good examples of it can be found in the works of Sufi 'Abd Allah, Zaynab Rushdi, and Fawziya Mahran.

The romantic trend was an expression of the rebellion and revolution against all types of authority as embodied in various types of institutions. An introspective tone that viewed society from a perspective of difference became prominent, but it was a difference that suggested an overwhelming desire to relate and belong. The stress on individualism and particularity was a means to exercise freedom and challenge restrictive frameworks. Some women writers chose poetry as a way to express the inflamed emotions of this period, fraught with hopes and aspirations. Some of the more prominent names in this regard are Amina Najib, Rawhiya al-Qallini, Jalila Rida, Malak 'Abd al-'Aziz, Jamila al-'Alayili, Safiya Abu Shadi, Hayfa' al-Shanawani, and Sufi 'Abd Allah. Despite the unevenness of their literary production, these poets all championed self-expression. They wrote about love and passion, advocated freedom, broke with the constraints of tradition, and often used images taken from nature. Some poets chose to avoid the forbidden zones in their poetry and restricted themselves to public issues, while others broke taboos and addressed topics that had long been inaccessible to women. The critical celebration of "women's poetry" illustrated the extent of society's acceptance or rejection of women's entry to the public sphere. On one hand, women poets were critically acclaimed the more they spoke in a confessional tone, rebelled, and broke taboos; on the other hand, they were also subjected to a critical-moral attack that ascribed the popularity of "the literature of the liberated, rebel women" to the control that restrictions and taboos exercised on their minds.[57] These conflicting views illustrate the difficulties faced by women poets in their attempts to storm the bastion of Arabic culture. They also had to confront a symbol of Arabic culture and a significant power center: al-'Aqqad, who never tired of disparaging women's ability to compose poetry.[58]

*

Mindful of the climate in which Egyptian women wrote poetry, Jamila al-'Alayili joined the Apollo Group in the 1930s and published her first collection of poetry, *Sada ahlami* (The Echo of My Dreams) in 1936. Al-'Alayili rebelled against the constraints of traditional poetry both in form and content, writing free verse and prose poetry. She also wrote lyric poetry that sang of the beauty of nature and the freedom of the universe and creation. Her passion for nature was not limited to tangible phenomena; rather, in her poetry, like that of other poets, nature became an approach and an inspiration for a philosophical treatment of existence, life, and death.

In addition to her poetry, Jamila al-'Alayili wrote novels, including *al-Ta'ir al-ha'ir* (The Confused Bird) 1935 and *Arwah tata'allaf* (Souls in Harmony) 1947, in which she addressed more directly the relationship between men and women in a society undergoing rapid change. In the latter novel, al-'Alayili engages in a cultural battle where she confronts a series of accepted ideas held about women by educated men. The novel is set up as a series of letters between an Egyptian writer named Mayy—

perhaps Mayy Ziyada?—and a revolutionary journalist named Sa'id.

The poet Jalila Rida was also associated with the Apollo poets. She was close to Ibrahim Naji and came to the attention of poetry circles when she composed an elegy for his funeral in 1953. Rida's poetry, written in the tradition of the classical Arabic ode, is characterized by its outpouring of emotion and its delicate sensibility, giving voice to a confused soul searching for herself in nature and the universe.

In the same vein, Malak 'Abd al-'Aziz wrote romantic poetry in the classical form to express rebellious emotion. Her poetry is inspired by ideas and trends surging with the desire for liberation and change. She then embarked on free verse and was one of the pioneers of the new form,[59] which, in the poet's own words, gave her "greater freedom" and the ability "to portray the emotions and sensations surging in one poem."[60] The battle for free verse was not an easy one, as 'A'isha 'Abd al-Rahman reminds us. In 1961, al-'Aqqad, the head of the poetry committee of the Higher Council for Arts and Literature, sent a telegram to the secretary-general of the council saying, "Please consider me as having resigned from the poetry committee, and my speech at the poetry festival in Damascus cancelled, if Salah 'Abd al-Sabur and Ahmad 'Abd al-Mu'ti al-Hijazi are allowed to recite their poetry at the festival or at the memorial celebrating [the ninth-century poet] al-Buhturi."[61] Malak 'Abd al-'Aziz's first collection of poetry, *Aghani al-siba* (Songs of Youth), appeared in the early 1960s; it contained both traditional poetry and free verse written in the late 1930s, the 1940s, and the 1950s. As she said in the introduction to her first collection, she was influenced by the Apollo poets. 'Abd al-'Aziz wrote about nature, politics, and national causes using an unsentimental, yet emotional style. Muhammad Mandur, known as "the shaykh of the critics" and also 'Abd al-'Aziz's husband, described her poetry as spiritual poetry, which inspired him to coin the term "whispered poetry"—a term he used to describe a style of Arabic poetry that was particularly prominent among the Mahjar poets, or poets of the Exile School. He remarked that he never felt "the whisper in poetry gliding into [his] soul except when [he] heard Malak's poetry."[62]

Malak 'Abd al-'Aziz shows a concern with national issues and gives voice to the sense of rebellion and liberation that prevailed in the 1960s. Her "Ughniya ila Jifara" ("A Song for Guevara") inspired an entire generation, and she composed elegies for martyrs and supported Palestinian revolutionaries—all in her "whispering" style, which rendered her expression free from ideological grandstanding and booming sloganeering.

*

In tandem with romantic tendencies, a social realism began to take shape, and the two styles intersected and merged in the works of many women writers. Realist works of this period engaged modern situations and contemporary events, both social and political, and particularly the problems facing women in the light of changing social circumstances. The focus was still on female characters through whose eyes the reader sees the world and approaches the character and her universe. It is noteworthy that women writers showed a close interest in social and domestic relationships, personifying many different types of women. It is also noteworthy that women writers were just as concerned with negative female types as with positive ones, or, more accurately, they were interested in critiquing those female models with whom they did not agree and whom they believed had abused the freedom given to women in the modern age. One finds many writings that are variations of central questions: questions about the limits of women's freedom, the meaning of freedom, the exercise of freedom in society, men's views, and the double standards applied to the two sexes. These are topics addressed by successive generations of women writers, starting with the generation of Jadhibiya Sidqi, Sufi 'Abd Allah, Najiba al-'Assal, Zaynab Sadiq, Ihsan Kamal, Asma Halim, Huda Jad, Iqbal Baraka, Sakina Fu'ad, and Fawziya Mahran, and up to the generation of Muna Rajab, 'A'isha Abu-l-Nur, and Muna Hilmi.

It is no accident that the early 1960s witnessed the publication of three important novels: *al-Bab al-maftuh (The Open Door)* 1960, by Latifa al-Zayyat; *I'tirafat imra'a mustarjila* (Confessions of a Masculine Woman) 1960, by Su'ad Zuhayr; and *Mudhakkirat tabiba (Memoirs of a Woman Doctor)* 1960, by Nawal al-Sa'dawi. These were followed by 'Inayat al-Zayyat's *al-Hubb wa-l-samt* (Love and Silence) in 1967. These four novels are an expression of the rebellion against various forms of oppression faced by women, both as women and as citizens, a bold confrontation of problems and faith in the possibility of changing society for the better. The four novels crown the burst of optimism that followed the years of struggle for liberation on all levels and the glimmering ray of hope that the fruits of work and struggle could be enjoyed.

Latifa al-Zayyat's *al-Bab al-maftuh* is an important marker in the development of the Arabic novel. The novel gives us an optimistic perspective on the future, both national and personal. As Latifa al-Zayyat said, "The open door was the people's door and the nation's door."[63] The novel begins in 1946 with the demonstration of February 21 in Isma'iliya Square and ends in 1956 with the popular resistance in Port Sa'id against the Tripartite Aggression on Egypt. It charts the unfolding fate of Layla, a girl from the rising middle class, in her journey to acquire a new consciousness. From the beginning, al-Zayyat links the public and the private; events take place on both levels, and the fate of Layla and her family is closely linked with the fate of the nation. After alluding to the events of 1946, the writer takes us into Layla's family, putting them center stage. Every phase in the national struggle represents a turning point in Layla's life and her journey toward knowledge and awareness. Layla rebels against the oppressive isolation that women face and their forced submission to rules and traditions, which, Layla discovers, have no real value, but have been transformed into masks for social hypocrisy. She faces a difficult moment on her developmental journey when she is beaten by her father for participating in a demonstration with other female students; when she appeals to her supportive brother, she finds that he, too, is against her and he raises the banner of tradition. Screaming in pain, Layla confronts her brother, Mahmud, with the contradictions in his thought, which supports women and recognizes their equal rights and duties "on paper" only. Mahmud is bewildered and silent after the argument because "it was not her problem, not hers alone anyway; it was his, he wanted to assure her; it was their whole generation's dilemma."[64] On another stop on her journey, Layla faces the pain of personal betrayal, when her sweetheart 'Isam cheats on her with Sayyida, the maid, and her cousin Jamila betrays her husband, whom she hates; all of this takes place in tandem with the Cairo fire and the betrayal of the nation. Yet Layla finds solace and strength against all the forms of oppression she endures as a woman through her involvement in the popular resistance in Port Sa'id and the fusing of the individual with the collective. Al-Zayyat's optimism infuses the text, in which events progress logically and inevitably toward completion and victory, on both the personal and national levels; the plot serves to uphold the spirit of resistance against the forces of imperialism, and Layla wins her freedom as a woman with status in society after she regains her self-confidence and her ability to engage in a balanced, egalitarian relationship with Husayn, her brother's friend and his comrade in the resistance. The novel embodies the peak of a period of optimism and faith in the future.

I'tirafat imra'a mustarjila was published in serial form in *Rose al-Yusuf* in 1959 and as a book in 1960.[65] In the novel, the author observes the discrimination faced by the protagonist because of her sex, starting in her childhood and continuing into adulthood. The heroine runs up against traditions and customs that throw obstacles in the face of girls and force them onto a path that is not freely chosen. The protagonist, who is making the eponymous confessions, discovers the yawning gulf between talk about freedom and equality and their actual application. She becomes known as a "masculine woman" despite herself, in order to protect herself in a society that makes fair game of women who depart from traditional feminine roles. She zealously adopts a stern, severe exterior and distances herself from all characteristics associated with femininity, not only to close the door on any suspicions or doubts, but also to compensate for the sense of weakness instilled in her. The heroine rebels against a society governed by values and traditions that serve men and their interests at the expense of women. She throws herself into heated battles with the men she meets, taking the advice of the proverb, "Eat him for lunch before he eats you for dinner."[66] The heroine continues to deny her womanhood until she meets a younger man, with whom she discovers love and emotional satisfaction. But society and its outdated customs and traditions triumph when the lovers are forced to end their relationship because of social pressures. In the introduction to the first edition, al-Zuhayr discussed the uproar that ensued when the novel was first serialized in *Rose al-Yusuf.* The publication of the "confessions" caused severe harm to the author since many readers and critics assumed that she was telling her own life story. As she said in the introduction, "These suspicious questions made some members of my family so angry that they threatened to sue me to stop the publication of the confessions, to protect the family name."[67]

Nawal al-Sa'dawi opens her *Mudhakkirat tabiba* with a return to the heroine's childhood, focusing on the psychological trauma she experienced because of the discrimination between her and her brother. The protagonist detests her femininity and despises the weakness of her gender, waging a battle against society, tradition, and men. In her clinic, she encounters life's tragedies and women's problems. After some time, she stops to reconsider her life and finds she wants to love a man who understands her and does not look at her only as a body. In this autobiographical novel, Nawal al-Sa'dawi confronts the repercussions of discrimination against women boldly and frankly, and her boldness is transformed into a positive energy that inspires hope in changing society for the better. Al-Sa'dawi has continued to write about discrimination against women in male-dominated societies, publishing several novels, short stories, and social and political essays that can all be considered variations on the same theme. Her works mercilessly expose the weak points of men in order to explain their oppressive behavior toward women, though some have criticized this severity as excessive and accused her of simplifying complex human relationships. In many of al-Sa'dawi's stories and novels, the reader meets a woman who has rebelled against her circumstances and begins her search for an identity that has been crushed by the detritus of custom and tradition. Often the protagonist is a doctor or a medical student, or a doctor who meets a female prisoner awaiting execution. These novels take a semi-autobiographical form that blends fiction with reality. In one of her best novels, *Imra'atan fi imra'a (Two Women in One)* 1971, the heroine, Bahiya Shahin, a medical student, questions her identity: is she a proper girl who bows to the directives of her family and others, or is she a free entity with her own desires, which differ from the mass of other people? In any case, she endures various forms of oppression—domestic, social, and political—but ultimately discovers herself. When she is told that she is "unnatural," she concludes this is a positive attribute in a society that represses human features. The novel ends as Bahiya takes matters into her own hands, willingly and fearlessly going to prison with the detainees she treats. She reshapes her identity, drawing the lines of her own life.

In *al-Hubb wa-l-samt*, 'Inayat al-Zayyat's only novel, we meet Najla', an eighteen-year-old girl from a well-off family who falls prey to depression and melancholy after her brother dies. She feels insignificant in a family that has lost a son and cares little for the daughter. The heroine talks about her perpetual sense of inferiority and desire to disappear; she is ultimately led to hate her femininity, which she holds directly responsible for her condition. She likes pastel colors "because they make me as invisible as possible."[68] In another section of the novel she says, "How I hate this beautiful body . . . I'm ashamed of it . . . Its overflowing femininity declares itself without asking for my opinion."[69] Najla' works at a company where she meets Ahmad, a leftist revolutionary journalist. She then truly embarks on life and gives up her pastel colors: "I want a positive color . . . a color that affirms me and makes him look at me."[70] The novel observes the evolution of the heroine's consciousness through important phases of self-confrontation and discovery, until she reaches the point when she affirms her awareness of her self, her individuality, and her independence from what she sees as the captivity of her femininity. She feels strong enough to meet the difficulties that face her, and her relationship with Ahmad is transformed, as she becomes the one who offers him a helping hand. Ahmad dies, and she decides to face life courageously. She enrolls in the College of Fine Arts, taking up art as a means to excite emotion and defend humanity. The novel ends with the July 23 revolution. Thus her new consciousness is born in tandem with the birth of a new nation, and once more we see that the liberation of the individual/woman intersects with the liberation of society.

*

In addressing women's place in society, one of the most compelling issues for women writers is the contradictions in modern society, particularly the conflict between new and old values. They balk at the paradoxes they find in the reality that surrounds them—paradoxes that strip the new model of its legitimacy and credibility and turn it into an abstract concept that has no relationship with real life. Women writers question the meaning of freedom and its significance for women: what are the limits to this freedom and the consequences of exercising it? How does society see the liberated woman and to what extent does it allow her to choose her own path and make her own decisions? Women writers point to the gap between the prevalent modernist discourse about the possibility of expanding liberty, both public and private, and the small margin of freedom actually allowed to women. Most of these writers address the contradiction between form and content, expectations and possibilities, and theory and practice to shed light on the dilemma of the contemporary woman in her relationship with society, with others, and with her self, which represents and reflects many of these external contradictions. Women writers highlight the dilemma of self-expression in a society that is searching for its own identity and takes women to be the symbol of that ideal identity. Within this framework, various stories and novels address the contradictions and conflicts inside the family. For example, contemporary marriage seems to differ from traditional marriage, but in fact it only illustrates the continuity of an imbalance of power in the relationship. Gradually the fiction of writers, both male and female, matures, and we begin to find better-crafted writing in terms of story, plot, and language.

A good example is the story, "Satr maghlut" ("A Mistake in the Knitting") by Ihsan Kamal.[71] Sawsan, the protagonist of the story, is ridden with anxiety because she wants to break her engagement to a man who she has discovered is unsuited to her, but she fears the rumors that she well knows will spread as a result. On the advice of her sister, Sawsan begins to knit a sweater for her fiancé, and the sweater becomes an objective measure of her relationship with him. She discovers a dropped stitch in the sweater, but she is too lazy to undo the stitch to correct it, trying to hide it instead by knitting more. Gradually, she comes to hate the sweater and rues the day she ever thought of making it, just as she despises her fiancé and feels trapped in the engagement. The story ends when her sister notices the dropped stitch and undoes it, causing the entire sweater to unravel. This symbolic action helps Sawsan confront herself, and she breaks the engagement and bears the consequences.

*

Alifa Rifaat began writing stories and publishing them in magazines in the 1950s; at her husband's request, she then stopped publishing for twenty years and only began again after his death. Rifaat probes the world of village women and storms taboo areas in the culture, describing the pain of female genital mutilation, forced marriage, rural marriage traditions such as the ritual of declaring and proving the bride's virginity and the family's honor, and repressed desires. She uses a language that is both realistic and sensual, calling things by their names and refusing to hide behind figurative images or symbols. Her story, "'Alami al-majhul" ("My World of the Unknown"),[72] sparked an uproar, receiving both praise and rebuke. It is the tale of a middle-class woman who moves to an abandoned house in a village with her husband and children. She sees a snake and is attracted to it despite herself. She loves it and, with it, she finds pleasure and perfect rapture. The woman speaks about her desire with a clarity and directness usually avoided by other women writers: "I would wish for her coil-like touch, her graceful gliding motion."[73] The snake and its parallel world embody the repressed world of women, which finds no outlet for expression despite its latent force. The deprived woman finds the love she lacks and craves in her own private world, off limits to the members of her family. But despite her desire to conceal and maintain her unknown world, the love is not safe from the real world's invasions on her privacy: her husband kills the snake, violating the sanctity of the place, and the family is forced to move to another house.

1967: All is not well

Very quickly there rose to the surface anxieties and apprehensions about the direction taken by the new order, particularly the gap between declared policies and rules and the actual application of these rules. In the 1960s, the various unspoken contradictions that accompanied the revolution began to emerge. While the revolution held aloft the banner of freedom, liberation, and social justice—and indeed began steering a socialist course to minimize the gaps between rich and poor and to push all segments of society toward progress and advancement—the Revolutionary Command Council began to eliminate the forums for political opposition and reduce the space for the exercise of freedoms, heralding the beginning of a one-party dictatorship. In August 1952, two textile workers were executed for taking part in a peaceful demonstration; in 1953, all political parties were dissolved; and in 1954, the Society of Muslim Brothers was outlawed after a failed assassination attempt on Nasser, who blamed the Brothers. The year 1959 witnessed a broad arrest campaign against communists, followed in 1960 by arrests and detentions of members of the Brothers, initiating an era of fear. In the 1960s, the idea of engagement was shaken as some of its oppressive repercussions were seen, including ideological propaganda and the abandonment of a critical spirit, a basic characteristic of literature. The contradiction between slogans about liberty and dignity and the institution of oppressive measures that violated the very heart of these slogans found its best expression in the novel *Tilka al-ra'iha (The Smell of It)* 1966, by Sonallah Ibrahim. This was followed by the defeat of 1967 and the shattering of all hopes.

Like political parties and associations, women's associations suffered from the restricted margin of liberty for people to express their opinions and interests. The revolution quashed associations and institutions that had some presence on the political stage, thus weakening popular forms of resistance, particularly for women. In the same year in which the constitution was amended to uphold equality between men and women

(1956), giving women political rights they had demanded for thirty-six years, the revolution disbanded the Egyptian Women's Union established by Huda Sha'rawi in 1923. The union became the Huda Sha'rawi Association, an N.G.O. involved in voluntary charity work. Its function thus changed: formerly an institution that demanded women's rights and worked to raise public awareness of women's issues—an essentially political function—it became a service-oriented association placed under the direct supervision of the Ministry of Social Affairs.

The incompatibility between the two faces of the revolution—which simultaneously granted and revoked liberties—is well illustrated in the fate of a pioneer feminist in Egypt, Doria Shafik (1908–1975). Shafik earned her doctorate from the Sorbonne in the 1940s, after which she returned to Egypt and established the magazine, *Bint al-Nil*, in 1945, followed by the Bint al-Nil Union in 1948 and the Bint al-Nil political party in 1953. In 1951, she led a women's march to demand changes in legislation. Doria Shafik was one of the first to question the revolution's repressive measures against civil society. She expressed her opposition and criticized Nasser, and in 1957, she launched a hunger strike to protest the dissolution of civic organizations. She also called on Israel to withdraw from Palestine. Her bold stance was met with a decisive severity that presaged the mass arrests and torture faced by opponents of the regime. She was placed under house arrest and banished from public life. Her name was banned from the press, and some of her colleagues informed on her, accusing her of conspiring with the forces of imperialism against the revolution. Doria Shafik entirely disappeared from public life, leaving only scattered poems and memoirs; she committed suicide in 1975.

On the private level, the legal changes that gave women many rights in public life were not accompanied by similar changes in the personal status laws. The constitutional amendments of 1956 gave women the right to vote and upheld gender equality, but the legislative changes that enshrined women's equal rights to education, work, and public office did not extend to personal status laws, thus preserving the non-egalitarian nature of the domestic relationship. As a result, women found themselves in a society suffering from a frightful split on the level of discourse and consciousness. On one hand, women were asked to share political and economic responsibilities with men, while on the other they were surrounded by a battery of laws and regulations that impeded their performance and made them less than men. Women writers of this time approached sociopolitical issues through eyes that also saw the particularity of women's place in the symbolic cultural order.

This period witnessed the beginning of writing about failure, loss, and fragmentation. The lovely dreams recede, replaced by a voice confused and at a loss before history's overpowering changes. We also see the beginning of the reification of the conscious self, related to the emergence of modernist tendencies in writing. Unlike realism, here the writer did not assume that reality had defined, specific features that she could embody or reflect in her writing. Rather, the writing woman found herself faced with an ambiguous, contradictory reality and she engaged it in a dialectical relationship, not relying on linear development or hanging any hopes on it. This modernist relationship gave rise to particular styles and perspectives. In the new writing, we can discern a tendency not to adhere to a strict chronology, the use of stream-of-consciousness narrative, the evocation of myth, and a probing of a fantastic world where the boundary between the real and the imagined is effaced. There is a noticeable state of fragmentation because of the loss of certainty; the heroine of these works is defeated from beginning to end, and she does not undergo some evolution from innocence to knowledge. In the late 1960s and early 1970s, we find novels and stories raising the alarm, to warn that all is not well.

*

Zaynab Sadiq's novel *Yawm ba'd yawm* (Day After Day) was first serialized in *Sabah al-khayr* from November 1964 to January 1965 and published in full by Hilal Novels in 1969. The novel tells the story of Amira, who feels that she is insignificant, suffers from depression and boredom, and fails to find any meaning in the life she lives. The author successfully conveys the protagonist's sense of ennui and futility. As the title suggests, the days pass, one after the other, bringing the same routine and more frustration and failure. Sadiq also manages to link the heroine's personal frustration with women's frustration in society. The reader encounters a group of women who have earned their degrees and joined the labor market. They have made sacrifices, only to confront the toils of routine, gender discrimination, and society's lack of appreciation of the roles they fulfill. The novel ends on a tone of resignation and hopelessness.

Hikayat 'Abduh 'Abd al-Rahman (The Tale of 'Abduh 'Abd al-Rahman) 1977, by Asma Halim, is a pioneering experiment in women's writing. The author adopts the point of view of a poor, desperate man and gives voice to his sense of oppression and defeat, a product of his poverty and exploitation. Creating a painful embodiment of oppressed manhood, Asma Halim successfully links personal defeat with the larger, national defeat.

In this tense climate, Safinaz Kazim published a series of articles in *al-Jil al-jadid* about hitchhiking around America in 1959. Kazim writes about her experiences and observations using various literary forms, including letters, essays, autobiographical short stories, fantasy, literary criticism, and the prose poem. In all her writings, we are struck by the uniqueness of Kazim's character, her views on art, people, love, and life, and her relationships with her family, her neighbors, her daughter, and her colleagues. "Safinaz is never impartial," as Amina Rachid tells us.[74] Indeed, her experience makes us question the very meaning of impartiality, its importance, and the possibility of actually achieving it. The writings of Safinaz Kazim are subjective impressions that take many forms, influenced by and exploring a variety of expressive and creative tools. Her impressions of color are perhaps indicative of her creative sensibility, as well as an apt comment on the times:

> The 1940s are the years of my childhood, and their color in my emotions is orange. The 1950s are cerulean blue, and the 1960s are red. The 1970s are purple, the color of bruises, that cousin of gray. The 1980s are white, overshadowed by dust clouds at the end to enter the 1990s as gray. A longing for orange: longing, longing, longing.[75]

*

The works of Latifa al-Zayyat remain one of the most eloquent and profound literary expressions of this period of angst in our political, social, and literary history. After the publication of her first novel, brimming with hope, optimism, and faith in a better future, al-Zayyat stopped publishing her writings—but she did not stop writing, something she considered "an act of freedom, a means of reformulating my self and my society."[76] Trying to answer the question of why she stopped publishing her work may give us the keys that will enable us to approach the concerns of literature in this period, particularly literature by women. Al-Zayyat's collection *al-Shaykhukha wa qisas ukhra* (Old Age and Other Stories), published in 1986, contains stories written in the early 1960s; parts of her *Hamlat taftish: awraq shakhsiya (The Search: Personal Papers)*, published in 1992, were written in the 1960s and 1970s; the play *Bi' wa shira* (Buying and Selling), published two years later, was also written in the 1960s, and she started writing her novel, *Sahib al-bayt (The Owner of the House)*, published in 1994, in 1962.[77] In these works, Latifa al-Zayyat leaves behind the optimism of *al-Bab al-maftuh*—where merging with the collectivity, the moment "I" is submerged into "we," is the moment of true freedom—to give voice to the painful contradictions between form and content, image and reality, the conscious, revolutionary intellectual and the false intellectual, enthusiastic slogans and their faulty application, truth and lie. Speaking of this period, al-Zayyat said:

> I personally actively contributed to this revolutionary moment. As a student, I was one of three officers of the National Council

for Students and Workers that led the struggle of the Egyptian people in 1946. In the street, I was a fully joined human being, with all my intellectual, emotional, and existential faculties. In the street, I was—we were—re-producing our society. I was us, which was me, and we were crafting tomorrow, feeling it as it took shape and came into being.[78]

Later in 1967, she notes "the margin narrows and things collapse."[79]

Why did Latifa al-Zayyat refrain from publishing her works? No sooner had she given voice to the peak of a national revival and hope in the future in *al-Bab al-maftuh*, than she began to sense the retreat and rupture that all of society would be forced to face sooner or later. In that period it was not permissible politically or ideologically to express fear or doubt the usefulness or credibility of the path chosen by the revolution's leaders and followed by a group of intellectuals and writers—some of whom became merely talking heads for the regime and its politics. This was the political repression that touched all members of society. In addition, Latifa al-Zayyat, by dint of her ideological leanings and her involvement in politics, was part of the nationalist, leftist movement that saw the cause of women in society as a secondary issue, not a social priority. They believed that liberation from imperialism and class oppression would bring about the liberation of women, and that movements demanding women's rights were divisive and would disperse efforts and weaken ranks. We can thus surmise some of the reasons that led al-Zayyat to imprison her writings, keeping them away from the light of day until some twenty-five years had passed. In the 1980s and 1990s, we can read in Latifa al-Zayyat the silences in the leftist political discourse of the earlier period, or what was not said about women's status—a condition that still affects some women writers of certain political affiliations.

In the early 1990s, Latifa al-Zayyat finished *Sahib al-bayt*, a novel which she had begun in 1962, weighting it with the depth of experience and insight acquired with the passing of time. Although the novel was published in the 1990s, it remains a fine expression of the stumblings of the 1960s. According to *Hamlat taftish*, the original title of the work was *Shajarat al-mishmish* (The Apricot Tree), then *al-Rihla* (The Journey), alluding to humankind's journey from birth to death.[80] Al-Zayyat said that she did not complete the novel due to a fundamental flaw, a flaw she only discovered after her divorce when she regained her "view of social and historical reality."[81] She added,

The vision of reality in *The Journey* is a painful one—it was mine at one point in my marriage—but strange, given the general direction of my life's development as a whole. In this novel, man is individual, not social, and his freedom is a burden which he alone has to bear. He is an ahistorical individial who finds himself thrown into an absolute, ahistorical situation, and his ahistoricality is brought out more strongly by his endless isolation and loneliness.[82]

What is the significance of this comment for the novel? *Sahib al-bayt* revolves around Samiya, who goes underground with her husband, Muhammad, a prison fugitive charged with a political crime, with the help of their friend, Rafiq. Although Samiya is involved in the prison escape and challenges her family by making the choice, she is not treated as an equal by Muhammad or Rafiq and is privy to none of the practical details about the escape or going underground. This engenders a perpetual terror in her and causes her to make a series of mistakes. Most of the time, Samiya is treated as an obstacle in the comrades' path, and her ability, as a woman, to withstand hardship is openly discussed. In a moment of clarity, Samiya discovers that always denying her knowledge has put her in a permanent second-class situation below her comrades. She finds that her desire to belong to the group and obey its directives has led her to shut her eyes to the methods of oppression and servitude that the collective has used against her, as a woman and a member of the group with rights on the collective. Samiya is torn between love and loyalty, between her attempt to cling to absolute values and her realization of the relativity of things, between her desire to belong and her overwhelming sense of her own individuality, between her submersion in the collective and her estrangement from it. In *Hamlat taftish*, Latifa al-Zayyat says that she realizes that she had spent her life "striving for the absolute and that the absolute is the spouse of death. I realize that there is no permanency and no stability in a life the nature of which is perpetual change."[83] Samiya enters the home/hideout/shelter to find that it has an owner, who bears down on them all. Latent conflicts and problems explode in Samiya's life, especially her marital life. In this oppressive, stifling house, Samiya hides with her husband and eludes the police, just as Latifa al-Zayyat hid with her husband in 1949 in the house in Sidi Bishr. In *Hamlat taftish*, al-Zayyat describes the house in Sidi Bishr as "my creation and my choice," while the ancient house in which she was raised is "my fate and my heritage."[84] In *Sahib al-bayt*, Samiya admits that the house which she imagines she has chosen still upholds the same values and traditions that oppressed her as a child. She still has not found the freedom for which she searches; the ideas and ideologies which she saw as a way to liberty are still betraying her. She wonders,

if she had become the monster they wanted her to be, a monster with no roots and no power to move? A lifetime of training had finally paid off, a lifetime spent hiding from other people's eyes and hearts, of isolation and deprivation, beating and intimidation, threats and promises, blame and punishment, of whispering in corners: Woe betide he who differs! . . . Mother, father, grandmother, the minaret that overlooks our old house, my friends, all of you who cleared a space for me among you, here I am poised on the brink of belonging, as you wanted me to, I have come to you as a monster with no roots and no power to move.[85]

Here the heroine abandons the illusion of dissolving in the collectivity as she discovers the falsity of ideologies that do not allow divergence from the group. In her attempt to escape the prison of the old house, despite its attraction and its poetic and emotional mythology, she entered the prison of another home that has its own warden and bars, though details and topography may differ. She looks on high and wonders; is it "a dove tower or an observation tower?"[86] In *Sahib al-bayt*, al-Zayyat confronts her silences of the 1960s: her ideology's oppression of her as a woman and the dictatorship's oppression of dissenting voices. Latifa al-Zayyat captures the human existential dilemma in which the individual tries to stand simultaneously with and against the collective, a human being's entanglement in the labyrinth of loneliness and conflict, trapped between necessity and freedom.[87] Samiya faces her life, recognizing that life's exigencies have forced her to adjust to the owner of the house and obey the rules of the game he and all those around him were playing. When she enters the house, she realizes that she

had always played that game [of the owner of the house] and, although she did not know when and where, she was able to sense that the owner of the house had always been with her in one way or another, always and forever dictating the rules of his game to her. What, or who, did this man remind her of, she wondered? The one and only sovereign? Her father? The preacher at the mosque who threatened hell-fire and damnation? The teacher as he asked her to spread out her hands?[88]

At the end of the novel, Samiya faces the owner of the house and defeats him in a battle that is both physical and symbolic, liberating herself from her restraints.

The novel embodies an era that combined the ideologies of liberation, nationalism, and Arab unity with the means of oppression practiced by a ruling elite that used emotive slogans, but only after emptying them of all meaning. Literature and writers were at the vanguard of those who rejected these tools of oppression. Just as in *al-Bab al-maftuh* Latifa al-Zayyat managed to blend revolutionary aspirations with women's emancipation, in *Sahib al-bayt* she is able to express the parallel nature of political and ideological oppression, on one hand, and sexual oppression, on the other. In both novels, she puts her finger on the conflicts and contradictions that informed women's status in society.

1976: The gods collapse

Economic liberalization and a new pro-Western politics brought back the values of capitalism and the power of money. The rise of neo-capitalism coincided with the collapse of the middle class, which sank into poverty and want. Egyptian society became a consumer society like those of the West, with the difference that it consumed goods it did not produce and enjoyed luxuries it had expended no effort to attain. A new, exploitative business class arose that monopolized capital and instituted a new value system whose pillars were quick profits, recklessness, and fraud. Egyptian society witnessed a new form of emigration as its sons and daughters headed in droves to the Gulf, particularly the oil-producing countries, looking for jobs to meet life's demands. Politically, the state made a fundamental shift: al-Sadat visited Israel, and yesterday's enemy became today's ally, at least officially. The dream of Arab unity took a final blow, and all familiar frames of reference collapsed. Leftist forces were defeated; conservative forces emerged to reshape values in accordance with the new circumstances. Although the beginnings of this general collapse lie in 1967, its consequences and manifestations came to the surface in the 1970s.

Realism and romanticism continued to be seen in the works of the generation of Jadhibiya Sidqi, Najiba al-'Assal, Fawziya Mahran, and Sufi 'Abd Allah. A second generation of women writers working in journalism appeared, including Iqbal Baraka and Sakina Fu'ad, followed by 'A'isha Abu-l-Nur, Muna Rajab, and Muna Hilmi. They continued the writerly journey through female eyes, observing reality and its consequences in the context of new social circumstances. The question of freedom continued to be pondered, as well as how to balance home and work; the problem of women torn between their view of themselves and society's expectations, and the difficult decisions that women make to protect themselves from being totally dissolved in the collective crucible. Women writers also explored human relationships from all perspectives. Iqbal Baraka wrote about the spirit of competition between working women and housewives, about the feelings of a teacher forced into retirement, about a married couple trying to regain moments of joy to resist the tedium of their lives, about the human interaction between a man and a woman in a moment of danger, trapped in a shelter during an air raid, about the feelings of a woman who is denied motherhood and the psychological and social pains she endures, about the role of work in a woman's life and the possibility of overcoming crises with strength drawn from career accomplishments,[89] and about the tragedy of a successful woman who discovers that she is still treated as a commodity by society.[90] 'A'isha Abu-l-Nur wrote about the difference between her public persona as a journalist, writer, and successful woman, and her persona at home with her husband and children,[91] and about Salwa, who chooses travel and exile to escape her reality.[92] Women writers thus continued to explore the boundaries of human relationships, particularly male-female relationships, in light of new social circumstances. In *Layla wa-l-majhul* (Layla and the Unknown) 1980, by Iqbal Baraka, Layla searches for the meaning of freedom and honor within the bounds of her relationship with Qays. Readers come to know the deprivations suffered by girls from poor families and the allure of economic liberalization, travel to the oil-producing countries, and marriage to a wealthy foreigner. Layla, a university student, comes to realize the importance of economic independence as a basic condition for a well-balanced love relationship. In *La tasriq al-ahlam* (Don't Steal the Dreams) 1978, by Zaynab Sadiq, the reader follows the developments of Amina's relationships through the wars of 1956, 1967, and 1973, while Wafiya Khayri makes the defeat of 1967 the center of events in her novel *al-Hayah fi khatar* (Life in Danger) 1983; in *Laylat al-qabd 'ala Fatima* (The Night Fatima Was Arrested) 1980, Sakina Fu'ad addresses political corruption.

*

Writing techniques evolved, and women writers continued to explore various ways and means of giving voice to the particularity of their experience. There was a tendency in this period to use symbolism, seen in I'tidal 'Uthman, Siham Bayyumi, Ibtihal Salem, and Sahar Tawfiq. In the introduction to her short-story collection, *Yunus al-bahr* (Jonah of the Sea) 1987, writer and critic I'tidal 'Uthman contemplates some features of the new writing, which breaks with the familiar and avoids the easy relationship between writer and reader that is based on perpetuating the expected in "fixed, obsolete molds,"[93] to offer instead stories that join poetry with prose and the lyrical with the narrative. In her stories, 'Uthman evokes a mythical age that intersects with and implicates the present, and the two dissolve in a melting pot of expressive allusions. The author weaves the story of the prophet Jonah into the tale of a village fighting to absorb the manifestations and consequences of modern urbanity, creating an air of myth that envelops the events and characters in an aura of poetry. In the story, "al-Sultana" (The Sultana),[94] myth meets contemporary Egyptian history in the tales of Aunt Sultana. In contrast to the affective words that penetrate the depths of a small child to shape and direct her, in a painful paradox the reader encounters the hollow words of an article written by the child when she grows up and becomes a journalist. Despite her break with the village and the era of Aunt Sultana and her stories, she, too, is stopped by the falsity of her words, "which have a ring without an echo."[95] She stops writing, tears up her papers, and remembers the truth and wisdom of Aunt Sultana's stories.

In "al-Ta'ir al-azraq" (The Blue Bird),[96] by Siham Bayyumi, the seagull becomes a symbol of the unattainable lover/dream; the bird flies to the heavens, foreboding loss and disappointment. In the stories of Ibtihal Salem, the seagull becomes a figure that embodies a longing for freedom and the simultaneous expectation that it will not come. The stories in her first collection, *al-Nawras* (The Seagull) 1989, take place in a coastal city after the 1967 war. They are linked by the voice of a narrator who witnesses the material and moral destruction of the city that touches her personally; she is not an outside observer of events but inside and involved in them. In "Madinat al-kartun" ("City of Cardboard"), the writer highlights some of the repercussions of economic liberalization, which turns her city into a city of cardboard boxes—a reference to the boxes used to smuggle goods from the free market to make huge profits for a group of opportunistic businessmen. At the end of the story, the narrator stumbles into "a large box of rubbish with a big cardboard carton on top."[97] She runs into the street, where she is deafened by the noise coming from the boutiques and overpowered by the ugliness of the boxes scattered about her; she hears only "the fluttering of the gulls plunging out to sea."[98] In contrast to the wide sea, the seagull spanning the sky, the fragrance of the sand, and the gentle sea breeze, the author observes a state of deprivation, loss, and frustrated dreams, using a poetic language that intersects with a hyper-realistic language. The bird's fluttering wings are coupled with a detailed, carefully chosen description of daily life to paint a living portrait of a popular neighborhood suffering the depredations of war. The stories are characterized by their brevity and profound allusiveness, approaching what Edwar al-Kharrat describes as "the story poem."[99] In her most recent collection, *Nakhb iktimal al-qamar* (A Toast to the Full Moon), Ibtihal Salem is even briefer; the stories are extremely short, more like fleeting glimpses that embody moments of pain, longing, and deprivation in a fierce reality stripped of human values.

In "al-Jihat al-arba'a" ("Points of the Compass"),[100] by Sahar Tawfiq, the author draws on folklore and the pharaonic heritage to create a world that blends the mythical and the real. The main character, the mother/goddess Mufida, embarks on journeys through time. The four points are the four pillars that hold up the sky in pharaonic tradition; they are also the topography surrounding the Nile River as it flows from south to north and floods both banks. They are the four limbs of the goddess of the heavens, Nut, who guards the land of Egypt and gives birth to the sun god every morning. Questions of emigration, belonging, and identity—

that is, contemporary issues—take on mythical, eternal dimensions. The mother mourns the departure of her children, for whom she sacrificed and gave everything, but they leave her to live alone in a state of permanent waiting. Her tragedy becomes the story of existence, the story of the bride of the Nile, who was given as an offering to the Nile every year to ensure the continuity of the floods, and life.

Ni'mat al-Buhayri also describes the effects of economic liberalization on Egyptian society, as well as the new values that came from the oil-producing region, through Egyptians who went there looking for a livelihood and fleeing deprivation and want. Social critique and a political sensibility are joined to a scrutiny of the soul. The writer describes confused spirits who hover in the sky looking for the familiar, a refuge, and containment, but connections are broken on the rocks of an oppressive, painful reality. In the story, "'Indama yasqut al-matar" (When It Rains),[101] a man and a women meet alone in the rain, brought together by circumstances, the pain of want, and what appears to be a shared awareness of values and problems. They find themselves in front of a café and go in for a tea. The couple watches the well-off café patrons—foreign and Gulf tourists—and the male and female waiters who have university degrees, but cannot find jobs in their field. The story ends with the man taking a job at the café as a waiter. Al-Buhayri presents social criticism indirectly, without sloganeering. Instead she alludes to the values of economic liberalization, which brought in foreign companies and ensured the supremacy of anything foreign; Egyptians, meanwhile, have become brokers, middlemen, and waiters. Al-Buhayri is brief and uses a conversational, self-revelatory style instead of direct narration.

"It had been a long winter and I could make myself wait no longer"— Radwa Ashour opens her story, "Ra'ayt al-nakhl" ("I Saw the Date-Palms"),[102] with these eloquently simple words to describe the sterility and emptiness that have afflicted people and become a chronic state of apathy, indifference, and even an inability to connect. Latifa al-Zayyat called this "a period story,"[103] and it is indeed suggestive with its profound symbolism and easy style, which completely eschews any directness in word or description. It is the story of Fawziya, who loves planting and tending plants. She goes into the street looking for tree blossoms, and people accuse her of madness. Using a saying of the prophet Muhammad—"Honour your paternal aunts the date-palms"—Ashour makes the palms a symbol of connection, mutual respect, and enduring ties over generations. The palm also becomes a symbol of the roots that link the past with the present. Fawziya's relationship with planting and the palm trees—"of straight stature and towering"—suggests the longevity and continuity of individual and collective memory,[104] despite attempts to break or fragment it, which lead to both a loss of memory and a dulling of the senses. Fawziya's efforts to link compassion with trees and people are not lost: the cactus planted by her grandmother still bears green leaves, despite the drought, and her neighbor visits to ask her to teach her how to tend to plants. In a ruined land, memory becomes the most important incentive to start on the road to deliverance.

*

That final observation leads us to one of the features of women's fiction of this period: the blend of history and literature, and private and public events. History here is the history of regular, simple people, not the history of the great and prominent. Can the palm tree in Radwa Ashour's story be interpreted as the Arab collective memory, striving against attempts to erase and distort it? In the dream, the tree stands lofty and tall, but what happens to it in reality? Women writers asked questions about history and memory in various ways in their works. In *al-Rihla* (The Journey) 1983, Radwa Ashour documents her experience as a graduate student in the U.S.; she finds that the discrimination endured by blacks and Indians in the land of dreams and liberty is equivalent to the discrimination and coercion experienced by people in the Third World. She offers a different perspective from that expressed in *'Usfur min al-sharq (A Bird from the East)* or *Qandil Umm Hashim (The Lamp of Umm Hashim)*. In those works, written in the early twentieth century, the male author focuses on the self and his inner experience; the theme is about being torn between traditional values and new values, represented by the Western world. The conflict in those texts is a conflict of loyalty versus a sense of awe, a choice between clinging to a romantic past and being prisoner to a tyrannical present. In contrast, in *al-Rihla*, Ashour evokes history to mix the events of her life with public events in the nation's life. Even in her early writings, Radwa Ashour has shown an interest in the relationship between collective and individual history, seeing them as organically bound up in a dialectical relationship that is always renewed: collective history reflects the lives of individuals, and the details of individual lives shape collective history and its course.

This is true for all of Radwa Ashour's works, including *Hajar dafi'* (A Warm Stone) 1985, *Khadija wa Sawsan* (Khadija and Sawsan) 1989, and particularly *Thulathiyat Gharnata* (The Granada Trilogy) 1994 and 1995, as well as the autobiographical *Atyaf* (Specters) 1999. The events of the trilogy begin in 1491, a few months before Granada is turned over to the Catholic monarchs Ferdinand and Isabella, and continue through 1609, the year the first expulsion order was issued for the Morisco Arabs in Andalusia. The trilogy documents the fall of Andalusia and the ensuing defeat, fragmentation, loss, and assaults designed to quash Arab-Muslim identity through forced conversion to Christianity, expulsion, the burning of books, and intimidation. Ashour presents her perspective on this period through the eyes of a family, that of Abu Ja'far, who inherits the job of safeguarding the community's books. By following the fate of this family, which runs parallel to the collapse of a civilization, the reader becomes familiar with documented historical events, but also experiences the minute details in the lives of the ordinary people who witnessed the fall. The trilogy manages to answer the question: how do people live and remain steadfast in the face of historical hardships and catastrophes that determine their fate? Radwa Ashour weaves a human tapestry in which she combines the public and private, the historical and the individual, in an integrated, well-ordered system. Did she intend the fall of Granada to represent the loss of Palestine? Or does the trilogy evoke the Gulf War and its repercussions, as the author says? It does not matter. In her autobiography, Radwa Ashour says that her absorption in the trilogy restored the balance to her personal life, which had been upset by the events of the Gulf War. She says her intent was to write "about people like [her] living in history's lethal grasp with no release."[105] Although her subject is endings, the act of writing and her engrossment in investigating historical facts "restored [her] sovereignty over the forces of [her] life."[106]

In *Atyaf*, autobiography becomes a mirror that reflects the history of an era and a country. The subject of this autobiography has an authorial double. We meet two female characters: Radwa, a professor of English literature at Ain Shams University, and Shajar, a professor of history at Cairo University. The two characters are, in fact, two faces of a shared fate and a common concern. The reader cannot miss the author's obsession with history and her belief in the close relationship between history and literature: it is significant that her double, Shajar, is a professor of history. She informs us of Aristotle's distinction between poetry and history: "One relates what has happened, the other what may happen."[107] She also quotes Aristotle's opinion that poetry is more sublime than history because "poetry is closer to universals, while history deals in particulars."[108] In *Atyaf*, Ashour comments on this expression, noting that, for Shajar, history is not limited to particulars. Speaking of Aristotle's law of probability, she says, "I interpret it as the logic of things, a law that links these events and extracts from their fierce chaos and riotous discord a thread of meaning and a light that allows humanity to understand its own stories. Do I mix literature and history, or do I turn my special enterprise over to Shajar?"[109] The name Shajar (literally, tree) evokes the plants, palm trees, and willows that the author so loves; they are the continuity of life that resists the ravages of time and its successive assaults. The characters are two sides of the same coin; both suffer from loss and imbalance in a society that has lost all its frames of reference. The most important feature of Ashour's autobiography is that it clearly aspires to blend public and personal history, assuming that people's personal histories may be more revealing than official history. Shajar is writing about Dayr Yasin and searches for "the truth," yet she does not turn to books written by Arab or Israeli historians, but rather to the survivors' testimonies of the massacre. Here Shajar's view of what constitutes history merges with the author's aspirations and her interest in fiction. The stories of Radwa and Shajar complement one another. Radwa's story revolves around events that actually happened to Radwa, the author of the autobiography, while Shajar's story is about events that could have happened and may have indeed happened, according to the law of probability. In this autobiographical novel, times meet and perspectives are deepened.

Hala El Badry explores the world and history of an Egyptian village in her novel *Muntaha (Muntaha)* 1995. The text contains such a wealth of information and detail about the daily life in a village society that it verges on being a work of sociology, as the author herself says.[110] El Badry writes a novel about Egyptian social history in the twentieth century. The reader becomes familiar with the customs and traditions of the villagers, and the confusion between fact and illusion, religion and custom. Through a close observation of the minute details of daily life, the author makes the reader understand the peasant's relationship to the authorities, and his defensive strategies or resistance to historical and social changes outside his will. In its aspiration to document, record, and understand history, the novel reveals an attempt to deal with the problems of alienation and belonging, and the loss of and search for identity, which is a central concern of writers of this and coming generations. Discussing the origin of *Muntaha*, Hala El Badry begins with a comment on the shock she experienced in 1980 upon returning from Baghdad to visit her village in Egypt. It was in this moment that she confronted the illusion of nostalgia and longing for an ideal past and a beautiful place and was forced to face the ugliness and deterioration that had touched the village and its inhabitants. In this moment, a desire was born to write a historical novel that searched for roots and examined historical changes and their impact on the lives of ordinary people.

*

Another characteristic of the works of women writers of the 1970s is their preoccupation with popular environments and ordinary characters from the downtrodden classes. We hear the voices of women who do not belong to the rising middle class in the stories of Ibtihal Salem, Siham Bayyumi, Salwa Bakr, and Ni'mat al-Buhayri. These stories stray far from the romantic perspective of earlier generations in their treatment of rural characters; the reader hears new voices expressing the concerns and problems of the poor, who suffer the most from social and political changes.[111] The stories of Salwa Bakr are characterized by their treatment of women characters from the lower classes who face life with a strength and awareness derived from the wisdom of experience and an instinct that manages to escape unscathed from the distortions and falsifications that have touched broad segments of society, especially the middle class. These characters express an awareness on many levels—an awareness of the general falsity, a political awareness, and an awareness of the various forms of coercion used against women. In "Nuna al-Sha'nuna" ("Dotty Noona"),[112] we meet an illiterate girl from the countryside who comes to Cairo to work as a servant for a wealthy family. The lady of the house thinks Nuna is a bit dotty because she is unable to understand her thirst for knowledge: Nuna spends her time listening to the math and Arabic classes that come through the kitchen window from the neighboring school. She repeats what she hears and imitates the girls during their physical education classes. Nuna becomes a symbol of the fate of many girls who fall prey to social and domestic injustice. She runs away, and Bakr leaves the door open on the possibility of deliverance. The point is that Nuna, the servant, proves better able to understand and absorb than the spoiled son of this middle-class family. In "al-Nawm 'ala-l-janib al-aryah" (Sleeping on the More Comfortable Side), Bakr draws an implicit comparison between Fatima, the illiterate servant, and a middle-class woman who turns to foreign books on modern childrearing. The result, as embodied in her two spoiled daughters, is abject failure. As for Fatima, her use of simple wisdom allows her to reveal the falsity latent in many prevailing ideas and attitudes, and she becomes capable of confrontation and change. We also encounter the political awareness of women from the popular classes in the form of Umm Shehta, a washerwoman who leads a popular uprising during what have come to be known as the "Bread Riots" of 1977, which erupted after the sudden increase in the price of bread and other staples. Just as the reader is struck by Fatima's wisdom compared to the lady of the house, she is struck by Umm Shehta's political sophistication and her understanding of the street. Umm Shehta stands in stark contrast to Husayn Diyab, the leftist intellectual who does nothing but repeat slogans and Marxist clichés about the imminent role of the proletariat, the weakness of the popular classes, and their inability to stand strong at this historical juncture against organized, armed force. Salwa Bakr resists widespread preconceptions about the awareness of intellectuals and the ignorance of the illiterate: after the demonstration, Husayn Diyab returns to his house where he is arrested; meanwhile, Umm Shehta hides until things calm down, thus avoiding arrest. In "Zinat fi jinazat al-ra'is" ("Zeenat Marches in the President's Funeral"),[113] we find another example of this type of female character who possesses political acumen and instinctive wisdom. Zinat embodies the disappointment and broken dreams of a generation that hung its hopes on the revolution's promises. Zinat belongs to the scattered remnants of the army that clung to the last fortress, represented by the person of President Gamal Abdel Nasser. Like many other Egyptians, Zinat loves the president and constantly writes to him about her problems, seeing him as her only aid and support in the world. The reader is struck by the painful contradiction between Zinat's boundless faith in Nasser and her desperate living conditions, which have not really been improved by the few pounds she receives in government aid. This faith is not shaken even after Zinat observes the armed guard accompanying the president's cavalcade. The climax comes when the president dies, and Zinat, along with thousands of others, takes part in the funeral procession and mourns him even after she is arrested during the demonstration. Zinat's political consciousness leads her take part in the Bread Riots of 1977, but she continues to pray for Nasser, clinging to the symbol of dreams and hopes and thereby representing the crisis of an entire generation. A political consciousness is not limited to women from the educated middle class; rather, in Salwa Bakr's stories, we meet women from both the middle and lower classes who try to overcome the various types of oppression they endure as women. A common theme in these stories is to accuse women of madness when they try to rebel against oppression. Women in Salwa Bakr's works feel alienated and estranged from their society. Here we must pause to consider the character of Sayyida in "Kull hadha-l-sawt al-jamil" ("Such a Beautiful Voice"). In the story, Sayyida, an illiterate woman ground down by the daily routine of housework, discovers she has a lovely voice that she uses to express her emotions. She runs up against the indifference of those surrounding her, followed by their attempts to force her to return to her former condition. Her husband takes her to a psychiatrist, and Sayyida imagines that this educated man might do her justice and explain the truth to her ignorant husband. But she is shocked by his apathy and by his diagnosis of her state as depression. Crestfallen, she returns home and throws his pills in the toilet. She chooses to act out her preordained role, but she does not give in to the attempts to question her sanity or her senses.

Sana' Sulayha also puts her finger on society's wounds and weak points. In her stories she gives us the tragedies of the downtrodden who inhabit the lowest rung of the social ladder, using a quiet language and a tight plot that avoids directness. In one story, she shows us the universe through the eyes of a child who enjoys watching the dancing colors and laughing puppets that play across the blackboard at school. The puppets disappear when she starts wearing glasses, and she is forced to see the world and people as they are, unwillingly entering the ugly world of reality.[114] The story can function as a fictional introduction to the narrative subject in Sulayha's stories.

1990: Fin de siècle

What does the map of contemporary writing look like? Many women writers have emerged on the scene who have managed to attract the attention of both readers and critics, including May Telmissany, Nura Amin, Amina Zaydan, Ghada 'Abd al-Mun'im, 'Afaf al-Sayyid, Miral al-Tahawy, Somaya Ramadan, Hana' 'Atiya, Siham Badawi, Bahija Husayn, Najwa Sha'ban, Najla' 'Allam, Amani Khalil, Muna Prince, and others. Women now write with confidence, and there is a wider space for the reception of works by women. There have been experiments in both language and content and the boundaries of literary genres have been overstepped. There is now a tangible celebration of women writers in Arabic culture, but there have also been repeated attacks on the idea of celebrating women's writing; some argue that focusing on this particularity will only heighten the walls erected around women, while others attack with the objective of impugning female writers' abilities. Assaults on fiction from the right use moral criteria to judge women writers and accuse them of moral laxity. The new generation of women writers is characterized by their lack of immersion in politics and national issues, a stance described by Muhammad Badawi as "a lack of concern with the big issues."[115] May Telmissany says that her concern is "writing on the margins of history": she does not address political events or social issues, such as women's issues, for example.[116]

*

We find in writing of the 1990s a language concerned with the small details of women's lives—details whose importance generations of women writers fought to win recognition. These are details that were largely ignored during women's attempts to belong to the world of men, when they threw themselves into "the big issues," leaving aside the small details that fill their world and give it meaning, emotion, and historic depth. In *Dariya* (Dariya) 1999, Sahar al-Muji speaks of orange cake, dusting, and bedtime stories in the life of a contemporary woman who is always forced to apologize for her interests and pursue them outside the bounds of the family. She is trapped in a spiral of guilt; her conflict is embodied in the details of her restricted daily life, details she unconsciously sacrifices to legitimize her existence and win sanction from the surrounding society. These details help to construct a well-rounded portrait of the protagonist that considers the character's various identities in a world veering toward generalization and homogeneity. Dariya is torn between society's view and expectations of her, and her own images of herself and her aspirations to fulfill them. "I see my face split vertically in two," Dariya says. "Each part has features that differ from the other. The two parts make a fearful face that is not me, but I know that it is me."[117] But does Dariya succeed in escaping the bonds of society's views of her? Does she free herself from prevailing molds and stereotypes? It may be that writing is a way for Dariya to connect with her interior world, a weapon to resist the reality imposed on her.

Nura Amin's novel, *Qamis wardi farigh* (An Empty Pink Shirt) 1997, verges on fantasy. The author intentionally seeks to blur the line between the experience of writing and writing about experience, between life and writing, putting the dialectic between the text and reality at center stage. On one interpretative level, the pink shirt is the actual experience of love, but it is also, simultaneously, writing about that experience. Amin uses the fantastic atmosphere to heighten the suggestiveness of the text. She uses cinematic terms such that the progression of events resembles a series of movie stills in which a spotlight is shined on certain feelings or on some aspect of the text's questioning subject. The confusion between reality and illusion is played out so that the main characters in life become the protagonists of the novel. Nura Amin shows such a profound concern with describing the minute details of her snapshots that we might even consider it "an obsession with details,"[118] despite the text's fast-paced rhythm. This obsession may be a passion for the act of writing and its permanence, the existence of an independent, physical text to contrast with the vagaries of reality. Is a passion for writing synonymous with alienation and fragmentation? But the pink shirt is ultimately just an empty shirt, "the story only a story,"[119] which translates the ruptures within the author/narrator into a novelistic form.

In a text that is new on more than one level, May Telmissany contemplates the act of writing and the repercussions of storytelling in *Dunyazad (Dunyazad)* 1997. The author involves the reader in the details of a painful experience she actually endured: a stillborn birth. The novel/autobiography is dominated by the pair of life and death. The womb becomes a tomb, the moment of birth a moment of death, and writing both a funerary memorial and a celebration. Dunyazad, the child's name, is also the name of Sheherazade's sister in *The Thousand and One Nights*, who hid under the bed and listened to her sister tell stories to escape death and save her sisters from Shahrayar's tyranny. Through the act of writing, the writer/mother seeks to overcome the dichotomy of life and death, writing stories that simultaneously struggle against death and contain it, just as Sheherazade tried to do in her stories in *The Thousand and One Nights*. Formally, Telmissany tries to overcome the first-person voice's dominance over the autobiographical narrative by giving us another voice, that of the father/husband, who tells the story from his point of view. The narrative contains other voices as well, which come from the world of dreams or the unconscious; the result is a multiplicity of voices, adding depth to the plot. The irony is that Dunyazad does actually die: "But she spent just one night in hospital. Was it my lot to spend the other thousand that lay ahead recalling a name that I only ever got to say once, or maybe twice?"[120] So did writing manage to interfere in the consequences of fate?

Intertextuality gives a distinctive depth to the stories of Somaya Ramadan in the collections *Khashab wa nuhas* (Wood and Brass) 1995 and *Manazil al-qamar* (Phases of the Moon) 1999. Perhaps the last sentence of her story, "Khashab wa nuhas," gives us the key to Somaya Ramadan's stories: "If you want to be a beautiful young woman again, just carry all the baggage of memory and don't forget a thing."[121] The narrating subject engages the author in an extended struggle against attempts at concealment that quash the self and distort its identity on the individual, social, domestic, historical, and political level. Using a densely intertextual writing that is laden with references to myths and texts from world literature, Ramadan tries to break the code of meaning and symbol and reach the authentic significance: the well of memory. Women occupy a pivotal spot in this process of construction; female characters dominate the narrative, their primary mission to revive memory and ensure the continuity of life. "Places are times that are revived by women by remembering them at the appointed date."[122] The character of the grandmother is a symbol of the good old days, which evoke conflicting feelings of rejection and nostalgia. In "Jaddati" (My Grandmother), the narrator rebels against the grandmother because of her excessive interest in details, which become "threads seen by no one else that she uses to choke anyone who dares to question her absolute authority."[123] At the same time, the author shows a pronounced interest in details herself, and we discover that they are the secret that protects memory from extinction and ensures survival. In many stories, details become a refuge for which the self yearns and around which it revolves. At other times, they are the secret of existence for women and the key to their hidden strength.

Bahija Husayn explores the shape and dimensions of alienation in her novel, *Ra'ihat al-lahazat* (The Scent of Moments) 1992. The heroine undergoes both physical and psychological alienation when she leaves her husband in Egypt to work at a school in Algeria. Physical exile—the fate of Egyptians seeking a livelihood outside their country—becomes the figurative equivalent of self-alienation in a time of loss and fragmentation. Husayn successfully depicts the contours of alienation and un-belonging in the beginning of the novel, using small details to reveal deep, painful emotions. After some time, the protagonist is able to establish human connections that help her overcome her self-alienation, but the primary issue is still the forced exile that is the fate of many due to specific historical events, which cannot be individually resisted but become individuals' inevitable destiny. These crushing historical events are the focus of *al-Bayt* (The House) 1999, also by Bahija Husayn. We meet

Robin, a doctor, a tragic hero, and a stranger both by birth and religion, who lives in an Egyptian village; he is bound to its inhabitants by various complex links. The author uses a stream-of-consciousness narrative to plumb the depths of Robin's memory—a nightmarish memory that records his journey to the village, which he in turn documents in paintings that he hides in a room no one enters, leaving them for future generations. There are multiple viewpoints and voices in the novel, but Robin remains the pivotal character who asks the pivotal question: who owns the house? Who is the Egyptian in the village where the events take place? What are the criteria of belonging and alienation?

Najwa Sha'ban offers a variation on the theme of identity and belonging in her ambitious novel, *al-Ghurr* (The Immigrant Bird) 1998, which traces the lives of Safiya and her grandchildren. As recorded in her deed of sale as a slave girl in the mid-nineteenth century, Safiya is "born in Nubia-Bajawiya, of reddish skin the color of coffee, with a birthmark on her left cheek."[124] Safiya comes to Egypt whereupon the plot branches out, taking her and her descendants across several countries where they encounter other characters, and move from place to place searching for belonging and stability. The novel examines the fate of ordinary people during history's grinding revolutions, and it strives to cross geographical boundaries in its examination of the question of identity. Various sub-plots, characters, generations, and points of view intersect in the novel, which is a fine novelistic experiment that observes the destiny of a family, or the descendants of a woman, across various historical periods. It thus links the lives of ordinary people with changing historical circumstances, and the characters' lives become an ongoing questioning of seemingly stable values and concepts that actually change with the fluctuations of history and fate.

In *al-Khiba'* (The Tent) 1996,[125] Miral al-Tahawy takes us to the world of the Bedouin, to explore untrodden places in women's fiction. Through al-Tahawy's dense, connotative language, we plunge into this old-new world, where the severity of reality intersects with the vastness of myth and we feel the contradictions of oppression, alienation, and resistance. We see things through the eyes of Fatima, "her father's gazelle," who stands by helplessly as her own gazelle, Zahwa, is slaughtered and roasted. She creates an imaginary world where she finds refuge from the harshness of her tyrannical grandmother and her persistent reproach of Fatima's mother for giving birth to evil—that is, to girls. Fatima seeks protection in her father, but his relationship with her mother—"the madwoman," as her grandmother calls her—remains inexplicable to her. Trying to run away, Fatima climbs a tree, flouting her grandmother's rules, but she falls and sprains her foot. She begins to see herself as lame and can only play with her gazelle, Zahwa, in her imagination. She seizes upon the arrival of

Anne, a foreigner who has come to study the lives of the Bedouin and acquire Arabian horses, to find an excuse to leave her grandmother's prison. Fatima loses her leg and becomes lame in reality; her sense of alienation and difference from her environment—her psychological lameness—becomes a tangible defect visible to all. In Anne's house, everyone gathers around her to listen to her stories, making her feel like "a frog in a crystal jar."[126] Anne and her friends watch her, and she decides to return home, where she meets the fate of her "deranged" mother, who lives in a world adjacent to, but outside the boundaries of the collective. The language plays an important role in constructing the novel's narrative and emotional charge. Al-Tahawy manages to create symbols that acquire their meanings as the narrative progresses, becoming objective equivalents of the development of the narrator's self-consciousness. In the first line of the novel, Fatima turns her hair over to Sardub, the henna woman, to let her dress it while she escapes to the world of imagination and the innocence of childhood. Then comes her harsh collision with reality, after which the length of her hair becomes a source of agony and a way of tightening control over her. When we reach the end of the novel, the moment of complete isolation and alienation, Fatima says, "No. I won't sleep. I know that you want to weave a tent out of my hair. You want Fatima to remain in the dark. I won't give up my plaits to you, ever. You just want me to die. I will die, ya-Sardoubh, but get your hands away from my hair."[127]

*

In poetry, female poets give us innovative poetic experiments; they do not just rebel against form, but establish a content that expresses a new reality and ascendant poetic visions. We have, for example, poets like Suhayr Musadafa, Ghada Nabil, Fatima Qandil, Iman Mirsal, Amal Farah 'Awad, Suhayr 'Ulaywa and 'Azza Badr. Using a poetic language that is eloquent in its brevity and deeply connotative, Fatima Qandil gives voice to conditions of human existence that cannot be summarized or conveyed using other means of expression. She weaves the strands of her lexicon with the utmost care and then scatters them on paper, creating meanings that quietly pierce deep into the walls of consciousness. In "Jawarib shafafa" (Pantyhose), she says:

> Small tensions. No emptiness, then, since the penknife turned
> And filled the room with all this delicately honed wood.[128]

The "delicately honed wood" is the words of the poem itself, but also the perceptions of a consciousness that observes itself through the pantyhose she puts on in the morning, along with her glasses and other masks.

The poetry of Iman Mirsal is some of the most powerful of the 1990s. In the poem, "al-Tafasil al-yawmiya" (Daily Details),[129] she creates a living embodiment of the vocabulary of the surrounding reality. Mirsal documents the dilemma of a self alienated from society and its all-consuming loneliness in a world in which connections are denied and the commonalities among people are hidden. In poetry that is almost celebratory and reverential, she magnifies this sense of alienation and loneliness, using it to challenge the monotony of the self and the ordinariness of the people around her, thus exploring the possibilities of identity opened to her because of her alienation, or her creative difference:

> I can't remember . . . when I discovered I had
> A musical name, suitable for signing
> Well-measured poems, and waving in
> The faces of friends with ordinary names.
> They don't understand the deep meaning, because
> Chance gives you an ambiguous name,
> Raising questions about you
> And suggesting that you be someone else,
> Like when new acquaintances ask you:
> Are you Christian?
> Or
> Do you have Lebanese roots?[130]

This same subject, who has grown used to loneliness and turned it into a weapon that she uses to cut off her desire for connection and belonging, has misgivings when a wise friend comes by. She expels her from her world then regrets her action, although she is still incapable of extending the hand of human connection:

> My friend, perfectly complete,
> Why don't you go
> And leave all this oxygen for me?
> The emptiness in your wake may make me
> Bite my lip in regret,
> When I see your toothbrush,
> Familiar . . . and wet.[131]

Final observations and questions

I would like to reiterate what I said earlier, that a discussion of women's fiction and creative writing is not about the innate differences between men and women, but is concerned rather with elucidating the significance of women's particular position in the symbolic order and its effect on their writing. I have sought to highlight some examples of women's writings in the modern era, focusing on the common characteristics between women's literary production and literature as a whole, since women's achievements are an inseparable part of the intellectual and cultural production of the twentieth century. Perhaps this historical discussion has captured some of the particularities in voice that arise from women's different position, but we still need to make detailed comparisons between particular texts written by men and women that appear at the same historical moment yet offer divergent points of view for reasons that need to be more fully understood. I will repeat some of the pivotal questions: when women write, who is speaking and what are the mechanisms of listening available to them? How do they face the ever-present drive to confiscate their voices and the power of representation as others speak for them? How do they deal with society's expectations of women? How do they stand up to these expectations, confuse them, or turn them on their heads? How do they manipulate the rules of language and mold it to serve their own points of view?

Finally, in the context of the questions raised during the course of this project, particularly since I have chosen to follow women's creative writing chronologically, here I shall record some thoughts on literary genres that are not addressed above: drama and autobiography.

On drama

In our attempt to assess women's contributions to dramatic writing, we must first stop at two major points: a definition of a dramatic text, and women's historical relationship with the theater. The theater was always "an integrated, collective activity, achieved through the conjunction and harmonization of a set of factors—of which the spoken, linguistic text is just one—all of which conjoin to produce the experience of the theater."[132] The arbitrary distinction between text and performance, or author and director, did not exist; indeed, the author of the text was its director and supervisor. Using this definition of a play, both as text and performance, the theater over the ages and in many civilizations was a site forbidden to women. At various historical periods, women who were associated in some way with the theater were held in contempt by society. In Arab culture, the most common image of women in the theater remains the dancing girl: a woman who is both desired and expelled, the available/taboo body. If Haykal did not sign the first printing of his first novel, *Zaynab*, with his real name, fearing for his social status, the status of those involved in the theater was much worse. When Yusuf Wahbi began working in the theater, his family disowned him; when the young Tawfiq al-Hakim showed an interest in the theater, his family shipped him off to France.

In general, women's contributions to drama came relatively late compared to other literary forms. It is noteworthy that the golden age of

Egyptian theater in the 1960s, when it became a pulpit for political expression, both opposition and pro-regime, did not manage to encourage women to embark on the experience of playwriting or directing, but left us only two texts written by women. Women's experiments with playwriting were very rare, even when we consider the texts that were never staged as performances.[133] *Kisibna al-brimo* (We Hit the Jackpot), the first theatrical production by a woman, Sufi 'Abd Allah, staged at the Opera House in 1951,[134] was followed by experiments by Saniya Qurra'a and Nadiya 'Abd al-Hamid, but these experiments never found their way to the stage. Adapting the novels of Naguib Mahfouz, Amina al-Sawi entered the world of the theater, after which she devoted herself to writing scripts for religious television serials. The 1960s saw the emergence of Layla 'Abd al-Basit and Fathiya al-'Assal, followed sometime later by Nihad Jad. Nawal al-Sa'dawi wrote a play, *Izis* (Isis), and Fawziya Mahran wrote two plays. They were followed by Na'ila Najib, Wafa' Wajdi, Fatima Qandil, and finally, Latifa al-Zayyat with *Bi' wa shira*. Most of the plays written by women were not staged, and many are experiments with the dramatic form that are still closer to novels or poems. Within this small corpus of works, Fathiya al-'Assal and Nihad Jad are distinguished by their proximity to the world of the theater, which gave them the opportunity to produce fine dramatic works. Fathiya al-'Assal began writing plays in the late 1960s with her *al-Murjiha* (The Swing) 1969, although this was never published, followed by *al-Basbur* (The Passport) 1972, which was staged under that name and only later, in 1997, published, as *Jawaz safar* (Passport), *Nisa' bila aqni'a* (Women Without Masks) and *al-Bayn bayn* (It Passes) in the 1980s, and finally *Sijn al-nisa'* (The Women's Prison) in 1993. Fathiya al-'Assal's own story is worthy of mention: she was raised in a family that did not believe in the education of girls. Her marriage to 'Abd Allah al-Tukhi, the well-known writer and journalist, had an important impact on her life. She learned how to read and write, circulated in a cultural milieu, and found the theater to be a means of expression that suited her. Al-'Assal's most recent play, *Sijn al-nisa'*, addresses the author's own prison experience, highlighting various examples of women who were imprisoned as a result of society's oppression and as a result of their own internalization of these forms of oppression and their use against themselves and others. The play is a collection of monologues by a set of characters. They reveal the characters' pain and suffering in the surrounding society, showing that the physical prison is only a metaphor for society's prison, which restricts women and puts them permanently in the defendant's chair.

Nihad Jad found her way to the theater in the 1980s after a long journey with the press. She was also influenced by her marriage to Samir Sirhan, a university professor and playwright. Nihad Jad contributed two fine texts to the theater. The first, *'Adila* ('Adila), was staged in 1981 in the Tali'a Theater; it was directed by Zaynab Shmays and starred Na'ima Wasfi. The second, *'Ala-l-rasif* (On the Sidewalk) 1989, was hugely successful. Nihad Jad's style is distinguished by its painfully honest, even severe, portrayal of female characters, who are presented without an iota of idealism or saintliness. She puts a magnifying glass before her characters, which reflects their flaws and the types of social hypocrisy that tighten the patriarchal control over their lives. Nihad Jad's career was cut short when she died an early death of cancer in 1989.

The 1990s witnessed the emergence of a new generation of young men and women involved in the theater. A director, male or female, would adapt more than one text, sections of many texts, or several disparate ideas, and forge them into a performance that went beyond the concept of the text and was more closely related to performance art. In this scenario, the director becomes the one who creates and envisions the performance. In this context, three young female directors—'Abir 'Ali, Caroline Khalil, and 'Iffat Yayha—presented fine theater performances. 'Abir 'Ali formed a theater troupe and experimented with children's theater. Caroline Khalil adapted a play by Caryl Churchill and staged it as *al-Qitt khall* (Vinegar Tom). She then took part in directing and acting in *Vienna* (Vienna), a play liberally adapted from a Jean Rhys story. 'Iffat Yahya stands out with her long-standing presence in the theater. She has directed three productions, the most important being *Sahrawiya* (Desert Woman), followed by *Iskitshat hayatiya* (Life Sketches). *Sahrawiya* was inspired from a text by English playwright Caryl Churchill, but the director intervened and set the drama in the desert, making the characters Arabs, including the dancing girl, the companion, and the modern girl. The play offers an innovative perspective on contemporary Arab reality. Exploring the boundaries of improvisation, in *Iskitshat hayatiya* 'Iffat Yahya collaborated with a group of actresses to write the dialogue and produce a collective performance. It is perhaps these new creative horizons sought by women in theater, in addition to similar experiments by young male directors, that are the lifeline and true hope for the current unfortunate state of Egyptian theater.

It is also worth noting that recently many women have produced texts for the cinema, television serials, and documentary films. These must be noted, although they lie outside our field of inquiry. One thinks of films by directors 'Atiyyat al-Abnudi, Asma' Bakri, and In'am Muhammad 'Ali, as well as a large group of young artists, like Hala Khalil, who have managed to create their own expressive language to give us fictional works that blend the visual, the written, and the aural.

On autobiography

It might be worthwhile to pause briefly at women's autobiographical writings. As much as successive generations of women felt the importance of documenting their experiences and asserting their presence, both physically and symbolically, on the cultural scene, they were not able to avoid the social and cultural complications and pitfalls that accompanied women's entry into the public sphere, where they were entangled in the dichotomies of concealment/confession and appearance/disappearance. Writing was, and still is, an act of resistance to the processes of marginalization and forced concealment that women have endured. If we accept Paul de Man's observation that every type of writing is some form of autobiography,[135] we can expand the concept of autobiography to include in our purview memoirs, diaries, letters, autobiography, biography, and autobiographical fiction. That is, we can speak of writing/autobiography and make similar, if not identical, conclusions and observations. Yet we are most concerned with autobiography due to its dense significations about the self and because it exercises such a pull on the critical field.

One of the most tangible contradictions to manifest and influence the concealment/confession dichotomy are those produced by cultural-literary circles in their reception of women's autobiographies. On one hand, women have often been accused of writing only about their own experiences, either because they are imprisoned in the self and unable to overcome it, or because of some flaw in their imaginative abilities, or because women, confined to the home, were not allowed the same interactions with the outside world as men. If a novel, short story, or poem contains an emotional tale or sexual allusion, it becomes a moral trial of the author. On the other hand, women's autobiographies, written since the early twentieth century, have been ignored in critical histories on the rise and development of the craft of autobiography.[136]

Women wrote autobiographies in different forms, fully aware of the attitudes lying in wait for them; their reactions varied according to their personal and historical choices. In her memoirs, Jalila Rida speaks of an article published in *al-Jil al-jadid* in December 1954, after the release of her first collection of poetry, *al-Lahn al-baki* (The Weeping Melody), which caused great embarrassment to her family and friends. The article appeared under a large headline that proclaimed, "An Egyptian female poet speaks about the taste of a kiss," followed by a subhead about the emergence of "a new type of Egyptian woman poet. . . who composes poetry about burning love and blazing kisses in a style new to Eastern female poets." The author of the article goes on to analyze the title of Rida's collection of poems and attributes it to her childhood and "her failed marriage."[137] In her memoirs, published in 1986, Jalila Rida chooses to speak about this tribulation in 1954, and she does not hesitate to reveal the particulars of her emotional relationships, entering into forbidden territory. Munira Thabit, in contrast, is excessively reticent about the details of her personal life, focusing on her public persona; as a result, her autobiography is dry and devoid of any significant human situations.

Women writers' reactions to the double standard applied to works by men and women were not limited to fear or rebellion. Some writers tried to exploit prevailing ideas about women's writing by directing the reader's attention to the similarity between their fiction and reality, perhaps noting that their stories are based on tales heard from real women in order to lend the credibility of autobiography to the topic at hand or to confirm the truth of their experiences. These writers intentionally used autobiographical styles and techniques in their novels, as seen in Su'ad Zuhayr's *I'tirafat imra'a mustarjila*, Asma Halim's *Hikayat 'Abduh 'Abd al-Rahman*, and Iqbal Baraka's *Yawmiyat imra'a 'amila* (Diaries of a Working Woman) 1993. The last work was a series of articles, published under the same title, that spoke of both real and fictional experiences. They contained snapshots from the lives of women who had gone out to work; despite the simplicity of the topic, they contained moments of profound significance about the hardships of public transportation, daily friction over life's details like cooking and childcare, and the emotions and fears of motherhood. Coming from the same standpoint, and in an experimental attempt, Asma Halim wrote *Arba'a zawjat wa rajul* (Four Wives and a Man) 1980, which contains a report about the dangers of polygamy and an analysis of the arguments used by both sides. The text reproduces the proposed personal status law of 1979 and discusses the points of view of its opponents. Finally, the book includes stories, or "a few entertaining amusements that are, in fact, slices of real life. There are not fictional additions; they come one hundred percent from the fabric of social reality."[138]

At the same time, autobiography has played a documentary role, highlighting experiences in the lives of Arab women that are worth preserving. The objective of documentation has varied, as have the modes of expression chosen by authors. In *Saqita fi ahdan al-radhila* (A Fallen Woman in the Bosom of Vice) 1927, Zaynab Muhammad uses an epistolary style, as two characters exchange letters that make us privy to details from the heroine's life. The letters are didactic and are essentially a work of guidance whose sole objective is to point out and warn against moral perils. In *Mudhakkirat mudarrisa* (Memoirs of a Woman Teacher) 1972, 'Awatif 'Abd al-Jalil gives the reader a historical documentation of the unnoticed details and difficulties faced by the first women pioneers who went out to work as teachers, a profession with which women have long experience. She also provides glimpses of the problems encountered by women who worked in journalism. Generally, memoirs are distinguished by boldness and frankness. Nawal al-Sa'dawi has written more than one autobiography or autobiographical novel, recording various phases of her professional and political life, for example in *Mudhakkirat tabiba, Imra'atan fi imra'a*, and *Mudhakkirati fi sijn al-nisa'* (*Memoirs from the Women's Prison*) 1984. We also recall Nabawiya Musa, who gave us *Tarikhi bi qalami*, as well as the memoirs of Huda Sha'rawi, Rose al-Yusuf, Madiha Abu Zayd,[139] Fatima Rushdi, 'Atiyyat al-Abnudi,[140] and others. There are also prison memoirs by Farida al-Naqqash, Zaynab al-Ghazali, Nawal al-Sa'dawi, and Safinaz Kazim.

Perhaps the most important point to note in the relationship between women and autobiography is the persistent tension in women's writings that revolves around the unsaid, or what is not said because it should not be said. These chronological or experiential lacunae can be even more eloquent than what is openly said and expressed. We can quote Sabry Hafez's remarks on Latifa al-Zayyat's *Hamlat taftish: awraq shakhsiya*, as an example of an autobiographical work that reflects the particularity of women's experience. Hafez identified three elements of the work: "liberation from chronology. . . the significance of gaps in personal writing. . . and the fact that autobiographies by writing women actually consist of sets of various papers that combine personal confession, memoir, and fiction."[141]

Latifa al-Zayyat's story, "al-Shaykhukha" (Old Age), for example, oversteps generic boundaries, and we are reminded of Paul de Man's comment about the non-distinction between writing and autobiography. The story, or novella, addresses a topic that is new to Arabic fiction on several levels. Al-Zayyat presents a virtual objective correlative of the writing woman's dilemma: her relationship with her own self-image and her social persona. Al-Zayyat opens the story by telling us that what we will read are diaries written in the mid-1970s—that is, ten years before the story was published. They are written from the perspective of a fifty-year-old woman, and the author now reads the memoirs and engages with them from the perspective of a sixty-year-old woman. Times intersect and meet in the consciousness of the subject/writer in her attempt to find the keys to a condition that has denuded her and dominated her relationship with her self and others. This condition, as the author herself describes it, is old age, or "an individual's sense that his existence is superfluous."[142] This state plunges the individual into a tempest in which he alternately clings to and disassociates himself from his surroundings. The diaries observe the relationship of the subject/protagonist with her daughter and son-in-law, revealing the implicit and explicit contradictions and conflicts in human relationships and exposing a psychological and life phase experienced by the subject in her attempt to reformulate her relationship with the self and others. The subject fingers through the pages of memory and recalls the feelings of old age that plagued her in her mid-fifties, embodied emotionally in her diaries. This is done indirectly, in the context of writing her diaries and analyzing the complexities of her relationship with her daughter, Hanan, after the latter marries and leaves home. The reader is faced with a two-sided consciousness: the consciousness of a fifty-year-old woman drowning in the details of the problem and the consciousness of a sixty-year-old woman going through a phase of self-exploration and engagement. She opens papers that have been cast aside and reads her diaries which "have fallen into the flurry of forgotten papers."[143] The story is about old age or how to form a consciousness that represents the condition of old age. Did Latifa al-Zayyat write simply about an experience limited to herself, or did she attempt to describe a universal condition, in which old age is also a metaphor for a period in the history of a collective? Or did she intend to generalize the dichotomy of concealment/confession, a keen dilemma facing women writers, and put it at the center of self-consciousness, making the process of self-exploration the inevitable road to maturity and insight?

Recalling what has been said here about the particularity of women writers' position in the symbolic cultural order, the pressures that lead them to assimilate to the prevailing power system, and the desire to clash with it or reveal the unsaid, again raises the same question: how can one portray difference and similarity? What counter-strategies do those who do not enjoy the authority to represent use to formulate their own representations and knowledge about the self and others? If writing is a locus for the construction of new identities, then it will become a field of conflict over the meaning and nature of reality itself. At this moment, we must remember and rethink and use lived relationships as the basis of knowledge. This might explain the special position of women's autobiographical writings in their various forms. Women writers have trodden many paths in their aspirations to participate in shaping their own identities. In the early phases, they overturned accepted meanings or used them in a new way, producing positive representations to replace negative ones; they then matured and began to put themselves in the center of the complexities and contradictions of the cultural order, showing an interest in form and deconstructing the intellectual foundations of the system itself.

Notes

1 Some literary historians consider the year 1798, the date of the French campaign on Egypt, to mark the true beginnings of modern Arabic literature; they maintain that this was the moment of the decisive encounter between Western and Eastern civilizations that brought with it the shock that pushed the Arab region out of the darkness of the Ottoman period to the light of civilization and progress. This historical narrative highlights the fact that the French brought the first press into Egypt, as well as social values and scientific advances that had a great impact on Egyptian society at the time. We must note, however, that the French took their press when they left and that this interpretation of the beginning of the Arab awakening is the object of much critical and historical debate.

2 In 1832, Muhammad 'Ali established the al-Muwallidat School, which enjoyed special status, followed by the al-Suyufiya School in 1873. Another school joined it in 1875, after which the institution was renamed al-Saniya School in 1889. These were official institutions run by the modern state, but when discussing girls' education, we cannot ignore the mission schools' role in producing a cadre of people with a largely Western education, though they were linked in complex, overlapping ways to traditional educational systems. We know from biographies and chronicles that some women received a religious education at home (a widespread practice for both men and women) or attended traditional institutions like the *kuttab*.

3 As noted above, Muhammad 'Ali's modernizations are controversial and the subject of critical debate; a reconsideration of the entire process is required. Yahya Haqqi notes in this regard, "You have before you, then, two different currents in education, which often diverge into completely separate paths and at times meet in a few individuals . . . I do not know of a more inauspicious day in Egypt's modern history than the day Muhammad 'Ali turned his back on al-Azhar . . . One of the consequences of this break was that the science coming from Europe did not enter al-Azhar and blossom as it should have." See *Fajr al-qissa al-Misriya* (Cairo: General Egyptian Book Organization, 1975), p. 16.

4 After Muhammad 'Ali, Khedive Isma'il (1863–1879) continued to promote the spread of modern education.

5 M. M. Badawi, *A Short History of Modern Arabic Literature* (Oxford: Clarendon Press, 1993).

6 Ibid. It is worth noting that Badawi does not mention one female writer who contributed to the translation movement or made any written contribution that might be considered a precursor of modern Arabic literature. Female voices begin to appear in his literary history with the advent of the generation of Suhayr al-Qalamawi and Amina al-Sa'id.

7 For example, *al-Firdaws* (1896), launched by Louisa Habbalin; *Mir'at al-hasna'* (1896), launched by Maryam Mazhar, a pseudonym of Salim Sarkis; *Anis al-jalis* (1898), launched by Alexandra Averino; *al-'A'ila* (1899), launched by Esther Azhari Moyal; *al-Hawanim* (1900), launched by Ahmad Hilmi; *al-Mar'a fi-l-Islam* (1901), launched by Ibrahim Ramzi; *al-Mar'a* (1901),

launched by Anisa 'Ata Allah; *al-Zahra* (1902), launched by Maryam Sa'd; *al-Muda* (1903), launched by Salim Khalil Farah; and *Shajarat al-Durr* (1901), launched by Sa'diya Sa'd al-Din. For more on the women's press in Egypt see Ijlal Khalifa, *al-Haraka al-nisa'iya al-haditha* (Cairo: al-Haditha Press, 1973) and Beth Baron, *The Women's Awakening in Egypt: Culture, Society and the Press* (New Haven and London: Yale University Press, 1994).

8 A journal by the title of *al-Sufur* (Unveiling) gives us a good indication of its editor's leanings, as well as those of many renaissance pioneers, who considered the veil (or lack of it) to be the touchstone of a society's liberation and advancement. This view links women's external appearance with issues of the development of society as a whole.

9 In addition to articles and books that diagnosed the problems and outlined means of reform, there are countless articles that admonish women for their laziness, ignorance, or inappropriate appearance when compared to their husbands. These articles maintained that an ignorant mother could not raise children, and was unable to communicate with her husband or win his respect; that the majority of traditional customs preserved by women were harmful and misleading; and that their external appearance was inappropriate and anathema to refined taste. They held women's "backwardness" to be the primary cause of failed marriages and many of the social ills then sweeping society. In general, they held women responsible for both society's backwardness and its advancement.

10 The concept of the modern society was wholly bound up with the form of contemporary Western societies. This view was based on several unspoken assumptions that can be summarized as: the adoption of the Western model of social progress and development; a faith in the linear evolution of civilization, such that it can be read as the journey of man's exit from darkness into the light of knowledge and civilization; the assumption that non-Western societies lag behind Western societies because they are still in the early stages of development; the adoption of an ideological construct that encourages a dichotomy between East and West, modernity and tradition, I and the Other, in such a way as to allow the West to maintain its difference and superiority to other societies. Critics of modernity have linked the concept of modernity itself and modern societies to the expansion of colonialism in the nineteenth century, positing that Western colonial societies needed to create another entity to stand in opposition to the Western self in order to reinforce and define Western subjectivity.

11 See for example the song by Sayyid Darwish, "Girls of Today": "This is your time, your day, O girl of today/Get up, wake up from your sleep, you've slept too long/Demand your rights and rid yourself of today/Why shouldn't we be like the Western woman and strive in our lives with freedom."

12 Labiba Hashim in the introduction to *Fatat al-sharq*, no. 1, 1906.

13 'A'isha Taymur, *Nata'ij al-ahwal fi-l-aqwal wa-l-afa'al* (Cairo: Muhammad Afandi Mustafa Press, 1887), p. 4.

14 'A'isha Taymur, *Mir'at al-ta'ammul fi-l-umur* (Cairo: al-Mahrusa Press, 1892), p. 7.

15 See the entry on 'A'isha Taymur in Zaynab Fawwaz, *al-Durr al-manthur fi tabaqat rabbat al-khudur*.

16 Ahmad Kamal Zada, 'A'isha's grandson, describes the latter two works as dramatic novels in *Hilyat al-tiraz: diwan 'A'isha al-Taymuriya* (1884) (Cairo: Dar al-Kitab al-'Arabi Press, 1952). The works are unavailable in libraries.

17 The pioneers who actively preserved the memory of 'A'isha Taymur include Zaynab Fawwaz, Mayy Ziyada, Malak Hifni Nasif, and Nabawiya Musa.

18 Mayy Ziyada, *'A'isha Taymur: sha'irat al-tali'a* (Beirut: Nawfal Foundation, 1975), p. 162.

19 Ibid., p. 206.

20 'A'isha Taymur, "La tasluh al-'a'ilat illa bi-tarbiyat al-banat," *al-Adab*, Jumada al-Thaniya 9, AH 1306.

21 Mayy Ziyada, *'A'isha Taymur*, p. 132.

22 Ibid., p. 167.

23 Al-'Aqqad, *Shu'ara' Misr wa bi'atuhum fi-l-jil al-madi* (Cairo: Maktabat al-Nahda, 1965), p. 153.

24 'A'isha 'Abd al-Rahman, *al-Sha'ira al-'Arabiya al-mu'asira* (Cairo: Committee for Composition, Translation, and Publication Press, 1962), p. 19.

25 'A'isha Taymur, *Hilyat al-tiraz*, p. 233.

26 'A'isha 'Abd al-Rahman, *al-Sha'ira al-'Arabiya*, p. 28.

27 Mayy Ziyada, *'A'isha Taymur*, p. 199.

28 M. M. Badawi, *A Short History*, p. 99.

29 Important exceptions include Muhammad Rushdi Hasan, *Athar al-maqama fi nash'at al-qissa al-Misriya al-haditha* (Cairo: General Egyptian Book Organization, 1974). As he follows the traces of the *al-maqama* form in the modern short story, the author points to *Nata'ij al-ahwal* and remarks on the "modern" elements that 'A'isha Taymur introduced into the traditional *al-maqama*. He notes, "When using rhymed prose and rhetorical figures, 'A'isha al-Taymuriya did not restrict or obscure the meaning; rather, she used them as a beautiful cloak ornamented with a feminine sensibility. Her language has none of the obscure, uncommon words found in *al-maqamat* because linguistic oddities are not the overwhelming, driving concern of the story form" (p. 137).

30 For quite some time, she was seen in the same light as al-Muwaylihi and his work, *Hadith 'Isa ibn Hisham*, which was also inspired by the *al-maqama* form, although his pioneering attempt to combine the old and new went unnoticed. Haykal's *Zaynab* became the exemplary novel that embodied the break with the past and inaugurated modern literature in the Arab world.

31 See Fawziya Fawwaz's introduction to Zaynab Fawwaz's *Husn al-'awaqib* and *al-Hawa wa-l-wafa* (Beirut: Cultural Council of Southern Lebanon, 1984), p. 14: "Egypt at that time was a refuge for those seeking knowledge and learning and a destination for Lebanese and Syrians seeking work in journalism and intellectual fields, since the Ottomans in the Levant were narrowing the field for Levantine thinkers and writers."

32 Ibid., pp. 16–17.

33 Alexandra Averino, *Anis al-jalis*, vol. 1, part one, 1898.

34 Labiba Hashim, "al-Mar'a al-sharqiya," *Fatat al-sharq*, 1918, p. 189.

35 See Ijlal Khalifa, *al-Haraka al-nisa'iya*, and Beth Baron, *Women's Awakening in Egypt*.

36 Fatima Rashid in *Tarqiyat al-mar'a*, vol. 1, 1908, p. 194.

37 For example, the owner of *Mir'at al-hasna'*, Salim Sarkis, who adopted the pseudonym Maryam Mazhar.

38 See Labiba Hashim, "Hunna yaktubna," *Fatat al-sharq*, 1910–11, p. 306. She refers to an article written by Jurji Niqula in *al-Hasna' al-zahira* in Beirut, in which he defended women's writing and notes that the articles signed with women's names were indeed written by women.

39 See M. M. Badawi, *A Short History*, for historical novels by Salim Bustani, Sa'id Bustani, Ya'qub Sarruf, Fatat Misr, Jurji Zaydan, Farah Antun, and others.

40 Labiba Hashim, "Hasanat al-hubb," *al-Diya'*, June 3, 1899, p. 634.

41 Hanna Afandi Sarkis, "Qalb al-rajul," *Anis al-jalis*, 1904, p. 1,794.

42 See 'Abd al-Hamid Ibrahim, *al-Qissa al-Misriya wa surat al-mujtama' al-hadith* (Egypt: Dar al-Ma'arif, 1973).

43 Albert Hourani, *Arabic Thought in the Liberal Age 1798–1939* (Oxford: Oxford University Press, 1970).

44 Qasim Amin's response to the Duke was a patriotic defense, but it was weak because he was unable to critique the colonial epistemological basis on which the Duke based his attack. He either denies the allegations about Egyptians or clings to the idea of Arab cultural particularity.

45 This is true of the character of Hamid in Haykal's *Zaynab* and Ibrahim in al-Mazini's *Ibrahim al-katib*, for example.

46 Although women were not allowed to register at the faculties, some women, like Mayy Ziyada, attended lectures. See Hala Kamal, "Muhadarat al-far' al-nisa'i fi-l-jami'a al-Misriya 1909–1912," in Hoda Elsadda, ed., *Min ra'idat al-qarn al-'ishrin* (Cairo: Women and Memory Forum, 2000).

47 Malak Hifni Nasif compared Western and Eastern women to highlight each one's strengths and weaknesses in "Muqarana bayn al-mar'a al-gharbiya wa-l-mar'a al-sharqiya," in *Nisa'iyat* (1910) (Cairo: Women and Memory Forum, 1998).

48 Mayy Ziyada, *Bahithat al-Badiya: bahth intiqadi* (Cairo: al-Muqtataf Press, 1920).

49 Introduction to *Diwan Nabawiya Musa*, p. 4.

50 Some of these essays and stories are reprinted with slight changes that deserve further examination.

51 Nabawiya Musa, *Tarikhi bi-qalami*, first and second editions undated; third edition published in Cairo: Women and Memory Forum, 1999.

52 Munira Tal'at, *al-Ba'isa* (Alexandria: al-Mustaqbal Press, 1931).

53 'A'isha 'Abd al-Rahman, *Sayyid al-'izba: qissat imra'a khati'a* (Cairo: al-Ma'arif Press, 1944).

54 Ibid., p. 99.

55 The stories were published in *al-Hilal* in the 1930s. They were republished in *Suwar min hayatihinna: fi jil al-tali'a min al-harim ila-l-jami'a* (Cairo: General Egyptian Book Organization, 1991).

56 See Mohammed Berrada, "al-Adabi wa-l-siyasi: jadaliya mu'aqa," in Sayyid Bahrawi, ed., *Latifa al-Zayyat: al-adab wa-l-watan* (Cairo: Nur and Dar al-Mar'a al-'Arabiya Publications, 1996), p. 40.

57 See 'A'isha 'Abd al-Rahman's view on this topic in her *al-Sha'ira al-'Arabiya al-mu'asira*, p. 57.

58 For 'Abbas al-'Aqqad's view of femininity and poetry, see his *Shu'ara' Misr wa bi'atuhum fi-l-jil al-madi*, p. 151: "Women's propensity to poetry is very rare . . . Women might be good at writing stories, but they are not good at poetry . . . for femininity in and of itself does not express its emotions nor can it conquer and possess the other character facing it."

59 Hilmi Salim believes that Malak 'Abd al-'Aziz is one of the true pioneers of free verse, on a par with Salah 'Abd al-Sabur and Ahmad 'Abd al-Mu'ti al-Hijazi but that she was slighted by critics who ignored her pioneering role and focused on the prominent male poets. He believes the reason is related to the timing of published collections. Salah 'Abd al-Sabur published his first collection, *al-Nas fi biladi*, in 1957, followed by Hijazi's first collection, *Madina bila qalb*, in 1959; Malak's collection, however, was only published in the early 1960s, although she had been writing free-verse poems since the 1950s. He adds that there are "other important reasons that the media attention went to 'Abd al-Sabur and Hijazi, but the slight of Malak 'Abd al-'Aziz nevertheless remains a mystery of our critical and literary lives." See Hilmi Salim, "Malak 'Abd al-'Aziz sha'irat al-qalb wa-l-iltizam matat . . . taht al-shajara," *al-Hayat*, December 16, 1999.

60 Malak 'Abd al-'Aziz in the introduction to *Aghani al-siba* in *al-A'mal al-kamila li-l-sha'ira Malak 'Abd al-'Aziz* (Cairo: Madbuli, 1990), p. 30.

61 'A'isha 'Abd al-Rahman, *al-Sha'ira al-'Arabiya al-mu'asira*, p. 125.

62 Muhammad Mandur, "al-Aghani wa-l-mughanniya," in *al-A'mal al-kamila li-l-sha'ira Malak 'Abd al-'Aziz*, p. 11.

63 Latifa al-Zayyat in *Alif*, no. 10, 1999, p. 139.

64 Latifa al-Zayyat in *Alif*, no. 10, 1999, p. 51; Latifa al-Zayyat, *The Open Door* (Cairo: American University in Cairo Press, 2000), p. 57.

65 Su'ad Zuhayr, *I'tirafat imra'a mustarjila* (1960) (Cairo: Arab Egyptian Center, 1994).

66 Ibid., p. 35.

67 Ibid., introduction, p. 9.

68 'Inayat al-Zayyat, *al-Hubb wa-l-samt* (Cairo: Dar al-Kitab al-'Arabi Printing and Publishing, 1967), p. 34.

69 Ibid., pp. 53–54.

70 Ibid., p. 72.

71 "Satr maghlut" was translated as "A Mistake in the Knitting," in *Arab Women Writers: An Anthology of Short Stories*, collected, translated, and introduced by Dalya Cohen-Mor (Albany: SUNY Press, 2005).

72 *Al-Zuhur* magazine, September 1974.

73 Alifa Rifaat, "'Alami al-majhul"; translated into English as "My World of the Unknown" in *Distant View of a Minaret and Other Stories* (London, Quartet Books, 1983), p. 71.

74 Amina Rachid, "Talabib al-kitaba am lubbuha," *al-Hilal*, March 1995, p. 175.

75 "Al-Ramadi," in *Talabib al-kitaba*, p. 51.

76 Latifa al-Zayyat, "al-Katib wa-l-hurriya," *al-Fusul*, vol. 11, no. 3, Fall 1992, pp. 237–39.

77 *Hamlat taftish: awraq shakhsiya* (Cairo: Dar al-Hilal, 1992), where she refers to a novel she began in the 1960s which evolved and changed its title many times and which bears close resemblance to *Sahib al-bayt*.

78 Latifa al-Zayyat, "al-Katib wa-l-hurriya," p. 238.

79 Ibid.

80 Latifa al-Zayyat, *Hamlat taftish*, p. 141.

81 Latifa al-Zayyat, *Hamlat taftish*, p. 142; translated into English as *The Search: Personal Papers*, trans. by Sophie Bennett (London: Quartet Books, 1996), p. 102.

82 Ibid.

83 Latifa al-Zayyat, *Hamlat taftish*, p. 55, and *The Search*, p. 39.

84 Latifa al-Zayyat, *Hamlat taftish*, and *The Search*, p. 200.

85 Latifa al-Zayyat, *Sahib al-bayt* (Cairo: Dar al-Hilal, 1994), p. 16; translated into English as *The Owner of the House*, trans. by Sophie Bennett (London: Quartet Books, 1997), pp. 31–32.

86 Latifa al-Zayyat, *Sahib al-bayt*, p. 24, and *The Owner of the House*, p. 38.

87 Latifa al-Zayyat, "al-Katib wa-l-hurriya," p. 238.

88 Latifa al-Zayyat, *Sahib al-bayt*, p. 27, and *The Owner of the House*, pp. 42–43.

89 Iqbal Baraka, *Li-nazall asdiqa' ila-l-abad* (Cairo: General Egyptian Book Organization, 1971).

90 Iqbal Baraka, *Kulluma 'ad al-rabi'* (Cairo: Kitab al-Yawm, 1985).

91 'A'isha Abu-l-Nur, "Imra'a didd imra'a," in *al-Hubb tifluna al-dall* (Cairo: A'isha Abu-l-Nur Publications, 1983).

92 'A'isha Abu-l-Nur, *al-Imda' Salwa* (Cairo: 'A'isha Abu-l-Nur Publications, 1985).

93 I'tidal 'Uthman, in the introduction to *Yunus al-bahr* (Cairo: General Egyptian Book Organization, 1987), p. 7.

94 I'tidal 'Uthman, "al-Sultana," in *Washm al-shams* (Cairo: General Egyptian Book Organization, 1992).

95 Ibid., p. 37.

96 Siham Bayyumi, "al-Ta'ir al-azraq," *Ibda'*, July 1991.

97 Ibtihal Salem, "Madiant al-kartun," in *al-Nawras*, p, 46; translated into English as "City of Cardboard" in *My Grandmother's Cactus: Stories by Egyptian Women*, trans. by Marilyn Booth (London: Quartet Books, 1991), p. 104.

98 Ibid.

99 Edwar al-Kharrat, "Ta'ir al-shi'r al-'anid," in *al-Nawras*.

100 Sahar Tawfiq, *An tanhadir al-shams* (Cairo: General Egyptian Book Organization, 1985); "al-Jihat al-arba'a" was translated as "Points of the Compass" in Sahar Tawfiq, *Points of the Compass: Stories*, trans. by Marilyn Booth (Fayetteville: University of Arkansas Press, 1995).

101 Ni'mat al-Buhayri, "'Indama yasqut al-matar," in *al-'Ashiqun* (Cairo: General Egyptian Book Organization, 1989).

102 Radwa Ashour, "Ra'ayt al-nakhl" in *Ra'ayt al-nakhl* (Cairo: General Egyptian Book Organization, 1989); translated into English as "I Saw the Date-Palms" in *My Grandmother's Cactus: Stories by Egyptian Women*, trans. by Marilyn Booth (London: Quartet Books, 1991), p. 147.

103 Latifa al-Zayyat in the introduction to *Kull hadha-l-sawt al-jamil* (Cairo: Nur and Dar al-Mar'a al-'Arabiya Publications, 1994), p. 15.

104 Radwa Ashour, "Ra'ayt al-nakhl," and "I Saw the Date-Palms," pp. 149 and 154.

105 Radwa Ashour, *Atyaf* (Cairo: Dar al-Hilal, 1999), p. 227.

106 Ibid., p. 227.

107 Ibid., p. 73.

108 Ibid.

109 Ibid., p. 74.

110 Hala El Badry, "Shahada 'an riwayat Muntaha," in *al-Mar'a al-'Arabiya fi muwajahat al-'asr* (Cairo: Nur and Dar al-Mar'a al-'Arabiya Publications, 1996), p. 322.

111 Ferial Ghazoul, "Balaghat al-ghalaba," in *al-Mar'a wa-l-fikr al-'Arabi al-mu'asir*, proceedings of a conference organized by the Organization for Arab Women's Solidarity, 1988.

112 "Nuna al-Sha'nuna," in *Zinat fi jinazat al-ra'is* (Cairo: n.p., 1986); translated into English as "Dotty Noona," in *The Wiles of Men and Other Stories*, trans. Denys Johnson-Davies (Cairo: American University in Cairo Press, 1997).

113 "Zinat fi jinazat al-ra'is," in *Zinat fi jinazat al-ra'is* (Cairo: n.p., 1986); translated into English as "Zeenat Marches in the President's Funeral," in *My Grandmother's Cactus: Stories by Egyptian Women*, trans. Marilyn Booth (London: Quartet Books, 1991).

114 Sana' Sulayha, "Arajuzat," in *Arajuzat* (Cairo: General Egyptian Book Organization, 1999).

115 Muhammad Badawi, "Fi kalam 'an al-kitaba," a documentary film directed by 'Aliya al-Biyali, 1999.

116 May Telmissany, "al-Kitaba 'ala hamish al-tarikh: Misr al-ghiyab," in *Latifa al-Zayyat: al-adab wa-l-watan*, pp. 97–106.

117 Sahar al-Muji, *Dariya* (Cairo: Dar al-Misriya al-Lubnaniya, 1998), p. 35.

118 Shakir 'Abd al-Hamid, "Hadha-l-haws bi-l-tafasil," *Akhbar al-adab*, November 9, 1997.

119 Nura Amin, *Qamis wardi farigh* (Cairo: Dar Sharqiyat, 1997), p. 29.

120 May Telmissany, *Dunyazad* (Cairo: Dar Sharqiyat, 1997), p. 11; translated into English as *Dunyazad*, trans. by Roger Allen (London: Saqi Books, 2000), p. 14.

121 Somaya Ramadan, *Khashab wa nuhas* (Cairo: Dar Sharqiyat, 1995), p. 64.

122 Ibid., p. 21.

123 Somaya Ramadan, "Jaddati," in *Khashab wa nuhas*, pp. 37–38.

124 Najwa Sha'ban, *al-Ghurr* (Cairo: al-Dar al-Misriya al-Lubnaniya, 1998), p. 13.

125 Miral al-Tahawy, *al-Khiba'* (Cairo: Dar Sharqiyat, 1996); second edition published in Beirut: Dar al-Adab, 1999.

126 Miral al-Tahawy, *al-Khiba'*, p. 125; Miral al-Tahawy, *The Tent*, trans. Anthony Calderbank (Cairo: American University in Cairo Press, 1998), p. 107.

127 Miral al-Tahawy, *al-Khiba'*, p. 148, and *The Tent*, p. 130.

128 Fatima Qandil, *Samt qutna mubtalla* (Cairo: Dar Sharqiyat, 1995), p. 71.

129 See the article by Sayyid al-Bahrawi on Mirsal's collection, *Mamarr mu'tim yasluh li-ta'allum al-raqs*, in *Nur*, no. 8, Summer 1996, p. 24.

130 Iman Mirsal, *Mamarr mu'tim yasluh li-ta'allum al-raqs* (Cairo: Dar Sharqiyat, 1995), p. 15.

131 Ibid., pp. 26–27.

132 Nehad Selaiha, in the introduction to *al-Masrah bayn al-nass wa-l-'ard* (Cairo: General Egyptian Book Organization, 1999), p. 11.

133 The first experiments were closer to novels and sometimes called "dramatic novels," which was the term Munira Tal'at used in 1931. Women writers who tried their hand at drama include Jadhibiya Sidqi, Nawal al-Sa'dawi, Fawziya Mahran, Wafa' Wajdi, Fatima Qandil, and Latifa al-Zayyat.

134 The text itself is unpublished, and critic Nehad Selaiha was unable to obtain a copy. She writes that drama historian Samir 'Awad saw the performance and came away with the impression that it was melodramatic and moralizing, and not technically well-crafted. See Nehad Selaiha, "The Voices of Silence: Women Playwrights in Egypt," in *Egyptian Theater: a Diary 1990–1992* (Cairo: General Egyptian Book Organization, 1993), p. 298.

135 See p. 922 of Paul de Man, "Autobiography as Defacement," *Modern Language Notes*, no. 94, 1979, pp. 919–30.

136 See my "Tatawwur nazariyat al-sira al-dhatiya: madha ta'ni bi-l-nisba li-kitabat al-mar'a," in *al-Mar'a al-'Arabiya fi muwajahat al-'asr*.

137 Jalila Rida, *Safahat min hayati* (al-Hilal Books, n.d.), pp. 84–85.

138 Asma Halim, *Arba' zawjat wa rajul* (Cairo: Dar al-Thaqafa al-Jadida, 1980), pp. 213–14.

139 Madiha Abu Zayd, *Mudhakkirat ikhsa'i fi-l-rif al-Misri* (Cairo: General Egyptian Book Organization, 1994).

140 'Atiyyat al-Abnudi, *Ayyam lam takun ma'ah* (Cairo: al-Fursan, 1999).

141 Sabry Hafez, "Bunyat al-khitab al-nisawi wa istratijiyat al-tatabu' al-kayfi," in *Latifa al-Zayyat: al-adab wa-l-watan*, p. 185.

142 Latifa al-Zayyat, "al-Shaykhukha," *al-Shaykhukha wa qisas ukhra* (Cairo: Dar al-Mustaqbal al-'Arabi, 1986), p. 55.

143 Ibid., p. 23.

4 Sudan

Haidar Ibrahim

Introduction

Sudanese women are victims of a double marginalization—once as citizens in a developing country and again as women in a male-dominated society—and this status is reflected in their cultural and artistic production. Sudanese literature, written by both men and women, is generally in short supply due to the conditions of Sudan's historical development. The country is economically underdeveloped despite its enormous resources, which are either unexploited or wasted, and with sporadic exceptions, it has also been involved in the quagmire of civil war since the 1950s because of an underlying identity conflict. As a result, Sudan has become the site of a false conflict between Islam and Arabism and other African cultures, a conflict exacerbated after the civil war in the south, which began in 1983, took on a religious dimension when the regime in Khartoum labeled it a "jihad." As a result of all this, Sudan is politically unstable and economically underdeveloped, conditions which are not conducive to the development and flourishing of a cultural infrastructure of publishing houses, museums, galleries, and theaters. Nor is there a favorable socio-cultural climate of continuity, liberty, openness, and cultural accumulation.

The overwhelming importance of politics in the life of the general populace has also had a negative impact on art and literature. Politics has attracted the abilities, potential, and interests of Sudanese intellectuals at the expense of literature, whether poetry, novels, drama, or criticism, and the result has been a great many politicians and would-be politicians. Politics occupies the lion's share of attention in the press, seminars, and conferences, while cultural and intellectual endeavors are neglected, as illustrated by the quantity of actual publications and works. Sudan's overwhelming concern with the political has given rise to a politics that has led the country into a spiral of military coups and popular uprisings against the military regime, followed by a brief return to a civic parliamentary life that is soon interrupted by another military coup. Politics has thus constituted a continual cultural drain, removing the cultural from the sphere of public influence and then absorbing it into the political. This process has been aided by the fact that many intellectuals have imagined themselves capable of resolving the dilemma of politics by participating in official institutions of authority or leading the struggle. An unthinking politics has swallowed culture and intellectuals, preventing intellectuals from producing literature or from exercising any refining influence over politics. They thus remain ineffective and impotent in both the cultural and political arenas.

This situation is most keenly felt by Sudanese women, who thought that their engagement with politics would improve their status and expand their rights. In fact, women's political influence in Sudan has been remarkable, and they obtained their electoral rights relatively early compared to other African and Arab nations. In 1965, Fatima Ahmad Ibrahim became the first female member of parliament, and Sudanese women have assumed senior positions, such as ministers, and work as judges and engineers. As the same time, however, personal status laws were not favorable, and women did not produce noteworthy writers. Most importantly, illiteracy among Sudanese women and the tradition of female genital mutilation remain to this day. In short, political gains were not accompanied by social and cultural development. Perhaps it can be said that the excessive interest in politics came at the expense of other, no less important achievements. Despite the considerable number of women journalists, researchers, and television and radio personnel, the article or essay remains the favored form of writing. A bibliography of women's works in magazines from 1975 to 1982 contains 646 citations for articles and essays written by Sudanese women, but only sixteen short stories and fourteen poems.[1]

Many speak of the inevitable impact that education is assumed to have on the educated, but it is not education in and of itself that is important, but the content and philosophy of the education—that is, what and how do we teach? Quantitative advances in the education of both girls and boys have not been matched by a similar advance in the creative capacities of male and female graduates. Girls' education in Sudan is further complicated by the fact that education often pushed women out of their traditional environment without equipping them with modern practices and mentalities. Thus Sudanese women have found themselves in an unspecified transitional state, what Durkheim termed "anomie." The old has been displaced, but the modern has not yet occupied its place. Paradoxically, women considered "traditional"—rural women or women who lived in previous centuries—manifested their creative abilities in society. History preserves the names of many female poets of panegyric and tribal poetry, such as Shaghba al-Marghumabiya, Bint Masimas, Bint al-Makkawi, Satna Bint Kanuna, and Mahira Bint 'Abbud. Women tribal poets were seen as the backbone of battle readiness. As one researcher writes, "In most cases, as warriors set out for battle, they were accompanied by the beating of drums and tins, and zealous war songs sung by the women and girls of the tribe. These songs were composed by the women themselves."[2] There was a break with this traditional creative legacy, but it was not replaced by a new legacy that could perform these and other functions in a transitional society. When tribal warfare ceased, so did the need for these women poets, although other forms of relations emerged that might have produced female artists of another type. Instead, with superficial social changes the role of Sudanese women became even more conservative, particularly in the countryside and outside urban centers. The social status of rural women who had worked in the fields and pastures and participated in many activities with men began to be measured by their distance or abstention from these activities. The activities of female pupils, for example, were limited to going to school, usually in girls' schools to prevent mixing with boys. The current form of education endowed Sudanese women with information and prepared them for modern jobs and positions, but they lost the wisdom and creativity that their grandmothers learned from life.

Creative expression is a basic spiritual necessity; Sudanese women thus found non-institutional channels for self-expression. Sudanese society has witnessed the rise of so-called "girls' songs." The songs, composed and arranged by girls, both individually and collectively—indeed, the original author is often lost—revolve around the desire for marriage and a longing for a gratifying domestic life that will fulfill their desires for consumption. One researcher categorizes girls' songs as part of folkloric literature because they reflect a folk sensibility and are inspired by the existing social structure. The authors of the songs are usually anonymous, and the lyrics themselves are often adapted from well-known songs which are then rearranged into poetic hemistiches.[3] Women Sudanese intellectuals have an ambivalent relationship with these songs. Some see them as a degraded art form that devalues and commodifies women for marriage or a passing affair. Yet at the same time, these songs are a permanent fixture of wedding ceremonies, and are admired and heard by all segments of society. This sort of creative production is the natural outcome of the narrow horizons for serious literature by women, as well as the general creative malaise that exists for objective reasons. The deteriorating standard of living and the absence of freedoms have impeded the formation of a middle class, an incubator for male and female writers alike. In addition, the Islamist political regime in power since June 1989 has tried to implement what it calls "an Islamic civilizational enterprise," declaring that it seeks to reshape the Sudanese individual. This totalitarianism and authoritarianism has killed what remained of the possibilities for the development of creative writing in Sudan.

Many researchers consider Sudanese culture an oral culture that relies heavily on unwritten speech and discussion. It is not difficult to prove this assertion; one need only review a bibliography of published Sudanese literature to see how lean it is, despite the great number of Sudanese who hold advanced degrees and are interested in public affairs. As a whole, Sudan is still closer to a Bedouin or rural society. It only witnessed the rise of cities a century ago, and even these were usually administrative centers created by the colonial regime to better manage the country. The ancient cities and cultural and commercial centers disappeared before the eighteenth century in the wake of conflicts and wars. Because culture and art develop and flourish in cities, this has necessarily influenced Sudanese literary production. Cities foster the rise of institutions that encourage art and cultural advancement, such as theaters, museums, publishing houses and printing presses, public libraries, festivals, and civic cultural organizations. Given the dearth, or sometimes complete absence, of these institutions, Sudanese intellectuals meet in homes—in what the Sudanese call "sittings." Such encounters have become a plague in the lives of intellectuals, where they fritter away time and energy almost addictively. Intellectuals spend much time talking in their sittings, but they do not find the time to write or compose, which requires a certain type of ordered, regulated life that is specifically urban.

Because of this cultural milieu there is little production and, even more important, literary careers tend to be short. Writer George Tarabishi, who is outside the Sudanese context, remarked on this point in a newspaper interview: ". . . even Sudanese poetry, which advanced in the 1960s and 1970s, has retreated and withdrawn, and I don't know why . . . Here things live and die quickly. Many of the names that rose to prominence in the cultural field quickly receded and waned."[4] This is an apt description of the state of Sudanese women writers; indeed, women usually stop writing after completing their higher education and certainly after marriage. Many intellectuals—men and women—consider writing poetry or stories to be a frivolity of youth. In press interviews, former or retired writers say they composed poetry or wrote literature at a certain point in their lives, giving the impression that they then wised up or even regret that period.

Another reason for the paucity of Sudanese literature can be found in the waves of Sudanese emigration, no longer only to nearby countries in the Gulf, the Arabian Peninsula, and Libya. Hundreds of thousands of Sudanese have left the country in the last decade, and the U.N. even has a resettlement program for Sudanese refugees, under which Sudanese in Cairo, for example, are resettled in the U.S., Canada, or Australia. Sudanese with rural backgrounds have not been able to easily adapt and acclimatize, and thus exile has not become an inspiration as it was for the Exile Poets of the Levant or those fleeing the Nazis, who established artistic and intellectual schools in their places of exile. Sudanese emigrants, particularly artists and writers, have felt uprooted by their forced, sudden departure.

Migration has also weakened the possibilities for literary development in Sudan itself; even those poets and writers who remain in the country have fled to history and the past, living in exile from their own time, if not the physical exile of refugees. Inside Sudan, poets have emerged who write about horses, swords, caravans of martyrs, and marriage to *huri*s. The Sudanese experience of 1989–1999 has proven the inability of Islamists in power to develop and foster a literature. The regime has shown no serious interest in culture in general, and a short time ago, the Sudanese minister of culture stated, "I aver and admit that culture in Sudan has not received its rightful share in the current period, although this year we staged several activities." He added, "I reviewed spending on culture and found that, on average, it was the equivalent of 0.036 percent of public spending. Of course, this is disgraceful and embarrassing."[5] All governments since independence in 1956 have evinced the same neglect of culture. Despite slight differences in degree, a dismissive view of culture and literature has been characteristic of all Sudanese national governments.

The beginnings of a women's literary renaissance were seen following independence, but it was cut short after the cap placed on liberties following the military coup of 1958, only two years after independence. The military regime ruled by emergency laws and impeded the activities of civil society. Before that, women's magazines appeared that were concerned about the cause of Sudanese women. In 1947, the first women's magazine appeared, *Bint al-wadi*, published by Takwa Sarkisian, a Sudanese woman of Armenian origin. Su'ad Fathi also contributed to the effort. In 1955, Professor Fatima Ahmad Ibrahim published the monthly *Sawt al-mar'a*; the journal published 120 issues despite repeated interruptions by the authorities. Professor Hajja Kashif published a monthly cultural magazine, *al-Qafila* in 1956, but it did not last long. Professor Thuraya Ambabi launched *al-Manar* in 1964. Other weeklies appeared, such as *al-Usra al-sa'ida*, 1974 and *Hawwa' al-jadida*, March 1969 to March 1970.[6] Many women writers also contributed to the literary pages and cultural supplements of newspapers. These gave some women the chance to hone their writing and the skills of self-expression.

On the state of culture and writing

We can date the inception of the short story in Sudan to the late 1920s when it began to appear in magazines of the day. Writing in the press of this period evinces preliminary attempts to improve the written language and address new topics. 'Abd al-Majid 'Abidin divides modern writing in Sudan into three types: first, descriptive writing, concerned with describing "life" directly in the form of a depiction of a psychological state, a natural landscape, or a human condition; second, fictional writing, which is part of writing that describes life. Sudanese writers used this type of writing in the form of the short story, the novel, and autobiography. The third type is critical writing, or literature that describes itself, which flourished in Sudan.[7]

Interest in these genres constituted a leap for Sudanese literature, particularly prose, when compared to the ancient literature "which knew official, didactic, and fraternal letters, as well as histories and biographical dictionaries."[8] Sudan began to communicate with the outside world after the break imposed during the Mahdiya period (1885–1898) and particularly after the reoccupation when the colonial authority attempted to assert its security presence. Sudanese began to initiate contact with other countries, especially Arab countries, seeking to catch up with modern developments. As Muhammad Ahmad al-Mahjub said,

> But the sincere man cannot help but remark, in pain and hope, that this country still lags behind the Arab caravan. It still needs revolutionary writers who can combine strong, coherent thought with a comely style and produce books that bear the imprint of this country.[9]

Egypt exercised a keen influence on the development of literature and fiction. One historian of Sudanese fiction notes, "With confused and stumbling steps, the Sudanese story began to adopt the form of the Egyptian story, sometimes romantic and at other times realistic."[10] Although some Sudanese writers were directly familiar with English literature, the Egyptian influence on literature in Sudan was very strong, disseminated through Egyptian newspapers and magazines such as *al-Siyasa al-usbu'iya*, which introduced the Sudanese to Muhammad Husayn Haykal, and *al-Balagh al-usbu'i*, which introduced Sudan to the influential 'Abbas Mahmud al-'Aqqad.

We cannot help but remark on the paucity of Sudanese novels and short stories, attributable to the factors discussed above. In his *al-Qissa al-haditha fi-l-Sudan* (Modern Fiction in Sudan), 'Ajuba counted the number of books that appeared up until 1970: forty-four novels and short-story collections, although this does not include short stories published in magazines and newspapers. Regardless of quality, the quantity of fiction produced was meager; the same number of publications might appear in one year in Arab countries such as Egypt or Lebanon. Writer 'Uthman 'Ali Nur initiated a fine enterprise with the launch of the magazine *al-Qissa* in January 1960. The same year, twelve issues of the journal appeared; in 1961, five issues appeared before the journal was suspended in May. The 1970s saw the emergence of cultural supplements to the daily papers, such as *al-Sahafa* and *al-Ayyam*. Some daily papers also had a cultural page, usually weekly. All of these featured some sort of creative writing, including fiction.

Despite the limited production, some names stand out in the novel and the short story. Although some see Tayeb Salih as dominating all the rest, one must also pause at the works of 'Isa al-Helw, Bushra al-Fadil, Ibrahim Ishaq Ibrahim, and Ahmad Hamd al-Mulk. These works encompass a great variety of fictional styles, despite the lack of cultural accretion and continuity needed to form broad, influential literary schools.

Women's writing is governed by this same context and the same conditions of Sudan's socio-cultural development. Women's voices appear, only to fade rapidly for reasons both objective and subjective. Political instability and a developmental crisis are reflected in the absence of a sustained Sudanese enterprise to resolve Sudan's complex problems, among them cultural. Artists and art suffered most of all. We must understand the paucity of women's writing within the general context: writing as a whole in Sudan has suffered because of lack of liberty, economic deterioration, social instability, cultural retreat, and obscurantist thought. Sudanese writers have begun to express their nostalgia for the past, seeing the golden age of the renaissance in the past rather than the future. They repeatedly express their wonder at the 1930s and later, the 1960s, all of which is indicative of a disappointment in the current cultural reality and its abject poverty and lack of depth. This attenuated reality may contribute to the overvaluation of those who try to create, write, and think despite the circumstances, which in turn might explain the overestimation of some writers. This study of women's writing aims more to define and introduce it than to evaluate it or issue critical judgments.

Sudanese women and fiction

A discussion of the pioneers of the novel and short story puts women at the forefront because writer Malakat al-Dar Muhammad 'Abd Allah was one of the first Sudanese of either sex to turn to the field. She is a pioneer, and not only among women. On the other hand, there is only a scattering of women fiction writers, and the careers of writing women have always been extremely brief. A woman writer might write once or only a few times, countable on the fingers of one hand. The author of *Adibat al-Sudan* (Women Writers of Sudan), Munir Salih 'Abd al-Qadir, mentions several names whose output is limited to one or two attempts. Such conditions do not allow any researcher to speak about literary schools or trends. Certainly there was an engagement with national events in the country in this period and the concomitant cultural and social changes resulting from local and external conditions. Women's writings from the 1950s are concerned with women going out to school and work, and fighting what their authors considered obsolete traditions that restricted women and prevented them from performing their necessary role in society.

Women writers showed a preference for directly didactic articles that conveyed a particular message, with the content of the message seen as more important than the literary tools used to convey it. As such, there was little concern with good artistic form. These writings may have contributed to defining the status of Sudanese women, which paved the way for an active, broad women's movement with much influence among educated women. In these early phases, any researcher will face the problem of generic classification using today's criteria. These are literary texts concerned with giving voice to certain causes. In his study of modern Sudanese fiction, 'Ajuba named only Malakat al-Dar Muhammad as a fiction writer, devoting only the following two lines to other women writers: "In 'Ahlam al-'adhra' (The Virgin's Dreams), Asma' Bint al-Shamaliya documents the memories of a Sudanese girl at the outset of girls' education in the early 1950s."[11] Critic Mu'awiya al-Bilal counts several women writers who contributed to the enrichment of women's writing in the 1950s, including Amal 'Abbas, who published the story "Masra' qalbayn" (The Death of Two Hearts) in *Sawt al-mar'a*. Amina Ahmad Yunus (later known as Amina Bint Wahb) wrote short stories for *al-Tilighraf*. Zaynab 'Abd al-Salam al-Mahbub wrote several stories, the most important being "al-Dahiya wa-l-khati'a" (The Victim and the Offense). Salma Ahmad al-Bashir published her works in *al-Manar* in 1957, including her most important story, "Yatiman" (Two Orphans).

Al-Bilal summarizes the characteristics of what he terms "traditional women's writing," which covered the 1950s until the mid-1970s. According to him, this writing is distinguished by a tight narrative structure, an expository language dominated by description, and an attempt to accurately reflect reality. The writing evinces a concern for social issues and aspires to be part of the liberation and renaissance enterprise. At the same time, al-Bilal notes the dominance of the character of the victimized, weak woman who reflects the hardships of bitter reality.[12] The writing of this period has clear pedagogical and didactic objectives, and it is noteworthy that most women writers worked as teachers, which influenced their style of writing; in addition, the nature of the topics at hand usually required a clear stance. Indeed critics of the period see all early writings— by both men and women—as marked by didacticism and protest.

The pioneer of the Sudanese short story: Malakat al-Dar Muhammad 'Abd Allah (1918–1969)

Malakat al-Dar Muhammad's beginnings were stunning: her first short story, "Hakim al-qarya" (The Village Doctor), won Sudanese Radio's short-story prize in 1947. The story was reprinted in *Kurdufan* newspaper and in the first issue of the journal, *al-Qissa*. Dr. Ihsan 'Abbas commented on the story,

> "Hakim al-qarya" shows an ability to construct a plot based on suspense; the mystery unfolds on the sidelines of the action and becomes almost a riddle. Nevertheless, the author has not carved out an independent style for herself, and the style of the student essay still dominates her writing. After the elements of suspense, the best thing in the story is the way she directs her subject—that is, the victory of good over self-doubt and uncertainty.[13]

"Hakim al-qarya" starts out well with its description of nature and the emotions of the story's characters. The story opens with an ironic tension: nature is tranquil, while the human element is agitated and filled with a desire for revenge and murder: "The sound of the thunder subsided and the clouds disappeared. The stars appeared, laughing and twinkling, and the moon began emitting its silver rays, which seeped into the narrow hut." The author then moves to the discussion underway inside the hut:

> A hoarse, emotional voice answered him: "The night is still long, so let us go now and take our vengeance on the interloper who disturbs our peace and steals our honor." No sooner had Bilal stopped speaking than they all leapt up, each fingering the dagger that hung at his arm, their voices quietly threatening.[14]

After this introduction, Muhammad turns to the main character of the story: Yusuf, the village doctor, giving us a description of him that highlights his total difference from the surrounding environment. Naturally, a conflict erupts between the newcomer to the village and the villagers, and woman is the symbol of this conflict, whether real or imagined.

Some critics believe the story refers to the problems associated with social change and the transition from a traditional society. The old (the village) stands against the new, represented by the doctor and his modern therapies. The fortune-teller, or the seer, represents the mystical mind, and he incites the youth against the doctor who would threaten the role of tradition in the village. The story ends with the victory of goodness and beauty over evil and ugliness. Evil is personified in characters like Yusuf, the one-eyed man, and 'Aqila, whose face is disfigured with burns. The story also holds an underlying conflict between the city and the village, a conflict that reappears in the story, "al-Majnuna" (The Madwoman). 'Ajuba remarks that Malakat al-Dar Muhammad's fiction is influenced by the films of the 1940s, which, much like her techniques, relied on the suspense of betrayal and surprise.[15]

The novel, al-Faragh al-'arid (The Vast Emptiness) 1970, published posthumously, sparked a broad debate among writers. Many celebrated the novel; for example, the poet Nur 'Uthman Abkar said:

As it sets out on its journey, the Sudanese novel is honored to have a female voice take part in opining on the social, cultural, and personal life of activist circles, both male and female, in Sudan in the period from the 1940s to the 1960s. This voice is rich in practical experience and endowed with a sharp awareness of reality.[16]

Meanwhile the critic and researcher Muhammad al-Mahdi Bushra notes,

Despite everything, al-Faragh al-'arid is a document of protest, but the overwhelmingly instructive nature of the text does not rob it of its vitality and structural cohesiveness. Thus, we can say that the novel, in both its artistic form and social content, is truly a candle in the darkness. At the same time, it is a courageous indictment of the social injustice endured by both women and men.[17]

The novel's protagonist, Muna, is an example of the new woman: she works, she is literate, takes political stances, and demands her rights to love and a happy marriage in exchange for the vast emptiness. Muna works as a teacher and writes for the press, and she criticizes her husband, Sayyid, for his lack of engagement with national issues. She is a strong, vital character and has a clear perspective in her dealings with people. Some critics have linked the author with the protagonist, saying that the novel is semi-autobiographical, and some attribute the novel's tone of protest to the fact that Muhammad sought directly to communicate stances on national issues in which she herself believed.

Buthayna Khidr Makki

Makki was active during a relatively short period of time and sent quite a few works to print; in the Sudanese context, she is considered a prolific author. In five years, she published the following works: a collection of short stories, *al-Nakhla wa-l-maghna* (Palm and Song) 1993; a children's novella, *Fatat al-qarya* (Village Girl) 1993; the short-story collection *Ashbah al-mudun* (Ghosts of the Cities) 1995; the short-story collection *Atyaf al-huzn* (Phantoms of Sorrow) 1996; *Ghita' al-samt* (The Cover of Silence) 1996; and a novel, *Ughniyat al-nar* (Fire Song) 1998. She received much attention and encouragement from the press and journals, making her the leading female short-story writer in Sudan. Despite her prominence in the media, her creative output needs to be reviewed, and not only in the context of Sudanese women's fiction, for women's literature in the Arab world has clearly evolved and many new writers have made fine contributions.

The reader of Makki's stories will notice the absence of social issues, although all of her works are grounded in the country with their descriptions of distinctly Sudanese natural and human landscapes. The problem is that Makki only touches her subjects on the surface and does not possess the patience to delve more deeply into one subject or one issue. In the novel *Ughniyat al-nar*, for example, the heroine proudly declares that she hates politics. She seems to be referring to party politics, but in the dialogue she shies away from any discussion of public issues. The characters and settings of the novel are largely upper class—doctors and senior officers— and set in places like London, Addis Ababa, and Saudi Arabia. When the protagonist wants to describe the lower classes living on the city's outskirts, she must disguise herself in different clothing.[18]

Love is at the center of the novel, but it is a strange, incomplete kind of love. We follow Raja', a married woman who meets her first love and becomes obsessed with him. Her husband, 'Asim, marries again in secret, though he is still desperately in love with her.[19] Her brother, 'Adil, falls in love at first sight with an Ethiopian secretary; he marries her and they have a child, whose story occupies a large portion of the novel. Makki could have given us a more profound portrayal of the people who feel these conflicting emotions, but she is more concerned with depicting the consequences of these feelings, packing the novel with surprises and action to compensate for a lack of character analysis and a probing of their interior lives that would answer the question of how they became the way they are in the first place.

The author possesses the ability to observe and construct events, and she uses a fine intermediate language that falls between the colloquial and standard Arabic. She is particularly expressive with the language in dialogue. What she lacks is a varied experience that is not derived solely from the lives of the upper classes. Significantly, she began with an interest in some social issues, as seen in her story, "al-Tuqus" (The Rituals), which deals with the Pharaonic custom of female genital mutilation as a social problem. She has the potential to make substantial contributions to the Sudanese novel if she makes her writing something more than an individual escape or mode of subjective expression. Like the protagonist of her novel, Makki is attempting to escape from the world and its problems through writing. There is nothing wrong with this as long as universal concerns lie at the center of the writing. Ultimately, the absence of literary criticism exacerbates the task of writers who seek to develop themselves and improve their craft. Most critics tend toward impressionistic criticism which often does not give writers new intellectual or literary knowledge.

Other writers
Several other women writers have added to the corpus of Sudanese literature, some of them writing from exile. Salma al-Shaykh Salama published a collection of short stories, *Matar 'ala jasad al-rahil* (Rain on the Body of the Departed) in 1998 and another collection, *Ibn al-nakhil* (Son of the Palm) in 1999. The writer's language approaches poetry at times. She gives the reader many examples of women's condition and more than once protests the authority to which women must bend, whether personified by the family, society, or the state. In *Atfal al-samgh* (Children of Glue), Salama addresses the conflict between the north and the south, which has generally been of only marginal interest in Sudanese fiction.

Malakat al-Fadil 'Umar published a novel, *al-Judran al-qasiya* (The Cruel Walls), in 1999, and Zaynab Balil published her novel, *al-Ikhtiyar* (The Choice), the same year. The impact of the current political situation is clear in the first novel; Malakat al-Fadil gives us a political novel, parts of which describe an interrogation by state security. Zaynab Balil's novel, with its 154 pages of continuous dialogue, is closer to a play.

The Sudanese press, both newspapers and magazines, have opened up a space for some women writers of the short story, including Nafisa al-Sharqawi (Umm Ahmad), 'Awadiya Yusuf, Amal Husayn, Fatima al-Sanusi, Maha al-Rashid, Su'ad 'Abd al-Tamm, In'am al-Hajj Babakr, and Sara Yusuf Khalil. From the south, the press has given us authors—Agnes Lakudu and Estella Catanio, for example—some of whom write in English. Critic Mu'awiya al-Bilal summarizes the formal features of modern fiction written by women from the 1970s through the 1990s as follows: 1) a use of modern fictional techniques, such as time intersection, the stream-of-consciousness, interior monologue, memory and recall, and disruption; 2) a poetic use of language; and 3) women's approach to fiction from subjective experiences and awareness of their independence and particularity, as well as their rejection of the various mechanisms of oppression that seek to control them.[20] Indeed we can detect the beginnings of a distinctive Sudanese women's literature that deserves the name in its themes, its language, and its view of the universe, life, and society.

Poetry

Women's contributions to poetry have been meager and weak; even considering the dearth of fiction, women have contributed more to the short story and novel. Anthologies of Sudanese poetry lack any women's names. In his *al-Shi'r wa-l-shu'ara' fi-l-Sudan 1900–1958* (Poetry and Poets in Sudan: 1900–1958), Ahmad Abu Sa'd lists no female name. The same is true for 'Abduh Badawi's *al-Shi'r al-hadith fi-l-Sudan 1840–1953* (Modern Poetry in Sudan 1840–1953) and 'Abd al-Majid 'Abidin's *Tarikh al-thaqafa fi-l-Sudan* (The History of Culture in Sudan). Similarly, 'Ali al-Makk's *Mukhtarat min al-adab al-Sudani* (Selections from Sudanese Literature) and 'Abd al-Hadi al-Siddiq's *Usul al-shi'r al-Sudani* (The Principles of Sudanese Poetry) make no mention of any female poets.[21] The corpus of Sudanese literature contains virtually no collections of poetry written by women, save *Iha'* (Inspiration), by Safiya al-Shaykh al-Amin and *Hataft la* (I Shouted No), by Rawda al-Hajj Muhammad 'Uthman. It is very difficult for the researcher to follow women's poetry closely because it is normally published in newspapers and magazines rather than in collections. These pages thus attempt to provide an incomplete documentation of women's attempts in the field of poetry.

Some poems written by Sudanese women appeared in the 1950s after the rise of the nationalist movement, as educated women entered the public sphere. This explains why women wrote for the papers, and also the dominance of certain themes in their poetry. One researcher notes that women's poetry in this period revolves around women's liberation and advancement, an engagement with national issues, and romantic tendencies.[22] We find poems like "Farha tammat" (A Joy Completed), by 'Alawiya al-Sayyid, about women seeking education; another poem by Zaynab 'Awad al-Karim, "Fatat al-jil" (Girl of the Generation), takes on the same subject.

Most of the poetry of this period is merely ordinary speech which has been rhymed and metered, particularly when the topic is a national issue. This is true of the poems of Amina Ahmad Yunus (Amina Bint Wahb) and Asma' Bint al-Shamaliya about Jamila Buhrayd (the Algerian freedom fighter), the aggression against Egypt (1956), and the Baghdad Pact (1954). Sentimental poetry was of no better quality than poetry addressing other themes. For the most part, these poems give voice to cold emotions that lack real experience, for Sudan was a closed, conservative society that did not allow women real, profound experiences that they could express in poetry.

In the midst of this poetic desert, a few short-lived flowers bloomed, but they did not grow into maturity. Critic Muhammad Mustafa Hadara celebrated a young poet by the name of al-Radiya Adam saying:

> There is a group of rising young women poets who believe in the cause of the new poetry. They engage with contemporary human issues and their nation's problems, particularly the cause of women. I would mention Fatima Babakr and al-Radiya Adam, in whom I find a delicate poetic sensibility, an intellectual outpouring, and a depth that heralds a shining future for contemporary Sudanese poetry. Thus far, neither poet has issued a collection of poems for readers.[23]

It remains true that neither poet published a collection; indeed, they both abandoned poetry, their talents being drawn to politics and academia.

Hadara examines six poems by al-Radiya Adam, saying he wished to encourage the budding poet "not, as the proverb says, out of compassion for women, but because the poet is taking her first steps into the world of literature. Her poems are merely attempts that do not claim perfection or maturity."[24] Al-Radiya Adam attempts to write free verse, but, as Hadara notes, she falls captive to ancient poetic meters. He points out her broken meters and rhyme schemes, but her linguistic and grammatical errors are relatively rare.

Safiya al-Shaykh al-Amin published the first collection of poetry written by a woman, *Iba'*, through a publishing house in Beirut. There is no date of publication, but it appears to date from the late 1960s. There is no sign of a grasp of, or talent for, poetry in the collection. She deals with several topics and addresses the nation in her poems. After this collection, al-Amin completely stopped writing poetry—or at least publishing it.

We can turn to contemporary poetry without having ignored any important milestones or influential figures in the evolution of poetry. All women poets have stopped writing after publishing only a few poems. I will deal with only two examples that have some hint of poeticity, despite their very different subject matter. This poetry is untraditional in both form and language, which tries to leave behind traditional vocabulary and formulations. Coincidentally, both of the poets, Huwayda 'Abd Allah 'Abd al-Qadir and Rawda al-Hajj Muhammad, were born in 1969. The latter published a collection of poems, while the former published her poems in several newspapers, including *al-Khartum*, the Lebanese *al-Safir*, and the Lebanese *al-Manabir*.

Huwayda 'Abd Allah 'Abd al-Qadir's poetry is self-revelatory. She often uses the first person, but at the same time she speaks of themes of common concern. The distress that appears repeatedly in her poetry is not simply a personal pain. She writes:

They have no father, no identity.
Happenstance, one woman, gave birth to them all
and they spread throughout the streets and the cattle ranches.
They bear the weight of goods and the weight of their cares
as they bear their weak bodies,
the crumbs of their souls.
These
do not sleep in their leisure like humans;
instead they
wander in the ruin of their street
to embrace, dying, their eyes' disappointments
and sell the remaining organs of their bodies,
so at night they can return with one drink,
one woman,
and share it in one room.
A salt-cured body that cannot reproduce:
This is their channel to the suspended spirit[25]

The language is sharp and shocking, and the harsh images capture a frustrating, absurd reality. But it is natural for the poet's experiences to be expressed in angry, severe texts. Before she reached the age of thirty, she was forced out of her homeland to live as a refugee in exile. Her poetry thus expresses this splintered reality and her language such emotion. At times it seems that the poem is totally fragmented and broken.

Rawda al-Hajj Muhammad represents another face of the Sudanese crisis; in her poetry she tries to uphold the Islamist discourse of the Sudanese regime. This complicity is found in her calls for jihad and calls to protect the Islamist regime, and thus her poetry is often clamoring and noisy, as the title of the collection, *Hataft la*, suggests. Her poetry glorifies death because it leads first to martyrdom and then paradise.

The works of these two poets illustrate the spiritual and intellectual division of Sudan into two different views of society and the nation. Sudan is currently experiencing an economic and political crisis and an acute identity conflict, torn between Arabism and Africanism. This has ramifications for writing in general, but women seem to be most keenly affected by the conflict and crisis.

Notes

1 'Uthman 'Awad 'Uthman, *Bibliyughrafiyat al-mar'a al-Sudaniya fi-l-majallat al-Sudaniya fi-l-fatra min 1975–1982* (Khartoum: Khartoum University Press, 1988), pp. 47–48.

2 'Izz al-Din Isma'il, *al-Shi'r al-qawmi fi-l-Sudan* (Beirut: Dar al-Thaqafa, 1988), p. 195.

3 Ni'mat 'Abd Allah Rajab, "Wad' al-mar'a fi Umm Durman min khilal dirasat aghani al-banat," in *Nisa' Umm Durman* (Umm Durman: Muhammad 'Umar Bashir Center, 1998), p. 168.

4 *Al-Khartum*, no. 17, 444, March 1998.

5 Interview with Ghazi Salah al-Din, minister of culture and information, in *al-Bayan*, August 29, 1999.

6 Qasim 'Uthman Nur, ed., *Dalil al-dawriyat al-Sudaniya* (Khartoum: n.p., 1999), p. 63.

7 'Abd al-Majid 'Abidin, *Tarikh al-thaqafa al-'Arabiya fi-l-Sudan* (Beirut: Dar al-Thaqafa, 1967), p. 326.

8 Ibid.

9 Muhammad Ahmad al-Mahjub, *al-Haraka al-fikriya fi-l-Sudan ila ayna tattajih* (Khartoum: n.p., 1941), p. 31.

10 Mukhtar 'Ajuba, *al-Qissa fi-l-Sudan* (Khartoum: Khartoum University, 1972), p. 16.

11 Ibid., p. 66.

12 Mu'awiya al-Bilal, "al-Kitaba al-qisasiya al-nisawiya fi-l-Sudan," paper presented at the conference, "Culture and Development," convened by the Center for Sudanese Studies, August 4–6, 1999, pp. 5–8.

13 Ihsan 'Abbas, "'Adadna al-madi fi ra'i," *al-Qissa*, vol. 1, no. 2, February 1960, p. 29.

14 *Al-Qissa*, vol. 1, no. 1, January 1960, p. 41.

15 Mukhtar 'Ajuba, *al-Qissa fi-l-Sudan*, pp. 63–64.

16 Al-Nur 'Uthman Abkar, "al-Faragh al-'arid," *Kitabat Sudaniya*, no. 6, September 1995, p. 117.

17 Muhammad al-Mahdi Bushra, "al-Faragh al-'arid . . . sham'a fi-l-zalam," *Kitabat Sudaniya*, no. 6, September 1995, p. 114.

18 Buthayna Khidr Makki, *Ughniyat al-nar* (Sharjah: privately published, n.d.), p. 178.

19 Ibid., p. 184.

20 Mu'awiya al-Bilal, p. 12.

21 Ahmad Abu Sa'd, *al-Shi'r wa-l-shu'ara fi-l-Sudan* (Beirut: Dar al-Ma'arif, n.d.); 'Abduh Badawi, *al-Shi'r al-hadith fi-l-Sudan* (Cairo: n.p., n.d.); 'Abd al-Majid 'Abidin, *Tarikh al-thaqafa*; 'Ali al-Makk, *Mukhtarat min al-adab al-Sudani* (Khartoum: 1997); and 'Abd Allah al-Siddiq, *Usul al-shi'r al-Sudani* (Khartoum: n.p., 1989).

22 Muhammad 'Abd al-Khaliq, unpublished manuscript on the features of early Sudanese women's writing.

23 Muhammad Mustafa Hadara, *Tayyarat al-shi'r al-'Arabi al-mu'asir* (Beirut: Dar al-Thaqafa, 1972), p. 195.

24 Ibid.

25 From "Shahqat akhira."

5 Iraq

Ferial J. Ghazoul

Introduction

I raqi women can draw on a rich literary tradition that stretches back to the
dawn of recorded civilization at Sumer and Babel, and continues up to the
pre-Islamic era (the poet Salma Bint Malik ibn Hudhayfa, for example)
and after the Islamic conquest, with figures such as Layla al-Akhyaliya
(who engaged in literary sparring with the governor of Iraq, al-Hajjaj ibn
Yusuf al-Thaqafi), Raya al-Salmiya, 'A'isha Bint al-Mahdi, al-Fari'a Bint
Tarif, Mahbuba, Dananir, the Sufi poet Rabi'a al-'Adawiya, and many
others. Nothing is more indicative of literary history's neglect of women's
literature than the fact that Zubayda Bint Ja'far was known primarily as the
wife of Caliph Harun al-Rashid and the mother of al-Amin, and recognized
for her charity and good deeds rather than for her literary works, which
included poetry, letters, and exhortations. After Baghdad fell to the
Mongols in the thirteenth century, the infrastructure of both civic life and
culture began to deteriorate, leading to decay and fragmentation. It is in
such times of deterioration and disintegration that the pressure increases
on the weaker segments of society, particularly women. The oppression
that accompanies cultural atrophy affects men but is compounded for
women, who become twice oppressed: once by their affiliation with an
occupied or defeated country, and again by their sex, seen by society as
lower and weaker. Thus, women become the group on which society vents
its rage. When learning and science retreated in Iraq under the Ottomans,
Iraqi cultural production and activity declined, and the limited activity that
existed was confined to men rather than women, the strong rather than the
weak, and the wealthy rather than the poor. Women were deprived of the

178

right to education; literature and debate were no longer parts of their lives as they had been in the golden age. As a result, women's literature became virtually extinct.

True, women continued to find windows of expression in even the darkest periods, illustrated in poetry and songs produced for both joyous and sad occasions, at weddings and funerals, as well as religious supplications and popular tales. Nevertheless, their contributions to "the higher arts" dwindled and we hear virtually nothing of any Iraqi woman writer for some six centuries. (The Iraqi poet Fad'a, known as Khansa' Khuza'a, who lived in the mid-eighteenth century, is perhaps the only exception.) Women began to speak again in the twentieth century when Iraq, as part of the Arab nation, regained its repressed identity and aspired to rise from its long slumber. During the nationalist awakening an intellectual renaissance took shape, a collective desire to advance society as a whole—men, women, and children. Since women's status was subordinate to men—for several reasons, some noted above—the literary and intellectual vanguard focused on freeing them from illiteracy and expanding their narrow cultural horizons, seeking to introduce them to more compassionate, welcoming spaces. Prominent Iraqi poets, among them Ma'ruf al-Rasafi and Jamil Sidqi al-Zahawi, demanded women's emancipation just as the Egyptian Qasim Amin and the Algerian Muhammad ibn Mustafa ibn al-Khuja had done before them. Jamil Sidqi al-Zahawi was known as "the partisan of women" because of his preoccupation with the cause of women in his poetry, and poetry, in Iraq, has a significant influence on thought. The attempts to remove obstacles to women's human and literary development coincided with the nationalist struggle against colonialism and the class struggle against exploitation. Indeed, some see women's status in any society as the most reliable indicator of that society's advancement.

The beginning of the road

In the early twentieth century, women were not part of the official educational system because of their lower, secondary status. Nevertheless, some wealthy, aristocratic families known for their learning sought to educate their daughters and encouraged them to write and compose poetry through private lessons or under the direction of a father or brother. Most women writers born in the first two decades of the century shared this supportive family environment: Salima 'Abd al-Razzaq al-Mala'ika (Umm Nizar), Fatina al-Na'ib (Saduf al-'Amiriya), Maqbula al-Hilli ('Afra'), Wadi'a Ja'far al-Shabibi, Hiyam al-Wiswasi, Ibtihaj 'Ata Amin, and Amira Nur al-Din.[1]

Undoubtedly, women from the wealthy classes and homes of literature and knowledge enjoyed greater social and literary rights than their peers from the middle and lower classes. At the very least, they had more spare time in which to educate themselves in language and literature, and they had greater access to books and manuscripts and witnessed intellectual debates and poetry readings in their homes. Literature is not only the fruit of innate talent, but also a product of practiced stylistic techniques and the assimiliation of other literary models, neither of which is easily attainable without some sort of direction or tutelage. This does not mean, however, that the dominant ruling class exercised a monopoly on literature. The tribal, religious nature of Iraqi society at the turn of the twentieth century meant that family and tribal occasions, as well as religious rituals, provided a space for creative expression. Women had an important mobilizing role, much like their role in Bedouin society in general. Bibliographies of women's literature are filled with the names of the *mullayat*, women who composed religious poetry known as *husayniyat* to commemorate the martyrdom of Husayn at Karbala.[2] Other women, known as '*addadat*, devoted themselves to dirges at funerals. Each had her own particular elegiac style, which she used to improvise a touching oratory appropriate to the status and characteristics of the deceased. Iraqi women also composed poems and songs to mark engagements, weddings, and circumcisions,[3] as well as poems during battle. More than twenty women recited their poetry during the 1920 uprising against the English occupation,[4] but the sources usually refer to them only by their first name or their agnomen (the mother of so-and-so). This is not uncommon in the male historical tradition: many women contributed to culture, but their names do not shine and sparkle like those of men in the history books. Al-Mubarrad (d. 898) mentions a female poet who wrote social poetry in his *al-Kamil* (The Complete), calling her only "the daughter of Labid al-'Amiri," without noting her given name.

In a tradition that intentionally or accidentally neglects the achievements of women, women's names and their individuality become an embarrassment. Thus, many Arab women writers, particularly in Iraq, used pseudonyms or signed their works only with their initials. So we find Saduf, Sarab, and 'Afra'. One Iraqi poet born in the 1920s explains how she chose her pen name:

> I am Khadija Mahmud 'Ali al-'Izzi al-Samirra'i . . . I was born in Baghdad and I grew up there. I called myself 'Sabira al-'Izzi,' and I used it to sign every poem I published. I liked this name very much, for it gives voice to my suffering and the patience with which I bore the calamities in my life and work ['Sabira' means patient]. I did not receive enough education. I learned the basics of reading and writing from my mother, may she rest in peace, in our home in Bab al-Shaykh. I longed to go to school and drink from the pure streams of knowledge, but my father

was very conservative and did not allow his daughters to go to school. Thus I grew up harboring much resentment toward my father in my heart and the notion that girls must be educated became fixed in my head.[5]

Taking the al-Mala'ika family as an example, we can discern a growing tendency to use one's real name. Salima 'Abd al-Razzaq al-Mala'ika signed her poems with the name "Umm Nizar," Nizar being the name of her oldest son; her daughter published her poems and articles under her real name, Nazik al-Mala'ika. Today, Iraqi women writers take pride in their works and are not ashamed to be known as writers and artists. In doing so, they are continuing the tradition of the oldest known Iraqi woman poet, Enheduanna (2370–2316 BC), the daughter of the Akkadian king Sargon, who signed her poem with her own name. Nevertheless, researcher and writer Lutfiya al-Dulaymi believes that much of Iraqi women's literature remains unsigned and anonymous.[6] In addition, many Iraqi women who began writing in the early twentieth century did not publish their works or collect their poems into published volumes. Luckily for Iraqi women's literature, there are those who have collected and published the works of the pioneers. Nazik al-Mala'ika collected and edited her mother's poetry in *Unshudat al-majd* (Hymn of Glory) 1968. 'Abd al-Rahman Muhammad 'Ali published a collection of poetry by another pioneer, *Rabab al-Kazimi: dirasa wa shi'r* (Rabab al-Kazimi: a Study and Poetry) 1969.

Early Iraqi women poets used traditional poetic styles and forms. They defended issues of concern to the Arab nation and addressed topics like the Palestinian dispossession, the Algerian war of liberation, and popular uprisings in Iraq and Egypt. They also drew attention to the injustices done to their sisters, giving voice to women's concerns in particular. Among the pioneers born in the second decade of the twentieth century is Saduf al-'Amiriya, the pen name of Fatina Husayn Na'ib (1917–1993), who came from a family known for its learning. Fatina was adept at expressing her feelings in poetry and spoke of her philosophy of existence in prose, using the metaphor of the book: "I love life, like a delightful book that must be read; I love death like a book I have not yet read, although at times I have felt it between my hands, as if I am on the verge of reading it."[7] Saduf al-'Amiriya's pride in herself and her people is clear in her texts.

The first women poets of the twentieth century maintained the traditional purity of style and the classical poetic form, following the manner of the great poets of the Arabic tradition, such as al-Mutanabbi, al-Buhturi, and al-Sharif al-Rida (or al-'Abbas ibn al-Ahnaf in the case of 'Atika al-Khazraji, who studied his poetry and edited his collection of poems). Nevertheless, some of the pioneers injected this generally male poetic tradition with female touches from their own environments and experiences, at times finding a way to forge a female voice that did not wear a male mask or speak in male tones. In a poem addressed to her son, Saduf al-'Amiriya brings the panegyric, a form traditionally associated with men, to bear on the largely female field of childrearing. Bakiza Amin Khaki uses the trope of mourning on a ruined abode with one's companions, a familiar conceit in the pre-Islamic poem, in a poem entitled "al-Rab' al-hazin" (The Melancholy Home), dedicated to "my homeless sisters from Jaffa," published in the Baghdad *al-Risala al-jadida* on November 1, 1953.

Cultural journals and the literary pages of newspapers were an important forum for the publication of the writings of Iraqi women at this historical juncture—and not only Iraqi periodicals, but Lebanese and Egyptian magazines as well. Iraqi women participated in the establishment of women's periodicals from 1923, much like Egyptian, Lebanese, and Syrian women some two or three decades earlier. Although Arab lands were colonized or under the mandate or control of foreign nations, Arab-Arab communications endured, at least on the cultural front. The poet Rabab al-Kazimi, for example, was born in Cairo and lived there for some time, considering it a second home.

Iraqi writing women did not undervalue themselves, but took pride in their capabilities. Rabab al-Kazimi did not hesitate to equate her poetry to her father's, refusing to confine herself to a lower status:

I am not the daughter of the exceptional poet
If I don't match him in passion,
And if I don't contend with him
In splendor and glory, in verse and prose.[8]

The family atmosphere was important in refining the talents of the first women writers. Rabab al-Kazimi was the daughter of a poet; Salma al-Mala'ika was the wife of a poet (Sadiq) and the mother of two poets (Nizar and Nazik). Saduf al-'Amiriya (known in some sources as Saduf al-'Abidiya) had a sister, Mahira al-Naqshbandi, who called herself Sarab al-'Amiriya (in some sources, Sarab al-'Ubaydiya), one of the first women short-story writers in Iraq. A literary collective—whether in the family or another context—is extremely important for the development of creative energies. Thus an environment that encourages women, whether on the domestic or national level, has a decisive impact on women's literature. Although male writers addressed women's status in society, their gendered social position made it difficult for them to express the particularity of women and explore the details of their lives. As Sarab al-'Ubaydiya, a pioneer of the short story, said in one interview,

A real writer can accurately portray the feelings of his characters and express their emotions and fears no matter how far removed he may be from them in social status, age, or sex. Nevertheless, I suspect that women may give the truest voice to what their sisters feel.[9]

Most of the early women pioneers had a dual education that was both traditional and modern. They studied the Islamic sciences, the Arabic literary tradition, and the canonical collections of poetry, and they were students at universities and institutes, where they specialized in modern sciences and literatures. Rabab al-Kazimi was a dentist who studied in Egypt, France, and the U.S.; 'Atika al-Khazraji studied in Iraq, France, and Egypt, and earned a doctorate; Amira Nur al-Din completed her higher education in Cairo, obtaining a master's degree in Iraqi folk poetry; Nazik al-Mala'ika studied in Iraq and the U.S. Clearly their firm grounding in the national tradition, their openness to other cultures, their awareness of the outside world, and their emergence from the shell of the home encouraged them to depict their own feelings, the sufferings of their nation, and the aspirations of their people. It is only natural that they would be influenced by prominent literary trends in the Arab world: the Romantic poetry of Egypt, the exile poetry of the Americas, and the works of the great writers like Taha Hussein, Tawfiq al-Hakim, Mahmud Taymur, and Mayy Ziyada. Although Iraqi women writers were relatively fortunate compared to other Iraqi women, they complained of their status and their lack of recognition, sometimes explicitly, as when Rabab al-Kazimi said:

My writing is my wound,
And my crime is my knowledge.[10]

Sometimes the complaints are indirect. As a response to their oppression, some women writers turned to melancholy love poetry or rebelled against the status quo, writing about general injustice and defending the spirit of revolution without addressing the particularity of their concerns and oppression. Sometimes, they turned to the ineffable, injecting their writing with a spiritualism that was above the contradictions of daily life.

Despite the significance of the first steps, only two women writers who walked that treacherous road survive in the collective memory: Nazik al-Mala'ika (1923–2007) and Lami'a 'Abbas 'Amara (b. 1929), who, along with Badr Shakir al-Sayyab, Buland al-Haydari, and 'Abd al-Wahhab al-Bayati, were part of the free-verse movement. Nazik al-Mala'ika was one of the founders of the movement, writing both poetry and theory to support it. She is a true pioneer in Iraq and across the entire Arab world: She exercised an influence on countless poets, both men and women, and her collections of poetry had a decisive impact on modern Arabic poetry. Along with contemporaries from Iraq, Lebanon, Syria, Palestine, and Egypt, she changed the face of Arabic poetry in the twentieth century. Although the beginnings of free verse were visible before Mala'ika wrote her famous poem, "al-Kulira" (Cholera) 1947, they only began to take shape as a movement that combined theory and practice in the person of Nazik al-Mala'ika.

In the second half of the twentieth century, Iraqi women's contributions to the literary arts were abundant and varied, and unlike the first half of the century, in which poetry dominated, they were not limited to one genre. Thus each genre will be addressed individually in this study (poetry, narrative, drama), although the more modern works, particularly those that came after Iraq's defeat in the 1991 Gulf War, go beyond traditional literary genres to combine narrative with poetry, drama with expository writing, and reality with myth. The increasing literary output of Iraqi women, both quantitative and qualitative, is attributable to the spread of women's education and employment. In addition, leftist politics and national liberation movements made women's cause and their equality a pivotal issue. The changes and rebellions in which women took part had a huge impact in shaking loose the traditional values dominant in the early twentieth century.

Iraqi women's literature is not limited to works in Arabic, but includes works in other Iraqi languages, most importantly Kurdish. Among the most prominent writers in this field are Sabriya Nuri Qadir (b. 1928), who has published several collections of poetry and is known for her children's literature; Nisrin Muhammad Fakhri al-Sabunji (b. 1937), a poet with a doctorate in linguistics; and Shafiqa 'Ali Husayn (b. 1940), known as "Laylan," who has written both poetry and drama. All three writers are from the province of Sulaymaniya.

Poetry
We cannot discuss modern Iraqi poetry without addressing Nazik al-Mala'ika and her poetic revolution, and we cannot discuss Nazik al-Mala'ika without considering her a poetic phenomenon, for she embodies "the consciousness of renewal and the pioneering spirit of poetry," to quote the poet Sami Mahdi.[11] The critic 'Abd al-Jabbar Dawud al-Basri calls the introduction to her collection, *Shazaya wa ramad* (Shrapnel and Ashes) 1949, "the first manifesto" issued by the free-verse movement. Remarkably, Nazik al-Mala'ika was only in her early twenties when she issued the first calls for change and rebelled against the old order of poetry in a domestic and social environment that was highly resistant to change. We must touch

on the conditions in which she composed her pioneering poem, "al-Kulira," to understand the poetic leap she represents.

As noted above, her domestic environment had a significant impact on Nazik al-Mala'ika. At family get-togethers, there were debates on linguistic and literary issues, and poems were composed collectively. Nazik's mother had the greatest impact on her, and Nazik considered her to be her major influence. In the dedication of her collection, *Qararat al-mawja* (Trough of the Wave) 1957, Nazik wrote: "To my mother . . . the first fertile poetic talent with whom I studied." Nazik wrote poetry in the colloquial Iraqi dialect when she was in primary school, moving on to poetry in classical Arabic when in preparatory school, and specializing in Arabic at the Higher Teachers' Institute. Nazik was thoroughly familiar with her national tradition, and she was open to other cultures as well. Her knowledge of foreign literatures, arts, and intellectual movements did not occupy an empty space, but interacted with the elements of Arabic civilization she had absorbed. Thus, her engagement with English poetry was not based on blind admiration, but was an interaction with what she viewed as a peer, psychologically and historically. Although Nazik did not deny the influence of Western poetry on her awakening, she justified the rules of free verse not by referring to Western poetry, but by looking to and contemplating unofficial, non-institutional forms of poetry such as *al-band*, which was widespread in Iraq. Nazik al-Mala'ika presented her experience not as a smashing of the traditional rules of prosody, but simply as a relaxation of them. She says in the introduction to *Shazaya wa ramad*:

> [The sensitive writer] must possess a deep culture, whose roots reach into the heart of the local literature, both ancient and modern, along with a broad familiarity with the literature of at least one foreign nation . . . We must not forget that this new style is not a rebellion against Khalil's traditional methods [of prosody], but a modification of them, dictated by the evolution of content and style over the ages.[12]

The abandonment of institutional poetic forms often directs the writer to popular traditions and sayings; similarly, the fall of the traditional poetic lexicon leads the poet to heed the colloquial eloquence of people's everyday speech. Aware that every liberation brings with it an obligation, this is what Nazik al-Mala'ika perceived, with her finely honed sensibility and her recognition of the complexity of literary creation. Her poetic revolution was not a rebellion against the past and the traditions of prosody as much as it was a rebellion against the monolithic form of traditional Arabic poetics. She advocated a multiplicity of forms rather than one stock model, although even the new form would be bound by the limits of meter, which Nazik believed was indispensable to poetry.

The poem, "al-Kulira," which researchers consider the opening shot of the free-verse movement in the Arab world,[13] grew out of the poet's grief for and sympathy with Egypt, then in the throes of a cholera epidemic. In particular, Nazik al-Mala'ika felt the pain of the poor and downtrodden, who always pay the highest price: "In the shack where grief lives/everywhere a spirit screams in the darkness." With her sensibility, her profound sense of her identity and belonging, and her sympathy with the weak and poor, al-Mala'ika was shaken to the core when faced with disease and death, and in turn, she shook the foundation of classical Arabic poetry, creating a new rhythmic language that could contain the present in all its complexity. When she read the poem to her father, he criticized her for abandoning the classical form and repeating the word "death" three times, but Nazik responded confidently that the poem was the beginning of a new Arabic poetry. She believed that renewal sprang from an urgent spiritual desire to mend a fissure in the community; the innovative artist may not be conscious of the fissure, but she senses it and spontaneously moves toward renewal.

Nazik al-Mala'ika was also interested in the psychological dimensions of poetry and published *Saykulujiyat al-shi'r wa maqalat ukhra* (The Psychology of Poetry and Other Essays) in 1993. Three decades earlier, spurred by her interest in prosody and the new poetry, she wrote *Qadaya al-shi'r al-mu'asir* (Issues in Contemporary Poetry), which went through several reprints. Nazik did not only write about poetic theory, but also about Arab society, having realized the intimate ties between the poet and society. She published *al-Tajzi'iya fi-l-mujtama' al-'Arabi* (Fragmentation in Arab Society) in 1974, a collection of articles first published in the Beirut journal, *al-Adab*, in which she exposes the double standards applied to men and women and how the dominant mentality and even language itself belittled and devalued women. Nazik al-Mala'ika expressed her stance on women in her poem, "Ghaslan li-l-'ar" (Washing Away the Shame).[14] It is a dramatic poem, in successive scenes, which offers an ironic critique of the traditional social order that allows a man to kill his sister or daughter "to wash away the shame" and preserve the family's reputation, even when the shame is only imagined and he himself cavorts with prostitutes. The poem opens with the dying rasp of a girl wrongly killed; she cries out "mother," but her executioner ignores her plea and shows her no mercy. He boasts of his deed, then spends the evening in a bar with a prostitute. The repetition of the phrase "washing away the shame" throughout the poem creates an ironic tension. A chorus of women, the neighbors, ask about the girl, tell her story, and sense that they might face a similar future. It is they who pay the price for false honor: "Our braids shall be shorn and our hands flayed/while their garments remain snow white and pure."

Just as she used dramatic poetry to portray social customs that victimize women, Nazik al-Mala'ika also used lullabies and baby talk in "Ughniya li-tifli" (A Song for My Child),[15] written for her son Barraq. She herself explained the poetics of the work after some critics disparaged it. Thus did Nazik al-Mala'ika use her experience as a woman and a mother as material for her poetry, writing poems in the new style that took women's concerns as a reference. But she did not limit herself to these themes. She pondered the nature of existence in her poem, "Ana" (I),[16] and gave expression to her philosophy of poetry in "Ila-l-shi'r" (To Poetry),[17] which alludes to myths and to Sheherazade; in "al-Khayt al-mashdud fi shajarat al-sarw" (The Taut Line in the Cyprus Tree) she turns to emotional themes.[18]

In many poems Nazik al-Mala'ika documented the major political events in Iraq and the wider Arab world. As successive defeats and calamities took their toll on her sensitive psyche, she withdrew from the world and began writing poems with a spiritual or Sufi bent, renouncing her former engagement and even occasionally denouncing her old rebellion. In this her experience mirrors that of the classically oriented poet 'Atika al-Khazraji, who gained renown in the salons of Baghdad before turning to Sufi poetry and withdrawing from the bustle of society.

Lami'a 'Abbas 'Amara, a contemporary of Nazik al-Mala'ika and Badr Shakir al-Sayyab, wrote tender poems of love and on the homeland, some of which were put to music. In one of her most famous love poems, "Law anba'ani al-'arraf" (If the Fortune-Teller Told Me), each stanza begins with the poem's title.[19] The poem's images and structure draw on the folk narrative style in depicting emotions: the princely lover comes "on a horse of rubies" and will carry "the sun" in his palm. These motifs are often found in folktales, especially those told by women, but here they are expressed with the lofty language of poetry and in one of the primary sub-genres of classical poetry, love poetry. The poet blends the oral and written poetic traditions, the popular imagination and the classical poetic lexicon, and women's oral heritage with the male tradition.

Men had long exercised a monopoly on love poetry; while countless men wrote love poems for women, only rarely do we find a woman poet writing love poetry for a man in the Arabic poetic tradition. For example, when the pioneering poet Fatina al-Na'ib (Saduf al-'Amiriya) wrote love poetry, she "did not explicitly address a man, but alluded to him with the word 'gazelle' or 'moon' or some such thing. She concealed her feelings toward the man because of prevailing social conditions."[20] Nevertheless, Lami'a 'Abbas 'Amara gives voice to emotions that for many ages only men had the right to proclaim. As if trying to redress this imbalance, another of her poems, "Sha'irat al-hubb?!" (The Poet of Love?!) describes a woman on the Atlantic coast, watching from her window in a Moroccan hotel as couples stroll on the beach in swimsuits: "naked but for two strips, the remnants of clothes."[21] The poetic persona calls the room "my prison" and the poem ends with the irony of her writing love poetry without ever having had the experience of love: "like a philosopher/describing wine/he has not sipped."

Lami'a 'Abbas 'Amara shares this vacillation between confession and suggestion, or between emotional expressiveness and submission to mechanisms of repression, with Nazik al-Mala'ika, who began with a powerfully rebellious spirit filled with existential angst, but with time lost her will to fight. The doubt and confusion of Nazik's early poems were replaced by a certainty and mastery of reality as she took spiritualism and Sufism as a refuge to protect her from conflicting pressures. In a paper presented at the conference, "One Hundred Years of Arab Women's Emancipation," convened in 1999 in Cairo, prominent poet and critic Salma Khadra Jayyusi lamented the fate of Arab women pioneers who paid a high price for their progressiveness and ambition, including Iraqi Nazik al-Mala'ika, Palestinian Mayy Ziyada, and Egyptian Doria Shafik.

Zuhur Dixon's poem, "al-Gharib" (The Stranger),[22] contains a motif that intersects with Lami'a 'Abbas 'Amara's "Sha'irat al-hubb," despite important differences in poetic perspective. Dixon concludes her poem, "As he waved at me, he climbed a hill . . . walked on/Leaving me watching the road/From a window in the wall!" In this excerpt, the observer in the poem looks outside and observes the goings on in the world while she is in a kind of prison, looking out "from a window in the wall," just as the subject of 'Amara's poem looked out from a window onto the outside world. This looking from the inside out, tinged with a sense of sorrow over the enforced seclusion, neatly summarizes the condition of Arab, and particularly Iraqi, women, who are forced to stay at home and get to know the world through a window. Zuhur Dixon's poem, however, is more complex than that of Lami'a 'Abbas 'Amara because of its references to other texts. She begins the poem by quoting a line from Walt Whitman (1819–1892), the father of modernism, about speaking to a passing stranger and the exhaustive search for him. She then refers to al-Suhrawardi (d. 1191), calling him "the stranger." (Al-Suhrawardi was a Sufi known for his work, *al-Ghurba al-gharbiya*, or 'The Western Exile). Western and Eastern references intersect in "al-Gharib," linked by the common theme of exile and strangeness, into which the subject of the poem sinks: she dreams of meeting this distant, yet familiar stranger—a stranger "on the road" who is nevertheless a familiar spirit. "If you would meet me," the poet says, but this fictional al-Suhrawardi merely waves, leaving her behind to watch him walk away. The poem's brilliance lies in the way it brings together strangers—particularly those people who are strangers in their corrupt societies—regardless of the cultures and eras to which they belong, as if there is a collectivity of outcasts who refer to one another, just like the intertextual references in the poem, without meeting or becoming one. It is a poem that speaks of alienation and the search for a fellow traveler, but it also says that fellowship is merely a wave from afar, no more.

Amal al-Zahawi's poem, "al-Tariqun bihar al-mawt" (Passengers on the Seas of Death),[23] found in her collection by the same name, is dedicated to her mother "who glided softly like the flow of water." Using the first person, the poet observes "the tranquil body" and asks the sort of questions raised by someone pained by the death of a loved one. Things are confused, between dream and reality, slumber and awe: "When I fell into the sea of unconsciousness/And had a vision of a magic carpet/The world around me shook." This comes after a mention of the phoenix, that mythical bird that rises from the ashes of death. The rejection of death here takes the form of describing it as a dream or a trance: "Are you in a dream, walking/Or am I dreaming/I think of the day when the riding mount of the night journey will whinny to me." In another poem, "Judran al-zi'baq" (Quicksilver Walls),[24] also about death and also dedicated to her mother, Amal al-Zahawi takes on the rituals of death and martyrdom to represent their cyclical nature. She imagines Karbala, using vocal rhythms that mimic the parade of mourners on 'Ashura', thus making aesthetic use of a religious scene that popular poets, the *mullayat*, and mourners have long sung about and referred to. Here, however, it becomes a poem—that is, a high art form—inspired by both religious and women's traditions. Using dense, economic references, the poet elliptically tells the story of al-Husayn's death. In presenting this slice of religious ritual, al-Zahawi does not neglect the women who fill out the procession, but in evoking the sad scene, she sees it not only as a historical event but links it to current events in the Arab world: "In yesterday's wound/In Jerusalem and Sinai/To the victor belongs the field." Referring to the Babylonian myth of the red anemones that grew out of the blood of Tammuz, the slain god, the poet adds, "She tries to make food burst forth . . . a goal/So that anemones will grow out of the incandescence of blood/And the nights of sin will spread over June's wound." The wounds of the past and the present are thus parallel in the poem. Evoking the past and the Shiite rituals of mourning indirectly refers to the rituals of martyrdom and their necessity for renewal and rebirth.

The theme of rebirth is also found in poet Dunya Mikhail, who uses the Christian tradition and that pressing human desire for man to rise from the dead. The poem, "Abyad . . . aswad" (White . . . Black),[25] opens with a quote from the Bible—"This is John the Baptist; he is risen from the dead"—and the entire poem is studded with Biblical verses. It mourns the death of a father, contrasting the white of the hospital with the black of mourning and employing the metaphor of chess. Mikhail compares her father to a king who is not dead, but merely sleeps. The poem is an attempt by the poetic persona to resist death by evoking images of rebirth and resurrection, on one hand, and the game of life and death as represented in chess, on the other. Figuring death as sleep has resonances in poetic traditions around the world, most famously immortalized in Hamlet's monologue.

Another poem by Dunya Mikhail, "Lastu ana . . . M" (I Am Not Me . . . M),[26] dedicated to Iraqi writer Lutfiya al-Dulaymi, manipulates language to make the strange familiar and the absent present. The motif of the lullaby is used as an allusion to motherhood when Mikhail says, "Don't rock the cradle/O mother of compassion/Don't rock the cradle/I am not strong enough for songs." Following the real mother addressed in Amal al-Zahawi's poem, here Lutfiya al-Dulaymi, to whom Mikhail dedicated the poem, becomes a figurative mother. More importantly, we observe how a female literary discourse takes shape that seeks to create a matrilineal genealogy for the woman writer. Indeed, we find many instances of poems dedicated to mothers or portrayals and representations of mothers. As noted above, Nazik al-Mala'ika collected and published her mother's poems. This indicates a certain awareness of women's inter-connectedness, part of which is a recognition of the mother's inspirational role and part of which springs from a desire to create a female literary tapestry to complement the dominant male model. Instead of defining themselves as the daughter of Labid al-'Amiri or 'Abd al-Muhsin al-Kazimi, our poets document their spiritual and genealogical filiation and affiliation to other women, not out of a desire to break away from the family tree with its male trunk, but as a reminder that the individual belongs to the mother as much as the father.

In the last two decades of the twentieth century, Iraq suffered from war and siege. The eight-year Iran-Iraq war (1980–1988) was followed by the Gulf War of 1991, and after both allied and enemy planes destroyed the country's infrastructure, a blockade was imposed on the Iraqi people, which led to the death of more than one million Iraqis, most of them women and children. It goes without saying that the weak and dependent segments of society suffer more than others in difficult conditions. This national tragedy gave rise to an explosion of literature, some of which falls between genres—between poetry and narrative, between myth and realism. Writing women felt the hardship with a special keenness, once as Iraqis and again as women. Amal al-Jabburi opens her "al-Huzn zakat al-qalb" (Grief is the Heart's Alms),[27] "From the longest war to the shortest wars/From your death to this destruction/Joy has disintegrated." The poet curses war, remembering "the tears of mothers, widows, and orphans." "Bi-intizar al-qasf" (Waiting for the Shelling), by Bushra al-Bustani, describes the moments accompanying the sirens announcing incoming enemy missiles. At the outset of the poem, the poet asks who will die at the end of the night: her child, her brother, or her neighbor? It is a description of the anticipation of an impending grief.

The poems written by Mayy Muzaffar after the Gulf War eschew directness, as in her poem, "al-Madina" (The City),[28] but they speak of pain in another way. The time is evening, the season winter, and "moans spill out of the homes' wounds." The poet alludes to the myth of the phoenix, the bird that rises from the ashes of death, and the brief poem—more like a poetic miniature—ends with a description of Baghdad and a desire for the return of its magnificence. In "al-Abwab" (The Doors),[29] Muzaffar speaks metaphorically about the siege and the sense of imprisonment. Here the prisoner is no longer a woman fated to disappear behind walls, but an entire people. The poet uses the traditional concealing garb of Iraqi women—the cloak and the veil—as a metaphor for the siege. She employs a lexicon drawn from the world of women to refer to the blockade, figuring it as a labyrinth ("a door behind a door . . . /Behind a door") and imbuing time with a fluidity ("No appointments define our day . . . /Or our sleep"). The closure and inability to escape from the existential crisis shake the solidity of time and make day like night.

In Siham Jabbar's prose poem, "Dhat infijar" (An Explosion),[30] the poet uses mythology and holy texts, particularly references to the book of Genesis and the Maryam chapter of the Quran—"Rise up and shake the udders for then life will be cast down in you"—in a brilliant play of intertextuality that suggests a resistance to the destruction and siege and holds out the possibility of escape. The poet uses the forces of compassion and motherhood, linked specifically with women, in the general context of national hardship, as the tremors that accompany the explosion are absorbed by Mother Earth: "Interpose blue tenderness and the motherhood of the wave to change the scene and smash the loneliness."

Fiction

The pioneering short-story writer Dalal Khalil Safadi published her collection, *Hawadith wa 'ibar* (Incidents and Lessons), in al-Najaf in 1937, although critic 'Umar Muhammad Talib believes that labeling them "short stories" is stretching the term, for, he says, they use "an oratorical language and a resounding tone to preach to her sisters and encourage them to hold to virtue, morals, and religious teachings. The writer tells stories of the wretched fates that are the end of deviant women."[31] The collection may be classified as a set of didactic tales that lack the artistry of fiction—a general characteristic of the modest beginnings of Iraqi fiction, which did not make an aesthetic leap until it matured in the 1950s.

Some ten years later, Maliha Ishaq published a novella entitled '*Aqli dalili* (My Mind Is My Guide) 1948. Although it is not finely crafted, the story gives us a positive portrayal of women and their characteristics over generations, conveying an implicit message of the need for women's economic and intellectual liberation.

Many of the narrative texts written by women are didactic and moralizing, which may be related to women's childbearing role and the domestic order in Iraqi society. The lesson or moral of stories and novels differs according to the writer's approach. Not all women writers have the same view of how society should progress. Some adopt a nationalist framework, others a Marxist view, and still others an Islamist perspective, but despite their ideological differences, they all agree on the centrality of women's role in building society.

'Umar Talib believes that "women's struggle against backwardness and injustice" emerges clearly in the stories of Safira Jamil, Samira al-Mani', Suhayla al-Husayni, Mayy Muzaffar, Lutfiya al-Dulaymi, Daisy Al-Amir, Buthaina Al Nasiri, Alia Mamdouh, Bilqis Ni'mat al-'Aziz, and Salima Salih.[32] In many narratives of the 1950s and 1960s, marital relationships are a favorite topic of description and critique, and men's betrayal of their wives is frequent. Amina Haydar al-Sadr's (Bint al-Huda) *al-Fadila tantasir* (Virtue Triumphs) 1969, contains two female models, one representing good and the other evil, and the good woman triumphs over the wicked. The novel has a clear didactic, moral value.[33]

Many of the short stories reveal the unpleasant reality of domestic relationships often presented to society as 'happy marriages,' as in Safiya al-Dibuni's ironic title "Zawaj mithali" (An Ideal Marriage). Or happy marriages end melodramatically with the death of a spouse, as in "Intifadat qalb" (An Eruption of the Heart) and "Azmat kibriya'" (A Crisis of Hubris), by Suhayla Dawud Salman, and "Min ahat al-qusur" (From the Palace Moans), by Maliha Ishaq. *Nadiya* (Nadiya) 1975, by Layla 'Abd al-Qadir, is one of the few novels to portray a positive, economically independent woman who meets a man who appreciates and loves her, after which they marry and live happily. An optimistic portrayal of a positive woman who ends up in a happy marriage is also found in the story, "Zawal al-nahs" (The End of Misfortune), by Salima Khudayr.[34] Many of these narratives are more important for their sociological significance than their artistic merit, for they indicate how rarely relationships between the sexes are successful, whether this is due to the pressure of tradition, the selfishness of men, or the intervention of fate. Women's experience of hardship is a frequent theme in these stories and novels, and the model of the westernized or bourgeois woman is often opposed to the authentic Iraqi woman or the working woman, with a clear preference expressed for the latter type. Women's sacrifice for their families and those they love is a recurrent theme as well. In "Ba'i'at al-dam" (Peddler of Blood) by Fatat Baghdad, a woman sells her blood to save her brother; in "'Asafat bi-ra'si" (It Made My Head Spin), by Salima Salih, a mother prostitutes herself to relieve her son's hunger; in "Thabat" (Stability), by Amina Haydar al-Sadr (Bint al-Huda), a wife sacrifices her human needs for the sake of her husband.

Those fiction writers who have proven themselves quantitatively and qualitatively include Daisy Al-Amir, who has given voice to Iraqi women's concerns and cares, their loneliness and alienation. She is an outstanding, prolific storyteller who is more concerned with the psychological dimension of fiction than with external action. She often describes social relationships and focuses on women's unease in their social surroundings. Although she was born in Alexandria, lived for a long period in Beirut, and spent a sizable amount of time in the West, she is closely tied to Iraq, her homeland, where she grew up and matured. Al-Amir was close to prominent poets and writers from the Arab world, including poet Nazik al-Mala'ika and the Lebanese poet Khalil Hawi. Her story, "al-Bakiya" ("Weeping"), written in the first person, opens with the protagonist waking up to the sound of crying, which she initially thinks is coming from the neighbor's house.[35] The next night, she hears the sobbing again and wonders if it is crying or the wind she hears. She is sure that "this was a woman's cry" and wonders about the cause of the woman's grief. The crying develops into what sounds like a cry for help. One day, the heroine goes out to a suburb where she sees a park being laid out to reduce pollution: "So it was that huge trucks came carrying tall, full-grown trees, complete with roots embedded in soil, to be set in deep gaping holes specially prepared for this purpose."[36] When at night the crying grows more intense, the heroine visits the park seeking comfort. One day, she comes across a tree with a bent trunk that seems to have some disease. It ultimately dies and the protagonist interprets it as suicide, brought on by the tree's forced uprooting and migration. That night, she does not hear the crying; rather, it is she who cries. The story has a symbolic dimension; with its clarity and unity, it is more like a parable. Like the tree, the protagonist feels alienated far from home, but the reader wonders whether the tree's suicide is a metaphor for the heroine's own condition or simply the imagination of a woman who is psychologically exhausted by her own alienation. Similarly, we wonder whether it is the heroine crying at night, even as she imagines it is someone else. The reader's questions add to the story and open up many possibilities. It is a story that speaks about the agony of being uprooted, on whatever level we choose to read that; it is an intense exploration of the state of Iraqi and Arab exiles.

If Daisy Al-Amir's story gives us a parable of alienation and exile, using natural symbols and leaving the conclusion open-ended, Haifa Zangana's "al-Mahatta" (The Station), in her collection, *Bayt al-naml* (The Ant Hill)

1996, gives us a different view of exile: a virtually deserted station in a faraway country.[37] The story revolves around an Iraqi refugee who has found work as a sweeper. In the station in London where he sweeps, he remembers his childhood—he used to live "near the railroad"—recalling the frivolity of youth in his carefree days in Iraq. When he was young, he played with a girl whom he promised to marry; now, in this strange city, he sees a woman and a girl sitting next to two young men. Using a stream-of-consciousness narrative, the author describes the scene of the mother and the girl from the perspective of the Iraqi sweeper, including the details of their conversations although he does not hear their exchange. They are on the opposite platform, and, as if watching a film, we see the images move, but do not understand the language, which only exacerbates the sense of alienation. A young man crosses the tracks in a way that reminds the refugee of his childhood, prompting him to recall what did not happen: "If he hadn't forced his wife to have an abortion . . . he would now have a twenty-year-old daughter, or a twenty-year-old son, or maybe both." In a rush, he recalls his journey from one country to another, how he applied for asylum and responded in writing to the investigators' questions. In exile he longs for his own city, having now forgotten all its flaws. He remembers how his wife wanted a child and how he objected, not wanting his children to endure what their parents had experienced. When he found that his wife was pregnant, he forced her to have an abortion, and when he left the city she refused to accompany him. The abortion here symbolizes a spiritual barrenness whose significance his wife intuitively understands. While watching ants, who instinctively give birth and procreate, the hero thinks of his empty life in exile. When the woman, the girl, and the two young men leave the station, the protagonist remains, alone, thinking he might leave for another city where perhaps he can forget his past: "Then he might be able to grip the eraser and wipe out his entire past."

Despite their differences in technique, both stories portray exile and conjure up a distant homeland—the first, by Daisy Al-Amir, through the portrayal of an alienated woman on the verge of a nervous breakdown; the second, by Haifa Zangana, through the portrayal of a refugee and stream-of-consciousness narrative. The first employs symbolism and figurative language, while the second relies on disruption and montage. In both, the protagonists are haunted by their homeland; their attempts to erase the past and take root in a new environment are almost impossible.

Many women have written novels, but the most brilliant is Alia Mamdouh, a writer of both short stories and novels. Her first novel, *Habbat al-naftalin (Mothballs)* 1986, a fictional portrayal of Iraq in the 1950s, views political events through the mirror of women's consciousness in Baghdad and Karbala and uses the Iraqi dialect to give the narrative a local flavor. This studding of classical Arabic with popular expressions and colloquial Iraqi is a distinguishing feature of the Iraqi novel, whether the author is a man or woman. We find the same thing with Iraqi novelists Fuad al-Takarli and Mahdi 'Isa al-Saqr, for example. What sets Alia Mamdouh apart is her ear for the female register of language and her rendering of dialogue that reflects the attitudes of various generations of women and reveals them to be politically involved and expressing their choices in their own ways. During a youth demonstration in support of Gamal Abdel Nasser, who nationalized the Suez Canal in 1956—when the Iraqi government was dependent on Britain and thus considered Nasser's bitter enemy—Alia Mamdouh portrays the role of women in supporting the demonstration, by preparing bread and water for the demonstrators and by readying first-aid supplies. Chapter fifteen of the novel, told through the eyes of the young heroine, describes her shock when Mahmud, a communist, gives her a flyer—it is as if he had kissed her. Since the political events of the novel are seen through the perspective of the protagonist, a young girl who does not know the meaning of politics, they are narrated in a naive, reportorial style, free of figurative language or rhetorical flourishes, which only increases their impact on the knowing reader, creating a sense of dramatic irony.

In her short stories and novels, Alia Mamdouh distinguishes herself with her ear for the details of life and its oddities. In the short story, "al-'Ubur" (The Crossing), written in the first person,[38] she gives us snatches of life in West Beirut in the early 1970s, with its fast cars and sophisticated women. When the protagonist senses that an attractive man is watching her through his thick black sunglasses, she feels "sexually flustered," but the story ends, like Maupassant's, with a twist that turns the heroine's expectations upside down.

Surprise is also used with great skill by Buthaina Al Nasiri to create a decisive, unexpected moment that reveals things hidden by one's daily perspective. Her "Hikayat Samah" ("The Story of Samah") revolves around a four-year-old girl,[39] the daughter of a doorman, who plays in the street and is hit by a speeding car—a frequent occurrence in cities packed with people and plagued by traffic. After her death, the child is bathed with perfumed soap for the first time, when her body is washed before burial. For the first time, the poor girl looks pretty and clean. The irony, of course, is that she only realizes her humanity and obtains her rightful share of attention when she is dead.

Ibtisam 'Abd Allah al-Dabbagh explores the world of children in "Fi-l-bustan" (In the Park).[40] She speaks through a mother whose son goes hungry while the mother works at a park where there is a restaurant that caters to the wealthy—something experienced by many Iraqi mothers during the siege, which exacerbated class divisions and affected the poor the most. The mother recalls a well-known tale from the Arab tradition, about a Bedouin woman who puts stones and water in a pot on the fire to make her children believe she is fixing a meal, giving them patience and the ability to bear their hunger. The mother ultimately prepares a simple meal of rice, which is devoured by both her child and the farm dog, and the surprise ending illustrates how man and animal are equalized by hunger. Statistics show that during the blockade on Iraq, when Iraqi children suffered from disease and hunger, the U.S. spent more on dog food than on feeding the children of the entire Third World.

Lutfiya al-Dulaymi's "Khusuf Burhan al-Kutubi" (The Eclipse of Burhan al-Kutubi) examines the hardship of the intellectual in an Iraq under siege.[41] The story uses well-crafted language, a complex construction, and free association to depict an intellectual forced to sell his most precious possessions—his books—in a time of hunger and sanctions. It is a breathtaking text that in many scenes blends the fluidity of poetry with apocalyptic dialogue, though it remains closely bound to reality. The protagonist is forced to sell his books, which represent more than paper between two covers; for him, they are the human values we absorb from books: "The library is the legacy of his father, passed down to him by his grandfather, a bookworm who learned from them the distinctiveness of ideas, the secret of conversation, and the sanctity of difference."

The objective of the continuous, six-week bombing of Iraq in 1991 was to bring the country to its knees and set it back centuries—this according to the aggressors themselves. More bombs were dropped on Iraq in 1991 than on Germany by the allies in the Second World War in six years, the equivalent of seven times the bombs dropped on Hiroshima. It is difficult for those who did not live those days and nights to imagine— simply imagine—what the war meant. For the artists and writers who experienced it, it was like an earthquake, a unique historical event. Some recorded the terrors and their own feelings in diaries, including Nuha al-Radi, the potter, whose *Yawmiyat Baghdadiya (Baghdad Diaries)* 1999 was her first work. In Dunya Mikhail's *Yawmiyat mawja kharij al-bahr (Diary of a Wave outside the Sea)* 1999, daily life intersects with the remembered past and visions of the future in a text that moves between the poetic, the mythical, and the documentary. These two works stand next to others written by both men and women who documented the tribulation—one of the most important being Warid al-Salim's memoir, *Infijar dam'a* (A Tear's Explosion).

Modern Iraqi history has witnessed extremely complex changes that have transformed its face more than once. Coups, revolutions, wars, sanctions, social unrest, and state violence have overturned many truisms in relatively short periods of time. Middle-aged and elderly Iraqis suddenly find themselves living in a world wholly different from that of their childhood and young adulthood. Iraqi writers often recall the past, using autobiography as a way to give voice to a collective memory that has almost been obliterated. Some of these works are semi-autobiographical, others partly fictional, but they all offer snapshots of a vanished world. Since women were often not able to give voice to the particularity of their lives, they have used this literary genre, bolstered by their own experiences and their imagination, to convey hidden worlds and untold experiences.

Salima Salih's *Zahrat al-anbiya': yaqzat al-dhakira* (Flower of the Prophets: Memory Awakened) 1994, a work that defies generic classification, is a collection of stories or scenes that come together to describe the Mosul of the writer's girlhood. In one chapter, "Shajarat al-tut" (The Berry Tree),[42] the narrator talks about her city, known as "the mother of the two springs" because both spring and autumn are especially long and beautiful and because of the city's spring festival. In describing spring and its pleasures, the author re-crafts a folktale told by women about their desire to leave their nests and enjoy nature, and the obstacles that stand before this very human desire. In a story the narrator hears from her mother, the reader can detect a liberating female logic. The story is about a woman who wants to leave the house and walk around in the springtime. Her husband asks her, "What does one find outside that one does not find inside the house?" Grass, she tells him. Her husband then brings a bag filled with grass clippings and empties them on the roof, telling her, "Here's the grass. You can stretch out on it." The narrator comments on this story about a woman's seclusion in her home by observing the difference between grass "that springs up vertically from the earth, whose roots stretch into it, that resists the hand that tries to uproot it" and cut grass that dries up in a few short hours. The story recalls Daisy Al-Amir's "al-Bakiya." With varying degrees of artistry, they both link women's desire for normal, natural development, figured by the growth of trees and grass in their own soil, and attempts to restrict and repress, represented by an artificial environment. The narrator also remarks on the differences between the stories of her mother and father. Her mother's stories gave voice to women's preoccupations and concerns, while her father's were more expressive of male anxieties: "My father's stories were not so sad, stories of knights crossing the deserts on the backs of their steeds, waging battles and performing noble deeds. But they would die alone in the desert or fortune would abandon them."

A childhood is recalled in *Kam badat al-sama' qariba!* (*A Sky So Close*) 1999,[43] by young writer Betool Khedairi, a work that could be described as a *bildungsroman*, along the lines of Flaubert's *Sentimental Education*, Charles Dickens' *David Copperfield*, Thomas Mann's *The Magic Mountain*, and Latifa al-Zayyat's *al-Bab al-maftuh*. What sets the novel apart is the clash of civilizations it contains, a cultural struggle between two models, one English and the other Iraqi. The novel's protagonist is the daughter of an Iraqi father and an English mother; her parents thus represent both the colonizer and the colonized. In his *Season of Migration to the North*, Sudanese writer Tayeb Salih tried to portray the impossibility of reconciling the culture of the colonized and the colonizer in the person of Mustafa Sa'eed. Betool Khedairi's novel encompasses these two clashing, yet intertwined worlds while showing us a more intimate side of cultural confusion. The child belongs to two sharply contradictory worlds, and she thus becomes the personal face of the confrontation. In contrast, Mahdi 'Isa al-Saqr in his novel, *Riyah sharqiya riyah gharbiya* (Eastern Winds, Western Winds), observes the public aspect of the conflict, focusing on politics and class.

Notably, Iraqi women writers make use of popular folktales in their works, perhaps because this literary heritage is part of a particularly female tradition. It may also represent an unconscious affiliation between marginalized groups and non-institutional literature. This solidarity among the subaltern—whether they are subordinated by structures of class or gender—is brilliantly wrought in the beginning of Betool Khedairi's novel: the child narrator enjoys the company of Khaduja, a barefoot girl who does not go to school and lives a simple life on a farm near the home of the narrator, who belongs to the professional middle class. The narrator's friendship with Khaduja angers her English mother, who fears the filth of the peasants; in contrast, the Iraqi father feels that his daughter is getting to know her environment by befriending the peasants. Speaking with an appealing style, the narrator describes Khaduja's creative attempts, which humanize her and illustrate her potential (similar to Buthaina Al Nasiri's "Hikayat Samah," in which the young girl's beauty is only discovered after she is washed for burial): "I watch Khaddouja sculpting her doughy gum into the shape of a fish or a bird. She adds two pebbles, one on either side of the creature's head, giving it colored eyes."[44] But the mother only wants her daughter to be involved in the 'high' arts, to go to music and ballet classes, to learn to dance and socialize. As the narrator says about her parents, "Your disagreement allowed me to mingle with both worlds. Just like our house, which was in itself two worlds."[45]

Iraq's history in the twentieth century brims with violence and tragedy, war and oppression, but it is also a history that allows moments of joy and connection. No story encapsulates the Iraqi condition like Buthaina Al Nasiri's masterful "Limadha la nadhhab ila-l-bahr kathiran?" (Why Don't We Go More to the Sea?).[46] The narrator recalls scenes from his family's past as he answers the questions of an interrogator. He recalls a happy day at the beach with his mother and siblings. Later, in passing, we find that his mother committed suicide one day without explanation, his younger brother died in the war, and another brother emigrated and has not been heard of since. The story, which could have been a novel if it had delved more deeply into the lives of the children and the mother, is an authentic expression of contemporary Iraqi life, and it presents woman as a mother and a symbol of Iraq.

Drama

Drama has received little attention from Iraqi women writers. One of the earliest examples is the poetic drama by 'Atika al-Khazraji, *Majnun Layla* (Crazy for Layla) 1954, but Iraqi women writers did not begin writing drama in earnest until television penetrated the country and needed plays to broadcast. Women playwrights include Salima Khudayr, Fakhriya 'Abd al-Karim, Lutfiya al-Dulaymi, and 'Awatif Na'im. The latter wrote the brilliant *al-Muharrij* (The Clown) 1998, which addresses a specifically female anxiety.[47] Women writers have often written about their childhood, their youth, and motherhood, about marital and work problems, and about liberation and self-expression, but they have rarely showed much concern with older women. Indeed, old age is a theme rarely addressed in Arab women's literature, with the exception of the writings of Egyptian author Latifa al-Zayyat.

Al-Muharrij is practically a monodrama: an old woman awaits a visit from her children and, in the meantime, death comes to her in the shape of a clown. She prepared for the visit of her children and grandchildren by making their favorite foods. She tries to speed up their impending arrival to avoid addressing the clown, but she finds no one to talk to but the sparrow in its cage, who, in turn, reflects her existence in a cage of another sort. The woman tries to prove to herself that her memory is still sound by recalling moments from her life, and in this way she relates pieces of her life, which grows lonelier by the day. She talks to herself about her son, who brought the caged bird to her as a gift after he moved far away with his wife. She talks about how initially he visited her every week, then monthly, then with every season, and finally began to make do with a telephone call. The play consists of an interior monologue in seven 'vigils' before the curtain is drawn on the woman's life. The woman alternately blames her son for his absence and find excuses for him: "I don't blame him. Yes, it's his right to build his family however he likes." He did stay with her during the bombing and the war: "He stayed with me for a few days then decided to return home. He asked me to go live with him instead of staying alone here, but I refused. I can't leave this place."

The play observes the hardship of women as they age and their children become independent; they lose their domestic foundation and remain alone, without companion or consort. This is exile inside one's country, the product of social and urban changes that have separated families. Younger family members are busy with work, which makes it difficult to constantly visit aging relatives. This is the price of entry to the modern world, with its fast-paced, industrial rhythm. The old woman's attachment to her home and unwillingness to leave it for her son's house are related: she inevitably feels no sense of belonging in a new place in a new neighborhood. This important psychological dimension might escape a generation accustomed to moving and roaming. Exile can exist at home as it does abroad. In *Yawmiyat Baghdadiya*, particularly in the chapter on exile, Nuha al-Radi discusses the problems of living abroad and being cut off from one's roots. She remembers what her friend, the poet and writer Mayy Muzaffar, told her:

> May told me the story of one of her Basra relatives who came to stay with them in Baghdad after the war. One of her daughters had a bad attack of asthma and died because they couldn't get her oxygen fast enough. Her mother's reaction in grief was, "Why did she have to die in foreign lands?" Baghdad is only a few hundred kilometres north of Basra yet she felt that she was not at home. Exile is a state of mind.[48]

A sense of alienation, then, may spring from the strangeness of place or time, or both.

Conclusion

Iraqi women's literature continued to evolve throughout the twentieth century. If women writers started out with traditional poetry and naive fiction, they soon grasped the tools of their trade, advocated modernizing it, and broke the restraints surrounding it. Women writers blazed trails in poetry and opened new doors in the short story and the novel. They were not afraid to reveal the concealed parts of the self and describe their world, leaving behind stock images and ready-made stereotypes. In drama, women have focused on women's concerns and their representation, showing a particular interest in marginalized women. In the important work, *Sawt al-untha: dirasat fi-l-kitaba al-nisawiya al-'Arabiya* (Woman's Voice: Studies in Arab Feminist Writing) 1997, Iraqi critic Nazik al-A'raji defines the dilemma of Iraqi women's writing:

> Regardless of the paths taken by Iraqi women writers, I believe that at some point all of them fell prey to the pressure of two seemingly contradictory factors: firstly, the desire of the writer to present herself as a writer, regardless of her sex, as equal to male writers; and secondly, their gravitation toward the world of women's hardships. They all felt the pressure—personal and public, individual and collective—of experiences that are

simultaneously frustrating and inspirational—frustrating regarding the first factor and inspirational for the second.[49]

The specificity of Iraqi women's writing, then, stems from Iraqi women's experience within Iraqi society as a whole. It does not stand in opposition to the writing and experiences of male authors, but complements them and adds another dimension that is shaped by women's conditions and their responsibilities, and drawn from their attitudes and sensibility. This specificity constitutes a branch among other branches of one order. In this context difference does not necessarily entail polarization, but it often highlights distinctive details and different responses. A society's portrait cannot be complete unless all segments of society—all its classes and both sexes—help to paint it. For an image to be grasped in all its perpetual movement and dynamism, it must be seen from a multi-dimensional perspective, which also deepens its meaning, with its complex, interwoven structure.

In this study we have discussed representative examples of Iraqi women's writing in the context of Iraqi men's writing and Arab women's writing as a whole, considering the particularity imposed by the Iraqi social and historical reality. A domestic, social, or national framework that supports women's literature and does not restrict women's potential is important for the emergence and development of women's writing everywhere and at all times.

Notes

1 Salman Hadi Al Tu'ma, *Sha'irat 'Iraqiyat mu'asirat* (Damascus: n.p., 1995) for a review of these poets on pp. 13, 169, 181, 209, 197, 9, and 35 respectively. Some women writers in the generation following Umm Nizar were educated in schools established in Iraqi cities in the early twentieth century. These were girls' schools that encouraged artistic activities. Some fathers supported their daughters' quest for knowledge, the best example being Sabiha al-Shaykh Dawud, the first Iraqi woman to enter the Faculty of Law and become a judge.

2 'Abd al-Hamid al-'Alwaji, *al-Nitaj al-nisawi fi-l-'Iraq khilal 1923–1974* (Baghdad: Ministry of Information, 1975), pp. 44–48.

3 See, as one of innumerable examples, Kamil Mustafa al-Shaybi, "'Adat wa taqalid al-wilada wa-l-khitan fi janub al-'Iraq," *al-Turath al-sha'bi*, vol. 9, no. 8 (1978), pp. 63–70.

4 'Ali al-Khaqani, *Sha'irat fi thawrat al-'ishrin* (Baghdad: al-Tadamun Press, n.d.).

5 Salman Tu'ma, *Sha'irat 'Iraqiyat*, p. 133.

6 Lutfiya al-Dulaymi, *Sharikat al-masir al-abadi* (Cairo: Dar 'Ishtar, 1999), pp. 11–12.

7 Ibid., p. 194.

8 Salman Tu'ma, *Sha'irat 'Iraqiyat*, p. 94.

9 "Liqa' ma'a al-sayyida Mahira al-Naqshbandi," *al-Kitab*, vol. 5, no. 4 (June 1971), p. 58.

10 'Abd al-Rahim Muhammad 'Ali, *Rabab al-Kazimi: dirasa wa shi'r* (Najaf: al-Ghurri Modern Press, 1969), p. 26.

11 Sami Mahdi, *Wa'i al-tajdid wa-l-riyada al-shi'riya fi-l-'Iraq* (Baghdad: Ministry of Culture and Information, 1993), p. 24.

12 Nazik al-Mala'ika, *Shazaya wa ramad* (Beirut: Dar al-'Awda, 1971), p. 8.

13 Ibid., pp. 136–40.

14 Nazik al-Mala'ika, *Diwan Nazik al-Mala'ika* (Beirut: Dar al-'Awda, 1979), vol. 2, pp. 351–54.

15 Ibid., pp. 552–54.

16 Ibid., pp. 114–17.

17 Ibid., pp. 557–62.

18 Ibid., pp. 187–96.

19 Lami'a 'Abbas 'Amara, *Law anba'ani al-'arraf* (Beirut: Arab Institute for Research and Publishing, 1980), pp. 6–8.

20 Salman Tu'ma, *Sha'irat 'Iraqiyat*, p. 170.

21 Lami'a 'Abbas 'Amara, *Law anba'ani al-'arraf*, pp. 98–99.

22 Zuhur Dixon, *Wahati halat al-qamar* (Baghdad: Dar al-Hurriya, 1990), pp. 115–18.

23 Amal al-Zahawi, *al-Tariqun bihar al-mawt* (Beirut: Dar al-'Awda, n.d.), pp. 7–9.

24 Ibid., pp. 28–46.

25 Dunya Mikhail, *Mazamir al-ghiyab* (Baghdad: al-Adib Press, 1993), pp. 37–41.

26 Dunya Mikhail, "Qasa'id," *Akhbar al-adab*, October 20, 1996, p. 22.

27 Amal al-Jabburi, *A'tiqini ayyatuha-l-kalimat* (Cairo: General Egyptian Book Organization, 1999), pp. 43–44.

28 Mayy Muzaffar, *Layliyat* (Amman: Dar al-Shuruq, 1994), p. 76.

29 Ibid., pp. 85–86.

30 Siham Jabbar, "Dhat infijar," *Sutur* no. 37 (December 1999), p. 77.

31 'Umar Muhammad Talib, *Mushkilat al-mar'a wa kitabat al-qissa fi-l-'Iraq* (Baghdad: General Union of Iraqi Women in conjunction with al-Sulaymaniya University, 1978), p. 3.

32 Ibid., pp. 5–6.

33 Ibid., pp. 8–9.

34 Ibid., pp. 11–12.

35 Daisy Al-Amir, *'Ala la'ihat al-intizar* (Baghdad: Bayt Sin Books, 1990), pp. 79–87; translated into English as *The Waiting List: An Iraqi Woman's Tales of Alienation*, trans. by Barbara Parmenter (Austin: The University of Texas at Austin, 1994).

36 Daisy Al-Amir, '*Ala la'ihat al-intizar*, and *The Waiting List*, pp. 67, 68.
37 Haifa Zangana, *Bayt al-naml* (London: Dar al-Hikma, 1995), pp. 11–19.
38 Alia Mamdouh, "al-'Ubur," *al-Aqlam*, vol. 9, no. 2 (June 1973), pp. 68–69.
39 Buthaina Al Nasiri, *Watan akhar* (Cairo: Dar Sina Publishers, 1994), pp. 13–15. "Hikyat Samah" has been translated into English as "The Story of Samah" in Buthaina Al Nasiri, *Final Night: Short Stories*, trans. by Denys Johnson-Davies (Cairo: American University in Cairo Press, 2002).
40 Ibtisam 'Abd Allah al-Dabbagh, "Fi-l-bustan," *Hin yahzun al-atfal tatasaqat al-ta'irat: qisas min al-'Iraq* (Cairo: Dar 'Ishtar Publishers, 1998), pp. 155–61.
41 Lutfiya al-Dulaymi, "Khusuf Burhan al-Kutubi," *Sutur* 37, December 1999, pp. 80–83.
42 Salima Salih, *Zahrat al-anbiya': yaqzat al-dhakira* (Damascus: Dar al-Mada, 1994), pp. 19–29.
43 Betool Khedairi, *Kam badat al-sama' qariba!* (Beirut: Arab Institute for Research and Publishing, 1999); translated into English as *A Sky So Close*, trans. by Muhayman Jamil (New York: Pantheon Books, 2001).
44 Betool Khedairi, *Kam badat al-sama' qariba!*, p. 10, and *A Sky So Close*, p. 7.
45 Betool Khedairi, *Kam badat al-sama' qariba!*, p. 13, and *A Sky So Close*, p. 11.
46 Buthaina Al Nasiri, "Limadha la nadhhab ila-l-bahr kathiran?" *al-Hayat*, August 25, 1998, p. 16.
47 'Awatif Na'im, "al-Muharrij," in *Masrahiyat 'Iraqiya* (Cairo: Dar 'Ishtar Publishers, 1998), pp. 223–48.
48 Nuha al-Radi, *Baghdad Diaries* (London: Saqi Books, 1998), p. 139; translated into Arabic as *Yawmiyat Baghdadiya* (London: Dar al-Saqi, 1999), 171.
49 Nazik al-A'raji, *Sawt al-untha* (Damascus: al-Ahali Printing, Publishing, and Distribution, 1997), p. 102.

6 Palestine and Jordan

Radwa Ashour

I t is generally difficult to separate writing from geography and
history, but in the case of Jordan and Palestine, it is impossible. The
geographical/historical fact of Palestine and Jordan should not be
ignored. Both part of the Levant, they were divided into two nation-states
as part of the colonial enterprise in the early twentieth century, but the
greater Levant (extending from the Taurus mountains in the north to
Rafah in the south, and from the Mediterranean coast to the Euphrates in
the west) was, since the Islamic conquest until the end of the First World
War—that is, for more than 1,200 years, with the exception of the
Crusader period—part of one nation, the Arab Islamic caliphate and later
the Ottoman state.

Under the Sykes–Picot Agreement of March 1916, signed by Britain,
France, and Czarist Russia, Iraq and the Levant were divided up between
France and Britain, who determined their respective shares using colors
drawn on a map. To France went "the blue area" (coastal Syria, currently
Lebanon, and part of northern Syria and southern Turkey) and Area A, the
white area surrounded by a blue belt (currently Syria and part of northeast
Iraq). Britain got "the brown area" (Palestine), "the red area" (the greater
part of Iraq), and Area B, a white area surrounded by a red belt (stretching
from al-'Aqaba in the east to Kirkuk in the northwest, and to Basra in the
west and south, passing through Amman).[1]

Our topic is women's writing in Palestine and Jordan—that is, in the
brown area and the eastern part of Area B surrounded by the red belt, areas
shaded in with a colored pen by a civil servant with the British Foreign
Ministry in 1916. In the same year, the World Zionist Organization's

204

political affairs committee sent a memo to Mark Sykes consisting of three articles: 1) the recognition of the Jewish people in Palestine, which would include those Jews currently located there and the Jews who will immigrate to Palestine in the future—as the kernel of the Jewish national homeland; 2) that the British government grant to all Jews the right to immigrate to Palestine, and that it facilitate for them the means to settle there and buy land; and 3) that the British government sanction the formation of a Jewish association whose objective is to organize and facilitate Jewish settlement in Palestine.[2] The following year, the British government responded in a letter from its foreign minister, Arthur Balfour, to Lord Rothschild: "His Majesty's Government view with favour the establishment in Palestine of a national home for the Jewish people"—a letter that was later to be known as the Balfour Declaration. The San Remo conference followed in 1920: maps were redrawn and a new agreement gave France a mandate over Syria and Lebanon and Britain a mandate over Iraq, Jordan, and Palestine. The Mandate government and its military forces remained in Palestine until May 14, 1948, the day of the declaration of the state of Israel; the next day, British forces left. A war erupted, the Arabs were defeated, and Zionists established their state on four-fifths of Palestine: the coastal strip and the Negev. Jerusalem was divided, the east going to the Arabs and the west to the Zionists. In Rhodes in 1949, truce boundaries were agreed upon, and Palestinian lands west of the Jordan River (the West Bank) became part of the Hashemite Kingdom of Jordan. In the Jericho conference the same year, it was decided to unite the two banks of the Jordan under the Hashemite crown in the Hashemite Kingdom of Jordan. Also in Rhodes, it was agreed that the Gaza Strip, from Rafah to Bayt Hanun, should come under Egyptian administration.

We shall not address in this article the consequences of the redrawn borders and the establishment of new states in the region, but we will make several brief observations about the situation that had cultural repercussions:

1. From the early twentieth century, an urban fabric of life was evident in Palestinian cities. Jerusalem, Haifa, Nablus, and other cities were relatively busy centers with presses, newspapers, schools, and associations. Jordan, on the other hand, was primarily a passage for trade caravans between the Hijaz and the Syrian coast. It possessed few resources and most of its population was Bedouin. Amman, which Prince 'Abd Allah (later King 'Abd Allah) chose as the capital of his new principality, was a village, dotted by a few administrative buildings left behind by the Ottomans. This difference helps explain the earlier emergence of Palestinian writing, particularly women writers.

2. Before the two banks of the Jordan were united, some 400,000 people lived on the East Bank. Three years later, by 1952–1953, this number had increased to 1,385,456, following the annexation of the West

Bank to Jordan and the migration of thousands of families who had left the villages and cities of occupied Palestine for both the West and East Banks. In 1948, Amman was a small city inhabited by some sixty thousand souls; by 1968, after two waves of occupation and forced migration, it was home to some half million people.

3. The occupation of the greater part of Palestine in 1948 resulted in the geographic dispersion of Palestinians. This affected writers and was reflected in how they identified themselves. 'Writers of Occupied Palestine' was a common term in the 1960s for writers who stayed on their land after the declaration of the state of Israel and became Israeli citizens. There were writers living in Jordan, including the West Bank, who are usually referred to as Jordanian writers, though sometimes they are described as Palestinian writers, particularly after the occupation of the West Bank in 1967. Finally, there were writers living in the Gaza Strip or various Arab and foreign countries who retained their identity as Palestinian writers.

4. In Jordan we find, in addition to writers from eastern Jordan or writers of Palestinian origin, writers of Syrian origin (a result of the historical fluidity of movement in the Levant) and others of Circassian origin, whose ancestors migrated to the region and settled there in the late nineteenth and early twentieth centuries. Because all these divisions are relatively new, we will come across writers who were born in Haifa and settled in Jordan, others of Jordanian origin who were born and educated in Palestine, and still others who are Palestinian but were born in Jordan and have Jordanian citizenship. The permutations are endless.

Women in Palestine, women in Jordan

Palestinian women's self-consciousness was shaped in the context of the collective confrontation with the colonial reality. Anger, and the means used to express it, touched everyone.

In 1920, all of Palestine saw demonstrations demanding the cancellation of the Balfour Declaration, and women took part in these demonstrations. Both Zulaykha al-Shihabi and Miliya al-Sakakini helped to organize women's protests. In 1924, the Society for Women's Advancement was founded in Ramallah. The association formed a team of nurses and collected funds to buy weapons for fighters and help victimized families. In Jerusalem in 1928, the Association of Arab Women was established, and it began setting up branches in various Palestinian cities. The association's charter upheld "the right of its women to take part in political activities." The establishment of women's organizations was not new to Palestine: in 1903, a women's association was founded in Acre. In 1910, another was established in Jaffa,[3] and Nablus had had a women's association since 1921.[4]

Following the Buraq Uprising,[5] a women's committee was founded that convened a conference on October 26, 1929, attended by some three hundred women from various Palestinian cities and villages. The conference ended with a set of resolutions, including the rejection of Jewish immigration and the Balfour Declaration, support for the establishment of a national government, encouragement of national trade and industry, a reinforcement of economic ties with Syria and other Arab countries, and the reiteration of the necessity of women's advancement. The conference elected a committee to represent Palestinian women, known as the Executive Committee for Arab Women:

> At the end of the conference, despite the opposition of the Mandate authorities, the women mounted a protest demonstration that filled the streets of Jerusalem with eighty cars that passed by the homes of the foreign consuls. When they reached the home of the British Lord Chancellor, five women handed him a memo containing the conference's demands.[6]

The Palestinian women's movement continued its political and social activities, crowning its efforts with an Arab women's conference convened in Cairo to discuss the Palestinian issue. The 1938 conference was headed by Huda Sha'rawi. In her autobiography, Fadwa Tuqan (1917–2003) writes about the late 1920s and the 1930s:

> At this time, the Palestine Women's Federation undertook the organisation of Palestinian women's participation in the political struggle in most of the cities and sometimes in the villages. The city women's activities were confined to demonstrations, to sending telegrams of protest and convening meetings, through the women's organisations which the bourgeoisie of that era had created. Being unveiled, the country women had greater and more effective freedom of movement. They were the ones who carried arms and food to the rebels hiding in the mountains.[7]

Educational opportunities were available to Palestinian women from the late nineteenth century. On the eve of the First World War there were ninety-two primary schools in Jerusalem, Nablus, and Acre, teaching 7,758 students, among them 1,480 female students.[8] In addition, some five hundred missionary and sectarian schools (including British, French, German, Russian, and American schools) provided education through the secondary phase. In the pre-war period, there were four hundred schools in Palestinian villages (both public and missionary schools), including forty-six girls' schools that taught 3,392 students. This is compared to 38,760 students registered at boys' schools. The ratio of girls to boys was thus less than 1:10, but in the cities there was one girl for every three students, with 11,911 female pupils and 17,599 male pupils.[9]

*

Jordan was not an independent entity before 1920. As of the academic year 1922–1923, the country had only two women teachers, and six primary schools teaching 318 female students and 2,182 male students. By 1945–1946, the number had increased to 1,956 female students and 7,918 male students. As of 1961, female illiteracy stood at 84.8 percent.[10] This naturally had consequences for women's participation in public life and their opportunities for cultural production. In 1944, the Social Association for Women's Solidarity was established, which aimed "to improve the status of the poor." The association was the first of its kind in Jordan. It was followed a year later by the Jordanian Women's Union, which sought to improve women's education. In 1949, the two associations merged into the Hashemite Jordanian Women's Association, but it was dissolved in the same year. In 1954, the Arab Women's Union was founded, headed by Emily Bisharat, the first female lawyer in Jordan. Its objectives included "fighting illiteracy, improving women's economic, social, and literary condition, and fully preparing them to exercise their complete rights as citizens," as well as "fostering friendly ties and mutual understanding with Arab women and women of the world to contribute to the improvement of national conditions in all vital fields."[11]

Writing in the beginning

Women writers appeared in Palestine from the early part of the century, but in Jordan they did not emerge until some four decades later. The reason for the disparity is not only Palestinian women's head start in education and the existence of relatively advanced civic associations in several Palestinian cities, but is also attributable to the challenges and confrontations imposed by Jewish immigration, and these challenges shaped both men and women.

From the early twentieth century, Palestinian women wrote articles, essays, letters, stories for radio, and speeches on every topic. Sadhij Nassar joined her husband, Najib Nassar, in putting out the paper, *al-Karmel*, established in Haifa in 1908, and she later published her own articles in the paper. Salma al-Nasr published an article on the education of girls in *al-Nafa'is al-'asriya* in 1909, and Rose Hassun published an article in the same journal the next year on Indian women. In the 1930s and 1940s articles were published by Mary Sarruf Shahhada (born in Jaffa in 1901), Asma Tubi (born in Nazareth in 1905), Sadhij Nassar, Qudsiya Khurshid, 'Anbara Salam al-Khalidi, Fadwa Tuqan, Shuhra Tawfiq al-Misri,

Najwa Kawar Farah, and Nimra Tannus; these women signed with their own names or used pseudonyms.[12]

In his study of modern Palestinian women's literature, Kamal al-Fahmawi writes:

> In the late 1930s, the Palestinian literary scene witnessed what might be called 'radio literature.' Although at that time, radio was a tool in the hand of the British Mandate authorities and under its direct supervision, it had a tangible impact on cultural life and gave rise to a new style of essay, the radio essay. In fact, in its general features this new type of essay did not depart from the familiar literary essay except in the way it was presented . . . It led writers to pursue a cultural, reformist path and choose more elegant phrases. Many Palestinian women writers participated in this field . . .[13]

Up until 1948, Palestinian women expressed themselves through the written or radio essay. In addition to the essay, Asma Tubi, Hadiya 'Abd al-Hadi, Najwa Kawar Farah, and others wrote short stories and "dramatic stories." Fadwa Tuqan also began publishing some of her poems in the late 1930s. These were poems written in the classical *'amudi* form that were inspired by traditional aesthetic values and sought to imitate them.

In the period before the *nakba*, Palestinian women made only modest achievements in the short story:

> [The stories] were dominated by an external description that preceded the action as if it were an introduction, although it had no real relation to it. In addition to these descriptive, expository prefaces, there was another style of introduction that sought to offer advice and truisms . . . [The stories] more closely resembled a descriptive essay that touched on subjective emotions.[14]

Usama Shihab summarizes the defining characteristics of the short story in the early phases as: the use of highly rhetorical flowery language; didacticism; authorial intervention; a view of the short story as a summary of a novel; the presentation of stock characters that do not develop through their interactions with events, but are usually either good or evil; the pervasiveness of romance.[15]

*

In December 1940, Taysir Zabyan, the owner of the Jordanian paper *al-Jazira*, published a series of letters in his paper under the title, "Where Are the Protectors of Virtue?" By way of introduction, he said the letters had come to him from a woman who wished to see them published, saying, "Open the arms of your newspaper to this deafening cry and exhausting story." In the letters, Abjad talks about the oppressive social conditions in which she lives—the pressure of poverty, the need to go out and work, her mother's pressure to marry a rich but dissolute man, and the pressures of the surrounding social environment. At the end of the series, the paper published its own happy addition: "*al-Jazira* is pleased to announce that the writer of these letters has succeeded in marrying the good man she had hoped for. In doing so, she has left behind her bitter life and embarked on a calm, assured existence."[16] The article has a clear social dimension and alludes to some details of the contemporary political reality—details that Taysir Zabyan later deletes in the book published in 1958.[17]

Did Taysir Zabyan write in a woman's voice and attribute the work to her to guarantee the text wide dissemination? Or did he use real letters from a female reader, publishing some as they were, adding to others, and in both cases, redacting and editing them? The text, attributed to a woman in 1940, was not directed at women, for the number of women readers at that time in Jordan was miniscule. It bears all the hallmarks of what was considered fine, elegant writing at the time: the tropes of high rhetoric, an expository mode of expression ornamented with truisms and exhortations, the dichotomy of good and evil, and the ultimate victory of truth.

In 1945, Ayman Abu-l-Shi'r founded the journal, *al-Ra'id*, dedicating a space to "Women's Affairs," "a milestone in the development of women's literature in Jordan."[18] The journal published thirty-two issues before suspending publication in 1947. Some of the articles were signed with the female author's real name, others with a pseudonym, and some with her initials.

Poetry

In her autobiography, Fadwa Tuqan relates how her brother and mentor, Ibrahim, cautioned her against reading modern poetry, with the exception of the poems he personally chose by Shawqi, Hafiz, Isma'il Sabri, and Mutran: "Ibrahim felt strongly that the Arab poetic heritage was sacred. He belonged to a generation that had grown up aware of a widespread movement to revive this heritage through restructuring its artistic values; its terseness of phraseology, its clarity of expression and its beauty of style." She continues, "I stuck to this poetic heritage for many years, during which it remained the pattern I followed in my attempts at poetry. Throughout the whole period between 1933 and 1940 my interest lay in what was termed a grandiose style and expression."[19]

Tuqan remembers that she signed her love poems with the name "Dananir," after the famed 'Abbasid-era slave-girl poet, and published them in the Beirut journal, *al-Amali*, and the Egyptian journal, *al-Risala*.

She adds that her compliance with the ready-made model of ancient poetry was confining and obstructed the flow of her emotions, until she read Dr. Muhammad Mandur's essays on Mahjar literature,[20] published in the 1940s in the Egyptian journal *al-Thaqafa*:

> I found the works of these North American poets closer to my psychological and mental make-up. During that period, I also chanced upon poets of the Apollo school, such as Ibrahim Naji, al-Shabbi, Ali Mahmud Taha and al-Tijani. From that time, I turned my back on the Abbasid style, my main ambition being to write poetry deriving its beauty from simplicity, flexibility, truthfulness, and poetical expression free of affectation.[21]

Not much later, Fadwa Tuqan discovered a new ability to write poetry when she read Nazik al-Mala'ika and other poets who had blazed new trails in Arabic poetry: "I was convinced of the viability of free verse," she writes. "I abandoned the traditional two-hemistich verse with its long lines and monotonous rhythm, and began applying myself to the writing of the new poetry." Tuqan says that her conviction with the new form did not mean that she abandoned rhyme and meter: "Poetry continues to be distinct from prose and there is nothing more charming than musical durations as they echo within lines of differing length, and nothing more beautiful than rhymes alternating in a free verse poem, sometimes appearing distinctly, and sometimes disappearing."[22]

Fadwa Tuqan's poems have a lyrical quality whether the theme is patriotism or love. In her early poems, the influence of Romantic poetry is clear in her lexicon and images (longing, passion, isolation, the overwhelming presence of nature and the desire to become one with it, and the glorification of imagination). In her first collection, *Wahdi ma'a al-ayyam* (Alone with the Days) 1952, Fadwa Tuqan largely observes the unity of the two-hemistich verse while in later works she turns to free verse, based on the unity of meter.

Salma Khadra Jayyusi (b. 1926?) first published her poems in the 1950s, then later collected them in *al-'Awda min al-nab' al-halim* (Return from the Dreaming Spring) 1960, her sole collection of poetry. After that, she only published individual poems in journals, dividing her energies between academia, criticism, and translation. Jayyusi wrote free-verse poems that went beyond direct lyricism, and she clearly draws on two poetic traditions, the Arabic and the European. Her texts are distinguished by their variety, complexity, and symbolism. She is inspired by cultural history and tradition, and includes colloquial expressions and popular folksongs in poems that have an organic structure, dramatic elements, and evocative images. She experimented with rhythm, changing meters in one poem, all of which was new to Arabic poetry of the period. In her first and only collection, Jayyusi includes poetic texts that carved out a pioneering spot for herself among the free-verse poets, both men and women, and gave her a place of distinction when compared to the poems of other Arab women of her generation.

Thuraya Malhas (b. 1925) was the first Palestinian woman poet to free herself from meter. She wrote prose poetry starting with her first collection, *al-Nashid al-ta'ih* (The Wayward Hymn), published in 1949. Her poetry is mostly lyrical, and it often gives voice to mystical experience using unfamiliar words and images.

Fadwa Tuqan occupied the preeminent spot in women's poetry in Palestine and Jordan over the second half of the twentieth century. She crossed three generations of poets—her own and two later generations—who are spread geographically over the Palestine occupied in 1948, the West Bank, Gaza, Jordan, Lebanon, and faraway places of exile. These women's works include the classical *qasida* poem, free verse, and the prose poem. National issues are a major theme in these poems, and women's poetry is mostly lyrical, at times leaning toward simplicity and at times toward complexity. The later generations of poets include Sulafa al-Hijjawi, Mayy Sayigh, Salwa Sa'id, Layla 'Allush, and Rajwa 'Assaf, all of whom are Palestinians who focused on the themes of Palestine, uprootedness, and resistance, and all of them write free verse. Overall, we can detect thematic, and even stylistic similarities in their works, despite the disparate quality of the texts. Layla al-Sayih wrote lyrical prose poetry, while Siham Dawud and Nida' Khuri wrote prose poems. All three are Palestinians. The first was born in 1936 and lived in Kuwait, the second was born in 1952, and the third in 1959; they all live in the Palestine occupied in 1948. Muna al-Sa'udi, Amina al-'Udwan, and Zulaykha Abu Risha—all three from Jordan—also wrote prose poetry. The poetry of Muna al-Sa'udi, a sculptor and painter, is distinguished by its plastic-arts sensibility. Her texts have a visual component that is formed through a sensory lexicon that comes together to create a spiritual experience with political and psychological dimensions. Amina al-'Udwan writes primarily political texts, usually direct, while Zulaykha Abu Risha takes a feminist stance, largely focusing on women's relationships with the Other and the experience of rebellion. Here, too, we notice clear differences between lyrical prose poetry *(al-shi'r al-manthur)* (the works of Layla al-Sayih, for example) and the prose poem *(qasidat al-nathr)*, more modern in its perspective and form (the works of Muna al-Sa'udi, for example).

A third generation of women poets began publishing in the late 1990s, including Ghada al-Shafi'i (born in Acre in 1977), who writes prose poetry. She follows a more modernist trend that goes beyond the direct lyrical poem to a more complex poetic form.

The novel

Who is Maryam Mash'al? There is no answer to this question in books on Palestinian literature. All we know about her is that she wrote a single novel, *Fatat al-nakba* (A Girl of the Dispossession) 1957, while a student in the 1950s and never took up writing again. The fact that we know nothing of her life makes her text the voice of a collective experience, recorded by an anonymous girl no different from the others who lived the same experience, save that it is she who speaks. She was not a professional writer, and her text might not, according to common criteria, qualify as literature. How could a schoolgirl write the experience of the *nakba*, the 1948 Palestinian catastrophe? But she did, recording what she lived.

She speaks, often fervently, and occasionally lapses into oratory and direct statement. She dedicates her text to Jamila Buhrayd—the Arab Joan of Arc, as she calls her—linking three models of heroism: the most famous European example of a heroine facing a foreign invasion, the most prominent Arab example of her time (the Algerian heroine), and the girl of the dispossession. Maryam Mash'al writes to record an experience she lived, most likely as a child. She names her protagonist Wafa'—literally, Faithfulness—and follows her through the Palestinian experience of war and forced migration, and through a love story with Diya' that represents the future. Despite its naive perspective and amateur composition, the text remains an authentic product of its context, blending a historical consciousness with an awareness of real-life's restrictions on girls. It reflects an aspiration for a love that will realize the dream of liberation, both collective and individual. The two lovers are united by their love, their common memory, and their dream of working for return.

We know nothing of Maryam Mash'al, but we do know Huda Hanna, who wrote her novel, *Sawt al-malaji'* (A Voice of the Refugee Camps), in the five years following the dispossession of 1948. She was born in the village of al-Rama in 1922 and forced out of Palestine when she was twenty-six. She then wrote her only novel, *Sawt al-malaji'*. She did not write either before or after it, but like Maryam Mash'al, she wanted to tell her story. She chose an epistolary form, pouring her experience into letters written to a friend who happened to be outside Palestine at the time. Huda Hanna starts with paradise before it was lost, relating good memories of now faraway cities: Safad, Acre, Haifa, al-Lydda, and others. She then talks about the fierce battles and the entry of Arab forces on May 15, 1948, followed by the experience of transfer and finally the refugee camps where she works. Here, too, is a text that lapses into oratory and direct expression, a significant historical topic in the hand of an unpracticed writer grasping at the still smoldering embers.

Despite their modest novelistic value and lack of artistry, these two texts share an obsession with documenting and recording, or mining one's memory, with other novels of artistic worth, whether written by men or women. From its first work—Khalil Baydas's *al-Warith* (The Inheritor) 1920—to the important examples of Ghassan Kanafani, Emile Habibi, and Jabra Ibrahim Jabra in the 1960s and 1970s, the Palestinian novel has been concerned with the fate of the collective and with observing and documenting the features of this fate, each in its own fashion.

The first novels written by a woman in Jordan are the texts of Julia Sawalha. Remarkably, Sawalha, who was born in Ma'daba in 1905, began publishing her works after she reached the age of seventy. She published her first novel when she was seventy-one and her last novel when she was eighty. Here, as in the early phases of the Palestinian novel, there is a clear tendency to trace the historical aspects of reality and record its details. *Salwa* (Salwa) 1976, which is, as far as I know, the author's first novel, revolves around rural life in Jordan before the establishment of the emirate, under Ottoman rule and during the First World War. In her second novel, *al-Nashmi* (A Man of Courage) 1978, Julia Sawalha moves on to a later period, ending the novel with the death of the hero in the 1948 war in Palestine. In her fourth novel, *al-Yatima* (The Orphan) 1985, she returns to a Jordanian village of the 1920s. In her works, Sawalha displays a keen awareness of women's oppression by poverty and unjust traditions. Her works have a doubly significant historical value: she explores Jordanian rural life in the first decades of the twentieth century, and she gives us novels that, despite their uneven quality, are the first to be written by a woman in Jordan. Esthetically speaking, we find a confused structure, a simple approach, an expository style, and a tendency to use rhymed prose and quote poetry. For example, she "closes her novel, *Hal tarji'in* (Are You Coming Back?), with a five-and-a-half-page poem, offered with no artistic justification."[23]

*

The 1970s witnessed the emergence of a generation of Palestinian women novelists who would continue to publish and gradually secure their place in Palestinian and Arab cultural life. Sahar Khalifeh, Liyana Badr, Salwa al-Banna, and, a few years later, Leila al-Atrash produced novels that would lay the foundations for future generations of women novelists in Palestine. The Palestinian diaspora endows these works with multiple perspectives, which, when taken together, create a sort of integrated whole. Writing from Nablus in the West Bank, Sahar Khalifeh explores Palestinian life under occupation. She also writes of the intifada and changes in society in the 1970s. From Amman and Beirut, Salwa al-Banna writes about the Palestinian resistance, along with Liyana Badr. Leila al-Atrash's experiences in the West Bank, where she was born and educated, and her life in Kuwait, where she settled and worked, enabled her to portray both with an especially critical eye.

Sahar Khalifeh's six novels and her firm grasp of the craft of writing put her at the forefront of Palestinian women novelists. In her duology, *al-Subbar (Wild Thorns)* 1976, and *'Abbad al-shams* (Sunflower) 1980, Khalifeh depicts the experience of the occupation with a fluid realism that combines the observation of external scenes with a probing of the interior lives of several characters who interact through the story, scenes, and dialogue, which is usually fast-paced and full of life. *Al-Subbar* revolves around the increasing numbers of West Bank residents who are forced to work in Israeli factories after the 1967 occupation, the confusion this creates for the freedom fighter coming from "abroad," and his painful transition from a naively romantic view of the homeland to a close familiarity with its harsh reality and the people living under an occupation.

In *'Abbad al-shams*, Khalifeh continues to follow the lives of some characters from *al-Subbar* while introducing a new cast as well, in an attempt to more fully encompass the interlocking elements of the reality of occupation: Israeli repression, the dream of individual redemption and its impossibility, the pressures of obsolete customs that refuse to die and only increase the burden of the occupation, and the obstacles to an active confrontation with the occupation. Women's concerns are not at the forefront of *al-Subbar*, but starting with *'Abbad al-shams*, they begin to occupy an increasing space in Khalifeh's novels, until in *Mudhakkirat imra'a ghayr waqi'iya* (Memoirs of an Unrealistic Woman) 1986, they become the center of the plot. In her first novel, too, *Lam na'ud jawari lakum* (We Are Your Slaves No More) 1974, she takes up the same issue. Indeed, in most of her novels, Khalifeh addresses women's issues from a feminist perspective, putting ideas familiar from the women's movement of the 1960s and 1970s into the mouths of her female characters and embodying these ideas in the plot and the characters' fates.

In *Bab al-Saha* (The Saha Gate) 1990, Sahar Khalifeh takes up both the confrontation between Palestinians and occupation soldiers in the years of the first intifada and women's oppression as well. The action is centered around the Saha Gate itself, where disparate characters meet and the threads of the story intersect to portray a Palestinian city constrained by both occupation and its own obsolete ideas. The plot develops along two parallel lines: the characters break the siege on their quarter by demolishing a gate walled up by the Israelis, while at the same time, women—under siege of a different kind—break the bonds imposed on them by undertaking an act of heroism. The two events take place simultaneously during a funeral procession for a martyr.

In Khalifeh's novel, *al-Mirath (The Inheritance)* 1997, we enter the West Bank in the 1990s, observing reality through the eyes of a Palestinian girl who grew up in America and has returned to her country to see it and take possession of her share of her father's legacy. This is the Palestinian reality of the 1990s that followed the first intifada, a collapsing and corrupt reality marked by the fierce struggle to divide the cake and take the biggest piece.

Sahar Khalifeh's texts rely on a central plot and usually end with a climatic final scene that is almost dramatic in nature, bringing together the major story lines and characters. She is a deft observer of collective scenes and character, particularly female characters. In her novels, she employs a set of images that become evocative metaphors, such as the land, the quarter, and the home. There is always a house, old or new, closed or open, whether it already exists or is an object of longing; it is either threatened with destruction or the focus of a dispute among relatives jockeying for their share of a bequest. In her most successful works, metaphor and figurative language have a tangible presence that encompasses the complexity of reality, creating a richly connotative chronotope of a present charged with history—thus intensifying a social reality whose elements are closely intertwined. For example, the Saha Gate, in the novel of the same name, is the site and object of the novel's conflict, a locus of both oppression and resistance, reflecting the contradictions of reality, positive and negative. In less successful instances, the metaphor becomes a direct representation that simplifies reality into an allegorical image. This is the case with *al-Mirath*, in which Khalifeh translates reality into simple symbols that are inserted into a plot brimming with details. Nevertheless, this novel was one of the first that dealt with the disintegration that followed the end of the first intifada.

In the novels of Liyana Badr the plot as a basic organizing principle of the novel recedes. Time is recreated through association or the succession of the seasons, and memory, fractured across place and time, plays a prominent role in the protagonists' experience. In her first novel, *Busla min ajl 'abbad al-shams (A Compass for the Sunflower)* 1978, Badr addresses the confrontation between the Jordanian regime and the Palestinian resistance in September 1970, which ended with the defeat of the resistance and its expulsion from Jordan. The novel's setting moves between the cities of the West Bank, Amman, and Beirut, depicting the Palestinian experience of the late 1960s and early 1970s: the occupation of the West Bank, the resistance, the September clashes between the Jordanian army and the Palestinian fedayeen, and the expulsion of the resistance and its transfer to Beirut.

In her most recent work, *Nujum Ariha* (The Stars of Jericho) 1993, an autobiographical novel, the narrator, living in exile, revisits her childhood memories, reviving the past through description and evocation and infusing it with the lived present. In *'Ayn al-mir'a (The Eye of the Mirror)* 1991, Badr gives the reader the siege of the Tall al-Za'tar refugee camp, a subject she had already addressed in her short-story collection, *Shurfa 'ala-l-fakihani (A Balcony over the Fakihani)* 1983. Here, too, historical reality replaces the novelistic plot: the situation in the camp, the lives of its inhabitants, the siege, the resistance, death, and defeat.

Liyana Badr uses personal witness and testimony—what the camp's inhabitants have seen both in their waking hours and in dreams—just as she employs popular songs and proverbs. The overlapping of time is also a marked feature of all of Liyana Badr's novels. The plot does not progress along a linear, chronological path, but is based on the fragmentation of place and the multifaceted nature of memory. The September events, the Tall al-Za'tar refugee camp, or the final journey in the three novels are only sites where the elements of the story meet; all of them are chronotopes charged with historical and personal significance.

In *Wa tushriq gharban* (And It Rises in the West) 1987, Leila al-Atrash gives us a *bildungsroman*, depicting the childhood of the protagonist in a city in the West Bank. The novel follows her development from childhood through young womanhood to maturity against the historical background of Palestine in the 1950s and 1960s, the occupation of the West Bank, and the resistance. In her next novel, *Imra'a li-l-fusul al-khamsa (A Woman of Five Seasons)* 1990, al-Atrash gives the reader a critical text that blends feminist with Palestinian concerns, bringing together the oil rich, their Palestinian middlemen, and the corrupt wings of Palestinian organizations. In her third novel, the action is focused on a meeting between two sisters, one coming from the West Bank and the other from the Gulf, the first a housewife and the second a working woman. Leila al-Atrash writes realistic novels with a critical spirit, bringing together a feminist and nationalist consciousness. In all her texts, she charts the evolution of Palestinian life with all its tragedies and hopes.

*

The 1990s witnessed the publication of two important novels by Jordanian writers: *al-Khuruj min Susruqa: riwayat al-shatat al-Sharkasi* (Out of Sosriqwe: a Novel of the Circassian Diaspora) 1992, by Zahra 'Umar, and *Shajarat al-Fuhud: taqasim al-hayah* (The Fuhud Family Tree: Improvisations of Life) 1995, by Samiha Khurays. Despite their differences, both texts engage in a similar historical project: they follow the fates of a collective, observing the particular details of their lives over successive decades. Both are generational, almost epic novels, although they differ in style.

Zahra 'Umar's novel opens with the death of a grandmother. Her daughters and granddaughters gathered around her do not understand her facial expressions, her mumbling, her widened pupils and nostrils, and her ears straining "like a cat snatching a sound from the depths of the unknown."[24] They are unaware that the grandmother's memories, the details of her life, are flowing out as she relives the collective departure from the Caucasus. She is speaking to her dead relatives, and they to her.

There are multiple story levels in *al-Khuruj min Susruqa*: the seemingly neutral voice of the narrator who relates the scenes and details, the voice of the grandmother, the voice of the dead relatives she summons, and the voice of Circassian folktales, myths, and epics—the council of the Narts, their gods, Sosriqwe —the mythic hero who was born of stone—and his mother Satanay. 'Umar breaks up the central story of the Circassian disapora—usually when the action bears down on the narrator and the listener—with long excerpts from translated epics or the women's gossip around the bed of the dying grandmother.

Zahra 'Umar records the history of the Circassians since their forced migration from their lands in the late nineteenth century, when they were trapped between the hammer of Czarist Russia and the anvil of the Ottoman Empire. She documents the journey of their diaspora until they reach Jordan and settle. Historical events are intertwined with myth and magical realism, at times evoking *The Thousand and One Nights* and at others the novels of Latin America. The novel encompasses the experience of the Circassian diaspora, and a common awareness of the Palestinian diaspora creates a bond between the author and her readers.

Zahra 'Umar's novel takes up a new subject, untouched by Arabic fiction. It is distinguished by the writer's bold experimentalism and her ability to blend myth and historical facts, realism and the fantastic, and her portrayal of individual characters and collective destiny. Let us take two examples here. The first describes the birth of Sosriqwe. Satanay, his mother, is washing on the river bank when a shepherd spots her and calls out to her. He looks at her and she at him and a fire burns her heart; she is no longer able to stand. She sits on a stone, which she then takes with her and hides in the corn bran. She later hears the stone making a noise, and it grows bigger every day:

> She took the stone out of the bran and put it in a warm place next to the hearth, where it stayed for nine months and nine days. Then she took it to the blacksmith god, and he spent seven full days breaking it.
>
> Satanay's heart burned every time the stone was struck until finally the stone split and a boy fell out of it. The boy's body was flaming like a fire, the sparks flying and steam rising off of him. Lepsh [the blacksmith god] gripped him with sturdy forceps on his knee and dunked him in the water seven times. The water boiled each time from the heat emanating from the boy's body. After that, his body was hardened like steel, except for the spot where Lepsh had gripped him with the forceps.[25]

The next excerpt takes us from the mythical to the historical: the migration of the Circassians from their homeland. The dying grandmother recalls her departure as a little girl. The large ox-drawn cart carries the family, and the girl—now the dying grandmother—wakes up frightened to see her dead brother chastising them for leaving without him. He wants to sleep next to her because he is tired and afraid:

> I went further away, and the distance between me and Jan grew. I asked him, choking down my tears, "But why is your body so crooked?"
> "When the bullets hit my chest they tore my body apart, and I felt my soul begin to exit from the holes. I bent over to try and close them, to prevent my soul from seeping away from me. Why does the soul long to flee from the body? I don't know. I wanted to grasp my soul, but I couldn't. It slipped off and left me a stranger, looking for a thread of light. Warm me up."
> I tried to touch his body. It was cold, cold.[26]

Samiha Khurays does not begin the first part of her novel, *Shajarat al-Fuhud: taqasim al-hayah*, at the end with the dying grandmother—she saves this moment for the conclusion of part two, *Shajarat al-Fuhud: taqasim al-'ishq* (The Fuhud Family Tree: Improvisations of Love) 1998. Here we start with the beginning: a boy, Fahd al-Rashid, "draws a broad circle with his hands and eyes, saying to himself, This land is Fahd's, and his children's, and for the Fahds that come after him." And so it is. He leaves his uncles and moves to a hilltop, which he sows and makes prosper. Khurays tells the story of Fahd al-Rashid's family, a history that begins with his relationship to the land, his four wives, and his children and grandchildren.

Shajarat al-Fuhud: taqasim al-hayah is a large tapestry bursting with details. An omniscient narrator relates the fate and deeds of the characters, and what goes on inside them, fleshing them out with events from modern Arab history: the end of the First World War, the establishment of the Emirate of Jordan, the Second World War, the coronation of Prince 'Abd Allah as king, the war for Palestine, nationalist aspirations, the 1967 defeat. The events take us briefly to a guesthouse for men. We hear them speak of these events and observe them from afar, and at times the events impose themselves on the plot and the characters involved in it, who face martyrdom, detention, or exile.

Samiha Khurays seems to have an urgent impulse to document history. In her most recent novel, *al-Qurmiya: al-layl wa-l-bayda'* (The Tree Stump: Night and the Desert) 1999, she seeks to record the history of the great Arab revolt, mixing fictional characters with historical figures like Prince Faysal and Lawrence, although this text and the second part of *Shajarat al-Fuhud* do not reach the artistic level of *Shajarat al-Fuhud: taqasim al-hayah*. In *Shajarat al-Fuhud: taqasim al-'ishq*, an unnecessary lyricism interrupts the flow of the narrative; in *al-Qurmiya: al-layl wa-l-bayda'*, in addition to this lyricism, there are difficulties and traps latent in the treatment of the historical subject, and she does not always manage to avoid them.

If in his trilogy Naguib Mahfouz described the history of the Egyptian middle class, its aspirations to liberation from colonialism, and the details of its social reality, what distinguishes Zahra 'Umar's *al-Khuruj min Susruqa* and Samiha Khurays's *Shajarat al-Fuhud: taqasim al-hayah* is their attempt to tell the story of a neglected history: the Circassian migration and settlement in Jordan in Zahra 'Umar's *al-Khuruj min Susruqa* and *Susruqa khalf al-dabab* (Sosriqwe Behind the Fog), and the reality of a Jordanian family in Irbid in *Shajarat al-Fuhud*. Neither writer addresses women's marginalization as an independent subject, but the marginalization which the two authors may have experienced more keenly than men expanded their knowledge and consciousness, which each has invested in writing the details of a marginalization that is shared by both men and women.

The short story

Najwa Kawar (later known as Najwa Kawar Farah, after she married Father Rafiq Farah) is the most prominent Palestinian woman story writer of the 1940s. In addition to the short story, she wrote articles for the press and radio. She published her works in *al-Adib*, *Sawt al-Mar'a*, *al-Muntada*, *al-Qafila*, and *al-Ghad*, and they were also broadcast by several radio stations. After the Palestinian *nakba*, Kawar remained in Nazareth while many of her colleagues were driven into exile. In 1954, a group of her friends (Isa al-Na'uri, Sami Habibi, and Rafiq Farah) collected fifteen of her stories, published or broadcast in the 1940s, and had them published by the Beirut-based al-Rayhani Publishers as *'Abiru al-sabil* (The Passersby) 1945. She wrote largely realistic stories on social themes with a moralistic bent; they are not free from direct, reportage style and some techniques of traditional rhetoric.

The same year that Najwa Kawar's first collection was published, a young Palestinian writer, aged twenty-nine, also published her first collection of stories, *Ashya' saghira* (Small Things) in 1954, followed two years later by *al-Zill al-kabir* (The Big Shadow) 1956. In these two collections, along with later collections such as *Qisas ukhra* (Other Stories) 1960, *al-Sa'a wa-l-insan* (The Clock and the Man) 1963, and *al-'Id la ya'ti min al-nafidha al-gharbiya* (The Holiday Doesn't Come from the Western Window) 1971, the last of which was published four years after her death, Samira 'Azzam gives us a model of the realist short story that distinguishes her as a pioneer of this literary genre. 'Azzam wrote stories with a cohesive structure based on unity of action and economy of language. She focused on ordinary people, their everyday cares, and their ongoing experience with various forms of repression, whether economic, social, or national:

> Among all of our women writers, Samira 'Azzam is the poet of everyday anxieties of all sizes. Small children are occupied by small worries, but they are typical cares that color their world. As for the problems of adults in the grown-up world, they are as big as their entire world.[27]

'Azzam's world is packed with people "who face not divided selves revealed by long monologues, but who respond to the attacks of a fiercely hostile classist society that crushes those who fall in the middle of the conflict."[28]

Samira 'Azzam wrote about Palestinians and non-Palestinians, and the reality of both men and women. The broad scope of her stories and the various human types she presents give them a variety. Women have a presence, but they are not alone on the plot's stage:

> We do not find one female model in her stories . . . there the anxieties of mother and wife meet those of the adolescent, the fighter, the orphan, the chewing gum vendor, and the thrown-away miserable woman who is body without soul. The problems are as varied as the situations and characters.[29]

*

The decades from the 1960s to the 1990s witnessed the publication of a significant number of stories by many Palestinian and Jordanian women writers, some of whom have published three, or more, collections. Of course, not all the stories are of the same quality, and there are clear differences in the writers' depth and range and their mastery of the techniques of the short story. In the best texts, we are first struck by the variety of subjects, characters, and approaches. In the stories of Suhayr al-Tall, Insaf Qal'aji, Hind Abu-l-Sha'r, Huzama Habayib, Maryam Jabr, Munira Shurayh, Munira Qahwaji, Basma al-Nusur, and Samiha Khurays, for example, the scene may be broad or narrow, but in both cases it carries complex elements that speak to the relationship of the individual with herself and the Other (man or woman), with society, with political reality, and with history. The first-person narrator may be male or female, the first-person plural may be used to relate a common experience, or the narrator may be totally effaced, with the action turned over to a seemingly neutral voice that speaks in the third person.

The writing styles are equally varied: some authors write the organically structured story, with a central action and a moment of illumination in the final paragraph (Suhayr al-Tall, for example, and some of the stories of Basma al-Nusur). Others try to write very short stories based on a brief moment of irony (some of the stories of Jawahir al-Rifay'a and Basma al-Nusur). Still others try to employ the folk tradition (Suhayr al-Tall and Jawahir al-Rifay'a have tried this technique in some of their texts). There is symbolic writing that revolves around a use of figurative language and dense signification (seen in some stories by Hind Abu-l-Sha'r, particularly in her collection, *al-Hisan* [The Horse] 1991). There are texts that focus on the interior experience of a particular character in a moment in which the feelings of a besieged, oppressed person reach a crescendo in the midst of a terrifying Arab reality (for example, the stories of Insaf Qal'aji and Jamila 'Amayira, although the first opens hers to the range of history, while the second focuses on the moment of terror arising out of this history). Finally, there are stories concerned with portraying a slice of human experience and observing its details, combining an observance of an external action with interior emotions. Here the stories of Huzama Habayib stand out, distinguished by their particular rhythm and her mastery of political expression in well-crafted texts that are as far removed as possible from the lexicon of political discourse. Habayib portrays ordinary, hardworking, beaten-down people, with the details of the scene illustrating the cruelty of their experiences. The story follows them to reveal a tough kernel of humanity, glimpsed in a fleeting moment that confirms their ability to dream, love, desire, sympathize, or engage with life.

In the most run-of-the-mill short stories, we find a clear tendency to direct self-expression, the use of the first person where the narrator is also the narrated object, the recurrent appearance of one character type with one voice across a collection of stories, and direct or sentimental modes of expression. These texts revolve around relationships with men: the love or hatred of men, and the burden of the restrictions they dictate or the hardship of losing them. In the worst cases, these texts seem set outside history, denying it and its contradictions and presenting male-female relationships as if they are not governed by historical conditions. Despite their modest value, some of these texts successfully depict women's alienated, besieged existence, although, in my opinion, they are often complicit in it and reinforce it by making male-female relationships their sole subject.

Both well-written and less well-crafted stories give voice to a sense of alienation and the fear of a constant threat; in some cases, these emotions become a sense of total isolation or an inescapable nightmarish existence. Dreams are reduced to small wishes, although they preserve their huge value precisely because they are so impossibly out of reach.

*

In the late 1960s, Ghassan Kanafani presented the writers of the occupied territories with the publication of his *Adab al-muqawama fi Filistin al-muhtalla* (The Literature of Resistance in Occupied Palestine).[30] This was followed by many other texts published across the Arab world that reflected joyous astonishment at discovering the literature of resistance that had emerged under the occupation and the hegemony of the Hebrew state. Arab readers took note of a set of fine poets, short-story writers, and novelists and were made aware of several prominent writers who would leave their mark on Arabic literature, perhaps the most important of them being Mahmoud Darwish and Emile Habibi. Neither Ghassan Kanafani nor any of the other critics writing on "the literature of the occupied territories" made any mention of women writers. Was this simply an oversight? Or are they excused by the fact that women writers in the occupied territories from the 1960s to the 1990s were unable to make their presence felt and did not produce enough, in quantity and quality, to bring themselves widespread Arab acknowledgement? Answering this question may require a full-length study that takes into consideration the reality of Palestinian women inside that part of Palestine occupied in 1948. We can note here that most of those who remained on their land, with the exception of the residents of Acre and Nazareth, were a rural population living in villages, where opportunities for girls' education were limited.

In his two-part work, *Antulujiyat al-qissa al-'Arabiya fi Isra'il 1948–1998* (The Arabic Story in Israel 1948–1998: An Anthology) 1987,[31] Habib Bulus includes seventy-one short-story writers in that part of Palestine occupied in 1948, among them nine women writers of three generations. There is Najwa Kawar Farah, born in 1920, who began writing and publishing before 1948. There is the generation born in the 1950s, most prominently Fatima Dhiyab and Shawqiya 'Uruq, and there is the third generation, born in the late 1960s and early 1970s, including Raja' Bakriya and Jacqueline Haddad. In his introduction, Bulus notes that "realism . . . was the school that encompassed most of these stories," and this is true for both male and female writers. A direct, expository style is prominent in the stories of many women writers, especially those belonging to the generation of the 1950s and 1960s. The stories address social situations and focus on women's lives and their problems; the narrator is usually a woman and so is the main character. Although younger writers continue to focus on women's experiences, their texts show a greater mastery of the tools of the craft and are thus distinguished by multiple levels of meaning, a fast pace, and overlapping time frames.

Autobiography

In 1947, the Cairo-based *al-Hilal* asked several Arab writers, men and women, How can one live contentedly? Among those who responded was Kulthum Nasr 'Awda, a professor of Arabic literature in the Soviet Union. Despite its brevity, her response is remarkable and is perhaps the first example of autobiographical writing by a Palestinian woman. Kulthum 'Awda was born in Nazareth in 1892 and was educated at the city's Russian school. She later married a Russian physician and went to Russia with him during the First World War.

She writes:

> I was born the fifth daughter in a family that longed for a boy with a mentality forged over seventy-three years . . . You can imagine the sort of reception I received that day . . . tears . . . My father's hatred stayed with me . . . I was dark-skinned, a fact held against me, and they called me "blackie." I became such an introvert that everyone in our house began to call me "the silent miss." I dedicated myself to learning, despite my father's wishes.
>
> I ran away from home to marry a Russian physician, and my father only forgave me years later . . . I traveled to Russia with my husband in 1914. The Great War erupted while we were on the waters of the Bosporus. As soon as I set foot on Russian soil I began to learn the nursing profession. When I completed my studies, I went to Serbia, and from there to the Black Mountain. After the retreat of the Russian army, I went via Albania to France, then to Norway and Finland and on to Russia. Six years after I was married, my husband died, leaving me with three children, the eldest aged three and the youngest two months . . . and leaving me alone in a strange environment. How did I feel that day?
>
> I was in the thick of the war in the Balkans and Russia, but wasn't I happy to nurse every soldier or relieve his pain . . . ? I taught . . . I visited the peasants in their homes . . . I treated them . . . I treated their children's eyes . . . I worked hard to feed myself and my three children. I rented four feddans of land to plant, and I did plant them, walking behind the reapers to gather the wheat tassels.[32]

Kulthum 'Awda continues:

> When my husband died, I heard one of the women teachers walking behind me in the funeral procession say to her companion, How miserable this woman must be. Now she has

no other choice but to carry a beggar's bag and go knocking on doors. She is a stranger with no helpmate and her children make it difficult for her to work, especially the young two-month-old girl . . . And she only arrived in this village three days ago. When my husband was alive, I did not work and they only knew me as my husband's wife. But no more than six months had passed until that same teacher told me, You're so happy and contented. I wonder what the reason for my happiness is? . . .

At every stage of my life, I have worked willingly, not despite myself . . . I only find comfort when I surmount difficulties . . . I was never ashamed of any sort of work, as long as it did not dishonor me or someone else. Finally, the great Orientalist Krachkovski taught me many lovely things about my people that I did not know, and I grew happier in the hope that we Arabs must have a future that is no less glorious than our past.[33]

*

One is struck by the links between Fadwa Tuqan's autobiography, *Rihla sa'ba rihla jabaliya (A Mountainous Journey)* 1985 and Najmiya Hikmat's (b. 1920) autobiography *65 'aman min hayat imra'a Urduniya: rihlati ma'a al-zaman* (Sixty-five Years in the Life of a Jordanian Woman: My Journey with Time) 1986. The two texts are incredibly complementary and engage in an implicit dialogue. The 1920s in Palestine; the 1920s in Jordan. A girl from Nablus born a year before the end of the First World War, and a girl who arrived in Jordan from Damascus in the early 1920s before she was even two years old. Both are forced to leave school at almost the same age, then their paths split. At age fourteen, Najmiya Hikmat was married off to a Jordanian army officer of Syrian origin; her creative energies found no outlet but inside the home, and she used them to raise her children.

In reading both texts, there is the pleasure of following the dialectic between the author's absence and her presence: how Fadwa Tuqan declared her presence with her first collection of poetry and her presence in cultural life, and how Najmiya Hikmat disappears into the details of her preordained life. She seems to be absent, but suddenly, in her sixties, she breaks her silence and seclusion to tell her story.

Both texts evince a keen sense of injustice. In Fadwa Tuqan's book, the house is stifling despite its spaciousness and cannot contain the energies of a growing child brimming with life and vitality. It is a metaphor of social reality:

The house is one of the most ancient of the old Nablus houses, reminding one of the palaces of the harem, adapted architecturally to the needs of the feudal system. In it could be seen arches, vaults, wide courtyards, gardens, water fountains, upper chambers and spiral staircases. . . .

In this house, within its high walls that shut off the harem society from the outside world, where it was buried alive, my oppressed childhood, girlhood and a great part of my youth were spent.

The man dominated family life, as in all homes of our society. The woman had to forget that the word 'no' existed in the language, except when she repeated, 'There is no god but God,' . . .

The right to express her feelings or views was prohibited. Laughing and singing were also taboo and could be indulged in only secretly, after the men, the lords and masters, left for work. Personal independence was a concept foreign to a woman all her life.[34]

Her brother Ibrahim notices her interest in poetry and begins to teach her, returning her to the world of notebooks and pens: "I was returning to my lost paradise."[35] She writes:

The words I had written in my bad handwriting on the cover of the exercise book for material to memorise caught my eye. It was the handwriting of the thirteen-year-old pupil:

Name – Fadwa Tuqan
Class – (I crossed out this word, writing in its place: Teacher – Ibrahim Tuqan)
Subject – Learning Poetry
School – The House.[36]

Ibrahim will teach her poetry before his untimely death. Her father expects her to write political poetry to fill the gap left by Ibrahim, but "how and with what right or logic does Father ask me to compose political poetry, when I am shut up inside these walls?"[37] She cries out of helplessness or rebels in protest, but in both cases her introversion increases. She stops writing, but "when the roof fell in on Palestine" in 1948 and with the death of her father the same year, Fadwa returned to writing (in these years, too, women in Nablus were taking off their veils; they had been preceded years earlier by women in Jerusalem, Haifa, and Jaffa). She writes patriotic and love poetry: " . . . my reaction to politics was no longer lacking. Although it was not strong, it still swayed me at different times, but lacked the quality of permanence. It would catch fire, on certain occasions, when things were inflamed, then die down when things were calm."[38] She writes, "Thus my poetry writing remained bound to my unpredictable moods. I did not experience a lasting sense of reality, nor an abiding emotional attachment to the communal cause, until after the June [1967] War."[39]

Najmiya Hikmat says, "It was decreed that I be deprived of education and stay at home because I had passed the age of twelve." She continues:

> After I was prevented from completing my education, I would devour books whole. I had nothing else to occupy me . . . and entertain me but books and reading. I read everything, even the papers that storms would blow into our garden or those the vendors used to wrap up their fruits, meats, and vegetables. As soon as I entered the house of a friend or relative, I would look around me to see if there were any books. My estimation of them would increase or diminish depending on how many books and magazines they possessed.[40]

There is a striking similarity here with Fadwa Tuqan:

> I read, so I exist. I continued to be a voracious reader and this voracity heightened my sense of deprivation from academic studies. Someone with high ambitions comes to harbour feelings of bitterness, arising from that vacuum left in the soul by being deprived when young of the chance to study. She becomes a bookworm.[41]

We return to Najmiya Hikmat, after her family brought her a violin:

> With much patience and practice I was able . . . to grasp the violin bow, pluck its strings, and play with full mastery . . .
> But how did I learn? And where did I play? It was taboo and sinful for the sound of musical instruments to be heard outside the house . . . When I played, I would first tightly shut the windows and doors and make for an interior room, so that the sound would not reach passersby on the street.
> I would often take the opportunity offered by rainy, stormy nights, when the melody would disappear into the sound of the wind and rain. Then I played freely, confident that there were no people or passersby, and no blame and reproach from my siblings and mother.[42]

The value of *Rihlati ma'a al-zaman* does not solely reside in the narrative of the oppression experienced by many of our mothers and grandmothers—

despite its centrality in the text—nor in the author's ability to convey this sense with affecting ease. It also lies in the care the author takes to describe places and record and document the details of a particular social reality. Najmiya Hikmat writes her autobiography and the biography of the places she saw in the 1920s and 1930s: Amman, Jarash, al-Karak, Ma'an, al-Tafila, al-'Aqaba, and Idlib, near Aleppo—all places in which she lived with her family or moved to with her husband. The pressing desire to capture the features of a disappearing world make the text a biography of place as much as the autobiography of a woman who lived on its margins, although as the wife of a senior officer she belonged to the upper echelons of Jordanian society.

Autobiography is not well-represented in Arab women's literature; the number of texts can almost be counted on the fingers of both hands. Fadwa Tuqan presents her story in the Palestinian context in the first half of the twentieth century. Her autobiography has double significance: she gives us the life of a pioneering Palestinian writer and documents the life of Palestine itself over seven decades of the twentieth century. I believe that Najmiya Hikmat's text is the first, and perhaps the only autobiography by a Jordanian woman. The book has a historical value in addition to the pleasure we feel as we come to know the stubborn insistence to maintain and realize the dream of reading and writing, even at the end of one's life.

*

We will move to two texts linked by one event: the Israeli invasion of Lebanon in 1982, as documented by Palestinian poet Mayy Sayigh and Jordanian physician Fathieh Saudi, both of whom lived and worked in Beirut. Mayy was the director of the al-Sumud children's home, a facility for the children of martyrs. Fathieh was a pediatrician. Both wrote their texts in the form of a diary.

Fathieh Saudi's work was first published in French as *L'oubli rebelle* (1985) and later in Arabic as *Ayyam al-jamr: hisar Bayrut 1982* (Days of Embers: The 1982 Siege of Beirut) 1990. The book contains diary entries from June 4 until her stay in Paris, where she went after the massacre of Sabra and Shatila in the fall of 1982. She records her experiences as a citizen and doctor in a Beirut besieged by the shelling, fires, and a shortage of water, food, and medical supplies. The text has its own aesthetic; its eloquence resides in its simple, moving style, both profound and remarkably sweet. She records the day's events and the reflections they inspire.

Mayy Sayigh's *al-Hisar* (The Siege) 1988, also takes the form of a diary, although hers uses a more rhetorical style to express her feelings. The book opens with an introduction, entitled "Beirut," followed by the diary entries, the first one documenting the first day of the invasion, June 6, 1982, and the last, August 26, 1982, the day she left the city with the fighters. The text describes events and some of the more significant statements that appeared in the press. With varying degrees of success, she blends the documentary form with a lyrical expression of her feelings about the experience. She often pauses to quote at length from a poem or even to include an entire poem. The book ends with a poetic epilogue entitled, "The Departure."

Al-Hisar links two separate experiences: the invasion of Beirut in 1982 and the Israeli occupation of Gaza in 1956.

Gaza, 1956:

They came at night. My mother hid me under the bed. They arrested all the young men of the family, then they arrested my cousin and my brother. They put out their cigarettes in his flesh. They plucked out his fingernails and flayed his back with whips, clubs, and the butts of rifles. They only stopped beating him when he passed out. He was young and thin and they showed no mercy on him . . . [after the brother's release] . . . My mother made a risky decision, preferring to see my brother and me drown than to fall in the hands of the enemy: she arranged for a fisherman to take us to Egyptian territory.

We hid in a cemetery on the beach, and when night fell, the sailor lit a small lamp. We ran toward it and plunged into the icy water up to our breasts to reach the small fishing boat. He indicated that we should stick to the bottom of the boat to avoid the intermittent enemy searchlights on the water's surface . . . [43]

Beirut, 1982:

Another raid and more planes. The young girl has become a woman of forty responsible for protecting children at the Sumud House. On the first day of the invasion, the shelling hits the house and throws the children into a panic. They have no refuge save the bodies of "the substitute mothers" and they cling to their clothes. Ahmad knows the raids very well: they killed his parents in Tyre. He came to al-Sumud House with his younger siblings, a girl not yet one and a three-year-old boy. His parents were killed in Tyre. Ahmad asks:
"Are you afraid?"
The planes are far away, I respond. But I am afraid. I love our house and I'm afraid they'll destroy it. If they destroy it, where will I go?[44]

Unexpectedly, the poetry of the work is not found in the poems cited in its pages, nor in the lyrical expression of the feelings of pain, anger, and bitterness, but in these powerful scenes.

Conclusion

Palestinian women have contributed to writing since the first decades of the twentieth century. This writing was limited to published or broadcast articles, and a few poems, stories, or plays, which were only very rarely given the opportunity to become actual productions. The most prominent writers before 1948 include Asma Tubi in the essay, poetry, and drama; Fadwa Tuqan in poetry; and Najwa Kawar Farah in the short story.

Jordanian women writers appeared later; with a few exceptions—newspaper articles and a text attributed to a woman but likely written by a man—it is difficult to write a history of Jordanian women's writing before the 1970s, when Jùlia Sawalha published her novels and the short story began to emerge. Thérèse Haddad published her first short-story collection, *Hatta naltaqi* (Until We Meet) in 1973 and her second collection, *al-Tahdiq fi malamih al-ghurba* (Scrutinizing the Features of Exile) in 1975.

The Palestinian *nakba* of 1948 was a pivotal event in the modern history of the Arabs, their culture, and their literature. Zionists occupied the greater part of Palestine, while the remaining part was annexed to the eastern bank of the Jordan River under the rule of the Hashemite family and Egypt assumed administrative responsibility for the Gaza Strip. Like the Palestinian people, Palestinian writers were divided into several categories: writers of the occupied territories (those carrying Israeli passports), Jordanians, or Palestinians living in Arab countries or abroad. Najwa Kawar Farah, who lived in Nazareth until the early 1960s, became a writer from the occupied territories, carrying an Israeli passport; Fadwa Tuqan, residing in Nablus in the West Bank, had a Jordanian passport and is often referred to as a Jordanian writer; Samira 'Azzam lived in Beirut, where she published all her short-story collections. The dispossession imbued Palestinian literature, by both men and women, with an active core, and it constituted a major theme of Palestinian poetry throughout the 1950s and 1960s. Novels by Palestinian women that appeared in the second half of the 1950s speak of the dispossession and tell some aspect of the story. The early examples were in keeping with the general concerns of the Arabic novel, and its preoccupation with the historical despite their literary shortcomings. Palestinian women's novels continued their engagement with history in better-crafted texts after 1967. Starting in the 1970s, and continuing in the 1980s and 1990s, Sahar Khalifeh, Liyana Badr, Salwa al-Banna, Leila al-Atrash, and others started to write novels examining various aspects of Palestinian life at home or in the diaspora, and confronting the injustice of the occupying powers, social backwardness and its contradictions, and corruption. Often in these novels, the narrators are women who speak of some aspect of collective experience, or women are central characters whose destinies we follow as they intertwine with the fate of other characters. We see women in their formative years or engaged in politics, as daughters, mothers, lovers, besieged in a refugee camps, yielding both figuratively and literally. These novels take us to the various places inhabited by Palestinians: the West Bank, Amman, Beirut, the Gulf, refugee camps, universities, and guerilla training camps. The novels may use a realism that relies on plot, panoramic views of several characters from various social classes, and an omniscient narrator who knows the details of their lives and fates, or the writing style may focus on the moment and speak in the first person, mixing time frames and using the stream of conciousness technique and documentary testimonies.

The 1990s witnessed the emergence of the novel in Jordan; with its documentary and historical concerns, it follows the general course of Arabic novel. Zahra 'Umar wrote the first Arabic novel about the Circassians and their migration to Jordan. Samiha Khurays wrote a generational novel, telling the story of a family from Irbid, as well as a historical novel about the Arab revolt.

The short story made qualitative leaps at the hands of Samira 'Azzam in the 1950s; she must take credit for establishing the foundations of the art in Palestinian literature. 'Azzam wrote realist stories about Palestinian concerns, although they were not limited to this theme. She wrote about men and women, the injustice of being uprooted from one's homeland, the oppression of poverty, and the human being toiling away in an alienating world, trying to realize his small hopes. 'Azzam paved the way for generations of women story writers, giving them a legacy to speak to, add to, or modify, whether they continued the tradition of realist fiction or broke with it to open new horizons, addressing the individual's relationship with the self and the Other, both male and female, and throwing the door open to history, whether to engage with it or to depict the feelings of alarm, fear, oppression, and incapacity arising from it. The 1980s and 1990s saw the emergence of an unprecedented number of Palestinian and Jordanian women short-story writers, some of whose texts followed familiar forms, while others were more experimental. In the last decade of the twentieth century, women writers inside the part of Palestine occupied in 1948 wrote stories that went beyond the directness that prevailed in previous decades. These texts indicate that these writers have now mastered the craft and possess the ability to forge complex perspectives.

In poetry, Fadwa Tuqan was the most prominent woman writer in Palestine and Jordan for more than half a century, but she had contemporaries and was followed by two generations of poets whose writings ranged from the classical *qasida* form to free verse to prose poetry. Poetic themes ran the gamut from political to emotional, employed direct expression and more complex forms, and included anthems glorifying the liberation movement as well as more introspective poems reflecting fragmentation and disintegration.

Although pioneering women writers in Palestine wrote plays and drama before 1948—for example, Asma Tubi, who started writing plays in 1925; Hadiya 'Abd al-Hadi, who wrote several texts published in Damascus after 1948; and Najwa Kawar Farah, who published two plays in Nazareth, in 1958 and 1961—drama is relatively underrepresented compared to other literary genres. This is quite understandable given the lack of a theater movement and the institutions necessary to foster its growth. As a result, with few exceptions plays remained written texts, trapped between the covers of a book. Some women poets, novelists, and short-story writers have also written dramas, but only a very few writers have devoted themselves entirely to playwriting, among them Maysun Hanna in Jordan and Samiya Qazmuz Bakri from 1948 Palestine, an actress who has published one play, *al-Zarub* (The Narrow Lane) 1998, a monodrama in which she performed.

Many poets, novelists, and short-story writers have also written children's literature, although, again, very few have devoted themselves exclusively to it. The few who have include Rawda al-Farkh Hudhud, most of whose stories touch on national issues and historical events. She has written children's books on Kafr Qasim and Dayr Yasin, 'Izz al-Din Qassam and Shaykh Hasan Salama, and the heroes of the 1936 revolt and the armed struggle. Munira Shurayh, a Palestinian who lives in Jordan, also writes children's theater.

Although there are very few autobiographies by Arab women, women from Palestine and Jordan have given us some of the most important of these; some deal with the author's entire life (the autobiographies of Fadwa Tuqan and Najmiya Hikmat) while others document a particular experience (the works of Mayy Sayigh and Fathieh Saudi on the invasion of Lebanon).

In closing, it should be noted that the nature of this rapid perusal of the achievements of women writers in Palestine and Jordan has imposed a degree of brevity and sometimes outright abridgement; similarly, it has meant that Palestine and Jordan have been dealt with singly at times and as one unit at others as a result of the special relation between the two countries.

Notes

1 See the map in *Milaff watha'iq Filistin* (Cairo: State Information Service, 1969), pt. 1, p. 195.

2 Ibid., p. 203.

3 'Izzat Daraghima, *al-Haraka al-nisa'iya fi Filistin 1903–1990* (Jerusalem: Maktab Diya' li-l-Dirasat, 1991), pp. 40–41.

4 Fadwa Tuqan, *Rihla sa'ba rihla jabaliya* (Acre: Dar al-Aswar, 1985), p. 132.

5 The Buraq Uprising (1929) touched various parts of Palestine. It lasted several days following clashes between Jews and Muslims at the Western Wall of al-Aqsa Mosque during the commemoration of the Prophet Muhammad's miraculous night journey from Mecca to Jerusalem.

6 *Al-Mawsu'a al-Filistiniya* (Damascus: Hay'at al-Mawsu'a al-Filistiniya, 1984), vol. 4, p. 380.

7 Fadwa Tuqan, *Rihla sa'ba*, p. 132; translated into English as *A Mountainous Journey: An Autobiography*, trans. by Olive Kenny; poetry trans. by Naomi Shihab Nye with the help of Salma Khadra Jayyusi (St. Paul, MN: Graywolf Press, 1990), p. 110.

8 Sati' al-Husri in *al-Thaqafa al-'Arabiya*, pp. 50–51, cited in Kamal Mustafa al-Shaykh Ahmad al-Fahmawi, *Adab al-mar'a al-Filistiniya al-hadith: 1914–1974*, Ph.D. dissertation, al-Azhar University, 1979, p. 20.

9 'Abd al-Latif al-Tibi, *al-Ta'lim al-'Arabi fi Filistin taht al-intidab*, cited in Kamal al-Fahmawi, *Adab al-mar'a al-Filistiniya*, p. 26. Also see Sarah Graham-Brown, *Images of Women: The Portrayal of Women in Photography of the Middle East 1860–1950* (London: Quartet Books, 1988).

10 Suhayr Salti al-Tall, *Muqaddimat hawl qadiyat al-mar'a wa-l-haraka al-nisa'iya fi-l-Urdun* (Beirut: Arab Institute for Research and Publishing, 1985), pp. 52 and 65.

11 Ibid., p. 126.

12 See Kamal al-Fahmawi, *Adab al-mar'a al-Filistiniya*, and Usama Yusuf Muhammad Shihab, *Adab al-mar'a fi Filistin wa-l-Urdun: 1948–1988*, Ph.D. dissertation, Ain Shams University, 1991, two volumes.

13 Kamal al-Fahmawi, *Adab al-mar'a al-Filistiniya*, p. 301.

14 Usama Shihab, *Adba al-mar'a fi Filistin*, p. 623.

15 Ibid.

16 Ibid., p. 393.

17 *Ayna humat al-fadila* (Amman: Dar al-Jazira Press and Publications, 1985).

18 Usama Shihab, *Adba al-mar'a fi Filistin*, p. 664.

19 Fadwa Tuqan, *Rihla sa'ba*, pp. 88–89, and *A Mountainous Journey*, pp. 72–73.

20 Literature produced by Lebanese immigrants in North and South America in the early decades of the twentieth century. Mahjar writers such as Gibran Kahlil Gibran, Iliya Abu Madi, Mikha'il Nu'ayma, and Amin Rihani contributed substantially to the innovation of modern Arabic poetry and prose.

21 Fadwa Tuqan, *Rihla sa'ba*, p. 91, and *A Mountainous Journey*, p. 74.

22 Fadwa Tuqan, *Rihla sa'ba*, p. 92, and *A Mountainous Journey*, p. 75.

23 Ayman al-Qadi, *al-Riwaya al-nisawiya fi bilad al-Sham: al-simat al-nafsiya wa-l-fanniya 1950–1985* (Damascus: Dar al-Ahali Press and Publishing, 1992), p. 303.

24 Zahra 'Umar, *al-Khuruj min Susruqa: riwayat al-shatat al-Sharkasi* (Amman: Dar al-Azmina, 1993), p. 11.

25 Ibid., p. 87.

26 Ibid., p. 53.

27 "Al-Taghrid kharij al-sirb al-nisa'i," in *al-Hurriya fi adab al-mar'a* (Beirut: Arab Research Institute, 1985, second edition), p. 203.

28 Ibid., pp. 203–204.

29 Ibid., p. 205.

30 Ghassan Kanafani, *Adab al-muqawama fi Filistin al-muhtalla: 1948–1966* (Beirut: Dar al-Adab, n.d.).

31 Habib Bulus, *Antulujiyat al-qissa al-'Arabiya fi Isra'il 1948–1998* (Sakhnin: Academic College, the Galilee Center, 1999), second edition; first edition published in Nazareth: al-Maktaba al-Sha'biya and Shafa 'Amr: Dar al-Mashriq, 1987.

32 Usama Shihab, *Adba al-mar'a fi Filistin*, pp. 700–701.

33 Ibid.

34 Fadwa Tuqan, *Rihla sa'ba*, p. 40, and *A Mountainous Journey*, p. 36.

35 Fadwa Tuqan, *Rihla sa'ba*, p. 69, and *A Mountainous Journey*, p. 58.

36 Fadwa Tuqan, *Rihla sa'ba*, p. 70, and *A Mountainous Journey*, p. 58.

37 Fadwa Tuqan, *Rihla sa'ba*, p. 131, and *A Mountainous Journey*, p. 107.

38 Fadwa Tuqan, *Rihla sa'ba*, p. 137, and *A Mountainous Journey*, p. 113.

39 Fadwa Tuqan, *Rihla sa'ba*, p. 152, and *A Mountainous Journey*, pp. 125–26.

40 Najmiya Hikmat, *65 'aman min hayat imra'a Urduniya: rihlati ma'a al-zaman* (Amman: privately published, 1986), p. 47.

41 Fadwa Tuqan, *Rihla sa'ba*, p. 153, and *A Mountainous Journey*, p. 126.

42 Najmiya Hikmat, *65 'aman min hayat imra'a Urduniya*, p. 48.

43 Mayy Sayigh, *al-Hisar* (Beirut: Arab Institute for Research and Publishing, 1988), pp. 53–54.

44 Ibid., p. 23.

7 Arab North Africa

Mohammed Berrada

Introduction

It is not necessary here to delve into the history of Arab North Africa in the twentieth century, its colonization, and the attempts to displace its national cultures and language.[1] Rather, we hope to stick close to the topic at hand: a review of the contributions of North African women writers to literature of all types written in Arabic and an examination of the distinguishing features of their contributions. Nevertheless, we must pause at certain factors that have had a special impact on the literature of North African women. First and foremost, we must note the disparities in the literary age of various regions in North Africa—that is, the different points at which they first opened up to foreign cultures and literatures and began to use modern forms of expression to give voice to the many changes experienced by Arab societies during the colonial and post-colonial periods. As literary experience accumulates, it encourages an exploration of new ground and the evolution of a new kind of literature freed from tradition, or a revival of models inspired by the great works of the past. This is clearly a historical process, and its consequences are illustrated in the relatively older literary age of Egypt, Syria, Lebanon, and Iraq when compared to the literary ages of Sudan, Libya, Algeria, Morocco, and Mauritania.

Here we are interested in linking this issue with the relatively late emergence of modern literary forms in Arab North Africa—delayed until the 1950s—and the ramifications for North African women writers. The relatively slow pace of literary accretion, as well as problems of education and Arabization after independence, was a factor in the slow emergence of women who turned to literature to address their circumstances and give voice to the self, forcibly displaced from all arenas of participation and expression. Other reasons, largely social, have compounded the problem; until very recently, North African societies did not have a favorable view of women who used literature as a means of making their voices heard and revealing the hidden things in their subjugated souls. The seeds of North African women's literature were sown as education became more accessible to girls, both during the periods of national anti-colonial struggles and in the post-independence eras when they entered universities. In addition, voices from women's liberation movements in the Arab East—Qasim Amin, Huda Sha'rawi, 'A'isha al-Taymuriya, Doria Shafik, Mayy Ziyada—always echoed across North Africa.

The first appearance of North African women writers was bound up with the appearance of national liberation movements and their social concerns. Educated women were always present at assemblies and celebrations to provide "the women's word" or recite poetry, usually neo-classical *qasida* poems (Arabian odes) glorifying the nation and its struggles. In this first phase, which lasted until the late 1950s, the few women's texts that exist do not go beyond national concerns and related social issues; as a consequence they are marked by a didactic realism aimed at shoring up morale and critiquing social ills. This is the case with the early works of Malika al-Fasi from Morocco, Khadija 'Abd al-Hayy from Mauritania, and Zuhur Wannisi from Algeria. While the works of North African male writers, including poets like al-Shabbi, Idris al-Jay, Muhammad al-Halwa, and Ramadan Mahmud, began to expand their concerns beyond national issues and draw on subjective experience and romantic themes and modes, circumstances did not yet allow for women writers' self-expression, particularly emotional expression.

After independence—Tunisia and Morocco in 1956, Mauritania in 1960, Algeria in 1962, and Libya in 1963—girls' education flourished, and women gradually came to occupy certain positions of responsibility. But the struggle over questions about the future and nature of North African societies clearly brought to light the male monopoly of authority and its institutions. The absence of democracy contributed greatly to sharpening the consciousness of the marginalized and highlighting class and social gaps between those men and women who had sacrificed for independence and those who benefited from it at the expense of the majority. In other words, the transition from a national consensus during the struggle against colonialism to the post-independence struggle for social justice and democracy convinced North African women of the need to forge their own voice to expose their reduced circumstances, the restrictions of male paternalism, and the law's erosion of their rights. This time, women's consciousness assumed a multi-dimensional form; it did not stop at the limits drawn by nationalist parties or, in the case of Algeria, revolutionary organizations. North African women no longer found themselves and their demands represented in the policies of post-independence governments, and voices began to be heard here and there, particularly from women educated in Europe and the Arab East. These voices began to break the dominance of traditional discourses or those that submerged the particularity of the women's cause in abstract demands to change or "revolutionize" society.

Since the late 1960s, women writers have appeared in Arab North Africa who no longer want their works to simply echo prevailing ideologies and discourses. The stories of Khunatha Bannuna and Rafiqat al-Tabi'a in Morocco have a different tone. We also have the poems of Mabruka Bu Saha, Ahlam Mosteghanemi, and Zaynab al-A'waj in Algeria, the poetry and novels of Fawziya Shlabi in Libya, and the stories of 'Arusiya al-Naluti and Na'ima al-Sayd in Tunisia. The features of North African women, previously hidden in the folds of political discourses, began to take shape in texts that addressed women's depths, emotions, moods, dreams, and stifled rebellions. In other words, North African women's literary discourse has illuminated and continues to illuminate women as real people, not merely as simultaneously exemplary and degraded symbols.

Since 1967, the best examples of modern Arabic literature as a whole have distanced themselves from explicit politics and ideological propaganda and have taken to revealing what is unsaid or concealed in dominant discourses. As such, there has been greater interest in the aesthetic conception and composition that enable literary works to rise above fleeting circumstances. Since the 1970s, several North African women writers have chosen this sort of writing, which allows greater self-expression, particularity of vision, and the freedom to experiment. Within this framework, however, there is much variation among writers in terms of the sophistication of the texts and the regularity with which they are produced

Keeping in mind the factors that distinguish North African women's writing in Arabic, we shall review and analyze several texts—poetry, short stories, and novels—to highlight their general features and artistic expressions. We shall not exclude traditional texts of limited sophistication, since understanding the changes in women's writing requires us to highlight the differences in form and content across the corpus of North African women's literature as a whole.

Poetry

A quick reading of the poetry of North African women reveals two major types: traditional, classical poems in the *qasida* form, and modern poetry that uses meter instead of the classical hemistich form or employs prose to render more closely the rush of emotion and sentiment, although poets are successful to varying degrees within these forms.

The first type includes the poetry of Habiba al-Sufi, Khadija ʻAbd al-Hayy, al-Sayyida Bint Ahmad, Amina al-Marini, Fawziya Haram Dayf Allah, and Imbaraka Bint al-Buraʾ. Although the last relies on meter, the structure and content of her poems are closer to the classical *qasida*. We shall examine examples of poems that represent these different trends and concerns.

In Habiba al-Sufi's poem, "Baʻd al-taʻafi" (Post-Recovery), the poet chides a friend who has reopened a wound she thought had healed: the experience of a failed love. Her reproach tells us that she is still attached to her lover and cannot forget him, even after her recovery. Despite its classical theme, the poem is imbued with a romanticism that depicts a woman who is absolutely, even unwillingly faithful, despite her claims that she has recovered from love.

Khadija ʻAbd al-Hayy's "Najwa al-asil" (Plaint of the Noble) gives us a voice remembering a dream that briefly shone in her life only to leave bitterness and anger in its wake. These feelings are reflected in the language of the classical poem, as it moves from contemplations, to truisms and maxims, to anger:

> Soothing draughts only increase our suffering
> No matter how long we sit alone among the ruins.

"Ta'ammaltu fatah halima" (I Pondered a Dreaming Girl), by al-Sayyida Bint Ahmad, illustrates the classical reliance on proverbs and truisms that efface the details of experience and the particularity of emotion:

> Such is the law of life: a ship,
> Its passengers without a grip on the helm,
> A road between pain and song,
> A battle between thorn and rose.

"Ta'awwuhat wa mawajid" (Lamentations and Glories), by Fawziya Haram Dayf Allah, begins with heartache and complaints of the torment of love, and ends up mourning an Arab civilization that has lost its glory. What are indeed lamentations are expressed in an emotive, facile language whose tone vacillates between grief and anger:

> Gather up your wounds and write a story in blood
> Collect your scattered self, my grief will retreat.
> . . .
> Oh heart, set fire to these flames of longing.
> Let me be, for storms of rage fill the heart's crevices.

If these poets blend pain and anger to express their disappointment in love and people, Amina al-Marini turns to Sufism to mix feelings of love with the spirit's desire for immortality and fusion with the ineffable—that higher thing that does not die. In "'Ashiqa" (Lover), she references Ibn Zaydun's (d. 1071) famous poem, "Adha al-tana'i badilan 'an tadanina" (Distance Replaced Our Nearness), while moving into the realm of Sufism:

In the presence of passion the spirit rises, drawn by
a flood of light that challenges bonds and clay.
It ascends and is united in goodness, effaced,
like perfume infused with basil and wild rose.[2]

Al-Marini is able to transform Ibn Zaydun's language and images into a spiritual lexicon that transcends the mortal pains of human love. It is a poem that has absorbed the modes of the classical *qasida* and its Andalusian romantic flavor.

In the second type of poetry, free verse or prose poems, we encounter individual experience, with each poet seeking to give voice to it through the use of detail and a language free from classical topoi and stock images. Poets of this school include Malika al-'Asimi, Najah Hadda, Fatima Mahmud, Zaynab al-A'waj, Rabi'a Jalti, Wafa' al-'Amrani, Thuraya Majdulin, Fadhila Chabbi, Ghaniya Sayyid 'Uthman, and al-Zuhra al-Mansuri.

Among these poems, two of them by Malika al-'Asimi are particularly striking—"al-Qasida al-mas'ura" (The Rabid Poem) and "Ziyarat al-faris al-qadim" (The Visit of the Ancient Knight)—because they suggest another horizon for women poets who want to make their voices heard and speak of their intimate feelings without false modesty or a romanticism that conceals carnal desires.[3] Malika al-'Asimi is perhaps one of the first Arab women poets to take the "woman's" poem to a zone of intimacy and bold introspection. She began to publish in the late 1960s as the modern poem made its presence felt in the Arab East and among pioneering North African poets like Ahmad al-Majati, Muhammad al-Sarghini, and 'Abd al-Karim al-Tabbal. Even now, Malika al-'Asimi continues to observe the interesting, confused, and usually impossible bonds between man and woman and between burning carnal desire and grief tinged by burning emotion.

In the same vein is Fatima Mahmud's "Dhabdhaba miqdaruha anta" (A Vibration the Size of You). It is a poem by a "complete" woman who observes her emotions and rebellion on all levels, starting with the body and love and ending with barriers that deaden the senses and bring loneliness and a longing for a lover who can reshape her:

My limbs are emptying themselves of you.
Something gently pulls you from

my marrow and stuffs me
with loneliness.
The winds come,
their emptiness rolling along,
and sweep me up like a field of ashes.

"Shizufriniya" (Schizophrenia), by Rabi'a Jalti, is perhaps an accurate diagnosis of the condition of the modern Arab woman who has rejected taboo, paternalism, and silence to face a tumultuous, terrifying world governed by patriarchy and the power of stifling tradition. The poem's female voice declares that she has been split in two in order to enable her to continue to exist amid the contradictions and coercions. The poet lives between two worlds, between the original and a copy of the lost original:

I have become two streets.
One looks over the apricot trees and narcissus,
and the morning of poems.
It enters the seas of language.
And the other
is he whose name is hung on the horizon and the color of bread,
whose face has fenced in all directions,
whose breaths have sealed all circles.
It nearly chokes me.[4]

The voice of Ghaniya Sayyid 'Uthman is frank and rebels against euphemism in her poem, "Atamada fi-l-balagha wa-l-samt" (I Push the Limits of Eloquence and Silence). She wants to expose herself and converse with what the body and memory conceal. In the beginning, she asks, "Do I have the right to love myself a little and speak a few flirtatious words?" As she recalls her dreams and her passion, she describes the relationship she would like to see between herself and her lover. Her words come in shrieking bursts:

A strange shiver takes hold of me/a mixture of joy and fear/approach/hesitation/your face disappears into the unknown. Your voice comes to me/piercing time and the tales of Sheherazade/I love you, come, my blue spring/Your gardens have produced apples and emeralds and stories I will write out of love for a twenty-eight-year-old child/her age is a breeze/her shade is exhausting, her shackles mind-boggling.

With Zaynab al-A'waj's poem, "Halat haml" (A Pregnancy), we leave the realm of self-exploration and its painful passion for a more comprehensive engagement with a reality characterized by deterioration, false values, and the burial of dreams:

> Blood is the parades
> in every square.
> Grief is the spaces
> burdening children with the heaviest slogans.
> A coffin there exploits funerals,
> they dressed it in blue and khaki
> and colors of darkness.
> What kind of democracy
> is the democracy of generals?[5]

Disappointment in the revolution of one million martyrs, as the war for Algerian independence is known, is also echoed in Najah Hadda's "Fi mawsim al-huzn al-mukaththaf" (In the Season of Intense Grief). The poem gives us dark, melancholic images, for things have not changed for the better and values continue to be eroded.

In "Maharib al-qamr" (The Moon's Prayer Niches), Jamila al-Majiri draws inspiration from the women of Qayrawan who weave beautiful carpets with a fascinating blend of colors that embodies their sensibilities, as if the carpets speak a language of love buried in their weavers' hearts as their voices chant their prayers in the moon's prayer niches:

> For the women of Qayrawan; when they speak in love riddles
> these talismanic wondrous twists come
> like knots that uttered things, but not in sin, for love
> has its own rules, its rituals described
> in ornament and incantation,
> a moon, a prayer niche, and Berber embroidery,
> maze upon maze[6]

With Wafa' al-'Amrani, Thuraya Majdulin, and al-Zuhra al-Mansuri we go back to the self, in its broadest, most profound sense; each of these poets plumbs the hidden, painful depths of the self that language can only encompass with difficulty. In "Fitnat al-aqasi" (The Seduction of Extremities), by Wafa' al-'Amrani, the poet faces herself and her explosive ambitions, which she wants to approach as easily as she approaches the images and words that give the text its existence.[7]

In contrast, Majdulin's voice is imbued with grief, distress, and longing. In "Jadhwat al-hulm" (The Dream's Firebrand), she tries to reclaim the final moments of a place that was flourishing and filled with her dreams and those of her loved ones. The poet observes the death of emotions and things, but she remembers the continuity of life when one clings to love, poetry, and dreams:

> Talk falls silent,
> the wonder of questions leaves my face,
> and the place remains quiet,
> like a seagull above.
> Suddenly it departs,
> suddenly it returns
> like the sun
> like the wind
> like tears.[8]

In the same vein, al-Zuhra al-Mansuri, in "Ghafwat al-ma'" (The Water's Slumber), gives us intertwined images of grief, loneliness, and a desire for love. In the poem a man addresses his lover, who has become a symbol of nature, existence, moments of waiting, and moments of transformation:

> Like the dead planted in the earth's flowerpots without revealing
> the bleeding of the dew, I travel in you.
> Perhaps I will become something other than myself.
> Perhaps I will again open up history and seek shelter in its sap,
> fenced in by names.
> . . .
> When I leave your body, blackened by isolation
> and exile,
> the dream seeps out of my walls . . . [9]

North African women's poetry can roughly be divided into poetry written in the classical mode, and free verse and prose poems. In the first type, the familiar themes of reproach, lamentation for the past, and patriotism are predominant. In the second type, women's voices seek to weave together details, illuminate subjective experience, and find a distinctive language. They express carnal desires, tortures of the spirit, and the melancholy of love. These poems do not deny the self; they are a declaration of the existence of North African women, made present through bold poetic expression that bears their own imprint instead of that of men writing on their behalf.

The short story

Among the twenty-four stories chosen as a representative sample of short-story trends in North Africa, more than ten are distinguished by their personal nature, their narrative variety, and the boldness of their subjects.

Other stories are more traditional, both in form and content, like the works of Malika al-Fasi, Najiya Thamir, Hayat Bint al-Shaykh, Fatima Salim, and Sharifa 'Arabawi. I will limit the analysis to stories defined by their experimental writing and their depiction of scenes and moments with existential dimensions that seek to expose the self and its hidden depths in the midst of changes and a troubled climate.

"Qabla an tutliq rasasat al-rahma" (The Bullet of Mercy), by Libyan Fatima Mahmud, is perhaps the most experimental story. Its structure is fragmented, overlapping, moving between distant spaces with an almost cinematic quality. The fragmented language, which alternates between an economic narrative and an associative poetic language, opens the story up to various elements and atmospheres. There are few elements in the story: a woman, the sultan's lover, looks out from a window on to the sea; a child, who asks odd, embarrassing questions; and a censor, who exercises his authority by monitoring immoral expressions that might offend the sultan's sensibilities. The use of the censor serves the writing style, achieving a cold, ironic tone that is consistent with the story's content, which rejects the objectification of women and their reduction to a source of pleasure.[10]

"Al-Masa' al-akhir" (The Last Evening), by Moroccan Khunatha Bannuna, also breaks with traditional narrative. The author uses only oblique, elliptical references to describe a woman pained and disappointed by her husband, who has abandoned her for the tumult of life, adventure, and fast cars. Her pain is compounded because her daughter also wants to leave in order to escape the perpetual tension between her parents. The wife/mother speaks, remembering and relating in short, incoherent snatches:

> Everything has to change. Didn't death intervene? Something from these beliefs is mine. They shouldn't be criminalized again. I decided: the true good is for me to be decisive and hide the murderous face of my emotions. Emotions, murder, decisiveness, concealment, and well-balanced emotions—what did all this produce?

But at times this choppy style tends toward a directness which undermines the rich ambiguity of meaning.

Three stories address the topic of alienation from a woman's perspective, depicting its manifestations at various moments. In "al-Ghuraba'" (The Strangers), Moroccan Zaynab Fahmi (Rafiqat al-Tabi'a) tells the story of a man and a woman stretched out on a bed in a closed room. Although the story is told in the third person, the woman intervenes from time to time to reveal a painful, yet refined sense of alienation lighting up her insides as the two bodies are conjoined. She lies next to him, but her mind is elsewhere; sex for her is an exhausting process, and she wants the impossible, something that goes beyond these fleeting meetings with her distant lover, who is the one who determines the nature of the relationship: he wants them to be friends! When they go their separate ways, he tells her, "We will miss one another when we meet." With this sentence, the woman feels that everything has died and been scattered; nothing can be repeated and loneliness is her fate. The story is successful and is cohesive in both form and content. It still possesses its freshness and penetrating perspective even thirty years after it was written.[11]

Similarly, "al-Zahf" (The March), by Tunisian Na'ima al-Sayd, portrays the alienation and loneliness of an impossible love. It is the story of a woman alone with her married lover in a room. They share love and its licentious rituals, but occasionally the woman remembers the other woman, her lover's wife. "Who is more pleasurable, me or her?" she asks. She knows that his answer will not change the nature of their relationship, and so she is determined to maintain her distance through this impossible love:

> She pressed her lips, then she rose and hurried straight to the door. She will not kiss him this time. She said goodbye with a long, long look, and nothing else. She locked him in her eyes, like a shot through a camera lens, then she opened the door and left.[12]

The theme of loneliness and alienation appears as well in "Tahawim layla barida" (Fitful Sleep on a Cold Night), by Moroccan Zuhra Zirawi. It tells the story of a man and a woman with totally different natures and sensibilities. He is carnal, and fond of drink and pleasure; she is an ascetic with a poetic sensibility. Being slightly advanced in years, the woman begins reading the works of al-Niffari, a tenth-century mystic, and talking to flowers. She has difficulty communicating with her lover and eventually she decides to leave him and embrace her isolation.[13]

"Ahzan qadima" (Old Griefs), by Tunisian Khayra al-Shaybani, contains a story within a story. The female narrator is involved with a married man, Majid, and through him she meets Ibn Nafi', who tells her that he has a daughter who looks like her. Ibn Nafi' tells the narrator about his life and his journeys around the world, and she finds in these tales elements of myth that are missing from her workaday life, consumed by classes and waiting for her rendezvous with a married man. Nothing she experiences can stave off loneliness at the end of the night:

> The loneliness of my house greeted me, and a cold bed embraced me. I heard the monotonous patter of the rain fall on the windowpane. I tried to trick my senses so as not to hear the rhythm of the rain and the sound of the alarm . . .

I pressed my head in my hands and changed my position in the bed. The empty spaces terrified me.[14]

Tunisian 'Arusiya al-Naluti, in "Yanfajir al-qitar dhat masa'" (The Train Explodes One Evening), mixes narrative with drama, and classical Arabic with colloquial to heighten the significance of context. The story recreates a state of waiting in a nightmarish atmosphere that is manifested in different scenes and inspires fear in those waiting, who are content to only sit and watch false heroes. Gradually, they are overwhelmed by a sense of incapacity as they wait for the train to explode.[15]

A nightmarish air also permeates "al-Hulm wa-l-kabus" (Dream and Nightmare), by Algerian Zuhur Wannisi, but her style differs from al-Naluti because she cleaves to reality and its paradoxes. She tells the story of an exemplary employee who does his job honestly, sincerely, and with a revolutionary spirit, but suddenly his boss informs him that the department will let him go. We encounter symbolic observations tucked in the folds of the narrative, with comparisons between pots of pure and fake brass and the impression that the latter more closely resemble antique furniture.[16]

"Al-Da'ira" (The Circle), by Tunisian Hafiza Qara Biban, evidences a tendency to formal experimentation. The story is divided into four sections, each with a subtitle: 'Days of the Past,' 'A Nightmare,' 'The Birth of Forgetfulness,' and 'The Circle.' We understand from the text that the female narrator, in addition to being a writer, is a labor activist who challenges officials. Dreaming of liberation and fighting, she neglects her body and health. A doctor informs her she must undergo an operation, and the nightmare pulls her in, but she continues to cling to life, caught in "the circle" between darkness and light. Through her poetic, emotive style and the images of nature she blends into the narrative, the author enriches her story with an ambiguity that compensates for the plot and opens up the text to various interpretations.[17]

"Imra'a ta'tarif" (A Woman Confesses), by the Tunisian writer, Shafiqa al-Sahili, brings us the voice of a woman whose relationship has failed because her lover deceived her. But she does not submit to failure and embarks on another experience, challenging both society and conservative women. Al-Sahili shows a mastery of narrative and dialogue.[18]

Tunisian Nafila Dhahab's "'Alaqa" (Relationship) is distinguished by its controlled structure, its precise, economic language, and the multivalency of its meanings. "'Alaqa" is part of the collection, al-Samt (Silence) 1993, in which Dhahab tries to create fictional variations on the theme of silence and its various manifestations. Here she tells the story of an accountant, a lonely, bored man who becomes addicted to detective novels. As he is absorbed in reading one evening, a beautiful woman knocks on his door and asks for his help because someone is following her. He lets her in, and during the brief encounter, both the man and the woman become someone else: she claims to be a philosophy student, while he says he is the manager of a publishing house. A friendly conversation ensues that revives the lonely man's soul, but soon the police raid the house: they had been following a drunk woman. The police take her away, and the man returns to his loneliness and his detective novels. Is this a story of hearts that lose their way to their soulmate? Or is it about laws that exercise their merciless authority, depriving people of the fleeting relationships that dispel their loneliness and relieve their boredom?[19]

Moroccan Leila Abouzeid's "al-Rihla" (The Journey) takes us to the world of childhood, mischief, and joy. Ruqaya's cousin, with whom she has a somewhat competitive relationship, comes to visit. Ruqaya's mother asks her to take her cousin with her to the fields to gather wild thyme, and their outing leads them to the cellar, where the visiting cousin takes garbanzo beans from a sack. A bean goes up her nose and nearly chokes her, but a woman suggests that she use snuff to extract it. The narrative is easy and light-hearted.

"Janah li-l-rih" (Wings for the Wind), by Moroccan Rabi'a Rayhan, takes place on a plane, as the female narrator relates her moments of fear during the trip. While she is alone with her anxieties, a woman approaches her, and discovering her fear of flight, she tells her to recite Qur'anic verses, which the woman has not fully memorized. The man sitting next to the narrator hears their conversation and shakes his head in disapproval. With its dialogue and precise language, the story observers a human moment that many might choose to ignore or rise above.[20]

"Mudhakkirat al-qa'a raqam thalatha" (Memories of Hall No. Three) by Layla al-Shafi'i steeps us in scenes of melancholy and grief, stemming from the narrator's experience during a stay in the hospital. At the hospital, she forges a friendship with a sick child named Ghazlan who does not survive the surgeon's knife, leaving the narrator to recall the experience. The story opens as if the narrator is looking out at the world from inside the grave and observing movements in the world of the living. She then returns to the hospital to recall Ghazlan's words and actions.[21]

Moroccan 'A'isha Mawqiz, in "Bard Disambir" (December Cold), uses an experimental approach, relying on fragmented writing and the alternation of the first- and third-person narrator. The story is divided into five parts: 'The Adversaries,' 'The Employee,' 'The Last Evening,' 'The Drummer,' and 'The Fish That Do Not Grow.' Each section, brief and allusive, speaks of different things and atmospheres. Two sections are told in the first person; the reader learns that the narrator has understood that her love story was a lie and she no longer has the strength to look in the eyes of the person next to her. Is the December cold responsible for the waning of emotions? The narrator says:

The light wind ripples the water's surface, and I—now looking at the small fish tank from this great height—feel a delicious shiver chafe my bones. I draw the folds of my pink coat to me and think: they just need a little bit of warmth to grow, these little old fish.[22]

After reading the story, the reader is left with the impression that the author is providing elements of an open structure that allow the reader to construct her own story or stories.

Also experimental, Moroccan Latifa Baqa's "Zaziya" (Zaziya) storms the depths of the soul, its dreams, and its black thoughts. Zaziya is the narrator's secret friend, invented out of the tales her mother used to tell her. Both the narrator and Zaziya have a phobia about people throwing themselves from others' windows, but the narrator is gripped by dark moments when she, too, wants to throw herself from the window, were it not for daydreams. The narrator discovers that daydreaming is necessary because it allows Zaziya, her twin spirit, to continue to exist. She puts her hand in Zaziya's and gives in to her dream, thus relieving her desperation. The story becomes a space for parallel dreams and poetic scenes that open a window on to an all-encompassing darkness.[23]

In this analysis, I have focused on those stories that are striking either in their form or content. Most of them tackle woman's fraught, difficult relationship with a married man or depict a woman's feelings as she discovers that a past relationship was based on deception and lies. Other stories explore human and social situations, such as those by Moroccan Layla al-Shafi'i, Tunisian 'Arusiya al-Naluti, Tunisian Hafiza Qara Biban, and Algerian Zuhur Wannisi. Most of the stories we have examined here constitute a step away from traditional narrative, a growing trend in the Arabic short story since the 1970s. Even if these stories represent nothing new in terms of their technique, they successfully reconcile the new form with their authors' sensibilities, allowing North African women to make their voices heard in these texts as they explore the self and the zones of conflict with social traditions.

The novel
North African women writers have produced barely twenty-five novels in Arabic. In addition to the factors noted above, the paucity of novels may be attributable to the fact that novel-writing requires stamina and the sort of life experiences long inaccessible to women. Nevertheless, some women writers have used the novel as a means of conveying their perspective and relating their stories and adventures. The first novels published by women in Morocco—Amina al-Luwa, *al-Malika Khunatha* (Queen Khunatha) 1954; Khunatha Bannuna, *al-Nar wa-l-ikhtiyar* (Fire and Choice) 1968;

and Fatima al-Rawi, *Ghadan tatabaddal al-ard* (Tomorrow the Earth Will Change) 1967—deal with history and social themes and are not remarkable for their freshness of either form or content. This traditionalism marks most novels published in Libya (Mardiya al-Na"as), Algeria (Zuhur Wannisi), and Tunisia (Zakiya 'Abd al-Qadir) up until the 1980s. Since then, novels with more striking form and content have begun to appear that address the particular features of North African women's experiences and lives. The most important of these texts are *Maratij* (Bolts) 1985, and *Tamass* (Contact) 1995, by 'Arusiya al-Naluti; *Rajul li-riwaya wahida* (A Man for One Novel) 1985, by Fawziya Shlabi; *Zahrat al-subbar* (Cactus Flower) 1991, by 'Aliya' al-Tabi'i; *Nakhb al-hayah* (A Toast to Life) 1993, by Amal Mukhtar; *Dhakirat al-jasad (Memory in the Flesh)* 1993, by Ahlam Mosteghanemi; and *al-Ruju' ila-l-tufula (Return to Childhood)* 1993, by Leila Abouzeid.

The most noteworthy development in North African women's novels is their exploration of emotions and subjective experience through the use of sophisticated techniques common in other modern Arabic novels (non-linear time frames, a multiplicity of narrative voices and perspectives, stream-of-consciousness narrative, and the use of individual memory). The early novels of Khunatha Bannuna, Zuhur Wannisi, Mardiya al-Na"as, and Leila Abouzeid are still bound to the traditional social climate, the nationalist struggle, and the ideals that constituted the frames of reference for North African women until the 1970s. Most of the female characters in these novels are traditional women who take part in the struggle, run households, and preserve sacred family values. The newer texts, on the other hand, engage with the rapid social transformations that have taken place since independence. These have had a clear impact on women's status and consciousness and have led them to begin expressing themselves through an anti-patriarchal discourse.

It is perhaps these social changes and the way they have sharpened women's consciousness that have fostered the appearance of problematic heroines in the more recent novels by North African women. Huda, the protagonist of Khunatha Bannuna's *al-Ghad wa-l-ghadab* (The Morrow and Anger) 1981, is a model of the conflicted heroine who tries to achieve self-fulfillment in accordance with values that do not exist in traditional society. The heroine develops a sense of alienation and deprivation because existing types of social bonds do not allow her to exercise her freedom, and she cannot have an active presence in a society that turns its back on women's questions and aspirations. In these sorts of novels, the scene expands to take in the café, the street, the shop, the prison, and even Western capitals. Their characters take shape through an introspective portrayal of their instincts, dreams, and desires—that set of characteristics that helps flesh out and capture a character's distinct features. Many pages are given over to depicting North African women's deepest desires and longings, and this expression of desire becomes a human component closely linked to woman's subjectivity and an integral part of her awareness of her particularity.

Two novels by 'Arusiya al-Naluti are striking for both their narrative and expressive strength and the areas into which they venture. The first, *Maratij*, is the story of Tunisian young people studying in Paris as they confront political responsibilities and experiment with love. Al-Mukhtar Jam'iya is an activist who tries to push his fellow students into taking a stance against the authoritarian repression of their fellow citizens in their homeland. A love story develops between al-Mukhtar and Jawda Mansur. She trusts and supports him, but al-Mukhtar buries his emotions and throws himself into the big political issues. At a certain point, during preparations for a huge student assembly, al-Mukhtar feels his emotions rebelling against his reason. He recalls scenes from his childhood, memories of his mother and his friend Yusuf. Through the process of remembering, he regains part of his lost self that was submerged under slogans and tumultuous meetings. Al-Mukhtar feels a yawning gap between his self and what he desired, and he is no longer satisfied with the speeches and resolutions made far from his country. At the same time, he cannot reveal his love for Jawda. He recalls his friend Yusuf, to whom he confides that he has committed no acts of heroism in Paris as he had claimed in his letters.

Maratij illuminates the moment of fragmentation that hits a revolutionary student who suddenly comprehends the emptiness of slogans that are so at odds with reality and realizes the importance of letting out the emotions buried deep inside himself. The writing is dense, using both the third- and then the first-person narration in interior dialogues that recall childhood memories and the homeland. Gradually, we begin to sense that *Maratij* seeks to portray an entire generation through the characters of al-Mukhtar, Jawda, and al-Hadi—a generation surrounded by questions and difficult choices.

In *Tamass*, 'Arusiya al-Naluti explores the depths of a woman through the experiences of love, sex, and motherhood. The writing brings together a multiplicity of times and narrative voices.

Zahrat al-subbar, by 'Aliya' al-Tabi'i is remarkable in both form and content. It seeks to capture features of Tunisian social life in the 1970s through the experience of Raja', the heroine, and her memories of love, oppression, and disappointment. Through three characters, al-Tabi'i observes moments of emotion and tension that allow us to see the mechanisms of oppression and class boundaries, as well as the moments of loneliness and alienation experienced by a woman who seeks self-fulfillment.[24]

In *Dhakirat al-jasad* and *Fawdat al-hawass (Chaos of the Senses)* 1998, Ahlam Mosteghanemi integrates issues and elements from modern Algerian history into a romance through her use of a passionate, poetic language that lends charm to the narrative and renders emotions and meanings ambiguous, riveting the reader to the interplay between bodily senses and the phantoms of a country whose very existence is threatened.

In contrast, in *Nakhb al-hayah*, Amal Mukhtar describes the experience of a rebellious woman, Sawsan Bin 'Abd Allah, who heads for Germany to forget a failed love affair and free herself from laws and traditions that force people in her country to live behind bars and bear injustice, hypocrisy, and repressed emotion. In Germany Sawsan lives with the utmost liberty, then she returns to Tunisia having realized what it means to be a woman responsible for her freedom and her choices.

Autobiography

No text produced by North African women bears the designation "autobiography" on the cover, but there are at least three works whose form and style qualify them as autobiographical novels.

In *al-Ruju' ila-l-tufula*, Leila Abouzeid speaks about her childhood, lived in various places (al-Quseiba, Sefrou, Rabat, and Casablanca) during the French Mandate, at which time many segments of society, both men and women, participated in the national resistance. Abouzeid talks about her father, Ahmad Abouzeid, and his involvement in the national struggle, his arrests, and the consequences for his family. The author seeks to settle a score with her father in the text, criticizing what she views as his extremist political behavior without giving us his point of view. The text is valuable, however, for its portrayal of women's society, women's conversations during family gatherings, and her mother's contributions to the national struggle. Leila Abouzeid published another autobiographical text in 2000, *al-Fasl al-akhir* (The Last Chapter), recalling her youth and her first experiences with writing.

The second text is Fatima Mernissi's *Dreams of Trespass: Tales of a Harem Girlhood*, first published in English in 1994 and later translated into Arabic in 1997 as *Ahlam al-nisa': qisas tufula fi kanaf al-harim*. Fatima Mernissi was drawn to literary narrative after having gained renown as a sociologist and researcher on Moroccan women. In this text, she draws on events from her childhood in Fez between 1940 and 1950 to portray the ancient city's social life, interspersing anecdotes and tales in the text. Having spent time among many women in a large family, she highlights the role of dreams in the imagination of the women of Fez, especially stories from *The Thousand and One Nights*, told to her by her Aunt Habiba. These scenes and tales are punctuated by the conflict between two generations of women, one traditional and the other contemporary. The first preserves tradition because it steers the family boat to safe shores; the second is attracted by Western products and Egyptian films, particularly the elegant, beautiful singer Asmahan, who has a great impact on many of the younger generation. The narrative, filled with descriptions of traditions, customs, and lifestyles, introduces the reader to the mind and imagination of the women of Fez in this period.

Jirah al-ruh wa-l-jasad (Wounds of the Spirit and Body) 1999, by Malika Mustazraf, takes the form of a testimonial. It is the story of the succession of rapes endured by the narrator-author from the age of four by Qaddur, a black youth, the local grocer, and a friend of her father. Having been beaten by her mother when she told her of the first rape, the child decides not to tell her family about the others. This is not the only aspect of the text; the narrator talks about her older sister, Khadija, who pretends to be visiting friends while going out to meet men. The younger sister accompanies her on these outings, and Khadija buys her silence with sweets and gifts. The father, who feigns piety while beating his wife, often frequents brothels. These episodes leave deep scars on the child Malika's psyche. Later, the author shows us how everything turns out when she grows up: her sister, Khadija, runs a brothel with her husband. Her mother dies, and her father marries a young woman who cheats on him with anyone she fancies. The narrator obtains a bachelor's degree, but her father refuses to allow her to travel to Rabat to continue her studies. She starts hanging around the streets of Casablanca, where she meets Ilham, who works in a bar and has a small child; Ilham was also raped at an early age. Qaddur travels to France where he marries and has three children, whom he sexually abuses; when he is exposed, he commits suicide. His French wife comes to Casablanca, where the narrator visits her and tells her about Qaddur and her past with him. His wife suggests that the narrator accompany her to France to help her run a center for rape victims.

The text contains violent, graphic scenes that portray the fragmentation and disintegration of the Moroccan poor and middle classes as a result of want, primitive laws, and faltering values.

The North African women's novel, in the few fine examples discussed here, shows its potential to give voice to North African women seeking liberty, equality, and self-expression in all its forms. In the context of rapid social changes and women's heightened awareness, the novel seems a particularly apt means of capturing interior experience through the various discourses available in the novelistic form. But the pace of novelistic production by North African women is sporadic, and the texts discussed here thus seem like the product of a few writers venting their frustration. It may be relevant to point out that no Arab writer is a full-time writer and that Arabic literary production as a whole has not managed to build a regular relationship between the writer and the public.

In this general survey, I have sought to highlight the basic features of literary texts produced by North African women. In general, these texts are part of two basic trends. The first is traditional, in which writing is considered a complement to or extension of a particular social, moral, or ideological discourse, which is used to moralize, stir emotion, or reinforce traditional values. The second is more modern. It is aware of the particularity of the literary text and recognizes its autonomy within the possible range of interaction between society and its questions. As such, it strives first and foremost to be a literary text, and an expression of the self and experiences that are absent from the dominant discourses.

The same distinction can be applied to modern Arabic literature as a whole, written by both men and women, but the goal of this analysis is to identify some of the features particular to North African women writers, since these are the elements of a distinctive voice that will relate the experience of North African women and their relationships with men, institutions, and various systems of authority, whether through poetry, short stories, or novels. A feminist discourse alone cannot defend the cause of women and their need for emancipation from all forms of patriarchy. Literature written by women themselves brings another dimension to women's experience and moves it from the realm of slogans to introspection, to real experience of life and hardship. This is literature's common horizon, regardless of male and female writers' different perspectives and conditions.

Significantly, despite the existence of texts remarkable in both form and content, the quantity of literature in Arabic produced by North African women is still limited, due to the many factors discussed at the outset of this chapter. Nevertheless, the paucity of works does not negate the symbolic value of the literature of North African women. They have used writing to open up horizons for confession, rebellion, and self-understanding, and their works are read and analyzed for a non-male perspective. The challenge now facing North African women writers is continuity—that is, maintaining a regular pace of production that will make them a permanent fixture of the literary scene and their voices a basic part of the equation between writers and the reading public.

Notes

1 See the Bibliography of Works in French for North African women who write in French.

2 Amina al-Marini, "'Ashiqa," recited at al-'Uyun Forum, April 3–4, 1997.

3 Malika al-'Asimi, *Kitabat kharij aswar al-'alam* (Baghdad: Dar al-Shu'un al-Thaqafiya, 1987).

4 Rabi'a Jalti, *Shajar al-kalam* (Meknes: Dar al-Safir, 1991).

5 Zaynab al-A'waj, "Halat Haml," *al-Tabyin al-Jahiziya* (1990), pp. 107–109.

6 Jamila al-Majiri, *Diwan al-nisa'* (Tunis: Tunisian Publishing Company, 1997).

7 Wafa' al-'Amrani, *Fitnat al-aqasi* (Casablanca: al-Rabita Publications, 1997).

8 Thuraya Majdulin, *Awraq al-ramad* (Rabat: Moroccan Writers' Union Publications, 1993).

9 Al-Zuhra al-Mansuri, "Ghafwat al-ma'" *al-Afaq*, no. 57, 1995: pp. 79–81.

10 Fatima Mahmud, "Qabla an tutliq rasasat al-rahma," *al-Fusul al-arba'a*, no. 25, 1984: pp. 106–14.

11 Zaynab Fahmi (Rafiqat al-Tabi'a), *Rajul wa imra'a* (Casablanca: Dar al-Kitab, 1969).

12 Na'ima al-Sayd, *al-Zahf* (Kuwait: Dar al-Rabi'an, 1982).

13 Zuhra Zirawi, *Nisf yawm yakfi* (Casablanca: al-Najah Modern Press, 1996).

14 Khayra al-Shaybani, "Ahzan qadima," *al-Qisas*, no. 29, 1973, pp. 61–67.

15 'Arusiya al-Naluti, *al-Bu'd al-khamis* (Tunis/Libya: al-Dar al-'Arabiya Books, 1975).

16 Zuhur Wannisi, "al-Hilm wa-l-kabus," *al-Musa'ala*, 1992, pp. 187–93.

17 Hafiza Qara Biban, *Fi zulumat al-nur* (Tunis: Qisas Magazine Publications, 1994).

18 Shafiqa al-Sahili, *Imra'a ta'tarif* (Tunis: al-'Asima Press, 1984).

19 Nafila Dhahab, *al-Samt* (Tunis: Dar al-Bahth 'an Tibr al-Zaman, 1993).

20 Rabi'a Rayhan, *Matar al-masa'* (Cairo: al-Dar al-Misriya al-Lubnaniya, 1999).

21 Layla al-Shafi'i, *al-Wahm wa-l-ramad* (Rabat: al-Mawja Publications, 1994).

22 'A'isha Mawqiz, "Bard Disambir," *al-Afaq*, no. 58, 1996, pp. 23–25.

23 Latifa Baqa, "Zaziya," typescript, courtesy of the author, n.d., pp. 1–7.

24 'Aliya' al-Tabi'i, *Zahrat al-subbar* (Tunis: Dar al-Janub Publishers, 1991).

8 The Arabian Peninsula and the Gulf

Su'ad al-Mana

T he appearance of women's creative writing in the Arabian Peninsula and Gulf area is linked with the rise of girls' education. In the first half of the twentieth century, only rarely do we find writing women of the likes of the Hijazi Khadija al-Shanqitiya, who published a collection of poetry in praise of the Prophet Muhammad in 1936.[1] The absence of women's writing prior to this does not mean that women in the Arabian Peninsula created no literature, for women played a role in oral composition, particularly colloquial poetry.[2]

Official education for girls was initiated at different times in the various countries of the region. In Bahrain, the first girls' school was established in 1928,[3] while in Kuwait education for girls began in 1937.[4] In Qatar, however, there were no girls' schools until 1954, followed by the Emirates in 1955, Saudi Arabia in 1960, and Oman in 1970.[5] Given the different dates at which girls' education was instituted, no written literature by women appears in the peninsula until the second half of the twentieth century. Indeed, there is hardly any record of a published book by a woman in the region until the early 1950s.

The rise of women's literature in the Arabian Peninsula is also linked to the press, where women first began publishing shortly in the 1950s. In Kuwait, for example, Hadiya Sultan al-Salim wrote an article in 1948 on the Palestinian *nakba* for *al-Bi'tha*, a magazine published by Dar al-Kuwait in Cairo.[6] The same year, Ibtisam 'Abd Allah 'Abd al-Latif published an essay entitled "Khawatir tifla" (A Child's Thoughts).[7] In Bahrain, Shahla al-Khulfan published an article in *al-Qafila* in 1952, and Mawza al-Za'id published a short story in *al-Watan* in 1955.[8]

In the 1960s, the Saudi press began publishing women's writings with some regularity. Each paper had a page devoted to women, and they sometimes carried women's literary writings as well.[9] Women wrote short stories, poetry, and literary essays, but many of the writers were just beginners and had not gone beyond secondary, or even middle school.[10] Women's writing began appearing in the presses of other countries in the region as well, although at various dates. In Qatar, women only started contributing to the press in the early 1970s,[11] but this does not seem to be a marker of women's condition since journalism in Qatar only began to take shape in the late 1960s.[12] Most likely, the first piece of women's writing published in the Qatari press was an article by Zahra Mal Allah about the poet Ibrahim Naji, entitled "Bulbul al-sharq rasam al-jamal fi kalimatih" (The Nightingale of the East Draws Beauty in His Words).[13] In the Emirates, the first story by a woman to appear in the press was "al-Rahil" (The Departure), by Shaykha al-Nakhi, in 1970.[14] This, too, is not indicative of women's status, for the short story only began to appear in the Emirates at this time.[15] Women began to publish poetry and articles at about the same time.[16] In Oman, women only began publishing in the 1980s, although 'A'isha Bint 'Isa ibn Salih al-Harithiya is known to have written poetry at a relatively early date, perhaps from as early as the 1950s. Yusuf al-Sharuni cites the names of several women who contributed to the early development of the short story and poetry in Oman, and none of their works were published before the 1980s.[17]

Generally speaking, we can take the 1950s and early 1960s as the starting point for women's literature in the Arabian Peninsula. It was at that time that Sultana al-Sudayri published a collection of poetry in Saudi Arabia, *'Abir al-sahra'* (Fragrance of the Desert), using the pseudonym Nida' in 1956.[18] Samira Khashuqji published her first work, a novel, *Wadda't amali* (I Bid My Hopes Farewell), under the name Samira Bint al-Jazira in 1958,[19] and Thuraya Qabil published a collection of poetry, *al-Awzan al-bakiya* (The Weeping Rhythms), in 1963.[20] In Kuwait, Su'ad al-Sabah published her poetry collection, *Wamdat bakira* (Early Gleams), in 1961,[21] while Hadiya Sultan al-Salim released a study, *al-Maqasid fi nawazi' al-'Arab wa sajayahum* (On the Traits and Disposition of the Arabs) in 1965.[22]

Genres in women's literature

An examination of the generic features of women's writing in the Gulf reveals that in the twentieth century women's literature was largely confined to poetry, the short story, and to a lesser extent, the novel. In total, 113 poetry collections, 115 short-story collections, and sixty-three novels were published up to about the late 1990s. With the exception of children's theater, drama accounts for only a very small part of women's literature, and autobiography is similarly rare in the writing of women of the Arabian Peninsula.[23] Finally, there are fifty works of children's literature of all kinds, including poetry, stories, and plays, and several women writers have devoted themselves exclusively to children's literature.

A consideration of trends in women's writing in the Gulf region thus requires us to pause at the most prominent features of poetry and short story in each country, with a brief overview of other literary genres. The treatment of each country will be ordered according to the first appearance of women's writing in the press.

Poetry

Poetry is the most deep-rooted art in the Gulf, and women have never stopped composing poems. Aside from their contributions to ancient and medieval poetry, there are several examples of colloquial poetry attributed to women in both desert and urban areas before the spread of girls' education.[24]

Kuwait

Poetry trails the short story in the literature of Kuwaiti women, with twenty-six collections of poetry and thirty short-story collections. Several Kuwaiti women poets are known throughout the Arab world, but the most well-known is Su'ad al-Sabah, one of the first women poets in the Arabian Peninsula. In addition, there is Khazna Bursili, whose first collection was published in the 1970s, Janna al-Qurayni, Sa'diya Mufrih, 'Aliya Shu'ayb, Ghanima Zayd al-Harb, and Nura al-Malifi, whose collections were published in the 1990s. Contemporary poetry by Kuwaiti women is dominated by prose poetry and free verse, although the classical *qasida* is found in a few collections.

Su'ad al-Sabah's prolific output requires some pause—she has published ten collections of poetry since the 1960s. As indicated by the titles of her collections, her poetry deals with various themes. Some poems address national or Arab issues, while others are about family and maternal feelings, and still others are about female experience and perceptions. Her poetry has been the subject of several academic studies and has been translated into more than one language. While some students of al-Sabah's poetry focus on her attitude to the dominance of tradition and backwardness in the Gulf,[25] it is nevertheless noteworthy that her first collection of poetry (1961) was published under her real name. The dominance of tradition and the sway of the family did not prevent her from signing her poems with her own name.

Examples of her poems dealing with women's view of men can be found in her collections *Fi-l-bad' kanat al-untha* (In the Beginning Was Woman), *Imra'a bila sawahil* (A Woman without Shores) 1994, and *Khudhni ila hudud al-shams* (Take Me to the Borders of the Sun) 1997. They largely revolve around female sentiment and are brimming with emotion, but they are not entirely free of conflict. On one hand, there is a conflict between expressions of love and traditions, symbolized by the tribe or clan; on the other hand, there is a conflict with the Other, the man, who is both the lover and the Other.

In many poems, the man appears as the woman's ideal lover, but at the same time he is portrayed as a dominant force who reduces woman to merely something pretty. This is true whether he is from the same or a different tribe, educated or non-educated. For example, the poem, "Kun sadiqi" (Be My Friend):

Why, oh man of the East, do you care about my looks?
Why do you look at the kohl on my eyes,
Not at my mind?
Like the earth, I need the water of conversation.
Why do you see only the bracelet on my wrist?
Why do you have traces of Shahrayar?[26]

In the poems of other Kuwaiti poets, like Khazna Bursili, we find examples of another kind of poetry, the classical *qasida*, and an almost mystical poetic expression.

Some of Sa'diya Mufrih's modern poems give voice to various anxieties, not necessarily those related to love between men and women; rather her poems touch on various aspects of life that trouble and concern the woman poet.

Bahrain

Poetry dominates the literature of Bahraini women; we find twenty-two poetry collections, compared to six collections of short stories and one novel. Indeed, women's poetry is flourishing in Bahrain, where women constituted one-sixth of all Bahraini poets from 1925 to 1985.[27] Bahraini women poets include Hamda Khamis, Iman Asiri, Fawziya al-Sindi, Fatima al-Taytun, and Fathiya 'Ajlan.[28]

Modern forms of poetry, including the prose poem and free verse, have been prominent in Bahraini women's poetry from its beginnings. Women first emerged on the scene in 1969, with the publication of "Shazaya" (Shrapnel), by Hamda Khamis. This was Khamis's first experiment with poetry, followed by a dramatic poem published in 1970,[29] although her first collection of poetry, *I'tidhar li-l-tufula* (An Apology to Childhood), did not appear until 1978.[30] Iman Asiri was the first poet, male or female, to write a prose poem in Bahrain; she began publishing her early efforts in the late 1960s. As such, she "represents the earliest embrace of prose poetry," although her collection, *Hadhi ana al-qubbara* (Here I Am, a Lark), was not published until 1982.[31]

It is striking that virtually no woman poet in Bahrain turned to classical forms of poetry in the beginning,[32] perhaps because modern trends in poetry were increasingly represented in the Arabic press at the time, and the younger generation, both men and women, embraced these new literary trends.

Among women poets in Bahrain, Hamda Khamis is noteworthy for her abundant, varied corpus of poetry; so far she has published six collections. The poems in *Masarat* (Byways) 1993 and *Addad* (Opposites) 1994 portray the concerns of a mature woman grappling with various life experiences.

Some of the poems in Fawziya al-Sindi's collection, *Akhir al-mahabb* (The Last of the Wind) 1998, speak about the nature of things, and the poetic imagination seems estranged from the self. Though some poems, such as "Riwaq awwal . . . li-l-ard li-yaqin al-wahm" (First Portico . . . to the Earth, to the Certainty of Illusion), use the first person, they are not subjective. The poem speaks of the earth and women's relationship with it, referring to war, grief, and the desperation that tribal warfare leaves in its wake.

Saudi Arabia

Women's poetry is flourishing today in Saudi Arabia, although in terms of quantity it trails the short story. As of the year 1999, forty-eight short-story collections, thirty poetry collections, and twenty-seven novels had been published.[33] The collection of Sultana al-Sudayri (known as Nida'), *'Abir al-sahra'* (1956), was the first modern work published by a woman in Saudi Arabia or anywhere in the Gulf. Composed of poems written at a very young age, the collection is of the utmost simplicity. It nevertheless contains lyrical love poems, which is perhaps why the poet published the collection under a pseudonym. It was unacceptable in Najd—especially at that time—for a woman to write openly about love, although the oral Nabati poetry of Najd, both ancient and contemporary, contains love poetry composed by women, particularly by Bedouin women.[34] Oral poetry is not viewed in the same light as written poetry, but even so, much of the corpus of oral love poems is attributed to anonymous women. Al-Sudayri's collection is important because it marks the beginning of published collections of poems in classical Arabic and contains love poetry written by a woman from the region.[35]

It is a paradox that although official girls' education was not established in Saudi Arabia until the relatively late date of 1960, Saudi women began publishing literary works before other women in the Gulf. Before the spread of official education, some areas had institutions of primary education for girls, and some affluent families—though very few—allowed their daughters to be educated in other Arab countries such as Egypt, Lebanon, and Iraq.[36] Sultana al-Sudayri was given a private education at home, and her collection of poetry was published in Beirut.[37]

Thuraya Qabil published her collection *al-Awzan al-bakiya* in 1963, the first published collection by a woman from Hijaz (apart from the limited circulation of Khadija al-Shanqitiya's work). The collection was also published in Beirut. Qabil studied in Lebanon, and she had already published several poems in Lebanese newspapers such as *al-Hayat* and *al-Anwar*. The poems in the collection address various topics, including national issues, as in "Biladi" (My Country), and larger Arab issues, seen in "Wa sha' al-jihad" (And the Struggle Willed), about the Algerian Jamila Buhrayd. Others, like "al-Hubb al-da'i'" (Lost Love), "Hubb amsi" (The Love of My Yesterday), and "Kitabi" (My Book), are about love.[38] Remarkably, Qabil published her collection under her real name, which illustrates the different levels of control exercised by tradition from one region to the next. Although the collection was critically acclaimed, Thuraya Qabil published no other collection.

Saudi women today write poetry in various forms, including the classical *qasida*, free verse, and the prose poem. In the 1970s, Fawziya Abu Khalid was the first woman poet in Saudi Arabia to write prose poetry. Her first collection, *Ila mata yakhtatifunak laylat al-'urs* (Until When Will They Kidnap You on the Wedding Night?) 1975, found a sizable audience outside Saudi Arabia in circles interested in women's poetry and modern Arabic poetry, and several of Abu Khalid's poems have been translated into English for poetry anthologies.[39] Women writers of classical poetry include Maryam Baghdadi, a university professor, in *'Awatif insaniya* (Human Emotions) 1980, and Ruqayya Nazir in *Khafaya qalb* (Secrets of the Heart) 1986, as well as in her later collections.

The 1980s witnessed the publication of a striking number of collections by women, including Huda 'Abd Allah al-Rifa'i's *'Ala shurfat al-azhar* (On the Balcony of Flowers) 1982, and Lulu Buqsh'an's *Thartharat al-buh al-samit* (The Chatter of the Silent Confession) 1989. Many women poets also published their works in newspapers and magazines and took part in poetry seminars. In the 1990s, other collections were published by women, some of them already well recognized, such as Thuraya al-'Urayyid, who published her first collection *'Ubur al-qifar furada* (Crossing the Wastelands One by One) in 1993, but had long contributed poetry to the press. Other collections published in the 1990s include Huda al-Daghfaq's *al-Zill ila a'la* (The Upward Shadow) 1993, Sara al-Khathlan's *Hara'iq fi da'irat al-samt* (Fires in the Circle of Silence) 1994, Ashjan al-Hindi's *Hurub al-ahilla* (Crescent Wars) 1997, Latifa Qari's *Lu'lu'at al-masa' al-sa'b* (Pearl of the Difficult Evening) 1998, Salwa Khamis's *Mithl qamar 'ala niyyatih* (Like a Gullible Moon) 1999, and Iman al-Dabbagh's *Taranim al-mays* (Hymns of the Proud) 1999.

Saudi women's poetry touches on many different themes; we shall have a closer look at three poems by three different poets.

In "Ayna ittijah al-shajar?" (Which Direction Are the Trees?), a long poem by Thuraya al-'Urayyid from her collection of the same name, a woman's voice speaks of national concerns. The poem's title evokes an ancient history, the myth of Zarqa' al-Yamama (an Arab semi-legendary figure whose sharp eyesight enabled her to warn her tribe of approaching enemies three days before they reached them). Zarqa' al-Yamama had already entered the world of modern poetry in Amal Dunqul's poem, "al-Buka' bayn yaday Zarqa' al-Yamama" (Crying in the Arms of Zarqa' al-Yamama), but the perspective here is different; it is the woman of the present, the one concerned by national issues, who evokes the figure of this ancient woman.

The female subject of the poem assumes the voice of Zarqa' al-Yamama, speaks to her, and finds herself in the same position. The poem connects current concerns about the Arab nation as a whole (not only the Arabian Peninsula) and woman's penetrating insight, which sees the dangers looming over her people though they are oblivious (the folkloric Zarqa' al-Yamama and the female subject speak in the poem in the present tense). Zarqa' al-Yamama's efforts to warn her people came to naught and she was accused of lying. Here, too, no one listens to her plea. An air of myth envelops the present in poem in the form of a woman who sees the danger in her people's negligence.

In another long poem "Hurub al-ahilla" (Crescent Wars) by Ashjan al-Hindi, found in her collection, *Li-l-hulm ra'ihat al-matar* (Dreams Have the Scent of Rain) 1998, a woman looks at her relationship with a man.[40] The poem speaks of a passionate relationship between a man and a woman, a purely physical relationship that seems devoid of true love. Through this perspective, an equivalency is made between the desires, feelings, and sins of man and woman.

The poem rebels against the stereotypical image of woman as a seductress and temptress of man, but it does not refute the charge. Rather, it makes men the source of this temptation. If Eve came from Adam then men are the source of temptation, and if men do injustice to women, it is no wonder that women seek revenge by turning the evil of temptation against them.

The entire poem has an evocative beauty, with images, allusions, and references that grip the listener or reader. But its perspective on women differs only superficially from the perspective of many male writers. Woman in the poem is subservient by nature, merely reflecting the good or evil attributed to her; she is not a human agent who bears responsibility for constructing her life and deciding what is best. When the poet alludes to child-bearing, it seems to be of benefit to men alone: "If injustice befalls me, I will only give birth to embryos ornamented by sin." The image of women in the poem is not one of a woman who is in charge of her own life or who seeks to build a better life. She is a dependent who rebels against the dominance of her master. Sin comes from man, and woman uses it against him to take revenge.

"Al-Shayb aw shuruq al-shams" (Old Age or Sunrise), by Fawziya Abu Khalid, also a relatively long poem, speaks of a woman's feelings about aging.[41] Old age as a theme in Arabic poetry has a long history, but most of it in the male, not female tradition.[42] The poem refers to the sudden approach of old age and is based on questions. Its structure relies on interrogative particles, used as headings in most of the stanzas (when, how, whence, who, why, which, wherefore, where, with what):

> Which?
> While I am still
> absorbed in weaving
> defiant dreams,
> I glimpse a thread of gray,
> and I do not know:
> From which of the two traps shall I flee?
> . . .
> When?
> When did the seasons take me unawares?
> And through its winters seeped
> into my night
> this early snow?

Some women poets, such as Khadija al-'Umari and Fatima al-Qarni, have not yet published collections but have nevertheless achieved some renown. Others have used pseudonyms and have not published collections of poetry, but were well-known at a certain point in time, such as Ghayda' al-Manfa (Young Lady of Exile) and Ghajariyat al-Rif (Countryside Gypsy).[43]

The Emirates

Poetry occupies the most prominent place in women's literature from the United Arab Emirates; Emirati women have published twenty-five collections of poetry, compared to nineteen short-story collections. Throughout the 1980s, several collections of poetry were published. In 1982, for example, Maysun Saqr al-Qasimi published her first collection, *Hakadha usammi al-ashya'* (That's How I Call Things), and Zabya Khamis al-Muslimani published *al-Thuna'iya ana al-mar'a, al-ard, kull al-dulu'* (The Dichotomy, I Am Woman, Earth, Every Rib) 1982, comprising several collections published under a single title. In the 1990s, Saliha Ghubaysh published more than one collection, starting with *Bi-intizar al-shams* (Waiting for the Sun) 1992; also published in the 1990s were Kulthum al-Shaybani's *Taranim al-khuzama* (Hymns of the Lavender) 1992, 'A'isha al-Busmayt's *Sayyidat al-rafd al-akhir* (The Woman of the Final Refusal), and Khulud al-Mu'la's *Huna dayya't al-zaman* (Here I Lost Time) 1997.

Women's poetry from the Emirates comes in many forms—the classical *qasida*, free verse, and the prose poem—and gives voice to different sensibilities, from a religious, pious poetic spirit, to a sense of wonder and contemplation of the universe, to a spirit that rebels against traditional values.

Some poetry gives expression to a connection with the Creator, such as Kulthum al-Shaybani's short poem, "Tasaddu'" (To Crack), in *Taranim al-khuzama*, a poem written in the classical *qasida* form.[44]

Saliha Ghubaysh's "Duwwamat al-shatat" (The Diasporal Whirlpool) is from her first collection, *Bi-intizar al-shams*, which includes both classical poems and free verse and is dominated by romanticism. The poem is an example of contemplative poetry; the poet's reflections on the universe are subtly woven with subejctive references. Dislocation in all its forms—literal, psychological, and social—dominates the poem, linked to fragmentation, scattered lives, the pains of the poor, and the transformation of the world into darkness through man's disfigurement of beauty in the world. The woman of the poem is not focused on personal concerns, and there is no place for subjective complaints. Rather, the poem recreates a universe threatened by darkness. The theme of dislocation is not uncommon in the poetry of Gulf women; we find the same tendency in the poetry of Janna al-Qurayni, from Kuwait.[45]

Zabya Khamis al-Muslimani's poem, "Kanari" (Canary), in the collection, *al-Sultan yarjum imra'a hubla bi-l-bahr* (The Sultan Stones a Woman Pregnant with the Sea) 1988, has a different poetic purpose: the portrayal of a modern Arab women's anxiety. The woman in the poem does not fit the average mold of most Arab women, and she is not the woman who appears in most men's poetry. Rather, she represents the exhausted, troubled human being of the modern age: she "smokes like a chimney," "is always on the move," and "walks in a minefield." She is also passionate, "carrying a pot of love and pot of spite," and "she dreams." She belongs to the desert—"her desert landscape"—and to the world of writing and struggle.

Khulud al-Mu'la's "Hakadha ara jaddati" (That's How I See My Grandmother), in *Huna dayya't al-zaman*, gives us a vision of a woman's relationship with time. The sympathetic perspective on the grief of an older woman who sees "time's receding ceiling" is mixed with a subtle sense of grief over the transformation of beloved things and their disappearance from the course of time.

Qatar
Qatari women have produced ten collections of poetry, six short-story collections, four novels, and one play, in addition to fourteen works of children's literature, including songs, stories, and plays. Clearly, then, in

terms of quantity, poetry dominates women's literature in Qatar. Indeed more than one study of this poetry, which occupies a generally prominent place in Qatari literature, has appeared.

The first collections of poetry by women in Qatar were published in the 1980s. In this period appeared the collections of Zakiya Mal Allah 'Abd al-'Aziz, the first being *Fi ma'bad al-ashwaq* (In the Temple of Desires) 1985,[46] as well as Su'ad al-Kawwari's *Taja'id* (Wrinkles) 1995, and Hissa al-'Awadi's *Milad* (Birth) 1998. Women's poetry in Qatar encompasses several different trends, touching on mysticism, the anxieties of writing, national concerns, and expressions of human suffering.[47]

Oman

Omani women writers have published four collections of poetry and only one collection of short stories. Much of women's literature in Oman finds its way to the reading public through newspapers and magazines.[48] Published collections include *Madd fi bahr al-a'maq* (Tide in the Sea of the Depths) 1986, by Sa'ida Bint Khatir al-Farisi, and *Ana imra'a istithna'iya* (I'm an Exceptional Woman) 1995, by Turkiya Bint Sayf ibn Ya'rub. We should pause at an Omani woman who wrote poetry at a relatively early date,[49] 'A'isha Bint 'Isa ibn Salih ibn 'Ali al-Harithi al-Qabili, born in the 1930s.[50] Her works include a lovely poem about the pilgrimage, which is infused with a religious sensibility.

Using the form of a narrative poem, the poet cites her age when she first undertakes the pilgrimage, then she speaks to us about the stages in her journey. Other lines allude to travel by both air and land and refer to the cities she visited. The poem is dominated by a deeply felt religious sensibility. The fact that she wrote the poem before the introduction of official girls' education in Oman and did not study abroad shows that some families did indeed give their daughters an education beyond the basics offered at traditional religious schools.[51]

The point of this brief review of women's poetry from the Arabian Peninsula is not to suggest that these are the only themes of women's poetry of the region. The objective was simply to pause at certain noteworthy perspectives, to give an idea of what is out there, and to highlight women poets' perspectives on themes that have often been read through the eyes of male poets. Judging by the number of collections, women's poetry is flourishing in the Gulf region. The prevalence of modern poetic forms—both free verse and the prose poem—is a product of the direct cultural contact with Arabic poetry in neighboring countries. Beirut and its cultural press played an especially important role in the 1960s and 1970s before the civil war, when it had strong links with Gulf Arabs who studied or spent their summers there.

The short story

The short story accounts for a sizable part of women's literature in the Gulf. Indeed, it was the first literary form used by women writers, emerging in the Arabian Peninsula in the 1950s. The first short-story collections were published in the 1960s. The following is a brief review of the short story in each country in the region.

Kuwait

The short story in Kuwait has gradually developed since the 1970s. The first collection published by a woman from Kuwait was Layla al-'Uthman's *Imra'a fi ina'* (Woman in a Jar) 1976. Women's short-story writing truly came into its own in Kuwait in the mid-1980s. During this period, Layla al-'Uthman published eight story collections, and Fatima al-'Ali, Thuraya al-Baqsami, Layla Muhammad Salih, Muna al-Shafi'i, and 'Aliya Shu'ayb each published more than one collection of stories. Other women writers, like Bazza al-Batini, published their first collections.

The early stories published in the press revolved largely around women's issues and social reform and were marked by a romantic melancholy. An example is Hayfa' Hashim's "al-Intiqam al-rahib" (The Terrible Retribution) 1953.[52] Stories published in the 1970s moved toward realism, at times blending it with fantasy or symbolism, such as Fatima al-'Ali's "Huwwa wa-l-'ukaz" (The Crutch and He) published in her collection, *Wajhuha watan* (Her Face Is a Homeland) 1995, where oddly shaped crutches are endowed with the ability to feel and grow. In Layla al-'Uthman's "al-Naml al-ashqar" (The Termite), from her collection, *Fi-l-layl ta'ti al-'uyun* (At Night the Eyes Come), the termite becomes a multivalent symbol, while the title story "Fi-l-layl ta'ti al-'uyun" moves between the world of *jinn* and the real world.[53]

The portrayal of women in the short story has evolved from its beginnings to the present day. The stories of Layla al-'Uthman, a prolific writer, provide a good example of the development of the female perspective in women's writing.[54] Women in the stories of *Imra'a fi ina'* are often passive; they cannot find happiness and cannot ward off evil unless a good man loves and marries them. In "'Aris fi hayy al-banat" (A Groom in the Girls' Quarter), a young woman assumed by everyone to be mad has no hope of happiness until an honorable young man falls in love with her and asks for her hand in marriage. In "al-Thawb al-akhar" (The Other Garment), a man leverages his wife's beauty to make several successful deals. Although the wife detests the situation, she can do nothing but hope for deliverance in the form of getting rid of her husband and finding an honorable man who loves her and has the power to protect her. This perspective, then, makes women's happiness dependent on men who love them, protect them, and honor them. It is perhaps a reflection of widespread views of women in general,[55] and it also reflects the portrayal of women in writings by men.

This image of women can be compared with that in "Ra'ihat al-jasad ra'ihat al-ramad" (The Scent of the Body, the Scent of Ash), in Layla al-'Uthman's *Yahduth kull layla* (It Happens Every Night) 1998. In this story, the woman is not passive when faced with a disagreeable situation, and the source of her happiness is not a man who loves her. The story depicts a woman's physical revulsion from a husband she did love once, but whom she has come to loathe through living with him. She feels terrible pain when he forcibly exercises his 'right' to her body, and she is overcome with humiliation when she sees him enjoy the thrill of victory with no regard to her feelings. The story portrays the woman's disgust at the scent that clings to her when her husband touches her—"I can't bear my own smell," she says. When she frees herself from him, she feels she has rid herself of an odious smell and begins to breathe in the fresh air, redolent with happiness.

The portrayal of a woman whose happiness springs from things in life other than a man who loves her and through whom she achieves her happiness, has come to the fore in the most recent stories written by women in Kuwait. Bazza al-Batini's collection, *al-Sayyida kanat* (The Woman Was) 1998, contains more than one story portraying such women, whose lives do not revolve entirely around men and who find happiness though they are not beautiful or young. This is seen in stories like "Min ayn yatasarrab al-bard?" (Where Is the Cold Coming From?), "al-Wajha al-thalitha" (The Third Direction), and "Wasalat wa lakin" (She Arrived, But). In the last, the female protagonist is a young, practical-minded woman who does not want to be a slave to the requirements of feminine beauty. The characters in the first two stories are middle-aged women from the educated generation who work for a living.[56]

These stories also give us a vision of women's feelings that are rarely found in the stories of male writers. Two of Layla al-'Uthman's most recent stories portray the feelings of a woman who, after a long interruption, meets a person she used to love or was infatuated with her from afar in her youth. In both stories, the man has been changed by time. In the first, she meets him when he is ill and old, and she is pained to see how this strong man who used to dazzle her has become ravaged by age. The story does not describe the woman physically; we only learn of her feelings toward the man, her old passion for him, and her sense of grief and compassion when faced with the transformation of once-beautiful things.[57]

Bahrain

After the early phase of women's short-story writing—in which Bahrain took the lead—more mature stories began to appear, and women remained a major element in most stories.[58] In 1983, Munira al-Fadil published her collection, *al-Rimura* (The Suckerfish), and Fawziya Rashid published *Maraya al-zill wa-l-farah* (Mirrors of Shadow and Joy) and *al-Hisar* (The Siege).[59] Many women who published individual stories in this period released them in collections only recently, such as 'A'isha Ghalum, who published her *Imra'a fi-l-dhakira* (A Remembered Woman) in 1990. Many of these stories focus on women's relationships with men, with the writers sympathizing with the women's problems. The husband emerges as the center of happiness. In Fawziya Rashid's "Wahshat al-aqbiya" (The Loneliness of the Cellars), he rescues a woman from her brother's injustice, and in "al-Wamd" (The Gleam) and "Nahnu nasriq al-hubb" (We Steal Love), both in *al-Rimura*, the man is the bestower of happiness.[60] Some stories, like those of Fawziya Rashid, address the issue of prisoners,[61] others the struggle with the sea—'A'isha Ghalum's "Fi-l-intizar" (Waiting)—or childhood emotions— Ghalum's "Hilm 'ala-l-rasif" (A Dream on the Pavement) and "Fi ghamrat al-farah al-kadhib" (In a Moment of False Joy).[62]

Saudi Arabia

Women's first published short stories in Saudi Arabia date to the 1960s, with the release of Najah Khayyat's *Makhad al-samt* (Labor Pains of Silence) 1966.[63] In the mid-1970s, women's short-story collections began to appear regularly, much as in Kuwait and Qatar.

The stories that appeared from the 1960s to the mid-1970s generally deal with women's problems and pains, but the portrayal of women's pains does not always entail complaint and passivity. Some writers link pain with resistance and attempts to change a bad situation. For example, Najah Khayyat's "Satushriq al-shams yawman" (One Day the Sun Will Rise) features a young woman suffering from the repression and coercion of her odious elderly husband. She decides not to give in to the hopeless situation and resists her husband's painful approaches. The story ends with her finding deliverance through resistance; although she is saved partly by happenstance, the idea of resistance is latent in the situation.[64] The story was hailed for its striking artistry, especially compared to similar stories written by male writers, as noted by some critics. Mansur al-Hazimi, for example, believed it was "honest and profound."[65] Jabra Ibrahim Jabra said, "When you read it, you find it a true story . . . with a language rich in details and painful metaphors."[66]

In the early stages, short stories were frequently published in the Saudi press. From the mid-1970s to the mid-1980s, a remarkable number of short-story collections by women were published, including Fatima Dawud Hinnawi's *A'maq bila bihar* (Depths without Seas) 1987, Khayriya al-Saqqaf's *An tubhir nahw al-ab'ad* (To Sail toward the Distances) 1982, Latifa al-Salim's *al-Zahf al-abyad* (The White March) 1982, and Ruqaya al-Shabib's *Hulm* (Dream) 1984. The common theme in all these stories is women's problems, but other themes are also there. Some stories experiment with different writing styles, such as "al-Arjuha fi muntasaf al-layl" (Seesaw at Midnight), in Khayriya al-Saqqaf's *An tubhir nahw al-ab'ad*, in which the author uses dreams and stream of consciousness.[67] In the stories of Ruqaya al-Shabib female historical figures like al-Zaba', Sheherazade, and Shajarat al-Durr are brought to bear on the current reality.[68] In this period, short stories are characterized by use of ambiguity, part of a general experimentation with new techniques, seen for example in the writings of Najwa Hashim, although this is not true for all stories of the period.[69] The short-story form flourished starting in the mid-1980s and up to the present day. In this period Sharifa al-Shamlan and Umayma al-Khamis each published three collections, Badriya al-Bishr and Nura al-Ghamidi published two collections,[70] and several other writers—Fawziya al-Jar Allah, Layla al-Uhaydab, and Wafa' al-Tayyib Idris—each published one collection. However many early short-story writers gave up writing for one reason or another, such as Hissa al-Tuwayjiri, who completely stopped publishing stories in the press, Latifa al-Salim, who published nothing after her first collection, and Fawziya al-Bakr, who focused on her academic work in the field of education and wrote only the occasional essay.[71]

The stories published after the mid-1980s employ different writing techniques and begin dealing with various aspects of life experience. Some address aspects of the relationship with the nation, while others deal with social issues, though the approach in both cases remains largely subjective.

In Sharifa al-Shamlan's "al-Naml al-abyad" (Termites) the perspective is subjective or individual, but the framework extends to encompass the nation and homeland in the broadest sense. The story is about a woman who has a recurring nightmare about a termite that comes and consumes everything. The woman's husband, father, and grandmother try to alleviate her fears, but the story ends with the terror even more deeply entrenched, as the woman sees the termite consume even her own brain. The nightmare does not stop at subjective experience, but has symbolic dimensions alluding to national threats.

The idea and image in al-Shamlan's story corresponds to Layla al-'Uthman's "al-Naml al-ashqar,"[72] which, along with other cases, is an indication of the mutual influence among women writers, whether conscious or unconscious, and an example of the threads that link them across the short story. This sort of inspiration is, of course, widespread in literature and does not necessarily mean that the later story is any less than the original. Sharifa al-Shamlan's story is dense, with a multivalent symbolism and a mixture of different moods—realistic, folkloric, and mythical. Despite its simple language, the story is well-crafted and mature.

Many stories by Fawziya al-Bakr, Badriya al-Bishr, and Layla al-Uhaydab contain repeated images of the hardships experienced by women raising children. Of course, these stories are not only noteworthy for their subject matter, but for the perspectives used to examine intimate aspects of women's lives; nevertheless, this remains a subject rarely addressed by male writers.[73] As an example, we can take Layla al-Uhaydab's story, "Nisa'" (Women), which portrays the daily hardship undergone by women in a style that blends the fantastic and the realistic.

In the story, the bus that takes women teachers home after work stops at Haya's house; she fails to notice it, and instead of her, a colleague who resembles her gets off the bus and opens Haya's front door. When the bus stops at this woman's house, Haya finds herself getting out, opening her co-worker's front door, and letting herself in. Later nothing seems out of the ordinary, except that Haya's voice begins to take on the sharp tone of her colleague. The children notice no difference, and Haya, too, sees nothing different from her own home. The children and the husband treat her the same as her own. The next day, the two women meet and laugh at one another. The story seems to say that common household and marital duties have turned women into carbon copies, indistinguishable from one another; even they barely notice the difference between one home and another, in which each woman plays out her preordained role.

In some recent stories, the portrayal of emotional relationships is neither romantic nor completely serious; it is often ironic and carries even a comic effect. In "Fi intizar al-nihaya" (Waiting for the End), Nada al-Tasan mixes the fantastic with the realistic. Set in London, the scene of the story is limited to a specific spot in Hyde Park. The anonymous narrator comments on a conversation between a forty-something man and a twenty-something woman, both of whom are spending the summer in London with their families. Their conversation takes place in an isolated corner of the park surrounded by trees.

In his comments, the narrator takes the position of an observer of events, making remarks that contain an undertone of subtle sarcasm. The narrator comments on the man's every word and gesture, noting that he is trying to pick the girl up. But the narrator also notices that the woman seems aware of the game. When the man proposes meeting in another place, safe from prying eyes, the woman hesitates, then postpones her answer until the next day at the same place. When the conversation ends, the narrator is eagerly awaiting the next day to see how the girl will respond. But the end remains a mystery for the reader, because the narrator turns out to be the seat upon which the man and woman sat, and it is later moved to another spot.

Another example of this type of narrative is "Rif'a" (Height), found in Badriya al-Bishr's collection, *Nihayat al-lu'ba* (Endgame) 1992. The story is set in a popular area in a village in Najd, and it portrays a day in the life of a young girl in a relationship with a boy of similar age and background.

She wants to see him after sunset and she prepares for the adventure the entire day. She is both happy and tense as she is about to succeed with her plan, but the story ends with her mother calling out to her as she is on the verge of stepping out the door. Her mother tells her that her father has guests coming in the evening and she needs to stay at home.[74] Despite their different styles, the two stories are related by their comic spirit and the complete separation between the author and the story's female protagonist.

Allusions to or portrayals of physical relationships were rare in earlier Saudi stories but have begun to appear in some women's stories today. Umayma al-Khamis's "al-Qamar al-fahim" (The Waning Moon), for example, refers quite transparently to a homosexual relationship in Riyadh, where people from various areas mix. The author uses an omniscient narrator, who adopts a critical social stance: "The doors swallow women at an early age, and they settle in at the back of the house until a marriage or a grave is prepared for them. Generally, the husband does not possess all the solutions." This fairly direct critique paves the way for an examination of marriage's repression and failures. "Kamira" (Camera), by Badriya al-Bishr, contains allusions to intimate marital moments. The story relies on the tension between the pleasure of having a video camera document these moments and the negligence that allows the film to reach the hands of strangers.[75] The fact that women writers have begun to broach such topics not only suggests that a segment of the reading public accepts or sees no harm in women writers discussing such things, but may also reflect the extent of women writers' freedom. Women writers are not refusing to address such topics in a largely conservative society, and no one from the family is pressuring them for raising the issue. Nevertheless, it should be noted that many of the story collections that contain topics unacceptable to a conservative society are published abroad. This is not so much indicative of women's status as the willingness or ability of publishers in Saudi Arabia to take on such subjects.

The Emirates

Today short stories written by women in the Emirates are flourishing. Thabit Malakawi notes that the number of women short-story writers even outweighs the number of male short-story writers,[76] and many studies have examined the literature of the Emirates, including short stories by women. Well-known women writers include Salma Matar Sayf, Maryam Jum'a Faraj, Zabya Khamis al-Muslimani, Shaykha al-Nakhi, Su'ad al-'Uraymi, and Asma' al-Zar'uni.

As was the case in other Gulf countries, women's short-story collections began appearing in the 1980s after first becoming common in the press. This period saw the publication of the collections by Zabya Khamis al-Muslimani: *'Uruq al-jir wa-l-hinna* (Veins of Lime and Henna), Salma Matar Sayf: *'Ushba*

(A Blade of Grass), and Maryam Jum'a Faraj: *Fayruz* (Fayruz). These were followed by further collections, some by previously published authors like Salma Matar Sayf and others by new authors like Shaykha Mubarak al-Nakhi, who published her first collection, *al-Rahil* (The Departure), in 1992, although she had published individual stories since the 1970s, and Su'ad al-'Uraymi, with *Tuful* (The Tender Ones) 1990.[77]

It is striking that many female writers from the Emirates have embraced the techniques of modern fiction, with a focus on ambiguity and the use of myth, symbolism, or dreams. In Salma Matar Sayf's *Hajar* (Hajar) 1991, for example, several stories entitled "Hummiyat" (Fevers) use elements of surrealism while portraying the madness of the characters. Her collection *'Ushba* draws on mythology, with women characters in many of the stories linked to images of women in ancient myth.[78] A similar tendency is noticeable in the writings of Maryam Jum'a Faraj. The use of a more direct symbolism appears in some stories by Su'ad al-'Uraymi. In her "al-Daqa'iq al-akhira qabl al-wahida" (The Final Minutes Before One) symbolism is used to portray a particularly female condition.[79] The story opens on a scene in a hospital delivery room, but instead of a birth that represents the beginning of new life, both the mother and child die, and the image of the tomb is contrasted with the scene of birth. Although some of the stories are marked by their use of ambiguity, they are all imbued with a local flavor, evoked by names, vocabulary, and social contexts.[80]

Qatar

After the early phase, several women writers published short-story collections in Qatar, including Nura Al Sa'd, Kulthum Jabr, Huda al-Na'imi, and Kulthum al-Ghanim. Muhammad Kafud considered Nura Al Sa'd's *Ba'i' al-jara'id* (Newspaper Seller) 1989 and Kulthum Jabr's *Waj' imra'a 'Arabiya* (The Pain of an Arab Woman) 1993, to be "a qualitative leap in the evolution of the short story in Qatar."[81] Comparing stories written by men with those written by women that address women's issues, he says, "Women's writings were better crafted and they had a better mastery of the various short-story styles and techniques."[82]

In several stories by Qatari women, the authors use various narrative styles and poetic language.[83] Two approaches in particular are employed by women writers in their portrayal of scene in the short story. One is to portray local cultural features, seen in some of Kulthum al-Ghanim's stories, such as "al-'Urs" (The Wedding), which alludes to slavery, and "al-Mahara" (Oyster), which gives us the image of a woman who makes face veils.[84] The second approach is to set the story in a European country. This is a common element in many Qatari stories; a woman is set in an alien environment and undergoes some sort of psychological or physical hardship.[85] An example is "Milad jadid" (New Birth) 1981, in Kulthum Jabr's collection, *Waj' imra'a*

'Arabiya, which revolves around a young girl in exile who decides to flee from all sense of belonging, but is ultimately overcome by nostalgia. The protagonist of the title story, "Waj' imra'a 'Arabiya," written in 1985, is a young woman from the Gulf who is married with a child. She is alone in Europe in a hospital suffering some sort of psychological trouble, plagued by feelings of grief, fragmentation, and unfulfilled emotion. The story's scattered allusions place responsibility for her grief and alienation on her husband, her society's traditions, and the dominant system, suggesting that they are the cause of her illness.[86] The theme is similar to that found in "al-Sharkh" (The Crack), by Huda al-Na'imi, in her collection, al-Makhala (The Kohl Jar), 1997, which tells the story of a pretty young woman from the Gulf who after her vacation returns to school in Europe for the winter. The first day, she goes walking along the river for a stroll and to experience the sting of winter. She heads for a bookstore she knows, but finds things are not as they should be. The guard tells her that the bookstore has moved. The woman recalls vague memories about the bookstore and the professor interested in philosophy and feels "bitter, frightened, and repelled by the vacant shelves and the mute walls." She connects the abandoned bookstore with her confused personal emotions and her feelings about her local and Arab identity. The story ends with the girl clinging to her Arab identity despite the burden involved: "I struggled to grasp my identity, this heavy Arab identity." Grasping this heavy identity is a process that involves "distress," "grief," and "pain."[87] The story contains a reference to Kulthum Jabr's "Waj' imra'a 'Arabiya," again indicating the connection between women's writings. The problem of a young Arab woman in a strange city is portrayed as a conflict between two different cultures, between the desire for seductive Western worlds and the need to cleave to one's roots. The story could be compared to Zabya Khamis's story set in London, although her heroine feels anxiety rather than a connection to her roots.[88]

Oman

The short story in the modern sense of the word, whether written by men or women, did not appear in Omani literature until the 1980s.[89] Nevertheless, several Omani women writers published short stories in the press, and students of Omani literature have pointed to writers like Badriya al-Shihhi,[90] Tiba Bint 'Abd Allah al-Kindi, 'A'isha Bint 'Ali ibn Sa'id al-Ni'mi, Zakiya Bint Salim al-'Ilwi, Safiya Bint Muhammad Sa'id al-Harithi, and Turkiya al-Busa'idi.[91] In 1998, Khawla al-Zahiri published her collection, Saba' (Sheba), which won a prize from the Girls' Clubs in Sharjah. Some of the stories in the collection mix the modern techniques of fiction with the private, feminine world of women. In "Hallaw" (Welcome), the narrator is the husband who tells us about about the stages of his wife's labor and the birth of his baby girl, who comes out strangely formed, an element used by the story to create a fantastic effect.[92]

The foregoing analysis has attempted to provide a framework from which to view women's short stories in the Gulf, although it does not represent all story writers or experiments. It is worth noting that although many women writers have published individual short stories, many have not published collections.[93] The main point to be made in the overall context is that after the early collections, which largely used simple techniques and openly advocated reform,[94] stories from the mid-1980s on began to make use of various writing styles and addressed different aspects of life experience, although a female subjective perspective continues to dominate the stories. Particularly feminine aspects of women's lives—puberty, pregnancy, birth, abortion—began to appear in some stories to document the psychological, emotional, or social changes they entail for women. It is also striking that many women who wrote short stories early on later stopped writing, including Hissa al-Tuwayjiri in Saudi Arabia and Mayy Salim and Maysa al-Khalifi from Qatar.[95]

The novel

Samira Khashuqji, known as Samira Bint al-Jazira al-'Arabiya (1940–1986), is the first women novelist from the Gulf area. She is from the Hijaz and was educated in Egypt. Her first novel, *Wadda't amali* (I Bid My Hopes Farewell), was published in 1958.[96] The Hijaz is thus the first area in the Arabian Peninsula from which a female novelist emerged.[97] Khashuqji published several novels, right up to her death. Mansur al-Hazimi classifies her works as "adventure novels" that try to excite the readers, featuring flat characters, and focus on an accumulation of action.[98] But this type of novel was prevalent in the region as a whole at the time, and novels written by men were no better.

The 1970s saw several novels published in Saudi Arabia by Hind Baghaffar, 'A'isha Zahir, and Huda al-Rashid. In Kuwait, Fatima al-'Ali published a novel and Nuriya al-Saddani published two. These novels are similar to those of the early period and are marred by artistic flaws.[99] Nevertheless, it is noteworthy that Fatima al-'Ali's first novel was the fourth novel written in Kuwait, the first three having been authored by male novelists.[100] This indicates that in Kuwait, men and women started writing novels at roughly the same time.

In the 1980s, more women started publishing novels in Saudi Arabia, among them Amal Shata, Raja Alem, and Safiya 'Anbar.[101] In Kuwait, Layla al-'Uthman published two novels, *al-Mar'a wa-l-qitta* (The Woman and the Cat) 1985, and *Wa Sumaya takhruj min al-bahr* (And Sumaya Emerges from the Sea) 1986. Until the late 1980s, the novel in the Arabian Peninsula was limited to Saudi Arabia and Kuwait. Although they were published in the same period, these novels are of varying quality and have different themes and structures, as seen in a comparison of Layla al-'Uthman's *Wa Sumaya takhruj min al-bahr* with *Arba'a/sifr* (Four/Zero) 1987, by Raja Alem, for example.[102]

In the 1990s, the number of published novels increased. In Saudi Arabia Salwa Damanhuri, Samira Lari, and Layla al-Jahani published novels. In Kuwait, several novels appeared by Khawla al-Qazwini, Tayba Ahmad al-Ibrahim, and others. In Bahrain Fawziya Rashid published *Tahawwulat al-faris al-gharib fi-l-bilad al-'Ariba* (Transformations of the Knight, a Stranger in Arab Lands) 1990. In Qatar, Shu'a' Khalifa and Dalal Khalifa published four novels.[103] The novels of Qatari women writers have received the attention of more than one student of Qatari literature. The sea is a common element in Qatari novels, showing the influence of the local environment. Dalal Khalifa's *Min al-bahhar al-qadim ilayk* (From the Ancient Mariner to You), 1995, was published without the author's name on the cover; it is not a subjective work and refers to women only in passing, although this is consistent with the content of the story itself: a sailor talking about his daily life on a boat. The narrative takes an epistolary form, in letters written to an anonymous figure, and uses simple language. Behind this simple language, however, the ship and the events on it become a symbol of the life of the nation in the current period. Khalifa, who appends her name to the end of the novel, notes on the last page that she used the ship as a symbol of society and that she was inspired by a Prophetic *hadith*.[104]

In contrast, the narrative is subjective in Layla al-Jahani's *al-Firdaws al-yabab* (The Desolate Paradise) 1998. The language is emotive, but is not limited to the interior world: Jeddah and its contemporary society are the setting. *Sidi Wahdanah (My Thousand and One Nights)* 1998, by Raja Alem, represents another type of novel that appeared in the 1990s, and it caught the attention of many. Alem is a good writer, but this novel is particularly well-crafted. In all her novels—*Tariq al-harir* (The Silk Road), *Masra ya raqib* (Happy, O Censor), and *Sidi Wahdanah*—she attempts to mix history and fiction, and intertextual references to classical texts are prominent. Her writing style relies on ambiguity and the interposition of things that spontaneously give rise to secondary meanings and allusions. The writing in *Sidi Wahdanah* is complex and brings together elements from books on magic and amulets, figures from *The Thousand and One Nights* like Hasan al-Basri, stories from the ancient tradition, Sufi worlds with their mystical numerology and symbolism, and the local folk heritage from the Hijaz, particularly Mecca.[105] The novel's setting alternates from the environs of Mecca from the early to mid-twentieth century, to the world of genies, spirits, and the fantastic. The world of women comes clearly to the fore; the storyteller is a young woman from a family who speaks about past events in her family's life and searches for secrets and the solutions to riddles. The action revolves around the narrator's aunt, Dambushi or Jamu, who died before the events recounted in the novel. The narrator tells stories about the aunt's life, brimming with vitality and strange happenings, which in turn contain other tales, filled with magic and ancient ritual, about other women—mothers, sisters, and strangers—whose stories are told from the perspective of the women themselves. Men, who represent the outside world, are also prominent in the novel. There is the father, the grandfather, and strangers, none of whom escapes the sway of the spirit world. Three men have a particularly strong love for Jamu: the mysterious prince, Sidi Wahdanah, who appears in various guises and disappears as soon as he appears; Miyajan, a young Khazar boy; and Hasan al-Sa'igh al-Basri, a character from *The Thousand and One Nights*. Love here is a circle that combines the worlds of the spirit and the flesh, and the novel's fantastic atmosphere emits a sort of magic in the soul.

Drama and autobiography

There are very few works written by Gulf women for the theater, but these include plays by Raja Alem, Malha 'Abd Allah, and Amina Sibyan al-Juhani in Saudi Arabia. Raja Alem's plays revolve around the intellectual contemplation of life. In Qatar, three plays by Dalal Khalifa were published in one volume, entitled *Insan fi hayz al-wujud* (A Person in the Sphere of Existence) 1995. In the Emirates, Bahrain, Oman, and Kuwait, we find hardly any published prose plays by women, with the exception of works for children's theater. Women have written plays in Oman, but they have not been published.[106]

Similarly, there is virtually no autobiography written by women from the Arabian Peninsula, although Zabya Khamis al-Muslimani, from the Emirates, has taken a stab at this literary genre. In *Ibtisamat makira wa qisas ukhra* (Deceptive Smiles and Other Stories) 1996, she appends a note to the title story, calling it "a chapter from an unfinished memoir," and she does the same thing in the story "al-Zinzana" (The Cell).[107]

Children's literature

With the increasing interest in children's education, women in the Gulf have recently shown a concomitant interest in writing for children. Children's literature is one of the most serious topics in Saudi Arabia and the Gulf, and only a few women from the area have turned to the field. During the 1970s in Saudi Arabia, Farida Farisi wrote more than ten children's stories. In the 1980s and 1990s, women continued to write books for children—short stories, poetry, and plays—in Saudi Arabia, Kuwait, the Emirates, and Qatar. These writers include Asma' al-Zar'uni, Iman al-Khatib, Hissa al-'Awadi, Dalal Khalifa, Sa'ida Bint Khatir al-Farisi, Fawziya Abu Khalid, and Hind Khalifa.

Conclusion

The foregoing essay has provided an outline of literature written by women from the Arabian Peninsula since the end of the Second World War to the end of the twentieth century, offering a brief sketch of the beginnings of the literary renaissance in the region. It is worth noting that the term 'pioneers' is not necessarily applicable to early women writers in the area. Short stories, poetry, novels, drama, autobiography, and other types of literature existed in the Gulf region and were accessible to local readers; women writers were not, then, pioneers in the sense of exploring utterly new ground. Nevertheless, pioneering efforts have recently been made in the field of children's literature, and engaging or educational books for children differ from the normal fare found in the wider Arab world.

It is also noteworthy that most women writers in the region are young. Nevertheless, it would be inaccurate to suggest that women's literature in the Gulf has followed a linear path of development, or that each decade represents a decisive point in its evolution and that women writers belong to clear-cut literary generations. Later generations of writers are not necessarily better than those who preceded them; rather, writers who continue to write improve with practice and experience, although this is certainly not inevitable. Some women writers published works in the 1990s that were neither serious nor authentic.

Notes

1 Ahmad Abu Bakr Ibrahim, *al-Adab al-Hijazi fi-l-nahda al-haditha* (Cairo: Dar Nahdat Misr, 1948), p. 58. Cited in Fawziya Baryun, "'An al-qissa al-nisa'iya al-qasira fi-l-adab al-Sa'udi," *al-Wahat al-mushmisha*, vols. 7 and 8, November 1999, pp. 16–45. Ibrahim mentions, "I heard during my stay there [the Hijaz] in 1938 about a poet called Khadija al-Shanqitiya and that she had written a collection of poetry in praise of the Prophet, but that the publication had gone out of print" (*al-Adab al-Hijazi*, p. 114).

2 Women's oral Nabati poetry has existed since ancient times in the desert. See for example 'Abd Allah ibn Muhammad ibn Raddas, *Sha'irat min al-badiya* (Riyadh: n.p., 1985), vol. 1, pp. 69–87 and 252.

3 Ibrahim Ghalum, *al-Qissa al-qasira fi-l-khalij al-'Arabi—al-Kuwayt wa-l-Bahrayn: dirasa naqdiya tahliliya* (Basra: Center for Arabian Gulf Studies Publications, 1947–81), p. 67.

4 Muhammad Hasan 'Abd Allah, *al-Haraka al-adabiya wa-l-fikriya fi-l-Kuwayt* (Kuwait: Authors' League in Kuwait, 1973), p. 157.

5 For the beginning of girls' education in Qatar, see Muhammad 'Abd al-Rahim Kafud, *al-Adab al-Qatari al-hadith* (Doha: Dar Qatari ibn al-Faja'a, 1982), p. 67; in the Emirates, see Thabit Malakawi, *al-Riwaya wa-l-qissa al-qasira fi-l-Imarat* (Abu Dhabi: Cultural Complex Publications, n.d. [after 1989]), p. 13; in Saudi Arabia, see Mudhi Bint Fahd al-Na'im, "al-Ta'lim al-'amm li-l-banat: bidayatuh, masiratuh, hadiruh, wa mustaqbaluh," in

Buhuth mu'tamar al-Mamlaka al-'Arabiya al-Sa'udiya fi mi'at 'am, proceedings of conference held in Riyadh, January 24–28, 1999, p. 16. She mentions the role of private, local education before the opening of government schools, pp. 26–42; in Oman, see Layla Salih, *Adab al-mar'a fi-l-jazira wa-l-khalij al-'Arabi/al-juz' al-thani: al-Yaman wa 'Uman* (Kuwait: Dhat al-Silasil, 1987), p. 318, where she says that "there was one small school for girls, then three government schools for girls opened in the academic year 1970/1971." But this does not tell us if the one small school was private or public. It is worth noting that many Omani women were educated long before this period in other Arab countries such as Kuwait and Egypt. See the same source, p. 319, and also see Nuriya al-Saddani, *Tarikh al-mar'a al-'Umaniya* (N.p.: n.p., 1984).

6 Sulayman al-Shatti, "Madkhal al-qissa al-qasira fi-l-Kuwayt," *al-Bayan*, no. 277, April 1989, pp. 72–169; 121, and Layla Salih, *Udaba' wa adibat al-Kuwayt a'da' al-rabita 1964–1996* (Kuwait: Authors' League in Kuwait, 1996), p. 79.

7 Sulayman al-Shatti, "Madkhal al-qissa," p. 121; see also the story in Khalid Sa'ud al-Zayd, *Qisas yatima fi-l-majallat al-Kuwaytiya 1929–1955* (Kuwait: al-Rabi'an Publishing, 1982), pp. 61–62.

8 Ibrahim Ghalum, p. 224 and Layla Salih, *Adab al-mar'a fi-l-jazira wa-l-khalij al-'Arabi: al-Mamlaka al-'Arabiya al-Sa'udiya, dawlat al-Bahrayn, dawlat Qatar, dawlat al-Imarat al-'Arabiya al-Muttahida* (Kuwait: al-Yaqza Press, 1983), pp. 164 and 171. Ghalum (pp. 58–59) refers to an article signed with the initial "A" in *al-Bahrayn* newspaper in 1939, as well as articles signed "Umm Usama" in *Kazima* in 1948–49, but there is no way knowing if the author was really a woman or if it was a man using a female pen name.

9 One of the first editors of such pages was Fatina Shakir, who worked at *'Ukaz* from 1961 to 1963, and Thuraya Qabil, who worked at *al-Bilad* and *'Ukaz*. Some editors of the women's page were still high-school students.

10 Although much of the material published on these pages was quite naïve, given the authors' youth and lack of education, there were several serious literary attempts.

11 Muhammad Kafud notes that the craft of the short story first emerged "in Qatar in tandem with the appearance of a local press" at the end of the 1960s, although there were some early precedents published in the early 1960s. See "Banurama li-l-qissa al-qasira fi Qatar: al-nash'a wa-l-tatawwur," in *al-Salun al-adabi: ibda'at Qatariya* (Doha: al-Jasra Cultural and Social Club, 1996), p. 67.

12 Muhammad Kafud, *al-Adab al-Qatari al-hadith*, p. 73.

13 *Al-'Uruba* magazine, no. 153, January 4, 1972. See Muhammad Kafud, *al-Adab al-Qatari al-hadith*, p. 95. Kafud also refers to a poem, "Asrar al-hayah," published under the pseudonym Fatat al-Khalij in *al-Dawha* magazine, p. 93.

14 Thabit Malakawi, *al-Riwaya wa-l-qissa*, pp. 118 and 163.

15 Muhammad Rashid, "al-Qissa al-qasira fi dawlat al-Imarat al-'Arabiya al-Muttahida," *al-Bayan*, no. 277, March 1989, pp. 17, 27, and 34, where he notes that on the eve of the establishment of the state in December 1971, the craft of the short story had taken shape in the Emirates.

16 I could find nothing in any sources on literature in the Gulf that indicates the emergence of women's literature in the Emirates before this period.

17 Yusuf al-Sharuni, *Fi-l-adab al-'Umani al-hadith* (London: Riyad al-Rayyis, 1990), pp. 48, 54, 69, 122–23, 136, 183, and 151–63. Al-Sharuni mentions that men began to write short stories in Oman in the early 1970s (p. 19).

18 *'Abir al-sahra'* (Beirut: al-Ahliya Foundation for Printing and Publishing, 1956). She published her second collection, *'Aynay fidak* (Beirut: Dar al-Kitab al-Jadid, 1964) under the same pen name. It contained most of the poems from the first collection. After that, she began publishing her collections under her real name.

19 I was not able to obtain a first edition of the novel, *Wadda't amali*, but the back cover of the most recent edition of Khashuqji's novel, *Wara' al-dabab* (Beirut: Zuhayr Ba'labakki Publications, 1979), refers to "her first book, *Wadda't amali,* [which] appeared in 1958."

20 *Al-Awzan al-bakiya* (Beirut: Dar al-Kutub, 1963).

21 The source of this information is the autobiography of Dr. Su'ad Muhammad al-Sabah, which she graciously sent to me in 1999.

22 'Abd Allah al-Mubarak, *Adab al-nathr al-mu'asir fi sharqi al-jazira al-'Arabiya* (Cairo: n.p., 1970), p. 97.

23 The figures were compiled by Manal al-'Isi in the course of preparing the bibliography of women's literature from the Arabian Peninsula and Gulf.

24 See for example, *Sha'irat min al-badiya.* Currently colloquial poetry is very widespread among educated women in Saudi Arabia, the Emirates, Oman, and Qatar. Some women poets compose in both colloquial and classical Arabic.

25 Muhammad al-Tunji, *Qira'at musafir fi shi'r Su'ad al-Sabah* (Kuwait: al-Nur Company, 1987) and Layla Salih, *Udaba' wa adibat al-Kuwayt,* pp. 141–42. Unsi al-Hajj refers to her as "a tribal princess who challenges the tribe: its customs, its men, its traditions, people of tradition, and an entire world of petrified customs." See the inside cover of Su'ad al-Sabah, *Fi-l-bad' kanat al-untha* (London: Riyad al-Rayyis, 1988).

26 Su'ad al-Sabah, *Fi-l-bad' kanat al-untha,* p. 12.

27 'Alawi al-Hashimi, *Shu'ara' al-Bahrayn al-mu'asirun: kashshaf tahlili musawwar 1925–1985* (Bahrain: n.p., 1988), p. 11.

28 Taha Wadi, "Tahawwulat al-azmina wa ta'arudat al-hadatha fi shi'r al-khalij al-mu'asir," from the proceedings of a seminar on literature in the Arabian Gulf, held on January 10–14, 1988 (Sharjah: Emirati Writers' and Authors' Union Publications, 1991), vol. 4, p. 60.

29 Ibid., p. 151. Also Jawad al-Tahir, "'An al-kitab al-adabi fi-l-khalij al-'Arabi," from the proceedings of a seminar on literature in the Arabian Gulf, held on January 10–14, 1988 (Sharjah: Emirati Writers' and Authors' Union Publications, 1990), vol. 1, p. 102, noting that a professor at the Art Academy in Iraq liked a poem by Hamda Khamis ("For You to Come . . . So the Wedding Started") and directed a stage adaptation of it.

30 Hamda Khamis wrote free verse and prose poems until her second collection of poems appeared in 1985, according to 'Alawi al-Hashimi, pp. 151–52. For more on the poet, see 'Alawi al-Hashimi, *Sukun al-mutaharrik: dirasa fi-l-bunya wa-l-uslub: tajribat al-shi'r al-mu'asir fi-l-Bahyrayn namudhajan* (Sharjah: Emirate Authors' and Writers' Union Publications, 1992), vol. 1, p. 383.

31 Her collection was published after Qasim Haddad had already gained some renown for the prose poem with his collection *Qalb al-hubb*. See 'Alawi al-Hashimi, *Sukun al-mutaharrik*, vol. 1, pp. 256–57.

32 Al-Hashimi categorizes Hamda Khamis and Fathiya 'Ajlan as "poets who never composed in the classical *qasida* form," along with Iman Asiri and Fawziya al-Sindi. See al-Hashimi, *Shu'ara' al-Bahrayn al-mu'asir*, p. 241.

33 There are also six plays and seventeen volumes of children's literature. See the bibliography.

34 'Abd Allah ibn Raddas, *Sha'irat min al-badiya*, vol. 1, for example, refers to poets Qamra' al-Da'janiya (p. 39), Sa'di al-Jihan (p. 218), Nura al-Sayhaniya (p. 271), Halla al-Hatimiya (p. 293), and Wadha' al-Harbiya (p. 339).

35 The small amount of women's poetry published in classical Arabic before this period tends toward religious themes, for example, the poetry of Khadija al-Shanqitiya. Sultana al-Sudayri published several subsequent collections, but then she focused on colloquial Nabati poetry.

36 'Abd Allah 'Abd al-Jabbar, *al-Tayyarat al-adabiya fi qalb al-jazira al-'Arabiya* (Cairo: Institute for Arab Studies at the Arab League, 1959), pp. 182–83.

37 Al-Sudayri comes from a well-known family, several of whose members have been prominent in the area of al-Qaryat in the north.

38 See her collection, pp. 43, 45, and 47.

39 Fawziya Abu Khalid may be the region's most internationally known poet. Her poetry has been translated into English in several books including K. Boullata, ed. and trans., *Women of the Fertile Crescent: an Anthology of Modern Poetry by Arab Women* (Washington D.C.: Three Continents Press, 1978); Salma Jayyusi, *The Literature of Modern Arabia* (London: Kegan Paul International, 1988); Saddeka Arebi, *Women and Words in Saudi Arabia: The Politics of Literary Discourse* (New York: Columbia University Press, 1994); and Carol Boyce Davies and Molara Ogundipe-Leslie, eds., *International Dimensions of Black Women's Writing* (London: Pluto Press, 1995).

40 She published the same poem in her second collection, *Hurub al-ahilla*.

41 She wrote the poem in 2000, but at the time of writing this survey it had not yet been published.

42 Another poem, "al-Ihtifal" by Saudi poet Fatima al-Qarni, is written in the *'amudi* (classical prosody) form and refers to old age: "Unwelcome greetings . . . you have taken me unawares, O gray, and begun to swagger about in my hair." *Al-Majalla al-'Arabiya*, Safar AH 1413, p. 71.

43 Ghayda' al-Manfa and Ghajariyat al-Rif are pseudonyms for the same female poet. For the poetry of Khadija al-'Umari, Ghayda' al-Manfa/Ghajariyat al-Rif, see "Mukhtarat min al-shi'r al-'Arabi al-hadith fi-l-khalij wa-l-jazira al-'Arabiya," *Mu'jam al-Babtin li-l-shu'ara' al-mu'asirin* (Kuwait: al-Qabas, 1995), pp. 420–24 and 443–46. Also Sa'd al-Bazi'i, *Thaqafat al-sahra': dirasat fi adab al-jazira al-'Arabiya al-mu'asir* (Riyadh: n.p., 1991), p. 20. Fatima al-Qarni published her poems in Saudi newspapers. She has two collections of poetry currently on press.

44 The collection is quite slim, composed of short poems in the *'amudi* form that address traditional themes, but it has a marked purity of style.

45 See what Su'ad 'Abd al-Wahhab has written about Janna al-Qurayni's poetry and the sense of alienation in "al-Ightirab fi-l-shi'r al-Kuwayti," *Annals of the College of Liberal Arts*, no. 14, letter no. 94, 1993–94, pp. 15–19 and 134–46.

46 Muhammad 'Abd al-Rahim Kafud has written about the poetry of Zakiya Mal Allah, seeing her first collection, *Ma'bad al-ashwaq*, as characterized by simplicity and fluidity and a gentle musical style dominated by romance. He notes that her second collection veered toward mystical poetry. He sees her most recent collections, *Min asfar al-dhat* and *'Ala shafa hufra min al-buh*, as representing a fundamental transformation of her style and poetic experience. See "al-Shi'r al-hadith fi Qatar," in *al-Salun al-adabi: ibda'at Qatariya* (Doha: al-Jasra Cultural and Social Club, 1996), pp. 37, 38.

47 For the anxieties of writing, see Zakiya Mal Allah's poem, "Hawajis," in *Najmat al-dhakira* (Doha: Dar al-Thaqafa), p. 67.

48 From personal telephone conversations with women writers in 1999, I concluded that many of them do not publish their writings in collections.

49 Muhammad ibn Rashid ibn 'Aziz al-Khasibi in *Shaqa'iq al-nu'man 'ala sumut al-juman fi asma' shu'ara' 'Uman* (Oman: Ministry of National Heritage and Culture, 1994) mentions her and includes some of her poems. He states that she "deserves to be called the only woman poet of our age" (vol. 2, pp. 13–16). Layla Salih in *Adab al-mar'a fi-l-jazira wa-l-khalij al-'Arabi/al-juz' al-thani: al-Yaman wa 'Uman* states that she published her poetry in local papers like *al-'Aqida* and *al-Usra* and that she had a collection of poems on press (p. 406). My research has turned up no published collection of her poems.

50 "Mukhtarat min al-shi'r al-'Arabi al-hadith fi-l-khalij wa-l-jazira al-'Arabiya," *Mu'jam al-Babtin li-l-shu'ara' al-mu'asirin* (Kuwait: al-Qabas, 1995) states that she was born in the early twentieth century (p. 485), while Layla Salih says she was born in Muscat in 1944 (p. 405) and al-Khasibi gives no date of birth. He only notes that she was among "those Omanis who recited poetry in the fourteenth and fifteenth centuries [AH]" (vol. 2, p. 13).

51 Layla Salih says that she received her early education in the *kuttab* (Qur'anic school) (p. 405), but she does not explain her later education, such as how she acquired her knowledge of prosody and Arabic grammar. I wrote to the poet asking for further information, but she did not respond.

52 This story is one of the first published by a woman. It focuses on the persecution of women and was published in *al-Ra'id*, May 1953. See Khalid Sa'ud al-Zayd, p. 195.

53 See Hanna Mina's comment on the first story in his introduction to the second edition of *Fi-l-layl ta'ti al-'uyun* (Beirut: Dar al-Adab, 1980; second edition, 1984), pp. 11–12. For the second story see Sulayman al-Shatti, "Madkhal al-qissa," p. 126.

54 For Layla al-'Uthman, see Sulayman al-Shatti, "Madkhal al-qissa," pp. 121–32.

55 Najma Idris links this story to women's status in society in "al-Untha wa-l-mujtama' fi-l-qissa al-Kuwaytiya," *Qawafil*, vol. 2, no. 3, 1994, pp. 55–78.

56 See the collection, *al-Sayyida kanat*, pp. 79–92, 33–52, and 113–20.

57 The first story is "al-Hubb fi-l-lahazat al-akhira," in *Yahduth kull layla*; the second is "Ghariban fi 'Uman," in the second edition of *al-Hawajiz al-sawda'* (Kuwait: n.p., 1997), pp. 73–82.

58 Ibrahim Ghalum (p. 224) notes that the idea of social reform dominated these stories. As an example of this early period, he cites "Tawaha al-nisyan," by Mawza al-Za'id, where a woman's fall is portrayed as a consequence of social injustice.

59 Some studies have addressed the stories of Fawziya Rashid, for example Walid Abu Bakr, "Athar al-bi'a wa-l-mutaghayyirat al-ijtima'iya fi-l-qissa al-qasira fi duwal majlis al-ta'awun," *al-Bayan*, no. 278, May 1989, pp. 142–53.

60 Studies that have addressed *al-Rimura* include Walid Abu Bakr, pp. 142, 145, and 148, and Sulayman al-Shatti, "Madkhal al-qissa," p. 72.

61 Ibrahim Ghalum states that Fawziya Rashid uses "the theme of prisoners and exiles as a means of critiquing reality." In "al-Qissa al-qasira fi duwal majlis al-ta'awun wa qadaya balwarat al-huwwiya al-qawmiya," *al-Bayan*, no. 278, May 1989, pp. 190.

62 *Imra'a fi-l-dhakira* (Bahrain: n.p., 1996), pp. 117–22, 137–41, and 69–74.

63 Su'ad al-Mana, "al-Qissa al-qasira wa tatawwuruha fi kitabat al-mar'a al-Sa'udiya," *al-Mar'a al-Sa'udiya fi mi'at 'am* (Riyadh: Research Center at the Girls Center for University Research, Humanities Section, King Sa'ud University, 2002), pp. 125–27.

64 Najah Khayyat, *Makhad al-samt* (1966), pp. 70–71.

65 Mansur al-Hazimi, *Fann al-qissa fi-l-adab al-Sa'udi* (Riyadh: Dar al-'Ulum, 1981), p. 121. He believed the story was more artistically mature than a similar story written by a male writer at that time.

66 "Qira'a naqdiya fi nukhba min al-qisas al-qasira," *al-Bayan*, no. 278, May 1989, pp. 232–33.

67 For this story, see Amal Amin al-Sabbagh, *al-Qissa al-qasira al-mu'asira fi-l-Sa'udiya*, Ph.D. dissertation, Damascus University, 1988, pp. 84–86. See also Ahlam 'Abd al-Latif Hadi, who mentioned it in her discussion of stream-of-consciousness writing in the short story in *Tayyar al-wa'i fi-l-qissa al-qasira al-Sa'udiya 1970–1995*, M.A. thesis, King Sa'ud University, 1996, pp. 250–57.

68 Amal Amin al-Sabbagh, pp. 82–84, and Ahlam 'Abd al-Latif Hadi, pp. 259–84.

69 Jabra Ibrahim Jabra has remarked on the heavy presence of allegory, surrealism, symbolism, and the fantastic in Gulf stories from the 1980s. See "Qira'a naqdiya," pp. 221, 224, and 247.

70 See the bibliography for these authors and al-Mana, "al-Qissa al-qasira."

71 One of Hissa al-Tuwayjiri's stories from the 1970s, "Tal sha'ri min jadid," is written from a perspective that examines hardship but does not give in to it. *Kitab al-qissa/millaf al-Ta'if: namadhij mukhtara min al-qisas al-Sa'udi* (N.p.: al-Ta'if Literary Club, Story Committee, AH 1398), pp. 57–60.

72 "Al-Naml al-abyad," *al-Qafila*, vol. 2, no. 3, 1994, pp. 173–75; "al-Naml al-ashqar," *Fi-l-layl ta'ti al-'uyun*, pp. 29–38.

73 See Su'ad al-Mana, "Kitabat al-mar'a: al-qissa wa hawajis al-mar'a," *Qawafil*, vol. 2, no. 4, 1995, pp. 20–49.

74 The first story is part of the collection, *Nabd wa irtijaf*, still unpublished; the second is from *Nihayat al-lu'ba* (Riyadh: Dar al-Ard, 1992), pp. 47–53.

75 "Al-Qamar al-fahim,"*Ayna yadhhab hadha-l-daw'* (Beirut: Dar al-Adab, 1996), pp. 19–30, and "Kamirat al-fidiyu," *Masa' al-Arbi'a'* (Beirut: Dar al-Adab, 1994), pp. 37–45.

76 Thabit Malakawi, *al-Riwaya wa-l-qissa*, pp. 132–35 and 159–68.

77 *Tuful* (Sharjah: Emirati Writers' and Authors' Union, 1990).

78 For more on the collection *'Ushba*, see Ibrahim Ghalum, "al-Tawzif al-usturi fi Tajribat fann al-qissa al-qasira bi-l-Imarat," *Fusul*, vol. 11, no. 2, 1992, pp. 264–89.

79 Su'ad al-'Uraymi, *al-Tuful*, pp. 9–10.

80 See for example "Min al-zawaya al-mutawadi'a," p. 67, and "'Abbar," pp. 15–17 in Maryam Ja'far Faraj, *Fayruz* (Sharjah: Emirati Writers' and Authors' Union, 1988).

81 Muhammad Kafud, *al-Qissa al-qasira*, p. 13.

82 Ibid., p. 63.

83 For examples see Kulthum Jabr, "al-Sunduq al-khamis," *Waj' imra'a 'Arabiya* (al-Dammam: Dar Umniya Publishing and Distribution, 1993) and Huda al-Na'imi, "al-Ashya'" and "Imra'a 'aqila," *al-Makhala* (Cairo: Amun, 1997).

84 *Shams al-yawm al-jadid* (Doha: Dar al-Sharq Press, 1998), pp. 37–45 and 73–79.

85 For example Umm Aktham, "Yawmiyat fi-l-manfa," published in Layla Salih, *Adab al-mar'a fi-l-jazira*, pp. 266–74. The action takes place in a mental sanitarium in Europe and highlights sharp contradictions between rich and poor, luxury and want, life and death. The world outside the homeland seems no better than the one inside.

86 Raja' al-Naqqash, in the introduction to *Waj' imra'a 'Arabiya*, pp. 8–12.

87 *Al-Makhala*, pp. 111–17. There are other examples in the collection of women in European environs. "Al-'Id" tells the story of a student in Montpellier passing the holiday in foreign lands (pp. 35–38); the main character of "al-Makhala" is a young married woman living in some European country. When she discovers her husband is cheating on her with a blonde woman, she decides to return home (pp. 61–65).

88 "Ba'd al-khamisa masa'an," *'Uruq al-jir wa-l-hinna*, pp. 7–18.

89 In *al-Adab al-'Umani al-hadith*, Yusuf al-Sharuni states, "We can confidently declare that 1983 is the year the Omani short story of all kinds was born" (p. 31). He says that before this date, in the 1970s, there was only "an embryo taking shape in the womb of the awakening (p. 48)."

90 Ibid., pp. 54, 122–23, 135–36, and 138.

91 Ibid., p. 48. Also Layla Salih, *Adab al-mar'a*, vol. 2, p. 321.

92 Khawla al-Zahiri, *Saba'* (Sharjah: Girls' Clubs of Sharjah and al-Dar al-Misriya al-Lubnaniya, 1998), p. 55

93 Examples in Saudi Arabia include Fawziya Bakr, who once wrote short stories but later stopped; she is currently a professor at the College of Education at King Sa'ud University; Nada al-Tasan, who is studying for a doctorate in genetics in Britain and has not yet published a collection of stories, though she still writes; and Munira al-Ghadir, who obtained a Ph.D. in the U.S. in English literature. She has not published a collection of stories although she still writes individual stories.

94 See Ghalum's comments on this type of writing in *al-Qissa al-qasira*, pp. 326–34.

95 There are quite a few Qatari women who wrote short stories early on; Kafud mentions their names. When I asked about their works today, I was told that they had abandoned writing for other activities.

96 See note 5 above. Sultan al-Qahtani, *al-Riwaya fi-l-Mamlaka al-Sa'udiya al-'Arabiya: nash'atuha wa tatawwuruha 1930–1989* (Riyadh: Matabi' Sharikat al-Safahat al-Dhabiya, 1998), notes that the Saudi women's novel emerged in the 1970s and makes no reference to Samira Khashuqji.

97 Her second novel, *Dhikrayat dami'a*, was published in 1962. See the new edition (Beirut: Zuhayr Ba'labakki Publications, 1979), p. 10, where the introduction is dated July 14, 1967, and refers to the first edition.

98 Al-Hazimi, *Fann al-qissa fi-l-adab al-Sa'udi al-hadith*, pp. 49–50.

99 Sultan al-Qahtani, *al-Riwaya fi-l-Mamlaka*, pp. 139–49 and 232, wrote about Hind Baghaffar's *al-Bara'a al-mafquda*, 'A'isha Zahir's *Wa basma min buhayrat al-dumu'*, and Huda Rashid's *Wa ghadan sayakun al-Khamis*. He says that the artistic structure of the last is good compared to novels of that period.

100 Fatima al-'Ali, in the introduction to her short-story collection, *Wajhuha watan* (Kuwait: n.p., 1995), p. 8.

101 Sultan al-Qahtani, *al-Riwaya fi-l-Mamlaka*, pp. 232–35, writes about Safiya 'Anbar's novel, *'Afwan ya Adam* (1988).

102 *Arba'a/sifr* received an honorary mention in the Ibn Tufayl competition of 1985, sponsored by the Spanish Arab Institute in Madrid. Sabry Hafez, "Surat al-rajul fi riwayat al-mar'a," *al-Mar'a al-'Arabiya fi muwajahat al-'asr* (Cairo: Nur and Dar al-Mar'a al-'Arabiya Publications, 1996), pp. 217–18, says that the author of *Wa Sumaya takhruj min al-bahr* reproduces the patriarchal discourse, but the passages he cites from the novel to support this are not consistent with what the novel says. For example, Sumaya does not sacrifice her life for a young man, but in fear of the scandal that will touch her and her family, and the mother of the child does not conceal what happened to protect the young man—for the young man committed no murder or moral crime—but to protect her daughter's and family's reputation and fearing that her husband will accuse her of negligence.

103 Muhammad Najib al-Talawi, *al-Riwaya al-'Arabiya fi Qatar: tahlil waza'ifi* (Doha: al-Jasra Cultural Club, n.d.), p. 111, says that *al-'Ubur ila-l-haqiqa* marked the dawn of the novel in Qatar.

104 *Min al-bahhar al-qadim ilayk* (Doha: Dar al-'Ulum, 1995), p. 211.

105 *Sidi Wahdanah*, pp. 5, 7, and 14, for example; translated into English as *My Thousand and One Nights: A Novel of Mecca* (Syracuse, NY: Syracuse University Press, 2007).

106 There are indications that Muhra al-Qasimi from the Emirates experimented with writing school plays early on, perhaps in the 1980s, but she later stopped. Saliha Ghubaysh, from the Emirates, is also currently writing a play.

107 She notes at the end of the first story that it was written in Sharjah, April 1989. To the second she appends the note, "September 1, 1991, Sharjah, Emirates, from the prison diaries, 1987." See pp. 5–48 and 85–90.

9   Yemen

Hatem M. al-Sager

To write about women's literature in the twentieth century in a country like Yemen is first to confront the many gaps in the historical record. The cultural ruptures and lacunae that are a product of Yemen's modern history, both in the north and the south, are reflected in the general conditions of Yemeni life and particularly in the cultural identity and literature of women. Indeed, it is difficult to talk about women's literature much before the 1960s, both in the south, where British colonial rule lasted until 1967, and in the north, which was under the rule of the Imamate until 1962. We cannot discuss, for example, the pioneering works of women in the early part of the century because, at that time, women had no education: they were not allowed to mix with men, to work, or to control important elements of their personal lives, such as marriage, place of residence, travel, and other basic rights theoretically granted to others by government, social, or religious institutions.

Women were also subjected to various types of social coercion. Specifically, the veil was forced on women, along with seclusion and sexual segregation. Women were even deprived of the rights prescribed for them by Islam: their share of the family inheritance was often confiscated by brothers or other male inheritors; most women did not see their husbands before their wedding night; their consent to become co-wives in a polygamous marriage was not asked; and often neither their husband nor family sought their opinion about divorce. Family disputes might even result in a forced divorce. In addition, women were forced to marry at an early age, at times before puberty.

But most damaging for Arab women, and particularly Yemeni women, was being deprived of an education. In Yemen, female illiteracy rates stood at 98 percent in 1971.[1] Despite the spread of schools and education, women themselves had little incentive to embark on an education, since they might marry young or discontinue their studies early in despair of finding a job or using their degrees if they continued. Although Yemen is renowned for the study of religious, linguistic, and legal sciences, and the education of boys begins at an early age in study groups in mosques and other prominent schooling centers, it was not until 1970 that Sana'a University and a few faculties in Aden University officially opened their doors, and this helps explain in large part why women were absent from the cultural and literary spheres and from various fields of work.

In addition to lack of education and female illiteracy, women's issues—to say nothing of writings by women themselves—were not given space in the Yemeni press. Although the Ottomans established the first Yemeni newspaper in Sana'a in 1887, followed by the establishment of *al-Iman* in Sana'a in 1926 and *al-Hikma al-Yamaniya* in 1937, women were completely absent from these papers both as writers and subjects. Women began to emerge socially with the appearance of radio in the early 1960s, bolstered by the increasing number of women university graduates, the expansion of universities in Sana'a and Aden and the inauguration of branches in the provinces, and the mixing of male and female students in classrooms and on university campuses. Some Yemeni women also traveled abroad to complete their studies and joined university faculties or the civil service upon their return.

Nevertheless, Yemeni women's literature does not have the same sort of roots as that of their Arab sisters in Egypt, Iraq, and the Levant. Rather—and this is a big difference—Yemeni women writers hark back to much more ancient foremothers, to women who are significant in the history of Yemen and the Arab world. Indeed, the reality of Yemeni women at the turn of the twentieth century and during its first half stood in complete contrast to the prominent role played by Yemeni women throughout history, with figures such as Queen Bilqis, the soothsayer Tarifa, Aslim, al-Zabba', and Arwa.[2]

During the Imamate period, women's cultural role was limited to memorizing or reciting poetry and copying manuscripts, but women were not authors, although, unlike most girls, the Imam's daughters were given some religious instruction.[3]

Many literary historians cite the names of women poets known for their popular poetry, particularly Ghazal al-Maqdashiya, who was illiterate. Her poetry, disseminated orally, was distinguished by its frankness and bite. In one poem, she even lampooned the collector of the tithe, one of the most dangerous men in the country. She also advocated equality regardless of class or sect, using the simple principle of the similarity and common origin of all humans[4]:

Same, same, God's servants, all alike
No one was born free, the other a slave.
Nine children—some are good people, they say,
And some are of another class, another type.

Undoubtedly two of the most important events for writing women were the establishment of a republic in northern Yemen (December 26, 1962) and the independence of the south from British colonial rule (November 30, 1967). This allowed women, in common with all Yemenis, to gradually win the rights that would foster the emergence of new generations of Yemeni women writers. These are rights that are still out of the reach of women in several neighboring countries, such as the right to mix freely with men at work and school, the right to vote and stand in elections in labor syndicates and local and national representative assemblies, the unlimited right to appear in the media, and the right to professional freedom. The union of the north and south (May 22, 1990) also contributed to women's cultural and literary advancement as women began to engage in political and party activities, appear in the media, and take part in the associations and institutions created by the union.

*

Socially and culturally, the tribe still plays an important role in Yemen. It is still generally recognized as a force by law and custom, and it has not kept pace with the political and cultural evolution of Yemen in recent decades. Although women's rights are enshrined in official legislation and the constitution guarantees them other basic rights, the Yemeni family has still not unleashed women's full energies. In reading the memoirs and testimonies of well-known Yemeni women writers, it becomes apparent that the family and society—and occasionally even official and party institutions—are obstructing women's full creative potential.

Society's traditional view of women was not easily amended by political change or constitutional laws. Armored with fixed principles and institutions that are imagined to be sanctified by time, religion and morality, society has resisted these changes and rejects women's new status, which includes the right of women to express themselves in literature. This was affirmed by several Yemeni women writers who gave important statements in a seminar, "Yemeni Women's Literature: Manifestations and Testimonies," held as part of the Yemeni literature festival organized by the Yemeni Writers' Union in Sana'a on April 1–4, 1997. If our critical reading of the texts of Yemeni women writers will shed light on women's social circumstances and the coercions to which they were subject, these testimonies, despite the unconscious and conscious revisions and omissions common to autobiography, also give us keys to explain certain elements common to Yemeni women's writings, such as the choice of one form or genre over another, their pronounced modernist tendency, and their rebellion against traditional literary forms.

In the seminar, seven female authors (six poets and one writer of fiction) spoke briefly of the difficulties facing Yemeni women writers. Some of these difficulties are particular to women *per se*, while others arise from social institutions, the world of publishing, and culture. The value of these testimonies is that these women are not pioneers from the early part of the century or the era before Yemen's political transformation. Most of them are under the age of forty, and matured or emerged on the literary scene in the 1970s and 1980s. Yet their choice to write and publish was accompanied by real struggle, hardship, and difficulty.

Poet Fatima al-'Ushbi, for example, discussed a real death experience she had when, at the age of twelve, she refused to marry a man three times her age. Her father had decided to marry her off when he learned that she was attempting to write colloquial poetry. "My beginning with poetry was my end with my father and the end of the future of which I dreamed," she said. His response to her early attempts at poetry was an attempt to ban her from writing it and to marry her off—an alternative to death in a grave that he had dug for her under the house.[5] At times marriage stands between women and writing, as was the case with poet Nabila al-Zubayr. The consequences are reflected in her testimony: "And . . . I married. This was my first encounter with a cloud that rained down ten years of stones of wrath. Every time I said 'Here,' he said 'No, there.' For years I wrote nothing but death notices, until I found that I had no need to write until my own funeral was concluded."[6]

Story-writer Arwa 'Abduh 'Uthman addressed the reasons for the disappearance of women writers, who emerge on the literary scene only to quickly fade away, whether temporarily or permanently. She cited social and domestic burdens, women writers' lack of stamina, insufficient depth and breadth of reading and self-enrichment, a lack of self-confidence, an absence of cultural institutions, and a dearth of serious criticism.[7] Some of these causes lie with women themselves, while domestic, social, and cultural institutions are responsible for others. Arwa believes the root of the problem is that women writers operate within a patriarchal society in which men are the foundation and women are marginal or dependent. Significantly, she noted that throughout her teaching experience she has met many female students who cannot make their writing public in fear of a father or husband, or occasionally an older brother or siblings. This is in addition to physical exhaustion; women writers are also wives, workers, and mothers. Their only time for writing and reading is what they can steal at the end of the day when the house is quiet, but by then, the energy of both body and mind has been exhausted.

Poet Ibtisam al-Mutawakkil cites another problem: the limited lexicon of women writers and their lack of rich and varied life experiences; as for subjects, women writers are limited to themselves and their own lives, topics which bring along with them the vocabulary of a bygone era.[8]

Poet and story-writer Azhar Fayi' observed that society may not overtly frustrate women's literary and intellectual production, but it does frustrate them by less direct means. Women are surrounded on all sides by responsibility, as if besieged by a thousand and one eyes. Fayi' recalled incidents from her own life. When on the day Yemeni unity was declared, she addressed the nation, saying—"And how long will you remain love and beloved?"—some dismissed her, thinking she was referring to an emotional crisis. When she wrote about her persistent, existential anxiety, one of her relatives responded violently, "Why are you whining like this? Did we tie you down?" A female friend also advised her not to publish her poetry in her own name, but to write it and then hide it.[9]

Writer Fatima Muhammad ibn Muhammad extended the scope of blame when she said, "My dilemma is complicated. I was rejected not only by male society, but male authority, of whatever kind and degree."[10] She spoke of how a progressive Marxist leader lined up with a shaykh to accuse her of treason and disloyalty. Men, she said, will immediately close ranks if a woman speaks a word of wisdom. Even if a female writer finds encouragement from family and society, as was the case with poet Huda Ablan, whose family helped her publish her poetry, she is the exception. Her family's encouragement still did not prevent Ablan from remarking on the "the dilemma of self-expression for the Yemeni woman writer. Her ability to lay bare her feelings, even as part of her dream system, will inevitably be met with lethal question marks . . . It is thus difficult to express intimate female experience in poetry, in this difficult, closed social climate."[11]

*

From these testimonies the researcher can isolate several common characteristics of Yemeni women's writing, some of which they share with other Arab women's literature to varying degrees depending on social awareness. These include the struggle involved in choosing to write: women must fight both family and society to win the right to write and publish. There is also an occasional use of pseudonyms.[12] Women complain both of the limited opportunities to publish in male-dominated forums and also about the automatic praise lavished on everything written by women even if it is weak (what Ibtisam al-Mutawakkil called in her testimony "gratuitous praise"). Arwa 'Abduh 'Uthman attributes this silence about women writers' shortcomings to a lack of self-confidence on the part of the writers themselves, which is then exploited by others to engage in "false compliments and naked hypocrisy" and avoid dealing with texts written by women as primarily texts. In addition, as Huda Ablan notes, there is a marked paucity of female writers; at times this means that women writers are too quickly celebrated, and this may ultimately have a negative impact on their writing, leading to unwarranted pride and a tendency to publish too soon.

On the positive side, Yemeni women's writing is marked by a spirit of ambition and rebellion. If these writers share common fears, they also share a space of hope and dreams. The dream of writing can be so strong that the death of the dream is tantamount to a real death. This dream is accompanied by a spirit of revolution and rebellion that starts somewhere in the depths of writing women and bubbles over to color their writing and texts. "Inside of me there is a repressed rebellion against all manner of injustice I encounter. The choice to write is a kind of challenge," says Azhar Fayi'. Huda Ablan says, "I decided to be a poet because I decided to live. I decided to live within the bounds of my humanity . . . to moisten the arid regions of life with water carved out of the spirit's stone." Arwa 'Abduh 'Uthman says, "The dream and the spirit of rebellion move along two lines; they meet and separate, and at the latter point they create my character." This dream of rebellion is also a summons to be: "what is inside me must flow out onto my notebooks," as Nabila al-Zubayr says. This urge to confess and write—that is, a rebellion against the sense of oppression and fear—explains the increasing willingness of Yemeni women to embark on the adventure of writing. In recent years, women have taken their natural place among male writers, their right to write and publish has become well-established, and their works are recognized by literary critics and even occasionally taught at state schools.[13]

*

Dreams and rebellion are the two primary motifs in Yemeni women writing. They are deployed to gain cultural rights as well as recognition in the cultural context. This is truly cause for optimism and wonder, although it is often not noted by women writers themselves, who tend to blame and complain. While there are ruptures in the female literary tradition and only in recent years have researchers begun to write histories of women's writing, this has proved to be an advantage from one perspective, for with their spirit of ambition it has led Yemeni women writers to embody their rebellion and rejection first and foremost in the choice of what to write. One will not find Yemeni women poets writing the traditional *qasida* poem; rather, their poetics is imbued with a sense of the modern, as if they have agreed to choose this style as a means of representing their rejection and rebellion.

Some researchers attribute Yemeni women's affection for modern poetry to a weakness in their educational formation, their lack of experience with and knowledge of the forms of traditional Arabic poetry, and their limited lexicon, all of which make it difficult to write the traditional *qasida* with its unified rhyme scheme. On the other hand, others explain the leap into modern poetry as a way of taking advantage of the poetic moment in which women writers emerged. When women began writing poetry seriously in the 1970s, modern poetry was easily accessible. In Yemen, as in other Arab countries, poets were quick to rally around the calls of pioneering poets in Iraq (Nazik al-Mala'ika, Badr Shakir al-Sayyab, 'Abd al-Wahhab al-Bayati) in the late 1940s to write modern free verse. Historians of modern literature note the early attempts by poet Ahmad al-Shami in the 1950s, although he later retreated into traditional forms. These were followed by the poems of 'Abd al-'Aziz al-Maqalih in the early 1960s, after which he turned irrevocably to the new poetry. His poems had an impact on several generations of Yemeni poets. Later, the poet Muhammad al-Sharafi also wrote free verse, alternating between the traditional and the new forms.[14] These local achievements in poetry reinforced the rise of modern Arabic poetry and ensured its victory in the debate about whether it should be accepted or rejected. Modern texts were introduced to school and university curricula, and collections of modern poetry reached readers through book fairs, distributors, cultural journals, and newspapers. It was in this climate that women poets engaged in their first experiments.

The reader of Yemeni women's poetry can discern a traditional strain in women's modern poetry. Their poems tend to rely on directness, clarity, and naked meaning. They employ a limited poetic lexicon and are marked by a musical and rhythmic regularity and a repetitive rhyme scheme, which creates a melodious, boisterous, lyrical atmosphere that recalls the early experiments in free verse and the traditional roots of the form.

This description is exemplified in the poetry of Fatima al-'Ushbi, one of the earliest women writers, who has shown an interest in both popular poetry and free verse. Al-'Ushbi's subjects are warm and vivid, and they find a fortuitously expressive vehicle in this directness and musical poetic rhythm. She has this in common with the early experiments of most female poets. Ibtisam al-Mutawakkil's collection, *Shadha al-jamr* (The Scent of Embers) 1998, contains some early experiments in the same vein, as do the early collections of Nabila al-Zubayr and Huda Ablan, two poets who are currently flourishing. In particular, Nabila al-Zubayr's first collection, *Mutawaliyat al-kidhba al-ra'i'a* (Successions of the Magnificent Lie), contains some elements of this direct discourse and its themes. Huda Ablan's first collection, *Wurud shaqiyat al-malamih* (Roses with Mischievous Features) 1989, contains several poems marked by their directness, repetitive rhyme scheme, and exalted lyricism.

Although many women poets have now forsaken this tendency, which was influenced by the early voices and the experiences of the pioneers, it is important to note it here in order to fully observe the transformations undergone by Yemeni women's writing. The observer may indeed be surprised to find how far many women poets have taken their modernist tendencies.

In much of her first collection of poetry, Nabila al-Zubayr tries to create a poetic language based on non-traditional systems. It picks at the readers' storehouse of familiar forms, propelling them to an exercise of effort that resembles the moment in which she wrote the poems. Indeed, I see her poems as an example of visual poems—that is, poems whose syntax, expressions, and images can only be understood through visualization and repeated reading because they are based on irony and on the fragmentation of the syntax of the normal sentence. This is especially apparent in her short poems, which require close reading to discover the transfer of meaning based on an ironic subversion of the sentence structure. Here we can take a look at her four-line poem, "Ma zal" (Still), where the transfer of meaning can be readily understood:

Every time my head smashes a wall
I say: I still have a head.
Every time a wall smashes my head
I say: I still have a wall in front of me.

Among her colleagues, al-Zubayr cleaves the closest to this particular type of metric rhythm. She does not make the reader aware of an external meter or an obvious rhyme scheme, but instead creates an internal rhythm from the juxtaposition of the sentence's two clauses. Many Yemeni women poets write similar poems: very short, with their rich economy of meaning stripped of any fluff or added weight. With its brevity and concentration of meaning, the poems are reminiscent of Japanese haiku.

Ibtisam al-Mutawakkil belongs to the same non-traditional, modern school, having evolved from the directness of some poems in her first collection toward a balanced, metered poem that does not rely on an overt metrical or rhyme scheme, and finally to the mature prose poems of her most recent period. Al-Mutawakkil is an example of the labor of poetry and the search for the new in both form and content. She devotes herself to poetic portraits of her fellow countrywomen (Hadramawti women, women from Aden), as well as Yemeni cities ("Every sea comes to Aden/they will cry out/only Aden"). This gives her two advantages: she avoids sentimentality and traditional discourse, and exploits her lexicon of faces and cities to give her poems a narrative dimension that dilutes the lyricism. This places her in a new locus of expression that allows her to write convincing, successful prose poems. Her most recent works evince a serious poetic and cultural awareness that eschews gratuitousness, prolixity, and sentimental soliloquies.

Like Nabila al-Zubayr and Ibtisam al-Mutawakkil, Huda Ablan has surpassed herself with her most recent poems, putting her first collection of poetry firmly in the past, unbecoming to the poet she has grown into. Her most recent works are touched by a sweet, poetic melancholy. Her sense of loss and disappointment in the world endows the poems with a beauty that narrows the distance between her and the reader.

Amina Yusuf Muhammad 'Abduh, a poet and fiction writer who, like many of her colleagues, does not hesitate to experiment with more than one literary genre, represents a midway point between the distinct modernism of Ibtisam al-Mutawakkil, Nabila al-Zubayr, and Huda Ablan and the conservatism of Fatima al-'Ushbi, with her preservation of the poem's external meter and direct discourse. I see her short poems as more representative of the current climate of modernism, rather than the facile modernism of some of the poems in her collection, *Qasa'id al-khawf* (Poems of Fear) 1997. Nadiya Mar'i, the newest poet among her colleagues, shows a clear affinity to the prose poem, choosing it as her sole means of expression to the exclusion of free verse. As such, her poems have an intentional narrative bent. Her text, "Rifqa" (Companionship), opens with a narrative framework, the characterization of a dog, and the observation of nearby places onto which the poet reflects herself. She then establishes a strange companionship between herself and the dog based on their common grief, ultimately seeing the dog as her twin spirit and their suffering as similar.

As they take confident strides toward modernism, Yemeni women reflect more general trends in Arab women's poetry. At times, their poetic consciousness displays a less than firm command of cultural and mythical symbols, and most of their poems are free of intertextual references. Thus, they lack the richness and added depth that can come with connotation and allusion, which are necessary to flesh out the modern features of the poems. This characteristic is, in turn, indicative of women poets' cultural formation.

We must make one final observation about Yemeni women's poetry: there has been a flood of unsophisticated "reflections" and "contemplations" written by women who believe they are writing poetry, but who are in fact living with a misapprehension of the concept of poetic prose. That is, any sort of reflective writing that does not conform to the rules of prosody is considered to be a kind of prose poetry. This trend has been fostered in recent years by the cultural pages of newspapers, which need writers of regular columns to fill their space. I do not think that such facile writing will have any sort of lasting influence because it is lost somewhere between poetry, prose, and hasty journalism.

One might not find the same modernist tendencies in the short story as in women's poetry, although the story is an extension of the collective memory. Yemeni culture boasts various types of popular or folk narrative, biography and legends being only one small part. Women assume the role of the narrator at female gatherings, telling their companions the popular tales and traditional stories they have memorized, accompanied by a dramatic narrative performance. Women may also speak of the tragedies of real life at these same gatherings, their audience listening with great interest and sympathy and at times commenting on the stories.[15]

The telling of folktales is part of women writers' cultural formation, learned in the family from childhood. This has had a clear impact on the story-writer Arwa 'Abduh 'Uthman, for example, who often draws on the popular tradition for material for her stories and imbues them with a folkloric or local flavor, evident in her choice of vocabulary, setting, and names. In the testimony referred to earlier, Arwa 'Abduh 'Uthman said that the folk tradition, myths, legends, and stories from her own life "led me to observe the particulars of image and scene and to imagine them with the consciousness of a child."[16] This oral folk tradition, like the oral poetic tradition, has been influential for Yemeni women writers, particularly since women were the producers of oral tales and poetry.

In addition, Yemeni society itself, with its firm traditions and inherited rules of life and culture, has encouraged writing women to take examples from the social body, fortified by tradition and custom that often exceed the authority of the law. Nevertheless, the fact that early narrative attempts were published prior to women's poetry raises further questions about the absence of a modernizing tendency in the fiction of Yemeni women.

The early 1960s saw the publication of some women's short stories, particularly in the press of southern Yemen, then under occupation. "Zalim ya mujtama'" (Cruel You Are, Society), by a writer who signed her name "F. Ahmad," was the first of these realistic stories to be published. This pioneering writer takes a clear stance and perspective on what she describes as an unjust, cruel society. She introduces the text with a short commentary that neatly summarizes the entire plot: society's injustice is passed down from mother to daughter through its portrayal of them as women lacking virtue. The writer boldly addresses one of society's biggest problems through the issue of choice in marriage. Muna's poor mother was married by her father to a rich man she did not love. Her father refused to marry her to her cousin, although she loved him and had slept with him, giving the young man his "right," as he called it, in advance. This incident constitutes the backbone of the story, which reaches its melodramatic climax when the same thing happens to the daughter, Muna, even as other social problems are addressed along the way. The conclusion proves the author's thesis, which attributes the reasons for "the fall," as she calls it, to the male persecution and coercion women endure. The narrative form is consistent with the story's social message. The author uses a third-person, omniscient narrator who tells the story in linear, chronological fashion, and the author shows no interest in other types of narrative. The third-person perspective does not allow the reader to locate a focal point through which to view the events. In terms of characterization, we only see the surface; there are no depths in which fates interact. Yet the writer may be forgiven these shortcomings on two counts: the relative novelty of story-writing, and both the burden and vitality of reality, which makes the critical, realistic style the most accessible.

The model of "Zalim ya mujtama'" was repeated, with variations in subject while maintaining the same direct, didactic style, in other stories from the 1960s written by Fawziya 'Abd al-Raziq, Samiya Mahmud, and Shafiqa Zawqari.[17] In addition to sharp social criticism, these stories show an interest in daily politics and contemporary national events, understandable given the struggle for independence and republicanism in both Yemens in the late 1960s. We find the same theme in stories by Thuraya Manqush and Ramziya al-Iryani.[18] Al-Iryani published the first novel by a Yemeni woman, *Dahiyat al-jasha'* (Greed's Victim), in 1971. She is thus an experienced writer, but readers will notice that from her first collection of stories, *La 'allahu ya'ud* (Maybe He'll Return) 1981, published in the early 1980s until her most recent collection, *al-Sama' tumtir qutnan* (It's Raining Cotton), released in 1999, she tends to stick to critical realism. Society and the cruelties of a reality that crush both men and women are constant themes in al-Iryani's stories.

We must wait another decade for the stories of Zahra Rahmat Allah, in her collection, *Bidaya ukhra* (Another Beginning) 1994, to find an interest in narrative techniques that partially overshadows the allure of social realism. Rahmat Allah's stories constitute a positive narrative leap that liberated language from its monotony and provided a variation on narratives that usually relied on description peppered with dialogue and a bit of internal tension for the characters. In contrast, she does not maintain a linear progression of events, but uses narrative 'tricks' such as analepsis and prolepsis, as well as narrative ruptures and interruptions and introspection or internal monologues.

We find more evolved traces of this poetic realism in texts by Azhar Fayi' (a poet and story-writer) and Bushra al-Miqtari. Fayi''s realism is marked by a use of symbolism. This manipulation of the power of symbol and her attempt to make it a stand-in, both in terms of structure and meaning, for the realistic event is attributable not only to Fayi''s poetic perspective, but also to the fact that her generation, writing in the 1970s, began to tire of naive forms of realism and started showing more interest in the craft of the story. Her story, "Limadha tatrud abna'aha" (Why Does She Drive out Her Children?), was an attempt to compare a cat's gruff handling of her kittens with emigration, a theme that weighs heavily on Yemeni women writers of the short story and novel. An innocent child's question about why cats carry their young in their teeth is juxtaposed to the question of a woman whose husband emigrates to realize his dreams of a better future: "The earth is a mother . . . so why does she drive out her children?" Azhar Fayi' maintains the rising tempo of the narrative action until the moment of tension and reconciliation between the symbol and the symbolized.

We find the same in Bushra al-Miqtari's "Dhikra yadayn" (The Hands' Memory). Narrated by the protagonist of the story, a man whose hands were burned in a fire twenty years ago, it is the story of the man, his mother who died in the fire, the ashes of his room, his books, and his furniture. The man is a prisoner of his memory of the fire and is afraid to look at his hands. Despite his grief and loss, he challenges himself and others and raises his hands up to symbolize his victory. Al-Miqtari preserves the flow of the narrative, its cohesiveness, and the perspective through which we observe the fire and the bitter, hellish memory without the use of any forced language or images. The monologue is carefully constructed and brings in elements from time and place that create an internal space in the narrative that we do not often find in stories by Yemeni women writers, who are more interested in abstracting or effacing time and place, often making do with an external, public, objective space.

The texts of Nadiya al-Kawkabani, a new writer who emerged in the late 1990s, take us to a more insightful realism. In "al-Nihaya" (The End), she examines the feelings of a grandfather returning home to see his grandchildren and die, observing his end with an honest humanity and sweet emotion. The story is brought to its sad climax by the son's wails of grief at the end and the grandfather's stifled response, "It's no use . . . no use. It's the end." The works of Arwa 'Abduh 'Uthman, a mature, experienced story-writer, give us another perspective on reality. Her realism is touched by irony and a critical spirit, her characters chosen from the dregs of society and put in the middle of contemporary situations to expose falsity. She avoids any particular female bias, for men in her stories suffer no less than women. She relies on irony in the narrative's action and plot, and even in the language of the story itself. Her stories are brimming with popular and colloquial usages, starting with names.

In contrast to the monotony of realism and its logic of directness, a counter-trend has emerged that strips and empties the action of its realistic frame of reference while enriching the text with figurative and expressive language. This trend is well represented by Huda al-'Attas in her short-story collection, *Hajis ruh, hajis jasad* (Anxiety of the Spirit, Anxiety of the

Flesh) 1995, as well as her more recent works. These texts use language and its figures as a skeleton for a narrative marked by brevity, tension, and verbal structure. That is, the events of the narrative recede or sometimes disappear altogether faced with a language that draws its mechanisms and meanings largely from poetry. In addition, Huda al-ʿAttas has a very conscious, evolved perspective and an astonishing energy of fiction characterized by her bold observation of the female body and male-female relationships. In "al-Maʿraka" (The Battle), two newlyweds become familiar with their bodies in a losing battle. In "Adwar" (Roles), a gigolo takes money from a woman for sleeping with her. In "Nutuʾat" (Protuberances), she associates a girl's physical maturity with being forced to wear the black veil. In that story, al-ʿAttas chooses an external perspective, since the objective narrative better allows her to observe and watch. Despite the abstraction and the non-action-based, cerebral bent of the story, Huda al-ʿAttas has managed to create a small, eloquent world to boldly and masterfully address one of the biggest problems of contemporary Yemeni women: their battle with the traditional veil, which custom imposes on many.

This intellectual abstraction is broadened by young writer ʿAfaf al-Bashiri. In her chosen text, a short story, "Asabiʿi" (My Fingers), she uses her fingers to symbolize her existence, closely and consciously observing what is happening in front of her eyes and using a sensual language that banishes all specificities and tangible elements from the narrative. There are no names here, no place or characters—only the shriek of the fingers and their furious dialogue with their owner. The story is based on dialogue with the exception of the introduction and conclusion. It is noteworthy that ʿAfaf al-Bashiri would choose this sort of poetic symbolism despite her proficiency with description, narrative, dialogue, and other modern narrative techniques such as analepsis and stream of consciousness.

In "Rahim Aflatuni" (Platonic Womb), by poet and fiction-writer Nabila al-Kabsi, we find another example of these spaces given over to language and emotional association. The lines of the fragmented story are arranged as if they are lines of poetry, relaying to us the thoughts of a fetus that thinks it is a king; after his descent to earth, he ends up buried alone and begins building a moat or a grave far from reality and people. The story's language suits the fantastic, unreal nature of the story. The reader is given over to poetic allusions and an evocative language, used to make up for the lack of action; the narrative line is fixed and limited, without development, digression, or progression. This narrative leanness and abstraction coupled with a poetic structure might be interpreted as a response to the realism of traditional stories, which is confirmed by another rising young author, Afrah al-Siddiq. Her texts also show escapist tendencies; the dialogue does not enlighten, but only further obscures the plot and breaks the connection with the reader. Perhaps the novelty of al-Siddiq's thought propels her toward concentration, leading her to use the energy of language to create a fantastic narrative that is nevertheless justified by the internal logic of the story that determines her protagonists' fates, the end of their stories, and the links between characters' acts.

At the end of this brief analysis, I can only declare my optimism at the variety evident in Yemeni women's short stories, as illustrated by the many published works. Nevertheless, the short story is at times confused with two types of writing that are foreign to it: expository or journalistic sketches, and imprecise writings. It is also unfortunate that realism in the short story is imagined to be the reflection of reality without embellishment, representation, or art.

*

The prominent poet and critic 'Abd al-'Aziz al-Maqalih believes that poetry has continued to dominate literary production in Yemen and other Arab regions, not because it is the first art of the Arabs and the most deeply rooted in our memories, but because of the Arab condition and the anxiety and turmoil of contemporary reality. Representing the aesthetic and intellectual aspects of this reality and producing a novel broad enough to contain its details and explore the depths of its characters is a task that will take many years.[19] He calls the novel "the missing literary genre" in Yemen,[20] although researchers have identified more than forty works since the publication in 1939 of the first Yemeni novel, *Sa'id* (Sa'id), by Muhammad 'Ali Luqman. Women's contribution to the Yemeni novel has been relatively meager. Indeed, there are only five such novels: *Dahiyat al-jasha'* by Ramziya al-Iryani, published in the early 1970s; the three works of 'Aziza 'Abd Allah Abu Lahum, *Ahlam wa Nabila* (Ahlam and Nabila) 1997, *Arkanaha al-faqih* (The Jurist Put Her Aside) 1998, and *Tayf wilaya* (The Semblance of a State) 1998; and a historical novel by al-Iryani, *Dar al-sultana* (The Sultana's Palace) 1998. We can add a sixth novel, forthcoming, by poet Nabila al-Zubayr, provisionally entitled *La . . . laysat ma'qula* (No . . . It's Not Reasonable).

Without going into the reasons for the scarcity of novels or attributing it to some failing of women writers or the dominance of poetry, it must be noted that women's novels are characterized by a direct, sincere realism that attempts to document events without artifice and neglects a variety of narrative techniques. This is true for the first women's novel, *Dahiyat al-jasha'* as well as the most recent works of 'Aziza 'Abd Allah. Female novelists are concerned with a variety of themes, first and foremost the migration of husbands looking for a livelihood, domestic coercion in the choice of a husband, divorce and its attendant problems, certain social issues such as the dangers of *qat*, and contempt for women.

We find a different narrative approach in the manuscript version of Nabila al-Zubayr's *La . . . laysat ma'qula*. The author uses her poetic energies to turn the novel's three sections (twelve chapters each) into a lengthy, raving monologue by the main character, Sakina 'Ali 'Umar, who is frustrated to the point of madness and delusion. The novel opens with Sakina's disjointed musings and her separation from Ahmad, who has disappointed her. In moments of lucidity, her musings recall various events, but without any chronology. All of this makes reading the novel a difficult task if the reader does not take note of the sudden transformation from madness to lucidity.

'Aziza 'Abd Allah's *Ahlam wa Nabila* is a bold treatment of the choice of one's husband, the problem of divorce, the dictatorship of the father, and women's general passivity. But Nabila al-Zubayr's approach is more profound and touching, not because of the nature of the main character (the poet Sakina) and her experiences with her family, men, job, and studies, but because of the novel's atypical style and its successful use of technique to link the multiplicity of voices, narratives, times, and situations. Examining Nabila al-Zubayr's language, we find she borrows much from poetry and its imagery, which at times makes the novel more abstract and cerebral and takes away from the tangibility of the novelistic narrative, its specificities, and the action. Al-Zubayr often executes her narrative enterprise through language rather than situations, actions, or events. It is as if the novel is one long nightmare, and when reading it, the reader feels the same sort of asphyxiation felt by the heroine.

Clearly, the rarity of women's novels compared to poetry and the short story, as well as the absence of drama (due to the dearth of theater as a cultural component) and the paucity of children's literature (with the exception of the modest attempts by Najiba Haddad) are all indicative of the difficulty of the task and the still shaky cultural foundation that affects women's lives. Although women's lives are undergoing enormous trans-formations, society and the male reader's view of women has not kept pace with these changes.

Notes

1 Ramziya al-Iryani, *Ra'idat Yamaniyat* (Sana'a: Ministry of Social Affairs and Labor, 1990), p. 82.

2 Ibid., p. 31. See also 'Abd Allah Muhammad al-Habashi, *Mu'jam al-nisa' al-Yamaniyat* (Sana'a: Dar al-Hikma al-Yamaniya, 1988), who has listings for dozens of prominent Yemeni women throughout history, arranged alphabetically.

3 Ramziya al-Iryani, *Ra'idat Yamaniyat*, p. 32.

4 Ibid., p. 33. The poetry comes from 'Abd Allah al-Barduni, *Rihla fi-l-shi'r al-Yamani: qadimih wa hadithih* (Damascus: Dar al-Fikr, 1995), p. 335. See also Kamal al-Din Muhammad, "al-Qawl al-mubah fi adab al-mar'a al-qisasi," *al-Thaqafa*, no. 227, November 1996, p. 85, where he mentions the names of women poets who recite oral, colloquial poetry, including Umm al-Sarikh al-Kindiya, Khadija al-Qudamiya, Sultana Bint 'Ali al-Zubaydi, Fatima al-'Amudi, and 'Aliya' al-Jabiriya.

5 Fatima al-'Ushbi, "Qissati ma'a al-shi'r," *al-Hikma*, July–September 1997, p. 93.

6 Nabila al-Zubayr, "'Indama ghannat bi-qalbi al-ru'ud," *al-Hikma*, July–September 1997, p. 99.

7 Arwa 'Abduh 'Uthman, "Tajribati al-adabiya," *al-Hikma*, July–September 1997, p. 107.

8 Ibtisam al-Mutawakkil, "Jamr al-kitaba," *al-Hikma*, July–September 1997, p. 113.

9 Azhar Muhammad Fayi', "'An al-tajriba al-adabiya wa ishkaliyat al-kitaba fi mujtama' dhukuri," *al-Hikma*, July–September 1997, p. 128.

10 Fatima Muhammad ibn Muhammad, "Tajalliyat wa shahadat," *al-Hikma*, July–September 1997, p. 120.

11 Huda Ablan, "al-Nabta al-'anida wa sukhur al-waqi'," *al-Hikma*, July–September 1997, p. 125.

12 This observation is supported by a review of the bibliography of Yemeni women writers prepared by Intilaq al-Mutawakkil; she lists many women who started writing under a pen name or simply their initials.

13 I presented an analytical reading of the testimonies of Yemeni women writers in "Shahrazad fi kalam mubah," *al-Quds al-'Arabi*, June 25, 1997.

14 'Izz al-Din Isma'il, *al-Shi'r al-mu'asir fi-l-Yaman: al-ru'ya wa-l-fann* (Cairo: Institute for Arab Research and Studies, 1972), pp. 222–27. Isma'il mentions other experiments in the early days of the renaissance by 'Abduh 'Uthman, 'Abd Allah Salam, Lutfi Ja'far Aman, and others, but he pauses at the poet 'Abd al-'Aziz al-Maqalih because of what he calls "the authentic poetic gift that he gave and gives every day; among contemporary Yemeni poets, he has the deepest understanding of the nature of the new poem, in terms of form and structure, as well as a clear, artistic, realistic vision" (p. 237).

15 Lanthe McClagan, "Nisa' 'Umran," in Lucine Taminian, ed. and Ahmad Jaradat, trans., *Surat al-mar'a al-Yamaniya fi-l-dirasat al-gharbiya* (Sana'a: American Institute for Yemeni Studies, 1997), p. 106 ff.

16 Arwa 'Abduh 'Uthman, "Tajribati al-adabiya," p. 102.

17 Stories by these writers and others can be found in Nahla 'Abd Allah, *Aswat nisa'iya fi-l-qissa al-Yamaniya* (Sana'a: n.p., 1991).
18 Kamal al-Din Muhammad, pp. 86–88, remarks on what he calls the simplicity and superficiality of all stories by women in the 1960s, adding that they were influenced by the Arabic romance novel and Egyptian cinema.
19 'Abd al-'Aziz al-Maqalih, *Dirasat fi-l-riwaya wa-l-qissa al-qasira fi-l-Yaman* (Beirut: al-Jami'iya Foundation, 1999), p. 11.
20 Ibid., p. 79.

Bibliography of Works in English

Writers in English *Ferial J. Ghazoul*

Arab women's writings in English grew out of a different context than their writings in French. Whereas French colonialism pursued a policy of cultural assimilation and tried to 'Francophy' its territories, expending great effort to repress the cultural specificity of dominated peoples, British colonialism eschewed such assimilation, not because it recognized the rights of conquered peoples, but due to a racist assumption that denied that Arabs and other colonized peoples could ever be a part of the British cultural fabric. As a result, we generally find that Arab women's Francophone literature is produced by women for whom French is their sole written language; these writers are familiar with spoken, colloquial Arabic, not the standard form of the language used in writing and literature. In contrast, Arab women who write in English are generally well acquainted with their mother tongue but have other reasons for writing in English, and usually grew up in areas or studied in institutions dominated by English.

Palestinian writer Soraya George Antonius, for example, recalls attending foreign schools since she was a child. These institutions imposed English as the medium of cultural and written expression, and thus the language was more accessible to her for novelistic expression. For her, writing in a foreign language does not entail the adoption of a foreign point of view, which is quite clear in her two novels and her devotion to the liberation of Palestine.

Egyptian novelist Ahdaf Soueif, whose novels and short stories have carved out a space on the stage of world literature, concurs with Antonius. Soueif lived much of her life, including part of her childhood, in Britain and later studied English literature. In turn, she found in the language a medium with which to address the English-speaking world. As English has become an international lingua franca and the most widespread global language of science and culture, this world goes beyond Britain and the U.S. Although Soueif is proficient in literary Arabic, she chose English, using the language of the colonizer to give voice to the colonized and positions of resistance. Soueif's injection of non-English terms and atmospheres and the way she formulates these in unfamiliar ways endow her literary English with a distinctiveness and strangeness, and readers have been surprised at how she is able to bend the English language to her own ends.

Syrian-Lebanese author Etel Adnan attended French schools and has produced works in French, among them *Sitt Marie Rose*, her most important work, which received both critical and popular acclaim. After a stint in California, she became more familiar with English and found in it a field open to free expression. As the language of both speech and writing, it can be used to depict lived experience with a greater immediacy. She has written poetry, short stories, and plays in English.

In times of war and other catastrophes, women may find themselves in a crisis and often document this in literature. During the Lebanese civil war, British colonial rule in Palestine, and the first Gulf War, stability was shaken and daily life became unbearable. These trials and tribulations led many women to transform the terrors of reality into powerful works of literature, among them Palestinians Yasmine Zahran and Jean Said Makdisi, Lebanese Mai Ghoussoub, Iraqi Noha al-Radi, and Jordanian Fadia Faqir.

Some of these writers were inspired to write in English after moving to the West to live, study, or work. Some, such as Sudanese Leila Aboulela and Tunisian Sabiha Khemir, chose the mediums of the novel and short story, while others, such as Egyptians Leila Ahmed and Samia Serageldin or Syrian Samar Attar, chose autobiography.

Many Arab women have written poetry in English, often publishing poems in literary periodicals but not a complete collection. Examples include Palestinian Hanan al-'Ashrawi, Syrian Mohja Kahf, and Egyptians Nadia Bishai and Pauline Kaldas.

While experiments in playwriting are rare among Arab women writers, whether in Arabic or a foreign language, there are some important exceptions. Egyptian Mary Massoud, a professor of English literature, wrote a play in English, which was then translated into ten languages, and Etel Adnan has written a play about the Gulf War. Both works are marked by irony and satire.

Many Arab Anglophone writers have also written literature, essays, or academic studies in Arabic, indicating that writing in English is not a repudiation, but a choice offered by the individual writer's background and sensibility, and reinforced by her study of the language and her familiarity with English literature.

To read testimonials by and interviews with Arab women writing in foreign languages, see *Alif: Journal of Comparative Poetics* 20 (2000), a special issue on "The Hybrid Literary Text: Arab Creative Authors Writing in Foreign Languages."

Also see *Jusoor* 11/12 (1999), a special issue on "Post Gibran: Anthology of New Arab American Writing," edited by Khaled Mattawa and Munir Akash (Syracuse, New York: Syracuse University Press, 1999). The issue includes texts and studies (all in English) about Arab-American writers and Arab writers who moved to North America.

Arab women writing in English: A selective bibliography

Aboulela, Leila. *The Translator* (novel). Edinburgh: Polygon, 1999.

Aboulela, Leila. *Coloured Lights* (short stories). Edinburgh: Polygon, 2001.

Adnan, Etel. *Five Senses for One Death* (poetry). New York: The Smith, 1971.

Adnan, Etel. *Pablo Neruda Is a Banana Tree* (poetry). Lisbon: De Almeida, 1982.

Adnan, Etel. *From A to Z* (poetry). Sausalito, California: Post-Apollo Press, 1982.

Adnan, Etel. *The Indian Never Had a Horse and Other Poems* (poetry). Sausalito, California: Post-Apollo Press, 1985.

Adnan, Etel. *Journey to Mount Tamalpais* (essay). Sausalito, California: Post-Apollo Press, 1986.

Adnan, Etel. *The Arab Apocalypse* (poetry). Sausalito, California: Post-Apollo Press, 1989.

Adnan, Etel. *The Spring Flowers Own and the Manifestation of the Voyage* (poetry). Sausalito, California: Post-Apollo Press, 1990.

Adnan, Etel. *Paris, When It's Naked* (novel). Sausalito, California: Post-Apollo Press, 1993.

Adnan, Etel. *Of Cities and Women* (letters). Sausalito, California: Post-Apollo Press, 1993.

Adnan, Etel. *Moonshots* (poetry). Beirut: 1996.

Ahmed, Leila. *A Border Passage* (memoir). New York: Farrar, Straus, and Giroux, 1999.

Antonius, Soraya. *The Lord* (novel). New York: H. Holt, 1986.

Antonius, Soraya. *Where the Jinn Consult.* London: Hamilton, 1987.

Faqir, Fadia. *Nisanit* (novel). New York: Penguin Books, 1987.

Faqir, Fadia. *Pillars of Salt* (novel). London: Quartet Books, 1996.

Farah, Najwa Kawar. *A Continent Called Palestine: One Woman's Story.* London: Triangle, 1996.

Ghoussoub, Mai. *Leaving Beirut* (novel). London: Saqi Books, 1998.

Kanafani, Fay Afaf. *Nadia: Captive of Hope: Memoir of an Arab Woman.* Armonk, New York: M.E. Sharpe, 1999.

Kashgari, Badia. *The Unattainable Lotus: A Bilingual Anthology of Poetry.* London: Saqi, 2001.

Khemir, Sabiha. *Waiting in the Future for the Past to Come* (novel). London: Quartet Books, 1993.

Makdisi, Jean Said. *Beirut Fragments: A War Memoir* (memoir). New York: Persea Books, 1990.

Massoud, Mary. *Our Father* (play). Singapore: The Way Press, 1979.

Mernissi, Fatima. *Dreams of Trespass: Tales of a Harem Girlhood* (autobiography). Reading, MA: Addison-Wesley Publishing, 1994.

al-Radi, Nuha. *Baghdad Diaries.* London: Saqi Books, 1998.

Sad, Maryam Qasim. *A Handful of Earth: Selected Poems.* London: Aurora Press, 1993.

Serageldin, Samia. *The Cairo House: A Novel.* Syracuse: Syracuse University Press, 2000.

Soueif, Ahdaf. *Aisha* (short stories). London: Jonathan Cape, 1983.

Soueif, Ahdaf. *In the Eye of the Sun* (novel). London: Bloomsbury, 1992.

Soueif, Ahdaf. *The Sandpiper* (short stories). London: Bloomsbury, 1996.

Soueif, Ahdaf. *The Map of Love* (novel). London: Bloomsbury, 1999.

Zahran, Yasmine. *A Beggar at Damascus Gate* (novel). Sausalito, California: Post-Apollo Press, 1995.

Works in translation

Abouzeid, Leila. *Year of the Elephant: A Moroccan Woman's Journey Towards Independence and Other Stories,* trans. by Barbara Parmenter. Austin: University of Texas Press, 1989.

Abouzeid, Leila. *Return to Childhood: The Memoir of a Modern Moroccan Woman,* trans. by Leila Abouzeid with Heather Logan Taylor. Austin: University of Texas Press, 1998.

Abouzeid, Leila. *The Last Chapter: A Novel,* trans. by Leila Abouzeid and John Liechety. Cairo: American University in Cairo Press, 2000.

Accad, Evelyne. *Wounding Words: A Woman's Journal in Tunisia,* trans. by Cynthia T. Hahn. Oxford: Heinemann, 1996.

Adnan, Etel. *Sitt Marie Rose: A Novel,* trans. by Georgina Kleege. Sausalito, California: Post-Apollo Press, 1982.

Alem, Raja and Tom McDonough. *My Thousand and One Nights: A Novel of Mecca.* Syracuse, NY: Syracuse University Press, 2007.

Al-Amir, Daisy. *The Waiting List: An Iraqi Woman's Tales of Alienation,* trans. by Barbara Parmenter. Austin: University of Texas Press, 1994.

Amrouche, Fadhma A.M. *My Life Story: The Autobiography of a Berber Woman,* trans. by Dorothy Blair. New Brunswick: Rutgers University Press, 1988.

Ashour, Radwa. *Granada: A Novel,* trans. by William Granara. Syracuse: Syracuse University Press, 2003.

Ashour, Radwa. *Siraaj: An Arab Tale,* trans. by Barbara Romaine, Austin: The University of Texas, 2007.

Assaad, Fawzia. *Layla: an Egyptian Woman,* trans. by Melissa Marcus. Trenton, N.J.: Africa World, 2004.

al-Atrash, Leila. *A Woman of Five Seasons,* trans. by Nora Nweihid Halwani and Christopher Tingley. New York: Interlink Books, 2002.

Attar, Samar. *Lina: A Portrait of a Damascene Girl,* trans. by Samar Attar. Colorado Springs: Three Continents Press, 1994.

Attar, Samar. *The House on Arnus Square,* trans. by Samar Attar. Pueblo, CO: Passaggiata Press, 1998.

Badr, Liyanah. *A Compass for the Sunflower,* trans. by Catherine Cobham. London: Women's Press, 1989.

Badr, Liyana. *A Balcony over the Fakihani: Three Novellas,* trans. by Peter Clark with Christopher Tingley. New York: Interlink Books, 1993.

Badr, Liana. *The Eye of the Mirror,* trans. by Samira Kawar. Reading, U.K.: Garnet Publishing, 1994.

El Badry, Hala. *A Certain Woman,* trans. by Farouk Abdel Wahab. Cairo: American University in Cairo Press, 2003.

El Badry, Hala. *Muntaha,* trans. by Nancy Roberts. Cairo: American University in Cairo Press, 2006.

Bakr, Salwa. *The Wiles of Men and Other Stories,* trans. by Denys Johnson-Davies. London: Quartet Books, 1992.

Bakr, Salwa. *The Golden Chariot,* trans. by Dinah Manistry. Reading, U.K.: Garnet Publishing, 1995.

Bakr, Salwa. *The Man from Bashmour,* trans. by Nancy Roberts. Cairo: American University in Cairo Press, 2007.

Barakat, Hoda. *The Stone of Laughter: A Novel*, trans. by Sophie Bennett. Reading: Garnet Publishing, 1994.

Barakat, Hoda. *The Tiller of Waters*, trans. by Marilyn Booth. Cairo: American University in Cairo Press, 2001.

Barakat, Hoda. *Disciples of Passion*, trans. by Marilyn Booth. Cairo: American University in Cairo Press, 2006.

Chedid, Andrée. *The Multiple Child*, trans. by Judith Radke. San Francisco: Mercury House, 1995.

Djebar, Assia. *A Sister to Scheherazade*, trans. by Dorothy Blair. Portsmouth, New Hampshire: Heinemann, 1987.

Djebar, Assia. *Fantasia: An Algerian Cavalcade*, trans. by Dorothy Blair. London: Quartet Books, 1989.

Djebar, Assia. *Women of Algiers in Their Apartment*, trans. by Marjolijn de Jager. Charlottesville: University Press of Virginia, 1992.

Djebar, Assia. *Far from Madina*. London: Quartet Books, 1994.

Djebar, Assia. *So Vast the Prison*, trans. by Betsy Wing. New York: Seven Stories Press, 1999.

al-Ghazali, Zaynab. *Days from My Life*. Delhi: Hindustan Publications, 1989.

Idilbi, Ulfat. *Sabriya: Damascus Bitter Sweet*, trans. by Peter Clark. New York: Interlink Books, 1997.

Idilbi, Ulfat. *Grandfather's Tale*, trans. by Peter Clark. London: Quartet Books, 1998.

Khaled, Leila. *My People Shall Live: Autobiography of a Revolutionary*. Toronto: N.C. Press, 1975.

Khalifeh, Sahar. *Wild Thorns*, trans. by Trevor Legassick and Elizabeth Fernea. London: Saqi Books, 1985.

Khalifeh, Sahar. *The Inheritance*, trans. by Aida Bamia. Cairo: American University in Cairo Press, 2005.

Khedairi, Betool. *A Sky So Close*, trans. by Muhayman Jamil. New York: Pantheon Books, 2001.

al-Kuzbari, Salma al-Haffar. *Love After the Fiftieth*, trans. by Shukrieh R. Merlet. Damascus: Dar Tlass, 1992.

Mamdouh, Alia. *Mothballs*, trans. by Peter Theroux. Reading, U.K.: Garnet Publishing, 1996.

Marouane, Leila. *The Abductor*, trans. by Felicity McNabb. London: Quartet Books, 2001.

Mikhail, Dunya. *Diary of a Wave Outside the Sea*, trans. by Louise I. Hartung. Cairo: Ishtar Publishing House, 1999.

Mosteghanemi, Ahlam. *Memory in the Flesh*, trans. by Baria Ahmar; revised by Peter Clark. Cairo: American University in Cairo Press, 2000.

Mosteghanemi, Ahlam. *Chaos of the Senses*, trans. by Baria Ahmar. Cairo: American University in Cairo Press, 2004.

Nana, Hamidah. *The Homeland*, trans. by Martin Asser. Reading, U.K.: Garnet Publishing, 1997.

Al Nasiri, Buthaina. *Final Night: Short Stories*, selected and translated by Denys Johnson-Davies. Cairo: American University in Cairo Press, 2002.

Nasrallah, Emily. *Flight Against Time*, trans. by Issa J. Boullata. Charlottetown, PEI: Ragweed Press, 1987.

Nasrallah, Emily. *A House Not Her Own: Stories from Beirut*, trans. by Thuraya Khalil-Khouri. Charlottetown, PEI: Gynergy Books, 1992.

Nasrallah, Emily. *The Fantastic Strokes of Imagination*, short stories, bilingual, trans. by Rebecca Porteous. Cairo: Elias Modern Publishing House, 1995.

Numani, Huda. *I Was a Point, I Was a Circle: An Elegaic Ode*, trans. by Huda Numani and Solomon I. Sara. Colorado Springs: Three Continents Press, 1993.

Rifaat, Alifa. *Distant View of a Minaret and Other Stories*, trans. by Denys Johnson-Davies. London and New York: Quartet Books, 1983.

El Saadawi, Nawal. *Woman at Point Zero*, trans. by Sherif Hetata. London: Zed Books, 1983.

El Saadawi, Nawal. *God Dies by the Nile*, trans. by Sherif Hetata. London: Zed Books, 1985.

El Saadawi, Nawal. *She Has No Place in Paradise*, trans. by Shirley Eber. London: Methuen, 1987.

El Saadawi, Nawal. *The Circling Song*, trans. by Marilyn Booth. London: Zed Press, 1989.

El Saadawi, Nawal. *Memoirs from the Women's Prison*, trans. by Marilyn Booth. Berkeley: University of California Press, 1994.

El Saadawi, Nawal. *A Daughter of Isis: The Autobiography of Nawal El Saadawi*, trans. by Sherif Hetata. London: Zed Books, 1999.

El-Saadawi, Nawal. *Love in the Kingdom of Oil*, trans. by Basil Hatim and Malcolm Williams. London: Saqi Books, 2001.

Sadawi, Nawal. *Two Women in One*, trans. by Osman Nusairi and Jana Gough. London: Saqi Books, 1985.

Sadawi, Nawal. *Death of an Ex-minister*, trans. by Shirley Eber. London: Methuen, 1987.

Sadawi, Nawal. *The Fall of the Imam*, trans, by Sherif Hetata. London: Methuen, 1988.

Sadawi, Nawal. *Memoirs of a Woman Doctor*, trans. by Catherine Cobham. London: Saqi Books, 1988.

Sadawi, Nawal. *Searching*, trans. by Shirley Eber. London: Atlantic Highlands, 1991.

Sadawi, Nawal. *The Well of Life and The Thread: Two Short Novels*, trans. by Sherif Hetata. London: Lime Tree, 1993.

Sadawi, Nawal. *The Innocence of the Devil*, trans. by Sherif Hetata. Berkeley: University of California Press, 1994.

al-Sabah, S.M. *Fragments of a Woman*, trans. by Nehad Selaiha. Cairo: General Egyptian Book Organization, 1990.

Samman, Ghada. *Beirut 75: A Novel*, trans. by Nancy N. Roberts. Fayetteville: University of Arkansas Press, 1995.

Samman, Ghada. *The Awakening of the Moon: A Selection of Poems*, trans. by Abdullah al-Shahhan and M.V. McDonald. Muscat: n.p., 1996.

Samman, Ghada. *Beirut Nightmares*, trans. by Nancy N. Roberts. London: Quartet Books, 1997.

Samman, Ghada. *The Square Moon: Supernatural Tales*, trans. by Issa Boullata. Fayetteville: University of Arkansas Press, 1998.

Samman, Ghada. *The Night of the First Billion*, trans. by Nancy N. Roberts. Cairo: American University in Cairo Press, 2005.

Sebbar, Leïla. *Sherazade: Missing, Age 17, Dark Curly Hair, Green Eyes*, trans. by Dorothy Blair. London: Quartet Books, 1991.

Sebbar, Leïla. *Silence on the Shores*, trans. by Mildred Mortimer. Lincoln: University of Nebraska Press, 2000.

Shaarawi, Huda. *Harem Years: The Memoirs of an Egyptian Feminist (1879–1924)*, trans. by Margot Badran. New York: Feminist Press at the City University of New York, 1987.

al-Shaykh, Hanan. *Women of Sand and Myrrh*, trans. by Catherine Cobham. London: Quartet Books, 1989.

al-Shaykh, Hanan. *The Story of Zahra*, trans. by Peter Ford. London: Quartet Books, 1991.

al-Shaykh, Hanan. *Beirut Blues: A Novel*, trans. by Catherine Cobham. New York: Anchor Books, 1996.

al-Shaykh, Hanan. *I Sweep the Sun Off Rooftops: Stories*, trans. by Catherine Cobham. New York: Doubleday, 1998.

al-Shaykh, Hanan. *Only in London*, trans. by Catherine Cobham. New York: Pantheon Books, 2001.

al-Tahawy, Miral. *The Tent: A Novel*, trans. by Anthony Calderbank. Cairo: American University in Cairo Press, 1998.

al-Tahawy, Miral. *Blue Aubergine*, trans. by Anthony Calderbank. Cairo: American University in Cairo Press, 2002.

Tawfiq, Sahar. *Points of the Compass: Stories*, trans. by Marilyn Booth. Fayetteville: University of Arkansas Press, 1995.

Telmissany, May. *Dunyazad*, trans. by Roger Allen. London: Saqi Books, 2000.

Tergeman, Siham. *Daughter of Damascus,* trans. by Andrea Rugh. Austin: University of Texas Press, 1994.

Tuqan, Fadwa. *A Mountainous Journey: An Autobiography,* trans. by Olive Kenny; poetry trans. by Naomi Shihab Nye with the help of Salma Khadra Jayyusi. St. Paul, MN: Graywolf Press, 1990.

Yarid, Nazik Saba. *Improvisations on a Missing String,* trans. by Stuart A. Hancox. Fayetteville: University of Arkansas Press, 1997.

Younes, Iman Humaydan. *B as in Beirut,* trans. by Max Weiss. Northampton, MA: Interlink Books, 2008.

Zangana, Haifa. *Through the Vast Halls of Memory,* trans. by Paul Hammond and Haifa Zangana. Paris: Hourglass, 1991.

Zayyat, Latifa. *The Search: Personal Papers,* trans. by Sophie Bennett. London: Quartet Books, 1996.

Zayyat, Latifa. *The Owner of the House,* trans. by Sophie Bennett. London: Quartet Books, 1997.

al-Zayyat, Latifa. *The Open Door,* trans., by Marilyn Booth. Cairo: American University in Cairo Press, 2000.

Anthologies

Attieh, Aman Mahmoud. *Short Fiction by Saudi Arabian Women Writers.* Austin: University of Texas, 1999.

Bagader, Abubaker, Ava M. Heinrichsdorff, and Deborah. S. Akers, eds. *Voices of Change: Short Stories by Saudi Arabian Women Writers.* Boulder: Lynne Rienner Publishers, 1998.

Booth, Marilyn, trans. *My Grandmother's Cactus: Stories by Egyptian Women.* London: Quartet Books, 1991.

Cohen-Mor, Dalya, ed. and trans. *Arab Women Writers: An Anthology of Short Stories.* Albany: State University of New York Press, 2005.

Glanville, Jo. *Qissat: Short Stories by Palestinian Women.* London: Telegram, 2006.

Handal, Nathalie. *The Poetry of Arab women: A Contemporary Anthology.* New York: Interlink Books, 2001.

Khalaf, Roseanne Saad, ed. *Hikayat: Short Stories by Lebanese Women.* London: Telegram, 2006.

Samaan, Angéle Botros, ed. *A Voice of Their Own: Short Stories by Egyptian Women.* Cairo: Ministry of Culture, 1994.

Bibliography of Works in French

Writers in French *Amina Rachid*

Francophone writing in the Arab world cannot be separated from colonialism, whether French is a necessity—in the case of a writer whose knowledge of Arabic is weak—or a choice—a writer with knowledge of both Arabic and French who prefers the latter. By the same token, the two languages can exist in happy confluence as part of a sense of a fully rounded hybrid identity, as in the case of Lebanese writer Nadia Tuéni and Andrée Chedid, a French author of Lebanese-Egyptian origin, or embody the gulf between two identities, as expressed by Tunisian writer Emna Belhaj Yahia.

In either case, an urgent question remains: what is the significance of this writing and to which culture does it belong? It is a hybrid form of writing whose subjects and concerns spring largely from the world in which the author was raised, but its language, aesthetics, and means of publication and distribution belong mainly to another culture and, at times, to its perspective and ideology.

Language is not an objective vessel: its letters and constructions bring with it the special world out of which it emerged, which in turn shapes a language's phraseology and features. Francophone writers, too, are engaging a foreign, French-speaking reader who has certain preconceptions about other worlds that might impinge on the writer herself when using this language. Is it, then, the fate of this writing to remain split between two worlds, a confused hybrid, marginalized both here and there? Or does it take part in forming what could be called world literature? In the best case, might it not help convey the experiences and reality of the Arab world to the foreign reader? These questions remain unanswered, as Francophone texts themselves have only recently come under close analysis.

The French language imposed itself on the world in the eighteenth century, the Age of Enlightenment, as the literary, cultural language par excellence, like Italian in the field of music, German in philosophy, and English in commerce. It soon became a language of social privilege as well, spoken by those who belonged, or wished to belong, to various national elites. In the nineteenth century, French spread among the Russian and German intelligentsia and aristocracy. The dissemination of French cannot be separated from France's expansionist, colonial objectives in the world, for France used its language to achieve its political ends. French became the language of administration and education in North Africa and several areas in sub-Saharan Africa; it also played a role in defining Christian and Muslim identity in Lebanon and supporting the nationalist movement against the English in Egypt. Certainly, this context had an influence on Francophone writing, both by men and women, giving rise to different kinds of writing, some of it marginalized and some of it achieving global recognition, part of it recognized in the nation of the writer and part of it simply ignored.

There are, of course, many differences in the French writings of women from the Arab world, but they are nevertheless linked by several factors, most important of which is the multiplicity of voices we find in these works. The linguistic registers and inspirations span diverse languages and local dialects, and the characters represent many nationalities. The style of writing, too, vacillates between history and myth, between nostalgia for an absent/present past and a preoccupation with a present torn asunder by events. These writings are remarkable for their depth of subjective experience and the richness of the female voice, whether it is a novel dealing with the oppression of women in traditional society or a text that addresses a longing for one's homeland through a specifically female perspective and experience in the form of autobiography, novelistic autobiography, or another type of literary text. Andrée Chedid's writings, set in Egypt and Lebanon, deal with misery and disease among the poorer classes in Egypt, women's oppression, and the atrocity of the civil war in Lebanon, while her autobiography tells the story of upper-class Levantine immigrants in Egypt between Cairo and Paris. Her semi-fictional writings vacillate between history and parable and give expression to the dream of reconciling class gaps in Egypt and the Muslim-Christian divide in Lebanon.

The writings of Algerian Assia Djebar, on the other hand, use subjective writing to remember the history of Algeria's colonization. They are dominated by women's voices, their stories, and their version of events, and combine the vernacular of women with narrative in French. Whereas Andrée Chedid admits her poor knowledge of Arabic, Assia Djebar declares her love for French, saying that she writes in the language by choice, not because she is "colonized." Despite this statement and Andrée Chedid's many declarations that she has gone beyond the issue of roots, we find in both writers' works a pressing return to roots. Using the symbol of the Nile and the story of Nefertiti, Chedid searches for Egypt's eternal existence, while Djebar returns to Algeria's recent history and even further back to narrate the glories of famous women at the dawn of Islam.

Between these two poles lie various types of writing, some giving voice to the rupture between language and identity and some making an explicit choice to go beyond the barrier of language to address history or accept a hybrid identity. While Tunisian author Emna Belhaj Yahia expresses the unequivocal rupture between the two worlds, between the language of authenticity and the homeland versus the language of modern culture and liberty, Lebanese writer Nadia Tuéni states that her works in French do not contradict her Arab identity and culture. The works of Etel Adnan and Dominique Eddé, both from Lebanon, bring us modernist writing with its multiplicity of voices and techniques and encompass the depth of the historical struggle lived by Lebanese society and the entire Arab world. Both authors champion the Palestinian cause and expose the violence of militias and the tragedy of a Beirut torn apart by civil war.

The basic problem of Francophone writing is that it lacks a context for its reception, with the exception of those texts that have achieved international recognition. The number of French readers in the Arab world remains small, despite the efforts of Francophone policy, illustrated in festivals, prizes, publishing opportunities, and the encouragement to teach French and improve its curricula. Literary texts in French remain unknown or marginalized among a limited readership in the Arab world, despite their clear literary value. They run the gamut of literary forms, from novels, to poetry, to drama, to autobiography, sometimes adding something truly innovative to these forms. They often pulse with a love for the author's homeland and are imbued with a profound awareness of its conflicts and problems. Arab women writing in French have also found various means and an aesthetic to represent Arabic colloquials, and they have succeeded in giving the French-speaking world some familiarity with both a traditional and modern Arab reality.

These texts are the object of important comparative research, between the individual texts themselves from one country to another and between the corpus of texts as a whole and other third world texts written in English or Spanish. Comparative studies focus on the aesthetics of the texts, their commonalities, and the features that distinguish texts in one language from another and one author from another. The question remains, however: will these works become better known through translation or will they remain a quaint treasure adorning the halls of literary history? In the best case, will they become a means of familiarizing the world with the Arab reality?

Abaroudi, Fatema Chahid (Abarudi, Fatima Shahid) (1965–) (see also: Bibliography of Works in Arabic), Moroccan poet born in Taroudant. She currently lives in Casablanca. She graduated from the King Muhammad V University in Rabat in 1990. She is a prolific poet and a founding member of the International Festival for University Theater in Casablanca. She is also the president of the Political and Literary Friendships Association in Morocco.

Imago (poetry), Imprimatic, Casablanca, 1983.

Songes de hautes terres, (poetry) Le Fennec, Casablanca, 1989.

Le Nouvel "IMAGO" (poetry), 1997.

Abdelnour, Elham Chamoun ('Abd al-Nur, Ilham Sham'un) (1953–), Lebanese poet born in Beirut. She has an M.A. in French from St. Joseph University in Beirut. She was a founder of *Wa tabqa al-kalima*, a journal published by the Word Movement in the greater Bikfaya area. She is a member of the al-Fikr Council, the International PEN Association, and the French Poets' Association in Paris.

Retraite des ombres (poetry). Beirut: Dar al-Nahar, 1992.

Fuite sans échos (poetry). Beirut: Librairie Sader, 1993.

Préludes (poetry). Lebanon: Dar Alam Alf Layla wa Layla, 1996.

Asma, une jeune fille du Liban (novel). Paris: L'Harmattan, 1999.

Abdessemed, Rabia ('Abd al-Samad, Rabi'a) (1930–), Algerian short-story writer born in Algeria. She was a secondary-school teacher and worked with Germaine Tillion in social centers in colonial Algeria. She was one of the first Algerian women to attend university.

La voyante du Hodna (stories). Paris: L'Harmattan, 1993.

Accad, Evelyne (al-'Aqqad, Evelyne) (1943–) (see also: Bibliography of Works in Arabic), Lebanese novelist born in Beirut. She began her university studies at the Beirut College for Women and continued them in the United States, where she received a B.A. in English literature from Anderson University in 1967, an M.A. in French from Ball State University in 1968, and a Ph.D. in comparative literature from Indiana University in 1973. She is a professor of French and comparative literature at the University of Illinois. She taught at Beirut University College in 1978 and 1984 and at Northwestern University in 1991. She has written several works of literary criticism and does research on women in Arab and African countries. Two of her novels have been translated into English, *L'Excisée (The Excised)* and *Coquelicot du massacre (Poppy from the Massacre)*. She won the France-Lebanon Prize in 1993. Her academic works in English include *Veil of Shame* (1978) and *Contemporary Arab Women Writers and Poets* (1986). She translated Noureddine Aba's dramatic poem, *Montjoie Palestine! ou L'an dernier a Jerusalem* (Montjoie Palestine! or Last Year in Jerusalem) into English.

Entre deux (stories). Sherbrooke, QC: Cosmos, 1976.

Veil of Shame: The Role of Women in the Contemporary Fiction of North Africa and the Arab World. Sherbrooke, QC: Naaman, 1978.

Montjoie Palestine! or Last Year in Jerusalem (bilingual edition, trans. of the dramatic poem by Noureddine Aba). Paris: L'Harmattan, 1980.

L'Excisée (novel). Paris: L'Harmattan, 1982.

Contemporary Arab Women Writers and Poets (monograph). Beirut: Institute of Women's Studies, 1986.

Coquelicot du massacre (novel). Paris: L'Harmattan, 1988.

Sexuality and War: Literary Masks of the Middle East. New York: New York University Press, 1990.

Des femmes, des hommes et la guerre: Fiction et réalité au Proche-Orient. Paris: Côté femmes, 1993.

Blessures des mots: Journal de Tunisie (novel). Paris: Côté femmes, 1993.

Adib, Hoda (Adib, Huda) (1943–) (see also: Bibliography of Works in Arabic), Lebanese poet and musician born in Beirut. She is the daughter of Albert Adib, the founder of *al-Adib* magazine. She received a degree in music from the National Conservatory and taught piano at the National Institute for Music in Beirut. She lives in London. She writes in both Arabic and French, and her second collection of poems in French received the Sa'id 'Aql Prize. She writes free verse and poetic prose.

Parenthèse (poetry). Beirut: Editions de la Revue al-Adib, 1968.

Demi-pause (poetry). Beirut: Editions de la Revue al-Adib, 1970.

A contretemps (poetry). Paris: Editions Saint-Germain-des-Prés, 1977.

Métamorphose de la mémoire (poetry). London: MECO, 1996.

Shahar et Shalim (poetry). Paris: L'Harmattan, 1997.

De rhapsode au zajal (poetry). Paris: L'Harmattan, 1998.

Adnan, Etel ('Adnan, Etel) (1925–), Lebanese poet, novelist, and artist born in Beirut to a Syrian father and a Greek mother. She attended the Ecole supérieure des lettres in Beirut and the Sorbonne. She also studied philosophy in the United States at Harvard University and Berkeley. She wrote for the Beirut-based paper, *L'Orient-Le Jour*. She moved to Paris in 1972 and lives between Paris and California. She writes in both French and English.

Jébu (poetry). Paris: P.J. Oswald, 1973.

Sitt Marie-Rose (novel). Paris: Des femmes, 1977.

L'Apocalypse arabe (poetry). Paris: Papyrus, 1980.

Ce ciel qui . . . n'est pas (poetry). Paris: L'Harmattan, 1997.

Ahdab, Joumana (Ahdab, Jumana) (1921–), Lebanese poet born in Beirut. She was educated at the Protestant College. She published often in the Francophone press in Lebanon, notably in *La Revue*

du Liban and *Le Jour*. In 1945 and 1946 she published several poems in *Le Cahier de l'Est*.

Vivre (poetry). Paris: Editions Debresse, 1951.

Ammoun, Denise ('Ammun, Denise) (?–), Lebanese novelist and journalist. She has a degree in law. She was a long-time contributor to the Beirut-based *Magasin*. She is currently a correspondent for *Le Croix* and *Le Point*, based in Cairo. She has published one work on Lebanese history, *Histoire du Liban contemporain, 1860–1943* (1997).

Le mors aux dents (novel). Beirut: privately published, 1973.

Histoire du Liban contemporain, 1860–1943. Paris: Fayard, 1997.

Amrouche, Fadhma A.M. ('Amrush, Fatima Ayt Mansur) (1882–1967), Algerian writer born in Tizi Hibel in Kabylie, Algeria. She converted to Christianity after her marriage and moved to Tunisia and then to France. She returned to Algeria in 1953 and later settled in France.

Histoire de ma vie (autobiography, followed by poems). Paris: Maspéro, 1968.

Amrouche, Marguerite Taos ('Amrush, Marguerite Tawus) (1913–1976), Algerian novelist and short-story writer born in Tunis. She was the first Algerian woman novelist to write in French. She devoted part of her life to collecting oral literature and music from Kabylie and made several recordings of Kabylie music and songs. She published *Le Grain magique* in 1976, a collection of Berber stories, poems, and proverbs.

Jacinthe noire (novel). Paris: Charlot, 1947.

Rue des tambourins (novel). Paris: La Table ronde, 1960.

L'amant imaginaire (novel). Paris: Nouvelle société Morel, 1975.

Solitude, ma mère (novel). Paris: Editions Joëlle Losfeld, 1995.

Aouad-Basbous, Thérèse ('Awwad-Basbus, Thérèse) (1934–) (see also: Bibliography of Works in Arabic), Lebanese poet and dramatist born in Bahr Saf. She received a B.A. in Arabic literature and French literature from the Sorbonne in 1964. She worked in French radio for six years, then as a lecturer in media studies at the Lebanese University from 1968. She has published studies on contemporary sculpture and writes in both Arabic and French. She has published Arabic poetry in the journals, *Shi'r* and *Mawaqif.* She staged her play, *al-Bakara,* about male–female relationships, at the House of Art and Literature, where it was directed by Fu'ad Na'im. Critic Khalida Sa'id argues that the show had a special impact on Beirut's cultural circles and went beyond the usual social or political drama. She has also written a work in Arabic about her late husband, the sculptor Michel Basbous. The book has appeared in English and French, as well.

Clair-obscur (poetry). Eygalières, France: Editions du Temps parallèle, 1983.

Michel Basbous: sculpture, texte auto-biographique (biography). Beirut: Université Libanaise, 1986.

H₂O (play). Paris: L'Harmattan, 1994.

La coincidence (play). Paris: L'Harmattan, 1994.

Seuls comme l'eau (play). Paris: L'Harmattan, 1994.

Mon roman (novel). Paris: L'Harmattan, 1995.

La nonne et le téléphone (play). Paris: L'Harmattan, 1996.

Aractingi, Andrée ('Araqtanji, Andrée) (?–), Lebanese author of crime novels.

Ballade pour un noyé (novel). Beirut: privately published, 1978.

Arcache, Jeanne (Arqash, Jeanne) (1902–1961), Lebanese poet and novelist born in Alexandria to a Lebanese father and a French mother. She wrote for several Francophone journals in Egypt, most notably the weekly *Image* and the monthly *La Revue du Caire.* In 1945 she married Charles Kuentz, the director of the Institut français d'archéologie orientale. Many of her works remain unpublished.

L'Egypte dans mon miroir (poetry). Paris: Editions des Cahiers libres, 1931.

La chambre haute (poetry). Paris: Corrêa, 1933.

L'Emir à la croix (novel). Paris: Librairie Plon, 1938.

Assaad, Fawzia (As'ad, Fawziya) (193?–), Egyptian novelist born in Cairo. She lives in Geneva. She received her B.A. and Ph.D. in humanities at the Sorbonne. She taught philosophy at Ain Shams University, as well as in Taipei and Dongyin in Taiwan. She has published many academic works on philosophy. She is active in both politics and literature. She defends imprisoned writers on behalf of the International PEN Association's human rights section at the U.N. She has twice received an award from the city of Geneva for her literary works. Her novel, *L'Egyptienne,* has been translated into Arabic as "Misriya."

L'Egyptienne (novel). Paris: Mercure de France, 1975.

Des enfants et des chats (novel). Lausanne, Switzerland: P.M. Favre, 1987.

Le grande maison de Louxor (novel). Paris: L'Harmattan, 1992.

Awad, Jocelyne J. ('Awwad, Jocelyne) (1949–), Lebanese novelist born in Beirut. She has a B.A. in literature. Her first novel in French was successful and was awarded the France-Lebanon Prize and the Prix Richelieu Senghor.

Khamsin (novel). Paris: Albin Michel, 1994.

Aziz, Désirée Sadek ('Aziz, Désirée Sadiq) (?–), Lebanese novelist. She is the editorial director of *Santé* magazine and the founder of the Scientific Agency for the Preservation of Lebanon's Cedars. She has published a historical-touristic work in French, *Liban terre éternelle*

(1995), as well as an album on the Lebanese cedar, *Le cèdre du Liban* (1991), which was awarded the Prix Félix de Beaujour by the Académie des sciences morales et politiques.
Le parfum du bonheur (novel). Paris: Robert Laffont, 1994.
Le silence des cèdres (novel). Paris: Robert Laffont, 1995.
L'enfant des cèdres (stories). Paris: Albin Michel Jeunesse, 1995.

Azzouz, Nassira ('Azzuz, Nasira) (1961–), Algerian poet born in Batna.
Les portes du soleil (poetry). Algiers: Entreprise nationale du livre, 1988.

Bahi, Jalila (?–)
Chapelles d'ombres. Tunis: L'or du temps, 1993.

Balabane-Hallit, Aïda (Halit, 'Ayida Balaban) (?–), Lebanese poet. She has lived in Paris since 1969.
La désertée (poetry). Paris: L'Harmattan, 1992.

Barakat, Leila (Barakat, Layla) (1968–), Lebanese novelist born in Kafr Qatra in al-Shuf. She has a B.A. in social sciences, literature, and education. She received a Ph.D. from the New Sorbonne in Paris for her thesis on Francophone cultural politics. She teaches French at the Lebanese University and is a consultant for the Lebanese minister of culture.
Sous les vignes du pays druze (novel). Paris: L'Harmattan, 1993.
Le chagrin de l'Arabie heureuse (novel). Paris: L'Harmattan, 1994.
Pourquoi pleure l'Euphrate . . . ? (novel). Paris: L'Harmattan, 1995.
Les hommes damnés de la Terre Sainte (novel). Paris: L'Harmattan, 1997.

Barakat, Najwa (1960–) (see also: Bibliography of Works in Arabic)
La locataire du pot de fer (novel). Paris: L'Harmattan, 1997.

Béji, Hélé (Baji, Hali) (1948–), Tunisian novelist born in Tunis. She currently lives in Paris. She has a degree in humanities. She has taught literature at the University of Tunis. She now works for U.N.E.S.C.O in Paris. Her non-fiction works include *Le désenchantement national* (1982), an essay on decolonization.
Le désenchantement national: Essai sur la décolonisation (essay). Paris: Maspéro, 1982.
L'oeil du jour (novel). Paris: Maurice Nadeau, 1985.
Itinéraire de Paris à Tunis (travelogue). Paris: Noël Blandin, 1992.
L'art contre la culture (essay). Paris: Intersignes, 1994.
L'imposture culturelle (essay). Paris: Stock, 1997.

Belghoul, Farida (Balghul, Farida) (1958–), Algerian novelist born in Paris. She is active in the Association of the Children of Emigrés.
C'est Madame la France que tu préfères? (short film), 1981.
Le départ du père, (short film), 1983.
Georgette! (novel). Paris: Barrault, 1986.

Belhaj-Yahia, Emna (Balhaj-Yahya, Yamina) (1936–), Tunisian novelist born in Tunis. She studied philosophy and managed the bilingual magazine, *Nissa*. Eight issues of the magazine appeared from April 1985 to March 1987.
Chronique frontalière (novel). Paris: Blandin, 1994.
L'étage invisible (novel). Tunis: Cérès, 1996.

Ben Mansour, Latifa (Bin Mansur, Latifa) (1950–), Algerian novelist and dramatist born in Tlemcen. She currently lives in Paris. She teaches linguistics in Paris and Orleans.
Le chant du lys et du basilic (novel). Paris: J.C. Lattès, 1990.
La prière de la peur (novel). Paris: Editions de la Différence, 1997.
Trente-trois tours à son turban (play). Arles, France: Actes Sud–Papiers, 1997.

Benmehdi, Yasmine (Bin Mahdi, Yasmin) (1957–), Algerian writer born in al-Ruwayba in eastern Algeria. She is a media technician.
Les rênes du destin (novel). Paris: L'Harmattan, 1995.

Boucetta, Fatiha (?–2007), Moroccan novelist who lived in Casablanca. She is a painter and writes in French.
Anissa captive (novel). Casablanca: Eddif, 1991.

Boukortt, Zoulika (Bukurt, Zulika) (?–), Algerian novelist.
Le corps en pièces (novel), Montpellier: Coprah, 1977.
Pétales éparpillés (poetry). Beirut: privately published, 1982.
A toi ma sympathie (poetry). Beirut: privately published, 1984.

Boumediène, Anissa (Bumadiyan, Anisa) (?–), Algerian poet and novelist born in Algiers. She is the widow of the late Algerian president, Houari Boumediène. She graduated from law school in Paris and works as an attorney in Algiers. She translated the poetry of al-Khansa' into French in 1978.
Le jour et la nuit (poetry). Paris: Editions Saint Germain des Prés, 1988.
La fin d'un monde (historical novel). Algiers: Bouchène, 1991.

Bouraoui, Nina (Burawi, Nina) (1976–), Algerian novelist born in Rennes, France, where she resides. She received the Prix de Livre Inter in 1991 for her novel, *La voyeuse interdite*.
La voyeuse interdite (novel). Paris: Gallimard, 1991.
Poing mort (novel). Paris: Gallimard, 1992.
La bal des murènes (novel). Paris: Fayard, 1996.
L'âge blessé (novel). Paris: Fayard, 1998.
Le jour du séisme (novel). Paris: Stock, 1999.

Boustany, Raya (Bustani, Raya) (1973–), Lebanese writer born in Beirut.
Papyrus religieux (prose). Adonis, Lebanon: privately published, 1992.

Bustros, Eveline Tuéni (Bustrus, Eveline Tuwayni) (1878–1971), Lebanese novelist born in Beirut, where she received her early education. She went to Egypt and from there on to Paris, where she studied French language and literature. She returned to Lebanon in the early 1930s and became involved in social and literary activities. She established an organization for the production and distribution of Lebanese and Syrian art and crafts, along with the Lebanese Pen Club (1945) and the Association for Rural Development (1953). She was the president of Friends of the Arts, the Women's Awakening Association (1934), the Writers' Association (1934), and the Arab Lebanese Women's Union (1942). She contributed to *Phoenica* magazine. She did research on traditional Arab costume and established al-Artizana, a crafts association and gallery. She published several works of non-fiction on French politics and tradition, including "Réminiscence" (1952) and *Michel Chiha* (1956).
La main d'Allah (novel). Paris: Bossard, 1926.
"Fredons" (political essay). Beirut: n.p., 1929.
"Réminiscence" (lecture). Beirut: Conferences du Cénacle, nos. 9–10 (1952).
Michel Chiha: Evocations (biography). Beirut: Editions du Cénacle libanais, 1956.
Sous la baguette du coudrier (novel). Beirut: privately published, 1958.
Romans et écrits divers (novels and selected writings): Beirut: Dar al-Nahar, 1988.

Chafik, Nadia (Shafiq, Nadiya) (1962–), Moroccan novelist born in Casablanca. She was raised in Rabat and studied art and French literature at the Université de Montreal, Canada, where she received an M.A. She is a professor at the Faculty of Humanities at Ibn Tufayl University in Qunaytira.

Filles du vent (novel). Paris: L'Harmattan, 1995.
Le secret des djinns (novel). Casablanca: Eddif, 1996.

Chaibi, Aicha (al-Shaybi, 'A'isha) (?–), Tunisian novelist. She is a French teacher.
Rached (novel). Tunis: Maison tunisienne de l'édition, 1975.

Chammam, Dorra (al-Shammam, Durra) (?–), Tunisian poet.
Le divan (poetry). Tunis: La N.E.F., 1989.
Profanation (poetry). Tunis: L'or du temps, 1993.

Chedid, Andrée (Shadid, Andree Sa'b) (1921–), Egyptian poet born to Lebanese parents in Cairo. She received her early education in French schools in Cairo and continued her studies at the American University in Cairo. In 1943 she published a collection of poems in English, *On the Trails of My Fancy*, using the pseudonym A. Lake. She moved to Lebanon and then to Paris, where she has lived since 1946. She has received several awards, including the Prix Louise Labé in 1966 for her collection *Double-Pays*, the Golden Eagle Award for poetry from the Nice Book Fair in 1972 for a collection of poetry, the Grand prix des lettres françaises from the Royal Belgian Academy in 1975, the Prix de l'Afrique méditéranéenne in 1975 for her novel *Néfertiti et le rêve d'Akhénaton*, the Goncourt Short Story Prize in 1979, the Paul Morand Prize from the French Academy in 1994, and the Mallarmé Prize for her collection, *Fraternité de la parole*.
Textes pour une figure (poetry). Paris: Editions Le Pré aux Clercs, 1949.
Textes pour un poème (poetry). Paris: Editions Guy Lévis-Mano (G.L.M.). 1950.
Le sommeil délivré (novel). Paris: Stock, 1952.
Textes pour le vivant (poetry). Paris: G.L.M., 1953.

Textes pour la terre aimée (poetry). Paris: G.L.M., 1955.
Jonathan (novel). Paris: Seuil, 1955.
Terre et poésie (poetry). Paris: G.L.M., 1956.
Terre regardée (poetry). Paris: G.L.M., 1957.
Seul le visage (poetry). Paris: G.L.M., 1960.
Le sixième jour (novel). Paris: Julliard, 1960.
Lubies (poetry). Paris: G.L.M., 1962.
Le survivant (novel). Paris: Julliard, 1963.
Double-pays (poetry). Paris: G.L.M., 1965.
L'étroite peau (stories). Paris: Julliard, 1965.
Contre-chant (poetry). Paris: Flammarion, 1968
Bérénice d'Egypte (play). Paris: Seuil, 1968.
Les nombres (play). Paris: Seuil, 1968.
Le personnage (play). Paris: L'Avant-Scène, 1968.
Le montreur (play). Paris: Seuil, 1969.
L'autre (novel). Paris: Flammarion, 1969.
Liban (prose). Paris: Seuil, 1969.
Visage premier (poetry). Paris: Flammarion, 1971.
La cité fertile (novel). Paris: Flammarion, 1972.
Le dernier candidat (play). Paris: L'Avant-Scène, 1972.
Fêtes et lubies (poetry). Paris: Flammarion, 1973.
Prendre corps (poetry). Paris: G.L.M., 1973.
Néfertiti et le rêve d'Akhénaton (novel). Paris: Flammarion, 1974.
Fraternité de la parole (poetry). Paris: Flammarion, 1976.
Cérémonial de la violence (poetry). Paris: Flammarion, 1976.
Grandes oreilles tout oreilles (children's literature). Paris: Laffont Robert, 1977.
Le corps et le temps suivi de l'étroite peau (stories). Paris: Flammarion, 1978.
Cavernes et soleils (poetry). Paris: Flammarion, 1979.
Les marches de sable (novel). Paris: Flammarion, 1981.
Le cœur suspendu (stories). Brussels: Casterman, 1981.
Epreuves du vivant (poetry). Paris: Flammarion, 1983.

Derrière les visages (stories). Paris: Flammarion, 1983.

La maison sans racines (novel). Paris: Flammarion, 1985.

Textes pour un poème, 1949–1970 (poetry). Paris: Flammarion, 1987.

Mondes miroirs magies (stories). Paris: Flammarion, 1988

L'enfant multiple (novel). Paris: Flammarion, 1989.

Les manèges de la vie (stories for young adults). Paris: Père Castor–Flammarion, 1989.

Poèmes pour un texte, 1970–1991 (poetry). Paris: Flammarion, 1991.

A la mort, à la vie (stories). Paris: Flammarion, 1992.

Géricault (biography/fiction). Paris: Editions Flohic, 1992.

Dans le soleil du père (novel). Paris: Flohic, 1992.

La femme de Job (novel). Paris: Maren Sell/Calman-Lévy, 1993.

La femme en rouge et autres nouvelles (stories). Paris: J'ai Lu, 1994.

Les métamorphoses de Batine (stories for young adults). Paris: Père Castor–Flammarion, 1994.

Par delà les mots (poetry). Paris: Flammarion, 1995.

Les saisons de passage (novel). Paris: Flammarion, 1996.

Compilation (science fiction). Paris: Flammarion, n.d.

Le jardin perdu (essay, stories; with calligraphy by Massoudy Hassan). Paris: Editions Alternatives, 1997.

L'enfant des manèges et autres nouvelles (stories). Paris: Flammarion, 1998.

Lucy: La femme verticale (science fiction). Paris: Flammarion, 1998.

L'artiste et autres nouvelles (stories). Paris: Flammarion, 1999.

Territoire du souffle (poetry). Paris: Flammarion, 1999.

Dabaneh, Frida Bagdadi (Dabana, Farida Baghdadi) (1947–), Lebanese poet born in Beirut. She is the sister of the late film director Marun Baghdadi. She was the long-time editor of the cultural page of Beirut's *Le Revue* and now covers youth affairs for the Beirut-based *L'Orient-Le Jour* and the bulletin, *Agenda Culturelle*. She received the Sa'id 'Aql Prize for her first collection of poetry in French.

Ailleurs (poetry). Beirut: privately published, 1967.

Enfance (stories). Beirut: privately published, 1974.

Débèche, Djamila (Dabish, Jamila) (1926–), Algerian novelist born in Satif. She currently resides in Paris. She was orphaned as a young girl and raised by her grandparents. Her grandfather maintained a friendship with Prince Louis of Monaco, so she often visited that country. In 1942 she started working for Algerian radio, preparing programs on women's development and demands for the education of Algerian women. She involved herself in journalism and began issuing a women's social, literary, and arts monthly, *L'Action*. Ten issues of the journal appeared starting on September 25, 1947. After 1962, she took part in the Paris-based Alliance of Algerian Women.

Leila, jeune fille d'Algérie (novel). Algiers: Imprimerie Charras, 1947.

Les Musulmans algériens et la scolarisation. Algiers: Imprimerie Charras, 1950.

L'enseignement de la langue arabe en Algérie et le droit de vote aux femmes algériennes. Algiers: Imprimerie Charras, 1951.

Aziza (novel). Algiers: Imprimerie Imbert, 1955.

Djebar, Assia (Jabbar, Asiya) (1936–), Algerian short-story writer and novelist born in Cherchell in western Algeria. Her real name is Fatima al-Zahra'. She currently resides in Paris. She was educated in Algeria. In 1955 she became the first Algerian woman to be admitted to the École normale supérieure in Paris. She has taught history in Rabat and Algeria and worked as a journalist in Tunisia. She has also written screenplays and produced several films. She received first prize at

the Venice Film Festival in 1979 for her film *La Nouba des femmes du Mont Chenoua* and the Prix Maurice Maeterlinck in 1995. She has devoted herself to literature since 1967. She contributed to the translation of Nawal al-Sa'dawi's novel *Ferdaous, une voix en enfer*, from Arabic to French.
La soif (novel). Paris: Julliard, 1957.
Les impatients (novel). Paris: Julliard, 1958.
Les enfants du nouveau monde (novel). Paris: Julliard, 1962.
Les alouettes naïves (novel). Paris: Julliard, 1967.
Poèmes pour l'Algérie heureuse (poetry). Algiers: Société nationale d'édition et de diffusion, 1969.
Femmes d'Alger dans leur appartement (stories). Paris: Des femmes, 1980.
L'amour, la fantasia (novel). Paris: J.C. Lattès, 1985.
Ombre sultane (novel). Paris: J.C. Lattès, 1987.
Loin de Médine (novel). Paris: Albin Michel, 1991.
Vaste est la prison (novel). Paris: Albin Michel, 1994.
Les nuits de Strasbourg (novel). Arles, France: Actes Sud, 1997.
Oran, langue morte (stories). Arles, France: Actes Sud, 1997.

Djura (1949–), Algerian writer born in Kabylie. She later moved to France, where she still resides. After a film experiment, in 1977 she and her sisters founded the music group Djurdjura, which performs Berber folksongs.
Le voile du silence (autobiography). Paris: Michel Lafon, 1990, trans. as *The Veil of Silence* by Dorothy S. Blair. London: Quartet Books, 1992.
La saison des narcisses (autobiography): Paris, Michel Lafon, 1993.

Douaïn Barakat, Mary (Duwayn Barakat, Mary) (?–), Lebanese poet born in Havana, Cuba.
Les ailes bleues (poetry). Beirut: Editions de la Fondation Melkart, 1979.

Poèmes de l'enfance (poetry). Beirut: Editions de la Fondation Melkart, 1979.

Doumet, Marie Claire (Dawmat, Marie Claire) (?–), Lebanese writer and the daughter of Michel Shiha.
Quand . . . (poetry): Paris: Editions Saint-Germain-des-Prés, 1974.
Mémoire du fil à plomb (poetry): Paris: Editions Saint-Germain-des-Prés, 1974.

Eddé, Carole (Edde, Carole) (1959–1981), Lebanese poet. She received a B.A. in anthropology from St. Joseph University in Beirut. She died in the bombing of Zahla in 1981 when she was twenty-two years old.
Musiques et couleurs (poetry). Beirut: n.p., 1982.

Eddé, Dominique (?–), Lebanese novelist born in Lebanon.
Lettre posthume (prose). Paris: L'Arpenteur-Gallimard, 1989.
Pourquoi il fait si sombre (novel). Paris: Seuil, 1999.

Efflatoun, Gulpérie (Aflatun, Gulpérie or Safeyah) (1921–), Egyptian writer. She was educated at a French school in Cairo and attended the American University in Cairo for a year. She worked at the archive for *Journal d'Egypte* and was a teacher at the al-Hurriya Lycée for eight years. Her first poem was published in *Image* magazine when she was fourteen. She has written many children's stories and published essays in several French magazines. Many of her short stories and poems have been published under the pseudonym Safeyah.
Pierres sur le chemin (poetry). Paris: Seghers, 1995.

Fakhoury, Tamirace (Fakhuri, Tamiras) (1974–), Lebanese poet born in Bayt Shabab in the Lebanon mountains. She is the daughter of writer and journalist

Riyad Fakhuri. She studied English literature and later international affairs. She published a collection of poems when she was nine years old.
Aubades (poetry). Beirut: Dar al-Nahar, 1996.

Farhoud, Abla (Farhud, 'Abla) (1945–), Lebanese dramatist. She lives in Montreal. Her plays have been shown in Canada, the United States, France, Belgium, and Lebanon. She received the Prix Arletty for Drama in French in 1993 and the Prix Théâtre et Liberté from the Société des auteurs et compositeurs dramatiques in France. Many of her plays have been translated into English.
Les filles du 5-10-15 (play). Carnières, Belgium: Lansman, 1993.
Quand j'étais grande (play). Solignac, France: Le bruit des autres, 1994.
Jeux de patience (play). Montreal: ULB Editeur, 1997.
Quand le vautour danse (play). Carnières, Belgium: Lansman, 1997.
Le bonheur à la queue glissante (novel). Montreal: L'Hexagone, 1998.
Maudite machine (play). Trois-Pistoles, QC: Editions Trois-Pistoles, 1999.

Farra, Sabine (?–), Lebanese poet, lawyer, and journalist. She is a journalist for *La Revue du Liban*, issued in Beirut.

Fassi, Nouzha (al-Fasi, Nuzha) (194?–), Moroccan novelist born in the early 1940s in Fez. She is a translator.
Le ressac (novel). Paris: L'Harmattan, 1990.
La baroudeuse (novel): Casablanca: Eddif, 1997.

Fathy, Safaa (Fathi, Safa') (?–) (see also: Bibliography of Works in Arabic)
Ordalie/Terreur (plays). Carnières, Belgium: Landsman, 2004.

Gaâloul, Béhija (Qa'lul, Bahija) (1946–), Tunisian poet and novelist born in Tabariya. She currently lives in Tunis. She studied French literature, sociology, and

law in Tunisia and France. She has been a flight attendant for Tunisair and the director of the Village Development Club in Nadur, Tunisia. She was a cultural attaché at the ministry of cultural affairs from 1982 to 1990. She currently teaches French at the secondary-school level and is interested in journalism. She is a member of the Union of Tunisian Writers, the Association des écrivains de langue française (A.D.E.L.F.), and the Union of French Teachers. She has published a collection of essays, *Voyages à travers la Tunisie* (1980).
Voyages à travers la Tunisie (essays). Tunis: Imprimerie Bouslama, 1980.
Mélodies enfantines pour enfants (children's poetry). Tunis: n.p., 1980.
Le lac en flammes (poetry). Tunis: Presses de l'imprimerie U.G.T.T., 1983.
Fruits perdus (novel). Tunis: n.p., 1983.
Les vapeurs de la ville (novel). Tunis: Imprimerie l'orient, 1994.
Mémoires d'une femme de plume (memoir). Tunis: privately published, 1994.

Gédéon, Nelly (Jad'un, Nelly) (?–), Lebanese poet.
Au rythme de l'instant (poetry). Beirut: Editions Liban, 1964.

Ghalem, Nadia (Ghalim, Nadiya) (1941–), Algerian writer born in Oran. She currently lives in Canada. She has been a radio and television correspondent in Niamey and Abidjan. In 1961 she went to France to continue her studies in philosophy, literature, and sociology. There, she married a Frenchman, which led to a break with her family. She later emigrated to Canada.
Exil (poetry). Montreal: Les compagnons du lion d'or, 1980.
Les jardins de cristal (autobiography). LaSalle, QC: Hurtubise HMH, 1981.
L'oiseau de fer (stories). Sherbrooke, QC: Naaman, 1981.
La villa Désir (novel). Montreal: Guérin littérature, 1988.
La nuit bleue (stories). Montreal: V.L.B., 1991.

Ghandour, Rim (Ghandur, Rim) (1960–1991), Lebanese poet born in Ankara, Turkey, where her father was the Lebanese ambassador. She spent her childhood in Morocco and Sweden and graduated with a B.A. in English literature from the American University of Beirut. She was a volunteer paramedic for the Red Cross during the Israeli invasion of Lebanon in 1982. She committed suicide in 1991.
Une nuit dans le Sahara (poetry). N.p.: Echoes, 1992.

Gholam, Nada (Ghulam, Nada) (1967–), Lebanese poet. Her first collection of poetry was published when she was sixteen years old.
Calcinations (poetry). Editions Saint-Germain-des-Prés, Paris, 1983.

Goraïeb, Carole (Ghurayyib, Carole) (?–), Lebanese poet.
Des chemins comme mémoire (poetry). Beirut: Les éditions nationales, 1973.

Guellouz, Soûad (Jalluz, Su'ad) (1937–), Tunisian novelist born in Ariyana. She is a French teacher. She received a prize for the best French novel by a Tunisian woman in the twentieth century.
La vie simple (novel). Tunis: Maison tunisienne de l'édition, 1975.
Les jardins du nord (novel). Tunis: Salammbô, 1982.
Myriam, ou, Le-rendez-vous de Beyrouth (novel). Tunis: Sahar, 1988.

Guendouz, Nadia (Qanduz, Nadiya) (1932–1999), Algerian poet born in Algiers to a French mother. She spent her childhood in the old city of Algiers. Starting in 1954, she fought in France along with her husband for the National Liberation Front. Until 1956 she worked as a nurse at the Francophone-Islamic Hospital in France. She was later arrested with her husband. In 1962, she returned to Askikda, Algeria, and continued her studies from 1966 to 1969. At the end of the 1970s she was in charge of social affairs in the Union of Algerian Writers.
La corde (poetry): Algiers: Société nationale d'édition et de diffusion, 1974.
Amal (poetry). Algiers: Société nationale d'édition et de diffusion, 1986.

el-Guoli, Safia (al-Qulli, Safiya) (1931–), Tunisian poet born in Susa. She currently resides in Tunis, where she was educated. She received a B.A. in French and English in 1955 and a Ph.D. in English and art history from the Sorbonne in 1974. She has worked as a teacher, in the cinema section of the ministry of cultural affairs, and in the Institute of Fine Arts in Tunis. She is a member of the Union of Tunisian Writers. She received the Culture Award for Cinema and the National Prize for criticism in 1991 and 1992. She writes poetry, short stories, and essays on art and literary criticsm. She also writes for the press.
Signes (poetry). Tunis: Société tunisienne de diffusion, 1973.
Vertige solaire (poetry). Tunis: Imp. Presse Presses Graphie Industrielle, 1975.
Nos rêves (poetry): Tunis: Union internationale de banques, 1980.
Le joueur d'échecs, le roi qui s'ennuyait, le soleil et la pluie (children's literature). Tunis: Salammbô, 1982.
Lyriques (poetry). Tunis: La N.E.F., 1989.
Les mystères de Tunis (novel). Tunis: Dar Annawras, 1993.

Hachemi, Frida (Hashimi, Farida) (?–), Tunisian novelist and poet.
Ahlem (novel). Paris: Pensée universelle, 1982.
Piège dans la nuit (novel): Tunis: Centre industriel du livre, 1986.
L'espoir d'un handicapé (autobiography). Tunis: Imprimerie centrale, 1989.

Hadad, Marie Chiha (Haddad, Marie Shiha) (1895–1973), Lebanese poet and artist.
Les heures libanaises (poetry). Beirut: Editions de la Revue phénicienne, 1937.

H

Haddad-Achkar, Marcelle (Haddad-Ashqar, Marcelle) (?–), Lebanese poet.
Papiers de guerre lasse (poetry). Eygalières, France: Editions du Temps parallèle, 1981.

Hafsia, Jélila (Hafsiya, Jalila) (1929–), Tunisian novelist born in Susa. She has published a collection of interviews titled *Visages et rencontres* (1981).
Cendres à l'aube (novel). Tunis: Maison tunisiénne d'édition, 1975.
Visages et rencontres (interviews). Tunis: Presses de la S.A.G.E.P., 1981.
La plume en liberté (stories). Tunis: Presses de la S.A.G.E.P., 1983.
Soudain la vie (stories). Tunis: Chama, 1992.

Houari, Leïla (Hawari, Layla) (1958–), Moroccan writer born in Casablanca. She spent her childhood in Fez then moved to Belgium with her family, where she resides today. Her novel, *Zeida de nulle part* (1985), received the Prix Laurence Tran in Brussels.
Zeida de nulle part (novel). Paris: L'Harmattan, 1985.
Quand tu verras la mer (stories). Paris: L'Harmattan, 1988.
Les cases basses (play). Paris: L'Harmattan, 1993.
Poème-fleuve pour noyer le temps présent (poetry). Paris: L'Harmattan, 1995.

Houfani-Berfas, Zehira (Birfas, Zahira Hufani) (1953–), Algerian novelist born in Kabylie. After her father was detained during the war of liberation, the family was forced to move to Algiers. She did not go to school until 1963. She managed a small trade-union paper and worked as a secretary at a gas company, and later in the media department of the same company. She retired early to devote herself to her family and writing. She writes poetry and children's stories.
Le portrait du disparu (novel). Algiers: Entreprise nationale du livre (E.N.A.L.), 1986.

Les pirates du désert (novel). Algiers: E.N.A.L., 1986.
L'incomprise (novel). Algiers: E.N.A.L., 1989.

Joumblatt, Amal (Junblat, Amal) (?–1982), Lebanese poet born in Beirut. She committed suicide after her marriage to the poet Sa'id 'Aql. She won the prize awarded in his name for her second and final collection of poetry.
Chant nocturne (poetry). Beirut: privately published, 1970.
L'absence ou anti-poésie (poetry). Beirut: privately published, 1974.

Ketou, Safia (Safiya Katu or Zawhara Rabihi) (1944–1989), Algerian poet and short-story writer born in 'Ayn Safra. She ended her education in the middle of secondary school. She worked as a teacher in her hometown from 1962 to 1969 and moved to Algiers in 1973. She contributed to educational radio programs and was a journalist and art critic. She committed suicide on January 29, 1989.
Amie cithare (poetry). Sherbrooke, QC: Naaman, 1979.
La planète mauve (stories). Sherbrooke, QC: Naaman, 1983.

Khabsa, Thérèse, Lebanese writer, poet, and interior designer.
Cicatrices (autobiographical novel). Beirut: privately published, 1995.

El Khayat, Ghita (al-Khayyat, Ghaytha, also known as Rita) (1944–), Moroccan researcher and psychoanalyst. She has published several psychoanalytical works on women in Morocco and the Arab world. She has published three collections of stories as *Les sept jardins* (1995).
Le monde arabe au féminin. Paris: L'Harmattan, 1985.
Le Maghreb des femmes. Casablanca: Eddif, 1992.
Le somptueux Maroc des femmes. Salé, Morocco: Dedico, 1994.
Les sept jardins (stories). Paris: L'Harmattan, 1995.

Kher, Amy (Khayr, Amy) (1882–?), Lebanese poet and novelist who lived most of her life in Cairo.
Salma et son village (novel). Paris: Editions de la Madeleine, 1933.
La traînée de sable (poetry). Cairo: Editions de la semaine égyptienne, 1936.
Méandres (poetry). Cairo: Editions de la semaine égyptienne, 1936.

Kherbiche, Sabrina (Kharbish, Sabrina) (1969–), Algerian novelist born in Algiers.
La suture (novel). Algiers: Laphomic, 1993.
Les yeux ternes (novel). Paris: L'Harmattan, 1995.
Nawel et Leila (novel). Paris: Présence africaine, 1997.

Khoury-Ghata, Vénus (Khuri-Ghata, Vénus) (1937–), Lebanese novelist and poet born in Beirut. She has lived in Paris since the 1970s. She has contributed to many Arabic and French literary journals. She has received several French awards for her works, including the Prix Apollinaire in 1980 for *Les ombres et leurs cris* (1979), the Prix Mallarmé in 1987 for *Monologue du mort*, and the grand prize for poetry from the Sociéte des gens de lettres for *Fables pour un peuple d'argile* in 1992. *Mon anthologie personnelle*, a selection of her previously published and new poems, was published in 1997.
Terres stagnantes (poetry). Paris: Seghers, 1969.
Les inadaptés (novel). Paris: Editions du Rocher, 1971.
Au sud du silence (poetry). Paris: Editions Saint-Germain-des-Prés, 1975.
Dialogue à propos d'un Christ ou d'un acrobate (novel). Paris: Editeurs Français Réunis (E.F.R.), 1975.
Alma, cousue main (novel). Paris: Editions Régine Deforges, 1977.
Les ombres et leurs cris (poetry). Paris: Belfond, 1979.
Qui parle au nom du jasmin (poetry). Paris: E.F.R., 1980.
Le fils empaillé (novel). Paris: Belfond, 1980.

Un faux pas du soleil (poetry). Paris: Belfond, 1982.
Vacarme pour une lune morte (novel). Paris: Flammarion, 1983.
Les morts n'ont pas d'ombre (novel). Paris: Flammarion, 1984.
Mortemaison (novel). Paris: Flammarion, 1986.
Monologue du mort (poetry). Paris: Belfond, 1987.
Bayarmine (novel). Paris: Flammarion, 1988.
Les fugues d'Olympia (novel). Paris: Ramsay, 1989.
La maîtresse du notable (novel). Paris: Seghers, 1992.
Fables pour un peuple d'argile (poetry). Paris: Belfond, 1992.
Mon anthologie (poetry). Beirut: Dar al-Nahar, 1993.
Les fiancées du cap Ténès (novel). Paris: J.C. Lattès, 1995.
La maestra (novel). Arles, France: Actes Sud, 1996.
Mon anthologie personnelle (poetry). Arles, France: Actes Sud, 1997.

Khoury-Mohasseb, Leila (Khuri-Muhassib, Layla) (1942–), Lebanese poet born in Beirut. She received a teaching certificate in languages from the Higher Language Institute. She worked for the economy page of the magazine *Le Commerce du Levant*. She is a member of the Nadia Tuéni Foundation, the Lebanese-German Cultural Association, and the Association of French Poets.
Capucines actualités (poetry). Paris: Cariscript, 1990.
Le Bonheur des mots (poetry). Beirut: Dar al-Nahar, 1992.

al-Kuzbari, Salma al-Haffar (1923–2006) (see also: Bibliography of Works in Arabic)
La rose solitaire (unknown). Paris and Buenos Aires: n.p., 1958.
Vent d'hier (poetry). Paris: n.p., 1966.

Latif-Ghattas, Mona (Ghattas, Muna Latif) (1946–), Egyptian poet, novelist, theater director, and popular musician. She lives in Montreal. She received her secondary-school education in Cairo. She emigrated to Canada in 1966. She received a B.A. in the dramatic arts from the University of Quebec in Montreal in 1976 and an M.A. in French studies from the University of Montreal in 1980. She taught dramatic expression at Selwyn House School, run by the program to teach French through theater. She taught theater at the Cégep level in 1977 and was a lecturer in theater at the University of Quebec in 1978. She has studied classical piano, song, ballet, and jazz. She has composed music for several rock singers and bands. She is a boardmember of the Quebec branch of the International PEN Association and a member of the Writers' Union in Quebec and the Association of Canadian Writers.

Nicolas, le fils du Nil (novel). Cairo: Elias Publishing House, 1985.

Les chants du Karawane (poetry). Cairo: Elias Publishing House, 1985.

Quarante voiles pour un exil (poetry). Laval, QC: Editions Trois, 1986.

Les voix du jour et de la nuit (novel). Montreal: Boréal, 1988.

Ma chambre belge (poetry). Amay, Belgium: Editions l'Arbre à Paroles, 1991.

Le double conte de l'exil (novel). Montreal: Boréal, 1993.

La triste beauté du monde (poetry). Montreal: Editions du Noroît, 1993.

Poèmes faxés, in coll. with Jean-Paul Daoust and Louise Desjardins (poetry). Trois Rivères, QC: Ecrits des Forges, 1994.

Lemsine, Aïcha L. (Lamsin, 'A'isha L.) (1942–), Algerian novelist born in Tabisa, Algeria. She spent her childhood in Tabisa and 'Anaba and currently resides in Algiers.

La chyrisalide: Chroniques algériennes (novel). Paris: Des femmes, 1976.

Ciel de porphyre (novel). Paris: J.C. Simoën, 1978.

Ordalie des voix (interviews with Arab women). Paris: Encre, 1983.

Beneath a Sky of Porphyry, trans. by Dorothy Blair. London and New York: Quartet, 1990.

The Chrysalis, trans. by Dorothy Blair. London: Quartet Books, 1993.

Maalouf, Andrée (Ma'luf, Andrée) (?–), Lebanese short-story writer and poet.

La magie de la vie (poetry). Beirut: Dar al-Nahar, 1961.

Eternel Liban (stories). Beirut: privately published, 1982.

Mabrouk, Alia ('Aliya Mabruk) (?–), Tunisian novelist.

Hurlement (novel). N.p.: Alyssa, 1992.

Blés de Dougga (novel). Tunis: L'or du temps, 1993.

Malak, Ezza Agha (Malak, 'Izza Agha) (1942–), Lebanese poet and novelist born in Tripoli. She received a Ph.D. in French literature and linguistics from the University of Lyon. She is a professor of linguistics at the Lebanese University. She has published works of literary criticism and has written a study on Su'ad al-Sabah in French, *Ambivalence amoureuse et multidimensionnalité dans "Une Fremme en miettes" de Souad el-Sabah* (1982).

Ambivalence amoureuse et mulitidimensionnalité dans "Une Femme en miettes" de Souad el-Sabah. Paris: Editions al-Mutanabbi, 1982.

Migration (poetry). Tripoli, Lebanon: privately published, 1985.

Entre deux battements de temps (poetry). Tripoli, Lebanon: privately published, 1991.

Quand les larmes seront pleurées . . . (poetry). Tripoli, Lebanon: privately published, 1992.

Récits bleus (stories). Paris and Beirut: Editions al-Mutanabbi, 1992.

La mallette (novel). Tripoli, Lebanon: Jarrous Press, 1996.

Mallat, Georgine (?–), Lebanese novelist. She is an attorney.

L'émeraude était bleue (novel). Beirut: Fiches du monde arabe (F.M.A.), 1995.

Massabki, Jacqueline (Masabiki, Jacqueline) (?–), Lebanese novelist. She is an attorney. In 1965 she became the first woman selected for the Council of State, the highest legal authority in Lebanon. She wrote her only novel in French with the French writer and journalist François Porel. The novel won the Press Prize and the Listeners' Prize from R.T.L. Radio in France.
La mémoire des cèdres (novel). Paris: Robert Laffont, 1989.

Mechakra, Yamina (Mushakira, Yamina) (1952–), Algerian novelist born in Maskiyana. She is a psychiatrist.
La grotte éclatée (novel). Algiers: Société nationale d'édition et de diffusion, 1979.

Menebhi, Saïda (al-Minibhi, Sa'ida) (1952–1977), Moroccan poet born in Marrakech. After graduating from secondary school, she continued her education at the College of Humanities in Rabat. She was a high-school teacher in Rabat. She was a member of the National Union for Moroccan Students and later the Moroccan Employment Union. She also joined Forward, a Marxist group. She was disappeared in 1976 and sentenced to seven years in prison in February 1977. She died in prison on December 11, 1977, after going on a hunger strike for more than a month. She published a collection of poems in French and a non-fiction work on prostitution and female detainees.
Poèmes, lettres, écrits de prison (poetry and letters). Paris: Comités de lutte contre la répression au Maroc, 1978.

Mernissi, Fatima (al-Marnisi, Fatima) (1940–), Moroccan researcher and writer born in Fez. She currently resides in Rabat. She studied in France and the United States. She is a research professor at the University Institute for Scientific Research at Muhammad V University in Rabat. She is a former member of the U.N. University Council. She writes in French and English, and all of her works have been translated into Arabic. She supervises several sociology research groups and many publication series on women and sociology. She is the recipient of several awards. Her academic and non-fiction works include *Le Maroc raconté par ses femmes* (1983), *Sexe, idéologie et Islam* (1983), *Chahrazad n'est pas Marocaine* (1988), *Le harem politique: Le prophète et ses femmes* (1987), and *Sultanes oubliées: Femmes chefs d'Etat en Islam* (1990). Her autobiographical novel, *Dreams of Trespass: Tales of a Harem Girlhood*, was translated into French (see below) and into Arabic, as *Ahlam nisa': qisas tufula fi kanaf al-harim* (Dubaya, Lebanon: Dar 'Atiya li-l-Nashr, 1997).
Sexe, idéologie et Islam. Paris: Tierce, 1983.
Le Maroc raconté par ses femmes. Rabat: Société marocaine des éditeurs réunis, 1983.
Le harem politique: Le prophète et ses femmes. Paris: Albin Michel, 1987.
Chahrazad n'est pas Marocaine; Autrement, elle serait salariée! Casablanca: Le Fennec, 1988.
Sultanes oubliées: Femmes chefs d'Etat en Islam. Paris: Albin Michel, 1990.
Rêves de femmes: Une enfance au harem (autobiographical novel), trans. by Claudine Richetin. Paris: Albin Michel, 1996.

Mokeddem, Malika (Muqaddim, Malika) (1949–), Algerian novelist born in Kandasa in southern Algeria. She currently lives in Montpellier, France, where she is a neurologist. She is a member of Intellectuals Against Religious Extremism. Her novel, *Les hommes qui marchent*, was awarded a literary prize from the Nureddine Aba Foundation in Algeria in 1994, and her *L'interdite* won the Prix Méditerranée in 1994.
Les hommes qui marchent (autobiographical novel). Paris: Ramsay, 1990.

M

Le siècle des sauterelles (novel). Paris: Ramsay, 1992.
L'inderdite (novel). Paris: Grasset, 1993.
Des rêves et des assassins (novel). Paris: Grasset, 1995.
The Forbidden Woman: L'Interdite (novel), trans. by Melissa Marcus. Lincoln: University of Nebraska Press, 1998.

Mourad, Farida Elhany (Murad, Farida al-Hani) (1945–), Algerian novelist born in al-Warza, Qasantina. She currently resides in al-Muhammadiya in Morocco. She graduated from high school and obtained Business English Certificates 1 and 2.
La fille aux pieds nus (novel). Casablanca: Imprimerie Eddar el Beïda, 1985.
Ma femme, ce démon angélique (novel). Casablanca: Imprimerie Eddar el Beïda, 1987.
Faites parler le cadavre (novel). Casablanca: Imprimerie Eddar el Beïda, 1990.
Dans l'ouragan des passions (novel). Casablanca: Imprimerie Les impressions atelier 26, 1996.

Mrabet, Aziza (al-Murabit, 'Aziza) (?–), Tunisian poet and artist. She is a teacher. She received the al-Tahir Haddad Prize in 1991.
Grains de sable (poetry). Tunis: L'or du temps, 1992.

Murr, Mayy (1929–2008), Lebanese poet and playwright born in Batagharin. She obtained a graduate degree in history and geography from the University of Lyon. She taught geography at the Lebanese University. She published a play and a collection of poetry in the Lebanese dialect. She was interested in research and publishing on history and Lebanon's Phoenician roots. Her first collection of poetry in French won the Sa'id 'Aql Prize, and her third collection was awarded a prize from the Société des Gens de Lettres in France.
Pourquoi les roses? (poetry). Paris: Jean Grassin Editeur, 1967.
Penchent leurs tête les épis (poetry). Paris: Jean Grassin Editeur, 1969.

Il s'agit d'un rien d'amour (poetry). Paris: Jean Grassin Editeur, 1970.
Quatrains (poetry). Paris: Jean Grassin Editeur, 1971.
Kamal ou l'hisoire d'un héros (journal). Beirut: Ishtar, 1987.
Poésie trismégiste (poetry). Beirut, privately published, 1994.

Nehmé, Lina Murr (Ni'ma, Lina Murr) (?–), Lebanese novelist.
Comme un torrent qui gronde (novel). Beirut: Ishtar, 1987.

Nigolian, Sonia (Niguliyan, Sunya) (?–), Lebanese poet and journalist born in Beirut. She is from an Armenian family and is an editor for the Beirut magazine *La Revue du Liban*.
J'ai jeté l'encre en terre sacrée (poetry). Antélias, Lebanon: Catholicossat arménien de Cilicie, 1993.
Images à contretemps (poetry). Antélias, Lebanon: Catholicossat arménien de Cilicie, 1995.

Nini, Soraya (Nini, Thuraya) (1961–), Algerian novelist born in southern France. She works at a girls' shelter.
Ils disent que je suis une beurette (novel). Paris: Fixot, 1993.

Out el Kouloub (al-Damardashiya, Qut al-Qulub) (1908–1992), Egyptian novelist born to a wealthy Muslim family affiliated with the Sufi al-Damardashiya order. Her novels deal with women's status in Egyptian society.
Au hasard de la pensée (novel). Cairo: Dar al-Ma'arif, 1934.
Harem (novel). Paris: Gallimard, 1937.
Trois contes de l'amour et de la mort (novel). Paris: Corra, 1940.
Zanouba (novel). Paris: Gallimard, 1947.
Le coffret hindou (novel). Paris: Gallimard, 1951.
La nuit de la destinée (novel). Paris: Gallimard, 1954.
Ramza (novel). Paris: Gallimard, 1958.

Hefnaoui le magnifique (novel). Paris: Gallimard, 1967.
Ramza, trans. by Nayra Atiya. Syracuse: Syracuse University Press, 1994.

Prince, Violaine (?–), Lebanese poet and novelist. She is an engineer.
Les marches du désert (poetry). Paris: Editions La Bruyère, 1983.
Le siège de Tyr (play). Paris: Editions La Bruyère, 1984.
L'Ougandais blanc (novel). N.p.: n.p., n.d.

Rabia, Ziani (Rabi'a, Ziyani) (1933–), Algerian novelist.
Le déshérité (novel). Algiers: Société nationale d'édition et de diffusion, 1981.
Ma montagne (novel). Algiers: Entreprise nationale du livre (E.N.A.L.), 1984.
Nouvelles de mon jardin (autobiographical novel). Algiers: E.N.A.L., 1985.
L'impossible bonheur (novel). Algiers: E.N.A.L., 1986.
La main mutilée (novel). Algiers: E.N.A.L., 1986.

Rezzoug, Leïla (Razzuq, Layla) (1956–), Algerian novelist born in Algiers. She currently lives in France. She obtained a degree in legal and political sciences.
Apprivoiser l'insolence (novel). Paris L'Harmattan, 1988.
Douces errances (novel). Paris: L'Harmattan, 1992.

Rohayem, Claudine (Ruhayyim, Claudine) (1957–), Lebanese poet.
Chute libre (poetry). Paris: Pensée universelle, 1983.
Entre la ville et un mur d'amour forcé (poetry). Beirut: privately published, 1986.

el Saad, Nouhad (al-Sa'd, Nuhad) (?–), Lebanese poet.
Itinéraires (poetry). Paris: Editions Saint-Germain-des-Prés, 1972.
Le chemin de ronde (poetry). Paris: Editions Saint-Germain-des-Prés, 1987.

Safa, Monique (?–)
Le violoniste au couvent de la lune (novel). Paris: Stock, 1991.

Saïd, Amina (Sa'id, Amina) (1953–), Tunisian poet born in Tunis. She currently resides in Paris. She graduated from the Sorbonne. She received the Prix Jean Malrieu, awarded by *Sud* magazine in Marseilles, in 1989 for her collection *Feu d'oiseaux*, and the Prix Charles Vildrac, awarded by the Société des Gens de Lettres in Paris, in 1994 for *L'une et l'autre nuit*. She translates and writes for the press and has translated a selection of stories by Francisco Sionil José into French as *Le dieu volé*.
Paysages, nuit friable (poetry). Vitry, France: Barbare, 1980.
Pour Abdellatif Laâbi, in coll. with Abdellatif Laâbi and Ghislain Ripault (anthology). Paris: Nouvelle Edition Rupture, 1982.
Métamorphose de l'île et de la vague (poetry). Paris: Arcantère, 1985.
Sables funambules (poetry). Trois-Rivières, QC: Ecrits des Forges, 1988.
"Feu d'oiseaux" (poetry). Marseille: *Sud* 84, 1989.
Nul autre lieu (poetry). Trois-Rivières, QC: Ecrits des Forges, 1993.
L'une et l'autre nuit (poetry). Chaillé-sous-les-Ormeaux, France: Le dé bleu, 1993.
Marcher sur la terre (poetry). Paris: Editions de la Différence, 1994.
Le secret (stories). Paris: Criterion, 1996.
Gisements de lumière (poetry). Paris: Editions de la Différence, 1996.
Le dieu volé (selected stories by Francisco Sionel José). Paris: Criterion, 1996.

Salameh, Nohad (Salama, Nuhad) (1947–), Lebanese poet born in Ba'labakk. She is the daughter of poet and journalist Yusuf Fadl Allah Salameh. She studied philosophy at the Ecole supérieure des lettres. She worked as a journalist and published several critical essays in Beirut's Francophone press, including in *Le Jour* and *al-Safa*. She married poet Marc Alyn and currently lives in France. She is a member of the judging committee for the Prix Louise Labé in France and is a member of the honorary commitee of the the Académie littéraire de France et d'outre-mer. She was awarded the Prix Louise Labé in 1988 and the Prix international des amitiés françaises in 1996. She has translated a collection of poetry by Shakib Khuri as *Le pouls du temps et de l'amour* (1979). She is the author of fifteen collections of poetry, including *L'autre écriture* (winner of the Prix Louise Labé in 1988).

L'écho des souffles (poetry). Beirut: privately published, 1968.

Lettres à ma muse (poetry). Beirut: privately published, 1971.

La frustrée (novel). Uzès, France: Actuelles formes et langages, 1973.

Le pouls du temps et de l'amour (poetry). Paris: Editions Saint-Germain-des-Prés, 1979.

Les enfants d'avril (poetry). Eygalières, France: Editions du Temps parallèle, 1980.

La folie couleur de mer (poetry). Eygalières, France: Editions du Temps parallèle, 1982.

L'autre écriture (poetry). Paris: Editions Dominique Bedou, 1987.

Chants de l'avant-songe (poetry). Paris: L'Harmattan, 1993.

Saleh, Christiane (Salih, Christiane) (?–), Lebanese poet and journalist born in Cairo. She worked as a journalist in Egypt and later in Lebanon, where she settled in 1956.

Les nuits parallèles (poetry). Beirut: privately published, 1968.

Médianes (poetry). Beirut: privately published, 1970.

L'autre mer (poetry). Paris: Editions Saint-Germain-des-Prés, 1975.

Sanbar, Shadia (Sanbar, Shadiya) (?–), Palestinian poet.

El Dar (poetry). Paris: Editions Galilée, 1978.

Saudi, Fathieh (Sa'udi, Fathia) (1949–) (see also: Bibliography of Works in Arabic) *L'oubli rebelle: Beyrouth 82* (journal). Paris: L'Harmattan, 1985.

Schehadé, Laurice (Shahhada, Laurice) (?–), Lebanese poet and the sister of poet George Shahhada.

Journal d'Anne (poetry). Paris: Editions Guy Lévi Mano (G.L.M.), 1947.

Récit d'Anne (poetry). Paris: G.L.M., 1950.

La fille royale et blanche (poetry). Paris: G.L.M., 1953.

Portes disparues (poetry). Paris: G.L.M., 1958.

Les grandes horloges (poetry). Paris: Julliard, 1961.

Le batelier du vent (poetry). Paris: G.L.M., 1961.

J'ai donné au silence ta voix (poetry). Paris: G.L.M., 1962.

Du ruisseau de l'aube (poetry). Paris: G.L.M., 1966.

Sebaï, Leila Ladjimi (al-Siba'i, Layla Lajimi) (?–), Tunisian poet. She worked with the Bolshoi Troupe in Moscow for two years and today is an archaeologist.

Chams (poetry). Paris: Pensée universelle, 1991.

Elisha (poetry). Tunis: L'or du temps, 1993.

Sebbar, Leïla (Sabbar, Layla) (1941–), Algerian novelist and short-story writer born in Aflu. She currently resides in Paris. She graduated from the University of Aix-en-Provence and is a teacher of French literature at a high school in Paris. She regularly publishes in several French journals, including *al-Azmina al-haditha*, *Bila hudud*, *al-Janub*, *Magazine littéraire*, and *Arabis*. She contributes to the cultural desk at Radio France and is interested in the status of immigrant women. She writes novels, short stories, and essays in French and has published several studies, anthologies, and photograph albums with accompanying text. Her writings focus on identity and memory.

She has published several collections of essays, including *On tue les petites filles* (1978) and *Le pédophile et la maman* (1980). Her novel, *Le silence des rives* (1993), received the Prix Kateb Yacine. She is a columnist for *Sans Frontières*, a journal on immigration and the third world, in which she publishes interviews under the title "Mémoires de l'immigration." She has contributed to a number of literary journals over the years, including *La quinzaine littéraire, Le magazine littéraire, Les moments littéraires,* and *Etoiles d'encre.* And from 1984 to 1999, she contributed to programs of the France-Culture service of Radio France: *Le panorama* with Jacques Duchâteau and *Antipodes* with Madeleine Mukamabano.

On tue les petites filles. Paris: Stock, 1978.

Le pédophile et la maman. Paris: Stock, 1980.

Fatima, ou, Les algériennes au square (novel). Paris: Stock, 1981.

Shérazade: 17 ans, brune, frisée, les yeux verts (novel). Paris: Stock, 1982.

Parle mon fils, parle à ta mère (novel). Paris: Stock, 1984.

Le chinois vert d'Afrique (novel). Paris: Stock, 1984.

Les carnets de Shérazade (novel). Paris: Stock, 1985.

J.H. cherche âme-soeur (novel). Paris: Stock, 1987.

Le fou de Shérazade (novel). Paris: Stock, 1991.

Le silence des rives (novel). Paris: Stock, 1993.

La jeune fille au balcon (stories). Paris: Seuil, 1996.

Le baiser (stories). Paris: Hachette, 1997.

Soldats (novel). Paris: Seuil, 1999.

Sebti, Fadéla (al-Sabti, Fadila) (1949–), Moroccan researcher and novelist born in Fez. She currently lives in Casablanca. She lived for some time in Paris, where she worked at Europe 1 Radio. She returned to Morocco in 1975 and continued her studies at the College of Legal, Economic, and Social Sciences in Casablanca. She

has worked as an attorney since 1983. She writes in French on both law and literature. Her legal works include *Répertoire de la législation marocaine* (1989) and *Vivre musulmane au maroc* (1986).

Vivre musulmane au maroc: Guide des droits et des obligations. Paris: Librairie générale de droit et de jurisprudence, 1986.

Répertoire de la législation marocaine: Novembre 1912–décembre 1988. Paris: Librairie générale de droit et de jurisprudence, 1989.

Moi Mireille, lorsque j'étais Yasmina (novel). Casablanca: Le Fennec, 1995.

Sefouane, Fatiha (Safwan, Fatiha) (1942–), Algerian writer born in western Algeria. She spent her childhood in difficult circumstances. She was involved in the struggle for liberation and was arrested, imprisoned, and tortured.

L'enfant de la haine (autobiography). Paris: L'Harmattan, 1990.

Shafik, Doria (Shafiq, Durriya) (1908–1975), Egyptian poet born in Tanta. She received her early education in Catholic convent schools. She went on to earn a Ph.D. at the Sorbonne for a thesis on women and Islam. She established the journal *Bint al-Nil* in 1945 and the Bint al-Nil Union in 1948. She was a feminist leader and one of the most fervent demanders of women's political rights. In 1956 she sharply criticized the July revolution and staged a hunger strike at the Indian embassy in Cairo, demanding democracy after the revolutionary government placed all non-governmental organizations under the supervision of the ministry of social affairs, which effectively led to the collapse of independent civil action. She was placed under house arrest and her name was banned from all newspapers. She lived in seclusion until she committed suicide in 1975. She published several essays and books on women's issues. Her works in Arabic include *Tatawwur* *al-nahda al-nisa'iya fi Misr* (Evolution of the Women's Awakening in Egypt, 1945, with Ibrahim 'Abduh) and *al-Kitab al-abyad li-huquq al-mar'a al-siyasiya* (The White Paper on Women's Political Rights). *La femme et le droit religieux de l'Egypte contemporaine*. Paris: Geunther, 1940. *L'art pour l'art dans l'Egypt antique*. Paris: Geunther, 1940. *Avec Dante aux enfers* (poetry). Périgueux, France: Fanlac, 1949. *La bonne aventure* (poetry). Paris: Seghers, 1949. *L'esclave sultane* (poetry). Paris: Latines, 1952. *L'amour perdu* (poetry). Paris: Seghers, 1954. *Larmes d'Isis: Poèmes des anneés 50* (poetry). Perigueux, France: Fanlac, 1971.

Stephen, Thérèse (Stifan, Thérèse) (?–), Lebanese poet. *Cri du silence* (poetry). Beirut: privately published, 1995.

Touati, Fettouma (Tawati, Fatima) (?–), Algerian novelist born in Kabylie. She worked in Algiers and later at the Mouloud Mammeri University of Tizi Ouzou. *Le printemps désespéré: Vie d'algériennes* (novel). Paris: L'Harmattan, 1984.

Toutounji, Samia (Tutunji, Samiya) (1939–1990), Lebanese poet, journalist, and artist. In the 1970s she published in the French-language *al-Safa*, based in Beirut. Through the Dar al-Fann Association she helped spread the plastic arts in Lebanon. She organized several art exhibits during the war, and lost her life in the conflict. Her sole collection of poetry has been translated into Arabic. *Multiples présences* (poetry). Beirut: privately published, 1968.

Trabelsi, Bahaa (Tarabulsi, Baha') (1966–), Moroccan novelist born in Rabat. She resides in Casablanca. She received her early education at French missionary schools in Rabat. She graduated from Grenoble University in France. She received a third-cycle doctorate in economics from the University of Aix-en-Provence. She has worked in the public and private sectors. She is active in non-governmental organizations in Morocco that work with women's issues and help fight HIV/AIDS. *Une femme tout simplement* (novel). Casablanca: Eddif, 1995.

Tuéni, Nadia (Tuwayni, Nadiya Hamada) (1935–1983), Lebanese poet born in Ba'aqlin in al-Shuf to a Lebanese father and a French mother. She was educated at the Bésançon convent school and the French mission in Beirut. She graduated from the Beirut College for Women (later the Lebanese American University of Beirut). She then studied at the French Institute in Athens, where her father, the diplomat and writer Muhammad 'Ali Hamada, represented Lebanon. She studied law at St. Joseph University in Beirut. She married journalist Ghassan Tuéni and worked for the cultural page at the Beirut-based *Le Jour*. In 1962 her seven-year-old daughter, Na'ila, died. Her collection, *Le rêveur de terre*, was translated into Arabic in 1983, and Roger 'Assaf brought her play, *Juin et les mécréantes*, to the stage in June 1966. She won several awards for her works, including the Sa'id 'Aql Prize for her collection *L'âge d'écume*, in 1966. *Les textes blonds* (poetry). Beirut: Dar al-Nahar, 1963. *L'âge d'écume* (poetry). Paris: Seghers, 1965. *Juin et les mécréantes* (poetry). Paris: Seghers, 1968. *Poèmes pour une histoire* (poetry). Paris: Seghers, 1972. *Le rêveur de terre* (poetry). Paris: Seghers, 1975. *Liban: 20 poèmes pour un amour* (poetry). Beirut: n.p., 1979. *Archives sentimentales d'une guerre au Liban* (poetry). Paris: Pauvert, 1982. *La terre arrêtée* (poetry). Paris: Belfond, 1984.

Au-delà du regard (poetry). Beirut: Dar al-Nahar, 1986.
Les œuvres poétiques complètes (poetry). Beirut: Dar al-Nahar, 1986.
La prose: œuvres complètes (collected prose). Beirut: Dar al-Nahar, 1986.

Zouari, Fawzia (al-Zawʻari, Fawziya) (1955–), Tunisian writer born in al-Kaf. She has a Ph.D. in comparative literature. She writes for the press and works in Paris for a bibliographical publication on the literary and artistic production of Arab women.

La caravane des chimères (novel). Paris: Olivier Orban, 1990.

Zouein, Sabah Kharrat (Zuwayn, Sabah Kharrat) (?–) (see also: Bibliography of Works in Arabic)
Sur un quai nu (poetry). Paris: Editions Saint-Germain-des-Prés, 1983.
Passion ou paganisme (poetry). Paris: Editions Saint-Germain-des-Prés, 1985.
Mais (poetry). Harisa, Lebanon: Imprimerie Antoine Chemali, 1986.
A partir, peut-être (poetry). Harisa, Lebanon: Imprimerie Antoine Chemali, 1987.

Z

Bibliography of Works in Arabic

A Note on the Bibliography

Writers are included in the bibliography if they have published literary works (poetry, short stories, novels, plays, memoirs, or biographies) in book form. An exception is made for Sudanese women writers, many of whom have not had the opportunity to publish books, and pioneering women writers, whose early endeavors in the areas of writing, publishing, education, and so on did not appear in book form but are regarded as having paved the way for other women to write or be published. All known literary works published until 1999 are listed for each author. While every attempt has been made to list the first edition of each literary work, this has not always been possible owing to the difficulty of access to archival data and the fact that the data accessed are not always complete or correct. Where the place of publication or the publisher of a title are not given in the edition cited, the abbreviation 'n.p.' is used; where the date of publication is not given, the abbreviation 'n.d.' is used. Translations of book titles in parentheses are rendered in roman type if there is no known published English-language translation, and in italic type if the book has been published in English translation. Differences in Arabic regional dialects and pronunciation and the variety of transliteration systems mean that the names of many authors in this guide can be and are written in various ways in English. In the interest of standardization and user-friendliness, however, all authors' names have been transliterated according to standard American University in Cairo Press style. The only exceptions are authors who have published translations in English or French, in which case their preferred spelling as it appears on their works in translation has been used. A wide range of sources was used to annotate the chapters preceding this bibliography; the bibliographical citations thus listed do not always correspond exactly to the information included in this bibliography since the same work may have been reprinted several times and by different publishers. Any corrections, comments, or updates can be sent to the co-editor Hasna Reda-Mekdashi: nour.writers@gmail.com.

Abaroudi, Fatema Chahid (Abarudi, Fatima Shahid) (1965–) (see also: Bibliography of Works in French)
Ibhar fi qila' al-ruh (Searching the Castles of the Soul, poetry). Rabat: n.p., 1997.

'Abbas, Amal 'Abbud (?–), Iraqi short-story writer.
al-Tanazzuh fi-l-jahim (A Stroll in Hell, short stories). Baghdad: al-Umma Press, 1971.

al-'Abbas, Dawla (1949–), Syrian poet born in al-Mashrafa in the province of Hama. She studied Arabic at Damascus University and law at the Beirut Arab University.
Qatarat jurh (Drops for a Wound, poetry). Damascus: n.p., 1982.

'Abbas, Intisar 'Abbas Mahmud (1967–), Jordanian short-story writer born in Irbid. She has a B.A. in English and works in education.
Li-l-shams junun akhar (The Sun Has Another Madness, short stories). Beirut: Arab Institute for Research and Publishing, 1997.

'Abbas, Sakina 'Abd al-'Aziz (?–), Egyptian novelist.
Hiba (A Gift, novel). Cairo: Dar al-Shuruq, 1976.

'Abbasi, Nawal (1936–), Jordanian short-story writer born in al-Hisn. She resides in Amman. She was educated in al-Hisn and Irbid. She has published several political and social criticism articles and short stories in the Jordanian press.
Sada al-mahattat (The Stations' Echoes, short stories). Amman: Dar al-Karmel, 1990.
Laylat al-hinna' (Henna Night, short stories). Amman: Dar al-Ibda', 1991.
Lahazat hiya al-'umr (Moments Are the Life, short stories). Irbid: al-Maktaba al-Zahiriya, 1994.

Shati' al-fayruz (The Turquoise Coast, poetry). Amman: al-Sha'b Press, 1994.

'Abbasi, Nuhad Tawfiq (1947–), Palestinian writer born in Safad. She has a B.A. in Arabic literature from Damascus University. She has worked as a teacher in Syria and the Gulf.
Abariq muhashamma (Smashed Jugs, short stories). Damascus: Karam Press, 1985.
Humq al-muthaqqafin (The Foolishness of Intellectuals, short stories). Beirut and Damascus: Karam Press, 1986.
Jazirat 'adala (Island of Justice, novel). N.p.: n.p., 1986.
Darat Matalun (Matalun's House, novel). Damascus: 'Akrama Press, 1987.
Husun al-mawta (Fortresses of the Dead, novel). Damascus: n.p., 1988.
al-Dumu' al-mutala'la'a (The Shimmering Tears, play). N.p.: n.p., n.d.
Muhakamat yamama 'Arabiya (The Trial of an Arab Dove, autobiography). N.p.: n.p., n.d.

'Abbud, Anisa (1958–), Syrian poet and novelist born in Jabla, where she lives. She graduated from the Agricultural Engineering College and works at the Citrus Research Center in Latakia. She writes a weekly column for *al-Thawra al-Suriya* and is a member of the Story and Novel Association.
Hin tunza' al-aqni'a (When the Masks Come Off, short stories). Damascus: Arab Writers' Union, 1991.
Hariq fi sanabil al-dhakira (A Fire in the Grain Spikes of Memory, short stories). Damascus: Dar al-Hisad, 1994.
Mishkat al-kalam (Lamp of Speech, poetry). Damascus: Ministry of Culture, 1994.
Ghasaq al-akasya (Acacia Twilight, short stories). Damascus: Arab Writers' Union, 1996.
al-Na'na' al-barri (Wild Mint, novel). Latakia: Dar al-Hiwar, 1997.
Qamis al-as'ila (Chemise of Questions, poetry). Latakia: Dar al-Hiwar, 1999.

'Abbudi, Henriette (?–), Syrian novelist. She has translated several books into Arabic, including *al-Fallahun wa harakat al-taharrur al-qawmi al-mu'asira* (Peasants and the Contemporary National Liberation Movement), Germaine Greer's *The Female Eunuch*, and Alexandra Kollontai's *The New Woman*.
al-Zahr al-'ari (The Exposed Back, novel). Beirut: Dar al-Adab, 1996.

'Abd Allah, Malakat al-Dar Muhammad (1918–69), Sudanese novelist born in al-Ubayyid. She received her early education at the al-Qubba School in al-Ubayyid, the first girls' school in western Sudan. She continued her education at the Teacher Training College in Umm Durman, from which she graduated in 1943. She worked as a teacher in several regions of Sudan and in 1960 became the school inspector in Kurdufan. She is a founding member of the al-Ubayyid Women's Charitable Association, as well as a member of the Sudanese Women's Union and the Teachers' Syndicate. She received first prize for her story, "Hakim al-qarya" (The Village Doctor), in a short-story competition sponsored by Sudanese radio in 1947. Her novel *al-Faragh al-'arid* was published posthumously.
al-Faragh al-'arid (The Vast Emptiness, novel). Khartoum: National Council for the Humanities and Arts, 1970.

'Abd Allah, Malha (?–), Saudi playwright. She received a B.A. in drama criticism from the Academy of Arts in Cairo in 1990. Her non-fiction works include *Athar al-badawa 'ala-l-masrah fi-l-Sa'udiya* (The Impact of Nomadism on Saudi Theater, 1994), *Adab al-mar'a fi-l-watan al-'Arabi* (Women's Literature in the Arab World), *Athar al-huwwiya al-Islamiya 'ala-l-masrah fi-l-Sa'udiya* (The Impact of Islamic Identity on Saudi Theater), *al-Fann wa-l-lawa'i* (Art and the Unconscious), and *al-Shakhsiya al-gha'iba al-hadira fi-l-masrahiya al-Sa'udiya* (The Present-absent Character in Saudi Theater). She

is a correspondent in Cairo for *Iqra'* magazine, published by the Saudi al-Bilad Foundation.
Finjan qahwa (A Cup of Coffee, play). N.p.: al-Madina Publications, 1995.
al-Maskh (The Deformed, plays). N.p.: n.p., 1995.
Umm al-fa's (Mother of the Axe, play). N.p.: al-Madina Publications, 1995.

al-'Abd Allah, Sikna (?–), Lebanese poet born in al-Khiyam in the south.
Mudhakkirat laji'a (Memoirs of a Refugee, poetry). Beirut: n.p., 1969.
Nihayat al-sada (End of the Echo, poetry). Beirut: Dar al-Kitab al-Lubnani, 1974.
Kalimat 'ala jidar al-dhakira (Words on Memory's Wall, poetry). N.p.: Dar al-Funun Press and Publishers, 1996.

'Abd Allah, Sufi (1925–), Pioneering Egyptian writer born in Fayyum. She had an English education at a school in Suez and then enrolled in the Good Shepherd School in Cairo, from which she graduated. She studied Arabic at home and was a student of al-'Aqqad, who called her "al-Sayyid Sufi." Her father and later her husband had an enormous impact on her as writer. She inherited her literary sensibility from her father, and her husband was always encouraging. Before her marriage, she was a teacher. In 1948, Dar al-Hilal announced a short-story competition in which Sufi took part. Although her submission was late, her stories so pleased the editor of *al-Musawwar* that he published them in the next issues. She held many positions at Dar al-Hilal. She was also an editor and had a weekly column at *Hawwa'*. She published a translation of Dostoevsky's *Poor Folk and Other Stories*, as *al-Masakin*, in 1952, and wrote *Nisa' muharibat* (Fighting Women, women's biographies). (Cairo: Dar al-Ma'arif, 1951.) In 1951 she wrote the drama, "Kisibna al-brimo" (We Hit the Jackpot) the first play by an Egyptian woman to be staged at the Opera Theater. She also wrote *Hawwa' wa arba'at 'amaliqa* (Eve and Four Giants), a work about

'Abbas al-'Aqqad, Taha Hussein, Tawfiq al-Hakim, and Naguib Mahfouz.

Nifirtiti: thawrat Akhnatun al-rawhiya (Nefertiti: Akhenaton's Spiritual Revolution, novel). Cairo: Dar al-Hilal, 1952.

'Arusa 'ala-l-raff (A Doll on the Shelf, novel). Cairo: Dar al-Ma'arif, 1954.

Kulluhunna 'Ayyusha (They Are All 'Ayyusha, novel). Cairo: Dar al-Jumhuriya, 1954.

Thaman al-hubb (The Price of Love, short stories). Cairo: Dar al-'Ubayd, 1955.

Baqaya rajul (Remnants of a Man, short stories). Beirut: al-Maktaba al-Tijariya, 1956.

La'nat al-jasad (Curse of the Body, novel). Beirut: n.p., 1956.

Dumu' al-tawba (Tears of Contrition, novel). Beirut: al-Maktab al-Tijari Press, 1958.

Madrasat al-banat (The Girls' School, short stories). Cairo: Rose al-Yusuf Foundation, 1959.

'Asifa fi qalb (A Heart Storm, novel). Cairo: Dar al-Hilal, 1960.

Nisf imra'a wa qisas ukhra (Half a Woman and Other Stories, short stories). Cairo: Rose al-Yusuf Foundation, 1962.

Layali laha thaman (Nights with a Price, short stories). Cairo: National Book Foundation, 1963.

Mu'jizat al-Nil (Miracle of the Nile, short stories). Cairo: al-Dar al-Qawmiya, 1964.

Nawabigh al-nisa' (Distinguished Women, short stories). Cairo: Dar al-Hilal, 1964.

Alf mabruk (Congratulations, short stories). Cairo: al-Dar al-Misriya, 1965.

Qusur 'ala-l-rimal (Castles on the Sand, novel). Cairo: Rose al-Yusuf Foundation, 1967.

Nabda taht al-jalid (A Pulse Beneath the Ice, short stories). Cairo: General Egyptian Book Organization, 1968.

Arba'at rijal wa fatah (Four Men and a Young Woman, short stories). Cairo: Dar al-Hilal, 1972.

Shay' aqwa minha (Something Stronger Than Her, novel). Cairo: al-Hilal Novels, 1975.

al-Qafas al-ahmar (The Red Cage, short stories). Cairo: Dar al-Ma'arif, 1975.

al-Lughz al-abadi (The Eternal Riddle, short stories). Cairo: Maktabat Gharib, 1978.

Arba' masrahiyat dahika (Four Comic Plays, plays). Cairo: General Egyptian Book Organization, 1979.

Hasab al-talab (Made to Order, play). Cairo: General Egyptian Book Organization, 1979.

A

'Abd al-'Ati, Fatima Fawzi (1959–), Egyptian short-story writer born in Tanta. She teaches at the College of Education at Tanta University.

Awraq mumazzaqa (Shredded Papers, short stories). Cairo: Dar al-Ahmadi Publishers, 1999.

'Abd al-'Ati, Hanan 'Abd al-Barr (?–), Egyptian writer.

Yawman sa'a'ud (One Day I Will Return). Cairo: Egyptian Association to Foster Talent, 1993.

'Abd al-'Aziz, Malak (1921–1999), Egyptian poet born in Tanta. She received a B.A. in Arabic in 1942. She was editor in chief of *al-Sharq* magazine from 1965 to 1985. She was a member of the Supreme Council for Culture (poetry committee), the Writers' Union, the Journalists' Syndicate, the Council for World Peace, the Arab Association for Cultural Integration, and the Committee to Defend National Culture. She was also a boardmember of the Cairo Atelier.

Aghani al-siba (Songs of Youth, poetry). Cairo: Dar al-Ma'arif, 1959.

al-Jawrab al-maqtu' (The Torn Sock, short stories). Cairo: Dar al-Fikr al-'Arabi, 1962.

Qal al-masa' (The Evening Said, poetry). Cairo: al-Dar al-Qawmiya Printing and Publishing, 1965.

Bahr al-samt (Sea of Silence, poetry). Cairo: Dar al-Kitab al-'Arabi, 1970.

Ughniyat al-layl (Night Songs, poetry). Cairo: General Egyptian Book Organization, 1978.

'Abd al-'Aziz, Yusriya (?–), Egyptian poet. *al-Fursan* (The Knights, poetry). Cairo: Dar al-Shuruq, 1990.
Ilayk wujudi (My Existence for You, poetry). Cairo: Maktabat Gharib, 1991.
Ash'ar mink (Poetry from You, poetry). Cairo: Dar al-Shuruq, 1992.

'Abd al-'Aziz, Zakiya Mal Allah (1959–), Qatari poet. She received a B.A. in pharmacy from Cairo University in 1980, an M.A. in 1985, and a Ph.D. in 1990. She is the head of the Pharmaceuticals Oversight Labs in Qatar. She has worked for the cultural desk at *al-Sharq* newspaper and taken part in several radio programs in Egypt and Doha. Her poems have been translated into English and Turkish. She received the Qatar Club Prize in Poetry in 1983.
Fi ma'bad al-ashwaq (In the Temple of Desires, poetry). Beirut and Cairo: Dar al-Shuruq, 1985.
Alwan min al-hubb (Colors of Love, poetry). Doha: Dawha Press, 1987.
Min ajlik ughanni (For You I Sing, poetry). Cairo: al-Shuruq Press, 1989.
Fi 'aynayk yuwarriq al-banafsaj (In Your Eyes the Violet Blossoms, poetry). Cairo: n.p., 1990.
Min asfar al-dhat (From Books of the Self, poetry). Qatar: n.p., 1991.
'Ala shafa hufra min al-bawh (On the Edge of a Hole of Confession, poetry). Damascus: Dar Hassan 'Atwan, 1993.
Hiwariyat al-hul wa-l-iqtiham (The Dialogue of Terror and Intrusion, poetry). N.p.: n.p., 1993.
Najmat al-dhakira (Star of Memory, poetry). Doha: Dar al-Thaqafa, 1996.

'Abd al-Baqi, Dawiya (1942–), Iraqi writer born in Basra. She graduated from the School of Domestic Arts in Basra in 1960. She worked in education and retired in 1982.
Nahr al-hanan wa-l-ahzan (The River of Compassion and Sorrows). N.p.: n.p., 1986.

'Abd al-Basit, Layla (1940–), Egyptian playwright born in Mansura. She has a B.A. in education from the department of Arabic literature at Ain Shams University. She was the chair of the department of educational activity at the Ministry of Education in 1987.
Azmat sharaf (Crisis of Honor, play). Cairo: General Egyptian Book Organization, 1988.
Waraqa (A Piece of Paper, play). Cairo: General Egyptian Book Organization, 1988.
Thaman al-ghurba (The Price of Exile, play). Cairo: General Egyptian Book Organization, 1989.

'Abd al-Dayim, Kawthar (?–), Egyptian short-story writer.
Shubbak wa sananir wa qisas ukhra (Nets and Hooks and Other Stories, short stories). Cairo: al-Istiqlal Press, 1972.
Hubb wa zilal (Love and Shadows, novel). N.p.: n.p., n.d.

'Abd al-Fattah, Ihsan Hanim (?–), Egyptian poet.
Ihtawini (Encircle Me, poetry). Cairo: Dar al-Hana' Press, 1982.

'Abd al-Ghani, Amina (?–), Egyptian short-story writer.
Rajul la yamshi 'ala-l-ard (A Man Who Walks Not on the Earth, short stories). Cairo: Dar 'Atwa Press, 1983.

'Abd al-Ghani, Salwa al-Sayyid Muhammad (1959–), Egyptian poet born in Port Said.
Sijn al-masha'ir (Prison of Feelings, poetry). Western Delta: General Authority for Culture Palaces, 1996.

'Abd al-Hadi, Fayha' (1951–), Palestinian writer and researcher born in Nablus. She received an M.A. and a Ph.D. in Arabic from Cairo University. Her non-fiction works include an academic study of Ghassan Kanafani, *Wa'd al-ghad* (Tomorrow's Promise, Amman, Dar al-Karmel,

1987), and a study of the Palestinian novel, *Namadhij al-mar'a/al-batal fi-l-riwaya al-Filistiniya* (Examples of the Woman/Hero in the Palestinian Novel, Cairo, General Egyptian Book Organization, 1997). She recently moved back to Palestine after living for years in Cairo. She is a member of the Palestinian Women's Union and responsible for the cultural committee of the union's branch in Cairo. She also oversees the 'Abbad al-Shams Children's Choir.

Hal yalta'im al-shatran (Will the Two Halves Join, texts). Ramallah: Dar al-Nashir, 1997.

'Abd al-Hadi, Hadiya (192?–), Palestinian poet born in 'Arraba, near Jenin. She studied in the traditional village school and continued her studies in Jenin. She graduated from Cairo University in 1966 and worked in education.

'Ala difaf al-Urdun (On the Banks of the Jordan). Jerusalem: Dar al-Aytam al-Islamiya Press, 1943.

Ghaliya (Beloved, novel). Amman: Dar Ibn Rushd, 1988.

Ma'an fi-l-qimma (Together on the Summit, plays and poetry). Jerusalem: al-Ma'arif Press Publications, n.d.

Rijal min sukhur (Men of Stones, play). Damascus: Palestinian Arab Theater Association, n.d.

'Abd al-Hadi, Siham (?–), Syrian novelist.
Lu'bat al-mazaj (The Mood Game, novel). Damascus: al-Katib al-'Arabi Press, n.d.

'Abd al-Hamid, 'Ayda (?–), Tunisian short-story writer.
Ishtaqtu ilayk (I Longed for You, short stories). Tunis: Bin 'Abd Allah Publications, 1986.

'Abd al-Hamid, Huda Mustafa (?–), Egyptian short-story writer.
Jumhuriyat Khanum (The Republic of the Lady, short stories). Cairo: al-Zahra' Arab Media, 1994.

'Abd al-Hayy, Khadija (1965–), Mauritanian short-story writer and poet born in al-Taraza. Her father instructed her in the religious sciences and language arts before she began her formal education. She received her preparatory school certificate in 1981 and a secondary-school diploma in literature in 1984. She graduated with a degree in Arabic literature from the Higher Teachers' School in Nouakchott in 1988. She worked as a high-school teacher and then became the head of the Library Authority in the Mauritanian Ministry of Culture. She writes poetry and short stories and has written literary and social essays. She won first prize in women's poetry in Nouakchott in 1989 and 1992 and took second place in the poetry competition sponsored by the Ministry of Information in Mauritania in 1990.

'Abd al-Hayy, Nadira (1973–), Palestinian poet born in al-Tira in the Triangle in the part of Palestine occupied in 1948. She finished primary and preparatory school in her village, but did not complete her formal education because of her health.

Zami'a al-shawq (Thirsty Passion, poetry). Haifa: Office of Arab Culture, 1995.

'Abd al-Husayn, Latifa (?–), Iraqi novelist.
Mat al-nahar (The Day Died, novel). N.p.: n.p., 1966.

'Abd al-Jalil, 'Awatif (1929–), Egyptian writer. She received a B.A. in sciences from Cairo University in 1951 and an M.A. in 1954. She also earned a Ph.D. in journalism from Cairo University in 1981. She was a teaching assistant at the School of Medicine at Cairo University and the School of Sciences in the Ministry of Education. She was the head of the foreign desk and a writer at *al-Qahira* (1955–1959) and a writer at *al-Masa'* and *al-Jumhuriya* in 1959. She is a member of the Journalists' Syndicate and the Teachers' Syndicate, and a boardmember of the World Federation of Scientific Workers (the first boardmember from Africa and the Arab world). She was awarded the Medal of Sciences, Arts, and Humanities in 1981, the gold medal on the hundredth anniversary of the national press in 1974, a medal of appreciation from the World Federation of Science Clubs in 1964, and a medal from the Ministry of Culture on International Women's Day in 1984. She has translated several works of popular science, including, *Kull shay' 'an 'aja'ib al-kimiya'* (Everything on the Wonders of Chemistry, 1959), *Dunya al-'ilm al-'ajiba* (The Wondrous World of Science, 1963, translated from English), *'Ilm wa tasliya* (Science and Fun, 1964, translated from English), and *Rijal ghayyaru wajh al-'alam* (Men Who Changed the World, 1985, translated from English).

Ghazw al-fada' (Conquest of Space, novel). Cairo: al-Ta'awun Publishers, 1966.

Ghazw al-mustaqbal (Conquest of the Future, novel). Cairo: al-Dar al-Qawmiya Printing and Publishing, 1969.

Mudhakkirat mudarrisa (Memoirs of a Woman Teacher, novel). Cairo: Dar al-Sha'b, 1972.

'Abd al-Karim, Ilham (?–), Iraqi novelist. She is a graduate of the Islamic Law College in Baghdad. She is active in women's organizations.

Khatim al-rabi' al-abadi (Ring of the Eternal Spring, autobiographical novel). Baghdad: General Union of Iraqi Women, 1994.

'Abd al-Karim, Sawsan (?–), Egyptian novelist. She received a B.A. in humanities from Alexandria University, and an M.A. in philosophy and a Ph.D. in sociology from the University of Paris.

Imra'a fi-l-zill (A Woman in the Shade, novel). Cairo: Rose al-Yusuf Foundation, 1979.

al-Janna al-mafquda (The Lost Paradise, novel). Cairo: Rose al-Yusuf Foundation, 1981.

'Abd al-Malik, Fluri (?–), Egyptian poet born in Mansura. She was educated at a convent school in an Upper Egyptian city for three years, after which she moved to the Girls' College in Cairo where she completed her high-school education. In 1965 she enrolled in the philosophy department at Alexandria University where she received a B.A. in philosophy and society.

Ruh ha'ima (A Perplexed Soul, poetry). Alexandria: Dar al-Ma'arif, 1969.

'Abd al-Malik, Raja' (?–), Egyptian short-story writer. She works for *al-Akhbar* newspaper.

La kibriya' fi-l-hubb (No Hubris in Love, novel). Cairo: Dar Nafi' Press, 1980.

Wa saqatat fi bi'r al-bitrul (And She Fell in an Oil Well, short stories). Cairo: al-'Asima Press, 1985.

'Abd al-Mun'im, Ghada (?–), Egyptian short-story writer.

Ana (I, texts). Cairo: Supreme Council for Culture, 1997.

'Abd al-Qadir, Huwayda 'Abd Allah (1969–), Sudanese poet born in Wad Madani, Sudan. She received a B.A. in the humanities from Cairo University in Khartoum in 1993 and a graduate degree from the Lebanese University in 1996. Her works have been published in Lebanese and Sudanese newspapers and journals.

'Abd al-Qadir, Layla (?–), Iraqi novelist.

Nadiya (Nadiya, novel). Baghdad: al-Mutanabbi Press, 1957.

'Abd al-Qadir, Zakiya (?–), Tunisian novelist born in Tunis. She is a professor of Arabic.

Amina (Amina, novel). Tunis: Qalam Publishers, 1983.

'Abd al-Rahman, 'A'isha (Bint al-Shati') (1912–1998), Egyptian writer, university professor, pioneering female jurist, and specialist in Islamic studies born in Damietta. She began her education at age five by memorizing the Qur'an and learning the art of Qur'anic recitation in traditional village schools. In 1920, she enrolled in the al-Luzi al-Amiriya School for Girls as a result of her insistence on continuing her education in public schools, with the support of her mother and grandfather. She received a teaching certificate and was a teacher at the girls' school in Mansura. In 1934, she enrolled in the Arabic department at Cairo University and received a B.A. in 1939, an M.A. in 1941, and a Ph.D. in 1950. She began to write for the press at age thirteen. After earning her teaching certificate, she met 'Ali Labiba Ahmad and worked with him on the magazine, *al-Nahda al-nisa'iya*, ultimately becoming the director of the magazine in 1933. She held many academic positions, including professor of Qur'anic exegesis and advanced studies at the College of Islamic Law at al-Qarawiyin University, professor of Arabic language and literature at Ain Shams University (1962–1972), professor at the Institute for Higher Arabic Studies at the Arab League in Cairo (1961–1974), and professor at the Institute for Editing the Tradition at the National Library in Cairo (1968–1974). She was a member of the Supreme Council for Islamic Affairs, the Supreme Council for Culture, and the National Specialized Councils. She was awarded several medals and distinctions, including the Medal of Intellectual Ability from King Hasan II of Morocco in 1967, the State Prize of Appreciation in Humanities in Egypt in 1972, a prize from the Language Academy in Cairo for textual editing in 1950 and the short story in 1953, a certificate of appreciation from the Arab Organization for Education and Culture in 1980, and the Egyptian State Prize for Social Studies for *al-Rif al-Misri* (The Egyptian Countryside) in 1980. Her name was given to the Bint al-Shati' Girls' Preparatory School in Damietta, a lecture hall at the Umm Durman Secondary School for Girls in Sudan, a lecture hall at the Teachers' Institute in Wad Madani in Sudan, and the Bint al-Shati' Cultural

and Intellectual Festival in Damietta. She published numerous academic and non-fiction works, including *al-Rif al-Misri* (1936), *Qadiyat al-fallah* (The Cause of the Peasant, 1939), *al-Hayah al-insaniya 'ind Abi-l-'Ala': lima khuliqna wa kayfa nahya wa ila ayna al-masir* (Human Life for Abi-l-'Ala': Why Were We Created, How Do We Live, and Where Are We Going, 1944), *Ard al-mu'jizat* (Land of Miracles, 1952, a journey to the Arabian Peninsula), *al-Ghufran* (Forgiveness, 1954, critical essay), *Banat al-nabi (nisa' al-nabi), radiya Allah 'anhunna* (The Prophet's Daughters, 1956), *al-Khansa'* (al-Khansa', 1957), *Umm al-nabi, salla Allah 'alayhi wa sallam* (The Prophet's Mother, 1961), *al-Sha'ira al-'Arabiya al-mu'asira* (The Contemporary Arab Woman Poet, 1962), *Madinat al-Salam fi hayat Abi-l-'Ala'* (Baghdad in the Life of Abi-l-'Ala', 1963), *Abu-l-'Ala' al-Ma'arri: a'lam al-'Arab* (Abu-l-'Ala' al-Ma'arri: Arab Luminaries, 1964), *al-Sayyida Zaynab batalat Karbala 'aqilat Bani Hashim* (al-Sayyida Zaynab: Heroine of Karbala and the Best of Bani Hashim, 1966), *Qiyam jadida li-l-adab al-'Arabi al-jadid wa-l-mu'asir* (New Values in Modern and Contemporary Arabic Literature, 1967), *Sayyidat bayt al-nubuwwa, radiya Allah 'anhunna* (Women of the House of the Prophet, 1967), *Turathuna bayn madin wa hadir* (Our Heritage Between Past and Present, 1967), *A'da' al-bashar* (Enemies of Humanity, 1968), *Ma'a al-mustafa 'alayhi al-salah wa-l-salam* (With the Chosen One, 1969), *Maqal fi-l-insan: dirasa Qur'aniya* (An Essay on Humankind: A Study of the Qur'an, 1969), *Masa'il Ibn al-Azraq* (Ibn al-Azraq's Theses, 1969), *al-Tafsir al-bayani li-l-Qur'an al-Karim* (An Interpretation of the Qur'an, two vols., 1969), *al-Qur'an wa-l-tafsir al-'asri: hadha balagh li-l-nas* (The Qur'an and Contemporary Exegesis: Here Is a Message for Mankind, 1970), *Lughatuna wa-l-hayah* (Our Language and Life, 1971), *Ma'a Abi-l-'Ala' fi rihlat hayatihi* (With Abi-l-'Ala' on His Life Journey, 1971), *Muqaddima fi-l-manhaj* (An Introduction to Methodology, 1971), *Risalat al-ghufran li-Abi-l-'Ala'* (Abi-l-'Ala''s Epistle of For-giveness, 1971, edited text), *Nisa' al-nabi* (The Prophet's Women, 1979), *al-I'jaz al-bayani li-l-Qur'an* (The Inimitability of the Qur'an), and *Muqaddimat Ibn al-Salah fi 'ulum al-hadith* (Ibn al-Salah's Introduc-tion to the Study of Prophetic Traditions, edited text).

Sayyid al-'izba: qissat imra'a khati'a (Lord of the Manor: The Story of a Fallen Woman, novel). Cairo: Dar al-Ma'arif, 1944.

Raj'at fir'awn (Pharaoh's Return, novel). Cairo: Dar al-Ma'arif, 1949.

Sirr al-shati' (Secret of the Shore, short stories). Cairo: Nadi al-Qissa, 1952.

Imra'a khati'a (A Fallen Woman, short stories). Cairo: The Story Club, 1958.

Suwar min hayatihunna (Pictures from Their Lives, short stories). Cairo: al-Maktaba al-'Arabiya, 1959.

'Ala-l-jisr (On the Bridge, autobiography). Cairo: Dar al-Hilal, 1967.

'Abd al-Rahman, Ghaniya (1958–), Egypt-ian poet born in Qina.

Uhawir fik al-sukun (I Speak to Tranquil-ity in You, poetry). Cairo: General Authority for Culture Palaces, 1996.

'Abd al-Sada, Hayat (?–), Iraqi poet.

Shu'lat al-hayah (The Flame of Life, poetry). Najaf: al-Adab Press, 1978.

'Abd al-Shahid, Olivia 'Uwayda (al-Zahra) (?–?), Egyptian writer born in Luxor. She used a pseudonym, al-Zahra, with her short stories and poems, which were published in Egyptian journals such as *al-Hilal*, *al-Risala*, and *al-Thaqafa*. She translated works from French and English into Arabic and published two works of non-fiction: *al-'A'ila al-Misriya* (The Egypt-ian Family, 1912) and *Malik al-mahabba: tarikh al-Masih* (The King of Love: The History of Christ, 1920, with Constance Baruk).

Khawatir fatah Misriya (Reflections of an Egyptian Woman, letters). Cairo: Young Christian Women's Press, n.d.

'Abd al-Tawwab, Mirvat Isma'il (1957–), Egyptian short-story writer, poet, and journalist born in Cairo. She received a B.A. in sciences from Cairo University in 1977 and a degree from the Institute of Arab Studies. She is a journalist at *al-Ahram* and a member of the Egyptian Writers' Union.

Qulub wast al-dabab (Hearts in the Fog, poetry). Cairo: Dar Lotus Printing and Publishing, 1985.

Hubb tawathu al-amwaj (Love Folded in the Waves, short stories). Cairo: Dar al-Sha'b, 1987.

Uhibbuhu wa lakin (I Love Him But, poetry). Cairo: Rose al-Yusuf Foun-dation, 1987.

al-Sharkh (The Crack, short stories). Cairo: al-Ahram Press, 1993.

Yawmiyat zawja sirriya (Diaries of a Secret Wife, novel). Cairo: al-Ahram Press, 1996.

al-'Abdan, Hind Nuri (1936–), Iraqi poet and novelist born in the Bab al-Shaykh district in Baghdad. She did not complete her university studies. She is fluent in English and has a familiarity with Russian. She has published prose poems in the Beirut-based magazine, *al-Adib*, as well as in the Iraqi press. She was active in the feminist movement. She participated in the Youth Festival in Moscow and the World Women's Conference in the 1960s. She has lived most of her life abroad with her husband, poet 'Abd al-Wahhab al-Bayati.

al-Ghasaq (Dusk, poetry). Cairo: al-Dumyati Printing and Publishing, 1971.

Wisal (Communion, novel). Baghdad: al-Jami'a Press, 1975.

'Abduh, Nahla 'Abd Allah (1956–), Yemeni playwright born in Aden. She has a B.A. in history. She is an editor for *Uktubir* magazine. She has taken part in many literary activities in Yemen and abroad and has received several awards about the relationship between women's writing and freedom. She has written many short stories, all of which were published in *14 Uktubir* magazine from 1996 to 1997.

Farfur wa-l-qird al-sahir (Farfur and the Magic Ape, play). Aden: Ministry of Culture, 1984.

Nashid al-mu'jiza (The Miracle's Anthem, play). Aden: Fourteenth of October, 1989.

Hajar (Stone, play). Aden: Ministry of Culture, 1993.

Abouzeid, Leila (Abu Zayd, Layla) (1950–), Moroccan short-story writer and author. She received a B.A. in English language and literature from Muhammad V University in Rabat and the University of Texas at Austin. She also received a degree in journalism from the International Journalism Institute. She is a former producer and journalist for Moroccan television and radio. She covered several government ministries in 1971, 1974, 1982, and 1991. She translates from English to Arabic. She translated Rom Landau's *The Sultan of Morocco* from English to Arabic as *Muhammad al-khamis mundhu tawallihi al-'arsh ila yawm wafatih*. Her *'Am al-fil* has been translated into English. *Malkum Iks* (*Malcolm X*, biography) (Beirut: Bisan Publishing and Distribution, 1996) is a translation from English.

Bid' sunbulat khudr 'an Lundun (A Few Green Spikes of Grain About London, memoirs). Tunis: al-Dar al-Tunisiya Publishers, 1978.

'Am al-fil (*Year of the Elephant*, short stories and novella). Rabat: Dar al-Ma'arif al-Jadida, 1983.

Amrika al-wajh al-akhar (America: The Other Face, travel literature, 1986). al-Muhammadiya: Fudala Press, 1986.

al-Ruju' ila-l-tufula (*Return to Childhood*, autobiography). Casablanca: al-Najah Modern Press, 1993.

al-Abrashi, 'Aziza (?–), Egyptian novelist.

Islah (Reform, novel). Beirut: Dar al-Fikr Printing and Publishing, n.d.

Abu Bakr, Mas'uda (1954–), Tunisian novelist, short-story writer, and children's writer born in Safaqis. Since 1986 she has published a weekly column for the cultural supplement of *al-Hurriya* newspaper, "'Iqd al-murjan" (Necklace of Coral). She was awarded the Medal of Cultural Achievement in 1997.

Ta'm al-ananas (The Taste of Pineapple, short stories). Tunis: al-Atlasiya Publications, 1994.

Laylat al-ghiyab (The Night of Absence, novel). Tunis: Dar Sihr Publishers, 1997.

Shahamat numayl (The Courage of a Little Ant, children's literature). Tunis: Dar al-Ithaf Publishers, 1999.

Tarshaqana (Gay, novel). Tunis: Dar Sahr Publishers, 1999.

Abu Bakr, Maymuna (1948–), Yemeni poet born in al- Makalla in the province of al-Khamisa. She was the first Yemeni woman to publish a collection of poetry in southern Yemen. She has two degrees, one in sociology and another in English. She attended special training sessions in television direction in Egypt. She is currently a television director. She has written songs, several of which have been recorded by various artists.

Khuyut fi-l-shafaq (Threads in the Twilight, poetry). Aden: Dar al-Tali'a, n.d.

Abu Dibs, Najwa Fakhuri (?–), Lebanese poet.

Hikaya wahida wa Bayrut (One Story and Beirut, poetry). Beirut: Ma'luf Press, 1985.

Abu Ghazala, Ilham (1940s?–), Palestinian short-story writer and researcher specialized in linguistics. She has a Ph.D. in linguistics and discourse analysis. She teaches at Birzeit University. She is active with non-governmental organizations working in the field of women's rights. She has published several critical studies, including *Ana wa anta wa-l-thawra: shi'r al-mar'a fi-l-'alam al-thalith* (You and I and the Revolution: Women's Poetry in the Third World, Kuwait, 1987). She is also a translator.

Nisa' min al-samt (Women of Silence, short stories). Jerusalem: Palestinian Writers' Union Publications, 1997.

Lawza tughanni li-l-shajar (Lawza Sings to the Trees, children's literature). N.p.: Tamir Foundation for Social Education, 1998.

Abu Ghazala, Raja' (1942–1995), Palestinian short-story writer and artist born in Beirut. She lived in Amman. She was educated in Beirut schools and attended the Jordanian University, from which she received a B.A. in English language and literature. In addition to being a writer, she was a photographer, painter, journalist, and translator. She translated several selections from Western women's literature. She had both group and individual art exhibitions in Jeddah, Oman, Jordan, al-'Aqaba, and Paris. She was a member of the League of Jordanian Writers and the officer of the league's women's committee. She received three certificates of esteem from the Office of Culture and Arts.

Ma'ak astati' ightiyal al-zaman (With You I Can Assassinate Time, poetry). Amman: Dar al-Sha'b Press, 1977.

al-Abwab al-mughlaqa (The Closed Doors, short stories). Amman: Dar al-Bahith, 1981.

al-Mutarada (The Chase, short stories). Amman: Dar al-Shuruq, 1988.

Karm bila siyaj (A Vineyard Without a Fence, short stories). Amman: Arab Institute for Research and Publishing, 1992.

al-Qadiya (The Cause, short stories). Amman: Ministry of Culture Publications, 1994.

Zahrat al-krayz (Cherry Blossom, short stories). Amman: Dar al-Karmel, 1994.

Imra'a kharij al-hisar (A Woman Outside the Siege, novel). Amman: Writers' League, 1995.

al-Hurub al-da'iri (The Circular Escape, prose poetry). Amman: Dar al-Sha'b Press, n.d.

Abu Ghazala, Samira (1928–), Palestinian writer born in Nablus. She attended school in Ramle and Jerusalem and university in Beirut and Cairo. She received an M.A. in Arabic literature in 1956. She resides in Cairo. She has taught at university and worked in the Higher Council to Foster the Arts and Humanities in Cairo. She has presented interviews and programs on Voice of the Arabs Radio in Cairo and on Ramallah radio. She is a member of the Palestinian National Council, a founding member of the Palestinian Women's Union, and the president of the union's branch in Cairo.

Mudhakkirat fatah 'Arabiya (Memoirs of a Young Arab Woman, memoir). Beirut: Dar al-Nashr li-l-Jami'iyin, 1960.

Nida' al-ard (Call of the Earth, poetry). Cairo: al-Dar al-Misriya Publishing and Distribution, 1989.

Abu Jawda, Maryam Shuqayr (1948–), Lebanese poet born in Mashghara. She studied media studies at Montpellier University in France. She has worked as a journalist and published in *Fayruz*, *al-Faris*, *Sahar wa Samar*, *al-Anwar*, *al-Kifah al-'Arabi*, and *Zahrat al-Khalij*. She established Maryam Publications in Beirut and is a member of the Family Planning Association.

Kalimat imra'a min burj al-hubb (Words of a Woman from the Star Sign of Love, poetry). Beirut: Dar al-Sayyad, 1986.

Khara'it wa 'asafir (Maps and Sparrows, texts). Beirut: Dar al-Sayyad, 1986.

al-Hubb yatakallam: sirat imra'a min burj al-hubb (Love Speaks: The Life of a Woman from the Star Sign of Love, poetry). Maryam Publications, 1989.

al-Lawn al-akhar (The Other Color, texts). Beirut: Maryam Publications, 1990.

Habibi (My Love, poetry). Beirut: Maryam Publications, 1993.

Ana al-'arrafa wardat al-dhahab (I Am the Soothsayer, Flower of Gold, poetry). Beirut: Maryam Publications, 1994.

Hadiqat Maryam (Maryam's Garden, poetry). Beirut: Maryam Publications, 1998.

Abu Khalid, Arlette (Anwar Abu Khalid) (1969–), Saudi children's writer born in Riyadh. She has a B.A. in sociology and a B.A. and an M.A. in psychology. She is a psychologist at the King Fahd National Guard Hospital and a lecturer in the special education department at King Sa'ud University. She worked in the office of *al-Riyad* from 1994 to 1997, and she writes a weekly column for the newspaper titled "Akhyilat al-tufula" (Chimeras of Childhood). She has written under the name Anwar Abu Khalid.

Hulm lujayn (A Silver Dream, children's literature). N.p.: Sultan Center for Publishing, 1998.

Sadiqi al-sukkar (My Friend Sugar, children's literature). N.p.: n.p., 1998.

Abu Khalid, Fawziya (1955–), Saudi poet and short-story writer born in Riyadh. She received a B.A. from the American University of Beirut in 1979 and an M.A. in sociology from King Sa'ud University in Riyadh in 1984. She is currently preparing her Ph.D. in Britain. She is a lecturer in sociology at King Sa'ud University. She is also a founder of, and an editorial consultant for, *al-Nass al-jadid* (established 1993). She writes regularly for the London-based *al-Hayat* and has a regular column in *al-Jazira al-Sa'udiya*. She has written on sociology, literature, and women in both Arabic and English. Her poems have been translated into French, Italian, and English.

Ila mata yakhtatifunak laylat al-'urs (How Long Will They Kidnap You on the Wedding Night, poetry). Beirut: Dar al-'Awda, 1975.

Ashhad al-watan (I Witness the Homeland, poetry). N.p.: n.p., 1984.

Qira'a fi-l-sirr li-tarikh al-samt al-'Arabi (A Secret Reading of the History of Arab Silence, poetry). Beirut: Dar al-'Awda, 1985.

Tayyarat al-waraq (Kites, children's literature). Jeddah: Tuhama, 1989.

Tifla tuhibb al-as'ila (A Child Who Loves Questions, children's literature). Riyadh: Dar al-Ard, 1990.

Ma' al-sarab (Water of the Mirage, poetry). Beirut: Dar al-Jadid, 1995.

Abu Lahum, 'Aziza 'Abd Allah (1945–), Yemeni novelist born in Naham in the generation prior to the revolution. She currently lives in Sana'a after residing in many Arab and other countries with her diplomat husband, Muhsin al-'Ayni. She has no formal academic degree, but her upbringing in an environment of awareness helped her. She later studied English and computers. She is considered a feminist pioneer. She helped found the Yemeni Women's Association in the 1970s. She has played a prominent role in the Arab Women's Council in the U.S. and was an active member in the Council of the Muslim Women's Union.

Ahlam wa Nabila (Ahlam and Nabila). Cairo: al-Madani Press, 1997.

Tayf wilaya (The Semblance of a State, novel). Sana'a: Armed Forces Moral Guidance Bureau Press, 1998.

Arkanaha al-faqih (The Jurist Put Her Aside, novel). Cairo: al-Dawliya Printing, 1998.

Abu Rashid, Renee (?–), Lebanese novelist.

Liman akun (To Whom I Belong, novel). Beirut: n.p., 1960.

'Adhra' wa sha'ir (A Virgin and a Poet, novel). Beirut: Arab Distribution Company, 1962.

Abu Rashid, Salma (Salima) (1887–1919), Lebanese writer born in the Shahrur valley. She was educated in her hometown and in Beirut, where she studied French, Italian, and English. She founded a school in her town and continued her education with the study of law. She founded the journal, *Fatat Lubnan*, in 1914, which suspended publication with the eruption of the First World War. She went to Egypt and after her return published her memoir of the trip. She published a work of non-fiction, *al-Ruznama al-Salimiya: taqwim li-mi'at sana* (Salima's Almanac: A Hundred-year Calendar).

Bayn al-qutrayn al-shaqiqayn (Between the Two Brother Countries, travel literature). N.p.: al-Nasir al-Bayruti, n.d.

Abu Risha, Zulaykha (1942–), Jordanian poet and short-story writer of Syrian origin born in Palestine. She received her early education in Damascus and Amman. She graduated from the Jordanian University with a B.A. in Arabic language and literature in 1964. She also received a degree in Islamic studies in Cairo and prepared an M.A. on children's literature. She has a book of non-fiction titled *al-Lugha al-gha'iba: nahw lugha ghayr janusiya* (The Absent Language: Toward a Non-gendered Language, Amman, 1996).

Almasatan (Two Diamonds, children's literature). Amman: Dar al-Hama'im for Children, Hayy Ibn Yaqzan Series, 1985.

Fi-l-zinzana (In the Cell, short stories). Cairo: General Egyptian Book Organization, 1987.

Tarashuq al-khafa' (Battle of Secrecy, poetry). Beirut: Arab Institute for Research and Publishing, 1998.

Ghajar al-ma' (Water Gypsies, texts). Cairo: General Egyptian Book Organization, 1999.

Abu Shadi, Safiya Ahmad Zaki (?–), Egyptian pioneering poet born in Cairo. She was educated in Cairo's schools and enrolled in the College of Liberal Arts at Cairo University in 1946. Her father, poet Ahmad Zaki Abu Shadi, immigrated to the U.S. with his family, where Safiya completed her studies at Georgetown University in Washington, D.C., earning a B.A. in literature and psychology. She only writes prose poetry.

al-Ughniya al-khalida (The Immortal Song, poetry). Cairo: League of Modern Literature, 1954.

Abu al-Sha'r, Hind (195?–), Jordanian short-story writer born in al-Hisn. She lives in al-Zarqa'. She attended school in al-Mafraq and Irbid. She has a B.A. and an M.A. in history from the Jordanian University, as well as a Ph.D. in modern Arabic literature. Her non-fiction works include *Harakat al-Mukhtar ibn Abi 'Ubayd al-Thaqafi min al-Kufa* (Movement of the Kufan Mukhtar ibn Abi 'Ubayd al-Thaqafi, historical study, al-Zarqa', Dar al-Shuruq, 1984) and *Irbid wa jiwaruha: 1850–1928* (Irbid and Its Environs: 1850–1928, Beirut, Arab Institute for Research and Publishing, 1995). In addition to short stories, she writes poetry and is an artist. She is a founding member of the Young Artists' Group and a member of the League of Jordanian Writers.

Shuquq fi kaff Khadra (Cracks in Khadra's Palm, short stories). Amman: al-Dustur Press, 1981.

al-Mujabaha (The Confrontation, short stories). Amman: Dar al-Shuruq and al-Zahra' Press, 1984.

al-Hisan (The Horse, short stories). Amman: League of Jordanian Writers Publications, 1991.

'Indama tusbih al-dhakira watanan (When Memory Becomes a Homeland, short stories). Amman: Ministry of Culture Publications, 1996.

Abu Shumays, Zinat (1948–), Palestinian short-story writer born in Jaffa. She lives in Amman. She was educated in Nazareth and Amman. She graduated from the Jordanian University in 1970. She has written articles for the cultural supplements of Jordanian newspapers.

Abjadiya 'ala jidar al-qalb (An Alphabet on the Walls of the Heart, short stories). Amman: Dar al-Karmel, 1989.

Abu Zayd, Madiha (1945–), Egyptian novelist born in Cairo's al-Darb al-Ahmar quarter. She has a B.A. in social studies from Cairo University. She is a social worker.
Mudhakkirat ikhsa'iya fi-l-rif al-Misri (Memoirs of a Social Worker in the Egyptian Countryside, novel). Cairo: General Egyptian Book Organization, 1994.
Za'ir ba'd muntasaf al-layl (A Late-night Visitor, novel). Cairo: al-Fajr Publications, 1998.

Abu Zayd, Nawal Muhanna Ahmad (1948–), Egyptian poet and playwright.
Dhat marra (Once, poetry). Cairo: Dar al-Fikr al-'Arabi, 1997.
al-Faris wa-l-amira (The Knight and the Princess, poetic drama). Cairo: Dar al-Fikr al-'Arabi, 1998.
Agharid al-rabi' (Warblings of Spring, poetry). Cairo: Dar al-Fikr al-'Arabi, 1999.

Abu Zayd, Wafa' (1967–), Egyptian short-story writer born in Cairo.
Ru'an janubiya (Southern Perspectives, short stories). Cairo: General Authority for Culture Palaces, 1996.

Abu-l-Naja, Zaynab (?–), Egyptian poet. She was educated in her hometown of Miyyat Ghamr and continued her education at the Higher Institute for Physical Education in Giza. After graduating in 1971, she joined the journalism department at the College of Media.
'Imlaq fi qalbi (A Giant in My Heart, poetry). Cairo: Maktabat Nahdat al-Sharq, 1985.

Abu-l-Nasr, Hayat (?–), Egyptian poet and short-story writer born in al-Qalyubiya. She has a high school diploma. She has composed songs for radio and television, in addition to several plays. She hosts a literary salon in Cairo.
Qataluk ya qalbi (They Killed You, My Heart, poetry). Cairo: n.p., 1980.

Nahr bila difaf (A River Without Banks, short stories). Cairo: Egyptian Company for the Art of Printing, 1982.
Li-annani untha (Because I'm a Female, poetry). Jounieh: International Center for Printing, Publishing, and Distribution, 1988.
Shay' min qadari: qisas Misriya (A Piece of My Fate: Egyptian Stories, short stories). Cairo: Dar al-Sha'b, 1988.
Afrah wa jirah (Joys and Wounds, poetry). Cairo: Maktabat Madbuli, n.d.

Abu-l-Nur, 'A'isha 'Abd al-Muhsin (1950–), Egyptian novelist and short-story writer. She received a B.A. in journalism from Cairo University in 1974. She works as a journalist for the Akhbar al-Yawm Foundation. She is a member of the Writers' Union, the Afro-Asian Peoples' Organization, and the UNDP working group on women. Some of her stories have been translated into English. Her non-fiction works include *Hiwarat sahafiya* (Press Interviews, 1978), *Irhal li-naltaqi* (Go So We Shall Meet, 1993), *Uhibbuk la uhibbuk* (I Love You, I Don't Love You, 1995), and *Qalu li 'an al-mar'a, al-hubb, al-hurriya* (They Told Me About Women, Love, and Freedom, 1997).
Rubbama tafham yawman (Perhaps You'll Understand One Day, short stories). Cairo: Maktabat Gharib, 1980.
Musafir fi dami (A Traveler in My Blood, novel). Cairo: Supreme Council for Culture, 1981.
al-Hubb tifluna al-dall (Love: Our Errant Child, short stories). Cairo: n.p., 1983.
al-Imda' Salwa (Signed, Salwa, novel). Cairo: 'A'isha Abu-l-Nur Publications, 1985.
Wa-l-rijal yakhafun aydan (And Men Also Fear, short stories). Cairo: 'A'isha al-Taymuriya Publications, 1989.

Abu-l-Rabb, Magdeline (1962–), Palestinian short-story writer born in Nablus. She received a B.A. in chemistry from the Jordanian University in 1985. She is a

teacher and has published several studies and articles in educational, developmental, and environmental journals.
Tishrin la yazul (October Still, short stories). Amman: Ministry of Culture, 1994.

Abu-l-Rus, Hanna (1880–1963), Lebanese novelist born in Beirut. She was educated in Beirut's Orthodox Christian School and taught at al-Aqmar al-Thalatha School, the Russian School in Damascus, and the Girls' School in Beirut.
'Awatif al-kibriya' (Feelings of Arrogance, novel, unpublished manuscript).
Murad fi-l-sijn (Murad in Prison, novel, unpublished manuscript).

Abu-l-Sha'r, Iman (?–), Palestinian poet.
al-Sada (The Echo, poetry). Acre: Abu Rahmun Library and Press, 1978.

Adam, Hikmat Kamil (?–), Egyptian short-story writer.
al-Nas wa-l-dunya (People and the World, short stories). Damanhur: al-Ahram Press, 1939.

Adam, al-Radiya (?–), Sudanese poet. She is interested in social and women's issues and has published in Sudanese newspapers and magazines.

al-'Adawi, Shirin Ahmad (1968–), Egyptian poet born in the province of al-Daqahliya. She teaches Arabic.
Dahaliz al-juruh (The Anterooms of the Wounds, poetry). Eastern Delta: General Authority for Culture Palaces, 1998.

Adib, Bahiya al-Filali (?–), Moroccan poet.
Waraqat min rihla samita (Papers from a Silent Journey, poetry). Casablanca: Dar al-Thaqafa, 1994.

Adib, Hoda (Adib, Huda) (1943–) (see also: Bibliography of Works in French)
Thalathat muka'abat (Three Cubes, prose poetry). Beirut: Commerical Organi-

zation for Printing and Publishing and *al-Adib* magazine, 1971.
al-Shari' al-madina al-raqm (Street, City, Number, poetry). Beirut: Commercial Organization for Printing and Publishing, 1979.

'Adli, 'Afaf (?–), Egyptian poet.
Wa anta ba'id (And You Are Far Away, poetry). N.p.: n.p., 1991.

Aflatun, Inji (1924–1989), Egyptian writer, artist, and political activist born in Cairo. She was a student at the School of the Holy Heart, known for its religious zealotry. Arabic was not well taught at the time so her mother insisted on hiring a private tutor to teach her the basics of Arabic and Islam. Aflatun later transferred to the French Lycée. Since her childhood, Aflatun had loved drawing and became a student of Kamil al-Tilmisani. She received a B.A. in philosophy in 1944. In the same year she joined the communist organization Iskra and began underground political work. In 1945, the League of Women University and College Students was established and Aflatun was one of its most important founders. She took part in the global women's conference held in Paris on November 26, 1945, and was arrested, along with her colleagues, as soon as she returned to Egypt. From that moment on, her name was on the blacklist and the security establishment maintained a political file on her. She took part in the women's conference in Paris in 1947, after which she wrote the pamphlet, *Thamanun milyun imra'a ma'ana* (Eighty Million Women with Us, 1948). The pamphlet was confiscated from the market as soon as it was released, but was redistributed after Aflatun sued the Ministry of Interior. In 1949, she published her second book, *Nahnu al-nisa' al-Misriyat* (We Egyptian Women). In January 1951 she helped found the Egyptian Committee for Peace. In 1959, a warrant was issued for her arrest and she decided to go underground to continue her political work. During this time, the

press announced that she had won first prize in a landscape painting competition sponsored by the Ministry of Culture and Information. She was arrested in June 1959. She painted several canvases in prison and was released on July 26, 1963. She was arrested again in 1981.
Sira dhatiya (Autobiography, autobiography edited and with an introduction by Sa'id Khayyal). Cairo: Dar Su'ad al-Sabah, 1992.

'Afra' (see: al-Hilli, Maqbula)

Ahmad, 'A'isha Zahir (?–), Saudi short-story writer.
Basma min buhayrat al-dumu' (A Smile from the Lakes of Tears, short stories). Jeddah: Literary Club, 1980.

Ahmad, Farida (?–), Egyptian novelist.
Akhaf 'alayk minni (I Fear for You from Myself, novel). Cairo: National Center for the Arts and Humanities, 1982.
al-Aruzz wa-l-barud wa-l-zaytun (Rice, Gunpowder, and Olives, short stories). Cairo: General Egyptian Book Organization, 1993.

Ahmad, Jamila Kamil (Mama Jamila) (1925–), Egyptian journalist and children's writer born in Cairo. She received a B.A. in English literature from Cairo University in 1948 and then traveled to England with her husband, where she studied social sciences. She was the editor of the family page at *al-Masa'* in 1956, an editor at *al-Idha'a al-Misriya* in 1962, and an editor at *Samir* in 1966. She is interested in women's issues and was a member of the Egyptian Women's Union. Along with Inji Aflatun and Sayza Nabrawi, she worked to create a youth committee in the union. She published the magazine, *Nawara*, as a practical example of publications that encouraged continued education for graduates of literacy classes. She has written and translated many children's stories, most of them published, including: *Nawadir Juha* (Tales of Juha, 1983), folklore; *Alf layla wa layla: hikayat al-amir*

Wardakhan (A Thousand and One Nights: The Story of Prince Wardakhan, 1984); *Alf layla wa layla: rihlat wa mughamarat al-Sindbad al-bahri* (A Thousand and One Nights: The Journeys and Adventures of Sindbad the Sailor, 1985); *Juha wa nawadir al-hamqa wa-l-mughaffalin* (Juha and Tales of the Foolish and Negligent, 1986); *Amthal wa hikayat* (Proverbs and Stories, 1987), folklore; and *Abtal baladna* (The Heroes of Our Country, 1989), history.
'Indama kunt saghiran (When I Was Young, memories of great writers, children's literature). Cairo: Dar al-Hilal, 1985.
'Arusatuna al-Misriya wa-l-arajuz (Our Egyptian Bride and the Puppeteer, children's literature). Cairo: Dar al-Hilal, 1988.
al-Fil yal'ab al-natta (The Elephant Plays Hopscotch, children's stories). Cairo: Dar al-Hilal, 1991.

Ahmad, Radiya (1959–), Egyptian short-story writer.
Hulm dafi' (A Warm Dream, short stories). Cairo: General Egyptian Book Organization, 1997.

Ahmad, Sawsan 'Abbas (1972–), Egyptian short-story writer born in the province of Qina.
al-Masa' (Evening, short stories). Upper Egypt: General Authority for Culture Palaces, 1998.
al-Fayruz (Turquoise, short stories). Upper Egypt: General Authority for Culture Palaces, 1999.

Ahmad, Surur (?–), Iraqi short-story writer.
Dukhan al-ghurfa (The Room's Smoke, short stories). Arbil: al-Thaqafa wa-l-Shabab Press, 1985.

al-'Ajab, Amal 'Abbas (?–), Sudanese writer. Her works have been published in Sudanese periodicals and journals published by the Sudanese Women's Union. She specializes in the popular tradition. She was the head of *al-Ra'i al-akhar* newspaper and is now a press consultant for *al-Hurriya*.

'Ajami, Mary (1888–1965), Syrian poet born in Damascus. She was educated at the Russian and Irish Schools. She translated short stories and essays from English into Arabic and is a pioneer of the Syrian press. She established the Literary League in Damascus in 1921, which lasted for three years, after which she opened her home to writers for literary and intellectual debate. She published the magazine, al-'Arus, from 1910 to 1914. It reappeared after the First World War, but suspended publication in 1926 for financial reasons, after eleven volumes. She worked as a teacher in Lebanon and Egypt and lectured in Iraq. She translated al- Majdaliya al-hasna' (The Lovely Magdalene Lady) in 1913.
Dawhat al-dhikra (The Great Tree of Memory, prose poetry). Damascus: Ministry of Culture, 1969.

'Ajlan, Fathiya 'Abd Allah (1953–), Bahraini poet born in al-Mahraq. She has a high-school diploma (literature section). She writes poetry in both classical and colloquial Arabic.
Ashri'at al-'ishq (Sails of Passion, poetry). Bahrain: n.p., 1984.
Shams al-dahari (Afternoon Sun, colloquial poetry). Manama: n.p., 1993.
Ji't fa-ghadarat hiya (I Came Then She Left, poetry). N.p.: n.p., n.d.

al-'Ajuri, Jamila (1969–), Jordanian poet born in Amman. She received a B.A. in Arabic from the Jordanian University in 1991.
Ana hakadha (That's How I Am, poetry). Amman: Dar al-Azmina, 1995.

Al Sa'd, Nura (1964–), Qatari short-story writer born in Doha. She has an M.A. in Arabic and works at the Foreign Ministry in Doha.
Ba'i' al-jara'id (Newspaper Seller, short stories). Doha: Dawha Press, 198?.

Al Sa'id, Janan al-Jarudi (?–), Lebanese journalist and novelist born in Beirut. She received a B.A. in English literature from the Beirut College for Girls. She won the Best Novel prize from *al-Nahar* newspaper in 1975 for *Hadha anta*.
Hadha anta (That's You, novel). Beirut: Dar al-Nahar Publishers, 1975.
La'la' barid al-shams (The Sun's Messenger Gleamed, novel). Beirut: Dar al-Afaq al-Jadida, 1980.
Istighathat al-fajr (The Dawn's Appeal, crime novel). Beirut: Dar al-Rayhani, 1989.
Man anta? (Who Are You, crime novel). Beirut: Dar al-Rayhani, 1990.

Al Yasin, Fa'ida (1959–), Iraqi poet born in Baghdad to a well-known secular, literary family in al-Kazimiya. She graduated from Baghdad University in 1978 with a B.A. in history. She has worked in journalism.
Da'irat al-lahw wa-l-alam (Circle of Pleasure and Pain, poetry). Baghdad: al-Umma Press, 1979.
Tada'iyat imra'a (Consequences of a Woman, poetry). Baghdad: n.p., 1986.

al-'Alayili, Jamila (1907–1991), Egyptian poet and novelist who was influenced in her early career by the writings of Mayy Ziyada. She published her works in *al-Nahda al-Misriya*, a women's magazine, and in *al-Mar'a al-Misriya*. Her poems were published in *Abullu*. In Mansura she formed a literary association, Family of Culture, and established the Writers of Arabism Association and *al-Ahdaf* magazine.
al-Nasamat (Breezes, poetry). Mansura: al-Haditha Press, 1929.
al-Ta'ir al-ha'ir (The Confused Bird, novel). Miyyat Ghamr: Wadi al-Nil Press, 1935.
Sada ahlami (The Echo of My Dreams, poetry). Alexandria: al-Ta'awun Press, 1936.
al-Amira (The Princess, novel). Cairo: Sa'd Misr Press, 1939.
Amani: qissa Misriya (Amani: An Egyptian Story, novel). Cairo: n.p., 1940.
al-Ra'iya (The Shepherdess, novel). Alexandria: King Faruq Press, 1942.
Arwah tata'allaf (Souls in Harmony, novel). Cairo: al-Haqa'iq Press, 1947.

Iman al-iman (Faith of Faith, novel). Cairo: Dar Nashr al-Thaqafa, 1950.
al-Nasik (The Hermit, novel). Cairo: General Egyptian Book Organization, 1972.
Hadhihi-l-aqasis (These Tales, short stories). Cairo: 'Abidin Press, 1977.
Bayn abawayn (Between Parents, novel). Cairo: Supreme Council for Culture and Arts, 1981.
Nabadat sha'ira (Heartbeats of a Woman Poet, poetry). Cairo: General Egyptian Book Organization, 1981.
Ana wa waladi (My Son and I, novel). Cairo: Dar al-Ta'lif, 1982.
al-Mar'a al-rahima: Misr (The Merciful Woman: Egypt, play). N.p.: n.p., n.d.

Alem, Raja ('Alim, Raja' Muhammad) (1963–), Saudi short-story writer, novelist, and playwright born in Mecca. She received a B.A. in English literature from King 'Abd al-'Aziz University in Jeddah in 1983. She is a teacher at the Training Center for Kindergarten Teachers in Jeddah. She received an honorary prize from the Spanish Arab Institute in the Ibn Tufayl competition in 1985.
Arba'a/sifr (Four/Zero, novel). Jeddah: Literary Club, 1987.
al-Mawt al-akhir li-l-mumaththil (The Final Death of the Actor, play). Beirut: Dar al-Adab, 1987.
al-Raqs 'ala sinn al-shawka (Dancing on the Tip of the Thorn, play). Beirut: Dar al-Adab, 1987.
Thuqub fi-l-zahr (Holes in the Back, play). Beirut: Dar al-Adab, 1987.
Nahr al-hayawan (River of Animals, short stories). Beirut: Dar al-Adab, 1994.
Tariq al-harir (The Silk Road, novel). Beirut and Casablanca: Arab Cultural Center, 1995.
Masra ya raqib (Happy, O Censor, novel). Beirut and Casablanca: Arab Cultural Center, 1997.
Sidi Wahdanah (My Thousand and One Nights, novel). Beirut and Casablanca: Arab Cultural Center, 1998.

'Ali, Buthayna (?–), Egyptian novelist.
Risala min jundi (Letter from a Soldier, novel). Cairo: n.p., n.d.

al-'Ali, Fatima Yusuf (1953–), Kuwaiti short-story writer and novelist. She received a B.A. in Arabic from Cairo University in 1987 and a graduate degree in Arabic literature from the same institution in 1989. She is a member of the Authors' League in Kuwait, the Kuwaiti Journalists' Association, the Human Rights Organization, the Women's Social and Cultural Association in Kuwait, and the Young Woman's Club in Kuwait. She has published a work of non-fiction: *'Abd Allah al-Salim: rajul 'ash wa lam yamut* ('Abd Allah al-Salim: A Man Who Lived and Did Not Die, 1970).
Wujuh fi-l-ziham (Faces in the Crowd, novel). Kuwait: Government of Kuwait Press, 1971.
Wajhuha watan (Her Face Is a Homeland, short stories). Kuwait: distributed by al-Rabi'an, 1995.
Dima' 'ala wajh al-qamar (Blood on the Face of the Moon, short stories). Cairo: General Egyptian Book Organization, 1998.
Awja' imra'a la tahda' (Ceaseless Pains of a Woman, short stories). Cairo: Dar Sharqiyat, 1999.

'Ali, Sayyida Faruq Muhammad (1967–), Egyptian poet born in Bani Suwayf. She has a B.A. in Arabic from Dar al-'Ulum.
Karakib (Stuff, poetry). Cairo: General Authority for Culture Palaces, 1999.

'Ali, Zahiya Muhammad (1964–1986), Libyan poet and short-story writer born in al-Marj. She studied at the media department at Qaryunis University.
Qisas qasira (Short Stories, short stories). Tripoli, Libya: al-Dar al-Jamahiriya, 1983.
al-Rahil ila marafi' al-hulm (Leaving for the Dream's Docks, texts). Libya: n.p., 1989.

A

'Allam, Najla' (1969–), Egyptian short-story writer. She has a B.A. in business from Ain Shams University and a degree in theater studies from the same institution. She works at the General Authority for Culture Palaces. She is a researcher at the University of Chicago.

Afyal saghira lam tamut ba'd (Little Elephants That Haven't Yet Died, short stories). Cairo: General Egyptian Book Organization, 1996.

'Allush, Layla (1948–), Palestinian poet and painter born in Amman. She lives in Jerusalem. She went to school in Amman and Jerusalem. She studied at the Beirut Arab University. She is a teacher and has staged painting exhibitions in Ramallah, Jericho, Haifa, Gaza, and Beirut.

Bahar 'ala-l-jurh al-maftuh (Spice on the Open Wound, poetry). Jerusalem: al-Wataniya Press, 1971.

Sinin al-qaht ya qalbi (Years of Drought, My Heart, poetry). Jerusalem: Dar al-Aytam Press, 1972.

Awwal al-mawwal ah (The Mawwal Starts with Oh, poetry). Jerusalem: Salah al-Din Publications, 1974.

al-Mawt wa-l-'ishq (Death and Passion, poetry). al-Sharq Cooperative Press, 1977.

al-Quds fi-l-qalb (Jerusalem in the Heart, poetry). Amman: Maktabat Amman, 1980.

al-Masafa bayn fuhat al-bunduqiya wa 'uyun habibi (The Distance Between the Rifle's Mouth and My Lover's Eyes, poetry). Amman: Office of Culture and Arts, 1983.

al-'Alyan, Qumasha 'Abd al-Rahman (?–), Saudi short-story writer born in Riyadh. She received a B.A. in chemistry from King Sa'ud University in 1991. She is a teacher and student counselor. She has worked as an editor for the Kuwaiti magazine, *al-Majalis*. She has received several awards for playwriting from King Sa'ud University.

Khata' fi hayati (A Mistake in My Life,

short stories). Riyadh: Tuhama Publishing and Distribution, 1992.

al-Zawja al-'adhra' (The Virgin Wife, short stories). al-Jum'a Press, 1993.

Dumu' fi laylat al-zifaf (Tears on the Wedding Night, short stories). N.p.: n.p., 1997.

'Amara, Lami'a 'Abbas (1929–), Iraqi poet born in Baghdad. She graduated from the Higher Teachers' Institute in 1950 and was appointed a teacher at the Primary Teachers' Institute. She began writing poetry at age fifteen and was at one point a classmate of the poet Badr Shakir al-Sayyab. She maintained cultural relations with many Arab poets and men of letters and exchanged letters with the exile poet Iliya Abi Madi. She was a member of the administrative organization of the Authors' Union in 1960. Iraqi singer Kazim al-Sahir has put some of her poetry to music.

'Awdat al-rabi' (Return of Spring, poetry). Baghdad: Iraqi Authors' Union Press, 1962.

Aghani 'Ishtar ('Ishtar's Songs, poetry). Beirut: al-Tijariya Press, 1969.

Yusammunahu al-hubb (They Call It Love, poetry). Beirut: Dar al-'Awda, 1971.

'Iraqiya (Iraqi Woman, poetry). Beirut: Dar al-'Awda, 1972.

Law anba'ani al-'arraf (If the Fortune-teller Told Me, poetry). Beirut: Arab Institute for Research and Publishing, 1980.

al-Bu'd al-akhir (The Final Dimension, poetry). Beirut: n.p., 1988.

Bi-l-'ammiya (Colloquially Speaking, poetry). N.p.: privately published, 1999.

'Amayra, Jamila (1963–), Jordanian short-story writer born in the village of Zayy in al-Salt. She was educated in Amman's schools.

Sarkhat al-bayad (The Shriek of the Emptiness, short stories). Amman: Dar al-Azmina, 1993.

Sayyidat al-kharif (Autumn Woman, short stories). Beirut: Arab Institute for Research and Publishing, 1999.

Amin, Badi'a (?–), Iraqi short-story writer and researcher. She has a B.A. in English literature from Baghdad University and a degree in plastic arts from the Institute of Fine Arts. She has published several books and studies on Zionism.

al-'Araba wa-l-matar (The Cart and the Rain, short stories). Baghdad: Dar al-Shu'un al-Thaqafiya, 1995.

Amin, Muna (1937–), Egyptian novelist and short-story writer. She published a collection of essays entitled *al-Fikr hamsa* (Thought Is a Whisper) in 1984.

Min al-fikr dharra (A Mote of Thought, short stories). Cairo: n.p., 1979.

Rifqan ayyuha-l-shawq (Take It Easy, Desire, novel). Cairo: Maktabat al-Nahda al-Misriya, 1982.

Muna Amin wa marhaban ayyuha-l-hubb (Muna Amin and Hello Love, novel). Cairo: Maktabat al-Nahda al-Misriya, 1983.

Rifqan ayyuha-l-hubb (Take It Easy, Love, short stories). Cairo: Maktabat al-Nahda al-Misriya, 1983.

Amin, Nura (1970–), Egyptian short-story writer and novelist born in Cairo. She received a B.A. in French from Cairo University in 1992. She is a teaching assistant at the Center for Languages and Translation at the Academy of Arts. She has translated several works from English and French into Arabic. She was awarded the short-story prize from the General Authority for Culture Palaces in 1996 for "Turuqat muhaddaba" and a prize for the best novel by writers under age forty from the Andalusiya Foundation for Culture and Arts in 1999.

Jumal i'tiradiya (Parenthetical Clauses, short stories). Cairo: Anglo Egyptian Bookstore, 1995.

Turuqat muhaddaba (Convex Roads, short stories). Cairo: Dar al-Thaqafa al-Jadida, 1995.

Qamis wardi farigh (An Empty Pink Shirt, novel). Cairo: Dar Sharqiyat, 1997.

Halat al-ta'attuf (Cases of Sympathy, short stories). Cairo: General Authority for Culture Palaces, 1998.

al-Amin, Safiya al-Shaykh (?–?), Sudanese writer

Iha' (Inspiration, poetry). Beirut: Dar al-Thaqafa, n.d.

'Amir, Amal 'Abd al-Karim (1964–), Egyptian colloquial poet born in Cairo. She has a secretarial degree and works for the Ministry of Electricity's Agency for New and Renewable Energy.

al-Shakmajiya (The Jewelry Box, poetry). Cairo: General Authority for Culture Palaces, 1999.

Al-Amir, Daisy (al-Amir, Daisy) (1935–), Iraqi short-story writer born in Alexandria. She lives in Beirut. She received a B.A. in Arabic language and literature in Baghdad and then began studying sculpture at the Institute of Fine Arts in Baghdad. She taught high school and later in the teachers' institute in Basra. She was a press attaché at the Iraqi embassy in Beirut and the director of the Iraqi Cultural Center in Beirut. She published the letters of Lebanese poet Khalil Hawi as *Rasa'il al-hubb wa-l-mawt* (Letters of Love and Death). She is currently writing her memoirs. Her short-story collection, *'Ala la'ihat al-intizar*, has been translated into English.

al-Balad al-ba'id alladhi tuhibbuh (The Distant Country You Love, short stories). Beirut: Dar al-Adab, 1964.

Thumma ta'ud al-mawja (And the Wave Returns, short stories). Beirut: Dar al-Adab, 1969.

al-Bayt al-'Arabi al-sa'id (The Happy Arab Home, short stories). Beirut: Dar al-'Awda, 1975.

Fi duwwamat al-hubb wa-l-karahiya (In the Vortex of Love and Hate, short stories). Beirut: Dar al-Nidal, 1979.

Wu'ud li-l-bay' (Promises for Sale, short stories). Beirut: Arab Institute for Research and Publishing, 1981.

'Ala la'ihat al-intizar (*The Waiting List*, short stories). Baghdad: Bayt Sin Books, 1988.
Jirahat tajmil al-zaman (Facelifts for Time, short stories). Beirut: Arab Institute for Research and Publishing, 1997.

'Amir, Madiha (?–), Egyptian poet born in Cairo. She has a B.A. in Arabic language and literature from Ain Shams University. She is the director of the general literature deparment at the Ministry of Culture's National Center for the Arts and Humanities. She is also the editor of the book series, al-Mawahib. She published a work of non-fiction, *Qiyam fanniya fi shi'r Salah 'Abd al-Sabur* (Artistic Values in the Poetry of Salah 'Abd al-Sabur), in 1984.
Tanahhudat 'ala-l-nahr (Sighs on the River, poetry). Cairo: General Egyptian Book Organization, 1981.
Ayna yadhhab al-hubb (Where Does Love Go, novel). Cairo: General Egyptian Book Organization, 1998.

'Amir, Ni'mat (?–), Egyptian poet.
Amwaj al-Suways (The Waves of Suez, poetry). Cairo: Anglo Egyptian Bookstore, 1968.
Zuhur al-nasr wa-l-Suways (Flowers of Victory and Suez, poetry). Cairo: Kamal Press, 1976.

al-'Ammar, Hissa Ibrahim Muhammad (?–), Saudi short-story writer born in Riyadh. She received a B.A. in English from the Liberal Arts College for Girls under the General Authority for Girls' Education in Riyadh in 1979. She has been a translator at the Ministry of Information since 1988.
al-Ibhar didd al-mustahil (Sailing Against the Impossible, short stories). Riyadh: n.p., 1991.

al-'Amrani, Wafa' (1960–), Moroccan poet born in al-Qasr al-Kabir. She received a B.A. in Arabic literature from Muhammad V University in Rabat in 1982 and an advanced studies degree in modern literature from the same institution in 1984. She is currently preparing an M.A. there. She is a professor at the College of Liberal Arts and Humanities at the Hasan II University in al-Muhammadiya. She received a certificate of merit from the Poeta Association in Salerno, Italy, in 1992 during the Arab Women Poets Forum. She helped organize the fifteenth Jarash Festival in Jordan in 1996 and the thirty-eighth round of the Susa International Festival in Tunisia in 1996. She was elected to the central bureau of the Moroccan Writers' Union for the 1993–1996 session. She has taken part in many cultural and poetry forums, Moroccan, Arab, and international. Her works have been published in several newspapers and periodicals and translated into English, Dutch, and Italian.
al-Ankhab (The Toasts, poetry). Rabat: Moroccan Writers' Union Publications, 1991.
Anin al-a'ali (Moan of the Heights, poetry). Beirut: Dar al-Adab Publications, 1992.
Fitnat al-aqasi (The Seduction of Extremities, poetry and audio cassette). Casablanca: al-Rabita Publications, 1997.

'Anani, 'Ahd Muhammad (?–), Saudi short-story writer born in Jeddah.
Ahdath mukhtasara (Events Abridged, short stories). N.p.: n.p., 1986.
Dhikrayat imra'a (Memoirs of a Woman, short stories). N.p.: n.p., 1987.
al-Rahma ya aba' (Mercy, Fathers, short stories). N.p.: n.p., 1989.
Ana al-rajul (I Am the Man, short stories). N.p.: n.p., 1992.

al-'Anani, Salwa (1947–), Egyptian short-story writer born in Cairo. She received a B.A. in journalism from Cairo University in 1968. She is the deputy editor of the *al-Ahram* weekly magazine supplement and is a member of the Journalists' Syndicate, the Writers' Union, and the International Board on Books for Young People (IBBY). She has published studies and interviews, including *Maw'id wa liqa'* (An Appointment and a Meeting) and *Kalam fi-l-hubb* (Talk About Love).

Ayyami 'ala-l-hawa' (My Days on the Air, autobiography). Cairo: Dar al-Ma'arif, 1977.

al-Amir wa-l-'arusa (The Prince and the Bride, children's literature). Cairo: Ministry of Culture, 1987.

Asatir Misriya qadima (Ancient Egyptian Myths, children's literature). Cairo: General Egyptian Book Organization, 1987.

Hikayat min alf layla (Stories from the Arabian Nights, children's literature). Cairo: Dar al-Lata'if, 1987.

Liqa' al-asdiqa' (A Meeting of Friends, children's literature). Cairo: General Egyptian Book Organization, 1987.

Ma'a al-hukama' al-'Arab (With Arab Sages, children's literature). Cairo: Dar al-Lata'if, 1987.

Muharib silahuhu al-kalima (A Fighter Whose Weapon Is Words, children's literature). Cairo: Dar al-Ma'arif, 1987.

Salam biladi (Peace, My Country, children's literature). Cairo: General Egyptian Book Organization, 1987.

al-Sunbula al-dhahabiya (The Golden Spike of Grain, children's literature). Cairo: General Egyptian Book Organization, 1987.

Tharthara ma'a al-hulm (Chattering with the Dream, short stories). Cairo: General Egyptian Book Organization, 1987.

'Anbar, Safiya (?–), Saudi novelist born in Medina. She lives in al-Dammam. She has a high-school diploma. With her sister, Hayat 'Anbar, she established the Women's Association in al-Dammam. She has published a collection of reflections titled *Awraq muba'thara fi zawba'at al-'umr* (Scattered Papers from the Cyclone of Life).

'Afwan ya Adam (Pardon Me, Adam, novel). Cairo: Dar Misr Press, 1986.

Wahaj, bayn ramad al-sinin (A Blaze Among the Ashes of the Years, novel). Beirut: al-Dar al-'Arabiya li-l-Mawsu'at, 1988.

Jama'atna al-sudfa wa faraqatna al-taqalid (Friendship Joined Us and Traditions Separated Us, novel). Cairo: al-Ahram Press, 1992.

Iftaqadtuk yawm ahbabtuk (I Missed You the Day I Loved You, novel). Cairo: al-Ahram Press, 1993.

Anta hubbi lan naftariq ma'an ila-l-abad (You Are My Love and We Will Never Part, novel). al-Dammam: Dar al-Rawi, 1999.

'Andani, Sabiha (?–), Syrian novelist born in Aleppo.

I'tirafat imra'a fashila (Confessions of an Unsuccessful Woman, novel). Aleppo: Dar al-Ra'id, 1983.

Anwar Abu Khalid (see: Abu Khalid, Arlette)

Anwar, Kalizar (?–), Iraqi short-story writer and novelist. She works at the Nineveh Department of Education.

Bi'r al-banafsaj (The Well of Violet, short stories). Baghdad: Dar al-Shu'un al-Thaqafiya, 1999.

Anwar, Samiya (?–), Egyptian writer.

Qalb laysa min al-zujaj (A Non-glass Heart). Cairo: Dar al-Thaqafa Printing and Publishing, 1992.

Aouad-Basbous, Thérèse ('Awwad-Basbus, Thérèse) (1934–) (see also: Bibliography of Works in French)

Buyut al-'ankabut (Spiderwebs, poetry). Beirut: n.p., 1967.

al-Bakara (The Pulley, play). Beirut: Gallery One Publishers, 1973.

Ana wa-l-hajar (The Stone and I, poetry). Beirut: privately published, 1993.

al-Katiba (The Writer, novel). Beirut: privately published, 1993.

al-'Aqil, Widad (?–), Yemeni poet.

Ahat 'ala jidar al-samt (Ahs on the Wall of Silence, poetry). N.p.: n.p., n.d.

'Arabawi, Sharifa (1950–), Tunisian short-story writer born in Nahala who currently resides in Tunis. She graduated from the English department at the Bourguiba Institute of Modern Languages in Tunis.

She is a member of the Story Club and the Tunisian Writers' Union.
al-Sa'b (The Difficult, short stories). Tunis: al-Akhla' Publications, 1983.

'Arida, Siham (1947–), Palestinian short-story writer and playwright born in Haifa. She lives in Jenin in the West Bank. She has a B.A. in Arabic from Cairo University. She is a teacher.
Durub al-shatat wa qisas ukhra (The Paths of Diaspora and Other Stories, short stories). N.p.: Palestinian Center for Culture and Media, 1995.
al-Ru'ya (The Vision, play). N.p.: n.p., n.d.
Masrah al-madrasa (The School Stage, play). N.p.: n.p., n.d.
Jamal al-mahamil (The Camel, short stories). N.p.: n.p., n.d.

'Arisha, Sumaya (1954–), Egyptian short-story writer. She attended a vocational school and took classes in film editing. She works as a film editor and is writing a screenplay. Two of her television scripts were filmed and aired as "al-Muttahama islah" (The Accused: Reform).
Judhur mutanathira (Scattered Roots, short stories). Cairo: General Egyptian Book Organization, 1992.

Armaniyus, Ikhlas 'Ata Allah (?–), Egyptian short-story writer born in Cairo. She received a B.A. in business in 1986, a diploma in art criticism from the Public Arts Academy in 1994, and a B.A. in journalism from the College of Communications at Cairo University in 1997. She heads the literature desk at *Watani* newspaper and is a member of the Journalists' Syndicate and the Writers' Union.
al-Shahid (The Witness, short stories). Cairo: General Authority for Culture Palaces, 1997.

al-Arna'ut, 'A'isha (1946–), Syrian poet of Albanian origin born in Damascus. She received a B.A. in 1965, a teaching certificate in 1966, a B.A. in French literature

from Damascus University in 1977, a diploma from the Sorbonne in 1985, and a degree in protocol in Paris in 1991. She worked as a teacher and supervised teaching programs for the Ministry of Education from 1969 to 1977. She is a member of the Arab Writers' Union and several literary judging committees. She began to publish in newspapers and literary magazines in 1960. She received the first prize in a short-story writing competition in Lebanon in 1961. Her poetry has been translated into English, Serbo-Croation, and Albanian. She also has published a collection of poetry in French, *Projet d'un poème*.
Projet d'un poème (Paris: privately published, 1979).
al-Hariq (The Fire, poetry). Beirut: Dar al-Kalima, 1981.
'Ala ghimd waraqa tasqut (On a Sheath of Falling Paper, poetry). Damascus: Arab Writers' Union, 1986.
al-Watan al-muharram (The Forbidden Homeland, poetry). Cairo: Dar al-Fikr Publishers, 1987.
Farasha 'ala-l-kitf (A Butterfly on the Shoulder, poetry). N.p.: n.p., n.d.
al-Qamar al-muhannat (The Mummified Moon, poetry). N.p.: n.p., n.d.

Arna'ut, Raja' (?–), Syrian poet and journalist born in Damascus. She is a journalist in Algeria and writes children's literature.
Mawj (Wave, poetry). Algeria: al-Dar al-Wataniya Books, n.d.
al-Namla (The Ant, children's literature). Algeria: al-Dar al-Wataniya Books, n.d.
al-Sahaba al-akhira (The Last Cloud, children's literature). Algeria: al-Dar al-Wataniya Books, n.d.

Arqash, Madeleine (?–), Lebanese novelist. She has also written three works of non-fiction: *al-Adab wa-l-lugha* (Literature and Language, 1942), *Rasa'il Mayy* (Mayy's Letters, 1948), and *Ukhtukum fa'ansifuha* (Your Sister, So Treat Her with Justice, 1948).

Muna: qissa fi samim al-hayah al-Lubnaniya (Muna: A Story from the Heart of Lebanese Life, novel). Beirut: al-Ittihad Press, 1952.

Taqaddum fi rihab al-haykal (Advancing in the Expanse of the Temple, novel). Beirut: n.p., 1955.

Arqash, Sufi (?–) , Lebanese short-story writer. She wrote several articles in *Sawt al-mar'a* in 1946. She is the daughter of writer Madeleine Arqash.

al-Kanisa al-qariba wa qisas ukhra (The Nearby Church and Other Stories, short stories). Beirut: Dar al-Ghad, 1969.

al-'Arusi, 'Afaf (?–), Egyptian novelist.

al-Muhawala al-ula (The First Attempt, novel). Cairo: al-Dar al-Qawmiya Press for Printing and Publishing, 1966.

al-As'ad, Su'ad (?–), Lebanese poet and short story writer.

Ghadan sa'a'ud (Tomorrow I Shall Return, short stories). Beirut: Arab Institute for Research and Publishing, 1983.

Ishraqat fajr (Dawn Rays, texts). Beirut: Arab Institute for Research and Publishing, 1983.

al-'Ashiq, Fayha' (1961–), Syrian poet born in Aleppo. She received a law degree from Damascus University in 1985. She works as an attorney.

'Indama tahlum Finus (When Venus Dreams, poetry). N.p.: n.p., 1993.

al-'Ashmawi, Fawziya (?–), Egyptian short-story writer born in Alexandria. She lives in Switzerland. She completed her high-school education in Alexandria in 1961 and received a B.A. in the humanities from Alexandria University in 1965. She earned an M.A. from the University of Geneva in 1972 and a Ph.D. in Arabic language and Islamic civilization from the same university in 1983. She has taught Arabic and Islamic studies at the University of Geneva since 1979. She

is an active member of several associations in Geneva, including the Islam and Arabs Association (since 1982), the Arabic and Islamic Studies Association, and the Switzerland and Islamic Culture Association. She has published several academic studies about Islam in English and French.

al-Ghurba fi-l-watan (Exile in the Homeland, short stories). Cairo: Maktabat Madbuli, 1995.

al-Qahira 60 (Cairo 60, short stories). Cairo: Maktabat Madbuli, 1996.

Ashour, Radwa ('Ashur, Radwa) (1946–), Egyptian novelist, short-story writer, and literary critic. She graduated from high school in 1963. She obtained a B.A. in English in 1967 and an M.A. in comparative literature from Cairo University in 1972, and a Ph.D. in African-American literature from the University of Massachusetts in 1975. She is a professor of English at Ain Shams University. She has published several critical studies and essays in both Arabic and English, including: *al-Tariq ila-l-khayma al-ukhra: dirasa fi a'mal Ghassan Kanafani* (The Road to the Other Tent: A Study of the Works of Ghassan Kanafani, 1977), *al-Tabi' yanhad: al-riwaya fi gharb Afriqiya* (The Rise of the Subaltern: The Novel in West Africa, 1980), and *Gibran and Blake*, 1978. The General Egyptian Book Organization awarded her the best novel prize in 1994 for *Gharnata* (Part 1 of *Thulathiyat Gharnata* ['The Granada Trilogy']). She received first prize in 1995 at the first Book Fair for Arab Women for *Thulathiyat Gharnata*.

al-Rihla: ayyam taliba fi Amrika (The Journey: A Student's Days in America, memoir). Beirut: Dar al-Adab, 1983.

Hajar dafi' (A Warm Stone, novel). Cairo: Dar al-Mustaqbal, 1985.

Khadija wa Sawsan (Khadija and Sawsan, novel). Cairo: Dar al-Hilal, 1989.

Ra'ayt al-nakhl (I Saw the Date Palms, short stories). Cairo: General Egyptian Book Organization, 1989.

Siraj (Lamp, novel). Cairo: Dar al-Hilal, 1992.

Gharnata (*Granada: A Novel*, novel). Cairo: Dar al-Hilal, 1994.

Maryama wa-l-rahil (Maryama and the Departure, parts 2 and 3 of The Granada Trilogy, novel). Cairo: Dar al-Hilal, 1995.

Atyaf (Specters, novel). Cairo: al-Hilal Novels, 1999.

al-Ashqar, In'am (1950–), Lebanese poet born in the village of al-Mitaylib. She has published several poems in *al-Udisiya* and other newspapers.

Sakrat al-hubb (The Intoxication of Love, colloquial poetry). Jounieh: al-Bulisiya Press, 1984.

Abad al-hubb (The Eternity of Love, colloquial poetry). Beirut: Mukhtarat, 1987.

Wa yabqa al-hubb (And Love Endures, colloquial poetry). Beirut: Mukhtarat, 1995.

Ashrawi, Ibtisam (?–), Moroccan poet born in Asila.

Lu'bat al-zill (Play of Shadows, poetry). Asila: Alumni Association of al-Imam al-Asili High School, 1998.

al-'Asimi, Malika (Rim Husam) (1946–), Moroccan poet born in Marrakech. She has a B.A. in Arabic literature and a graduate degree. She is currently preparing a state Ph.D. in literature. She is a university professor and a researcher at the University Institute for Academic Research at Muhammad V University in Rabat. Before that she was a high-school principal and an inspector of Arabic language and literature at the secondary level. She is a member of the Moroccan Writers' Union and a founder of the union's branch in Marrakech. She is the president of the Sada Hawwa' Association, one of the oldest women's groups in Moroccan. She is a member of several professional, cultural, women's, and social organizations. She is a leading member of the Independence Party. She served as the deputy mayor of Marrakech for sixteen years. She has participated in many cultural, social, and political conferences in Morocco and abroad, as well as in several Moroccan, Arab, and international poetry festivals. She published *al-Ikhtiyar*, a newspaper, and a magazine by the same name. Her non-fiction works include *al-Mar'a wa ishkaliyat al-dimuqratiya: qira'a fi-l-waqi' wa-l-khitab* (Women and the Problematic of Democracy: A Reading of Reality and Discourse, 1991, a sociopolitical study), *Jami' al-fana' jami' al-katabiyin* (al-Fana' Mosque, al-Katabiyin Mosque, 1993, urban anthropology), and *Su'al al-'asr (al-dhat wa-l-akhar)* (Question of the Age: The Self and the Other, 2000). Her poems have been translated into French, Spanish, Italian, Dutch, Chinese, Macedonian, Flemish, German, and Portuguese. She is also known as Rim Husam.

Aswat hanjara mayyita (Sounds of Dead Throat, poetry). Rabat: Kitab al-'Ilm, al-Silsila al-Jadida, 1980.

Kitabat kharij aswar al-'alam (Writings from Outside the World's Walls, poetry). Baghdad: Dar al-Shu'un al-Thaqafiya, Afaq 'Arabiya, 1987.

Shay' lahu asma' (A Thing With Names, poetry). Casablanca: Arab Foundation for Publishing and Art, 1997.

Asiri, Iman (1952–), Bahraini poet born in Manama. She has a high-school degree and graduated from the Higher Teachers' Institute in 1986. She is a teacher and has been published in the Bahraini, Iraqi, and Emirati press.

Hadhi ana al-qubbara (Here I Am, a Lark, poetry). Beirut: Dar al-Farabi, 1982.

'Assaf, Layla Muhammad Fath Allah (1958–), Lebanese poet born in Sidon. She received a B.A. in painting and photography from the College of Fine Arts at the Lebanese University in 1990, as well as a teaching certificate in the natural sciences from the College of Education at the Lebanese University the same year. She was a member of the Lebanese Writers' Union from 1995 to 1997 and a member of the Artists' Association. She worked as a middle school and high school teacher in Lebanon from 1982 to 1992. Since 1992, she has taught in Riyadh, Saudi Arabia, at the Najd School. She has published poems in *al-Safir*, *al-Nahar*, and *al-Tariq*.

Zill la yadhub (An Indissoluble Shadow, poetry). Beirut: Dar al-Hamra' Printing and Publishing, 1991.

'Assaf, Rajwa (1948–), Palestinian poet born in Jenin and educated in its schools. She enrolled in the Jordanian University in 1970. She works in teaching. She is active in charitable and cultural associations.

al-Khubz fi baladi (The Bread in My Country, poetry). Amman: Maktabat Amman, 1969.

al-'Assal, Fathiya (1933–), Egyptian playwright born in Cairo. She audited classes at the Screenplay Institute. From 1957 to 1967 she wrote for radio. Since 1967 she has written television dramas. She is a boardmember of the Egyptian Women Writers' Union and a member of the Union of Filmmakers, the Cairo Atelier, the Writers' Union, the Filmmakers' Syndicate, the Actors' Syndicate, the Union of Progressive Women, and the Committee to Defend National Culture. She is a member of the secretariat of the al-Tajammu' Party and the secretary of the party's writers' and artists' bureau. She was awarded a prize at the Lahore Conference in 1978 and a theater prize from the College of Liberal Arts at Alexandria University. She also received a prize from Arab Television for the drama, "Hiya wa-l-mustahil" (She and the Impossible). Her plays have been translated into Russian, French, and Finnish, and she has written many works for radio and television. Although her play was published in 1997 as *Jawaz safar*, it was first staged as *al-Basbur*.

Nisa' bila aqni'a (Women Without Masks, play). Cairo: Dar al-Thaqafa al-Jadida, 1981.

al-Bayn bayn (It Passes, play). Cairo: General Egyptian Book Organization, 1989.

Sijn al-nisa' (The Women's Prison, play). Cairo: General Egyptian Book Organization, 1993.

Jawaz safar (Passport, play). Cairo: General Egyptian Book Organization, 1997.

al-'Assal, Najiba (1921–1992), Egyptian novelist. With Ihsan Kamal and Huda Jad, she founded a weekly literary salon for young writers at Dar al-Udaba' in 1969. She was a member of the Committee for Cultural Integration in the Authors' Association and a member of the Artists' Association. She had two radio programs, "Yawmiyat Jadda" (Diaries of a Grandmother) and "Li-l-kibar wa-l-sighar" (For Young and Old). Her novel, *Bayt al-ta'a*, received a prize from the Story Club and the al-Qabbani Prize.

Bayt al-ta'a (House of Obedience, novel). Cairo: Rose al-Yusuf Foundation, 1962.

al-Gha'iba (The Absent One, short stories). Cairo: al-Dar al-Qawmiya Printing and Publishing, 1962.

al-A'maq al-ba'ida (The Distant Depths, novel). Cairo: Dar al-Hilal, 1964.

al-Hasa wa-l-jabal (The Pebble and the Mountain, novel). Cairo: al-Dar al-Qawmiya Printing and Publishing, 1966.

Satr maghlut (A Mistake in the Knitting, short-story anthology), co-edited with Huda Jad. Cairo: General Egyptian Book Organization, 1971.

Kull hadha li-annaha Hawwa' (All of This Because She Is Eve, short stories). Cairo: General Egyptian Book Organization, 1981.

al-Yamama al-hakima (The Wise Dove, children's literature). Cairo: al-Sha'b Publications, 1982.

Taj al-dhahab (The Golden Crown, children's literature). Cairo: Dar al-Hilal, 1985.

Wa tarakat hams al-sukun (And She Left the Whisper of Silence, short stories). Cairo: Dar al-Hilal, 1985.

al-Kura bi-titkallim (The Ball Speaks, children's literature). Cairo: Dar al-Hilal, 1987.

al-Amir wa-l-liss (The Prince and the Thief, children's literature). Cairo: Dar al-Hilal, 1988.

al-Tha'lab al-makkar wa-l-dhi'b al-maghrur (The Sly Fox and the Vain Wolf, children's literature). Cairo: Dar al-Hilal, 1989.

al-Ha'it al-rabi' (The Fourth Wall, novel). Cairo: General Egyptian Book Organization, 1990.

al-Tha'lab fat (The Fox Went By, children's literature). Cairo: Dar al-Hilal, 1990.

al-Asyuti, Lawra (?–), Egyptian poet born in Asyut. She wrote poetry in French and later in Arabic.

Marfa' li-l-dhikrayat (A Mooring for Memories, poetry). Cairo: n.p., 1990.

Misr al-khalida (Egypt the Immortal, poetry). Cairo: General Egyptian Book Organization, 1990.

'Atiya, Farida Yusuf (1867–1917), Lebanese novelist born in Tripoli. She was educated and later taught at the American College. She was fluent in both Arabic and English. She translated Edward Bulwer Lytton's novel, *The Last Days of Pompeii* (*al-Rawda al-nadira fi ayyam Pompeii al-akhira*, 1981).

Bayn al-'arshayn (Between the Two Thrones, novel). Tripoli: al-Najah Press, 1912.

'Atiya, Hana' (1959–), Egyptian short-story writer. She received her B.A. from the Higher Institute for Cinema, screenwriting department, in 1988. She is a writer and screenwriter. She is a member of the Filmmakers' Syndicate. She has published short stories in *Adab wa naqd*, *al-Qahira*, *al-Sharq al-Awsat*, and London-based *al-Hayat*.

Shurufat qariba (Nearby Balconies, short stories). Cairo: Dar Sharqiyat, 1993.

Hiya wa khadimatuha (She and Her Maidservant, short stories). Cairo: General Authority for Culture Palaces, 1997.

al-Atrash, Leila (al-Atrash, Layla) (1951–), Palestinian novelist and short-story writer born in Bayt Sahur. She went to school there until the 1967 defeat, when she left and continued her schooling in Amman. She received a B.A. in Arabic literature from the Beirut Arab University in 1972, followed by a degree in law. She is an announcer on Qatari television and she produces cultural programs. She received three cultural television awards from Cairo, Carthage, and the Foundation for Joint Programming in the Gulf. She has published many cultural essays.

Wa tushriq gharban (And It Rises in the West, novel). Beirut: Arab Institute for Research and Publishing, 1987.

Imra'a li-l-fusul al-khamsa (*A Woman of Five Seasons*, novel). Beirut: Arab Institute for Research and Publishing, 1990.

Laylatan wa zill imra'a (Two Nights and a Woman's Shadow, novel). Beirut: Arab Institute for Research and Publishing, 1998.

Sahil al-masafat (Whinny of the Distances, novel). Cairo: Dar Sharqiyat, 1999.

Yawm 'adi wa qisas ukhra (A Regular Day and Other Stories, short stories). Beirut: Arab Institute for Research and Publishing, n.d.

'Atsha, Zayda (1964–), Palestinian poet born in Daliyat al-Karmel, near Haifa. She received her early education in her hometown and continued her studies at the Teachers' Academy in Haifa. She is a teacher.

al-Dumu' al-bakiya (The Weeping Tears, poetry). Daliyat al-Karmel: Dar al-'Imad, 1995.

al-'Attar, Najah (?–), Syrian short-story writer and literary critic born in Damascus. She graduated from high school in 1950 and received a B.A. in Arabic literature from Damascus University in 1954 and a Ph.D. from Edinburgh University in 1958. She taught high school and then worked in the translation department at the Syrian Ministry of Culture. She became the director of that department and later the minister of culture (1976–2000). She has published literary studies on poetry and theater, including *Shu'ara' mu'asirun* (Contemporary Poets) and *Adab al-harb* (War Literature, with Hanna Mina, 1976). She published a collection of essays, *Min mufakkirat al-ayyam* (From the Notebook of Days). Her other non-fiction works include *As'ilat al-hayah* (Life Questions, 1982), *Kalimat mulawwana* (Tinted Words, 1986), and *Isbanya wa Himingway wa-l-thiran* (Spain, Hemingway, and the Bulls).

Man yadhkur tilka-l-ayyam (Who Remembers Those Days, short stories, with Hanna Mina). Damascus: Ministry of Culture, 1974.

Attar, Samar (al-'Attar, Samar) (1940–), Syrian novelist born in Damascus. She received a Ph.D. in comparative literature from Binghamton University in the U.S. and has taught at universities in Canada, the U.S., Algeria, Germany, and Australia. She writes in Arabic and English. Her non-fiction works include *al-Bitriq li-l-sha'irat* (The Penguin to the Poets) and *al-'Arabiya al-mu'asira* (Contemporary Arabic), an introduction for non-native speakers.

Lina: lawhat fatah Dimashqiya (*Lina: A Portrait of a Damascene Girl*, novel). Beirut: Dar al-Afaq al-Jadida, 1982.

al-Bayt fi sahat 'Arnus (*The House on Arnus Square*, novel). Australia: Charbel Baini Publications, 1988.

Khawatir min asfal al-'alam (Reflections from the Bottom of the World, novel). Sydney: Ralya Press, 1999.

al-'Attas, Huda (1970–), Yemeni short-story writer born in Daw'an in Hadramawt. She resides in Aden. *Al-Hikma* magazine published some of her short stories in 1997 and the story, "Adwar" (Roles), in 1998. She received the al-'Afif Cultural Prize in 1997. She currently works in the Cultural Office and has made several cultural contributions.

Hajis ruh, hajis jasad (Anxiety of the Spirit, Anxiety of the Flesh, short stories). Aden: Ministry of Culture and Tourism, 1995.

'Attaw, Walida (?–), Syrian novelist born in Aleppo.

Imra'a la ta'rif al-khawf (A Fearless Woman, novel). Damascus: Dar al-Kunuz al-Adabiya, 1991.

al-'Atum, Lamis (1951–), Jordanian poet and novelist born in al-Zarqa'. She is a journalist.

Adabiyat imra'a rafida (The Writings of a Dismissive Woman, poetry). Amman: Dar Tubas, 1994.

'At'ut, Samiya (1958–), Palestinian short-story writer born in Nablus. She lives in Amman. She received her early education in Nablus schools and received a B.A. in modern mathematics from al-Mustansiriya University in Baghdad in 1979. She is a computer programmer, systems analyst, and researcher for the Arab Bank in Amman. In addition to fiction, she writes articles and critical studies and has published in newspapers and magazines such as the London-based *al-Manabir* and *al-Naqid* and the Jordanian *Najmat al-Maghrib* and *Afkar*. She is a member of the League of Jordanian Writers. She was co-recipient of the first prize in the Su'ad al-Sabah youth competition for literary and scientific works in 1989. She also was awarded a fiction prize by the League of Jordanian Writers in 1986.

Judran tamtass al-sawt (Sound-absorbent Walls, short stories). Amman: al-Sharq al-Awsat, 1986.

Tuqus untha (A Woman's Rituals, short stories). Cairo and Amman: General Egyptian Book Organizattion and Arab Thought Forum, 1990.

Tarbush Muzart (Mozart's Tarboosh, short stories). Beirut: Arab Institute for Research and Publishing, 1998.

Averino, Alexandra Khuri (1873–1937), Lebanese pioneer and poet born in Beirut. She was educated at convent schools in Lebanon before moving to Alexandria, Egypt, where she studied Arabic and married an Italian. She established the monthly magazine, *Anis al-jalis*, in Alexandria (1898–

1908) and the French-language *Lotus*. She has many published poems and also translated the story, "Shaqa' al-ummahat" (The Hardship of Mothers), from French. She was close to Khedive 'Abbas Hilmi and later with the English. After the First World War, her papers were confiscated and she was ordered to leave Egypt. She went to England and died in London.

Amanat al-sha'b (The Trust of the People, play). N.p.: n.p., n.d.

'Awad, Amal Farah (1968–), Egyptian poet. She received a B.A. in Arabic from Cairo University in 1990. She worked in journalism from 1991 to 1996 as a cultural editor for *al-Kifah al-'Arabi* magazine. She writes poetry, children's stories, television screenplays, and children's songs. She has received several prizes from the General Authority for Culture Palaces.

Ghazala wa sayyad (A Gazelle and a Hunter, children's literature). Cairo: Dar al-Shuruq, 1998.

Muthallith wa da'ira (A Triangle and a Circle, children's literature). Cairo: Dar al-Shuruq, 1999.

'Awad, Nayfa (1959–), Palestinian poet born in Kafr Yasif. She attended school in Bethlehem. She has been an actress at the al-Karma Theater and currently works at the Tales of Hamama and Zaghlul Children's Theater.

al-Bahth 'an safar al-rijal (Look for the Book of Men, poetry). Shafa 'Amr: Dar al-Mashriq, 1986.

Rijal hawl shams al-nahar (Men Around the Day's Sun, poetry). Shafa 'Amr: Dar al-Mashriq, 1987.

al-'Awadi, Hissa (1956–), Qatari poet and short-story writer born in Doha. She studied radio and television at Cairo University (1984–1985) and completed her studies at New York State University. She has been the head of family programming for Qatar television. She writes children's literature and was previously an editor for *Hamad* and *Sahar* magazines.

She was also an editor for "Iftah ya simsim" (Sesame Street).

Unshudati (1) (My Anthem 1, children's songs). N.p.: n.p., 1983.

Unshudati (2) (My Anthem 2, children's songs). Qatar: Qatar National Press, 1987.

Kalimat al-lahn al-awwal (Words of the First Melody, poetry). Doha: Ministry of Information, Deptartment of Culture and Arts, 1988.

al-Shams la tazal na'ima (The Sun Is Still Sleeping, children's literature). N.p.: n.p., 1995.

Hawl ma'idat al-ahlam (Around the Table of Dreams, children's literature). Beirut: Dar al-'Awda, 1996.

Fi daw' al-qamar (In the Moonlight, children's literature). N.p.: n.p., 1996.

Kharuf al-'id (The Holiday Sheep, children's literature). N.p.: n.p., 1996.

Nura wa rasm al-hinna' (Nura and the Henna Drawing, children's literature). Beirut: Dar al-'Awda, 1996.

Yasamin (Yasamin, children's literature). N.p.: n.p., 1996.

al-Ghazala li-man? (Who Owns the Gazelle?, children's literature). N.p.: n.p., 1997.

al-Atfal yuhibbun al-ghuyum (Children Love the Clouds, children's literature). N.p.: n.p., 1998.

Lulu yanhad min jadid (Lulu Rises Up Again, children's literature). N.p.: n.p., 1998.

Milad (Birth, poetry). Qatar: n.p., 1998.

Sani'at al-ahlam (The Maker of Dreams, children's literature). N.p.: n.p., 1998.

al-A'waj, Zaynab (?–), Algerian poet. She received a state Ph.D. in humanities and is a researcher in Algiers. She founded and managed the Dafatir Nisa'iya series, produced by a research group on women's issues. The first book in that series was published in 1991. Her non-fiction works include *al-Simat al-waqi'iya fi-l-tajriba al-shi'riya bi-l-Jaza'ir* (Realism in Experimental Poetry in Algeria, 1985).

Ya anta! Man minna yakrah al-shams? (You There! Who Among Us Hates the

Sun?, poetry). Damascus: Arab Writers' Union Publications, 1979.
Arfud an yudajjan al-atfal (I Reject the Domestication of Children, poetry). Damascus: Ministry of Culture Publications, 1981.

al-A'war, Nada Amin (?–), Lebanese short-story writer.
Laytaha sabi (I Wish She Were a Boy, short stories). Beirut: Dar al-Hamra', 1993.
Qarawiyun wa dhikrayat (Villagers and Memories, memoir). Beirut: Dar al-Hamra', 1993.

'Awn, Maggie (?–), Lebanese poet born in Beirut. She received a B.A. in media studies and an M.A. in philosophy. She worked as a radio announcer for the Voice of Lebanon and published several articles in *al-Nahar*. She has also worked as a television announcer at the Lebanese Broadcasting Company and Future Television.
Alf imra'a wa jasad (A Thousand Women and One Body, poetry). Beirut: Mukhtarat, 1995.

'Awni, Jihan Ghazawi (1918–1956), Lebanese short-story writer born in Tripoli. She was educated at the Italian Institute in Tripoli and taught Arabic at several schools from 1946 to 1956. She wrote several articles about Mayy Ziyada and published her work in *Sawt al-mar'a*, *al-Risala*, *al-Adib*, and *al-Adab*.
"Hibat al-qadar" (Gift of Fate, short story). *Sawt al-mar'a*. Beirut: 1951.
"Al'ubat al-hayah" (Life's Plaything, short story). *Sawt al-mar'a*. Beirut: 1952.
"Su'ad" (Su'ad, short story). *Sawt al-mar'a*. Beirut: 1952.

'Awwad, Hanan (1951–), Palestinian poet born in Jerusalem, where she resides. She received a teaching certificate in Ramallah in 1971 and a B.A. in Arabic literature from the Beirut Arab University in 1974. She is the president of the Palestinian branch of the International League of Women for Peace and Freedom and a lecturer at Birzeit University. She has published several critical studies, including a study of Ghassan Kanafani, one on the impact of the *nakba* on the literature of Samira 'Azzam, and one on Palestinian women's poetry. Her other non-fiction works include *Min dami aktub: mawaqif siyasiya* (From My Blood I Write: Political Essays, Jerusalem, 1983) and *al-Faris yuzaff ila-l-watan: mawaqif siyasiya* (The Knight Marches to the Homeland: Political Essays, Acre, 1988).
Ikhtart al-khatar (I Chose Danger, poetry). Jerusalem: Writers of Palestine Union, 1989.
Sada al-hanin (The Echo of Yearning, poetry). Shafa 'Amr: Dar al-Mashriq, 1992.

'Ayyad, Kawthar (?–), Jordanian short-story writer.
Rajul fi mataha (A Man in a Maze, short stories). Amman: Dar al-Karmel, 1993.

al-Ayyubi, Yusra (?–), Syrian novelist.
Bustan al-burtuqal (The Orange Orchard, novel). Damascus: Dar al-Jumhuriya, 1990.

al-'Aziz, Bilqis Ni'ma (?–), Iraqi short-story writer.
Zifaf al-ayyam al-mubhira (Wedding of the Sailing Days, short stories). N.p.: al-Gharri Modern Press, 1969.
al-Rafiq (The Comrade, short stories). Baghdad: Ministry of Information, 1974.

'Azzam, Samira (1927–1967), Palestinian short-story writer and translator born in Acre. She went to Lebanon in 1948, then to Iraq, and later to Cyprus. She attended school in Acre and later schooled herself in culture and academic subjects. She became a teacher when she was just sixteen years old and later became a school principal. She was also the announcer for the program, "Rukn al-mar'a" (The Women's Corner), on Near East Radio in Cyprus and Beirut. She wrote short stories and published them in the press under the pseudonym Fatat al-Sahil. She wrote many stories and articles and translated several literary works, among them *Candida* (1955) by George Bernard Shaw, *East Wind: West Wind* (1958) by Pearl Buck, *The Short Story in America* (1961) by Ray West, and *The Winter of Our Discontent* (1962) by John Steinbeck. She was posthumously awarded the Jerusalem Medal for Culture and the Arts in January 1990.

Ashya' saghira (Small Things, short stories). Beirut: Dar al-'Ilm li-l-Malayin, 1954.

al-Zill al-kabir (The Big Shadow, short stories). Beirut: al-Sharq al-Jadid and Dar al-'Ilm li-l-Malayin, 1956.

Qisas ukhra (Other Stories, short stories). Beirut: Dar al-Tali'a, 1960.

al-Sa'a wa-l-insan (The Clock and the Man, short stories). Beirut: al-Ahliya Foundation for Printing and Publishing, 1963.

al-'Id la ya'ti min al-nafidha al-gharbiya (The Holiday Doesn't Come from the Western Window, short stories). Beirut: Dar al-'Awda, 1971.

Asda' (Echoes, short stories). Beirut: Union of Writers and Journalists of Palestine and Bisan Publishing and Distribution, 1997.

'Azzuz, Hind (Fatat Bani Sulayman) (1926–), Tunisian writer born in Tunis. She is an announcer and the head of the projects department at Tunisian radio. She is a member of the Tunisian Writers' Union and the Story Club in Tunis and the secretary of the women's bureau of the Tunisian al-Tajammu' Party. She has published short stories and essays in *al-Hayah al-thaqafiya*, *al-Fikr*, *Qisas*, *al-Idha'a*, *al-Mar'a*, and *al-Tarbiya al-shamila*, as well as in newspapers such as *al-'Amal* and *al-Sabah*, all published in Tunisia. She received the Medal of Culture, the Medal of Employment, and the Medal of National Struggle, as well as many certificates of appreciation from party and press organizations in Tunisia.

Fi-l-darb al-tawil (On the Long Road, short stories). Tunis: al-Dar al-Tunisiya Publishers, 1969.

Badawi, Fabyula (1960–), Egyptian poet born in Cairo. She has a B.A. in business administration and a graduate degree in accounting. She is a journalist at the Saudi newspaper, *al-Madina*.

Mahlan ayyuha-l-rajul (Take It Easy, Man, poetry). Cairo: n.p., 1989.

Qasa'id zami'a (Thirsty Poems, poetry). Cairo: n.p., 1990.

al-Washm (The Tattoo, poetry). Cairo: n.p., 1992.

Badawi, Siham (?–), Egyptian novelist.

Mushtahayat (Objects of Desire, novel). Cairo: General Authority for Culture Palaces, 1997.

al-Badi, Nura 'Abd Allah (1969–), Omani poet born in Oman. She currently resides in al-Brimi. She studied at 'Ajman University for Sciences and Technology, the College and Languages and Translation. She works in education. She writes a weekly column for the Emirati paper, *al-Khalij*. She has written a radio series for Abu Dhabi radio, "Kalimat al-haqq" (The True Word), and an operetta about the environment, "Sawt al-ard" (Voice of the Earth).

Li-l-shahin jinah hurr (The Falcon Has a Free Wing, poetry). Cairo: Dar al-Shuruq, n.d.

Badr, 'Azza (1961–), Egyptian poet. She received from Cairo University a B.A. in media studies in 1983, an M.A. in journalism and media in 1990, and a Ph.D. in journalism and media in 1995. She is a journalist for *Sabah al-khayr* magazine and was awarded the Journalism Dialogue Prize in 1999.

Alf muttaka' wa bahr (A Thousand Cushions and a Sea, poetry). Cairo: Rose al-Yusuf Foundation, 1989.

Haqq al-luju' al-'atifi (The Right to Emotional Asylum, texts). Cairo: n.p., 1997.

Badr, Layali (195?–), Palestinian children's writer born in the West Bank. She has worked in journalism and the media in Kuwait.

Lubana wa-l-qamar (Lubana and the Moon, children's literature). Amman: League of Jordanian Writers Publications, 1984.

Badr, Liyana (1951–), Palestinian novelist and short-story writer born in Jerusalem. She went to school in Jerusalem and Jericho. She was a student at the Jordanian University and the Beirut Arab University, from which she received a B.A. in philosophy and psychology in 1973. She also earned an M.A. in psychology from the Lebanese University in 1975. She volunteered with women's organizations in the resistance of 1969–1970 in the al-Baq'a refugee camp in Jordan and from 1973 to 1976 in Sabra and Shatila in Beirut. She was a journalist for a year in 1977 with *al-Hurriya* magazine in Beirut, Damascus, and Tunis. She currently works at *Dafatir Filistiniya* and is based in Ramallah. Her novels have been translated into English and several of her short stories into French, Dutch, German, Polish, and English. She is the author of *Fadwa Tuqan: zilal al-kalimat al-mahkiya* (Fadwa Tuqan: The Shadows of Spoken Words, interview with Fadwa Tuqan). (Cairo: Dar al-Fata al-'Arabi, 1996.)
Busla min ajl 'abbad al-shams (*A Compass for the Sunflower*, novel). Beirut: Dar Ibn Rushd, 1979.
Firas yasna' bahran (Firas Creates a Sea, children's literature). Beirut: Arab Institute for Research and Publishing, 1981.
Rihla fi-l-alwan (A Journey in Colors, children's literature). Beirut: Dar al-Ruwwad, 1981.
Fi-l-madrasa (At School, children's literature). Beirut: Dar al-Fata al-'Arabi, 1983.
Qisas hubb wa-l-mulahaqa (Stories of Love and Pursuit, short stories). Aden: Dar al-Hamadhani, 1983.
al-Qitta al-saghira (The Kitten, children's literature). Beirut: n.p., 1983.
Shurfa 'ala-l-fakihani (*A Balcony over the Fakihani*, short stories). Damascus: Media and Culture Office, 1983.
Ana urid al-nahar (I Want the Day, short stories). Latakia: Dar al-Hiwar, 1985.

Hikayat al-banafsaj (The Violet's Tale, children's literature). N.p.: n.p., 1986.
Tayyarat Yunus (Yunus' Kite, children's literature). Cairo: n.p., 1990.
'Ayn al-mir'a (*The Eye of the Mirror*, novel). Casablanca: Dar Tubqal, 1991.
Jahim dhahabi (A Golden Hell, short stories). Beirut: Dar al-Adab, 1992.
Nujum Ariha (The Stars of Jericho, novel). Cairo: Dar al-Hilal, 1993.
Zanabiq al-daw' (Lilies of the Light, poetry). Cairo: Dar Sharqiyat, 1998.
al-Asdiqa' ya'burun al-nahr (The Friends Cross the River, children's literature). Ramallah: Tamir Foundation, 1998.

Badran, Nabila (?–), Egyptian writer.
Muhakamat Si al-Sayyid (The Trial of Male Chauvinism). Cairo: al-Ahram Press, 1992.

al-Badri, Huriya (1952–), Egyptian poet and short-story writer born in Alexandria. She has a Ph.D. in microbiology from Alexandria University.
Akhrijni min 'ayanayk (Take Me Out of Your Eyes, short stories). Alexandria: al-Fanniya Printing and Publishing, 1986.
Ihtiraq qaws quzah (A Rainbow Burns, short stories). Alexandria: Qasr al-Thaqafa al-Hurriya, 1988.
Tarnimat al-kanariya wa aswat al-hawari (The Canary's Song and the Sounds of the Slums, short stories). Cairo: Nafix Agency, 1995.
Zilal bila rijal (Shadows Without Men, short stories). Cairo: General Egyptian Book Organization, 1995.
Marafi' al-tih (Docks in the Wilderness, short stories). Cairo: n.p., 1988.

El Badry, Hala (al-Badri, Hala) (1954–), Egyptian short-story writer and novelist. She received a B.A. in business administration from Cairo University in 1975 and a degree in journalism and media from Cairo University in 1985. She is the head of the cultural desk at *al-Idha'a wa al-talafizyun* magazine. She received a prize for her novel, *Imra'a ma*. Her non-fiction works include *Hikayat min al-Khalisa* (Stories from

B

al-Khalisa, 1976, about the experience of Egyptian farmers in an Iraqi village), *Fallah Misri fi ard al-'Iraq* (An Egyptian Farmer in the Land of Iraq, 1980), and *al-Mar'a al-'Iraqiya: shahadat wa mashahid* (Iraqi Women: Testimonies and Scenes, 1980).

al-Sibaha fi qumqum 'ala qa' al-muhit (Swimming in a Bottle on the Ocean Floor, novel). Cairo: Dar al-Ghad, 1988.

Raqsat al-shams wa-l-ghaym (The Dance of Sun and Clouds, short stories). Cairo: Dar al-Ghad, 1989.

Ajnihat al-hisan (The Horse's Wings, short stories). Cairo: General Egyptian Book Organization, 1992.

Muntaha (*Muntaha*, novel). Cairo: General Egyptian Book Organization, 1995.

Laysa ana (Not I, novel). Cairo: General Egyptian Book Organization, 1998.

Imra'a ma (*A Certain Woman*, novel). Cairo: Dar al-Hilal, 2001.

Baghaffar, Hind Salih Ahmad (1954–), Saudi short-story writer and novelist born in Jeddah. She received a B.A. in sociology from King 'Abd al-'Aziz University in 1982. She has contributed to newspapers, radio, and literary clubs. She has written several works of non-fiction, including *al-Aghani al-sha'biya fi-l-Mamlaka al-'Arabiya al-Sa'udiya* (Folksongs in the Kingdom of Saudi Arabia), *Mahattat musafira* (A Traveler's Stations, essays), *Nafidha 'ala-l-ha'it al-mahdum* (A Window onto a Demolished Wall, essays), and *Sahil al-qalam* (The Pen's Whinny, essays). She is a member of the al-Wafa' Women's Charitable Association in Jeddah.

al-Bara'a al-mafquda (Lost Innocence, novel). Beirut: al-Misri Press, 1972.

Juruh fi jabin al-hayah (Wounds in Life's Brow, novel). N.p.: n.p., 1978.

al-'Ata' al-akbar (The Greatest Giving, novel). N.p.: n.p., 1979.

al-Hadiya (The Gift, short stories). N.p.: n.p., 1979.

al-Rihla al-akhira (The Final Journey, novel). N.p.: n.p., 1980.

Ribat al-walaya (The Bond of the Weak, novel). N.p.: n.p., 1987.

Da'i'a fi khutut yadayk (Lost in the Lines of Your Hands). N.p.: n.p., 1988.

I'tirafat imra'a, Dar al-Qadisiya (Confessions of a Woman, The al-Qadisiya Home). N.p.: n.p., 1999.

Baghdadi, Maryam Muhammad (?–), Saudi poet born in Mecca. She received a Ph.D. in Arabic literature from the University of Paris in 1972. She is a professor at the College of Liberal Arts at King 'Abd al-'Aziz University. Her academic writings include *Shu'ara' al-trubadur* (The Troubadour Poets, 1981) and *al-Madkhal fi dirasat al-adab al-Sa'udi* (Introduction to the Study of Saudi Literature, 1982).

'Awatif insaniya (Human Emotions, poetry). Tuhama and Jeddah: al-Kitab al-'Arabi al-Sa'udi, 1980.

Bahi al-Din, Amira (1959–), Egyptian novelist born in Cairo. She received a law degree from Cairo University in 1980. She works as an appellate lawyer and is interested in women's issues.

al-'Id (The Holiday, novel). Cairo: Dar Horus Publishers, 1996.

al-Bahi, Fadla' (?–), Algerian short-story writer and novelist.

al-'Ulayqi (The Ivy, novel). Algeria: al-Wataniya Book Foundation, 1985.

Daqqat al-sa'a (The Clock Chimed, short stories). Algeria: al-Wataniya Publishing and Distribution, 1986.

Bahithat al-Badiya (see: Nasif, Malak Hifni)

Bahithat al-Hadira (see: al-Fasi, Malika)

Bahlul, Zaha (1946–), Palestinian poet born in Haifa. She received her early education in Haifa. She graduated from Haifa University with a degree in political science and economics. She has worked in social services.

Mama li-alf tifl (Mother to One Thousand Children, poetry). Shafa 'Amr: Dar al-Mashriq, 1985.

Bahna, Collette Na'im (?–), Syrian short-story writer.

al-I'tiraf al-awwal (The First Confession, short stories). Dar al-Tali'a al-Jadida and Dar Kan'an Publishers and Printers, 1995.

Waw (W, short stories). Damascus: Dar al-Jundi, 1997.

Takharif (Delusions, play). N.p.: n.p., 1999.

al-Bakr, Fawziya Bakr Rashid (1959–), Saudi short-story writer born in Riyadh. She received a B.A. in education and psychology in 1978, an M.A. in school management and educational counseling from King Sa'ud University in Riyadh in 1983, and a Ph.D. in education in developing countries and comparative education from the University of London in 1989. She works in the education department at King Sa'ud University. She has published a work of non-fiction, *al-Mar'a al-Sa'udiya wa-l-ta'lim: bahth fi-l-tatawwur al-tarikihi li-ta'lim al-mar'a* (Saudi Women and Education: A Study of the Historical Development of Women's Education, 1988).

Yahduth kayf? (How Does It Happen?, short stories). N.p.: n.p., n.d.

Bakr, Salwa (1949–) , Egyptian novelist and short-story writer. She received a B.A. in business administration from Ain Shams University in 1972 and a B.A. in theater from the Higher Institute for the Dramatic Arts in 1976. She was a supplies inspector for the Ministry of Supply in Cairo for six years, after which she worked five years in Lebanon and Cyprus as a theater, film, and literary critic for the press. After that, she devoted herself entirely to writing. Along with Hoda Elsadda, she edits a series of books, *Hajir*, on women's issues. Her stories and novels have been translated into German, English, and Dutch, and part of her novel, *al-'Araba al-dhahabiya la tas'ad ila-l-sama'*, was adapted as the film, *Kart ahmar* (Red Card). Her story, "Nuna al-sha'nuna" ("Dotty Noona") was adapted for television.

Maqam 'Atiya ('Atiya's Shrine, short stories and a novella). Cairo: Dar al-Fikr Research, Publishing, and Distribution, 1986.

Zinat fi jinazat al-ra'is (Zeenat Marches in the President's Funeral, short stories). Cairo: n.p., 1986.

'An al-ruh allati suriqat tadrijiyan (On a Soul Gradually Stolen, short stories). Cairo: Misriya Publishing and Distribution, 1989.

al-'Araba al-dhahabiya la tas'ad ila-l-sama' (*The Golden Chariot*, novel). Cairo: Sina Publishers and al-Saqr al-'Arabi li-l-Ibda', 1991.

'Ajin al-fallaha (The Peasant Woman's Dough, short stories). Cairo: Sina Publishers, 1992.

Wasf al-bulbul (Description of the Nightingale, novel). Cairo: Sina Publishers, 1993.

Aranib (Rabbits, short stories). Cairo: Sina Publishers, 1994.

Iqa'at muta'akisa (Contrasting Rhythms, short stories). Cairo: Dar al-Nadim Journalism and Publishing, 1996.

Layl wa nahar (Night and Day, novel). Cairo: Dar al-Hilal, 1997.

Bashmuri (*The Man from Bashmour*, novel). Cairo: Dar al-Hilal, 1998.

Bakri, Iman (1955–), Egyptian poet born in Cairo. She received a B.A. in Arabic and Islamic studies from Cairo University in 1977. She teaches Arabic on the secondary school level and is a member of the Poets of Arabism group.

al-'Azf 'ala awtar al-qalb (Playing the Heart Strings, poetry). Cairo: Rose al-Yusuf Foundation, 1988.

Wamdat qalb yahtariq (Glimmers of a Burning Heart, poetry). Cairo: Rose al-Yusuf Foundation, 1991.

Imra'a fi sijill al-zaman (A Woman in Time's Archives, poetry). Cairo: General Egyptian Book Organization, 1993.

'Ajayib ya zaman (What a World, colloquial poetry). Cairo: General Authority for Culture Palaces, n.d.

Bakri, Samiya Qazmuz (1952–), Palestinian actress and playwright born in Acre in the part of Palestine occupied in 1948. She received a high-school diploma from al-Tarasanta in the old city. She studied Arabic language and literature and educational counseling at Haifa University. She worked in education for thirteen years until she was fired by the Israeli authorities. She lectured at the Dar al-Tifl for Preschool Teachers for eight years. She has published short stories and literary reflections and has made audio recordings of short stories and poetry. She currently devotes herself to the theater.

al-Far wa-l-fara (The Male and Female Mouse, adapted folktale). Shafa 'Amr: Tal al-Fakhkhar Foundation, Hikayat Sitti Series, 1995.

al-Zarub (The Narrow Lane, monodrama). Acre: Dar 'Akka Publishing and Distribution, 1998.

al-Bakri, Zahra Umm Hasan (?–), Iraqi poet.

al-Rawda al-Haydariya al-jadida (The New Haydar Garden, folk poetry). Najaf: al-Nu'man Press, 1973.

Bakriya, Raja' (1970–), Palestinian novelist born in the Galilee in the part of Palestine occupied in 1948. She studied plastic arts and Arabic literature at Haifa University and is preparing a Ph.D. at Tel Aviv University. She has lived in Haifa since 1989. She has participated in several art exhibitions and was awarded the Short Story Prize for Women of the Mediterranean Rim in 1997.

Mazamir Aylul (September Psalms, prose collection). Shafa 'Amr: Dar al-Mashriq, 1991.

'Uwa' al-dhakira (Howl of Memory, novel). Nazareth: Office of Arab Culture, 1995.

Ba'labakki, Layla (1934–), Lebanese novelist and short-story writer born in the district of al-Nabatiya in southern Lebanon. She received a B.A. in Oriental civilizations from St. Joseph University and worked as a secretary in the Lebanese parliament from 1957 to 1960. She wrote for Lebanese newspapers and magazines, including al-Usbu' al-'Arabi, al-Dustur, al-Hawadith, and al-Nahar. She was published in al-'Irfan magaine in 1963. She was brought to trial because of her short-story collection, *Safinat hanan ila-l-qamar*, on charges of harming public morals, but she won the case against the Ministry of Information. She lived in London from 1975 to 1989.

Ana ahya (I Live, novel). Beirut: Dar Majallat Shi'r, 1958.

al-Aliha al-mamsukha (The Deformed Gods, novel). Beirut: Dar Majallat Shi'r, 1960.

Safinat hanan ila-l-qamar (A Spaceship of Tenderness to the Moon, short stories). Beirut: al-Wataniya Foundation for Printing and Publishing, 1963.

al-Baladawi, Fawziya Faraj al-Hasun (?–), Iraqi poet.

Diwan majra al-madami' (The Course of Tears, folk poetry). Najaf: al-Gharri Modern Press, 1974.

al-Balghithi, Asiya al-Hashimi (al-Tilmisani) (1942–), Moroccan poet and writer born in Tetouan. She currently resides in Rabat. She received a degree in French from the French Cultural Center in Tetouan in 1964. She also studied at the Higher Professors' School in Tetouan (1965), the College of Legal, Sociological, and Economic Sciences in Casablanca (1971), the College of Humanities in Fez (1975), the College of Humanities in Rabat (intensive study of ancient literature, 1976), and the Dar al-Hadith al-Hasaniya in Rabat (1982), where she defended her thesis in 1995. She has taught at both primary and secondary school levels. She was the director of a secondary school in Casablanca from 1968 to 1978 and of another school in Rabat from 1985 to 1995. She was also an attaché at the State Ministry's Office, supreme leadership

(1983–1985). She is a member of the Moroccan Scientists' League, the National Council in Rabat (where she is a scholar), and the International Union for Family Planning (the regional office for the Arab world, Rabat section, women's committee). She has trained Arab women government and popular leaders for the Arab League. She publishes her poetry in Arab and international newspapers and magazines. She also writes in Spanish and is proficient in French and Persian. She published a non-fiction work, *al-Majalis al-'ilmiya al-sultaniya 'ala 'ahd al-dawla al-'Alawiya al-sharifa* (Royal Academic Councils under the 'Alawids), in 1996. Her collection of poetry, *Fajr al-milad*, was translated into Spanish in 1989. She is also known as al-Tilmisani.

Fajr al-milad (Dawn of Birth, poetry). Casablanca: Banshara Foundation for Printing and Publishing, 1986.
Falaq al-asbah (Dawn of Mornings, poetry). Casablanca: Banshara Foundation for Printing and Publishing, 1996.

Balil, Zaynab (?–), Sudanese novelist and short-story writer. Her works have been published in local periodicals.
al-Ikhtiyar (The Choice, novel). Khartoum: n.p., 1999.

Balshaykh, Hayat (1943–), Tunisian short-story writer and poet born in Tunis. She graduated with a B.A. and worked as a civil servant in several positions. She later joined the Tunisian Women's Union, where she worked at *al-Mar'a* magazine and in Tunisian radio. She has written poetry, essays, journalistic articles, short stories, and novels. Her works have been published in Tunisian journals. She has taken part in many literary seminars and forums in Tunisia and abroad. She is a member of the Story Club, the New Pen Association, and the Tunisian Writers' Union.
Bila rajul (Without a Man, short stories). Tunis: Ibn 'Abd Allah Foundations for Publishing, 1979.

Wa ghadan tushriq shams al-hurriya (And Tomorrow the Sun of Freedom Rises, short stories). Tunis: Dar al-Qalam, 1983.
Hubbuk qadari (Your Love Is My Fate, poetry). Tunis: al-Dar al-Tunisiya Publishers, 1990.
Intizar alf sana (A Thousand-year Wait, poetry). Tunis: al-Dar al-Tunisiya Publishers, 1990.
Wa kan 'urs al-hazima (And It Was the Wedding of Defeat, short stories). Tunis: Dar al-Akhla', 1991.

al-Banhawi, Nadiya (1944–), Egyptian short-story writer and playwright born in Cairo. She received a B.A. in classics from Cairo University in 1969, a degree from the Institute for Art Criticism in 1975, an M.A. in theater criticism from the Institute for Art Criticism in 1975, and a Ph.D. from the same institution in 1990. She is editor in chief of *al-Masrah al-'Arabi* journal, which is published by the General Egyptian Book Organization. She has translated several plays for the Egyptian Channel Two Radio. Several of her plays have been staged, among them *Sunata al-hubb wa-l-mawt* and *al-Wahaj*. She wrote *Khams masrahiyat tajribiya li-Samawil Bikit* (Five Experimental Plays by Samuel Beckett, 1992), *al-Mar'a fi masrah Tawfiq al-Hakim wa Rashad Rushdi wa tahliluha 'ala daw' al-bina' al-musiqi* (Women in the Drama of Tawfiq al-Hakim and Rashad Rushdi in Light of Musical Composition, 1994), and *Budhur masrah al-'abath fi-l-trajidiya al-Ighriqiya wa atharuha 'ala masrah al-'abath* (Seeds of the Theater of the Absurd in Greek Tragedy and Its Impact on the Theater of the Absurd, 1998).

al-Lawha al-naqisa wa qisas ukhra (The Unfinished Painting and Other Stories, short stories). Cairo: General Egyptian Book Organization, 1992.
Sunata al-hubb wa-l-mawt (Sonata of Love and Death, play). Cairo: General Egyptian Book Organization, 1998.

al-Wahaj wa masrahiyat ukhra (The Blaze and Other Plays, plays). Cairo: General Egyptian Book Organization, 1999.

al-Banna, Maryam (?–), Egyptian short-story writer. She received a B.A. in business from Cairo University in 1984. She is an editor at *al-Ahram*. Her stories have been published in *al-Ahram* and *al-Jumhuriya* newspapers and in *Sabah al-khayr* and *Rose al-Yusuf* magazines. She is a member of the Journalists' Syndicate and the Egyptian branch of the PEN association.
Tasmah katifak min fadlik (Kindly Watch Your Shoulder, short stories). Cairo: Maktabat Madbuli, 1990.
Ra'ihat al-wajh al-qadim (The Scent of an Ancient Face, short stories). Cairo: Dar Sharqiyat, 1999.

al-Banna, Salwa (1948–), Palestinian novelist and short-story writer born in Jaffa. She went to school in Nablus and attended the Beirut Arab University. She has lived in Amman, Beirut, and Nicosia. She worked in journalism and publishing. She is a member of the Palestinian Journalists' and Writers' Union and the Arab Authors' Union.
'Arus khalf al-nahr (A Bride Beyond the River, novel). Beirut: Dar al-Ittihad Printing and Publishing, 1970.
al-Wajh al-akhar (The Other Face, short stories). Beirut: Arab Institute for Research and Publishing, 1974.
al-Ati min al-masafat (Coming from the Distances, novel). Beirut: Palestinian Journalists' and Writers' General Union, 1977.
Matar fi sabah dafi' (Rain on a Warm Morning, novel). Beirut: Dar al-Haqa'iq, 1979.
Kawabis al-farah (Nightmares of Joy, short stories). Damascus: Dar al-Jil, 1984.
al-'Amura 'arus al-layl (al-'Amura, Bride of the Night, novel). Nicosia: Manar Press Journalism, Printing, and Publishing, 1986.

Bannuna, Khunatha (1940–), Moroccan short-story writer and novelist born in Fez. She was educated at the Primary Teachers' School at the Higher Iraqi Institute in Fez, from which she graduated in 1963. She worked in high-school education. In 1968 she was appointed the director of the Wallada High School in Casablanca. She is a member of the Moroccan Writers' Union and the Independence Party. In 1965 she founded *Shuruq* magazine, the first women's cultural magazine published in Morocco. She has attended various cultural and literary seminars and forums in North Africa. She was awarded the Moroccan Book Prize in 1971 by the Ministry for Cultural Affairs and the P.L.O. Medal in appreciation of her support for the Palestinian cause and for donating to the P.L.O. the auction proceeds of her book, *al-Nar wa-l-ikhtiyar*.
Li-yasqut al-samt (May the Silence Fall, short stories). Casablanca: Dar al-Kitab, 1967.
al-Nar wa-l-ikhtiyar (Fire and Choice, short stories and novella). Rabat: al-Risala Press, 1968.
al-Sura wa-l-sawt (Image and Sound, short stories). Casablanca: Dar al-Nashr al-Maghribiya, 1975.
al-'Asifa (The Storm, short stories). Rabat: al-Risala Press, 1979.
al-Ghad wa-l-ghadab (The Morrow and Anger, novel). Casablanca: Dar al-Nashr al-Maghribiya, 1981.
al-Samt al-natiq (Speaking Silence, short stories). Casablanca: 'Uyun al-Maqalat Publications, 1987.

Baqa, Latifa (1964–), Moroccan short-story writer born in Sala. She received a B.A. in sociology. She is a counselor for the Office of Professional Development and Employment. She is a member of the Moroccan Writers' Union, the Union of Women's Work, and the Moroccan Organization for Human Rights. Her short stories have been published in Moroccan periodicals. She received the Moroccan Writers' Union Prize for Young Authors in 1992 for her collection, *Ma alladhi naf'aluh*.

Ma alladhi naf'aluh (What Are We Doing, short stories). Rabat: Moroccan Writers' Union Publications, 1993.

al-Baqsami, Thuraya (1952–), Kuwaiti short-story writer born in Kuwait. She receved an M.A. in plastic arts, with a specialization in book illustration, from the Sirkov Academy of Arts in Moscow in 1981. She has worked at *al-Watan* newspaper and *al-'Arabi* magazine. She is a founding member of the Gulf Friends of Art Group and a member of the Handcrafts' League. She won two prizes for short-story writing, one in 1968 and one in 1969. She has published a work of non-fiction, *al-Marsam al-hurr wa rihlat al-25 'aman* (The Open Atelier and a Journey of Twenty-five Years).

al-Sidra (The Lotus Tree, short stories). Kuwait: n.p., 1988.

Mudhakkirat Fattuma al-Kuwaytiya al-saghira (Memoirs of the Young Kuwaiti Fattuma, children's literature). Kuwait: Kuwaiti Association for the Advancement of Arab Childhood, 1992.

Shumu' al-saradib (Cellar Candles, short stories). Kuwait: Maktabat Dar al-'Uruba, 1992.

Rahil al-nawafidh (The Windows' Departure, short stories). Kuwait: al-Manar Press, 1994.

al-'Irq al-aswad (The Black Vein, short stories). Kuwait: Ministry of Information, 1997.

Baradha, Nazaha (?–), Moroccan novelist. *Rahil qamar* (The Moon's Departure, novel). Casablanca: al-Najah Modern Press, 1994.

Baraka, Iqbal (1942–), Egyptian journalist and novelist. She received a B.A. in English from Alexandria University, as well as a B.A. in Arabic. She has worked in public relations for Philips, as a simultaneous interpreter, for an English-language

school in Kuwait, and as an announcer in English-language radio. She was an editor at *Sabah al-khayr* and in June 1993 became editor in chief at *Hawwa'*, where she still works. She is a member of the Journalists' Syndicate, the Writers' Union, and the Association of Women Writers. She also founded the Association of Egyptian Women Filmmakers and has written many works for the big and small screens. Her novels have been translated into Japanese, Chinese, English, and French. She published the non-fiction work, *Hiwar hawl qadaya Islamiya* (A Conversation on Islamic Issues).

Li-nazall asdiqa' ila-l-abad (Let's Remain Friends Forever, novel). Cairo: General Egyptian Book Organization, 1971.

al-Fajr li-awwal marra (Dawn for the First Time, novel). Beirut: Dar al-Quds al-'Arabiya, 1975.

Layla wa-l-majhul (Layla and the Unknown, novel). Isma'iliya: Maktabat Qanat al-Suways, 1980.

al-Sayd fi bahr al-awham (Fishing in the Sea of Illusions, novel). Cairo: General Egyptian Book Organization, 1981.

Rihla ila Turkiya (A Journey to Turkey, travel literature). Cairo: Maktabat Gharib, 1983.

Timsah al-buhayra (Crocodile of the Lake, novel). Cairo: Maktabat Gharib, 1983.

Kulluma 'ad al-rabi' (Whenever Spring Returns, novel). Cairo: Akhbar al-Yawm Foundation, 1985.

Hadithat ightisab (An Incident of Rape, short stories). Cairo: Akhbar al-Yawm Foundation, 1993.

Yawmiyat imra'a 'amila (Diaries of a Working Woman, novel). Cairo: Dar al-Ma'arif, 1993.

Barakat, Hoda (Barakat, Huda) (1952–), Lebanese novelist and short-story writer born in Basharri. She received a degree in French literature in 1974 and has worked in teaching, journalism, translation, and radio. She works as a journalist in Paris and has been a guest lecturer at several universities, including the Sorbonne and the Higher Teachers' Institute in Paris. Her novels have been translated into French, English, Italian, Spanish, Dutch, German, and Norwegian. She received the Critics' Prize in 1990 for her novel, *Hajar al-dahk.*

Za'irat (Visitors, short stories). Beirut: Dar al-Matbu'at al-Sharqiya, 1985.

Hajar al-dahk (The Stone of Laughter, novel). London: Riyad al-Rayyis Books and Publishing, 1990.

Ahl al-hawa (Disciples of Passion, novel). Beirut: Dar al-Nahar Publishers, 1993.

Harith al-miyah (The Tiller of Waters, novel). Beirut: Dar al-Nahar Publishers, 1998.

Barakat, 'Iffat al-Rifa'i Khalil (1970–), Egyptian poet born in Damietta.

Nuqisha lahu fi dhakirati (He Was Etched in My Memory, poetry). Damietta: General Authority for Culture Palaces, 1992.

Barakat, Najwa (1960–) (see also: Bibliography of Works in French), Lebanese novelist born in Beirut. She received a B.A. in theater from the Lebanese University in Beirut and a B.A. in film studies in Paris. She works as a journalist and radio scriptwriter. She won the prize for the best Lebanese work of fiction in 1996 for her novel, *Bas al-awadim.* She was also awarded a prize by the Lebanese Cultural Forum in Paris in 1997. She has written a novel in French, *La locataire du pot de fer* (1997).

al-Muhawwil (The Transformer, novel). Beirut: Mukhtarat, 1986.

Hayat wa alam Hamad Ibn Silana (The Life and Pains of Hamad Ibn Silana, novel). Beirut: Dar al-Adab, 1995.

Bas al-awadim (A Busload of Folks, novel). Beirut: Dar al-Adab, 1996.

Ya Salam (Wow, novel). Beirut: Dar al-Adab, 1998.

Barakat, Ruqaya (1952–), Lebanese poet born in Sidon. She received her primary and secondary education at Sidon's public schools and taught at schools run by the al-Maqasid Islamic Charitable Associa-tion from 1979 to 1986. She completed three years of university study in Arabic literature and then went to Saudi Arabia with her family. She has published poems in Lebanese and Egyptian newspapers.

Baqat al-baqat (Bouquet of Bouquets, poetry). Sidon: al-Maktaba al-'Asriya, 1991.

Barghuth, Shadha (1958–), Syrian novel-ist and poet born in the province of Dayr al-Zur. She is a member of the Story and Novel Association.

Lawhat 'ala jidar rifi 'atiq (Paintings on an Old Country Wall, novel). Damas-cus: n.p., 1996.

Sawalif furatiya (Euphrates Sideburns, folk poetry). N.p.: n.p., n.d.

al-Barghuthi, Widad (1958–), Palestinian poet and novelist born in the village of Kubar in the vicinity of Ramallah in the West Bank. She received an M.A. in jour-nalism from the Moscow Government University in 1984. She works as a journalist. She was awarded the Feminist Novel Prize by the Palestinian Ministry of Culture.

Suqut al-zill al-'ali li-l-fuqara' faqat (Fall of the High Shadow—Only for the Poor, poetry). Jerusalem: Writers' Union, 1991.

Dhakira la takhun (Memory Doesn't Lie, novel). Ramallah: n.p., 1999.

Barudi, Fatima (1965–), Moroccan poet. She received a degree from the Higher Journalism Institute and a graduate degree in political science from Muhammad V University in Rabat. She currently works in Moroccan television.

Ibhar fi qila' al-ruh (Boating in the Spirit's Sails, poetry). Rabat: n.p., 1997.

al-Baruni, Za'ima Sulayman (1910–1976), Libyan literary pioneer and short-story writer born in Jadu, located in Libya's western mountains. She is the daughter of anti-colonial fighter Sulayman al-Baruni. She received her early education in Turkish in Istanbul and then returned to Libya, where she completed her studies in the field of Arabic. She witnessed the various phases of her father's struggle and after his death settled in Tripoli. She worked in education after Libyan independence and published her literary works in Libyan newspapers and magazines. She collected and edited critical editions on her father's life and poetry. She participated in the Afro-Asian Women's Conference held in Cairo in 1960.

al-Qasas al-qawmi (The National Narrative, short stories). Cairo: al-'Alamiya Press, 1958.

Basha, Majida Musa (?–), Syrian novelist born in the province of Hama.

al-Tabib al-muhajir (The Immigrant Doctor, novel). Damascus: n.p., n.d.

Bashir, Thuraya Najah (1964–), Palestinian poet and novelist born in the village of al-Faradis near Haifa in the part of Palestine occupied in 1948. She went to primary school in her village and to high school in Haifa. She works in nursing.

Nadam dam'a (Regret of a Tear, novel). Acre: al-Jalil Press, 1982.

Ghurub al-amal (The Vanishing of Hopes, poetry). Acre: al-Jalil Press, 1987.

Tuqus fi zifaf al-mawt (Rituals in the Procession of Death, poetry). Haifa: al-Karma Press, 1996.

Bashir, Zubayda (1938–), Tunisian poet born in Saqiyat Sidi Yusuf. She currently resides in Tunis. She has worked in Tunisian radio and was the producer of the program, "Aghani li-l-mustami'in" (Songs for Listeners). She is considered a pioneer of Tunisian poetry and contemporary Tunisian women's literature. She began publishing her poems at the age of fourteen. She was the first Tunisian woman to publish a collection of poetry. After being subjected to a campaign of slander, she retired. A literary prize was named in her honor in 1994.

Hanin (Longing, poetry). Tunis: al-Dar al-Tunisiya Publishers, 1968.

Basikri, Khadija al-Sadiq (1962–), Libyan poet born in Benghazi. She graduated from the French language department at Qaryunis University. She was the vice president of the Libyan Writers' and Authors' League for several years.

Layl qaliq (A Restless Night, poetry). Beirut: Dar al-Ward, 1992.

Basir, Iman (?–), Palestinian short-story writer born in al-Tiba near Ramallah. She has a B.A. in nursing and works at the Augusta Victoria Hospital in Jerusalem.

Marfa' farah (Dock of Joy, short stories). N.p.: al-Mashriq Center for Media and Research, 1994.

Jasad min bukhur (A Body of Incense, short stories). Jerusalem: Palestinian Journalists' and Writers' Union Publications, 1997.

al-Bassam, Sajida (?–), Iraqi short-story writer.

al-Hayah al-ba'isa (The Wretched Life, short stories). Baghdad: al-Najah Press, 1953.

Basyuni, Amal (?–), Egyptian poet.

Amal fi-l-hawa (Hopes in Passion, poetry). Alexandria: Authors of the People Association, 1993.

Bat Bint al-Bura' (see: Bint al-Bura', Imbaraka)

al-Batini, Bazza (1945–), Kuwaiti short-story writer. She received her high-school diploma in 1972. She works at the Ministry of Information's Center to Foster Folk Arts. She is a member of the children's programs committee at Kuwait television, the Kuwait museum committee, and the Film Club's cultural committee. She has participated in programs for "Iftah ya simsim" (Sesame Street). Her story, "al-Bayt al-kabir", won the prize of the Arab Educational Office of the Gulf States in 1997.

al-Ard al-khadra' (The Green Earth, children's literature). Kuwait: Kuwaiti

Environmental Protection Association, 1994.

Kulluna al-yawm kabarna (All of Us Have Grown Up Today, children's literature). N.p.: n.p., 1996.

al-Bayt al-kabir (The Big House, children's literature). Riyadh: Arab Educational Office of the Gulf States, 1997.

al-Sayyida kanat (The Woman Was, short stories). Kuwait: n.p., 1998.

Batuli, Basima (?–), Lebanese poet and artist born in Beirut. She received her primary education at a foreign school and studied Arabic at a government school. She earned her high school degree from home. She earned a teaching certificate in Arabic language and literature and a degree in sociology from the Lyon University (Lebanon branch). Her poetry has been translated into English, French, and Turkish.

Ma'a al-hubb hatta-l-mawt (With Love until Death, poetry). Beirut: privately published, 1978.

Mukallala bi-l-shawq (Crowned with Desire, poetry). Beirut: privately published, 1996.

Bayraqdar, Maha (1947–), Syrian poet born in Damascus. She received a degree from the Center for Plastic Arts in Damascus in 1967 and a B.A. in business administration from the Advanced Translation College in Munich, Germany, in 1969. She worked at *Fayruz* magazine and has presented programs for Damascus television. She has written several children's songs. She has had several exhibitions and runs Gallery One with her husband, poet Yusuf al-Khal.

'Ushbat al-milh (The Salt Plant, poetry). Beirut: Dar al-Nahar Publishers, 1987.

Rahil al-'anasir (Departure of the Elements, poetry). Beirut: Dar Sadir, 1997.

Bayruti, Hanan (1968–), Jordanian short-story writer born in al-Zarqa'. She received a B.A. in Arabic literature from the Jordanian University in 1990. She has published various articles in the press and works in teaching.

al-Ishara laysat hamra' da'iman (The Light Isn't Always Red, short stories). Amman: Dar al-Yanabi' Publishing and Distribution, 1993.

Li-'aynayk ta'wi 'asafir ruhi (The Sparrows of My Soul Take Refuge in Your Eyes, prose texts). Amman: Dar al-Azmina, 1995.

Futat (Crumbs, short stories). Amman: Dar al-Faris Publishing and Distribution, 1999.

Bayruti, Sunya (1934–), Lebanese short-story writer and journalist born in Beirut. She received her primary and secondary education in Sisters of the Holy Family schools in Beirut and earned a B.A. in Eastern civilizations from the St. Joseph University in Beirut in 1957. Since 1962 she has worked as a television announcer and has presented several noteworthy programs. She has worked in journalism since 1961. She has worked at *al-Anwar* and *al-Hasna'* and was the chief editor at *al-Sharqiya* from 1974 to 1976. She currently works at *al-Mustaqbal* newspaper.

Mawa'id ma'a al-bariha (Appointments with Yesterday, memoir). Beirut: Nawfal Foundation, 1987.

Hibal al-hawa' (Ropes of Air, short stories). Beirut: Bahsun Foundation, 1991.

Madar al-lahza (Circuit of the Moment, short stories). Beirut: Dar al-Nahar Publishers, 1994.

al-Bayyati, Kalshan (?–), Iraqi short-story writer.

al-Hisan al-ta'ir (The Flying Horse, short stories). Baghdad: Dar al-Shu'un al-Thaqafiya, 1991.

Bayyumi, Siham (1949–), Egyptian novelist born in Cairo. She received a B.A. in social service from Helwan University in 1974 and works as a journalist for *al-Jumhuriya*. Her works of non-fiction include *Fi-l-thaqafa al-Bur Sa'idiya* (On the Culture of Port Said, a sociological study) and *9 nisa' Misriyat fi-l-mukhayyamat al-Filistiniya fi Lubnan* (Nine Egyptian Women in Palestinian Refugee Camps in Lebanon, 1989). She is a member of the Committee to Defend National Culture and the Egyptian Women Writers' Association.

al-Musalaha (The Reconciliation, novel). Cairo: General Egyptian Book Organization, 1980.

Khara'it li-l-mawj (Maps to the Waves, novel). Cairo: al-Hilal Novels, 1997.

al-Khayl wa-l-layl (Horses and the Night, novel). N.p.: Dar al-Mustaqbal al-'Arabi, n.d.

al-Baz, Ni'am (Mama Ni'am) (1935–), Egyptian journalist and short-story writer. She has a column in *al-Akhbar*. She published the non-fiction work, *al-Baquri: tha'ir taht al-'imama* (al-Baquri: A Revolutionary under the Turban), in 1998. She also published a collection of her articles as *Zawjatuhum wa ana* (Their Wives and I).

Sanawat al-hubb (The Love Years, short stories). Cairo: Akhbar al-Yawm Foundation, 1980.

Ummat al-Razzaq (Nation of God the Provider, novel). Cairo: Akhbar al-Yawm Foundation, 1988.

al-Aswar al-bayda' (The White Walls). N.p.: n.p., n.d.

Biban, Hafiza Qara (Bint al-Bahr) (1951–), Tunisian short-story writer born in Binzart. She received a B.A. in classical literatures and studied at the College of Humanities, University of Tunis. She is a member of the Tunisian Writers' Union and was elected the vice president of the union's branch in Binzart. She is a member of the Story Club in Tunisia. She has published her works in several Tunisian newspapers, including *al-Sabah, al-Sada, al-Ra'i al-'amm, al-Sahafa, Biladi,* and *al-Ayyam*. She has also published in magazines such as *al-Fikr* (before its suspension), *Qisas, al-Hayah al-thaqafiya, al-Idha'a,* and *Lutis*. She writes in both Arabic and French and some

of her works have been translated into French and Chinese as part of anthologies of Arab women's writing. She is also known as Bint al-Bahr.

al-Tifla intaharat (The Child Killed Herself, short stories). Tunis: al-Dar al-Bayda' Books, 1983.

Rasa'il la yahmiluha al-barid (Dead Letters). Tunis: Tunisian Company for Publishing and Distribution, 1989.

Fi zulumat al-nur (In the Darkness of Light, short stories). Tunis: Qisas Magazine Publications, 1994.

Bibawi, Tiri (1939–), Egyptian poet born to Sudanese parents in Cairo. She attended high school in Khartoum. She is a journalist and has published in several newspapers and magazines, including *Hawwa', Nisf al-dunya, Sabah al-khayr,* and *al-Hayat*.

Lahzat sidq (A Moment of Truth, poetry). Cairo: n.p., 1981.

Baqat hubb (A Bouquet of Love, poetry). Cairo: n.p., 1982.

'Umr min al-hubb (A Life of Love, poetry). Cairo: n.p., 1983.

al-Mar'a wa-l-zaman (Woman and Time, poetry). Cairo: Maktabat Madbuli, 1984.

al-Farashat (Butterflies, poetry). Cairo: Maktabat Madbuli, 1986.

al-Hanan (Tenderness, poetry). Cairo: Maktabat Madbuli, 1986.

Ahla min al-kalimat (Sweeter Than Words, poetry). Cairo: Maktabat Madbuli, 1987.

Imra'a min burj al-amal (A Woman Whose Sign Is Hope, poetry). Cairo: Maktabat Madbuli, 1988.

al-Matar suhba (Rain Is Companionship, poetry). Cairo: Maktabat Madbuli, 1990.

Huruf mulawinna (Tinted Letters, poetry). Cairo: Maktabat Madbuli, 1993.

Wurud wa yasamin (Roses and Jasmine, poetry). Cairo: Maktabat Madbuli, 1996.

Qalbi madinat hubb (My Heart is the City of Love, poetry). Cairo: Maktabat Madbuli, 1997.

Bidaywi, Fatima (1929–), Syrian poet born in Hama. She was educated in Aleppo and Hams and received a teaching certificate in 1961. She has worked in education and founded a kindergarten in Hams in 1955. She also founded the School Theater in 1956. Several of her plays were staged between 1956 and 1963. She is a member of the Poetry Association.

Qiyam al-thawra (Values of the Revolution, play). N.p.: n.p., 1956.

Bayn al-khayr wa-l-sharr (Between Good and Evil, play). N.p.: n.p., 1957.

Bayn al-fadila wa-l-radhila (Between Virtue and Vice, play). N.p.: n.p., 1958.

Agharid al-tufula (Warblings of Childhood, poetry). Hams: Dar al-Andalus, 1962.

Awladuna dahayana (Our Children Are Our Victims, play). N.p.: n.p., 1963.

Dumu' tahtariq (Burning Tears, poetry). Hams: Dar al-Andalus, 1981.

al-'Ishq al-Qudsi (Jerusalem Passion, poetry). N.p.: n.p., 1998.

'Arus (Bridegroom, novel). N.p.: n.p., n.d

Bilal, 'Ammariya (Umm Siham) (?–), Algerian short-story writer born in Morocco. She currently resides in Oran. She has a B.A. in Arabic literature. She is a member of the Algerian Writers' Union. Her nonfiction publications include *Shazaya al-naqd wa-l-adab* (Slivers of Criticism and Literature, 1989, essays) and *Jawla ma'a al-qasida* (A Journey with the Poem, 1986, criticism).

'Ala-l-rasif al-Bayruti (On the Beirut Sidewalk, short stories). Algeria: al-Wataniya Book Foundation, 1986.

Zaman al-hisar wa zaman al-wilada al-jadida (Time of Siege and Time of New Birth, poetry). Damascus: Arab Writers' Union, 1989.

Min yawmiyat Umm 'Ali (From the Diary of Umm 'Ali, short stories). Algeria: al-Wataniya Book Foundation, 1990.

Bilyazid, Farida (1948–), Moroccan short-story writer and filmmaker born in Tangier. She received a B.A. in humanities in 1970. She then moved to Paris to study film at the University of Paris VIII and the Higher Film Studies School, from which she graduated in 1974 and received a degree in film direction in 1976. In 1977 she took part in training sessions on film specializations in Paris. She is a screenwriter, director, and journalist. She received the Bronze Award at the 'Anaba Festival in Algeria in 1988 for her film, *Bab al-sama' maftuh*, and the Best Screenplay award at the third National Film Festival in Morocco in 1991 for the same film. She also received the Best Screenplay award at the fourth National Film Festival in Tangier in 1992 for the film, "al-Bahth 'an zawj imra'ati."

"Huwiyat al-mar'a" (Woman's Identity, documentary film). 1979.

"'Ara'is min qasab" (Sugarcane Dolls, screenplay). 1980.

"Badis" (Badis, screenplay). 1986.

"Bab al-sama' maftuh" (The Door to the Sky is Open, film direction and screenplay). 1988.

"al-Bahth 'an zawj imra'ati" (Looking for My Wife's Husband, screenplay). 1993.

"Amina Tarawari: imra'at al-sahil" (Amina Tarawari: Woman of the Coast, documentary film). 1993.

"al-Suq al-sawda'" (The Black Market, reportage). 1994.

"'Ala-l-shurfa" (On the Balcony, short-film direction and screenplay). 1995.

"Sariq al-ahlam" (The Thief of Dreams, screenplay). 1995.

Bin Dawud, Su'ad (1958–), Moroccan poet born in Rabat. She received a B.A. in Arabic literature and is a primary-school teacher. She takes part in many professional, literary, and educational seminars and forums. Her literary works have been published in the Moroccan press. She received the Best Recitation Award at the Sala Poetry Festival in 1996 and the Egyptian Cultural Week Prize in the city of Khouribga in 1997.

Tadaris al-jasad al-jarih (Contours of the Wounded Body, poetry). Rabat: Fidbrant Press, 1996.

Bint Ahmad, al-Sayyida (1972–), Mauritanian poet and short-story writer born in al-Rashid. She continued her education in Mauritania and received a B.A. in Arabic literature in 1991. She publishes and is the editor in chief of *al-Shumu'* newspaper.

Bint al-Bahr (see: Biban, Hafiza Qara)

Bint Barada (see: al-Husni, Amira)

Bint al-Bura', Imbaraka (Bat Bint al-Bura') (1956–), Mauritanian short-story writer, poet, and novelist born in al-Mazarzara. She received her early education in al-Mahraza and graduated from high school in 1979. She received an M.A. in humanities from the Higher Teachers' School in 1983 and an advanced studies degree from Muhammad V University in Rabat in 1987. She worked in education and literacy projects and taught at the university from 1987 to 1990. She is a consultant at the Ministry for Rural Development and Environment. She has published two works of non-fiction: *al-Bina' al-masrahi 'ind Tawfiq al-Hakim* (Dramatic Structure in the Works of Tawfiq al-Hakim) and *al-Mar'a fi-l-mujtama' al-Muritani* (Women in Mauritanian Society). She is also known as Bat Bint al-Bura'.
Taranim li-watan wahid (Hymns to One Homeland, poetry). Nouakchott: al-Wataniya Press, 1991.
al-'Ubur ila-l-jisr (Crossing to the Bridge, novel). N.p.: n.p., n.d.
al-Azafir al-hamra' (The Red Fingernails, short stories). N.p.: n.p., n.d.

Bint al-Huda (see: al-Sadr, Amina Haydar)

Bint al-Jazira (see: al-Hammud, Nawwar)

Bint al-Shamaliya, Asma' (?–), Sudanese short-story writer. She published her stories in the Sudanese press. Her first story was "Mashi al-Shamal" (Traveling North) and her most recent was "al-Nashid" (The Anthem).

Bint al-Shati' (see: 'Abd al-Rahman, 'A'isha)

Bint al-Waha (see: Thamir, Najiya)

Bint al-Yaman (see: al-Shami, Amal Muhammad 'Ali)

Biqa'i, Iman Yusuf (1960–), Syrian novelist born in Damascus. She obtained an M.A. in Arabic language from the Beirut Arab University in 1983. She lives in Beirut. She has published several literary studies, including *al-Fituri: al-da'i' alladhi wajad nafsahu* (al-Fituri: The Lost Man Who Found Himself, 1994), *Sulayman al-'Isa: munshid al-'Uruba wa-l-atfal* (Sulayman al-'Isa: Singer of Arabism and Children, 1994), *Ilyas Abu Shabaka wa-l-firdaws al-mushtaha* (Ilyas Abu Shabaka and the Longed-for Paradise, 1995), *Mikha'il Na'ima* (Mikha'il Na'ima, 1995), and *Nazik al-Mala'ika* (Nazik al-Mala'ika, 1995).
Fi-l-wafa' (On Fidelity, novel). Beirut: n.p., 1983.
al-Armala (The Widow, novel). Beirut: Arab Center for Culture and Science, 1996.
'Azza ('Azza, novel). Beirut: Arab Center for Culture and Science, 1996.

Biqa'i, Marah (1959–), Syrian poet born in Damascus. She received a B.A. in French literature from Damascus University. She is a member of the Poetry Association.
al-Hurub ilayh (Fleeing to Him, poetry). Damascus: al-Thaqafa Magazine Publishers, 1987.
Wajh al-nar al-akhar (The Other Face of Fire, poetry). Damascus: al-'Ajluni Press, 1988.
Ma' wa lugha (Water and Language, poetry). Beirut: al-Warif, 1989.

al-Bishr, Badriya 'Abd Allah (?–), Saudi short-story writer born in Riyadh. She received a B.A. in sociology from King Sa'ud University in 1989 and an M.A. in sociology from the same institution in 1997. She was an editor at *al-Riyad* from 1983 to 1987. She was a social worker at King Fahd Hospital in Riyadh and since 1997 has been a lecturer at King Sa'ud

University. She has won gold and silver medals in short-story competitions at King Sa'ud University. She writes a regular column for *al-Riyad*.

Nihayat al-lu'ba (Endgame, short stories). Riyadh: Dar al-Ard, 1992.

Masa' al-Arbi'a' (Wednesday Evening, short stories). Beirut: Dar al-Adab, 1994.

al-Bisi, Sana' (1937–), Egyptian novelist, short-story writer, and journalist. She received a B.A. in journalism from Cairo University in 1958. She was an editor for the women's page of *al-Ahram* and the deputy editor of *al-Ahram* in 1980. She is currently editor in chief of the magazine, *Nisf al-dunya*. She is a member of the Journalists' Syndicate.

Huwa wa hiya (He and She, short stories). N.p.: al-Ahram Commercial Press, 1984.

Imra'a li-kull al-'usur (A Woman for All Ages, short stories). N.p.: al-Ahram Commercial Press, 1984.

al-Kalam al-mubah (Permissible Talk, short stories). Cairo-Kuwait: Dar Su'ad al-Sabah, 1989.

al-Bitar, Hayat (?–), Syrian novelist.
Nihaya wa 'ibra (An End and a Lesson, novel). Beirut: Byblos Press, 1964.

Bitar, Hayfa' (1959–), Syrian short-story writer and novelist born in Latakia. She is a doctor specializing in ophthalmology and ophthalmic surgery. She writes for many Arab and local newspapers and journals.

Wurud lan tamut (Undying Roses, short stories). Latakia: Dar al-Manara, 1992.

Qisas muhajira (Stories of an Emigré, short stories). Damascus: al-Ahali Press and Publishing, 1993.

Yawmiyat mutallaqa (Diary of a Divorcée, novel). Damascus: al-Ahali Press and Publishing, 1994.

Khawatir fi maqha rasif (Reflections in a Sidewalk Café, short stories). Damascus: Arab Writers' Union, 1995.

Qabw al-'Abbasiyin (The Cellar of the 'Abbasids, novel). Damascus: al-Ahali Press and Publishing, 1995.

Afrah saghira, afrah akhira (Small Joys, Final Joys, novel). Damascus: al-Ahali Press and Publishing, 1996.

Zill aswad hay (A Living Black Shadow, short stories). Damascus: Ministry of Culture, 1996.

Mawt al-baja'a (Death of the Swan, short stories). Damascus: Arab Writers' Union, 1997.

Nasr bi-janah wahid (A One-winged Eagle, novel). Latakia: Maktabat Palmyra, 1998.

Imra'a min tabiqayn (A Woman from Two Floors, novel). Latakia: Maktabat Palmyra, 1999.

al-Biyali, Zahira (1945–), Egyptian short-story writer. She received a B.A. in French and a certificate in French translation from Cairo University. She earned a Ph.D. in journalism at the Sorbonne. She works as a writer and journalist at *Uktubir*. Her brother's death in the War of Attrition in 1969 had a great impact on her, and the pain was channeled into her first poem. She has taken part in many conferences on women and children and is involved in several other activities. She is a boardmember of the Writers' Union and a member of the Egyptian Women Writers' Association, Dar al-Udaba', the Foreign Press Association, and the Huda Sha'rawi Association. She is an honorary member of the Pen Club in Paris. She has published several works of non-fiction, including *Rasa'il ila ibnati: mashakil al-hubb wa-l-zawaj wa-l-jins* (Letters to My Daughter: Problems of Love, Marriage, and Sex, n.d.), *Hiwar al-sharq wa-l-gharb* (A Dialogue of East and West, n.d.). Her translations include, *Mon chere inconnu* (translation of Anis Mansour's *'Azizi fulan*) and *Laylat al-qadar* (translation of Tahar Ben Jelloun's *La nuit sacrée.*).

Hiwar al-hubb (A Dialogue of Love, short stories). Cairo: General Egyptian Book Organization, 1986.

'Id milad al-amira (The Princess' Birthday, children's literature). Cairo: General Egyptian Book Organization, 1987.

Man ana? (Who Am I?, novel). Cairo: General Egyptian Book Organization, 1990.

'Asima bila rutush wa riyah al-janub (A Capital without Makeup and the Southern Winds, novel). Cairo: General Egyptian Book Organization, 1995.

al-Tifla al-mudallala (The Spoiled Child, children's literature). Cairo: Dar al-Ma'arif, 1995.

al-Himar al-nafi' (The Useful Donkey, children's literature). Cairo: Dar al-Ma'arif, 1996.

Jism al-insan (The Human Body, children's literature). Cairo: Dar al-Ma'arif, 1996.

Sa'diya (Sa'diya, short stories). Cairo: Dar Madbuli Publishers, n.d.

Bu Saha, Mabruka (1943–), Algerian poet born in Tiaret. She studied journalism and media in Cairo. She works as a producer and announcer.

Bara'im (Blossoms, poetry). Algiers: al-Wataniya Publishing and Distribution, 1969.

Bubsit, Bahiya (1967–), Saudi short-story writer born in al-Ahsa'. She received her secondary-school diploma in 1976. She works in administration at the Educational Counseling Office in al-Ahsa'. She is a member of the Women of al-Ahsa' Charitable Association and the Culture and Arts Association in al-Ta'if. She received the Abha Cultural Prize in 1991.

Imra'a 'ala fuwahat burkan (A Woman on the Mouth of a Volcano, short stories). N.p.: Dar 'Alam Books, 1985.

Durra min al-Ahsa' (A Pearl from al-Ahsa', short stories). Riyadh: al-Jazira Foundation Press, 1987.

Ma'sat Nura wa akharin (The Tragedy of Nura and Others, short stories). Riyadh: Dar al-Raya, 1990.

Wa tasha' al-aqdar (And the Fates Wish It, short stories). Riyadh: al-Jazira Foundation Press, 1990.

al-Masyada (The Trap, short stories). N.p.: n.p., 1993.

Budayr, 'Azza Muhammad (1964–), Egyptian short-story writer born in Tukh. She is a social worker at the Ministry of Youth and Sport.

Maqam al-khawf (The Stage of Fear, short stories). Cairo: General Authority for Culture Palaces, 1997.

al-Buhayri, Ni'mat (1953–), Egyptian short-story writer born in Shibin al-Qanatir. She received a B.A. in business from Ain Shams University in 1976 and works as an administrative specialist. Many of her stories have been translated into English. She was married to an Iraqi and was in Iraq during the first Gulf War. The wartime climate did not allow her marriage to develop and had a negative effect on her writing. She asked for a divorce so that she could continue her writing, which had a great impact on her works.

Nisf imra'a (Half a Woman, short stories) Cairo: Dar al-Thaqafa Printing and Publishing, 1984.

al-'Ashiqun (The Lovers, short stories). Cairo: General Egyptian Book Organization, 1989.

Dil' a'waj (A Bent Rib, novel). Cairo: General Egyptian Book Organization, 1997.

Irtihalat al-lu'lu' (The Pearl's Wanderings, short stories). Cairo: General Authority for Culture Palaces, 1997.

al-Buhi, Fawziya Labib (?–), Egyptian novelist.

al-Shahid al-'azim (The Great Martyr, novel). Cairo: Supreme Council to Foster Arts and Humanities, 1970.

Bulhajj, Lamiya' (?–), Tunisian poet.

Mir'a wa imra'a wa-l-bahr (A Mirror, a Woman, and the Sea, poetry). Tunis: n.p., 1993.

B

Buqsh'an, Lulu Salih (1965–), Saudi poet born in Jeddah. She received a B.A. in English literature from King Sa'ud University in 1987. She is an editor for *al-Riyad* and an announcer for the English section of Riyadh radio.
Thartharat al-bawh al-samit (The Chatter of the Silent Confession, poetry). Riyadh: al-Sharif Press, 1989.

Burayk, Samira (1953–), Syrian short-story writer born in Kharba (al-Suwayda'). She received her primary and secondary education in al-Suwayda' and received a degree in dentistry from Damascus University. She has been a dentist since 1977. She has translated a work on the novel in Latin America into Arabic, *al-Riwaya fi Amrika al-Latiniya*. She is a member of the Story and Novel Association.
Ahzan shajar al-laymun (The Lemon Tree's Woes, short stories). Beirut: Dar al-Masira, 1979.

Bursili, Khazna Khalid (1946–), Kuwaiti poet. She received a B.A. in Arabic and Islamic studies in 1970 and she has a degree in education. She was the department head of school activities at the Ministry of Education's Curriculum Research Center from 1980 until she retired. She is a member of the Kuwaiti Authors' League. She has published in several Kuwaiti and Gulf newspapers and magazines.
Azhar Ayyar (May Flowers, poetry). Kuwait: Ministry of Information, 1976.
Jirahat Kuwaytiya (Kuwaiti Wounds, poetry). N.p.: n.p., n.d.

al-Busmayt, 'A'isha (1965–), Emirati poet. She has a B.A. in media from Emirates University. She has worked as a program researcher for Sharjah television. She is a member of the Emirati Writers' and Authors' Union and the Emirati Women Authors' League.
Sayyidat al-rafd al-akhir (The Woman of the Final Refusal, poetry). Sharjah: Emirati Writers' and Authors' Union Publications, 1995.

al-Bustani, Alice Butrus (1870–1926), Lebanese novelist.
Sa'iba (Correct, novel). Beirut: al-Adabiya Press, 1891.

al-Bustani, Bushra (1950–), Iraqi poet born in Mosul. She received a Ph.D. in Arabic literature for her dissertation, *Naqd al-shi'r al-hadith: al-bina' al-fanni li-shi'r al-harb fi-l-'Iraq* (Critique of Modern Poetry: The Artistic Structure of War Poetry in Iraq). She has published several academic and cultural works and studies in literary criticism in Iraq and abroad. She is currently a professor of Arabic literature at Mosul University.
Ma ba'd al-huzn (After Sorrow, poetry). Beirut: Maktabat al-Nahda, 1973.
al-Ughniya wa-l-sikkin (The Song and the Knife, poetry). Baghdad: Ministry of Information, 1976.
Ana wa-l-aswar (The Walls and I, poetry). Mosul: Mosul University, 1979.
Zahr al-hada'iq (Flower of the Gardens, poetry). Baghdad: Ministry of Culture and Information, 1984.
Uqabbil kaff Baghdad (I Kiss Baghdad's Palm, poetry). Baghdad: Ministry of Culture and Information, 1989.

Buzu, Majida (?–), Syrian poet and novelist who lives in Latakia. She established a publishing house, Dar al-Majd, to publish her works.
Sada ruhi (The Echo of My Soul, poetry). Damascus: al-'Ilmiya Press, 1976.
Sajina bayn al-zahir wa-l-batin (Imprisoned Between the Exterior and the Interior, novel). Latakia: Dar al-Majd, 1991.
al-Mawt al-hadi' (The Quiet Death, novel). Latakia: Dar al-Majd, 1993.
Hubb wa ashya' ukhra (Love and Other Things, short stories). Latakia: Dar al-Majd, 1995.

Chabbi, Fadhila (Shabbi, Fadila) (1946–), Tunisian novelist and poet born in 24 Tawzar. She is a graduate of the College of Liberal Arts and Humanities in Tunis and teaches Arabic in high schools. She was awarded the Wallada Poetry Prize in 1984 by the Arab Spanish Cultural Institute in Madrid. She is also the recipient of the prize for the best collection of poetry published by a woman in Arabic in Tunisia in the twentieth century.

Rawa'ih al-ard wa-l-ghadab (The Scents of Earth and Anger, poetry). Beirut: Arab Institute for Research and Publishing, 1973.

al-Layali taht al-ajras al-thaqila (Nights Under the Heavy Bells, poetry). Tunis: n.p., 1988.

al-Hada'iq al-handasiya (Geometric Gardens, poetry). Tunis: n.p., 1989.

Shamarikh (Date Clusters, colloquial poetry). Tunis: n.p., 1991.

al-Ism wa-l-hadid (The Name and the Lowland, novel). Tunis: n.p., 1992.

al-Kawakib al-ma'iya (The Watery Planets, children's poetry). Tunis: n.p., 1995.

Miyah nisbiya (Relative Waters, poetry). Tunis: Dar Aqwas Publishers, 1998.

al-Uf'uwan (The Viper, poetry). Tunis: n.p., 1999.

al-Dabbagh, Ibtisam 'Abd Allah (1943–), Iraqi novelist and short-story writer born in Kirkuk. She received her early education in Kirkuk and Mosul. She graduated from the English literature department at Baghdad University in 1964. She headed the news and translation department at Baghdad television. In 1968 she was appointed head of the oversight department at the General Institution of Journalism. In 1969 she was an editor for the weekly *Alif ba'* and later settled at *al-Jumhuriya* newspaper as a translator and editor. She was a television presenter on her famed program, "Sira wa dhkirayat" (Life Story and Memories) from 1967 to 1987. She published many translations, most famously Mikis Theodorakis's *Journal de résistance (Yawmiyat al-muqawama fi-l-Yunan)* and the autobiography of Angela Davis *(Mudhakkirat Anjila Dafiz)*. She also translated the screenplay of Ingmar Bergman's film, "Autumn Sonata." She belongs to the Union of Authors and Writers in Iraq and

was a boardmember of the Journalists' Syndicate for three terms, from 1984 to 1990.

Fajr nahar wahshi (Dawn of a Wild Day, novel). Baghdad: Dar al-Adib, 1984.

Mamarr ila-l-layl (A Passage to the Night, novel). Baghdad: Dar al-Shu'un al-Thaqafiya, 1988.

Matar aswad matar ahmar (Black Rain, Red Rain, novel). London: Dar Mawaqif 'Arabiya, 1994.

Bukhur (Incense, short stories). Baghdad: Dar al-Shu'un al-Thaqafiya, 1998.

al-Dabbagh, Iman, Saudi poet. She works at al-Jazira newspaper.

Taranim al-mays (Hymns of the Proud). N.p.: N.p., 1999.

al-Dabuni, Safiya (1931–), Iraqi short-story writer born in Mosul. She studied in Iraq and Egypt and has a B.A. in Arabic from Cairo University.

Mas'alat sharaf (A Matter of Honor, short stories). Cairo: al-Dar al-Qawmiya, 1967.

al-Daghfaq, Huda 'Abd Allah (1967–), Saudi poet born in al-Mujammi'a. She lives in Riyadh. She received a B.A. in Arabic and education from the College of Education for Girls run by the General Office of Girls' Education in Riyadh in 1990. She has taught Arabic since 1991.

al-Zill ila a'la (The Upward Shadow, poetry). Riyadh: Dar al-Ard Publishers, 1993.

Daghir, Katherine Ma'luf (?–?), Lebanese novelist.

Ghussa fi-l-qalb (A Lump in the Heart, novel). Beirut: Dar Maktabat al-Hayat, 1965.

Kifah imra'a (A Woman's Struggle, novel). Beirut: Dar Maktabat al-Hayat, 1965.

Dahir, Hanina (?–), Lebanese poet born in the district of al-Nabatiya.

Kukh wa alam (A Hut and Pain, folk poetry). N.p.: n.p., 1952.

Iman (Faith, folk poetry). N.p.: n.p., 1956.

Dahla, Ghada (1964–), Palestinian poet born in the village of Qar'an in the part of Palestine occupied in 1948. She went to school in her village and enrolled in the Teachers' Academy. She is a teacher in the Bedouin sector in Beersheba.

al-Bahth fi-l-'uyun al-sahira (Searching in Wakeful Eyes, poetry). Nazareth: n.p., 1983.

Dakarmanji, 'A'ida (?–), Lebanese short-story writer.

Ghadan yawm akhar (Tomorrow Is Another Day, short stories). Beirut: al-Maktaba al-Sharqiya, 1983.

La taghib 'anni (Don't Leave Me, short stories). Beirut: Dar al-'Ilm li-l-Malayin, 1994.

al-Dalati, 'Alya' Huju (1932–), Lebanese poet and novelist born in Tripoli. She is also an artist. She has worked for the press and has published in *al-Bayraq*, *al-Kamira*, and *al-Raqib*. She has worked at Lebanese radio since 1964.

'Alya' ('Alya', poetry). Beirut: Lebanese Arab Company, 1968.

Khada'atni al-mir'a (The Mirror Deceived Me, novel). Beirut: 'Ashtarut Publications, 1968.

Batal 'ala sadri (A Hero on My Breast, novel). Beirut: al-Sharqiya Company, 1969.

Layali al-hubb (Nights of Love, novel). Beirut: United Commercial, 1969.

Nisa' min jahannam (Women from Hell, novel). Beirut: al-Sharqiya Company, 1969.

al-'Ashiqa (The Lover, poetry). Beirut: al-Sharqiya Company, 1970.

Murahiqa hatta ish'ar akhar (An Adolescent until Further Notice, poetry). Beirut: al-Sharqiya Company, 1970.

Qamus al-hubb (Dictionary of Love, novel). Beirut: al-Sharqiya Company, 1972.

Shari' al-'ushshaq (Lovers' Lane, novel). Beirut: al-Sharqiya Company, 1972.

Ta'iha fi Bayrut (Lost in Beirut, novel). Beirut: Maktabat al-Ma'arif, 1973.

Hariba min al-qadar (Fleeing from Fate, novel). Beirut: Dar al-Masira, 1977.

Lan aqtul watani (I Will Not Kill My Homeland, novel). Beirut: Dar al-Masira, 1977.

Anta wa ana (You and I, novel). Beirut: Maktabat al-Ma'arif, 1982.

Dam'at hubb fi Baris (A Tear of Love in Paris, novel). Beirut: Maktabat al-Ma'arif, 1995.

Damanhuri, Salwa 'Abd al-'Aziz (?–), Saudi novelist.

al-La'na (The Curse, novel). Mecca: al-Safa Press, 1994.

Sira' 'aqli wa 'atifati (A Conflict of My Mind and My Emotion, novel). Jeddah: Dar al-Khashrami Publishers, n.d.

Damuni, Nihay (1953–), Palestinian short-story writer born in Shafa 'Amr in the part of Palestine occupied in 1948. She received her high-school diploma in night school. She lives in Shafa 'Amr.

Rihlat al-'adhab (The Journey of Suffering, short stories). Haifa: Office of Arab Culture, 1993.

Sira' ma'a al-zaman (A Conflict with Time, short stories). Kafr Kanna: Hisham Press, 1994.

Darqawi, Hanan (1971–), Moroccan writer born in Tangier. She received a B.A. in philosophy in 1995 and a degree in advanced studies from Muhammad V University. She is a philosophy teacher in a secondary school.

Tuyur bayda' (White Birds, short stories). al-Qunaytira: al-Bukili Printing, Publishing, and Distribution, 1997.

al-Darraji, Samira (?–), Iraqi short-story writer and novelist.

Risalat ghufran (An Epistle of Forgiveness, short stories). Mosul: al-Zawra' Modern Press, 1969.

Ashwak fi tariq al-shabab (Thorns on the Path of Youth, novel). Mosul: al-Jumhuriya Press, 1970.

Darwish, Anisa (1941–), Palestinian poet born in the village of al-Maliha in

Jerusalem. She has a high-school diploma.

Saf'at wa qubal (Slaps and Kisses, poetry). Jerusalem: Dar al-Katib Publications, 1991.

Wa ahun 'alayk (And I Am Unimportant to You, poetry). Jerusalem: Dar al-Katib Publications, 1992.

Sitr al-layl (The Night Curtain, poetry). Jerusalem: Dar al-Katib Publications, 1994.

Anisiyat (Intimacies, colloquial poetry). Jerusalem: Dar al-Katib Publications, 1995.

al-Nada al-jabali ya'raq (Mountain Dew Sweats, poetry). Jerusalem: Dar al-Katib Publications, 1995.

Man minkum habibi (Who Among You Is My Beloved, poetry). Jerusalem: Dar al-Katib Publications, 1996.

Min milaff rasa'ili (From My Letter File, prose letters). Jerusalem: Palestinian Writers' Union Publications, 1996.

Nawma 'ala khadd al-shi'r (A Nap on Poetry's Cheek, colloquial poetry). Jerusalem: Dar al-Katib Publications, 1996.

Tasabih (Songs of Praise, prose letters, part two of *Min milaff rasa'ili*). N.p.: Dar al-Faruq, 1998.

Raqsat al-khaliya (Dance of the Beehive, poetry). N.p.: Dar al-Faruq, 1998.

Shams 'ala-l-nabi (Sun on the Prophet, autobiography). N.p.: n.p., 1999.

Darwish, Hanan (1952–), Syrian short-story writer and journalist born in Misyaf. She was educated at the Teachers' Academy and works at the Misyaf Cultural Center. She writes for Syrian and Arab newspapers and magazines, including *al-Usbu' al-adabi*, the Kuwaiti *al-Siyasa*, *al-Fida'*, *al-Ba'th*, and *al-Thawra*.

Dhalik al-sada (That Echo, short stories). Misyaf: Dar al-Sarmad, 1994.

Fada' akhar li-ta'ir al-nar (Another Sky for the Bird of Fire, short stories). Aleppo: n.p., 1995.

Bawh al-zaman al-akhir (Confession of the Final Time, short stories). Damascus: Arab Writers' Union, 1997.

Wa 'adat al-'asafir (And the Sparrows Returned, short stories). N.p.: n.p., n.d.

Darwish, Usayma (1939–), Syrian novelist born in Damascus. She received a B.A. in Arabic language from King Sa'ud University in Riyadh. She published the non-fiction work, *Masar al-tahawwulat* (Road of Transformations) in 1992.

Shajarat al-hubb, ghabat al-ahzan (Tree of Love, Forest of Sorrows, novel). Beirut: Dar al-Adab, 2000.

al-Dawi, Zaynab Mar'i (1952–), Lebanese poet born in Mashghara. She received her primary and secondary education at public schools in her hometown. She received a degree from the Teachers' School in Beirut in 1972 and completed two years at the Lebanese University studying Arabic literature. She teaches in public schools in Beirut. She has published critical essays in *Nida' al-watan* and is a member of the Lebanese Writers' Union, the Cultural Council for Southern Lebanon, and the Tuesday Cultural Forum. She is a founding member of the Friday Cultural Forum and Friends of Writers and Books.

Fasila bayn al-ma' wa-l-nar (An Interval between Water and Fire, poetry). Beirut: Friends of Writers and Books, 1991.

Nayat ka'annaha al-zaynab (Flutes Like the Zaynab Tree, poetry). Beirut: Dar al-Katib al-'Arabi, 1996.

Dawud, Siham (1952–), Palestinian poet born in Ramle. She went to school in Ramle and Jaffa. She worked at Dar al-Nashr al-'Arabi and at *al-Ittihad* newspaper, becoming the editorial secretary in 1978. She was then the editorial director of the Palestinian magazine, *Masharif*. She translated many Arabic poems into Hebrew and published a collection of poems in Hebrew titled *Ani ohevet bi-deyo levana* (I Love in White Ink, Tel Aviv, 1984).

Hakadha ughanni (That's How I Sing, poetry). Jerusalem: Salah al-Din Publications, 1979.

al-Daylami, Munira (?–), Yemeni poet and journalist. She writes for *al-Mar'a* newspaper. In the introduction to her poetry collection, *Taranim wajd Yamaniya*, the well-known Yemeni poet Dr. 'Abd al-'Aziz al-Maqalih described her as "a poet of the generation of the revolution who loved poetry and began writing it." Her poetry has been published in the local and Arab press.

Taranim wajd Yamaniya (Yemeni Hymns of Love, poetry). Sana'a: Dar al-Tawjih al-Ma'nawi, n.d.

Dhahab, Nafila (1947–), Tunisian short-story writer born in Tunis. She was educated in Tunis. She has a B.A., a law degree, and two degrees from the Academy for Journalism and Media Sciences. She was a division head at the Esparto and Paper Company and a civil servant at the Ministry of Culture. She received a prize for her first collection of short stories and a national prize for a children's story. She also received a prize for the best short-story collection published in Tunisia in the twentieth century. She is interested in translation and has made contributions to poetry.

A'mida min dukhan (Pillars of Smoke, short stories). Tunis: Dar Safa' Publishing and Journalism, 1979.

Ahlamuna (Our Dreams, children's literature translated from French). N.p.: Dar Malika Publishers, 1979.

Rihlat Yabusa al-najma Sina (Yabusa's Journey, Sina the Star, children's literature). Tunis: Tunisian Distribution Company, al-Dar al-Tunisiya Publishers, and Dar al-Janub Publishers, 1980.

al-Shams wa-l-asmant (Sun and Cement, short stories). Tunis: Dar Safa' Publishing and Journalism, 1983.

Mughamarat al-qird Mukhmakh (The Adventures of Mukhmakh the Monkey, children's literature). Tunis: Tunisian Distribution Company, 1986.

al-Samt (Silence, short stories). Tunis: Dar al-Bahth 'an Tibr al-Zaman, 1993.

al-Ghaba al-sajina (The Imprisoned Forest, children's literature). Tunis: Dar al-Janub Publishers and Amnesty International, 1994.

Dhiyab, Fatima (1951–), Palestinian writer born in the village of al-Tamra. She was educated in her village and in Nazareth. She works with the cultural committee of the Popular Cultural Center in al-Tamra. She has published several types of works, among them novels, drama, children's stories, and reflections. She was the recipient of a prize from Bayt al-Karma for her play, *Ghaltat 'umr* (Mistake of a Lifetime).

Rihla fi qitar al-madi (A Journey on the Train of the Past, novel and short stories). Acre: al-Qabas al-'Arabi, 1972.

'Ali al-sayyad ('Ali the Fisherman, children's literature). Tamra: privately published, 1982.

Tawbat na'ama (An Ostrich Repents, children's literature). Tamra: privately published, 1982.

Jurh fi-l-qalb (A Wound in the Heart, reflections and illustrations). 'Iblin: printed by poet George Najib Khalil, 1983.

al-Khayal al-majnun (The Mad Phantom, short stories). 'Iblin: printed by poet George Najib Khalil, 1983.

Qadiya nisa'iya (A Woman's Cause, novel). Shafa 'Amr: Dar al-Mashriq, 1987.

Sirruk fi bir (Your Secret Is Safe, play). Shafa 'Amr: Dar al-Mashriq, 1987.

Jalid al-ayyam (The Ice of Days, short stories). Nazareth: Office of Arab Culture, 1995.

al-Khayt wa-l-tazziz (The Thread, play). N.p.: privately published, 1996.

Dhu-l-Fiqar Majida (?–), Egyptian poet.

Tarnimat ha'ira (Confused Hymns, poetry). Cairo: General Egyptian Book Organization, 1990.

Dimashqiya, Julia Tu'ma (1883–1953), Lebanese pioneer in education, social affairs, and journalism born in al-Mukhtara. She was one of the first Christian girls to receive an education at the American School for Girls in Sidon, the Kafr Shima School, and the al-Shuwayfat School. She taught at schools in Barmana and Shafa 'Amr in Palestine before returning to Beirut. She met al-Sayyid Badr Dimashqiya (whom she later married), who, with al-Sayyid 'Ali Salam, was responsible for the education department in the al-Maqasid Islamic Charitable Association. He asked her to direct the first girls' school for the association in 1914. She established the Women's Association and the Women's Club in Beirut in 1917, whose objective was to "bring Syrian women to a level appropriate to them, encourage them to work in the modern renaissance, and create a real spirit of understanding between Syrian women of all confessions." Well-known members of the Women's Association include Amira Zayn al-Din, Salma Junblat, Badriya Zantut, Huda Dumat, 'Afifa Sa'b, Amina Khuri, Mari Yani, and Najla Abi-l-Lam'a. She issued and served as the editor from 1921 to 1928 for the monthly magazine, *al-Mar'a al-jadida*, the organ of the Women's Association, whose objective was to disseminate "a spirit of independent education, improve family life, and elevate Syrian women literarily, scientifically, and socially." This was one of the first women's magazines in Lebanon and it carved out a venerable space for itself. She published in *Sawt al-mar'a*, *al-Hasna'*, *al-Fatah*, *al-Fajr*, and *al-Nadim*, and she published children's stories in the children's magazine, *Samir al-sighar*. She represented the Association for Young Women's Enculturation and the Women's Union at the Global Women's Conference held in Istanbul in 1935. She published a work of non-fiction, *Mayy fi Suriya wa Lubnan* (Mayy in Syria and Lebanon), in 1924. She received the Lebanese Gold Medal of Achievement in 1947.

Dixon, Zuhur (1933–), Iraqi poet born in Abu-l-Khasib in the province of Basra. She completed her primary and preparatory education there and graduated from the Teachers' Institute. She educated herself in language and literature. She was a teacher and later a school principal. She also worked in the General Union of Iraqi Women and was a desk chief at *al-Mar'a* magazine. She is a member of the Authors' Union.

Khalf al-dhakira al-thaljiya (Behind Frozen Memory, poetry). Beirut: Dar al-'Awda, 1975.

Sada' al-sada wa asfar al-layl (The Echo's Rust and Journeys of the Night, poetry). Baghdad: Ministry of Information, 1975.

Wa li-l-mudun sahwa ukhra (And Cities Have Another Awakening, poetry). Baghdad: Ministry of Information, 1976.

Fi kull shay' watan (In Every Thing Is a Homeland, poetry). Baghdad: Ministry of Culture, 1979.

Marrat amtar al-shams (The Sun's Rains Passed, poetry). Baghdad: Ministry of Culture and Information, 1988.

Wahati halat al-qamar (My Oasis Is the Moon's Halo, poetry). Baghdad: Dar al-Hurriya, 1989.

Laylat al-ghaba (Forest Night, poetry). Baghdad: Dar al-Shu'un al-Thaqafiya, 1994.

Maraya al-a'asir (The Whirlwinds' Mirrors, poetry). Cairo: al-Dar al-Misriya al-Lubnaniya, 1998.

Dudin, Rifqa (?–), Jordanian novelist and short-story writer.

Qalaq mashru' (Legitimate Anxiety, short stories). Amman: Kitabukum Press, 1991.

Majdur al-'Urban (Among Pockmarked Bedouin, novel). Amman: Ram Foundation for Technology and Computers, 1993.

al-Dulaymi, Lutfiya (1943–), Iraqi writer born in Baghdad. She received a B.A. in Arabic literature in 1966. She also attended English literature classes at Gold-smiths College, University of London. She was a teacher and later the editorial secretary of *al-Thaqafa al-ajnabiya*. She was the president of the Women's Cultural Forum in Baghdad. In 1984 she devoted herself to writing full time. In 1993 she wrote a weekly literary column in *al-Qadisiya al-thaqafiya*. In 1994 she wrote for *al-Quds al-'Arabi*. She has published translations of several books, including *Snow Country*, a novel by Japanese writer Yasunari Kawabata (1985), and *Clear Light of Day*, a novel by Indian writer Anita Desai (1989). She wrote about writing women in ancient Iraqi civilizations in a pamphlet titled *Sharikat al-masir al-abadi* (Partners of the Immortal Destiny, 1999). Her stories have been translated into European and Asian languages. Her collection, *Musiqa sufiya*, won the Best Fiction Prize in Iraq in 1994, and her play, *al-Layali al-Sumiriya*, won a prize for the best play adapted from the Iraqi tradition. She has published a collection of essays as *al-Mughlaq wa-l-maftuh* (The Closed and the Open, 1997). The journal *Difaf* dedicated to her its fifth issue, "Lutfiya al-Dulaymi fi maraya al-ibda' wa-l-naqd" (Lutfiya al-Dulaymi in the Mirrors of Fiction and Criticism, 2000).

Mamarr ila ahzan al-rijal (A Corridor to the Sorrows of Men, short stories). Baghdad: Dar al-Jahiz, 1969.

al-Bishara (Glad Tidings, short stories). Baghdad: Dar al-Hurriya, 1975.

al-Timthal (The Statue, short story). Baghdad: Ministry of Information, 1977.

Idha kunt tuhibb (If You Love, short stories). Baghdad: Dar al-Rashid Publishers, 1980.

'Alam al-nisa' al-wahidat (World of Lone Women, novel and short stories). Baghdad: Dar al-Shu'un al-Thaqafiya al-'Amma, 1986.

Man yarith al-firdaws (He Who Tills Paradise, novel). Cairo: General Egyptian Book Organization, 1987.

Budhur al-nar (Seeds of Fire, novel). Baghdad: Dar al-Shu'un al-Thaqafiya, 1988.

Musiqa sufiya (Sufi Music, short stories). Baghdad: Dar al-Shu'un al-Thaqafiya, 1994.

Ma lam yaqulhu al-ruwah (What the Story-tellers Do Not Say, short stories). Amman: Dar al-Azmina, 1999.

al-Kura al-hamra' (The Red Ball, play). N.p.: n.p., n.d.

al-Layali al-Sumiriya (Sumerian Nights, play). N.p.: n.p., n.d.

Qamar Ur (The Moon of Ur, play). N.p.: n.p., n.d.

al-Shabih al-akhir (The Final Resemblance, play). N.p.: n.p., n.d.

al-Duraydi, Fatima (1952–), Tunisian poet born in Tunis. Her education ended in the last year of high school. She took a job at the Postal Ministry. She joined Tunisian radio as an employee and later became an announcer. She worked in the humanities section of the Ministry of Cultural Affairs and the Arab Organization for Education, Culture, and Sciences in the 1980s. She has written poetry, essays, short stories, songs, and children's songs, and her work has been published in Tunisian and Arab magazines and newspapers. She has taken part in many poetry festivals and events in Tunisia.

Dahkat 'uyun bakiya (Smiles from Crying Eyes, poetry). Tunis: al-Dar al-Tunisiya Publishers, 1977.

al-Durdunji, Hiyam Ramzi (1942–), Palestinian writer born in Jaffa. She resides in Amman. She went to school in Tripoli, Libya, and later enrolled in Benghazi University, from which she graduated in 1976. She is a member of the Writers' League and the Jordanian Authors' and Writers' Union. She published a critical study titled *Fadwa Tuqan: sha'ira am burkan* (Fadwa Tuqan: Poet or Volcano, Amman, Dar al-Karmel, 1994).

Zahrat fi rabi' al-'umr (Flowers in the Spring of Life, poetry). Tripoli, Libya: Dar al-Fikr, 1966.

Alhan wa ahzan (Melodies and Sorrows, poetry). Tripoli, Libya: Libyan Ministry of Culture, 1969.

Dumu' al-nay (Tears of the Flute, poetry). Tripoli, Libya: Dar al-Fikr, 1969.

Ila-l-liqa' fi Jaffa (Goodbye in Jaffa, novel). Tripoli, Libya: Dar al-Fikr, 1970.

Wada'an ya ams (Farewell Yesterday, novel). Tripoli, Libya: Maktabat al-Fikr, 1972.

Ughniyat li-l-qamar (Songs for the Moon, poetry). Tripoli, Libya: Dar al-Fikr, 1973.

al-Nakhla wa-l-i'sar (The Palm Tree and the Cyclone, short stories). Tripoli, Libya: Maktabat al-Fikr, 1974.

'Abir al-kalimat (Scent of Words, poetry). Amman: Dar al-Ufuq al-Jadid, 1982.

Rasamtuk shi'ran (I Drew You in Poetry, poetry). Amman: al-Sharq Press, 1984.

Qasa'id rihlat sayf (Poems of a Summer Journey, poetry). Amman: Dar al-Karmel, 1985.

Mazamir fi zaman al-shidda (Psalms in a Time of Difficulty, poetry). Amman: al-Sharq Press, 1987.

Buhur bila mawani' (Seas Without Ports, poetry). Amman: Dar al-Karmel, 1989.

Humum imra'a sha'ira (Concerns of a Woman Poet, poetry). Amman: Dar al-Karmel, 1992.

al-Tahliq bi-ajnihat al-hulm (Flying on the Wings of a Dream, poetry). Amman: Dar al-Karmel, 1996.

al-Duwayk, Almas Salman (1904–1978), Lebanese poet, children's writer, and artist born in al-Shuwayfat. She was educated at the Sisters of Nazareth School and the Zahrat al-Ihsan convent school in Beirut. She studied Arabic with Shaykh Ibrahim al-Mundhir. She published several articles in the Lebanese journals *al-Mar'a al-jadida*, *Minirfa*, *al-Fajr*, *al-Khidr*, and *al-Jumhur*. She published one work of non-fiction, *'Ala durub al-hayah* (On the Paths of Life, 1978), containing her articles on literary and social issues, as well as essays on women's issues and rights.

Balabil al-rabi' (Spring Nightingales, children's literature). Beirut: Samir Press, n.d.

Hilat Abu Zahra (Abu Zahra's Ruse, children's literature). Beirut: Samir Press, n.d.

Sawsan wa ummuha (Sawsan and Her Mother, children's literature). Beirut: Samir Press, n.d.

Diyafat al-'Arab (Hospitality of the Arabs, children's literature). Beirut: Samir Press, n.d.

Quwat al-ta'awun (The Power of Cooperation, children's literature). Beirut: Samir Press, n.d.

al-Fadil, Munira Khalifa (1958–), Bahraini short-story writer. She has a B.A. in English literature from Kuwait University and a Ph.D. in comparative literature from the University of Essex in Britain. She is an assistant professor at the University of Bahrain. She is a member of the Writers' and Authors' League in Bahrain and the National Council for Culture, Arts, and Literature. She has published a full-length study of Arab women novelists.

al-Rimura (The Suckerfish, short stories). Kuwait: al-Rabi'an Publishing Company, 1983.

al-Fahd, Hayat Ahmad (?–), Kuwaiti novelist.

'Itab (Rebuke, novel). Kuwait: Sawt al-Khalij Press, n.d.

Fahim, Izis (?–), Egyptian short-story writer.

Bayn zawji wa ummi (Between My Husband and My Mother, short stories, with Samiya Anwar and Tawfiq Lutf Allah). Cairo: Dar al-Thaqafa al-Masihiya, 1974.

Fahmi, Asma' (?–1956), Pioneering Egyptian writer. She graduated from al-Saniya School in 1920 and enrolled in the Egyptian University, where she attended evening lectures. She was part of an academic mission to England and studied Islamic history at the University of London. She taught in various secondary schools and published many essays and short stories in Egyptian newspapers and journals in the early twentieth century.

Fahmi, Matilda Halim (?–), Egyptian short-story writer.
Rabi' al-hayah (The Spring of Life, short stories). Cairo: Misr Modern Press, 1954.

Fahmi, Siham (?–), Egyptian novelist.
Azwaj wa zawjat 'arafathum al-Qahira (The Husbands and Wives of Cairo, novel). Cairo: al-Dajwa Press, 1959.
Hubbuk nar (Your Love Is Fire, novel). Cairo: Atlas Press, 1960.
Lan abki ya ummi (I Will Not Cry, Mother, novel). Cairo: Atlas Press, 1960.

Fahmi, Zaynab (Rafiqat al-Tabi'a) (1941–), Moroccan short-story writer born in Casablanca. She was a high-school teacher and later a principal at a Casablanca high school. She has been a member of the Moroccan Writers' Union since June 1968. She is considered a pioneer of the short story in Morocco, but she stopped publishing in the 1980s after she wrote a series of articles dealing with aspects of the Prophet's life. She is also known as Rafiqat al-Tabi'a.
Rajul wa imra'a (A Man and a Woman, short stories). Casablanca: Dar al-Kitab, 1969.
Taht al-qantara (Under the Bridge, short stories). Casablanca: Dar al-Kitab, 1976.
Rih al-sumum (Winds of the Sandstorm, short stories). Casablanca: Dar al-Nashr al-Maghribiya, 1979.

al-Faqih, Jamila (?–), Syrian novelist born in al-Suwayda'. She lives in London.
'Ala darb al-sa'ada (On the Road of Happiness, novel). Damascus: Dar al-Hijaz, 1977.
Satafhamuni akthar (You Will Understand Me More, novel). Damascus: Damascus Press, 1979.

Wa yabqa khayt min al-amal (A Thread of Hope Remains, novel). Damascus: Damascus Press, 1981.

Farah, Najwa Kawar (Farah, Najwa Qa'war) (1923?–) (see also: Bibliography of Works in English), Palestinian writer born in Nazareth. She attended school in Nazareth and later attended the Teachers' Academy in Jerusalem. She was a teacher in Nazareth in 1943. With her husband, Father Rafiq Farah, she put out the magazine, *al-Ra'id*, in 1957. In 1965 she published several articles on political, social, and literary issues in the press. She lived in Haifa until the mid-1960s and then moved abroad.
'Abiru al-sabil (The Passersby, short stories). Beirut: Dar al-Rayhani, 1954.
Durub masabih (Lamp Paths, short stories). Nazareth: al-Hakim Press, 1956.
Mudhakkirat rihla (Memoirs of Journey, autobiography). Nazareth: al-Hakim Press, 1957.
Sirr Shahrazad (Sheherazade's Secret, play). Nazareth: al-Hakim Press, 1958.
'Abir wa asda' (Scent and Echoes, illustrations). Nazareth: al-Hakim Press, 1959.
Malik al-majd (The King of Glory, play about Jesus Christ). Nazareth: al-Hakim Press, 1961.
Li-man al-rabi'? (Who Owns Spring?, short stories). Nazareth: al-Hakim Press, 1963.
Silsilat qisas li-l-ashbal (A Series of Stories for Young Ones, children's literature, 3 vols.). Nazareth: n.p., 1963–1965.
al-Liqa' (The Meeting, short stories). Beirut: Dar al-Nahar, 1972.
Ummat al-rabb (Nation of the Lord, play). Beirut: Dar al-Nafir, 1972.
'Ahd min al-Quds (A Vow from Jerusalem). Beirut: Palestinian Journalists' and Writers' Union, 1978.
Rihlat al-huzn wa-l-'ata' (Journey of Sadness and Giving). Beirut: Dar al-Kalima, 1981.
Intifadat al-'asafir (The Sparrows' Uprising, short stories). Amman: Dar al-Jalil and the Office of Culture, 1991.

Sukkan al-tabiq al-'ulwi (The People Up-stairs, novel). Amman: Jordanian Artistic Committee to Support the Intifada, 1996.

Faraj, 'Aziza Zaki (?–?) , Egyptian novelist.
Nuwwar al-azhar (The Flowers' Blossoms, novel). Cairo: al-Taqaddum Modern Press, 1927.
Zinat al-azhar (The Flowers' Ornament, novel). Cairo: al-Taqaddum Modern Press, 1927.

Faraj, Maryam Jum'a (?–), Emirati short-story writer.
Fayruz (Fayruz, short stories). Sharjah: Emirati Writers' and Authors' Union Publications, 1988.
Ma' (Water, short stories). Beirut: privately published, distributed by Dar al-Jadid, 1994.

Faraj, Sana' Muhammad (1961–), Egyptian novelist and short-story writer.
Sabah fi-l-mukhayyam (Sabah in the Camp, novel). Cairo: General Egyptian Book Organization, 1991.
Tifl al-jabal al-multahib (Child of the Flaming Mountain, short stories). Cairo: General Authority for Culture Palaces, 1994.
al-Daw' al-akhdar (Green Light, short stories). Cairo: n.p., 1996.

Farid, Amani (1926–), Egyptian poet born in Cairo. She received a diploma from the Institute for Education in 1945 and continued her studies in history and English literature. She has worked in teaching and journalism. She also took part in the Arab Women's Conference in Palestine in 1947 and joined the sit-in for women's political rights in 1954. Her non-fiction works include *al-Mar'a al-Misriya wa-l-barlaman* (Egyptian Women and Parliament, 1947).
Hamasat wa lafatat (Whispers and Gestures, poetry). Cairo: n.p., 1947.
Fikr wa ruh (Thought and Spirit, poetry). Cairo: Anglo Egyptian Bookstore, 1949.

Qalb yatahaddath (A Heart Speaks, poetry). Cairo: Anglo Egyptian Bookstore, 1992.
Misriya fi Amrika (An Egyptian Woman in America, autobiography). Cairo: Anglo Egyptian Bookstore, 1997.
Thalathat amwaj wa rimal (Three Waves and Sand, short stories). N.p.: n.p., n.d.

Farisi, Farida Mahmud 'Ali (1945–), Saudi children's writer born in Mecca. She received a B.A. in public administration from King 'Abd al-'Aziz University in Jeddah in 1980. She has been the director of al-Hamra' Schools in Jeddah since 1993. She is a member of the Umm al-Qura Women's Charitable Association in Mecca and the Faysaliya Association in Jeddah.
al-Dik al-maghrur (The Proud Rooster, children's literature). N.p.: n.p., 1970.
al-Hadiqa al-mahjura (The Abandoned Garden, children's literature). N.p.: n.p., 1972.
Nazima wa ghanima (Nazima and the Prey, children's literature). N.p.: n.p., 1972.
al-Zahra wa-l-farasha (The Flower and the Butterfly, children's literature). N.p.: n.p., 1972.
Zuhur al-babunaj (Chamomile Flowers, children's literature). N.p.: n.p., 1973.

al-Farisi, Sa'ida Bint Khatir (1956–), Omani poet born in the province of Sur in Oman. She received a B.A. in Arabic and Islamic law from Kuwait University in 1976. She also has a degree in education. She is currently preparing an M.A. in Arabic literary criticism. She is the assistant dean for student affairs at the Sultan Qabus University. She is a boardmember of the Cultural Club and the editor in chief of the *al-'Umaniya* magazine. She has received several local prizes and was awarded the Medal of Kings and Princes of the Gulf Cooperation Council in literature.
Madd fi bahr al-a'maq (Tide in the Sea of the Depths, poetry). Muscat: n.p., 1986.
Ughniyat li-l-tufula wa-l-khadra (Songs to Childhood and Greenery, children's poetry). Muscat: n.p., 1990.

al-Farshishi, Rabi'a (?–), Tunisian short-story writer.
al-Rajul al-dabab (The Fog Man, short stories). Tunis: Dar al-Jil al-Jadid, 1992.
Fi tilka-l-layla (On That Night, short stories). Tunis: Dar Saras Publishers, 1995.

al-Fasi, Malika (Bahithat al-Hadira; al-Fatah) (1919–2007), Pioneering Moroccan writer born in Fez. She published under two pseudonyms, Bahithat al-Hadira and al-Fatah. She was the first woman writer in Morocco in the modern period. She began publishing her articles and literary works in 1935. She was educated in a traditional Islamic school, Dar Faqiha, and was later instructed by her father and her husband, the late research professor, Muhammad al-Fasi. She took part in the nationalist movement and was a member of the women's bureau of the Independence Party. She was the only woman to sign the 1944 document demanding Moroccan independence. She published articles in the Moroccan press, including "Hawl tahafut al-fatayat 'ala-l-lisseh" (On Young Women Flocking to the Lycée), published in *al-Maghrib* (1938); "Ta'lim al-fatah" (The Education of Girls) and "Sawt al-fatah" (The Voice of Young Women) for *al-Maghrib* magazine (1938); "al-Fatah al-Maghribiya bayn marahil al-ta'lim" (Moroccan Women Between Phases of Education), published in *Risalat al-Maghrib* magazine (1952); and "Ta'lim al-mar'a" (Women's Education) for *Risalat al-Maghrib* (1952). She wrote a book for young women, *Dhikrayat bi-mathabat sira dhatiya* (Memories as Autobiography), which was also published in a series of articles in the supplement to *al-Maghrib* newspaper in May–June 1938.

Fatani, Jamila Yasin (1952–), Saudi short-story writer born in Mecca. She received a B.A. in Arabic from King Sa'ud University in Riyadh in 1980. Since 1993 she has been a member of the training unit at the educational supervision department of the General Authority for Girls' Education in Riyadh.
al-Intisar 'ala-l-mustahil (Triumph Over the Impossible, short stories). al-Ta'if: Literary Club, 1990.

al-Fatah (see: al-Fasi, Malika)

Fatat Baghdad (see: Nuri, Huriya Hashim)

Fatat Bani Sulayman (see: 'Azzuz, Hind)

Fatat al-Khalij (see: al-Harb, Ghanima Zayd)

Fatat al-Muhit (see: al-Marini, Amina)

Fath al-Bab, Manar Hasan (1964–), Egyptian short-story writer. She has a B.A. in humanities from Oran University in Algeria. She received an M.A. in Arabic from Ain Shams University in 1994. She contributed the story, "Shabah al-qamar" (The Moon Ghost), to the collection, *20 qisat hubb* (Twenty Love Stories), which was published in 1995 as part of the *Kitab al-Yawm* series. Since 1983 she has published her stories and critical articles in various Egyptian and Arab newspapers and magazines.
Lu'bat al-tashabbuh (The Game of Resemblance, short stories). Cairo: General Egyptian Book Organization, 1993.
Mughamarat al-safina (The Ship's Adventures, children's literature). Cairo: Dar al-Jihad Publishers, 1998.

Fathi, Sharifa (1923–), Egyptian novelist, poet, and painter born in Helwan. She was educated at the School of Fine Arts in Cairo. She is a boardmember of the Association of the Lovers of Fine Arts and a member of the National Arts Association, the Story Club, Dar al-Udaba', and the Poets of Arabism Forum. She illustrates her collections of poetry and since the 1950s has staged many exhibitions of her oil, watercolor, and pastel paintings.

Min shi'r al-mahrajan (Festival Poetry, poetry). Damascus: n.p., 1961.

Lahab wa amwaj (A Blaze and Waves, poetry). Cairo: General Egyptian Foundation for Composition, Translation, Printing, and Publishing, 1964.

Alhan fi qalb imra'a (Melodies in a Woman's Heart, poetry). Cairo: al-Balagh Press, 1968.

Fi mihrab al-jamal: sufiyat (In Beauty's Prayer Niche: Sufi Poems, poetry). Cairo: n.p., 1975.

Rihla fi qalb imra'a (Journey in a Woman's Heart, poetry). Cairo: n.p., 1975.

'Alaqa ghayr bari'a (A Not So Innocent Relationship, novel). Cairo: n.p., 1978.

Kibriya' (Hubris, novel). Cairo: n.p., 1979.

Hadath dhat layla (It Happened One Night, short stories). Cairo: General Egyptian Book Organization, 1987.

Shahrazad lam ta'ud jariya (Sheherazade Is No Longer a Slave, novel). Cairo: n.p., 1988.

Taghrid (Warbling, poetry). Cairo: General Egyptian Book Organization, 1990.

Fathy, Safaa (Fathi, Safa') (see also: Bibliography of Works in French), Egyptian poet and playwright. She received a Ph.D. in the humanities from the Sorbonne in 1993. She has written a play in French, *Terreure*, and has co-directed several documentary films in London and Paris.

. . . *Wa layla* (And a Night, poetry). Cairo: Dar Sharqiyat, 1995.

'Ara'is khashabiya saghira tasbah fi samawat Almaniya wa Birlin (Small Wooden Dolls Float in the Skies of Germany and Berlin, poetry). Cairo: Dar Sharqiyat, 1998.

Fatima Rif'at (see: Rifaat, Alifa)

Fattuh, Rafif (1954–), Lebanese short-story writer and novelist born in Beirut. She graduated from the Beirut National School and continued her education at the Lebanese University. She worked in Lebanese journalism and has published

in *Kull shay'*, *al-Hawadith*, and *al-Watan al-'Arabi*.

La shay' yahummuni (Nothing Concerns Me, novel). Beirut: al-Maktab al-Tijari, 1971.

Bayrut: al-aziqqa wa-l-matar (Beirut: Alleys and Rain, short stories). Beirut: Zuhayr Ba'labakki Publications, 1974.

Tafasil saghira (Little Details, short stories). Beirut: Arab Institute for Research and Publishing, 1980.

Fawwal, Munawwar (1932–), Syrian short-story writer born in Damascus. She received a degree in journalism in Cairo and has published in the Arab press. In 1952, she taught high school in Damascus. She helped establish the League of Arabic Literature (1951–1954).

Dumu' al-khati'a (The Fallen Woman's Tears, short stories). N.p.: n.p., 1951.

Kibriya' wa gharam (Pride and Passion, short stories). N.p.: n.p., 1951.

Ghadan naltaqi (Tomorrow We Meet, short stories). Damascus: Dar al-'Umri, 1959.

Fawwaz, Zaynab (1846–1914), Pioneering Lebanese poet, novelist, and historian of famous women, as well as one of the most prominent figures in the early modern Arab press. Born in Tabnin in southern Lebanon to a poor family, she grew up and worked in the home of Fatima Khalil al-As'ad, a prominent figure in Mount 'Amil at the time who was proficient at poetry and loved literature and learning. Al-As'ad was struck by Fawwaz's talent at memorizing the Qur'an and she took her in and supervised her education. Fawwaz married a worker at Fatima al-As'ad's house but the marriage failed because of differences in thought. She joined the family of a prominent Egyptian, Yusuf Hamdi, in Beirut and moved with them to Alexandria, Egypt, where she met Hasan Husni al-Tuwayrani, the owner of *al-Nil* magazine and a poet of Turkish extraction. She became al-Tuwayrani's student until she had mastered writing and poetry and began to write valuable articles for *al-Nil, al-Fatah, Anis al-jalis, Lisan al-hal, al-Bustan, al-Hilal, al-Mu'ayyad, al-Liwa'*, and *al-Ahali*. Most of her articles touched on social issues and advocated women's education and the advancement of women. Hers was the first woman's voice calling for women's awakening and defending their rights, humanity, and equality with men. She even preceded Qasim Amin in this regard. She published several historical and social works, including *al-Rasa'il al-Zaynabiya* (The Zaynab Epistles, 1904), a collection of her articles and essays on women's rights and their place in society; *al-Durr al-manthur fi tabaqat rabbat al-khudur* (Scattered Pearls in the Lives of the Harem Dwellers, 1895), a 552-page collection of the biographies of 456 famous women in ancient and modern history from around the world; *Madarik al-kamal fi tarajim al-rijal* (Perfect Discernment in the Biographies of Men, manuscript); *al-Durr al-nadid fi ma'athir al-Malik Hamid* (Arranged Pearls on the Exploits of King Hamid, manuscript); and *Kashf al-izar 'an mukhabba'at al-zar* (Removing the Cloak from the Inner Workings of the *Zar*), a collection of essays critiquing occult values in Egyptian society.

al-Hawa wa-l-wafa' (Love and Fidelity, poetic drama). Cairo: al-Jami'a Press, 1893.

Husn al-'awaqib aw Ghada al-zahira (Fine Consequences, or Radiant Ghada, novel). Cairo: Indian Press in Azbakiya, 1899.

al-Malik Qurush (King Cyrus, novel). Cairo: Indian Press in Azbakiya, 1905. Untitled collection of poetry (manuscript).

Fawzi, Zaynab (?– ?) , Egyptian novelist and pioneer.
Mawt Hafiz Bakhit (Hafiz Bakhit's Death, novel). Cairo: al-Maktaba al-Tijariya, 1921.

Fayyad, Dunya (1952–), Lebanese poet born in Ansar in the south. She attended the Sisters of Charity Secondary School and went on to receive a B.A. in Arabic language and literature from the Institute for Eastern Literatures at St. Joseph University in 1975, as well as a B.A. in Arabic literature from Lyon II University in France in 1977. She earned a Ph.D. in ethnic and social studies from Nice University in 1986. She worked in the Women's Affairs Ministry in Ivory Coast from 1979 to 1982. She is a member of the Bayt al-Mar'a al-Janubi Association.

Majamir al-hanin (The Hot Coals of Longing, poetry). Beirut: Dar al-Rayhani, 1993.

Mayasim al-nawa (The Hot Irons of Distance, poetry). Jounieh: Dynamic Graphic Press, 1999.

Fayyad, Muna (1950–), Lebanese novelist born in Ansar in southern Lebanon. She received a diploma in rural economy from Irchonwelz, Belgium in 1974 and a Dipôme d'étides approfondies (DEA) in psychology from the Lebanese University, Beirut in 1977. In 1980 she received a Ph.D. in pyschology from the Sorbonne. She worked in art education from 1975 to 1980, and since 1980 has been an assistant professor of psychology at the Lebanese University. Her non-fiction and academic works include *al-Tifl al-mutakhallif 'aqliyan fi-l-muhit al-usari wa-l-thaqafi* (The Mentally Disabled Child in the Family and Cultural Environment, 1983), *al-Murshid al-ghidha'i* (The Guide to Nutrition, 1986), *al-'Ilm fi naqd al-'ilm* (The Science of Science Criticism, 1996), and *al-Sijn mujtama' barri* (Prison: An Untamed Society, 1999).

Ta'akhkhar al-waqt (The Time Grows Late, novel). Beirut: Dar al-Masar, 1997.

Fu'ad, Sakina (1940–), Egyptian short-story writer and journalist born in Port Said. She received a B.A. in journalism from Cairo University in 1965 and writes for *al-Ahram* newspaper. She is a member of the Shura Council (the upper house of parliament) and the Egyptian National Committee. She is vice president of the Building and Urban Development Association and a member of the Association to Maintain Monuments and Heritage. Her story, "Laylat al-qabd 'ala Fatima," was translated into French in 1986.

Muhakamat al-Sayyida S. (The Trial of Mrs. S., short stories). Cairo: Akhbar al-Yawm Foundation, 1975.

Milaf qadiyat al-hubb (Papers in a Case of Love, short stories). Cairo: Akhbar al-Yawm Foundation, 1977.

Laylat al-qabd 'ala Fatima (The Night Fatima Was Arrested, short stories). Cairo: Akhbar al-Yawm Foundation, 1980.

Dawa'ir al-hubb wa-l-ru'b (Circles of Love and Terror, short stories). Cairo: Maktabat Madbuli, 1984.

Tarwid al-rajul (Taming of the Man, novel). Cairo: Akhbar al-Yawm Foundation, 1986.

9 Sh. al-Nil (No. 9 Nile Street, short stories). Cairo: Akhbar al-Yawm Foundation, 1987.

Imra'at Yunyu (A June Woman, short stories). Cairo: Akhbar al-Yawm Foundation, 1997.

Ghadat al-Sahra' (?–), Iraqi poet and novelist. Her pen name is Ghadat al-Sahra' and her real name is unknown.

Shamim al-firar (The Smell of Flight, poetry). Beirut: Dar al-Kitab al-Lubnani, 1964.

Hal min ma'bad akhar (Is There Another Temple, novel). Beirut: al-Ma'arif Foundation for Printing and Publishing, 1965.

Ashri'at al-layl al-mansiya (Sails of the Forgotten Night, poetry). Beirut: Ha'ik wa Kamal, 1969.

Ghalib, Samiha (?–), Egyptian short-story writer.

al-Sayf wa-l-hikma (The Sword and Wisdom, short stories). N.p.: n.p., n.d.

Ghalum, 'A'isha 'Abd Allah (1952–), Bahraini short-story writer. She received a B.A. in Arabic from Kuwait University in 1983. She received a degree in education from the University College for Sciences, Humanities, and Education in Bahrain in 1980. She later obtained an M.A. in education and curriculum development, with a specialization in Arabic. She is a specialist in Arabic-language curricula at the curricula department of the Bahraini Ministry of Education.

Imra'a fi-l-dhakira (A Remembered Woman, short stories). N.p.: n.p., 1996.

al-Ghamidi, Maryam Muhammad 'Abd Allah (1949–), Saudi poet and short-story writer born in Asmara, Eritrea. She lives in Riyadh. She received a B.A. in English literature from King 'Abd al-'Aziz University in Jeddah in 1990. She works at Riyadh radio. She has been an announcer, program preparer, and radio actress at Jeddah radio since 1962.

Uhibbuk wa lakin (I Love You But, short stories). Jeddah: Literary Club, 1987.

Wa iftaraqna 'ashiqin (And We Parted Lovers, poetic prose). Riyadh: n.p., 1993.

al-Ghamidi, Nura (?–), Saudi short-story writer born in Bisha. She received a B.A. in Arabic from the College of Education in Bisha in 1998. She is an administrator in educational counseling in Bisha.

'Afwan la zilt ahlum (Sorry, I Still Dream, short stories). Cairo: Dar Sharqiyat, 1995.

Tahwa' (Tahwa', short stories). Beirut: Arab Institute for Research and Publishing, 1996.

Ghanim, Iqbal al-Shayib (1949–), Syrian poet and short-story writer born in Damascus. She received a teaching certificate in English language and literature and an M.A. in linguistics from the Lebanese University. She has published several literary essays in *al-Nahar, al-Hayat,*

G

al-Anwar, and *Fayruz*. She has lived in Lebanon since 1972.

Li-l-nay lahn akhar (The Flute Has Another Melody, poetry). N.p.: privately published, 1986.

Rihlat shafaq (A Twilight Journey, poetry). Beirut: Friends of Writers and Books, 1992.

al-Hassa al-sabi'a (The Seventh Sense, short stories). Beirut: Dar al-Fikr al-Lubnani, 1997.

'Abbud ('Abbud, short stories). Beirut: Nawfal Foundation, 1998.

al-Ghanim, Kulthum 'Ali (?–), Qatari short-story writer born in Doha.

Shams al-yawm al-jadid (Sun of the New Day, short stories). Doha: Dar al-Sharq Press, 1998.

al-Ghanim, Nujum Nasir (1962–), Emirati poet. She has a B.A. in media from Ohio University and a B.A. in political science from Indiana University. She is a journalist at *al-Ittihad*.

Masa' al-janna wa Fi malakut al-tawila (Evening of Paradise and In the Realm of the Table, poetry). Dubai: n.p., 1989.

al-Jara'ir (Outrages, poetry). Bahrain: Family of Writers and Authors, 1991.

Rawahil (Riding Camels, poetry). Beirut: Dar al-Jadid, 1996.

al-Gharaballi, Iqbal 'Abd al-Latif (1952–), Kuwaiti novelist. She received a B.A. in computer science and worked as a computer programmer for Kuwaiti Airlines. She currently works at the Kuwaiti Transportation Company. She has published in *al-Nahda* and *al-Yaqza* magazines.

Shadha al-ayyam (The Scent of Days, novel). Kuwait: Dhat al-Salasil Publications, 1979.

Adab bila marafi' (Literature Without Docks, novel). Kuwait: Dar al-Siyasa Press, n.d.

Mudhakkirat muwazzafa (Memoirs of a Woman Civil Servant, memoir). Kuwait: n.p., n.d.

Ghaybur, Fadiya (1948–), Syrian poet born in Silmiya, Hama. She received a B.A. in Arabic and teaches Arabic literature in secondary schools in Silmiya and Hama. Her first poems were published in Syrian newspapers and magazines. She is a member of the Poetry Association.

Li-l-mar'a lugha ukhra (Woman Has Another Language, poetry). Damascus: Arab Writers' Union, 1993.

Lakinni 'ashiqt al-ard wa-l-insan (But I Loved the Earth and Humankind, poetry). Damascus: Arab Writers' Union, 1994.

Mazidan min al-hubb (More Love, poetry). Damascus: Arab Writers' Union, 1997.

Li-dam ka hadha (For Blood Like This, poetry). Tartus: Arwad, 1998.

Ghazal, Muna (1946–), Syrian poet born in Damascus. She was educated in Damascus and received a B.A. in Arabic language from the Beirut Arab University. She has worked in the Bahraini Ministry of Information and in literary journalism. She is a member of the Poetry Association. Her non-fiction works include *al-Sha'ir Ibrahim al-'Arid ma bayn marhalatay al-rumansiya wa-l-klasikiya* (The Poet Ibrahim al-'Arid Between Romanticism and Classicism, 1990) and *Tarikh al-'Atub Al Khalifa* (History of the Blameless Khalifa Clan, 1991).

Tamarrud al-shawq (Passion's Rebellion, poetry). Bahrain: n.p., 1974.

al-Majnuna ismuha zahrat 'abbad al-shams (The Madwoman's Name Is Sunflower, poetry). Jeddah: Dar Tuhama, 1983.

Ramad al-sunbula (Ashes of the Grain Spike, poetry). Cairo: n.p., 1988.

Lughat al-tasa'ulat al-dababiya (The Language of Foggy Musings, poetry). Damascus: n.p., 1990.

al-Ghazali, Sawsan (?–), Egyptian writer.

Hadith lam yahduth ma' al-shams (A Conversation with the Sun That Did Not Happen). Cairo: Egypt Press Company, 1995.

al-Ghazali, Zaynab (1917–2005), Egyptian writer and pioneering activist born in Miyyat Ghamr. She received her education from al-Azhar scholars and joined the Muslim Brothers. In 1938 she established the Muslim Women Group and headed it until her arrest in 1964. She had already been arrested for her political activities and spent time in prison in the 1950s. She published the magazine, *al-Sayyidat al-Muslimat*, in 1950. Her non-fiction works include *Nahw ba'th jadid* (Toward a New Awakening, 1986), *Humum al-mar'a al-Muslima wa-l-da'iya Zaynab al-Ghazali* (Concerns of the Muslim Woman and the Preacher Zaynab al-Ghazali, 1990), and *Min khawatir Zaynab al-Ghazali fi shu'un al-din wa-l-dunya* (Zaynab al-Ghazali's Thoughts on Religion and the World, 1996).
Ayyam min hayati (*Days from My Life*, autobiography). Cairo-Beirut: Dar al-Shuruq, 1989.

al-Ghazzi, Nadiya (1935–), Syrian poet born in Damascus. She received a law degree from Damascus University. Her non-fiction works include *al-'Ubur ila-l-sharr: milaffat wa qadaya qanuniya* (Crossing Over to Evil: Legal Cases, 1982), *Qadaya khassa jiddan* (Very Special Cases, 1991), and *Shirwal Barhum: ayyam safar barlik* (Barhum's Pants: Days of Forced Conscription 1993).
Ismuha Layla al-'Arab (Her Name Is Layla al-'Arab, poetry). Beirut: n.p., 1979.

Ghubaysh, Saliha 'Ubayd (1960–), Emirati poet born in Kuwait. She received a B.A. in Islamic studies and Arabic from the Emirates University in 1987. She oversees the cultural section of the Girls' Clubs in Sharjah. She is a member of the Emirati Writers' and Authors' Union and of the Arab Writers' Union, and the former head of the Emirati Women Authors' League. Her poems have been translated into English and Italian.

Bi-intizar al-shams (Waiting for the Sun, poetry). Sharjah: Emirati Writers' and Authors' Union Publications, 1992.
al-Maraya laysat hiya (The Mirrors Are Not She, poetry). Sharjah: Emirati Writers' and Authors' Union Publications, 1997.

Ghurayyib, Rose (1909–2006), Lebanese pioneer, novelist, short-story writer, and researcher born in al-Damur. She received her primary education in the convent school in her town then moved to Sidon where she continued her education in the American Anglican School. She attended university at the Beirut College for Women. She then traveled to Iraq and taught Arabic literature at Iraqi universities from 1937 to 1941, after which she returned to Lebanon and continued her studies at the American University of Beirut. She received a B.A. and then an M.A. in 1945 in literary criticism. She taught Arabic literature at the Beirut College for Girls (later the American Lebanese University) for more than forty years. She published several works of criticism, most importantly *al-Naqd al-jamali wa atharuhu fi-l-naqd al-'Arabi* (Aesthetic Criticism and Its Impact in Arabic Criticism, 1952), *al-Tawahhuj wa-l-uful: Mayy Ziyada wa adabuha* (Stars Flicker and Set: Mayy Ziyada and Her Works, 1978), *Nasamat wa a'asir fi-l-shi'r al-nisa'i al-'Arabi al-mu'asir* (Breezes and Cyclones in Contemporary Arab Women's Poetry, 1980), and *Aswat 'ala-l-haraka al-nisa'iya al-mu'asira* (Voices on the Contemporary Women's Movement, 1988). She also published more than fifty books for children and youth. She was a member of the Children's Literature Committee, the Women's Union, and the Village Revival Association. She received the National Cedar Medal (knight's rank) in 1972 and the Lebanese Gold Medal of Achievement in 1980.
Aghani al-sighar (Songs of the Young, poetry). Beirut: Catholic Press, 1948.
Laylat al-milad (Christmas Night, children's literature). Beirut: Maktabat al-Mash'al, 1957.

Khutut wa zilal (Lines and Shadows, short stories). Beirut: Dar al-Rayhani, 1958.

Hadiqat al-ash'ar li-l-awlad (The Garden of Children's Poetry, poetry). Beirut: Dar al-Kitab al-Lubnani, 1964.

Sunduq Umm Mahfuz (Umm Mahfuz's Box, children's stories). Beirut: Bayt al-Hikma, 1970.

al-Ma'ni al-kabir (The Great Amir, novel). Beirut: Bayt al-Hikma, 1971.

Nur al-nahar (Light of Day, short stories). Beirut: Bayt al-Hikma, 1974.

Ruwaq al-lablab (The Ivy Curtain, short stories). Beirut: Dar al-Fikr al-Lubnani, 1983.

Habash, Zaynab (1941–), Palestinian poet and short-story writer born in Bayt Dajan, Jaffa. She attended Nablus schools and graduated from Damascus University in 1965. She lives in Ramallah and works in education. She has published a work on academic curricula in the West Bank and the Gaza Strip.

Li-madha ya'shaq al-awlad al-barquq (Why Do Children Like Plums, short stories). Ramallah: Dar al-Katib Press, 1992.

Qalat li al-zanbaqa (The Lily Told Me, short stories). Ramallah: n.p., 1993.

Qawli li-l-raml (My Words to the Sand, poetry). Ramallah: Dar al-Katib, 1993.

al-Jurh al-Filistini wa bara'im al-dam (The Palestinian Wound and Blossoms of Blood, poetry). Ramallah: Maktabat al-Karmel Advertising and Design, 1994.

Ughniyat hubb li-l-watan (A Love Song for the Homeland, reflections). Jerusalem: n.p., 1995.

La taquli mat ya ummi (Don't Say He Is Dead, Mother, poetry). Ramallah: Maktabat al-Karmel, 1996.

Rasa'il hubb manqusha 'ala jabin al-qamar (Love Letters Etched on the Moon's Brow, reflections). Jerusalem: Palestinian Writers' Union Publications, 1996.

Hafaru mudhakkirati 'ala jasadi (They Etched My Memoirs on My Body, poetry). Ramallah: al-'Anqa' Foundation, 1997.

Li-annahu watani (Because It Is My Homeland, poetry). Ramallah: al-'Anqa' Foundation, 1999.

Habayib, Huzama (1965–), Palestinian short-story writer born in Kuwait. She was educated in Kuwaiti schools and received a B.A. in English language and literature in Kuwait. She then moved to Amman, where she worked in translation, teaching, and journalism. With Basma al-Nusur, she was co-recipient of the Jerusalem Festival for Youth Literature Award in 1993. She was awarded the Sayf al-Din al-Irani Short Story Prize by the League of Jordanian Writers in 1994.

al-Rajul alladhi yatakarrar (The Man Who Is Repeated, short stories). Beirut: Arab Institute for Research and Publishing, 1992.

al-Tuffahat al-ba'ida (The Distant Apples, short stories). Amman: Dar al-Karmel, 1994.

Shakl li-l-ghiyab (A Shape for Absence, short stories). Beirut: Arab Institute for Research and Publishing, 1997.

al-Habib, Hamida (?–), Iraqi short-story writer.

Fawq al-masarih (On Stage, short stories). Baghdad: n.p., 1940.

Haddad, Da'd (?–), Syrian poet and playwright born in Latakia. She was educated at Damascus University and worked in journalism. Her plays include *Ba'i' al-zuhur al-mujaffafa* (The Peddler of Dried Flowers), *Ithnatan fi-l-ard wa wahid fi-l-sama'* (Two Women on Earth and One Man in the Heavens), *Sa'ahki lakum qissati* (I Will Tell You My Story), and *Fuqqa'at sabun* (Soap Bubble), all of which are unpublished manuscripts.

Tashih khata' al-mawt (Correcting the Error of Death, poetry). N.p.: Ministry of Culture and National Guidance, 1981.

Kasrat khubz takfini (A Piece of Bread Is Enough, poetry). Damascus: Ministry of Culture, 1987.

al-Shajara allati tamil nahw al-ard (The Tree That Leans toward the Earth, poetry). Damascus: Ministry of Culture, 1991.

Haddad, Fatima (1925–2000), Syrian poet born in Latakia. She received a preparatory school certificate. Her first poems were published in the Cairo-based *al-Risala al-jadida* in the 1950s. She was a member of the Poetry Association.

Sadiqi (My Friend, poetry). Damascus: Dar al-Anwar Press, 1976.

Ghazal al-ramad (Spinning Ashes, poetry). Damascus: n.p., 1984.

Raha al-ayyam (The Mill of Days, poetry). Damascus: Arab Writers' Union, 1991.

Haddad, Habbuba (1897–1957), Lebanese pioneering journalist and novelist born in al-Baruk. She was educated at the English School in Shamlan and later studied political science at the American University of Beirut. She was one of the most prominent pioneers of the women's liberation movement in Lebanon. She worked as a radio announcer for children's programs and published in *al-Hakim* and *al-Sha'b* in 'Ayn Zahlata. She established the journal, *al-Hayah al-jadida*, in France and began publishing it in Beirut in 1921. She headed the Working Women's Association in Beirut at the beginning of the French Mandate. The French Mandate authorities banned her journal in 1929 after she began having an impact and her editorials embraced resistance to the occupation. She sponsored a salon from 1920 to 1930 where literary and political figures met. A book of her collected articles was published as *Nafathat al-afkar* (Thought Emissions). She also published the non-fiction work, *Taqalid wa 'adat Bayrut qabl mi'a wa khamsin sana* (The Traditions and Customs of Beirut from One Hundred and Fifty Years Ago).

Dumu' al-fajr (Dawn Tears, novel). N.p.: n.p., n.d.

Haddad, Jacqueline (1965?–), Palestinian short-story writer born in al-Jishsh in the part of Palestine occupied in 1948. She attended school in her village and studied psychology at Haifa University. She lives in her village and works in education.

Khutut al-suf (Lines of Wool, short stories). Nazareth: Office of Arab Culture, 1997.

al-Haddad, Ma'suma Rida (?–), Iraqi poet.

Tuhfat al-bakin fi ritha' wa madh al-a'imma al-Mayamin (The Mourners' Treasure in the Elegy and Praise of the Blessed Imams, folk poetry). Najaf: Maktabat Dar al-Ma'arif, 1973.

Haddad, Nabiha (1920–1977), Syrian poet born in Latakia. She received a B.A. in literature from Damascus University in 1969. She runs a private preparatory school for girls in Latakia.

Azhar laylak (Lilacs, poetry). Damascus: Moral Guidance, 1970.

Haddad, Najiba Mahmud 'Ali (1950–), Yemeni short-story writer born in Aden. She resides in Sana'a. She has a B.A. and has completed several training sessions in Egypt, Hungary, Germany, and Cyprus. She received the highest medal from the National Center for Children's Culture in Egypt, in addition to several other medals from Arab countries. She is a member of the Permanent Office for Children's Literature in the Arab World, the Authors of Yemen Union, the Journalists' Organization, the Yemeni Women Writers' Association, and Friends of the Book. Some of her children's stories have been translated into English and Russian. Her "Sariq al-'asal" has been translated into fourteen languages. She received the Gold Prize from the Soviet Union. Her story, "Nihayat al-ahlam," was included in the anthology, *Aswat nisa'iya fi-l-qissa al-Yamaniya* (Women's Voices in the Yemeni Short Story, 1992).

Lawn li-l-atfal (A Color for Children, children's literature). Aden: Dar al-Hamdani, 1979.

Lu'bati (My Toy, children's literature). Aden: Dar al-Hamdani, 1980.

Risalat Waddah al-Yaman (Waddah al-Yemen's Message, children's literature). Aden: Dar al-Hamdani, 1983.

Sariq al-'asal (The Honey Thief, children's literature). Aden: Dar al-Hamdani, 1985.

"Nihayat al-ahlam" (The End of Dreams, children's literature). In *Aswat nisa'iya fi-l-qissa al-Yamaniya*. (Women's Voices in the Yemeni Short Story). Sana'a: n.p., 1992.

al-'Usfur al-jarih (The Wounded Sparrow, children's literature). Aden: Dar al-Hamdani, n.d.

Rusum Nasir (Nasir's Drawings, children's literature). Aden: Dar al-Hamdani, n.d.

Haddad, Therese Farid (1948–), Palestinian short-story writer born in Amman, where she resides. She was educated in Damascus, where she graduated with a degree in political science in 1972. She has published many articles in the Jordanian and Arab press and has published several books on social and political topics, most important *al-Qararat wa-l-mubadarat al-khassa bi-l-qadiya al-Filistiniya bayn 'amm 1947–1988* (Resolutions and Initiatives on the Palestinian Cause 1947–1988). She is a member of several associations and unions and is the former head of the women's committee in the Jordanian Journalists' Syndicate.

Hatta naltaqi (Until We Meet, short stories). Amman: Jordanian Press Foundation, 1973.

al-Tahdiq fi malamih al-ghurba (Scrutinizing the Features of Exile, short stories). Amman: al-Tawfiq Press, 1975.

al-Hayah wa-l-nas (Life and People, short stories). Amman: Dar al-Sha'b, 1994.

Hadi, Maysalun (1954–), Iraqi novelist and short-story writer born in Baghdad. She received a B.A. in statistics from the College of Management and Economics in 1975 and a degree in English from the International School of Languages in Exeter in 1980. She was the editorial secretary for *al-Mawsu'a al-saghira* and at the magazine, *al-Tali'a al-adabiya*. She was also the head of the cultural desk at *Alif ba'* magazine. She currently resides in Jordan. She translated *Asatir al-Hunud al-Humr* (Baghdad, 1983). Her stories have been translated into Spanish, English, and Chinese. She has written several collections of short stories and children's novels, some of them science fiction. Her novel, *al-'Alam naqisan wahid*, was named the best book in a poll conducted by *al-'Iraq* newspaper.

al-Shakhs al-thalith (The Third Person, short stories). Baghdad: al-Iqtisad Press, 1985.

al-Farasha (The Butterfly, short stories). Baghdad: Dar al-Shu'un al-Thaqafiya, 1986.

Ashya' lam tahduth (Things That Didn't Happen, short stories). Cairo: General Egyptian Book Organization, 1992.

Rajul khalf al-bab (A Man Behind the Door, short stories). Baghdad: Dar al-Shu'un al-Thaqafiya, 1993.

al-Ta'ir al-sihri wa-l-nuqat al-thalath (The Magic Bird and the Three Points, short stories). Amman: Ministry of Culture, 1995.

al-'Alam naqisan wahid (The World Minus One, novel). Baghdad: Dar al-Shu'un al-Thaqafiya al-'Amma, 1996.

La tanzur ila-l-sa'a (Don't Look at the Clock, short stories). Baghdad: Dar al-Shu'un al-Thaqafiya, 1999.

al-Haffar, Nadira Barakat (1951–), Palestinian novelist and short-story writer born in Jerusalem. She attended the Sisters of Nazareth School in Amman. She has a law degree from Damascus University.

al-Ghurub al-akhir (The Final Sunset, novel). Damascus: Arab Writers' Union, 1985.

Imra'a fi 'uyun al-nas (A Woman in the Eyes of the People, novel). Damascus: Dar Tlas, 1988.

al-Hawiya (The Abyss, novel). Damascus: Arab Writers' Union, 1990.

H

Hafiz, Ratiba Muhammad (?–), Egyptian poet.

Idha ma aqbal al-layl (When the Night Comes, poetry). Cairo: al-Shini Center for Printing and Publishing, 1991.

Hafiz, Safira Jamil (1926–), Iraqi short-story writer.

Duma wa atfal (Dolls and Children, short stories). Baghdad: al-Ma'arif Press, 1956.

al-Hafiz, Thuraya (1911–2000), Syrian short-story writer born in Damascus. She graduated from the Teachers' Academy in Damascus. She was fluent in both French and Turkish and worked as a teacher for fifty years in primary and secondary schools. She wrote for the Arab and Syrian press and presented social issues on Arab and Syrian radio. She established and headed the Female Graduates of Teachers' Academies Association, the Girls' Home, the Soldiers' Care Association, and the Sukayna Literary Forum. She stood in the parliamentary elections of 1952 but did not win. She ran for office again during the union with Egypt and won, but she was not admitted into the parliament on the grounds that "her voice would ring out" and create problems for the state.

Hadath dhat yawm (It Happened One Day, short stories). Damascus: I'tidal Press, 1961.

al-Hafiziyat (The al-Hafiz Papers, memoir). Damascus: al-Thabat Press, 1979.

al-Hajj, Maggie al-Ashqar (1912–), Lebanese short-story writer born in France. She received her primary and secondary education at the French Holy Family School in Beirut and attended university at the Lebanese Academy.

'Indama atadhakkar (When I Remember, memoir). Beirut: Dar 'Awwad, 1995.

al-Hajj, Nada Unsi (1958–), Lebanese poet born in Beirut. She received her primary and secondary education at the Lazarene School of the Sisters of Love. She studied philosophy at the Sorbonne for two years, then returned to Beirut and began stage acting with director Raymond Jabbara. She published several literary articles and prose poems in the early 1980s and translated French dramas to colloquial Lebanese, which were staged at al-Masrah al-Baladi theater.

Salah fi-l-rih (A Prayer in the Wind, poetry). Beirut: Dar al-Nahar Publishers, 1988.

Anamil al-ruh (Fingertips of the Spirit, poetry). Beirut: Dar al-Nahar Publishers and the Nadia Tuéni Foundation, 1994.

Rihlat al-zill (Journey of the Shadow, poetry). Beirut: Dar al-Nahar Publishers, 1999.

al-Hajj, Samira al-Ghali (1962–), Sudanese poet born in northern Kurdufan. She received a B.A. in Arabic from Cairo University in Khartoum in 1985, an M.A. in Arabic from the Girls' College at the Islamic Umm Durman University in 1987, and an M.A. in teaching Arabic as a foreign language from the International Khartoum Institute for Arabic in 1993. She earned a Ph.D. in education from the World African University in 1999. She is a lecturer in Arabic at the University of Sudan for Science and Technology, an Arabic teacher, and since 1985 has been a newspaper editor. She is a member of the Literary Forum at Cairo University in Khartoum, the Sudanese Journalists' Union, the Literature of Sudanese Children Group in the National Organization for Culture and Arts, and the Teachers' Union at the University of Sudan for Science and Technology. She is also a member of the executive committee of the Sudanese Writers' and Authors' Union.

Idhak ayyuha-l-qalb al-jarih (Laugh, You Wounded Heart, poetry). Libya: al-Dar al-Jamahiriya Printing and Publishing, 1992.

Li-l-nawras ughniya ukhra (The Seagull Has Another Song, poetry). Sudan: Khartoum University Publishers, 1993.

Maqati' li-l-bahr wa-l-luqya (Passages for the Sea and the Encounter, poetry). N.p.: n.p., n.d.

Hakim, Jihan (?–), Saudi short-story writer born in Jeddah. She received her B.A. from the College of Sciences at King 'Abd al-'Aziz University in 1986.
Wajh fi imra'a (A Face on a Woman, short stories). Jeddah: al-Madina Foundation, 1994.

al-Hakim, Nur al-Huda (?–), Pioneering Egyptian short-story writer.
Qisas al-hayah (Life Stories, short stories). N.p.: al-Nass Press, 1935.

Halawa, Basima (1949–1979), Palestinian short-story writer born in Nablus, where she received her early education. She graduated from the sociology department at the Jordanian University in 1972. She suffered from heart disease as a child and it plagued her throughout her life. After her death her writings, including those published in newspapers and magazines, were collected and published in two volumes. She was posthumously awarded the Jerusalem Medal in Culture and the Arts in December 1990.
Lawz akhdar (Green Almond, short stories). Amman: Jordanian Popular Committee to Support the Intifada, 1993.
Taratil shi'riya (Poetic Recitations, poetry). N.p.: n.p., n.d.

al-Halila, al-Jawhara 'Abd al-Rahman al-Hamad (?–), Saudi poet born in al-Dammam. She received a B.A. in sociology from Colorado University in 1983. She has been the director of the al-Amal Institute for Deaf Girls in al-Dammam since 1991. She is a founding member of the Prince Sa'ud Ibn Nayif Center for the Rehabilitation of Deaf Girls and a member of the al-Dammam Women's Charitable Association.
Sawt maksur (A Broken Sound, poetry). N.p.: n.p., 1990.

Halim, Asma (1921–2003), Egyptian writer. She obtained a B.A. in English from Cairo University in 1941 and an ad-vanced degree in editing, translation, and journalism in 1943. She worked as a teacher for the Ministry of Education for many years and as a translator. She translated Elmer Rice's drama, *Dream Girl*, into Arabic in 1965, as well as Elena Dmitrievna Modrzhinskaia's *Leninism and the Battle of Ideas* in 1975. She wrote *8 ayyam fi-l-Sa'id* (Eight Days in Upper Egypt, Cairo, Dar al-Fajr, 1944), and *Tard al-Injliz min qanat al-Suways* (Expulsion of the English from the Suez Canal, Cairo, Dar al-Fajr, 1950). She was arrested and remained in detention for five years, from 1959 to 1964.
Fi sijn al-nisa' (In the Women's Prison, short stories). Cairo: Dar al-Misriya Books, 1958.
Hikayat 'Abduh 'Abd al-Rahman (The Story of 'Abduh 'Abd al-Rahman, novel). Cairo: Dar al-Thaqafa Printing and Publishing, 1977.
Arba' zawjat wa rajul (Four Wives and a Man, novel). Cairo: Dar al-Thaqafa al-Jadida, 1980.
Mu'jizat al-qadar (Miracle of Fate, novel). Cairo: Dar al-Thaqafa al-Jadida, 1985.
Ikhwan al-Safa wa khullan al-wafa (Brethren of Purity and Friends of Fidelity, short stories). Cairo: Dar al-Sha'b Foundation, 1998.

Hamad, 'A'isha 'Abd al-Qadir (?–), Egyptian novelist.
Bayn 'ahdayn (Between Two Eras, novel). Cairo: al-Dar al-Qawmiya Press for Printing and Publishing, 1963.

al-Hamamsi, Salwa (?–), Egyptian writer.
Quyud al-ahlam (Bonds of Dreams). Cairo: General Egyptian Book Organization, 1993.

Hamarna, Wafa' (?–), Syrian novelist. She has a B.A. from the Liberal Arts College at Damascus University.
Mamlakat al-hubb al-damiya (The Bloody Kingdom of Love, novel). Damascus: al-Maktaba al-Adabiya, 1990.

Maw'id ma'a al-sa'ada (A Date with Happiness, novel). Latakia: Dar al-Majd, 1991.
Sira' ma'a al-nisa' (A Conflict with Women, novel). Damascus: Maktabat Filistin, 1999.

Hamdan, 'Abir (1973–), Lebanese poet born in Shamstar in Ba'labakk. She received a B.A. in business and works at the Kuwaiti newspaper, *al-Siyasa*.
Abwab al-asil (Gates of the Authentic, poetry). Beirut: Dar al-Hadatha, 1996.

Hamdan, Umayya (1923–), Lebanese poet, writer, and dramatist born in Sawfar. She received her primary and secondary education at the English School and earned a B.A. in philosophy from the American University of Beirut in 1966, followed by an M.A. in Arabic literature in 1974. She worked as a teacher and a journalist. She published *al-Ramziya al-rumantiqiya fi-l-shi'r al-Lubnani* (Romantic Symbolism in Lebanese Poetry) in 1980 and has worked as a high school teacher for the Ministry of Education since 1966.
Antazir (I Wait, novel). Sidon: al-Maktaba al-'Asriya, 1966.
Majnun Shaniya (Crazy for Shaniya, play). Beirut: Dar al-Ittihad, 1972.
Nuqtat al-bikar (The Compass Point, novel). Beirut: Dar al-Ittihad, 1978.
al-Azraq al-qadim ma'a al-rih (The Blue Coming with the Wind, novel). Beirut: Dar al-Afaq al-Jadida, 1979.

al-Hamdan, Wafa' (?–), Kuwaiti short-story writer.
al-Tayaran bi-jinah wahid (Flying with One Wing, short stories). Kuwait: al-Khatt Press, 1988.
al-Shams la taghrub marratayn (The Sun Does Not Set Twice, short stories). Kuwait: al-Khatt Press, 1994.

Hamid, Masarra (?–), Iraqi poet.
Kull yujaddif kull yulqi bi-hajar (Everyone Rows, Everyone Throws a Stone, poetry). Amman: Dar al-Karmel, 1994.

al-Hammud, Nawwar (Bint al-Jazira) (1943–), Kuwaiti poet. She began writing poetry after the 1967 War. She has written many songs for Kuwaiti radio. She is also known as Bint al-Jazira.
Rabi' al-nuwwayr (Spring of the Blossom, colloquial poetry). Kuwait: Government of Kuwait Press, 1975.
Diwan Bint al-Jazira (The Poetry of Bint al-Jazira, poetry). Kuwait: Ministry of Information, 1980.
Jadayil al-layl (Tresses of the Night, poetry). Kuwait: Government of Kuwait Press, 1980.
Naqsh al-hinna' (Henna Tracing, poetry). Kuwait: Dhat al-Salasil Publications, 1983.

Hammud, Nuha Tabbara (1933–), Lebanese short-story writer born in Beirut. She received a degree in children's literature and a B.A. in fine arts from the Beirut College for Girls. She worked in children's cultural journalism. She is a member of the Lebanese Agency for Children's Books, a branch of the World Agency for Youth Books. She has written puppet dramas and television puppet shows. She also writes crime short stories and is a screenwriter.
Rabi' bila wurud (Spring without Flowers, short stories). Beirut: Dar Maktabat al-Turath al-Adabi, 1992.
Suhd wa zilal (Insomnia and Darkness, novel). Beirut: Dar al-Jadid, 1996.

Hammud, Zaynab (?–), Lebanese poet born in Beirut. She writes for *al-Anwar* and edits the journal, *Sahar*. She has published a two-part work, *al-Wajh al-akhar lahum: dirasat wa hiwarat fi-l-sira* (Their Other Face: Studies and Conversations about Autobiography, 1993).
Kalimat 'ala-l-shifah al-janub (Words on the Lips of the South, poetry). Beirut: Dar al-Bahith, 1987.

Hammuda, Layla (?–), Egyptian novelist.
Nabadat ka'in hayy (Heartbeats of a Living Being, novel). Cairo: General Egyptian Book Organization, 1991.

H

Hamza, Du'a' al-Mutawalli (?–), Egyptian short-story writer.
Iqa' al-rih: qisas qasira jiddan (Rhythm of the Wind: Very Short Stories, short stories). Cairo: al-Amal Publications, 1994.

Hamza, Jilan (?–), Egyptian novelist. She received first prize for youth literature for her novel, *al-La'ba wa-l-haqiqa*. Some of her works have been translated into English.
Ulamlim 'iqdi bi-ghadab (I Gather My Necklace in Anger, novel). Baghdad: Dar al-Ma'arif, 1970.
al-La'ba wa-l-haqiqa (The Game and the Truth, novel). Cairo: Dar al-Fikr al-'Arabi, 1970.
Qadar al-akharin (The Fate of Others, novel). Cairo: General Egyptian Book Organization, 1974.
al-Zawja al-hariba (The Fugitive Wife, novel). Cairo: Akhbar al-Yawm Foundation, 1974.
Zawj fi-l-mazad (A Husband at the Auction, novel). Cairo: Dar al-Sha'b Foundation, 1976.
Musafira ma'a al-jirah (Traveling with the Injury, novel). Cairo: Akhbar al-Yawm Foundation, 1981.
al-Habiba (The Beloved, novel). Cairo: Akhbar al-Yawm Foundation, 1988.
Kawalis Munt Karlu (Monte Carlo Backstage, short stories). Cairo: General Egyptian Book Organization, 1988.
al-Mu'jiza (The Miracle, short stories). Cairo: General Egyptian Book Organization, 1994.
al-A'mal al-riwa'iya (The Novels, anthology). Cairo: General Egyptian Book Organization, 1996.

Hanna, Huda (1922–), Palestinian novelist born in the village of al-Rama in northern Palestine. She completed her primary education in the village and graduated from the Teachers' Academy in Jerusalem in 1937. After the *nakba*, she moved to Damascus, where she was the principal of a school run by the U.N.R.W.A.

Sawt al-malaji' (Voice of the Refugee Camps, novel). Damascus: Damascus Press, n.d. (The author notes that the novel was written in the five years following the *nakba*.)

Hanna, Maysun (?–), Palestinian playwright born in Jerusalem. She is a physician in the province of al-Zarqa' in Jordan.
Shubbak al-hulwa (The Beauty's Window, play). Amman: Dar Jad Publications, 1987.
Kahin al-ma'bad (The Temple Priest, play). Amman: Dar Jad Publications, 1989.
Maqtal Shahrazad (The Murder of Sheherazade, play). Amman: Dar al-Karmel, 1991.
al-Shahhadh hakiman and *'Azif al-nay* (The Beggar As a Ruler, and The Flute Player, two plays). Amman: privately published, 1993.

Hannush, Georgette (1930–), Syrian novelist born in Aleppo. She is fluent in French.
Dhahab ba'idan (He Went Away, novel). Beirut: Dar al-Andalus, 1961.
'Ashiqat habibi (My Beloved's Lover, novel). Beirut: al-Maktab al-Tijari, 1964.

al-Harb, Ghanima Zayd 'Abd Allah (Fatat al-Khalij) (1949–), Kuwaiti poet. She received a B.A. in psychology and sociology from Kuwait University in 1974. She was a social worker before her retirement. She writes poetry in both classical and colloquial Arabic and some of her lyric poetry has been put to music under the pseudonym Fatat al-Khalij (Young Woman of the Gulf).
Qasa'id qafas al-ihtilal (Poems on the Cage of the Occupation, poetry). Kuwait: al-Khatt Press, 1991.
Hadil al-hamam (The Dove's Coo, poetry). Kuwait: al-Khatt Press, 1993.
Ajnihat al-rimal (Wings of the Sands, poetry). Kuwait: al-Khatt Press, 1993.
Fi khaymat al-halak (In the Tent of the Pitch Black, poetry). Kuwait: al-Khatt Press, n.d.

Harb, Rim (1959–), Palestinian poet born in Gaza. She is a refugee from 'Iraq Suwaydan in the part of Palestine occupied in 1948. She has a degree from the College of Sciences at Cairo University. She works in journalism.

Min tajalliyat huriyat al-buhur al-sab'a (Manifestations of the Nymph of the Seven Seas, poetry). Jerusalem: Palestinian Writers' Union Publications, 1998.

Thamarat li-l-'ishq (Fruits for Love, poetry). N.p.: Ugharit Palestinian Cultural Center, 1999.

Harun, 'Aziza (1923–1986), Syrian poet born in Latakia. She did not continue her studies because of an early marriage. She worked as a civil servant for Damascus radio and began writing poetry in the late 1950s. Starting in 1945 she was a correspondent for the Damascus publications, *al-Asda'*, *al-Sabah*, and *al-Tamaddun al-Islami*, as well as the Lebanese *al-Adib* and *al-Adab*. Her works were not published in her lifetime. After her death in 1986, her friend, the poet 'Afifa al-Hisni, collected her poems and published them in 1992.

Diwan 'Aziza Harun (The Poetry of 'Aziza Harun, poetry). Damascus: Women's Forum Publications, 1992.

Harun, Hind (1928–1996), Syrian poet born in Latakia. She had a teaching certificate and worked in education. She was the director of the al-Karama Secondary School for Girls in Latakia. She wrote and published poetry in several Arabic newspapers and magazines. From 1981, she was a boardmember of the Arab Writers' Union. Her poems have been translated into French, English, and German.

Sariqat al-ma'bad (The Temple Thief, poetry). Damascus: Dar al-Anwar, 1978.

Diwan 'Ammar ('Ammar's Poems, poetry). Damascus: Arab Writers' Union, 1979.

Shams al-hubb (Love's Sun, poetry). N.p.: Dar al-Su'al Press and Publishers, 1983.

Bayn al-marsa wa-l-shira' (Between the Dock and the Sail, poetry). Damascus: Ministry of Culture, 1984.

'Ammar fi damir al-umuma ('Ammar in the Conscience of Motherhood, poetry). Damascus: Arab Writers' Union, 1988.

Hasan, Bilqis Hamid (?–), Iraqi poet. She lives in the Netherlands.

Makhad Maryam (Maryam's Labor Pains, poetry). Damascus: Dar al-Tali'a al-Jadida, 1998.

Hasan, Faliha (?–), Iraqi short-story writer.

Li-annani fatah (Because I'm a Young Woman, poetry). Baghdad: n.p., 1991.

Hasan, Khadija Muhammad (?–), Sudanese poet. Her poems have been published in Sudanese and Egyptian journals. Her earliest published poem was "Hal ansa?" (Do I Forget?) and her most recently published was "Hadath dhat yawm" (It Happened One Day).

al-Hasan, Lina Hawiyan (?–), Syrian novelist and artist. She received her university education at Damascus University.

Ma'shuqat al-shams (Beloved of the Sun, novel). Damascus: Dar Tlas, 2000.

Hasan, Sabah Muhammad (1954–), Egyptian short-story writer.

Fi-l-layl tarhal al-sufun (At Night the Ships Leave, short stories). Alexandria: al-Safir Newspaper Press, 1987.

al-Qitar yughayyir ittijahah (The Train Changes Direction, short stories). Riyadh: al-Farazdaq Commercial Press, 1987.

Iftitahiya li-l-samt wa-l-surakh (A Prelude to Silence and Screams, short stories). Beirut: Dar al-Adab, 1988.

Hasan, Zaynab 'Abd al-Ghani (?–), Egyptian poet.

Ashtaq ila-l-hanan (I Long for Tenderness, poetry). Cairo: Egyptian Association to Foster Talent, 1995.

Hashim, 'Alaya (?–), Egyptian novelist. *Sira' fi-l-a'maq* (A Conflict in the Depths, novel). Cairo: n.p., 1967.

Hashim, Labiba Madi (1882–1952), Pioneering Lebanese journalist and novelist born in Beirut. She was educated at the Sisters of Love School and the English Missionary School. She moved with her family to Cairo in 1900, where in the literary salon of Warda al-Yaziji she met men of literature and thought. Ibrahim al-Yaziji taught her the fundamentals of Arabic language and literature. She published the magazine, *Fatat al-sharq*, in Egypt from 1906 to 1935. The Egyptian University invited her to be a lecturer in 1911 and 1912, and she was the first Arab woman to hold this position. The government of King Faisal I appointed her in 1919 as the general inspector of girls' schools in Damascus, the first woman to hold the post. After the battle of Maysalun, the fall of King Faisal's government, and the entry of invading French forces, Hashim went to Egypt. In 1921 she immigrated to Chile, where she published the magazine, *al-Sharq wa-l-gharb*. In 1924 she returned to Egypt to continue publishing her first magazine, *Fatat al-sharq*, which she issued for twenty-four years. The magazine was well known for its columns on famous women and aphorisms. Her non-fiction works include *Kitab al-tarbiya* (The Book of Education), a collection of her university lectures from 1911, as well as her writings on the difference in men's and women's treatment of women's issues.
"Hasanat al-hubb" (The Merits of Love, short story). *al-Diya'*. Cairo: 1898.
"al-Fawz ba'd al-mawt" (Victory After Death, short story). *al-Diya'*. Cairo: 1899.
"Jaza' al-khiyana" (The Recompense of Betrayal, short story). *al-Diya'*. Cairo: 1902–1903.
Qalb al-rajul (A Man's Heart, novel). Cairo: al-Ma'arif Press, 1904.
Shirin (Shirin, novel). Cairo: al-Ma'arif Press and *Fatat al-sharq* magazine, n.d.

"Jaza' al-ihsan" (Charity's Reward, short story). *Fatat al-sharq*. Cairo: n.p., n.d.

Hashim, Najwa Muhammad (1960–), Saudi short-story writer born in Jizan. She received a B.A. in sociology from King 'Abd al-'Aziz University in Jeddah in 1985. Since 1991, she has been the director of a school in Jeddah. She writes a regular column for *al-Riyad* and is a counselor for the General Office of Girls' Education.
al-Safar fi layl al-ahzan (A Journey through the Night of Sorrows, short stories). Jeddah: al-Dar al-Sa'udiya Publishing, 1986.

Hatim, Dalal (1931–), Syrian short-story writer born in Damascus. She received a B.A. in history from Damascus University and works as editor in chief for the children's magazine, *Usama*. She writes for the newspapers *al-Ba'th* and *al-Thawra* and has published several studies on Arab children's culture. In 1984 she received a prize from the Arab Organization for Education, Culture, and Science for her story, *Hadath fi yawm rabi'i*.
al-Hamama al-bayda' (The White Dove, children's literature). Damascus: Ministry of Culture, 1974.
al-Sama' tamtur khirafan (The Sky Rains Sheep, children's literature). Damascus: Ministry of Culture, 1976.
al-'Ubur min al-bab al-dayyiq (Passing through the Narrow Door, short stories). Damascus: Ministry of Culture, 1979.
al-Dik al-aswad (The Black Rooster, children's literature). Beirut: Dar al-Fata al-'Arabi, 1980.
Hanun al-Qurtaji (Hanun of Carthage, children's literature). Damascus: Ministry of Culture and Usama Books, 1981.
Balun Rima (Rima's Balloon, children's literature). Beirut: Dar al-Fata al-'Arabi, 1982.
Ma ajmal al-'alam (How Beautiful the World Is, children's literature). Beirut: Dar al-Nawras, 1982.

Shajarat zaytun saghira (A Little Olive Tree, children's literature). Damascus: Ministry of Culture and Usama Monthly Books, 1982.

Dars istithna'i (An Exceptional Lesson, children's literature). Damascus: Ministry of Culture and Usama Monthly Books, 1983.

Hadath fi yawm rabi'i (It Happened on a Spring Day, children's literature). N.p.: General Department of Archaeology and Museums, 1984.

Mudhakkirat 'asharat qurush (Memoirs of a Ten-piaster Coin, children's literature). Damascus: Arab Writers' Union, 1984.

Adfa' makan fi-l-'alam (The Warmest Place in the World, children's literature). Damascus: Ministry of Culture and Usama Monthly Books, 1985.

al-Zahra wa-l-hajar (The Flower and the Stone, children's literature). Damascus: Ministry of Culture and Usama Monthly Books, 1989.

Halat araq (A Case of Insomnia, short stories). Damascus: Ministry of Culture, 1990.

Juha fi-l-fada' (Juha in Space, children's literature). Damascus: Dar Sahari, 1993.

Qasr al-marmar (The Marble Palace, children's literature). Kuwait: Kuwaiti Association for the Advancement of Arab Childhood, 1994.

Hayat al-Nahr (see: al-Zubaydi, Hayat)

al-Hayb, Ghada (1950–), Syrian short-story writer born in Aleppo. She studied Arabic at Aleppo University in 1968.

Safina bila shira' (A Ship Without a Sail, short stories). Damascus: n.p., 1971.

al-Hayik, Renée (1959–), Lebanese novelist and short-story writer born in Beirut. She received a B.A. in philosophy from the Lebanese University. Since 1980, she has taught at the Anglican Secondary School in Beirut. She publishes her essays in literary criticism in *al-Nahar* and *al-Hayat*. She has translated

works by European poets and won a prize at the Arab Book Fair in Beirut in 1995 for *Burtrayh li-l-nisyan*.

Burtrayh li-l-nisyan (A Portrait of Forgetting, short stories). Beirut: Arab Cultural Center, 1994.

Shita' mahjur (A Forsaken Winter, novel). Beirut: Arab Cultural Center, 1996.

al-Bi'r wa-l-sama' (The Well and the Sky, novel). Beirut: Arab Cultural Center, 1997.

Buyut al-masa' (Evening's Houses, short stories). Cologne: al-Jamal Publications, 1997.

al-'Abir (The Passerby, novel). Beirut: Arab Cultural Center, 1999.

Hayrab, Hanan Amin (?–), Syrian poet.

al-Nakhil (The Palm Tree, poetry). Damascus: Dar Hittin Research, 1991.

Hazza', Fatima 'Abd al-'Al Muhammad (1968–), Egyptian poet born in Shibin al-Qanatir.

Wanas al-suqut (The Comfort of Falling, poetry). Giza: General Authority for Culture Palaces, 1999.

al-Hifnawi, Hala (?–), Egyptian short-story writer born in al-Isma'iliya. Her first novel, *al-'Abir al-ghamid*, was published when she was sixteen years old. She has published several articles and stories in *Akhir sa'a*, *al-Maw'id*, *Dunya al-fann*, and *Rose al-Yusuf*.

Min fam al-rajul (From the Mouth of a Man, short stories). Cairo: Dar al-Katib al-'Arabi Printing and Publishing, 1968.

Hal akhla' thawbi (Should I Take Off My Clothes, novel). Beirut: al-Maktab al-Tijari Printing and Publishing, 1969.

Layla fi sarir rajul (A Night in a Man's Bed, short stories). Beirut: al-Maktab al-Tijari Printing and Publishing, 1969.

al-Rajul yuhibb marratayn (Men Love Twice, novel). Cairo: Rose al-Yusuf Foundation, 1977.

Wasit al-jinn: dastur ya asyadi (The Medium: Excuse Me, Spirits, novel). Riyadh: al-Sharqiya Global Company, 1982 (second printing).

Qisas al-hubb wa-l-rahil (Stories of Love and Departure, short stories). Cairo: Akhbar al-Yawm, 1993.

Atwal risalat 'ishq (The Longest Love Letter). Cairo: Akhbar al-Yawm, 1995.

Hazimati anta (You Are My Defeat). Cairo: Akhbar al-Yawm, 1995.

Illa al-hubb (Except for Love). Cairo: Akhbar al-Yawm, 1995.

al-'Abir al-ghamid (The Mysterious Scent, novel). Cairo: Fann al-Tiba'a Foundation, n.d.

Hifni, Zaynab Ahmad (?–), Saudi short-story writer born in Jeddah. She received a B.A. in liberal arts from King 'Abd al-'Aziz University in Jeddah in 1993. She has worked in the school administration department at the General Office for Girls' Education in Jeddah since 1976.

Risala ila rajul (Letter to a Man, short stories). Jeddah: Matabi' Dar al-Bilad, 1993.

Qayduk am hurriyati (Your Fetter or My Freedom, short stories). Beirut: Lebanese Foundation for Publishing, 1994.

al-Hijjawi, Sulafa (1934–), Palestinian poet and researcher born in Nablus. She was educated in that city's schools. She lived in Iraq and married Iraqi poet Kazim Jawad. She has published several studies and translations, most importantly, *Poetry of Resistance in Occupied Palestine* (1982). She has also translated a work into Arabic as *al-Tajriba al-ibda'iya* and poems by Federico García Lorca.

Ughniyat Filistin (The Song of Palestine, poetry). Baghdad: Ministry of Information, 1977.

Hikmat, Najmiya (1920–), Jordanian writer of Syrian origin born in Damascus. She moved to Amman with her family

when she was two years old. She had only reached sixth grade when she was forced to leave school. She is self-educated. Her only published work is her autobiography.

65 'aman min hayat imra'a Urduniya: rihlati ma'a al-zaman (Sixty-five Years in the Life of a Jordanian Woman: My Journey with Time, autobiography). Amman: privately published, 1986.

Hilal, Rabab (?–), Syrian short-story writer born in Safita. She studied French at Damascus University.

Dawa'ir al-ma' wa-l-asma' (Circles of Water and Names, short stories). Damascus: Dar al-Shadi, 1992.

Taranim bila iqa' (Hymns Without a Rhythm, short stories). Damascus: Arab Writers' Union, 1995.

al-Hilli, Maqbula ('Afra') (1929–1979), Iraqi poet born in Baghdad to a prominent family from al-Hilla. She graduated from the Queen 'Aliya College, humanities, in 1953 and was appointed a teacher of Arabic in the province of Diyala. Three years later she returned to Baghdad where she taught high school until her death. She wrote descriptive and reflective poetry, as well as sentimental poems and nationalist poems about Palestine and the Algerian revolution.

al-Hubb al-kabir (Big Love, poetry). Baghdad: n.p., n.d.

Hilmi, Muna (1958–), Egyptian short-story writer born in Cairo. She received a B.A. in economics from Cairo University in 1977 and an M.A. in urban planning and development from the University of London in 1982. She was awarded the Taymur Story Prize in 1993 for the collection, *al-Bahr baynuna*. She writes for the press and composes programs for Egyptian radio. She is the secretary of the Association of Women's Solidarity. Her non-fiction works include *Rajul jadid fi-l-ufuq* (A New Man on the Horizon, 1990, essays) and *al-Hubb fi 'asr al-'awlama* (Love in the Age of Globalization, 1999, essays).

Ajmal yawm ikhtalafna fih (The Most Beautiful Day We Argued, short stories). Cairo: Maktabat Madbuli, 1987.

Bidun awraq (Without Papers, short stories). Cairo: Maktabat Madbuli, 1990.

Hatif al-sabah (The Morning Caller, poetry). Cairo: al-Maliji Press, 1991.

al-Bahr baynuna (The Sea Between Us, short stories). Kuwait-Cairo: Dar Su'ad al-Sabah, 1993.

Hilmi, Su'ad (1929–), Egyptian writer. She has a law degree from Cairo University. She was editor in chief of *Hawwa'* from 1980 to 1991, where she became known for her column, "Whisper of Honesty." She helped translate the series of 'Abir novels, issued by al-Ahram. She received the medal of the Supreme Council for Culture in 1975 for a collection of stories on the October War. She is a member of the Supreme Council for Journalism.

Da'ni li-zawji (Leave Me to My Husband, short stories). Cairo: Dar al-Kitab al-'Arabi Printing and Publishing, 1967.

Arjuk ifhamni (Please Understand Me, short stories). Cairo: al-Ahram Center for Translation and Publication, 1992.

al-Hindi, Ashjan (1968–), Saudi poet born in Jeddah. She has a B.A. in Arabic from King 'Abd al-'Aziz University in Jeddah. She received an M.A. in Arabic from King Sa'ud University in 1994 for her thesis, *Tawzif al-turath fi-l-shi'r al-Sa'udi al-mu'asir* (The Use of Literary Tradition in Contemporary Saudi Poetry). She is currently preparing a Ph.D. in London.

Hurub al-ahilla (Crescent Wars, poetry). Beirut: Dar al-Adab, 1997.

Li-l-hulm ra'ihat al-matar (Dreams Have the Scent of Rain, poetry). Syria: Dar al-Mada for Culture and Publishing, 1998.

Hinnawi, Fatima Dawud (1949–), Saudi short-story writer born in Mecca. She received an M.A. in philosophy from Cairo University and a Ph.D. in Arabic

literature from the same institution in 1988. She has worked in journalism and is currently a businesswoman.

A'maq bila bihar (Depths Without Seas, short stories). Jeddah: Culture and Arts Association, 1987.

al-Hisni, 'Afifa (1918–2003), Pioneering Syrian poet born in Damascus. She received a B.A. in Arabic literature from the Institute of Education in Cairo (later the Girls' College at Ain Shams University). She taught Arabic and was the director of a secondary school. During the Egyptian–Syrian union (1958–1961), she worked in the Central Ministry of Education in Cairo, planning curricula in Arabic language and literature for the preparatory and secondary levels. She wrote several textbooks, including *al-Qira'a al-muwahhada* (Unified Reading) for the high-school level. She also wrote non-fiction works, including *al-Mar'a fi shi'r Abi-l-'Ala'* (Women in the Poetry of Abi-l-'Ala'), *Maraya wa nisa'* (Mirrors and Women), and *Risalat al-mar'a* (The Woman's Message). She published in Arab newspapers and magazines and was a member of the Arab Writers' Union in Damascus and the Women's Culture Association.

Wafa' (Fidelity, poetry). Cairo: al-Dar al-Qawmiya, 1966.

Shahid al-tadhiyat (Martyr of Sacrifices, poetry). Cairo: al-Nashir al-'Arabi Press, 1970.

Wala' (Loyalty, poetry). Cairo: al-'Asima Press, 1971.

'Azifat al-qithara (The Lyre Player, poetry). Damascus: Arab Writers' Union, 1979.

Sarab al-bahr (Phantom of the Sea, poetry). Damascus: Arab Writers' Union, 1989.

al-Hissu, Sabriya 'Abd al-Raziq (1931–), Iraqi poet born in al-'Amara. She was raised in a conservative family. She lost her parents when she was five years old. She began writing poetry at the age of fifteen. In 1948 she took part in the popular uprising and recited fiery poems that led to her suspension from school.

Qayd wa lahn (A Fetter and a Melody, poetry). Baghdad: al-Wafa' Press, 1959.

al-Qamar fi shawari' Baghdad (The Moon in the Streets of Baghdad, poetry). Baghdad: Iraqi Authors' Union Press, 1961.

Hudhud, Rawda al-Farkh (1946–), Palestinian short-story writer who specializes in children's literature. She was born in Jaffa and lives in Amman. She attended school in Ramallah and enrolled in Cairo University, but the 1967 war prevented her from finishing university at the College of Pharmacy. She transferred to the Beirut Arab University, graduating from the School of Law in 1972. After graduation, she worked as a teacher for a year. She was the officer of the children's literature committee in the League of Jordanian Writers and the editor of the children's supplement of the Jordanian *al-Dustur*. She has published many stories in children's magazines and is the founder of Dar Kinda Publishers.

Fi ahraj Ya'bad (In the Woods of Ya'bad, children's literature). Amman: Dar Kinda, 1976.

Munqidh al-qarya Ibrahim Abu Diyya (The Village Savior Ibrahim Abu Diyya, children's literature). Amman: League of Jordanian Writers, 1980.

Qafilat al-fida' (Caravan of Sacrifice, children's literature). Amman: League of Jordanian Writers, 1980.

Sa'im fi sijn 'Akka (Fasting in the Acre Prison, children's literature). Amman: League of Jordanian Writers, 1980.

Rihlat al-nidal: al-Shaykh Hasan Salama (The Journey of Struggle: Shaykh Hasan Salama, children's literature). Amman: Dar Kinda, 1982.

Sirr al-qanabil al-mawquta (The Secret of the Ticking Bombs, children's literature). Amman: League of Jordanian Writers, 1983.

Kafr Qasim wa-l-muhakama al-'adila (Kafr Qasim and a Fair Trial, children's literature). Amman: Dar Kinda, 1984.

Asad fawq Hayfa (A Lion Above Haifa, children's literature). Amman: Dar Kinda, 1985.

Lughz al-atfal fi mukhayyam al-Duhaysha (The Children's Riddle in the Duhaysha Camp, children's literature). Amman: Dar Kinda, 1987.

Sirr al-shayatin al-humr fi-l-Bira (The Secret of the Red Devils in Bira, children's literature). Amman: Dar Kinda, 1987.

Hal yakfi al-hazz (Is Luck Enough, children's literature). Amman: Dar Kinda, n.d.

Sira' fi-l-ghaba (Struggle in the Forest, children's literature). Amman: Dar Kinda, n.d.

al-Zaman al-hazin fi Dayr Yasin (Sad Days in Dayr Yasin, children's literature). Amman: League of Jordanian Writers, n.d.

al-Hufi, Iman Muhammad al-Sayyid (1978–), Egyptian poet born in Cairo. She graduated from a vocational college in 1995.

Hakaya wa shatat (Stories and Fragments, poetry). Western Delta: General Authority for Culture Palaces, 1997.

Yutubiya (Utopia, poetry). Cairo: General Authority for Culture Palaces, 1999.

al-Humani, Amira (?–), Lebanese *zajal* poet born in southern Lebanon. She received her high-school education in Lebanon and studied musical education in Cairo. She worked as a teacher in Kuwait and first began writing lyrics and songs in Kuwait in 1962. She has published several anthems and children's songs in classical Arabic, the *zajal* poetic form, and Egyptian colloquial, and she has been heard in Lebanon and various parts of the Arab world. She is a member of the Lebanese Poetry League and the Association of Writers and Composers in Paris.

Hayk ghanayna (That's How We Sang, *zajal* poetry, two vols.). Lebanon: Center for Training in Active Teaching Methods, 1967 and 1968.

al-Humani, Bilqis (?–), Lebanese novelist and short-story writer born in the southern town of al-Nabatiya. She studied nursing in London and worked as a nurse and a journalist. She has published a work of non-ficiton, *Innaha hayatuki ya ukhtah* (It's Your Life, Sister, 1979).

al-Lahn al-akhir (The Final Melody, short stories). Cairo: n.p., 1961.

Hayy al-Lija (The Lija Quarter, novel). Beirut: Hamad Publications, 1967.

Sa'amurr 'ala-l-ahzan (I Will Pass through the Sorrows, novel). Beirut: Maktabat al-Ma'arif, 1975.

Khubz zayt wa karama (Bread, Oil, and Dignity, short stories). N.p.: al-'Alamiya Books, n.d.

al-Hummusani, 'Atiya (?–), Egyptian novelist and playwright.

Last nadima (I Have No Regrets, novel). Cairo: Maktabat al-Zanadi, 1965.

Hubbi habibi (My Love My Beloved, play). Cairo: General Egyptian Foundation for Printing and Publishing, 1967.

al-Hurr, Zahra (1917–2004) , Pioneering Lebanese poet born in Tyre to a family of jurists and writers. She received her primary education in the *kuttab*, a traditional Islamic school, in Tyre before enrolling in the official girls' school in 1927. She completed her intermediate education in 1932 before continuing her higher education at the Teachers' School and the French Medical School in Beirut. She received a degree in obstetrics and gynecology in 1937. She taught in Tyre and later in Iraq from 1940 to 1941. She contributed to the founding of the Cultural Council for Southern Lebanon in 1964, as well as the Working Literary League, the Association of the Women of Mt. 'Amil, the Women's Awakening Association in Sidon, the Young Muslim Women's Association, and the National Council for Public Development. She published poems in the Lebanese journal, *al-'Urfan*, and the Egyptian journal, *al-Risala*. She was known as "the poet of Mt. 'Amil." She wrote about women and their concerns in everyday life, as well as the revolution of Imam al-Husayn at Karbala. She received the Medal of Labor in 1971 and the Medal of the Cultural Council for Southern Lebanon in 1984.

Qasa'id mansiya (Forgotten Poems, poetry). Beirut: Dar Ghandur Printers and Publishers, 1970.

Riyah al-kharif (Autumn Winds, poetry). N.p.: Cultural Council for Southern Lebanon, 1992.

Husayn, Bahija (1954–), Egyptian novelist born in Kafr Saqr in the province of al-Sharqiya. She received a B.A. in philosophy from Ain Shams University in 1979. She worked as a philosophy teacher in Egypt and Algeria. She is currently a journalist. Her stories have been published in many magazines. She was arrested in 1975 for her political activities in the student movement.

Ra'ihat al-lahazat (The Scent of Moments, novel). Cairo: Dar al-Thaqafa al-Jadida, 1992.

Ajnihat al-makan (Wings of Place, novel). Cairo: Dar al-Thaqafa al-Jadida, 1995.

Maraya al-ruh (The Soul's Mirrors, novel). Cairo: Dar al-Thaqafa al-Jadida, 1997.

al-Bayt (The House, novel). Cairo: General Authority for Culture Palaces, 1999.

Husayn, Hadiya (?–), Iraqi short-story writer and novelist.

A'tadhir niyabatan 'ank (I Apologize for You, short stories). Baghdad: Waraq Press, 1993.

Qab qawsayn minni (Very Close to Me, short stories). Baghdad: Dar al-Shu'un al-Thaqafiya, 1998.

Husayn, Huda (1972–), Egyptian poet and novelist. She received a B.A. in French from Cairo University. She is a translator and has cooperated on translation projects with the Centre d'Etudes et de Documentation Economique, Juridique, et Sociale and the publishing house Dar Sharqiyat. She translated a collection of short stories by Marguerite Duras published in 1996 as *al-Kitaba: majmu'a qisasiya* (Writing: A Collection of Stories). She has published translations and other writings in *al-Hayat*, *al-Quds*, *Ibda'*, *Adab wa naqd*, *al-Jarad*, and *Akhbar al-adab*.

Li-yakun (Let It Be, poetry). Cairo: Supreme Council for Culture, 1996.

Dars al-amiba (The Amoeba's Lesson, novel). Cairo: General Egyptian Book Organization, 1998.

Qasa'id bayn al-harbayn (Interwar Poems, poetry). Cairo: al-Kitaba al-Ukhra Publications, 1998.

al-Husayni, Layla (?–), Iraqi poet.

Risalat al-as (The Myrtle's Message, poetry). Baghdad: Shafiq Press, 1971.

al-Husayni, Suhayla (1942–), Iraqi novelist and short-story writer born in Mosul. She received her education at the Secondary School for Domestic Arts in Mosul. She is self-educated. She has taught in primary and preparatory schools in Baghdad and Kuwait. She lives in Cairo. She published a non-fiction work about Shaykh Muhammad al-Ghazali in Cairo, *al-Mar'a fi manhaj al-Imam al-Ghazali* (Women in the System of Thought of Imam al-Ghazali, 1998).

al-Dafn bila thaman (Burial Free of Charge, short stories). Baghdad: Rashid Press, 1968.

Antum ya man hunak (You There, novel). Beirut: Dar al-Ittihad Printing and Publishing, 1972.

al-Husni, Amira (Bint Barada) (?–), Syrian novelist and the daughter of Taj al-Din Husni, the second president of the Syrian Arab Republic. Also known as Bint Barada.

al-Azahir al-humr (The Red Flowers, novel). Damascus: Ibn Zaydun Press, 1961.

Lahib (Blaze, novel). Damascus: n.p., 1962.

al-Qalb al-dhahabi (The Golden Heart, novel). Damascus: Ibn Zaydun Press, 1963.

Husni, Layla (?–), Egyptian short-story writer. She is an editor at *al-Jumhuriya* newspaper.

Sahra khassa jiddan (A Very Exclusive Get-together, short stories). Cairo: Dar al-Diya' Printing, Publishing, and Distribution, 1992.

Husni, Rasha Samir (?–), Egyptian short-story writer.

Hawadit 'arrafa (A Fortune-teller's Tales, short stories). Cairo: General Egyptian Book Organization, 1995.

Ibn Ya'rub, Turkiya Bint Sayf (1964–), Omani poet born in Muscat. She has a B.A. in law.

Ana imra'a istithna'iya (I'm an Exceptional Woman, poetry). Muscat: n.p., 1995.

Ibrahim, Arij 'Abd al-Hamid (1972–), Egyptian short-story writer born in Giza. She earned a Ph.D. in English and comparative literature and teaches in the English department at Helwan University.

Ansaf hikayat (Half-baked Stories, short stories). Cairo: General Authority for Culture Palaces, 1997.

Zaman Qaraqush (The Age of Qaraqush, novel). Cairo: General Egyptian Book Organization, 1999.

al-Ibrahim, Tayba Ahmad (?–), Kuwaiti short-story writer and novelist. She has a degree in pure mathematics. She has worked as a math teacher for the Ministry of Education and in the Libraries Department. She currently reviews literary texts for the Ministry of Information. She is a member of the Authors' League in Kuwait.

al-Insan al-muta'addid (The Manifold Human Being, novel). Cairo: al-'Arabiya al-Haditha Foundation, 1991.

Inqirad al-rajul (The Extinction of Men, novel). Cairo: al-'Arabiya al-Haditha Foundation, 1992.

al-Insan al-bahit (The Pale Human, novel). Cairo: al-'Arabiya al-Haditha Foundation, 1992.

Mudhakkirat khadim (Memoirs of a Servant, novel). Cairo: al-'Arabiya al-Haditha Foundation, 1995.

Zilal al-haqiqa (Shadows of the Truth, novel). Cairo: al-'Arabiya al-Haditha Foundation, 1995.

Hadhar an taqul (Don't You Dare Say, short stories). N.p.: n.p., n.d.

La'nat al-mal (The Curse of Money, novel). Cairo: al-'Arabiya al-Haditha Foundation, n.d.

al-Qalb al-qasi (The Cruel Heart, novel). N.p.: n.p., n.d.

'Id, Nada (1967–), Lebanese poet born in al-Damur. She received a B.A. in journalism from the Lebanese University. She works as a journalist and television announcer. She has published in *al-Anwar* and works at *Dalal* magazine. She has been editor in chief at *Dunya al-ahdath* since 1995.

Kitab al-nawras (Book of the Seagull, poetry). Jounieh: Dar Kan'an, 1994.

'Id, Nahid (?–), Egyptian novelist.

Ashjan (Sorrows, novel). Cairo: al-Dar al-Misriya Composition and Translation, 1965.

Idilbi, Ulfat (al-Idlibi, Ulfat) (1912–2007), Syrian novelist and short-story writer. She received a preparatory school diploma and took part in early feminist demonstrations during the great Syrian rebellion against the French occupation. She began writing short stories in 1947. She was a member of the Women's Cultural Symposium and worked on the publications committee of the Higher Arts Council for seven years. Several of her stories have been translated into other languages. She also wrote several works of non-fiction: *al-Manulya fi Dimashq wa ahadith ukhra* (Magnolia in Damascus and Other Stories, 1970), *Nazra ila adabina al-sha'bi* (A Look at Our Folk Literature, 1974), *Naghamat Dimashqiya* (Damascus Melodies, 1990), *Wada' al-ahibba* (The Loved One's Farewell, 1992), and *'Adat wa taqalid al-harat*

al-Shamiya al-qadima (Customs and Traditions from Ancient Damascene Alleys, 1996).

Qisas Shamiya (Damascene Stories, short stories). Damascus: Dar al-Yaqza, 1954.

Wada'an ya Dimashq (Farewell, Damascus, short stories). Damascus: Ministry of Culture, 1963.

Yadhak al-shaytan (Satan Laughs, short stories). Damascus: Maktabat Atlas, 1970.

'Asiy al-dam' (The Recalcitrant Tears, short stories). Damascus: Arab Writers' Union, 1976.

Dimashq ya basmat al-huzn (*Sabriya: Damascus Bitter Sweet*, novel). Damascus: Ministry of Culture, 1980.

Hikayat jaddi (*Grandfather's Tale*, novel). Damascus: Dar Tlas, 1991.

Ma wara' al-ashya' al-jamila (Behind the Beautiful Things, short stories). Damascus: Ishbiliya Research and Publishing, 1993.

Idris, 'A'ida Matarji (1934–), Lebanese short-story writer, editor, and publisher born in Tripoli. She received a B.A. in philosophy from the Lebanese University. She is a founder of the pioneering Arab publishing house, Dar al-Adab, and has published several essays in literary criticism. She is also the editorial secretary for the Lebanese journal, *al-Adab*. She has translated works by Albert Camus, Jean Paul Sartre, and Simone de Beauvoir into Arabic.

al-Ladhin la yabkun (Those Who Do Not Cry, short stories). Beirut: Dar al-Adab, 1966.

Idris, 'Awatif Sinnu (?–), Lebanese poet and short-story writer.

al-Yanbu' al-jadid: fi-l-'awatif al-Lubnaniya (The New Spring: On Lebanese Sentiments, poetry). Beirut: Dar al-Ittihad, 1988.

Harb wa sha'b aw rihla ila Bari Lutshi (A War and a People, or a Journey to Perry Lucci, reflections and poetry). Beirut: al-Dar al-Haditha, 1989.

'Abarat wa 'ibar min al-yanbu' al-jadid (Tears and Admonitions from the New Spring). Beirut: n.p., 1990.

Bayrut fi-l-'ishrinat (Beirut in the Twenties, short stories). Beirut: al-Dar al-Haditha, 1990.

Idris, Wafa' Muhammad al-Tayyib (1960–), Saudi short-story writer born in Medina. She received a B.A. in English literature from the College of Education at King 'Abd al-'Aziz University in Medina in 1990. She is a teaching assistant at the same institution and an administrator for the Qur'an Memorization Group.

Lan a'ud ilayk (I Will Not Come Back to You, short stories). Medina: Literary Club, 1996.

al-Ihsa'iya, Fatima al-Wusaybi'i (?–), Iraqi poet.

Kanz al-akhira fi marathi al-'itra al-tahira (Treasure of the Afterlife in Elegies for the Noble Companions, poetry). Najaf: Maktabat Dar al-Ma'arif, 1975.

Ilyas, Alice (1961–1988), Syrian short-story writer born in Marjarita. She was educated at Aleppo University.

al-Rimal al-mutaharrika (Shifting Sands, short stories). Damascus: Arab Writers' Union, 1992.

Imam al-Jisr, Kinana (1941–), Lebanese short-story writer born in Tripoli. She received a B.A. in psychology and philosophy from Cairo University and a degree from the Faculty of Education at the Lebanese University.

Rajul fi mataha (Man in a Labyrinth, short stories). N.p.: n.p., 1993.

'Imara, Ikhlas Fakhri (1940–), Egyptian poet born in al-Qalyubiya. She received her M.A. and Ph.D. from the Academy of Sciences in Cairo and has taught at the girls' college at Umm al-Qura University. She has published several works of non-fiction, including *al-Shi'r al-jahili bayn al-qabaliya wa-l-dhatiya* (Pre-Islamic Poetry

Between the Tribal and the Subjective, 1991), *al-Islam wa-l-shi'r* (Islam and Poetry, 1992), and *Qira'a naqdiya fi-l-shi'r al-'Arabi al-mu'asir* (A Critical Reading of Contemporary Arabic Poetry, 1992).

al-Ta'ir al-muhajir (The Migratory Bird, poetry). Jeddah: Dar al-Shuruq Publishers, 1986.

Wa kadha al-rijal (And That's Men, poetry). Cairo: Dhat al-Nitaqayn Press and Publishing, 1990.

al-Iryani, Ramziya 'Abbas (1955–), Yemeni novelist and short-story writer born in Iryan in the province of Ibb. She has a B.A. in philosophy and an M.A. in Arabic literature. She is currently preparing her Ph.D. in Arabic literature in the U.S., where she is a minister plenipotentiary. She is the first Yemeni woman novelist. Her first novel was published in the 1970s. She is also the first Yemeni woman to publish a collection of short stories in northern Yemen. She is an active feminist. She has published a work of non-fiction, *Ra'idat Yamaniyat* (Yemeni Women Pioneers), and she has written several academic papers on women's issues. She is one of the few Yemeni women writers who has not stopped writing and publishing.

Dahiyat al-jasha' (Greed's Victim, novel). Ta'z: Dar al-Qalam, 1970.

'Allahu ya'ud (Maybe He'll Return, short stories). Damascus: Dar al-Mukhtar, 1981.

Dar al-sultana (The Sultan's Palace, novel). Sana'a: n.p., 1998.

al-Qanun 'arus (The Law Is A Bridegroom, short stories). Sana'a: al-Offset Printers, 1998.

al-Sama' tumtir qutnan (It's Raining Cotton). N.p.: n.p., 1999.

al-Iryani, Salwa Yahya 'Abd al-Rahman (1967–), Yemeni short-story writer born in Cairo, where her father worked was the Yemeni ambassador. She has a B.A. in English literature from Sana'a University. She is currently a homemaker living in Sana'a. She first published in the press.

Lahzat shajan (A Moment of Grief, short stories). Sana'a: n.p., 1992.

al-'Isawi, Rim (1948–), Tunisian short-story writer born in Hamam al-Anf. She is a graduate of the Higher Teachers' Academy in Tunis and is a high-school teacher. She is a member of the Story Club and the Tunisian Writers' Union.
Limadha tamut al-'asafir (Why Do Sparrows Die, short stories). Tunis: Qisas Magazine Publications, 1988.

Ishaq, Maliha (1925–), Iraqi short-story writer born in Baghdad.
'Aqli dalili (My Mind Is My Guide, short stories). Beirut: Munaymina Press, 1948.
Layali milah (Nice Evenings, short stories). Cairo: Fann al-Tiba'a, 1950.
Ra'i'a (Magnificent, short stories). Cairo: n.p., 1952.

Isma'il, Dunya al-Amal (197?–), Palestinian poet from Gaza. She studied in Cairo and works as a journalist. She published a work of non-fiction, *Ra'aytu fi Ghazza* (I Saw in Gaza, Cairo, 1995), on her impressions of Gaza after her return from Cairo.
Ranin al-'uzla (The Ring of Loneliness, poetry). Ramallah: Palestinian Authority Ministry of Culture Publications, 1999.
Kull 'ala hida (Each Individually, poetry). Cairo: Dar al-Fursan, n.d.

'Izz al-Din, Umayma (?–), Egyptian short-story writer.
al-Ta'ir al-abyad (The White Bird, short stories). Cairo: Egyptian Association to Foster Talent, 1994.

'Izzat, Amira (?–), Egyptian short-story writer.
Qabl an tasqut al-'asafir (Before the Sparrows Fall, short stories). Cairo: al-Nashir al-'Arabi Press, 1985.

al-'Izzi, Khadija Mahmud (1928–1995), Iraqi poet. She had no formal education.

Her mother taught her to read and write. She began writing poetry in her early fifties.
Nafahat al-iman (Scents of Faith, poetry). N.p.: Ministry of Culture and Information and Dar al-Rashid Publishers, 1980.
Arij al-rawda (Fragrance of the Garden, poetry). Baghdad: n.p., 1982.
Nasa'im al-sihr (Breezes of Magic, poetry). Baghdad: al-Awqaf Press, 1985.

al-Ja"ar, 'Aliya (1935–2003), Egyptian poet born in Tanta. She received her early education from her father and graduated from the Faculty of Law at Cairo University in 1960. She practiced law before starting to work in television. She wrote religious programs and dramas adapted from Islamic history for television. She was a member of the Bar Association, the Supreme Council for Islamic Affairs, and the cultural committee at the Cairo Opera House. She was awarded the 'Abd al-'Aziz Sa'ud Prize for Poetry for the best poem of 1995.
Inni uhibb (I Love, poetry). Cairo: al-'Alamiya Press, 1968.
Atahadda bi-hawak al-dunya (With Your Love I Challenge the World, poetry). Cairo: al-Misriya Printing and Publishing, 1977.
Gharib anta ya qalbi (You Stranger, My Heart, poetry). Cairo: Dar al-Ma'arif, 1983.
Ibnat al-Islam (Daughter of Islam, poetry). Cairo: al-Maktab al-Misri al-Hadith, 1987.
'Ala a'tab al-rida (On the Thresholds of Contentment, poetry). Cairo: n.p., 1993.

Jabbar, Siham (1963–), Iraqi poet born in Baghdad. She has an M.A. and a Ph.D. in Arabic literature from Baghdad University. She writes prose poetry. Her research focuses on literary forms and mixtures of genre. She won *Aqlam* magazine's poetry prize in 1992 and the Hasab al-Shaykh Ja'far Prize from the Iraqi Writers' and Authors' Union in 1995 for her collection

'An sarab al-mir'a. She has worked in journalism and teaching and has done research on literature and literary criticism.
al-Sha'ira (The Poet, poetry). Baghdad: Dar al-Shu'un al-Thaqafiya, 1995.
'An sarab al-mir'a (On the Mirror's Mirage, poetry). N.p.: n.p., n.d.
'Arabati al-sahira (My Magic Carriage, poetry). N.p.: n.p., n.d.
Abwab kharijiya (Outside Doors). N.p.: n.p., n.d.
Adwar al-'alam (Floors of the World, poetry). N.p.: n.p., n.d.
Awanuha (Her Times, poetry). N.p.: n.p., n.d.
Ila-l-awghad al-awlad al-makirin (To the Scoundrels Belong Devious Children, poetry). N.p.: n.p., n.d.
Min nasl al-ma' (From the Water's Spawn, poetry). N.p.: n.p., n.d.

Jabbarin, Umayma Rafiq (1967–), Palestinian poet born in Umm al-Fahm in the part of Palestine occupied in 1948. She has a B.A. in Arabic and education.
Imra'at al-rih (Woman of the Wind, poetry). Nazareth: al-Tala'i' Journalism and Publishing, 1994.

Jabbur, Muna (1942–64), Lebanese novelist.
Fatah tafiha (Silly Girl, novel). Beirut: Dar wa Maktabat al-Hayat, 1962.
al-Ghirban wa-l-musuh al-bayda' (The Ravens and the White Gowns, novel). Beirut: Dar wa Maktabat al-Hayat, 1966.

al-Jabburi, Amal (1965–), Iraqi poet born in Baghdad. She received a B.A. in English literature from Baghdad University. She has worked as a translator, journalist, and cultural correspondent. She now resides in Germany. She has translated two books by Herbert Mason from English into Arabic: *The Death of al-Hallaj* (1979) and *Gilgamesh: A Verse Narrative* (1970).
Khamr al-jirah (Wine of the Wound, poetry). Baghdad: n.p., 1986.

A'tiqini ayyatuha-l-kalimat (Free Me, Words, poetry). Amman: Dar al-Shuruq, 1994.
Laka hadha-l-jasad la khawf 'alayha (This Body Is for You, She Is Safe, poetry). London: Saqi Books, 1999.

al-Jabburi, Irada (1966–), Iraqi novelist and short-story writer born in Karbala. She received a B.A. in translation and an M.A. in media studies. She worked as a translator and journalist. She has written screenplays for documentary films, including the award-winning "Hawl atfal al-'Iraq" (On the Children of Iraq). She now teaches at Sana'a University in Yemen.
Shajarat al-umniyat (The Wish Tree, short stories). Baghdad: Dar al-Shu'un al-Thaqafiya, 1990.
Ghubar al-mudun (Dust of the Cities, short stories). Baghdad: Dar al-Hamid, 1993.
'Itr al-tuffah (The Scent of Apple, novel). Baghdad: Dar al-Shu'un al-Thaqafiya, 1996.
Inana ibnat Babil (Inana the Daughter of Babel, children's literature). Baghdad: Dar Thaqafat al-Tifl, 1996.

al-Jabburi, Siham (?–), Iraqi poet.
Imra'a sharqiya min al-'alam al-thalith (An Eastern Woman from the Third World, poetry). Baghdad: al-Adib Press, 1986.

Jabir, 'Inaya (?–), Lebanese poet and journalist born in southern Lebanon. She studied political science at the Faculty of Law at the Lebanese University. She works for *al-Safir* newspaper and is a member of the Traditional Songs music group.
Taqs al-zalam (The Ritual of Darkness, poetry). Beirut: Maryam Publications, 1994.
Mazaj khasir (The Disposition of a Loser, poetry). Beirut-Damascus: Dar al-Mada, 1995.
Umur basita (Simple Things, poetry). Beirut: Dar al-Nahar Publishers, 1997.
Asta'idd li-l-'asha' (Preparing for Dinner, poetry). Beirut: Riyad al-Rayyis Books and Publishing, 1999.

al-Jabiri, Shaykha (1966–), Emirati short-story writer born in al-ʿAyn. She has a B.A. in media studies and Arabic from the Emirates University. She is the head of cultural relations at Emirates University. She used to work as a journalist and now writes a regular newspaper column.

Sindirilla al-Khalij (Cinderella of the Gulf, short stories). U.A.E.: privately published, 1993.

Jabr, Kulthum (1958–), Qatari short-story writer. She graduated from high school and continued her studies at Qatar University. Since 1972, she has worked in journalism and published many articles and stories in local magazines and newspapers.

Anta wa ghabat al-samt wa-l-taraddud (You and the Forests of Silence and Hesitation, short stories). Doha: al-ʿAhd Journalism Foundation, 1987.

Wajaʿ imraʾa ʿArabiya (The Pain of an Arab Woman, short stories). al-Dammam: Dar Umniya Publishing and Distribution, 1993.

Jabr, Maryam (1962–), Jordanian short-story writer born in Kafr Naja in ʿAjlun. She attended school in her village and later in ʿAjlun. She received a B.A. in Arabic language and literature from al-Yarmuk University. She was the recipient of the Young Authors Fiction Prize from the League of Jordanian Writers in 1985 and the university short-story award from al-Yarmuk University in 1988. Her nonfiction works include *Shakhsiyat al-marʾa fi-l-qissa al-qasira fi-l-Urdun* (Female Characters in the Jordanian Short Story, Irbid, Dar al-Kindi, 1995).

Akhir ahadith al-ʿarrafa (The Fortune-teller's Last Sayings, novel). Amman: al-Shaʿb Press, 1996.

Jad, Huda (1933–), Egyptian short-story writer and novelist. She graduated from high school. She is a boardmember of the Story Club and a member of the Writers' Union, the Authors' Association, and the Egyptian Women Writers' Association. She began to publish under an assumed name in 1961 in the Cairo-based *al-Hayat*. She began using her own name in contributions to *Hawwaʾ*, *al-Kawakib*, *al-Musawwar*, and *al-Hilal*. Her story, "al-Silah al-azraq" (The Blue Gun), has been translated into English, and some of her stories have been translated into Chinese and German. She has written several works for radio, including "Fulla wa Umm Hasan" (Fulla and Umm Hasan).

Kaffuk (Your Palm, short stories). Cairo: al-Thaqafa al-Jamahiriya, 1964.

al-Washm al-akhdar (The Green Tattoo, novel). Cairo: General Egyptian Book Organization, 1965.

Satr maghlut (A Mistake in the Knitting, short-story anthology), co-edited with Najiba al-ʿAssal. Cairo: General Egyptian Book Organization, 1971.

ʿAynaki khadrawan (Your Eyes Are Green, novel). Cairo: Dar al-Hilal, 1974.

Jarima lam turtakab (An Uncommitted Crime, novel). Cairo: Dar al-Hilal, 1976.

Sukkar nabat (Sugar Candy, short stories). Cairo: Dar al-Maʿarif, 1979.

Taʿwidhat hubb (Love Charms, short stories). Cairo: Akhbar al-Yawm Foundation, 1983.

Bayn shatiʾayn (Between Two Coasts, novel). Cairo: General Egyptian Book Organization, 1986.

Jad, Nihad (?–1989), Egyptian playwright born in Asyut. She received a B.A. in English from Cairo University and an M.A. in drama from Indiana University in 1968. She was the director of *Sabah al-khayr* magazine and wrote more than five plays and ninety short stories for children. Her plays, *ʿAdila wa mahattat al-utubis* and *ʿAla-l-rasif*, were staged. She published a collection of articles entitled *Ayyam wa ahlam* (Days and Dreams).

Hamada fi-l-sirk (Hamada at the Circus, children's literature). Cairo: Dar al-Hilal, 1969.

'Adila wa mahattat al-utubis ('Adila and the Bus Stop, play). Cairo: Maktabat Gharib, 1985.
'Ala-l-rasif (On the Sidewalk, play). Cairo: General Egyptian Book Organization, 1989.

al-Jadayid, Naziha (1957–), Tunisian poet born in Sidi 'Umur. She is a teacher.
al-Rasm bi-mahar al-bahr (Painting With Seashells, poetry). Susa: Sa'idan Publications, 1993.

al-Jahmi, Khadija Mahmud (1921–1996), Libyan short-story writer and social re-seacher born in Benghazi. She studied the Qur'an before studying formally. She went to Egypt in 1952 and received her primary and preparatory education at the 'Abidin Evening School in Cairo. Upon her return from Egypt, she worked in radio and journalism. She presented several radio programs and wrote several well-known Libyan songs. For many years she was the head of the Woman's Association. She established *al-Mar'a* magazine in 1965 and *al-Amal* children's magazine in 1970.
Amina (Amina, short stories). Tripoli, Libya: al-Dar al-Jamahiriya, 1978.

Jalal, Salma (1947–), Egyptian short-story writer. She received a B.A. in medicine in 1972, an M.A. in sociology in 1976, and a Ph.D. in medical sociology in 1987. She is a professor of social medicine and a development consultant. She is a member of the Egyptian branch of PEN. and the Egyptian Women Writers' Association, as well as a founding member of the Forum for Women's Development Agencies. She is also the vice president of the Women's Medical Association. Her non-fiction works include *Sihhat al-umm wa-l-tifl* (Maternal and Infant Health, 1991), *Sihhat al-mar'a al-Misriya min Nayrubi ila Bakin* (The Health of Egyptian Women from Nairobi to Peking, 1994), *Talabat al-tibb ka-du'ah li-l-sihha wa-l-bi'a* (Medical Students as Advocates of Health and the Environment, 1996), and *Dalil jam'iyat al-Katibat*

al-Misriyat (The Guide of the Association of Egyptian Women Writers, 1998).
Wa qal Abu-l-Hul (And the Sphinx Said, short stories). Cairo: 'Uyun Jadida, 1995.
Rihlat al-hayah (Life's Journey, short stories). Cairo: Dar al-Thaqafa al-Jadida, 1997.

Jalasi, al-Zawhara (1950–), Tunisian short-story writer born in Susa. She is a teacher of Arabic at the high-school and university levels. She has produced radio programs for literature lovers. After a writing hiatus of fourteen years, she re-sumed writing and publishing in the Tunisian press.
In'ikasat 'ind al-zawiya (Reflections at the Corner, short stories). Tunis: al-Dar al-Tunisiya Publishers, 1990.

Jalti, Rabi'a (1954–), Algerian poet born in Bu'anan, Algeria. She currently resides in France. She earned a state Ph.D. in modern literature and is a lecturer at the Algerian University in Oran. She writes and presents the program, *Hawwa' wa dunya* (Eve and the World), for Algerian radio and *'Atabat* (Thresholds) for Algerian television. She received the Ministry of Higher Education and Scientific Research Poetry Prize. Her poems have been published in the Lebanese *al-Safir*, the Syrian *al-Ma'rifa*, the Libyan *al-Fusul al-arba'a*, the Algerian *Amal*, and the Jordanian *Afkar*.
Tadaris li-wajh ghayr Barisi (The Contours of a Non-Parisian Face, poetry). Damascus: al-Karmel, 1981.
al-Tuhma (The Charge, poetry). Oran University, Algeria: University Center for Research, Documentation, and Media, 1984.
Shajar al-kalam (The Tree of Words, poetry). Meknes: Dar al-Safir, 1991.
Kayf al-hal? (How's It Going?, poetry). Damascus: Dar Huran, 1996.

Jamal, Amal Muhammad (1968–), Egypt-ian short-story writer born in al-Daqahliya. She received a degree in education from

Mansura University in 1991 and a degree in art criticism in 1999.

La usammik (I Do Not Name You). Cairo: General Egyptian Book Organization, 1995.

Min ajl sahaba (For a Cloud). Cairo: General Authority for Culture Palaces, 1998.

al-Jamili, Rabiha Ahmad (?–), Iraqi novelist.

Shay' minh (Something from Him, novel). Beirut: Dar al-Hayat Press, 1989.

Jamjum, Jamila Saqr (?–), Egyptian poet.

Ashki li-min al-ah (To Whom Shall I Cry, colloquial poetry). Cairo: Lotus Press, 1992.

Khayfa ahibb (I'm Scared to Love, colloquial poetry). Cairo: n.p., 1993.

al-Janabi, Su'ad 'Abd al-Hurr (?–), Iraqi short-story writer.

Samt wa 'unfuwan (Silence and Vigor, short stories). Baghdad: Dar al-Shu'un al-Thaqafiya, 1998.

Janim, 'Itaf Sa'id (1953–), Palestinian poet born in East Baqa, near Tulkarm. She lives in Irbid, Jordan. She attended U.N.R.W.A. schools in Irbid and Tiberias. She received a B.A. in Arabic from al-Yarmuk University in 1983. She is a teacher. She has written a collection of stories, *Sharat al-khalas* (Badge of Deliverance), which has not been published because of circumstances beyond her control.

Li-zaman sayaji' (For a Time to Come, poetry). Amman: League of Jordanian Writers, 1983.

Bayadir li-l-hulm ya sanabil (Wheat Bundles for a Dream, O Grain Spikes, poetry). Amman: Ministry of Culture, 1993.

al-Jar Allah, Fawziya (?–), Saudi short-story writer born in Riyadh. She received a B.A. in administrative sciences from King Sa'ud University in 1982 and a translation degree from the same institution in 1998. She works in the Training and Delegation Department of the Ministry of Health.

Fi-l-bad' kan al-rajul (In the Beginning Was Man, short stories). Riyadh: Story Club, 1991.

al-Maq'ad al-khalfi (The Back Seat, short stories). Beirut: Dar al-Jadid, 1999.

Jarju'i, Maha (?–), Lebanese poet born in Tyre. She graduated from the Liberal Arts College of the Lebanese University in Sidon.

Qasa'id imra'a mansiya (Poems of a Forgotten Woman, poetry). n.p., n.d.

Jarrah, Amal (?–), Syrian poet and novelist born in Damascus. She worked in journalism.

Khudhni bayn dhira'ayk (Take Me in Your Arms, novel). Beirut: n.p., 1967.

Rasa'il imra'a Dimashqiya ila fida'i Filistini (Letters of a Damascene Woman to a Palestinian Freedom Fighter, poetry). Beirut: Dar al-'Awda, 1969.

Safsafa taktub ismaha (Safsafa Writes Her Name, poetry). Beirut: Arab Institute for Research and Publishing, 1976.

Sah 'andalib fi ghaba (A Nightingale Shrieked in the Forest, poetry). Beirut: Arab Institute for Research and Publishing, 1978.

Imra'a min sham' wa shams wa qamar (A Wax Woman, a Sun, and a Moon, poetry). Kuwait: Dar Su'ad al-Sabah, 1992.

Jasim, Hayat (al-Zahra al-Bayda') (1936–), Iraqi poet and short-story writer born in Baghdad. She graduated from the Liberal Arts College at Baghdad University and received an M.A. in 1971. She published *al-Drama al-tajribiya fi Misr wa-l-ta'thir al-gharbi 'alayha (1960–1970)* (Experimental Drama in Egypt and Western Influence: 1960–1970) in Beirut in 1983. She also translated Martin Wallace's *Recent Theories of Narrative (Nazariyat al-sard al-haditha)* and published it in Cairo in 1998. She has written poetry since the mid-1950s, which has been published in Beirut and

Baghdad journals. She published her M.A. thesis, *Wihdat al-qasida fi-l-shi'r al-'Arabi hatta nihayat al-'asr al-'Abbasi* (Unity of the Poem in Arabic Poetry through the End of the 'Abbasid Period), in Baghdad in 1972. She earned a Ph.D. from Indiana University in 1978.

Sizif yatamarrad (Sisyphus Rebels, poetry). Baghdad: al-Jumhuriya Press, 1970.

Li-l-farah ughniya ukhra (Joy Has Another Song, short stories). Damascus: n.p., 1998.

al-Qafz fawq al-mawja (Jumping On the Wave, poetry). Rabat: al-Mawja Publications, 1999.

al-Jawahirji, Nabila (1945–), Egyptian poet. She has a B.A. in psychology and a graduate degree in education and psychology.

Shawq al-muhibbin fi hadrat sayyid al-mursalin salla Allah 'alayhi wa sallam (The Passion of the Lovers of the Master of Prophets, Peace Be Upon Him, poetry). Cairo: al-Dar al-Misriya al-Lubnaniya, 1993.

al-Jayyar, Sawsan (?–), Egyptian novelist. She published the non-fiction work, *Ahasis imra'a* (A Woman's Senses), in 1966 and a book of biographies, *Ad'iya' al-nubuwwa* (Pretenders to Prophethood), in 1987.

Uriduk ma'i (I Want You with Me, novel). Cairo: Everest and al-Wikala al-'Arabiya for Journalism and Publishing, 1990.

Jayyusi, Salma Khadra (al-Jayyusi, Salma al-Khadra) (1926–), Palestinian poet, researcher, translator, and professor born in al-Salt in eastern Jordan. She resides in the U.S. She received her early education in Jerusalem and Acre. She graduated with a B.A. in Arabic from the American University of Beirut in 1946. She earned a Ph.D. in Arabic literature from the School of Oriental and African Studies at the University of London in 1970. She taught at American universities until 1980, when she devoted herself full time to the Project for the Translation of Arabic (PROTA). She has published several academic works, among them *Mawsu'at al-adab al-Filistini al-mu'asir* (Encyclopedia of Contemporary Palestinian Literature, Beirut, Arab Institute for Research and Publishing, 1997) in two volumes, one on poetry and one on prose. She has translated many works, including the first two volumes of Lawrence Durrell's Alexandria Quartet (*Justine* and *Balthazar*) into Arabic. Her academic studies in English include *Trends and Movements in Modern Arabic Poetry* (Leiden, 1997). She has edited several valuable books, the most prominent being *Anthology of Modern Palestinian Literature*, (1992); *The Legacy of Muslim Spain* (1992); *Modern Arabic Poetry: An Anthology* (1987); *Modern Arabic Drama: An Anthology* (1995); and *The Literature of Modern Arabia* (1988).

al-'Awda min al-nab' al-halim (Return from the Dreaming Spring, poetry). Beirut: Dar al-Adab, 1960.

Jubran, Nadiya Husayn (?–), Egyptian poet born in Ra's Gharib on the Red Sea.

Ahasis wa asda' (Sensations and Echoes, poetry). N.p.: Writers of the Red Sea Association, 1980.

Hamasat al-bahr (The Sea's Whispers, poetry anthology). Hurghada: General Authority for Culture Palaces, 1998.

al-Juhani, Amina Sibyan (?–), Saudi playwright.

al-Hubb alladhi la yantahi (Never-ending Love, play). Riyadh: General Youth Authority, n.d.

al-Juhani, Layla (1969–), Saudi novelist born in Medina. She has a B.A. in English from King 'Abd al-'Aziz University in Medina. Her novel, *al-Firdaws al-yabab*, won first prize in the Sharjah Literary Competition in 1997.

al-Firdaws al-yabab (The Desolate Paradise, novel). Sharjah: Da'irat al-Thaqafa Publications, 1998.

Jum'a, Muna 'Abd al-'Azim (1958–), Egyptian poet. She has a B.A. in English from the College of Languages and works as a journalist for the Middle East News Agency.
'Ala bu'd haffa min jasad (At the Distance of a Body's Edge, poetry). Cairo: Dar Sashat Publishing and Distribution, 1995.

al-Junaydi, Amira (?–), Egyptian short-story writer.
Qadirun 'ala-l-hubb (Able to Love, short stories). Cairo: n.p., 1991.
al-Rihla (The Journey, novel). Cairo: n.p., 1995.

al-Jurani, Widad (1940–), Iraqi poet born in Baghdad. She finished her primary and secondary schooling in Baghdad and graduated with a degree in Arabic from Baghdad University in 1962. She has an M.A. in Arab intellectual history from the Institute of Arab History. She worked in teaching and was later appointed to the newspaper, *al-Jumhuriya*. She also worked at *Alif ba'* and the House of Culture for Children. She has written a study on heaven, hell, myth, and the epics of ancient Iraq.
Ya' nun al-sayyida (The Woman's Y.N., poetry). Baghdad: Dar al-Shu'un al-Thaqafiya al-'Amma, 1993.
Ahad 'ashar wataran fi qithara sumiriya (Eleven Strings on a Sumerian Lyre, poetry). Baghdad: Dar al-Shu'un al-Thaqafiya al-'Amma, 1995.

Juwaydi, Imtithal (194?–), Palestinian novelist born in Jaffa. She went to Lebanon after the *nakba*.
Shajarat al-subbayr (The Cactus Tree, novel). Beirut: Dar al-Tali'a, 1972.

al-Ka'bi, Ma'ida 'Abd al-Husayn (1942–), Iraqi writer of children's stories.
al-Asira al-bari'a (The Innocent Prisoner, children's literature). N.p.: n.p., n.d.

Kahili, Cecile (1958–), Palestinian poet and set designer born in Tarshiha in the part of Palestine occupied in 1948. She studied in schools in her village and enrolled in Haifa University, where she majored in the art of applied planning. She has designed the sets of several plays and art works, as well as the covers of literary works. She has published a collection of essays as *al-'Anqa'* (The Griffon, 1985).
al-Zill (The Shadow, poetry). Haifa: Ibrahim Salama Press, 1983.
Takwin (Creation, poetry). Haifa: al-Wadi Press, 1992.
Shazaya al-nur (Slivers of Light, poetry). Nazareth: Office of Arab Culture, 1994.

Kahluni, Samiha (1934–), Lebanese novelist. She published *Layinat al-malamis* (Soft to the Touch) in 1970, a work in which she analyzes women's character and proclivities.
Imra'a da'i'a (A Lost Woman, novel). Beirut: al-Wafa' Press, 1960.
I'tirafat qadin (Confessions of a Judge, novel). Beirut: Dar al-Jil, 1972.
I'tirafat tabib nafsi (Confessions of a Psychiatrist, novel). Beirut: Dar al-Jil, 1974.
'Adhdhabuni (They Tormented Me, novel). n.p., n.d.

Kalash, Ghada (1963–), Lebanese poet born in Beirut, where she received her secondary education. She worked in journalism and is the cultural editor for the newspaper, *al-Kifah al-'Arabi*.
Madarat al-ruh (Orbits of the Spirit, poetry). Beirut: Dar al-Hamra', 1991.
'Asafir al-qudban (Sparrows of the Tracks, texts). Beirut: Dar al-Hamra', 1995.

Kamal al-Din, Camilia (?–), Egyptian short-story writer.
al-Ta'ibun (The Repentent, short stories). Cairo: General Egyptian Book Organization, 1989.
Buyut bila abwab (Houses Without Doors, short stories). Cairo: Nahdat Misr Printing and Publishing, 1991.

K

Kamal al-Din, Madiha (?–), Egyptian poet.
al-Ahlam ghayr mu'ajjala (Undeferred Dreams, poetry). Cairo: n.p., 1993.

Kamal al-Din, Samiha (?–), Egyptian poet.
Sa'at al-hubb wa-l-alam (Hours of Love and Pain, poetry). Cairo: Maktabat Madbuli, 1986.
Qalbi ladayk (My Heart Is Yours, poetry). Cairo: Maktabat Madbuli, 1989.

Kamal, Ihsan (1935–), Egyptian short-story writer born in Jirja in Upper Egypt. She received a degree in embroidery arts in 1956. She has been awarded many prizes, including the Short Story Club Prize in 1958 and 1960, the Ihsan 'Abd al-Quddus Prize for the Short Story in 1991, and the Mahmud Taymur Prize for the Short Story, awarded by the Supreme Council for Culture, in 1994. She also received a medal from the Supreme Council for Arts and Humanities for the best short stories on the October War in 1974. She has adapted fifteen of her stories for television and cinema, some of which have been awarded prizes and which represented Egypt in international festivals. Many of her works have been translated into English, Russian, Chinese, Dutch, and Swedish.
Sijn al-malika (The Queen's Prison, short stories). Cairo: General Egyptian Book Organization, 1960.
Satr maghlut (A Mistake in the Knitting, short story anthology). Cairo: General Egyptian Book Organization, 1971.
Ahlam al-'umr kullih (An Entire Life's Dreams, short stories). Cairo: Dar al-Hilal, 1976.
al-Hubb abadan la yamut (Love Never Dies, short stories). Cairo: Dar al-Hilal, 1981.
Aqwa min al-hubb (Stronger Than Love, short stories). Cairo: Akhbar al-Yawm Foundation, 1982.
Lahn min al-sama' (A Melody from the Heavens, short stories). Cairo: General Egyptian Book Organization, 1987.

Mamnu' dukhul al-zawjat (No Entry for Wives, short stories). Cairo: Akhbar al-Yawm Foundation, 1988.
Dayfat al-fajr (A Dawn Guest, short stories). Cairo: General Egyptian Book Organization, 1992.
Basmat shifah (Lip Print, novel). Cairo: Akhbar al-Yawm Foundation, 1998.
Qabl al-hubb ahyanan (Before Love Sometimes, short stories). Cairo: Dar al-Qiba', 1998.

Kamal, Karima (1949–), Egyptian journalist. She works at *Sabah al-khayr* magazine. She published a work of non-fiction, *Madha yahduth fi-l-saraya al-safra'* (What Goes on in the Insane Asylum), in 1981.
Bint Misriya fi Amrika (An Egyptian Girl in America, travel literature). Cairo: Maktabat Gharib, 1983.
Khataya wa aliha: rihla ila-l-sharq al-ba'id (Sins and Gods: A Journey to the Far East, travel literature). Cairo: Maktabat Gharib, 1990.

Kana'ana, Lamis (1961–), Palestinian poet born in Nazareth. She was educated in that city. She studied journalism and media.
Qasa'id sadiqa (Sincere Poems, poetry). Nazareth: al-Nahda Press, 1992.

Kan'an, Evelyne Hitti (?–), Lebanese novelist.
Bayda' (A White Girl, novel). Beirut: Dar Majallat Shi'r, 1963.

Karam, 'Afifa Salih (1883–1924), Pioneering Lebanese novelist and journalist born in the village of 'Amshit. She was educated at the village convent school and the Sisters of the Holy Family School in Jubayl. She married at the age of thirteen and immigrated to the U.S. with her husband in 1897. She enriched her knowledge of culture with extensive reading and wrote for the diaspora press, including the journal *al-Huda*. She established the journal, *al-Mar'a al-Suriya* (1911–1913), after which she published the monthly *al-'Alam al-jadid* (1913). She was also a correspondent for *al-Mar'a al-jadida*. She translated Alexander Dumas' novel, *The Regent's Daughter* (Ibnat na'ib al-malik), as well as the novel, *Malika li-yawm* (Queen for a Day).

Badi'a wa Fu'ad (Badi'a and Fu'ad, novel). New York: al-Huda Press, 1906.

Fatima al-badawiya (Bedouin Fatima, novel). New York: al-Huda Press, 1906.

Ghadat 'Amshit (The Beauty of 'Amshit, novel). New York: al-Huda Press, 1914.

Muhammad 'Ali al-kabir (Muhammad 'Ali the Great, novel). n.p., n.d.

Cliyubatra (Cleopatra, novel). n.p., n.d.

Karam, Hana' (?–), Kuwaiti short-story writer.

Wurud al-iyyab (Roses of the Return, short stories). Kuwait: al-Risala Press, 1989.

Karnik, Lily Kamil (1939–), Palestinian poet born in Tulkarm, where she went to school. She moved to Ramallah with her family and completed high school there. She was a teacher at a U.N.R.W.A. school in Dayr 'Ammar and a school in al-Jalzun. She later moved to Lebanon.

Ajnihat al-qamar (The Moon's Wings, poetry). Jerusalem: al-Ma'arif Press, 1973.

Qatarat shawq fawq rasif al-'ubur (Drops of Passion on the Crosswalk, poetry). Jerusalem: Salah al-Din Publications, 1978.

al-Karrad, Nazmiya (?–), Syrian short-story writer born in Dir'a. She was educated in Damascus and received a B.A. in literature from St. Joseph University in Beirut. She is a member of the Children's Literature Association in Damascus.

al-Af'a wa-l-ra'i (The Snake and the Shepherd, children's literature). Damascus: Arab Writers' Union, 1985.

al-Hisan al-azraq (The Blue Horse, children's literature). Damascus: Arab Writers' Union, 1988.

Kashghari, Badi'a (?–), Saudi poet born in al-Ta'if. She received a B.A. in English from King 'Abd al-'Aziz University in Jeddah in 1977. She is an editor for *al-Qafila* magazine, published by Aramco.

al-Raml idha azhar (When the Sand Blooms, poetry). Beirut: Arab Institute for Research and Publishing, 1995.

Maqamat kharij al-zaman (Episodes outside Time, poetry). N.p.: n.p., n.d.

al-Kasrawi, Samira (1950–), Tunisian poet born in Sars.

Balaghat shi'riya fi-l-rafd wa-l-hurriya wa-l-rasas (Poetic Notices on Rejection, Freedom, and Bullets, poetry). Tripoli, Libya: n.p., 1982.

Malhamat al-mawt wa-l-milad fi sha'bi (Epic of Death and Birth Among My People, poetry). N.p.: n.p., 1983.

al-Kawwari, Shama Shahin (?–), Qatari short-story writer. She has a B.A. in organic medical sciences. She has worked in journalism and published in several Qatari newspapers, including *al-Raya*, *al-'Arabi*, and *al-Maraya*. She writes a weekly column for *al-Sharq*. She is active in social and women's activities in Doha.

Nahnu nazra' al-hubb (We Sow Love, short stories). Doha: Doha Youth Center's Forum for Writers and Authors, 1995.

al-Kawwari, Su'ad (1965–), Qatari poet. She graduated from the College of Education with a specialization in Arabic. She is a cultural official at the Ministry of Education and Higher Education.

Taja'id (Wrinkles, poetry). Doha: n.p., 1995.

al-Kayid, Rawda (?–), Syrian novelist.

Risala fi-l-tariq (A Letter on the Road, novel). Damascus: Dar al-Hayat Press, 1973.

al-Kayyali, Da'd (1935–), Palestinian poet born in Ramle. She was educated in that city's schools. After the fall of Ramle in 1948, she and her family went to Gaza.

She received a B.A. in English literature from Cairo University in 1963. She resided in Kuwait, where she taught.

Wa lima tamturi ya ghuyum (Why Are You Raining, Clouds, poetry). Beirut: Dar al-'Ilm li-l-Malayin, 1970.

Agharid al-hanin ila-l-watan (Songs of Longing for the Homeland). N.p.: n.p., n.d.

Sakinat al-iman (The Serenity of Faith, novel). Cairo: Matba'at al-Sidq al-Khayriya, 1954.

al-Kayyali, Shahla (1941–), Palestinian poet born in al-Lud. She was forced out of the city in 1948 and resides in Amman. She went to school in al-Zarqa'. She earned a B.A. in Arabic from the Arab University in Beirut in 1977. She teaches in schools run by U.N.R.W.A. In addition to poetry, she has published short stories and reflections in newspapers and journals. In conjunction with Amina al-'Adwan, she translated an anthology, *Rebellious Voices: Selections of Poetry by Arab Women Writers in Jordan.*

Kalimat fi-l-jurh (Words in the Wound, poetry). Beirut: Arab Institute for Research and Publishing, 1985.

Wa inqata'at awtar al-samt (And the Chords of Silence Ceased, poetry). Beirut: Arab Institute for Research and Publishing, 1988.

Khatawat fawq al-mawj (Footsteps on the Wave, poetry). Beirut: Arab Institute for Research and Publishing, 1992.

Wajhi alladhi hunak (My Face There, poetry). Beirut: Arab Institute for Research and Publishing, n.d.

Kazim, Safinaz (1937–), Egyptian writer and journalist. She received a B.A. in journalism from Cairo University in 1959 and an M.A. in theater criticism from New York University in 1966. She is the assistant editor of *al-Musawwar*. She was awarded the 'Ali and Mustafa Amin Journalism Prize in 1996. She considers all of her writings to be creative writing, even if the subject is literary criticism or politics.

Her non-fiction works include *al-Khadi'a al-Nasiriya* (The Nasserist Ruse, 1983), *Masrah al-masrahiyin* (Stage of Thespians, 1984), *Yawmiyat Baghdad, Lundun* (Diaries of Baghdad, London, 1984), *al-Haqiqa wa ghasil al-mukhkh fi qadaya mu'asira* (The Truth and Brainwashing in Contemporary Issues, 1985), *'An al-sijn wa-l-hurriya* (On Prison and Freedom, 1986), *Risaliyat fi-l-bayt al-nabawi* (Essays on the House of the Prophet, 1987, trilogy), *Milaff masrah al-sitinat* (Theater in the 1960s, 1991), *Fi mas'alat al-sufur wa-l-hijab* (On Veiling and Unveiling, 1995), *al-Muqawama wa irhab al-fikr al-Sihyuni* (Resistance and the Terrorism of Zionist Thought, 1996), and *Min daftar al-mulahazat* (From the Notebook of Observations, 1997).

Rumantikiyat (Romantic Texts, texts). Cairo: Dar al-Hilal, 1970.

al-Bu'd al-khamis (The Fifth Dimension, play). Cairo: al-Zahra' Arab Media, 1987.

Talabib al-kitaba (The Collars of Writing, texts). Cairo: Dar al-Hilal, 1994.

Khaldun 'Ayda (?–), Algerian short-story writer.

Rabi' Ghajariya wa matar (Spring, a Gypsy Woman, and Rain, short stories). Algiers: n.p., 1998.

Khalid, Ni'mat (1958–), Palestinian short-story writer and novelist born in 'Ayn Ziwan, al-Qantara, Syria. She studied at the Teachers' Preparatory Institute and received a law degree from Damascus University in 1991. She has written several critical studies, among them *al-Takhyil al-riwa'i li-l-jasad* (The Novel's Imagining of the Body).

al-Muwajaha (The Confrontation, short stories). Damascus: n.p., 1992.

Wahshat al-jasad (Loneliness of the Body, short stories). Latakia: Dar al-Hiwar, 1996.

al-Badad (Power, novel). Latakia: Dar al-Hiwar, 1998.

Nisa' (Women, short stories). Latakia: Dar al-Hiwar, 1999.

Khalid, Wisal (1943–), Lebanese short-story writer born in Beirut. She received a teaching certificate in philosophy from the Lebanese University and an M.A. from the Sorbonne in Paris. She taught French at the al-Irshad School for Girls. During the Lebanese civil war, she moved to London. She has published in the Lebanese *al-Diyar* and *al-Kifah al-'Arabi*, as well as in *al-Hayat* and *al-Khalij*.

Tadhkara li-matahat al-qarya (A Ticket to the Village Maze, short stories). Beirut: Dar al-Afaq al-Jadida, 1973.

Dumu' al-qamar (The Moon's Tears, short stories). Beirut: Dar al-Afaq al-Jadida, 1980.

al-Khalidi, 'Anbara Salam (1898–1986), Lebanese social pioneer born in Beirut. She received her primary education from a *shaykha*, studying the Qur'an, and later at a girls' school run by the Thamrat al-Ihsan Association, prominent Muslims in Beirut who believed in girls' education. She was forced to wear the veil at age ten, but her father enrolled her in the French St. Joseph School in Beirut (girls' section) for two years. When her father established the department for girls' education at the al-Maqasid Islamic Charitable Association, run by Julia Tu'ma Dimashqiya, 'Anbara transferred to that school. After her graduation, she continued studying Arabic language and literature with author 'Abd Allah al-Bustani in 1913. She helped found the Awakening of Young Arab Women Association to help young Arab women receive an education. When she visited Egypt with her father in 1920, she attended the ceremony sponsored by the Egyptian University to honor Qasim Amin and she met Huda Sha'rawi and her colleagues in the women's movement. In 1928, she removed her veil at a public party in Beirut. She moved to Jerusalem in 1929 with her Palestinian husband, Ahmad Samih al-Khalidi, and lived there until 1948. She returned to Beirut with her family after the Palestinian *nakba* and founded an orphanage for the children of Palestinian fighters. She published articles on women's emancipation in the Egyptian newspaper, *al-Muqattam*, and from 1944 to 1946 she translated *The Iliad* and *The Odyssey* into Arabic. In 1917, along with five other women, she founded the Literary Club for Muslim Girls. In 1924 she established the Women's Awakening Association with her teacher, Salma Sa'igh, to foster the development of national industry.

Jawla fi-l-dhikrayat bayn Lubnan wa Filistin (A Tour of Memories between Lebanon and Palestine, autobiography). Beirut: Dar al-Nahar Publishers, 1979.

Khalifa, Dalal (?–), Qatari novelist and playwright born in Doha. She has a B.A. in English from Qatar University and an M.A. in translation from Heriot-Watt University. She is the head of the Foreign Publications Unit. She is also the head of Marasina, a women's cultural forum, part of the al-Jisr Cultural and Social Club.

Insan fi hayz al-wujud (A Person in the Sphere of Existence, play). Qatar: 'Ali Ibn 'Ali Press, 1992.

Kitab al-duma (vol. 1) (The Book of Dolls, vol. 1, children's literature). N.p.: n.p., 1992.

Kitab al-duma (vol. 2) (The Book of Dolls, vol. 2, children's literature). N.p.: n.p., 1992.

Usturat al-insan wa-l-buhayra (The Legend of the Man and the Lake, novel). Qatar: Dar al-'Ulum Foundation, 1993.

Min al-bahhar al-qadim ilayk (From the Ancient Mariner to You, novel). Qatar: Dar al-'Ulum Foundation, 1995.

Khalifa, Hind Khalid Muhammad (1958–), Saudi short-story writer born in Riyadh. She has a B.A. and an M.A. in sociology and is currently studying for a Ph.D. in Britain. She has been a lecturer at King Sa'ud University in Riyadh since 1987.

Jawhara bi-l-'amal talma' (With Effort a Gem Shines, children's literature). N.p.: n.p., 1993.

Khalid 'ala-l-qamar (Khalid on the Moon, children's literature). N.p.: n.p., 1994.
al-Qalam (The Pen, children's literature). N.p.: n.p., 1994.
al-Risha al-dhahabiya (The Golden Feather, children's literature). N.p.: n.p., 1994.
Dinasur Ibrahim (Ibrahim's Dinosaur, children's literature). N.p.: n.p., 1995.
Qaryat al-asmak (Village of Fish, children's literature). N.p.: n.p., 1996.

Khalifa, Shu'a' (?–), Qatari novelist born in Doha.
al-'Ubur ila-l-haqiqa (Crossing to the Truth, novel). Qatar: Dar al-'Ulum Foundation, 1993.
Ahlam al-bahr al-qadim (Dreams of the Ancient Sea, novel). Qatar: Dar al-'Ulum Foundation, 1993.

Khalifeh, Sahar (Khalifa, Sahar) (1941–), Palestinian novelist born in Nablus, where she still resides. She received her early education in Nablus and Amman and graduated from the English department at Birzeit University in 1976. She continued her studies in the same field in the U.S. She has done translation, management, and secretarial work. She manages the Center for Women's Studies. Her novels have been translated into several languages, including French, German, Dutch, Italian, and Hebrew. She has written a novel in English, *Women in No Man's Land* (1988).
Lam na'ud jawari lakum (We Are Your Slaves No More, novel). Cairo: Dar al-Ma'arif, 1974.
al-Subbar (*Wild Thorns*, novel). Jerusalem: al-Sharq Cooperative Press, 1976.
'Abbad al-shams (Sunflower, novel). Jerusalem: Dar al-Katib, 1980.
Mudhakkirat imra'a ghayr waqi'iya (Memoirs of an Unrealistic Woman, novel). Beirut: Dar al-Adab, 1986.
Bab al-Saha (The Saha Gate, novel). Beirut: Dar al-Adab, 1990.
al-Mirath (*The Inheritance*, novel). Beirut: Dar al-Adab, 1997.

Khalil, Amani (1954–), Egyptian short-story writer and novelist. She received a B.A. in sciences from al-Azhar University.
Washish al-bahr (Whisper of the Sea, novel). Cairo: Supreme Council for Culture, 1998.

Khallaf, Raniya (1967–), Egyptian short-story writer. She received a B.A. in media from Cairo University and works as a journalist at *Ahram Weekly*. She is also a translator.
Jasad akhar wahid (Another Lone Body, short stories). N.p.: n.p., n.d.

Khalusi, Sada (?–), Iraqi poet.
Asda' al-ightirab (The Echoes of Alienation, poetry). Baghdad: Dar al-Shu'un al-Thaqafiya, 1987.

Khamis, Hamda (1946–), Bahraini poet born in Manama. She currently resides in Sharjah. She received a B.A. in political science from Baghdad University in 1969. After graduation she worked for British Airways and as a correspondent for several newspapers. She also worked as a teacher in Bahrain for nine years. She has worked at several Gulf newspapers, including *al-Azmina al-'Arabiya, al-Ittihad al Zabyaniya*, and *Abu Zabi al-Yawm*. She is a founding member of the Family of Writers and Authors in Bahrain and a member of the Emirati Writers' Union and the Arab Writers' Union.
I'tidhar li-l-tufula (An Apology to Childhood, poetry). Bahrain: Dar al-Ghad, 1978.
Masarat (Byways, poetry). Latakia: Dar al-Hiwar Publishing and Distribution, 1993.
Addad (Opposites, poetry). Amman: Arab Authors' General Union, 1994.
'Uzlat al-zaman (The Loneliness of Time, poetry). Beirut: al-Kunuz al-Adabiya, 1999.
Taranim (Hymns). (Beirut: Dar al-Farabi; Bahrain: al-Maktaba al-Wataniya, 1985).

Khamis, Salwa, Saudi poet, who works at *'Uqaz* newspaper.

Mithl qamar 'ala niyyatih (Like a Gullible Moon). Beirut: Dar al-Jadid, 1999.

al-Khamis, Umayma 'Abd Allah (1964–), Saudi short-story writer born in Riyadh. She received a B.A. in Arabic from King Sa'ud University in 1988. She is a high-school Arabic teacher. She is a former columnist for *al-Riyad* and currently writes a column for *al-Jazira*.

al-Dil' hin istawa (The Rib When It Was Straightened, short stories). Riyadh: Dar al-Ard, 1993.

Ayna yadhhab hadha-l-daw' (Where Does This Light Go, short stories). Beirut: Dar al-Adab, 1996.

Majlis al-rijal al-kabir (The Great Council of Men, short stories). Beirut: Dar al-Jadid, 1996.

al-Khani, Mallaha (1938–), Syrian short-story writer and novelist born in Damascus. She received a B.A. in history from Damascus University. She worked as a program presenter on radio and television and as an editor at *al-Mu'allim al-'Arabi* magazine. She published her first stories in Syrian newspapers and magazines. She is a member of the Story and Novel Association.

Kayf nashtari al-shams (How Do We Buy the Sun, short stories). Damascus: Arab Writers' Union, 1978.

al-'Araba bila jawad (The Cart Without a Horse, short stories). Damascus: Arab Writers' Union, 1981.

Khatawat fi-l-dabab (Steps in the Fog, novel). Damascus: Arab Writers' Union, 1984.

Imra'a mutalawwina (A Fickle Woman, short stories). Damascus: Ministry of Culture, 1987.

Banat haratina (The Girls of Our Alley, novel). Damascus: Arab Writers' Union, 1998.

al-Kharsa, Ghada (1947–), Lebanese poet and novelist born in Beirut. She received her primary and secondary education at schools run by Franciscan nuns and at the Zahrat al-Ihsan convent school in Beirut. She received a B.A. from Montreux College in Switzerland in 1973 and studied Arab literature at Cairo University. She moved to Cairo and worked for Kuwaiti television and radio doing family programs.

Lu'bat al-qadar (Fate's Plaything, novel). Cairo: al-Ahram Commercial Press, 1974.

Hariq fi-l-janna (A Fire in Paradise, novel). Cairo: al-Ahram Commercial Press, 1976.

al-Harb wa-l-hubb (War and Love, novel). Kuwait: Dar al-Siyasa, 1982.

Li'annak al-hubb (Because You Are Love, poetry). Beirut: privately published by the Arab International Press for Publishing and Printing, 1994.

al-Khashin, Adele (1923–), Lebanese poet born in al-Shuwayfat. She went to school there and earned her high school diploma in 1945. She taught in the first official girls' school and worked at Near East radio (1950) and Lebanese radio. She is a founding member of the Women's Agency in the Druze Charitable Association and a member of the Lebanese Writers' Union. She has published in *al-Adib* and *al-Adab* magazines and written for *al-Nahar*, *al-Anwar*, *al-Sharq*, and *al-Liwa'*. She and her husband selected and translated poems for two anthologies, *Antulujiyat al-shi'r al-Bulghari al-hadith* (An Anthology of Modern Bulgarian Poetry) and *Antulu-jiyat al-shi'r al-Sufiyati* (An Anthology of Soviet Poetry). She was a teacher at a girls' school and later emigrated to Venezuela to work with her husband.

Asda' (Echoes, poetry). Beirut: Dar al-'Awda, 1988.

Ashwaq al-layl (Yearnings of the Night, poetry). Beirut: n.p., 1999.

al-Khashin, Wafa' (?–), Syrian poet.

La tadkhul yafi'an ila qalb al-majzara al-wadi' (Do Not Enter As a Boy the Heart of Calm Slaughter, poetry). Damascus: Dar al-Majd, 1984.

Khashuqji, Samira Muhammad (Samira Bint al-Jazira al-'Arabiya) (1940–1986), Saudi novelist and short-story writer born in Mecca. She was educated in Egypt and received a B.A. in economics from Alexandria University. She published *al-Sharqiya* magazine and was a founding member of the Young Women of the Arabian Peninsula Club and the Saudi Awakening Association in Riyadh. She published several essays, including *Rihlat al-hayah* (Life's Journey) and *Yaqzat al-fatah al-Sa'udiya* (Keenness of the Young Saudi Woman). She is also known as Samira Bint al-Jazira al-'Arabiya.

Wadda't amali (I Bid My Hopes Farewell, novel). Beirut: Zuhayr Ba'labakki Publications, 1958.

Dhikrayat dami'a (Tearful Memories, novel). Alexandria: Dar Luran Printing and Publishing, 1961.

Bariq 'aynayk (The Gleam of Your Eyes, novel). Beirut: al-Maktab al-Tijari, 1963.

Wa tamdi al-ayyam (And the Days Go By, short stories). Beirut: Zuhayr Ba'labakki Publications, 1969.

Wara' al-dabab (Beyond the Fog, novel). Beirut: Zuhayr Ba'labakki Publications, 1971.

Ma'tam al-wurud (The Roses' Funeral, novel). Beirut: Zuhayr Ba'labakki Publications, 1973.

Qatarat min al-dumu' (Drops of Tears, novel). Beirut: al-Maktab al-Tijari, 1973.

Wadi al-dumu' (The Valley of Tears, short stories). Beirut: Zuhayr al-Ba'labakki Publications, 1979.

Talal fi rimal (Hills in the Sands, novel). Riyadh: Dar al-Sharqiya, 1983.

al-Khathlan, Sara Muhammad (?–), Saudi poet born in Riyadh. She resides in al-Dammam. She received her high-school diploma in 1986. She is a member of the Women's Charitable Association in al-Dammam and she hosts a literary salon for Saudi women poets and fiction writers. She writes a column for *al-Sharq* magazine, published in the Eastern Province.

Hara'iq fi da'irat al-samt (Fires in the Circle of Silence, poetry). al-Dammam: al-Ibtikar, 1994.

Wa laysa ay imra'a imra'a (Not Any Woman Is a Woman, poetry). Beirut: Dar al-Kunuz, 1996.

Mubajjal fi hudur al-warda (Honored in the Presence of the Rose, poetry). Egypt: Dar Sama', 1997.

Wa tahab al-bahr (And She Gives the Sea, poetry). Egypt: Dar Sama', 1999.

Khatib, 'Ayda (?–), Palestinian poet born in Shafa 'Amr in the part of Palestine occupied in 1948. She received her primary and secondary education in her hometown.

al-Juri 'umruhu qasir (The Damask Rose's Life Is Short, poetry). Shafa 'Amr: Dar al-Mashriq Translation and Publishing, 1991.

Hamama muntasaf al-layl (The Midnight Dove, poetry). Nazareth: Office of Arab Culture, 1994.

al-Khatib, Iman Fu'ad (1959–), Saudi children's writer born in Jeddah. She received a B.A. in English language from the College of Education for Girls in Riyadh in 1976 and an M.A. in English from the University of Iowa in 1980. She has been a lecturer at the European languages and translation department at the Languages and Translation Colleges of King Sa'ud University in Riyadh since 1993. Before that she was a lecturer at King 'Abd al-'Aziz University in Jeddah.

Shaja'at al-'alim al-Hasan al-Basri (The Courage of the Scholar al-Hasan al-Basri, children's literature). Kuwait: al-Islah Association, 1989.

al-Khatib, Samira (1948–) (Layla al-Maqdisiya), Palestinian poet and journalist born in Jerusalem. She attended al-Ma'muniya College in Jerusalem and continued her studies in the U.S. She helped found *al-Fajr* newspaper in 1972. She has published some of her works as Layla al-Maqdisiya. She lives in the U.S.

al-Qarya al-zaniya (The Fornicating Village, poetry). Jerusalem: al-Fikr al-Jadid, 1971.

al-Khatib, Suzanne (?–), Lebanese poet.
Wa yabqa al-athar (And the Trace Remains, poetry). Beirut: Dar al-Jadid, 1996.

al-Khatib, Tahiya (1942–), Iraqi poet born in Basra. She completed her primary and secondary education there then moved to Baghdad, where she joined the College of Medicine. She graduated in 1965 and returned to Basra to work as a physician. She ardently defends women's causes in her works. She has translated the work, *Marad fuqdan al-mana'a al-muktasaba* (Acquired Immune Deficiency Syndrome). She has written about the illness of poet Badr Shakir al-Sayyab and her experiences in clinics and hospitals.
Haqibat al-ruh (The Spirit's Bag, poetry). N.p.: n.p., n.d.

Khattab, Fadiya 'Abd al-Mun'im (1947–), Egyptian short-story writer born in al-Minufiya.
'Ala difaf al-sharqawiya (On Eastern Shores, novel). Cairo: General Authority for Culture Palaces, 1997.
Sahil al-dhikrayat (The Whinny of Memories, short stories). Cairo: General Authority for Culture Palaces, 1998.
Satabqa baynana al-ashya' (Things Will Remain Between Us, short stories). Cairo: General Authority for Culture Palaces, 1998.

Khatun, Hana' al-Amin (?–2006), Lebanese poet born in Shaqra. She received a teaching certificate in Arabic language and literature from the Lebanese University. She published in several Arab and Lebanese newspapers, including *al-Safir*, *al-Nahar*, and the Emirati *al-Ittihad*. She was a member of Friends of Writers and Books and the Friday Cultural Forum.
Lugha tahull jada'ilaha (A Language That Loosens Its Braids, poetry). Beirut: Arab Institute for Research and Publishing, 1991.

Li-ghayr hadha-l-hawan (For Anything But This Shame, poetry). Beirut: Friends of Writers and Books, 1993.

Khawja, Ghaliya (1968–), Syrian poet born in the province of Aleppo. She received a degree in law. She publishes essays on criticism of poetry, fiction, and the plastic arts in the Arab press and participates in various social seminars and forums.
al-Faris al-azraq (The Blue Knight, novel). N.p.: n.p., 1997.
Ilyadhat al-dam (The Iliad of Blood, poetry). N.p.: n.p., 1997.
Nushur al-azraq (The Resurrection of Blue, poetry). Latakia: Dar al-Mirsah, 1998.
Jahimiyat al-arjawanfasaj (The Hellfires of Purple-violet, poetry). N.p.: n.p., 1999.

al-Khayr Salwa (?–), Syrian short-story writer.
Khuyul al-dhakira al-sawda' (The Black Horses of Memory, short stories). Latakia: Dar al-Hiwar Publishers, 1993.

Khayri, Wafiya (1931–), Egyptian novelist and short-story writer raised in Cairo. She received a B.A. in English from Cairo University in 1953, a degree from the Screenwriting Institute in 1964, and a degree in dramatic writing in 1972. She writes television dramas. She is a board-member of the Association of Female University Graduates and a member of the Egyptian Women Writers' Association, the Writers' Union, and the Film Professionals' Syndicate. She worked as a translator at the Ministry of Economy and was the head of the development department at the Capital Market Authority. She has written dramas for television since 1965, and some of her works have been translated into English.
Akthar min shay' (More Than a Thing, short stories). Cairo: General Egyptian Book Organization, 1983.
al-Hayah fi khatar (Life in Danger, novel). Cairo: Dar al-Hurriya, 1983.

Imra'a bi-dakhili (A Woman Inside Me, short stories). Cairo: General Egyptian Book Organization, 1989.

Za'ir al-sa'a al-tasi'a (The Nine O'Clock Visitor, short stories). Cairo: General Egyptian Book Organization, n.d.

K

al-Khayyat, Najah 'Umar (1944–), Saudi short-story writer born in Jeddah. She received a B.A. in Beirut. She is a pioneer of Saudi women's literature. She has written literary essays and short stories. She took first place in a short-story competition organized by the Medina Literary Club in Jeddah in 1993.

Makhad al-samt (Labor Pains of Silence, short stories). Jeddah: Maktabat al-Fikr, 1966.

Khayyat, Salam (1934–), Iraqi poet and novelist born in Basra. She received a law degree from Baghdad University in 1965 and practiced law while writing for Iraqi and Arab newspapers. She was the editorial secretary of *al-Mar'a* and later *al-Ajyal*, both published in Baghdad. She has taken part in Arab and international conferences. She currently lives in London. She has published a work of non-fiction, *al-Bigha' 'abr al-'usur* (Prostitution Throughout the Ages). She also published *Iqra'* (Read), on the art of writing. Both books were published by Riyad al-Rayyis Books and Publishing in London.

Mamnu' al-dukhul mamnu' al-khuruj (No Entry, No Exit, novel). London: Moody Press, 1984.

Ma'zufat (Recitals). London: n.p., 1986.

al-Khazin, Hind Rashid (1884–?), Lebanese literary pioneer.

Mufakkirat Hind (Hind's Journal, memoir). Harisa: St. Paul's Press, 1924.

al-Khazraji, 'Atika Wahbi (1924–1997), Iraqi poet and playwright born in Baghdad. She received a B.A. in Arabic literature from the Higher Teachers' Institute in 1945 and worked as a teacher. She then went to Paris where she enrolled in the Sorbonne in 1950. She received a Ph.D. in 1955 for her work on the poet al-'Abbas ibn al-Ahnaf. She published her edition of the poet's works in Cairo in 1954. She was a teacher of Arabic at the Higher Teachers' Institute. She composed poetry and published some of it in the Iraqi press when she was just fourteen years old. She also published a work on the poet Isma'il Sabri.

Majnun Layla (Crazy for Layla, poetic drama). Cairo: Fann al-Tiba'a Foundation, 1954.

Anfas al-sihr (Breaths of Magic, poetry). Cairo: Fann al-Tiba'a Foundation, 1963.

La'la' al-qamar (The Moon Shimmered, poetry). Cairo: n.p., 1965.

Afwaf al-zahr (The Flower's Membranes, poetry). Kuwait: al-'Asriya Press, 1975.

al-Majmu'a al-shi'riya al-kamila (The Complete Works of Poetry, six collections of poetry and a play). N.p.: n.p., 1986.

Khedairi, Betool (Khudayri, Batul) (1965–), Iraqi novelist born in Baghdad. She received a B.A. in French literature from al-Mustansiriya University in Baghdad. She translated Graham Greene's *Dr. Fischer of Geneva or the Bomb Party* into Arabic (Dar Manarat, 1990).

Kam badat al-sama' qariba! (*A Sky So Close*, novel). Beirut: Arab Institute for Research and Publishing, 1999.

Khudayr, Salima (?–), Iraqi writer.

Thawrat al-a'maq (Rebellion of the Depths, short stories and a play). Basra: Haddad Press, 1963.

Nakhil wa qithara (Palm and Lyre, novel). Beirut: Maktabat al-Nahda, 1973.

Khurays, Samiha (1956–), Jordanian novelist born in Amman. Her father worked for the Foreign Ministry and so she was educated in several places. She received a B.A. in social sciences from Cairo University in Khartoum in 1978. She lived for five years in Sudan, seven years in Qatar, and seventeen years in the

U.A.E., where she worked for many years at *al-Ittihad* newspaper. She moved back to Jordan and currently works for the Jordanian *al-Ra'i*. She received the State Encouragement Prize in 1997 for her novel, *Shajarat al-Fuhud: taqasim al-hayah*. She has written a manuscript for a novel titled *al-Khishkhash* (The Poppy). She has contributed children's literature to several magazines and oversees the publication of *al-'Unud*, a children's magazine that also publishes writing by children.

Ma'a al-ard (With the Earth, short stories). Khartoum: Dar al-Ayyam, 1978.

Rihlati (My Journey, novel). Beirut: Dar al-Haytham, 1980.

al-Madd (The Expanse, novel). Amman: Dar al-Shuruq, 1986.

Shajarat al-Fuhud: taqasim al-hayah (The Fuhud Family Tree: Improvisations of Life, novel). Amman: Dar al-Karmel, 1995.

Urkistra (Orchestra, short stories). Amman: Dar al-Kindi, 1996.

Shajarat al-Fuhud: taqasim al-'ishq (The Fuhud Family Tree: Improvisations of Love, novel). Cairo: Dar Sharqiyat, 1998.

al-Qurmiya: al-layl wa-l-bayda' (The Tree Stump: Night and the Desert, novel). Amman: Amanat 'Amman al-Kubra Publications, 1999.

Khuri, Collette (1937–), Syrian short-story writer and novelist born in Damascus. She is the granddaughter of Faris al-Khuri. She was educated at the Arab French Institute in Damascus and later studied law at the Weekly University in Beirut. Years later she returned to Damascus University to obtain a B.A. in French literature. She currently works as a lecturer in French at Damascus University and has published two collections of poetry in French. She published her first work when she was fifteen years old. She collected and edited her grandfather's papers in *Awraq Faris al-Khuri* (The Papers of Faris al-Khuri, 1993).

Ayyam ma'ah (Days with Him, novel). Beirut: Dar al-Kutub, 1959.

Layla wahida (One Night, novel). Beirut: al-Maktab al-Tijari, 1961.

Ana wa-l-mada (The Expanse and I, short stories). Beirut: al-Maktab al-Tijari, 1962.

Dimashq bayti al-kabir (Damascus Is My Big House, short stories). Beirut: Dar al-Kutub, 1969.

Kayan (Entity, short stories). Beirut: Zuhayr Ba'labakki Publications, 1969.

al-Marhala al-murra (The Bitter Period, short stories). Beirut: Zuhayr Ba'labakki Publications, 1969.

al-Kalima al-untha (The Feminine Word, short stories). Damascus: n.p., 1972.

Qissatan (Two Stories, short stories). Damascus: Arab Writers' Union, 1972.

Aghla jawhara fi-l-'alam (The Dearest Gem in the World, play). Damascus: Arab Writers' Union, 1975.

Wa marr al-sayf (And the Summer Passed, novel). Damascus: Arab Writers' Union, 1975.

Da'wa ila-l-Qunaytira (An Invitation to al-Qunaytira City, short stories). Damascus: Arab Writers' Union, 1976.

Ayyam ma'a al-ayyam (Days with Days, novel). Damascus: al-Kitab al-'Arabi, 1979.

al-Ayyam al-mudi'a (The Illuminating Days, short stories). Damascus: Dar Tlas, 1984.

Ma'ak 'ala hamish riwayati (With You on the Margin of My Novels, poetry). Damascus: Arab Writers' Union, 1987.

al-Khuri, Mahat Farah (1930–), Syrian poet born in old Damascus. She was educated in convent schools and at a girls' secondary finishing school, from which she graduated in 1948. She enrolled in the Liberal Arts College at the Syrian University in 1952. She taught Arabic to French students at the Institute for Oriental Studies in Damascus and later worked as a translator for the Ministry of Information, the French press, and the Polish embassy in Damascus. She founded a branch of the Lebanese Family Library in 1981 and has run it since then. She published several essays under the pseudonym "M." Her non-fiction works include *al-Haraka al-niqabiya fi-l-'alam* (The Trade Union Movement Around the World, 1967), *al-Quds al-qadiya* (The Cause of Jerusalem, 1971), *Niqula Kubirnik* (Nicolaus Copernicus, 1973), and *al-Fann fi-l-qarn al-'ishrin* (Art in the Twentieth Century).

Wa kan masa' (And It Was Evening, poetry). Damascus: Alif Ba' Press, 1965.

al-'Usfur al-bishara (The Good News Sparrow, reflections). Damascus: Alif Ba' Press, 1979.

Khuri, Nida' (1959–), Palestinian poet born in the village of Fassuta in the part of Palestine occupied in 1948. She graduated from Tarshiha High School. She writes prose poetry.

U'lin lak samti (I Declare My Silence to You, poetry). Acre: Abu Rahmun Press, 1987.

Jadilat al-ra'd (The Thunder's Braid, poetry). Shafa 'Amr: Dar al-Mashriq Printing, Translation, and Publishing, 1989.

al-Nahr al-hafi (The Barefoot River, poetry). Jerusalem: n.p., 1990.

Zunnar al-rih (The Wind's Sash, poetry). Acre: Abu Rahmun Press, 1992.

Thaqafat al-nabidh (Culture of Wine, poetry). Jerusalem: Office of Arab Culture, 1993.

Khawatim al-milh (Rings of Salt, poetry). Beirut: Arab Institute for Research and Publishing, 1998.

al-Khuri, Violet Tarrad (1930–), Lebanese short-story writer born in 'Ayn al-Qabw in the north. She was educated at the Zahrat al-Ihsan convent school. She was influenced by the Mahjar (exile) school of literature.

Zuhur al-uqhuwan (Daisies, short stories). N.p.: Dar 'Awn and al-Jabal Press, 1987.

Hayfa' (Slender, novel). Beirut: Dar al-Mashriq, 1988.

Huzn al-madina (The City's Melancholy, novel). Beirut: Nawfal Foundation, 1995.

Wisadat al-hajar (The Stone Pillow, short stories. Beirut: Nawfal Foundation, 1997.

al-Khush, Umayma (1948–), Syrian short-story writer and novelist born in Misyaf. She received a B.A. in Arabic language from Damascus University in 1970 and taught Arabic. She established the private Isis Press in 1990. She is a member of the Story and Novel Association, part of the Arab Writers' Union.

Da'wa ila-l-raqs (An Invitation to Dance, short stories). Damascus: Dar al-Ahali, 1991.

Zahrat al-lutus (The Lotus Flower, novel). Damascus: Dar al-Mustaqbal, 1993.

In'itaq (Emancipation, short stories). Damascus: n.p., 1995.

al-Tawq (Yearning, novel). Beirut: Dar al-Kunuz al-Adabiya, 1997.

Khust, Nadiya (1935–), Syrian novelist and short-story writer born in Damascus. She received a B.A. in philosophy from Damascus University and a Ph.D. in comparative literature from Moscow University for her dissertation, *Adab Tshikhuf wa atharuhu 'ala-l-adab al-'Arabi* (Chekhov's Works and Their Impact on Arabic Literature). She studied French at Strasbourg University. She works in the media and has presented several television dramas. She is a member of the executive bureau of the Arab Writers' Union and a founding member of the Old Damascus Organization. She has published several non-fiction works, including: *Kuttab wa mawaqif* (Writers and Stands, 1983), critical studies; *al-Hijra min al-janna* (Out of Paradise, 1989), on the relationship between humankind and the Arab city; and *Dimashq dhakirat al-insan wa-l-hajar* (Damascus: Memory of People and Stone, 1993), on memory, identity, and Arab architecture.

Uhibb al-Sham (I Love Damascus, short stories). Damascus: n.p., 1967.

Fi-l-qalb shay' akhar (In the Heart Is Something Else, short stories). Damascus: Ministry of Culture, 1979.

Fi sijn 'Akka (In the Acre Prison, short stories). Damascus: Ministry of Culture, 1984.

La makan li-l-gharib (No Place for the Stranger, short stories). Damascus: Arab Writers' Union, 1990.

'Ashiyat laylat al-harb (Eve of the War, novel). Damascus: n.p., 1995.

Hubb fi bilad al-Sham (Love in the Levant, novel). Damascus: Arab Writers' Union, 1996.

Mamlakat al-samt (Kingdom of Silence, short stories). Damascus: Arab Writers' Union, 1997.

A'asir fi bilad al-Sham (Cyclones in the Levant, novel). Damascus: Arab Writers' Union, 1998.

Kilani, Amal (?–), Egyptian short-story writer.

Ard al-qamar wa qisas ukhra (Land of the Moon and Other Stories, short stories). Cairo: Dar al-Amal Printing and Publishing, 1978.

Asabi' bila basamat (Fingers Without Prints, short stories). Cairo: Dar al-Amal Printing and Publishing, n.d.

Kilani, Lina (1957–), Syrian short-story writer and novelist born in Damascus. She received a B.A. in agricultural engineering and an M.A. in agricultural economy from the American University of Beirut. She works as an agricultural specialist for the Arab Organization for Agricultural Development, which is part of the Arab League. She has published several essays on literary criticism and children's literature. Her stories were first published in Syrian magazines. She founded the publishing house, Qaws Quzah, in 1988. She is a member of the Association for Children's Literature.

al-'Asafir la tuhibb al-zujaj (Sparrows Don't Like Glass, children's literature). Damascus: Arab Writers' Union, 1979.

al-Jazira al-sa'ida (The Happy Island, children's literature). Damascus: Arab Writers' Union, 1981.

al-Ta'ir alladhi wajad sawtah (The Bird Who Found His Voice, children's literature). Damascus: Dar al-Jalil, 1984.

Magharat al-kanz (The Treasure Cave, children's literature). Damascus: Dar al-Jalil, 1985.

Asdiqa' al-tabi'a (Friends of Nature, children's literature). Damascus: Dar al-Jalil, 1986.

al-'Asafir ta'qid mu'tamaraha (The Sparrows Hold Their Conference, children's literature). Damascus: Dar al-Jalil, 1987.

al-Samaka al-maghrura (The Vain Fish, children's literature). Damascus: Ministry of Culture, 1988.

Akhi Muhammad (My Brother Muhammad, children's literature). Damascus: Dar Qaws Quzah, 1989.

Ana 'Arabi (I Am an Arab, children's literature). Damascus: Dar Qaws Quzah, 1989.

al-Dafda' rawgh (Rawgh the Frog, children's literature). Damascus: Arab Writers' Union, 1989.

Faris shuja' (A Brave Knight, children's literature). Damascus: Dar Qaws Quzah, 1989.

al-Khubz al-murr (Bitter Bread, children's literature). Damascus: Dar Qaws Quzah, 1989.

Rima wa-l-batta Umm al-Khayr (Rima and the Duck, Umm al-Khayr, children's literature). Damascus: Dar Tlas, 1990.

al-Ghazala Rim (Rim the Gazelle, children's literature). Damascus: Arab Writers' Union, 1991.

al-Qitta Miyaw (Meow the Cat, children's literature). Damascus: Dar Qaws Quzah, 1991.

al-Samaka Sira (Sira the Fish, children's literature). Damascus: Arab Writers' Union, 1995.

K

al-Sulhufah Nasma (Nasma the Turtle, children's literature). Damascus: Ministry of Culture, 1995.

Kilani, Nahid (?–), Syrian poet born in Hama. She has published several articles and poems in the Damascus newspaper, *al-Thaqafa*.
Awwal al-ghayth (First Rain, poetry). Damascus: al-Thaqafa Magazine Publishers, 1984.

Kilani, Qamar (1932–), Syrian novelist and short-story writer born in Damascus. She received a B.A. in Arabic language from Damascus University and a degree in pedagogy in 1954. She worked as a teacher in teaching academies and in Syrian and Moroccan secondary schools. She is a member of the executive bureau of the Arab Writers' Union and editor in chief of the foreign literatures review, *al-Adab*. She is also a member of the Story and Novel Association. She began publishing in the 1950s and her interests include history and literary criticism. She writes for the Syrian press and Arabic journals. Her non-fiction works include *Usama ibn Munqidh* (Usama ibn Munqidh), *Imru' al-Qays* (Imru' al-Qays), and *al-Tasawwuf al-Islami* (Sufism).
Ayyam Maghribiya (Moroccan Days, novel). Beirut: Dar al-Katib al-'Arabi, 1964.
'Alam bila hudud (A World Without Borders, short stories). Baghdad: Ministry of Information, 1972.
Bustan al-karaz (The Cherry Orchard, novel). Damascus: Arab Writers' Union, 1977.
al-Sayyadun wa lu'bat al-mawt (The Hunters and the Game of Death, short stories). Damascus: Arab Writers' Union, 1978.
al-Hawdaj (The Camel Litter, novel). Damascus: Arab Writers' Union, 1979.
I'tirafat imra'a saghira (Confessions of a Young Woman, short stories). Damascus: Ministry of Culture, 1980.
Imra'a min khazaf (A Porcelain Woman, short stories). Damascus: Dar al-Anwar, 1980.

al-Ashbah (Ghosts, novel). Tripoli, Libya: al-Munsha'a al-Sha'biya Publications, 1981.
Ta'ir nar (Bird of Fire, novel). Damascus: Arab Writers' Union, 1981.
Hubb wa harb (Love and War, novel). Damascus: al-Idara al-Siyasiya, 1982.
Hulm 'ala judran al-sujun (A Dream on the Prison Walls, short stories). Tunis: al-Dar al-'Arabiya Books, 1985.
al-Duwwama (The Whirlpool, novel). Damascus: Ministry of Culture, 1987.
al-Mahatta (The Station, short stories). Damascus: Arab Writers' Union, 1987.

Kiram, Zuhur (1961–), Moroccan novelist born in Satat. She is a university professor. She graduated from high school in 1980 and received a B.A. in Arabic literature in 1985, followed by an advanced degree in modern Arabic literature. She received a third-cycle doctorate. She was the secretary of the Rabat branch of the Moroccan Writers' Union (1996–1999). She was a member of the organizing committee of the first and second Arab Video Festival. She is a member of the national bureau of the Center for Research and Cultural Continuity. She is a member of the editorial staff of *al-Katib* and the cultural committee of Jusur, the Moroccan Women's Forum. She took part in the Conference of Arab Writers and Authors in Casablanca in January 1990 and participated in a panel on Arabic literary discourse between the stable and the changing. She has participated in many national, Arab, and international conferences in Morocco and abroad and has published several critical essays on the novel. She has written two columns for the Moroccan *Anwal* newspaper, "Shahrazad" and "Readings in Arab Women's Narrative." She has published in several periodicals.
Jasad wa madina (A Body and a City, novel). Rabat: al-Ghani Publications, 1996.
Safar fi-l-insan (A Journey Into the Human Being, texts). al-Qunaytira: al-Bukili Printing and Publishing, 1998.

Kubba, Rim Qays (1967), Iraqi poet born in Baghdad. She received a B.A. in translation from al-Mustansiriya University in 1989. She was awarded a prize from the Girls' Clubs of Sharjah for Arab women's literature.

Nawaris taqtarif al-tahliq (Seagulls Commit the Crime of Soaring, poetry). Baghdad: n.p., 1991.

Aghmud ajnihati wa astariq al-kitaba (I Draw in My Wings and Snatch Some Writing, poetry). Baghdad: Dar al-Shu'un al-Thaqafiya, 1997.

Ihtifa' bi-l-waqt al-da'i' (Celebrating Lost Time, poetry). Baghdad: Dar al-Shu'un al-Thaqafiya, 1999.

al-Kurdi, Zaynab (?–), Sudanese short-story writer born in Wadi Halfa. She received a B.A. in humanities and history from Alexandria University in 1975. She has worked as a journalist in Kuwait since 1986. Her works have been published in many periodicals, including *Sayyidati*, *Hayatuna*, *al-Siyasa*, and *al-Qabas*. She also has written dramas for radio and television.

'Uyuni al-layla la tu'ti dam'an (My Eyes Tonight Will Not Shed a Tear, short stories). Cairo: al-'Arabi Publishers, 1985.

Zahrat al-janub (Flower of the South, short stories). Cairo: General Egyptian Book Organization, 1997.

al-Kuzbari, Salma al-Haffar (1923–2006) (see also: Bibliography of Works in French), Syrian short-story writer, novelist, and poet born in Damascus. She received her secondary education at convent schools in Damascus and received a B.A. in political science from the Jesuit University in Beirut. She was fluent in French and Spanish and published two collections of poetry in French. She contributed to the creation of an Arab historical cultural program and translated stories from French into Arabic. She also wrote several works of non-fiction, including: *Fi zilal al-Andalus: muhadarat* (In the Shadow of Andalusia: Lectures, 1971), *Jurj Sand: hubb wa nubugh*

(George Sand: Love and Genius, 1979), *al-Shu'la al-zarqa': rasa'il Jubran ila Mayy Ziyada* (The Blue Flame: Gibran's Letters to Mayy Ziyada, 1979), *Mayy Ziyada wa a'lam 'asriha: watha'iq jadida* (Mayy Ziyada and the Leading Lights of Her Age: New Documents, 1982), *Mayy Ziyada aw ma'sat al-nubugh* (Mayy Ziyada, or the Tragedy of Genius, a complete biography of Mayy and the Renaissance in Egypt, 1987), *Basamat 'Arabiya wa Dimashqiya fi-l-Andalus* (Arab and Damascene Imprints in Andalusia, 1993), and *Lutfi al-Haffar: mudhakkiratuhu wa hayatuhu wa 'asruhu* (Lutfi al-Haffar: His Memoirs, His Life, His Age). She received the Spanish Lady's Ribbon: Queen Isabelle's Medal in 1964 and the Mediterranean Literature Award from the University of Palermo in 1980.

Yawmiyat Hala (Hala's Diary, novel). Beirut: Dar al-'Ilm li-l-Malayin, 1950.

Hirman (Deprivation, short stories). Cairo: Dar al-Ma'arif, 1952.

Zawaya (Corners, short stories). Beirut: Dar al-'Ilm li-l-Malayin, 1955.

'Aynan min Ishbiliya (Two Eyes from Seville, novel). Beirut: Dar al-Katib, 1965.

al-Ghariba (The Stranger, short stories). Damascus: Maktabat Atlas, 1966.

'Anbar wa ramad (Ambergris and Ashes, autobiography). Beirut: Dar Beirut Publishers, 1970.

al-Burtuqal al-murr (Bitter Orange, novel). Beirut: Dar al-Nahar Publishers, 1974.

Huzn al-ashjar (The Melancholy of Trees, short stories). Beirut: Nawfal Foundation, 1986.

al-Hubb ba'd al-khamsin (*Love after the Fiftieth*, autobiography). Damascus: Dar Tlas, 1989.

al-Labbudi, Zuhur (?–), Egyptian poet.

Mink wa ilayk (From You and to You, poetry). Cairo: 'Uyun Jadida Publishing, 1995.

Lahham, Salma (1942–), Palestinian short-story writer born in Haifa. Following the *nakba*, she moved with her family to Damascus, where she was educated. She

has published several articles on politics.
A'wad al-thiqab (Matchsticks, short stories).
Damascus: Barakat Press, 1971.
al-Intizar (Waiting, short stories). N.p.:
n.p., n.d.

Lari, Samira Ahmad (1949–), Saudi poet
and novelist born in Jeddah. She has a
B.A. in journalism from Cairo University.
Hafiya ila-l-shams (Barefoot to the Sun,
novel). N.p.: n.p., n.d.
Hisan min al-qamar (A Horse from the
Moon, novel). N.p.: n.p., n.d.
al-Ziba' tahlum (Gazelles Dream, poetry).
N.p.: n.p., n.d.

al-Lawwa, Amina (1926–), Moroccan
short-story writer and playwright born in
al-Hasima, Morocco. She grew up in
Tetouan and received her primary and
secondary education there. She received a
B.A. in humanities from Madrid University in 1957, an M.A. from Madrid
University in 1965, and a state Ph.D. from
the same institution in 1968. She was a
teacher and later a director and inspector at the secondary-school level. She is
currently a research professor at the University Institute for Academic Research at
Muhammad V University in Rabat. She
has taken part in many conferences,
debates, and cultural, social, national, and
international activities. She prepared a
series of radio talks on the advancement of
Moroccan women. She has published her
articles and essays in Moroccan magazines,
including *al-Mu'tamid*, *al-Anis*, *Da'wat
al-haqq*, and *al-Manahil*. She received the
Moroccan Prize for Humanities in 1954 for
her *al-Malika Khunatha*.
al-Malika Khunatha (Queen Khunatha,
novella). Tetouan: Mawlay al-Hasan
Institute, 1954.
Kitab Muhammad aw ila Dar al-Arqam
(Muhammad's Book or To the Dar
al-Arqam, school play). *Da'wat al-haqq*,
no. 4 (February 1968).

Layla al-Maqdisiya (see: al-Khatib, Samira)

al-Ma'dul, Fatima (1948–), Egyptian author
of children's literature. She received a B.A.
in theater from the High Institute of
Theater Arts in 1970. She has worked as a
director of children's theater at the Palace
of Culture for the Child. She became
the director of the Culture Palace in 1980
and the head of the National Center for
Children's Culture in 1998. She has
written short plays that are performed in
popular quarters and schools, including
Mughamarat Tik al-'ajib (The Adventures of
the Marvelous Tik, 1973) and *al-Muharrij
wa-l-asad* (The Clown and the Lion, 1980),
both unpublished.
Dunya khamisa (A Fifth World, poetry).
Cairo: Egyptian Council for Children's
Books, 1998.
Khutut wa dawa'ir (Lines and Circles,
pre-school textbook). Cairo: Association for Integrated Care, 1998.
Qit'a min al-sama' (A Piece of Sky, children's literature). Cairo: al-Thaqafa
al-Jamahiriya, 1998.
al-Warda al-zarqa' (The Blue Flower,
children's literature). Cairo: al-Thaqafa
al-Jamahiriya, 1998.
'Usfur yajid 'ishshah (A Sparrow Finds Its
Nest, children's literature). Cairo:
National Center for Children's
Culture, 1999.
Ghanni ma'i ya ummi (Sing with Me,
Mama, folklore). N.p.: n.p., n.d.

al-Maghribi, 'A'isha Idris (1956–), Libyan
poet born in Benghazi. She received an
M.A. in philosophy from Qaryunis University in 1996. Her literary works have
been published in Libyan and Arab
newspapers and journals.
al-Ashya' al-tayyiba (The Good Things,
poetry). Tripoli, Libya: al-Dar al-
Jamahiriya, 1986.
al-Bawh bi-sirr al-untha (Confessing the
Female's Secret, poetry). Tripoli, Libya:
al-Dar al-Jamahiriya, 1995.
Amirat al-waraq (The Princess of Paper,
poetry). Tripoli, Libya: al-Dar al-
Jamahiriya, 1998.

Mahir, Ni'mat Fahim (?–), Egyptian writer.
Min al-a'maq (From the Depths). Alexandria: al-Ma'arif Institution, 1985.

Mahmud, Fatima (1954–), Libyan poet and short-story writer born in Tripoli. She graduated from the Teachers' Academy. She has worked as a journalist for *al-Fajr al-jadid*, *al-Usbu' al-thaqafi*, and *al-Jamahiriya*. She published the magazine, *Shahrazad*, in Cyprus.
Ma tayassar (What Is Possible, poetry). Tripoli, Libya: al-Dar al-Jamahiriya, 1985.

Mahmud, Hala 'Arabi Isma'il (1977–), Egyptian poet born in Suez.
Ummi al-Suways (My Mother Suez, poetry). Cairo: General Authority for Culture Palaces, 1998.
al-Madi (The Past, poetry). Cairo: General Authority for Culture Palaces, 1999.

Mahmud, Masarra (?–), Egyptian novelist.
Qulub min zujaj (Glass Hearts, novel). Cairo: n.p., n.d.

Mahran, Fawziya (1931–), Egyptian novelist and short-story writer born in Alexandria. She has a B.A. in English literature from Cairo University. She is a boardmember of the Rose al-Yusuf Foundation. A collection of her stories, *Bayt al-talibat*, was translated into Russian. She has worked at *Sabah al-khayr* magazine and is the author of *Ta'ammulat mawaqif dramiya fi qisas al-Qur'an* (Contemplating Dramatic Scenes in Stories of the Qur'an, Cairo, Dar al-Ma'arif, 1987).
Bayt al-talibat (The Girls' Dorm, short stories). Cairo: Rose al-Yusuf Foundation, 1961.
Najmat Sina' (The Sinai Star, short stories). Cairo: privately published, 1968.
Jiyad al-bahr (Sea Horses, novel). Cairo: Rose al-Yusuf Foundation, 1984.
Hajiz amwaj (A Barrier of Waves, novel). Cairo: Rose al-Yusuf Foundation, 1988.

Ughniya li-l-bahr (A Song for the Sea, short stories). Cairo: Dar 'Uyun Jadida, 1994.
al-Tamathil tantasir: al-Mutran Kabutshi (The Statues Prevail: Archbishop Cappuci, play). Cairo: General Egyptian Book Organization, 1995.

Mahran, Rashida (?–), Egyptian novelist.
'Asharat ayyam takfi (Ten Days Are Enough, novel). Alexandria: Giza Press, 1980.
al-Hubb wa-l-nar (Love and Fire, novel). Beirut: Filistin Magazine Publications, 1981.
Da'iman ma'ak (Always with You, novel). Cairo: n.p., 1990.

Maja'is, Josephine Mar'i (?–?), Lebanese novelist. She published the essay, "Lughati wa biladi" (My Language and My Country, 1927).
Ghada al-Shuwayr (Ghada of Shuwayr, novel). Beirut: al-Adabiya Press, 1930.

Majdulin, Thuraya (1967–), Moroccan poet born in Satat. She received a B.A. in Arabic literature in 1982 and a degree in intensive studies in 1988. She is a high-school Arabic teacher and a member of the Moroccan Writers' Union. She published a critical study of 'Abd al-Rahman Majid al-Rabi'i's novel, *al-Anhar* (The Rivers), in *'Abd al-Rahman Majid al-Rabi'i riwa'iyan* ('Abd al-Rahman Majid al-Rabi'i as a Novelist, 1984), an edited volume. She has published her poems in the Casablanca paper, *al-Ittihad al-ishtiraki*. She has been publishing in *al-Muharrir* since 1987.
Awraq al-ramad (Papers of Ash, poetry). Rabat: Moroccan Writers' Union Publications, 1993.

Majid, Na'ima (?–), Iraqi short-story writer.
Zuhur thaljiya (Snow Flowers, short stories). Baghdad: al-Umma Press, 1979.

Majid, Shahira (?–), Egyptian poet.
Rihla fi a'maq al-banafsaj (A Journey into the Depths of Violet, poetry). Cairo: al-Kamaliya Press, 1978.

Wa tahda' al-'uyun (And the Eyes Abate, poetry). Cairo: al-Nahda al-'Arabiya Press, 1987.

al-Majiri, Jamila (?–), Tunisian poet.
Diwan al-wajd (The Passion Collection, poetry). Tunis: Umiqa Press, 1995.
Diwan al-nisa' (The Women Collection, poetry). Tunis: Tunisian Company for Publishing and the Development of Illustration, 1997.

al-Makkawi, Jihan (?–), Egyptian novelist.
Mashru' zawaj (A Marriage in the Works, novel). Cairo: Dar Usama Printing and Publishing, 1987.
Hawiyat al-sihr (The Abyss of Sorcery, novel). Cairo: General Egyptian Book Organization, 1994.

Makki, Buthayna Khidr (1948–), Sudanese novelist and short-story writer born in Shandi. She currently resides in Sharjah. She received a B.A. in English from King 'Abd al-'Aziz University, a teaching certificate in English from Khartoum University, and a degree in folklore from the African and Asian Studies Institute at Khartoum University. She teaches secondary school in the U.A.E. She writes for the Sudanese press and has regular columns in *al-Siyasa*, *al-Adwa'*, and *al-Ittihad*. Her short stories have been published in the Sudanese and Arabic press in *al-Sharq al-Awsat*, *al-Khalij*, and the Abu Dhabi-based *al-Ittihad*, as well as in *al-Muntada* and *al-Bayan* magazines. She is a member of the Sudanese Writers' Union, the League of Women Writers in Sharjah, and the Emirati Writers' Union.
Fatat al-qarya (The Village Girl, children's literature). Sharjah: n.p., 1993.
al-Nakhla wa-l-maghna (Palm and Song, short stories). Sharjah: n.p., 1993.
Ashbah al-mudun (Ghosts of the Cities, short stories). Sharjah: n.p., 1995.
Atyaf al-huzn (Phantoms of Sorrow, short stories). Sharjah: n.p., 1996.
Ghita' al-samt (The Cover of Silence, texts). Sharjah: n.p., 1996.

Ughniyat al-nar (Fire Song, novel). Sharjah: privately published, 1998.

al-Mala'ika, Nazik (1923–2007), Iraqi poet and critic born in Baghdad to a household interested in poetry and literature. Her father and mother were both poets. Her brother, Nizar al-Mala'ika, was a poet as well. She graduated from the Higher Teachers' Institute in 1944 with a B.A. in Arabic. Wanting to study music, she enrolled in the Academy of Fine Arts. She graduated from the music department (lute playing) in 1949. She studied Latin, French, and English, and completed her studies in the U.S., where she received an M.A. in comparative literature from the University of Wisconsin in 1956. She taught at universities in Baghdad, Basra, and Kuwait. She lived in Cairo before her death. She was a pioneer of free verse in the Arab world. She published many academic studies on Arabic poetry and social issues, including *al-Adab wa-l-ghazw al-fikri* (Literature and the Cultural Invasion, Baghdad, 1965, research study and essays), *Muhadarat fi shi'r 'Ali Mahmud Taha* (Lectures on the Poetry of 'Ali Mahmud Taha, Institute of Arab Studies, Cairo, 1965), *al-Sawma'a wa-l-shurfa al-hamra'* (The Hermitage and the Red Balcony, Cairo, 1965, literary criticism), *al-Tajzi'iya fi-l-mujtama' al-'Arabi* (Fragmentation in Arab Society, Beirut, Dar al-'Ilm li-l-Malayin, 1974), and *Saykulujiyat al-shi'r wa maqalat ukhra* (The Psychology of Poetry and Other Essays, Baghdad, Dar al-Shu'un al-Thaqafiya, 1993). Her pioneering study, *Qadaya al-shi'r al-mu'asir* (Issues in Contemporary Poetry, Beirut, Dar al-Adab, 1962), was reprinted several times. Her collection of poetry, *Yughayyir alwanahu al-bahr* was reissued in Cairo by the General Authority for Culture Palaces in 1998. It contains an appendix by Nazik titled "Lamahat min masirat hayati wa thaqafati" (Glimpses of My Life and Culture).
'Ashiqat al-layl (The Night's Lover, poetry). Baghdad: al-Rumman Press, 1947.

Shazaya wa ramad (Shrapnel and Ashes, poetry). Baghdad: al-Ma'arif Press, 1949.

Qararat al-mawja (Trough of the Wave, poetry). Beirut: Dar al-Adab, 1957.

Shajarat al-qamar (The Moon Tree, poetry). Beirut: Dar al-'Ilm li-l-Malayin, 1968.

Ma'sat al-hayah wa ughniya li-l-insan (The Tragedy of Life and a Song for Human Beings, poetry). Beirut: Dar al-'Awda, 1970.

Diwan Nazik al-Mala'ika (The Poetry of Nazik al-Mala'ika, poetry, two vols.). Beirut: Dar al-'Awda, 1971.

Yughayyir alwanahu al-bahr (The Sea Changes Its Colors, poetry). Baghdad: Dar al-Hurriya Press, 1977.

Li-l-salah wa-l-thawra (For Prayer and the Revolution, poetry). Beirut: Dar al-'Ilm li-l-Malayin, 1978.

al-Shams allati wara' al-qimma (The Sun behind the Peak, poetry). Cairo: Supreme Council for Culture, 1997.

al-Mala'ika, Salima (Umm Nizar) (1909–1953), Iraqi poet born in Baghdad. She married her cousin, Sadiq al-Mala'ika, also a poet, at an early age. She is the mother of famed Iraqi poet Nazik al-Mala'ika. She was taught by her family and is self-educated. She wrote poetry at an early age and published it in Iraqi and Arab newspapers. She adopted the causes of liberation, Palestine, and women's emancipation in her poetry.

Unshudat al-majd (Hymn of Glory, poetry). Baghdad: al-Tadamun Press, 1968.

Malas, Sahar (1958–), Jordanian short-story writer of Syrian origin born in Damascus. She resides in Amman. She attended school in Amman and graduated from the College of Pharmacy at Damascus University in 1979. She is a pharmacist at the network of al-Husayn al-Hashimi Workers' Clinics and a department head at al-Mujtama' College, where she teaches pharmacy courses. She is a former member of the scientific committee in the

Pharmacists' Union and the publications committee of *al-Saydali*, the syndicate's journal. In addition to fiction, she has written on pharmaceuticals and published articles in the press. She was the recipient of a short-story award for youth authors from the League of Jordanian Writers. She also won the Queen Nur Prize for Children's Literature in the field of educational literature.

Shaqa'iq al-Nu'man (Anemone, short stories). Amman: Dar al-Karmel, 1989.

Iklil al-jabal (Rosemary, novella). Amman: Dar al-Bashir, 1990.

Daj'at al-nawras (Sleep of the Seagull, short stories). Amman: Dar al-Bashir, 1991.

Maskan al-salsal (The Clay House, short stories). Amman: Dar al-Bashir, 1995.

al-Wajh al-muktamil (The Perfect Face, short stories). Amman: Ministry of Culture Publications, 1997.

Malhas, Thuraya (1925–), Palestinian writer and researcher born in Nablus. She was educated in Amman and Jerusalem and attended university in Beirut. She received an M.A. in Arabic literature in 1964 for her thesis, *al-Qiyam al-ruhiya fi-l-shi'r al-'Arabi qadimihi wa hadithih* (Spiritual Values in Arabic Poetry, Ancient and Modern). She was a professor and the head of the Arabic literature section at the Beirut College for Girls. She has published several collections of poetry, both prose poetry and verse, as well as short stories. She also published many essays and studies in Arabic and English, as well as a collection of poetry in English, *Prisoners of Time*.

al-Nashid al-ta'ih (The Wayward Hymn, poetry). Beirut: Dar al-Kitab al-Lubnani, 1949.

Qurban (Sacrifice, poetry). Beirut: Dar al-Rayhani, 1952.

Prisoners of Time (poetry collection). Beirut: n.p., 1956.

Malhamat al-insan (The Epic of Man, poetry). Beirut: Dar al-Kitab al-Lubnani, 1961.

M

al-'Uqda al-sabi'a (The Seventh Knot, short stories). Beirut: Karam Press, 1962.

al-Khalil ibn Ahmad al-Farahidi: al-'alim alladhi hasara lughat al-'Arab wa shi'rahum (al-Khalil ibn Ahmad al-Farahidi: The Scholar Who Compiled the Arabs' Language and Poetry, play). N.p.: n.p., 1963.

Khaba'na al-sawarikh fi-l-hayakil (We Hid the Missiles in the Temples, poetry). Beirut: Dar al-Kitab al-Lubnani, 1968.

Mahajir fi-l-kuhuf (Quarries in the Caves, poetry). Beirut: Dar al-Kitab al-Lubnani, 1970.

Qadaya wa majamir (Causes and Braziers, poetry). Beirut: n.p., 1970.

Dhikrayat shabb lam yaghtarib (Memoirs of a Young Man Who Did Not Leave Home). Acre: n.p., 1989.

Hawajis yawmiya (Daily Apprehensions, short stories). Acre: n.p., 1989.

Araqim mu'allaqa 'ala maqbarat al-kawn (Poems Hung in the Universe's Cemetery, autobiography). Amman: Dar al-Azmina, 1998.

al-Thuluj al-hamra' tarakamat 'ala-l-ru'us (The Red Snow Collected on the Heads, poetry). Amman: Dar al-Bashir, 1999.

al-Malifi, Nura (1966–), Kuwaiti poet. She received a B.A. in liberal arts from Cairo University in 1990. She is an Arabic teacher. She won first place in several competitions organized by Kuwait University, including the classical poetry competitions of 1990, 1992, and 1995.

al-'Azf 'ala awtar al-jurh (Playing on the Wound's Strings, poetry). Kuwait: n.p., 1991.

Malik, Fayruz (?–), Syrian novelist.

al-Sadafa wa-l-bahr (The Seashell and the Sea, novel). N.p.: n.p., 1977.

al-Malluhi, Salwa Harmaz (?–), Syrian novelist.

al-Mutamarrida (The Rebel, novel). Beirut: Center for Christian Publications, 1966.

Da'i'a fi-l-madina (Lost in the City, novel, with Mazhar al-Maluhi). Beirut: Center for Christian Publications, 1967.

Maryam (Maryam, novel). Beirut: Center for Christian Publications, 1968.

Ma'luf, Hala (1899–1969), Lebanese pioneer and novelist born in Dayr al-Ahmar in the Biqa' valley. She received her primary and secondary education at the English School in Beirut and graduated in 1916. She worked at al-Amrikiya Press in Beirut from 1917 to 1927. She married Palestinian Iskandar Saba and moved to Jerusalem, where she was active in Palestinian women's associations. After her husband died in 1949, she returned to Beirut and worked as a secretary at the American University Hospital.

al-Janiya (The Criminal, novel). Beirut: al-Amrikiya Press, 1922.

Atmamt al-wajib aw 'Aqiba Bint al-Han (I Did My Duty, or 'Aqiba Bint al-Han, novel). Beirut: n.p., 1931.

Mama Jamila (see: Ahmad, Jamila Kamil)

Mama Lubna (see: Rashid, Natila)

Mama Ni'am (see: al-Baz, Ni'am)

Mamdouh, Alia (Mamduh, 'Aliya) (1944–), Iraqi novelist and short-story writer born in Baghdad. She received a B.A. in psychology and currently lives in Paris. She has published in several papers and magazines, including *Mawaqif*, *al-Karmel*, *al-Mawqif al-adabi*, *al-Safir*, and *al-Quds al-'Arabi*. Her novel, *Habbat al-naftalin*, has been translated into English, French, Dutch, German, and Italian. She also wrote the non-fiction work, *Musahibat: qira'a fi-l-hamish al-ibda'i* (Keeping Company: Reading on the Creative Margin), published by Dar 'Ukaz in Rabat.

Iftitahiya li-l-dahk (Preface to Laughter, short stories). Beirut: Dar al-'Awda, 1973.

Hawamish ila-l-Sayyida B. (Footnotes to Mrs. B., short stories). Beirut: Dar al-Adab, 1977.

Layla wa-l-dhi'b (Layla and the Wolf, novel). Baghdad: Dar al-Hurriya, 1980.

Habbat al-naftalin (*Mothballs*, novel). Cairo: General Egyptian Book Organization, 1986.

al-Wala' (Burning Desire, novel). Beirut: Dar al-Adab, 1995.

Mami, Layla (1944–), Tunisian short-story writer born in Djerba. She was educated in Tunis. She received a B.A. in Arabic language and literature and continued her studies at the Journalism Institute. She has worked as a journalist for newspapers and magazines and was part of the African Tunisian News Agency. From November 1974 to August 1976, she founded and published *Femina* magazine, a French-language publication that specialized in women's affairs. Her work has been published in Tunisian and Arab newspapers and journals. She has taken part in many seminars and forums on women's social status. She is a member of the Tunisian Writers' Union.

Sawma'a tahtariq (A Hermitage Burns, short stories). Tunis: General Tunisian Employment Union, 1968.

al-Mani', Samira (1935–), Iraqi novelist and short-story writer born in Basra. She studied Arabic literature at Baghdad University. She has lived in London since 1965. She is currently the deputy editor of the London-based *al-Ightirab al-adabi*. In 1990 she spent three months at the International Writing Program at Iowa University. She also took part in the World Writers' Fair in Toronto.

al-Sabiqun wa-l-lahiqun (The First and the Last, novel). Beirut: Dar al-'Awda, 1972.

al-Ghina' (Singing, short stories). Baghdad: Dar al-Hurriya, 1976.

al-Thuna'iya al-Lunduniya (The London Duology, novel). London: Ithaca Press, 1979.

Habl al-surra (Umbilical Cord, novel). London: al-Ightirab al-Adabi Publications, 1990.

al-Nisf faqat (Only Half, play). London: Panorama Ltd., 1994.

al-Qami'un (The Subduers, novel). Damascus: Dar al-Mada, 1997.

al-Ruh wa ghayruha (The Spirit and Other Things, short stories). Beirut: al-Intishar al-'Arabi Foundation, 1999.

Mansi, Su'ad (?–), Egyptian novelist.

al-Dima' (Blood, novel). Cairo: al-Hurriya Press, 1942.

Ghadba malakiya fi ard al-rasul (Royal Rage in the Land of the Prophet, novel). Cairo: al-Bayan al-'Arabi Committee, 1960.

Jisr min al-awham (Bridge of Illusions, prose poetry). Cairo: al-Bayan al-'Arabi Committee, 1964.

Mansur, Ahlam (1951–), Iraqi short-story writer born in Khaniqayn in the province of Diyala. She graduated from the Kurdish department at Baghdad University. She worked in journalism and has published her stories in the Kurdish and Arabic press.

al-Jisr (The Bridge, short stories). N.p.: n.p., 1981.

Mansur, Ilham (1944–), Lebanese novelist born in Ra's Ba'labakk. She received a Ph.D. in philosophy from the Sorbonne in 1975. She worked as a researcher at the Lebanese Ministry of Foreign Affairs' Center for Research and Documentation (1970–1976) and is a professor at the Liberal Arts College at the Lebanese University. She has published a work of non-fiction, *Nahw tahrir al-mar'a fi Lubnan* (Toward the Emancipation of Women in Lebanon, 1996).

Ila Hiba: sira ula (To Hiba: A First Story, novel). Beirut, Dar al-Farabi, 1991.

Hiba fi rihlat al-jasad: sira thaniya (Hiba on a Journey of the Body: A Second Story, novel). Beirut: Mukhtarat, 1994.

Sawt al-nayy aw sirat al-makan (Sound of the Flute, or a Biography of Place, novel). Beirut: Mukhtarat, 1996.

al-Mansuri, al-Zuhra (1961–), Moroccan poet. She has a B.A. in Arabic literature and a degree from the Higher Professors' Institute. She is a high-school teacher and a member of the Moroccan Writers' Union and the House of Poetry.
Taratil (Recitations, poetry). Casablanca: Dar Tubqal Publishers, n.d.

al-Maqdisi, Amina al-Khuri (1876–1951), Pioneering Lebanese story writer born in Tripoli. She received her primary and secondary education at the American School and graduated in 1896. She was taught by poet Labiba Sawaya. She taught at several schools in Cairo and Lebanon and founded the children's magazine, *Mawrid al-ahdath*, in Beirut (1923–1926). She published in *al-Mar'a al-jadida*, *Sawt al-malak*, and *Lisan al-hal*. She translated several books, including *Arba' min shahirat al-nisa'* (Four Famous Women, 1926), and she introduced theater into the schools at which she taught, writing songs for children. She was a member of the Young Women's Christian Association, the Lebanese Women's Association, and the Lebanese Women's Union.
"al-Hasna' al-mutabakkira" (The Haughty Beauty, children's literature). *al-Mar'a al-Jadida*. Beirut: 1921.
"Hikayat al-namla" (The Story of the Ant, children's literature). *al-Mar'a al-Jadida*. Beirut: 1921.

al-Mar'i, Fawziya Jum'a (?–), Syrian novelist born in al-Riqqa.
Ghariba bayn al-shahid wa-l-qabr (A Stranger Between the Tombstone and the Grave, novel). Damascus: Dar al-Maqdisiya, 1999.

al-Marini, Amina (Fatat al-Muhit) (1955–), Moroccan poet born in Fez, where she lives. She has a degree in Arabic literature. She works in education and educa-

tional counseling. She is a member of the World Islamic Literature League. She was awarded the Poetry First Prize in the province of Fez in 1991 and the Fourth Prize of the Hasan II Mosque in 1994. She is also known as Fatat al-Muhit.
Wurud min Zanata (Roses from Zanata, poetry). Casablanca: n.p., 1997.

Marrash, Maryana (1848–1919), Syrian poet and literary pioneer born in Aleppo. She was educated at a convent school and by her brother, Francis Marrash. She learned French and was instructed in grammar and prosody by her father. She wrote poetry and published it in *al-Janan*, a magazine run by Butrus al-Bustani. She published the first collection of poetry by a Syrian woman in the nineteenth century, and her home was a meeting place for literary figures. Her non-fiction works include *Tarikh Suriya al-hadith* (The History of Modern Syria), the first book in this field.
Bint fikr (A Girl of Thought, poetry). Beirut: al-Adabiya Press, 1893.

Mash'al, Maryam (?–), Palestinian writer.
Fatat al-nakba (A Girl of the Dispossession, novel). Amman: al-Sha'b Press, 1957.

al-Masri, Maram (1962–), Syrian poet born in Latakia. She studied English literature at Damascus university before moving to Paris in 1984 where she now lives.
Andhartuk bi-hamama bayda' (I Warned You with a White Dove, poetry). Damascus: Minstiry of Culture, 1984.
Karaza hamra' 'ala balat abyad (A Red Cherry on White Tile, poetry, with Muhammad Sayyida and Mundhir al-Misri). Tunis: Tibr al-Zaman, 1997.

Mas'ud, Mary (1932–), Egyptian playwright. She completed her undergraduate studies at Cairo University and obtained a Ph.D. in English literature. She has taught at American and British universities and was the chair of the English literature department at Ain Shams University from 1984 to 1990. She is a member of the executive committee of the International Biographical Center in Cambridge.

Tamthiliyat 'asriya (Modern Dramas, play). Cairo: Dar al-Ta'lif wa-l-Nashr of the Episcopal Church, 1972.

Our Father (play). Singapore: The Way Press, 1979.

al-Kalima hall baynana wa masrahiyat ukhra (The Word Dwelt Among Us and Other Plays, play). Cairo: Dar al-Thaqafa al-Masihiya, 1980.

Matarid, Thana' 'Ali (1969–), Egyptian poet born in Kafr al-Zayyat. She has a degree in business.

Shumu' al-watan (Candles of the Homeland, poetry). Western Delta: General Authority for Culture Palaces, 1998.

Ma'tuq, Hala Hamid (1952–), Emirati poet.

Qitar layli (Night Train, children's literature). N.p.: privately published, 1986.

al-Ma'ushi, Ibriza (?–), Lebanese journalist and novelist born in the district of al-Shuf. She obtained a B.A. in Arabic from the College of Liberal Arts at the Lebanese University. She has worked at several Lebanese newspapers, including *al-'Amal*, *al-Bayraq*, and *al-Hasna'*, as well as at the Voice of Lebanon and Lebanese radio. She published a collection of articles, *Lubnan jabin la yanhani* (Lebanon of the Unbowed Head), in 1978.

Hal aghfir lah (Do I Forgive Him, novel). Beirut: Dar al-Thaqafa, 1962.

Ana min al-sharq (I Am from the East, novel). Beirut: Dar Lubnan, 1966.

al-Thalj al-aswad (Black Snow, novel). Beirut: Lebanese Company for Publishing and Printing, 1980.

Wa yabqa al-su'al (And the Question Remains, novel). Beirut: Dar Sadir, 1988.

Shamsuhu la taghib (His Sun Does Not Set, novel). Beirut: Dar al-Jil, 1995.

Mawardi, Fatima (?–), Syrian novelist.

al-Saqi' yahriq al-bara'im (The Frost Burns the Blossoms, novel). Latakia: Dar al-Mirsah, 1996.

Mawqiz, 'A'isha (1968–), Moroccan short-story writer born in al-Jadida. She has a B.A. in Arabic literature.

al-Bum (The Owl, narrative text). Casablanca: al-Rabita Publishers, 1995.

Mi'dad, Insaf al-A'war (?–), Lebanese poet born in the village of al-Qal'a. She received a B.A. in media studies in Cairo and has worked as a radio announcer and journalist since 1960. She has published in the journal, *al-Hasna'*, as well as in several Lebanese newspapers. She has written for the children's press and has presented children's radio programs. She has been a member of the Lebanese Writers' Union since 1972 and is a member of the Arab Writers' Union and the Mountain Authors' League. Her literary salon, the Meeting Place, held in her home, attracts many writers and poets.

Allah wa-l-hubb al-yabis (God and Dessicated Love, poetry). Beirut: 'Uwaydat Publications, 1961.

Ruffat hubb (The Remains of Love, poetry). Beirut: Dar al-Hikma, 1961.

Hiya al-ula huwwa al-awwal (She Is the First, He is the First, poetry). Beirut: Dar al-'Awda, 1972.

al-Wahaj (Incandescence, poetry). Beirut: Dar al-Afaq al-Jadida, 1977.

Kull qadim huwwa (Every Looming Figure Is He, poetry). Beirut: Dar al-Afaq al-Jadida, 1982.

Ishti'al (Flame, poetry). Beirut: al-Multaqa al-Adabi Publications, 1987.

Mikhail, Dunya (Mikha'il, Dunya) (1965–), Iraqi poet born in Baghdad. She received a B.A. in English literature from Baghdad University in 1987. She is currently a graduate student in the Middle Eastern Studies Department at Wayne State University in Michigan. She has worked as a journalist and translator for the Iraqi

Baghdad Observer and the Jordanian *al-Mashriq*. She has published several cultural articles in Arabic and English and has been published in Iraq and abroad.

Nazif al-bahr (Bleeding of the Sea, poetry). Baghdad: 'Ishtar Press, 1986.

Mazamir al-ghiyab (Psalms of Absence, poetry). Baghdad: al-Adib Press, 1993.

Yawmiyat mawja kharij al-bahr (*Diary of a Wave outside the Sea*). Baghdad: Dar al-Shu'un al-Thaqafiya al-'Amma, 1995.

'Ala washk al-musiqa (On the Edge of Music, poetry). Tunis: Dar Nuqush 'Arabiya, 1997.

Miqati, Huda (1954–), Lebanese poet and journalist born in Beirut. She received her primary education at schools run by the al-Maqasid Islamic Charitable Association in Beirut and earned a teaching degree in Arabic literature from St. Joseph University in Beirut. She has published several articles in the Lebanese press and works with *Lubnan al-'aqari* magazine. She is a member of the Lebanese Writers' Union, the U.N. Lebanon Organization, Dawhat al-Biqa', and Friends of Writers and Books.

'Aba'at al-muslin (Cloak of Muslin, poetry). Beirut: Dar al-Nahda, 1985.

Sanabil al-Nil (Spikes of Grain on the Nile, poetry). Beirut: Dar al-Fikr al-'Arabi, 1989.

Illa habibi (Except My Beloved, poetry). Cairo: Dar Qiba', 1999.

Hadil al-manabir (The Pulpits' Cooing, poetry). Beirut: Dar al-Fikr al-'Arabi, 2000.

al-Mirghani, Amal (?–), Egyptian short-story writer.

Jabal wa bahr wa warda (Mountain, Sea, Flower, short stories). Cairo: al-Jirad Books, 1998.

Mirsal, Iman (1966–), Egyptian poet born in Mansura. She has an M.A. in Arabic from Cairo University. She worked as the edito-

rial secretary for *Adab wa naqd* magazine.

Ittisafat (Character Marks, poetry). Cairo: Dar al-Ghad, 1990.

Mamarr mu'tim yashluh li-ta'allum al-raqs (A Dark Alley Suitable for Learning to Dance, poetry). Cairo: Dar Sharqiyat, 1995.

Misbah, Munira (?–), Palestinian poet and journalist born in Beirut. She has worked in education and journalism. She currently lives in the U.S.

Sayyidat al-bara'im (Woman of Blossoms, poetry). Beirut: Arab Institute for Research and Publishing, 1988.

Khitab al-nada (The Dew's Discourse, poetry). Amman: Dar Azmina, 1995.

al-Shajara (The Tree, children's literature). Nicosia: Dar Anahid, n.d.

Mosteghanemi, Ahlam (Mustaghanami, Ahlam) (1953–), Algerian poet, novelist, and researcher born in Tunis. She currently lives between Paris and Beirut. She received a B.A. in humanities in Algeria and a state Ph.D. in sociology from the Sorbonne. She received the Naguib Mahfouz Medal for Literature in 1998 for her novel, *Dhakirat al-jasad*. She published a work of non-fiction, *al-Mar'a fi-l-adab al-jaza'iri al-mu'asir* (Women in Contemporary Algerian Literature), in 1981.

'Ala marfa' al-ayyam (On the Dock of Days, poetry). Algiers: al-Wataniya Publishing and Distribution, 1973.

al-Kitaba fi lahzat 'uriyy (Writing in a Moment of Nakedness, poetry). Algiers: al-Wataniya Publishing and Distribution, 1975.

Dhakirat al-jasad (*Memory in the Flesh*, novel). Beirut: Dar al-Adab, 1993.

Fawdat al-hawass (*Chaos of the Senses*, novel). Beirut: Dar al-Adab, 1998.

al-Muflih, Hiyam Hasun (?–), Saudi short-story writer born in Syria. She resides in Riyadh. She received a B.A. in agricultural sciences in Aleppo, Syria, in 1985. She is an editor at *al-Riyad* newspaper.

Safahat min dhakira mansiya (Pages from a Forgotten Memory, short stories). Damascus: Dar Daniya, n.d.

Mufrih, Sa'diya (1964–), Kuwaiti poet born in al-Jahra'. She received a B.A. in Arabic from Kuwait University in 1987. Starting in 1988 she worked as a cultural editor for *al-Watan* newspaper. In 1993 she moved to *al-Qabas*. She received the Su'ad al-Sabah Prize for Literature in 1992.
Akhir al-halimin kan (The Last Dreamer Was, poetry). Kuwait: Dar Su'ad al-Sabah, 1992.
Taghib fa-usarrij khayl zununi (You Vanish So I Saddle the Horse of My Doubts, poetry). Beirut: Dar al-Jadid, 1994.
Kitab al-atham (The Book of Misdeeds, poetry). Cairo: General Egyptian Book Organization, 1997.

Mughith, Fadiya (?–), Egyptian poet.
al-Hubb hadha-l-zaman (Love in This Age, poetry). Cairo: n.p., 1992.

Muhammad, Amina (1928–), Iraqi short-story writer born in Basra. She is a graduate of the Teachers' Institute in Baghdad. She worked in education.
al-Harf J (The Letter J, short stories). Baghdad: al-Irshad press, 1976.
Abadan tasta' al-adwa' (The Lights Always Shine, short stories). Baghdad: al-Irshad Press, 1977.
Asfar al-ruh (Books of the Spirit, short stories). N.p.: n.p., 1987.
al-Shams allati taghrub (The Setting Sun, short stories). N.p.: n.p., 1988.
al-Shams allati tushriq (The Rising Sun, short stories). N.p.: n.p., 1988.

Muhammad, Fatima Isma'il (?–), Egyptian poet. She received a degree in humanities in 1975 and works as an art critic at the Arts Academy in al-Zamalik, Cairo.
Jidar min al-hubb (A Wall of Love, poetry). Cairo: Egyptian Association to Foster Talent, 1994.

Athar 'ala nafidha (Traces on a Window, short stories). Cairo: Tiba'at al-Watan Printing, Publishing, and Distribution, 1995.

Muhammad, Hala (?–), Syrian poet and filmmaker.
Laysa li-l-ruh dhakira (The Soul Has No Memory, poetry). Damascus: Ministry of Culture, 1994.
'Ala dhalik al-bayad al-khafit (On That Pale White, poetry). N.p.: n.p., 1997.

Muhammad, Harbiya (?–), Iraqi short-story writer.
Jarimat rajul (A Man's Crime, novella). Baghdad: al-Jami'a Press, 1953.
Man al-jani (Who Is the Criminal, novella). Baghdad: al-Jami'a Press, 1954.

Muhammad, I'tidal Dayriya Khayri (1948–), Yemeni short-story writer born in Aden. She received a B.A. in English literature in 1984. She is the director of public relations at the General Communications Institution and the assistant director at the Women's Professional Training Association. She has written on women and on development. She also writes poetry, children's literature and songs, and short stories. She is publicly active as a founding member of the Women's Union and as a women's representative in health activities. She is also active in teaching and supervising literacy efforts.
"Sawt min al-madi" (A Voice from the Past). In *Aswat nisa'iya fi-l-qissa al-Yamaniya* (Women's Voices in the Yemeni Short Story). N.p.: n.p., n.d.
"'Azif al-nay" (The Flute Player, children's literature). In *Aswat nisa'iya fi-l-qissa al-Yamaniya* (Women's Voices in the Yemeni Short Story). N.p.: n.p., n.d.

Muhammad, Samiya Sulayman (1944–), Egyptian poet born in Alexandria.
Jisr al-hubb (The Bridge of Love, poetry). Alexandria: General Authority for Culture Palaces, 1996.

M

Naghm (A Tune, colloquial poetry). Alexandria: General Authority for Culture Palaces, 1998.

Muhammad, Wahiba Shawkat (?–), Syrian novelist. She has a medical degree.
al-Intisar mawtan (Victory at Death, novel). Damascus: Dar Petra, 1996.

Muhammad, Zaynab (?–?), Egyptian novelist and literary pioneer. Her non-fiction works include *Asrar Ramadan* (Secrets of Ramadan, 1927), *Butulat Sa'd fi hayatihi aw tarikh hayat al-faqid* (Sa'd's Heroism in His Life, or the Life History of the Deceased, 1927), *Dustur al-ajinna* (Embryos, 1927), *Dalil al-sa'ada al-zawjiya: kayf yanaluha kull rajul wa imra'a* (A Guide to Marital Bliss: How Every Man and Woman Can Attain It, 1927).
Mudhakkirat wasifa Misriya (Memoirs of an Egyptian Lady in Waiting, written in novel form by following the form of novelists Muhammad al-Hidi and Muhammad Kamil Farid). Seven vols.: *Baris wa malahiha* (Paris and Its Nightclubs), *'Ashiq ukhtih* (In Love with His Sister), *Dahaya al-qadar* (Victims of Fate), *Akhirat al-malahi* (The End of the Nightclubs), *al-Fadila sirr al-sa'ada* (Virtue Is the Secret of Happiness), *Ila rahmat Allah ya za'im al-sharq* (To God's Mercy O Leader of the East), *'Awatif al-aba'* (The Sentiments of Fathers). Cairo: n.p., 1927.
Saqita fi ahdan al-radhila (A Fallen Woman in the Bosom of Vice, N.p.: n.p., 1927).

Muhanna, Duha (1947–), Syrian short-story writer born in al-Haska. She received a degree in Arabic language and works as an Arabic teacher. She is currently the librarian of the al-Asad School in Latakia. She published her first stories in newspapers and journals. She is a member of the Children's Literature Association.
al-Janahan (The Two Wings, children's literature). Latakia: Dar al-Hiwar, 1986.

al-Hukm al-batil (The Baseless Judgment, children's literature). Latakia: Dar al-Hiwar, 1987.
al-Sibaq (The Race, children's literature). Latakia: Dar al-Hiwar, 1987.
Hasan wa-l-farasha (Hasan and the Butterfly, children's literature). Damascus: Dar al-Mutanabbi, 1988.
Huriyat al-nahr (The River Nymph, children's literature). Damascus: Dar al-Mutanabbi, 1988.
al-Jadila (The Braid, children's literature). Damascus: Dar al-Mutanabbi, 1988.
al-Muhasibun al-sighar (The Little Accountants, children's literature). Damascus: Dar al-Mutanabbi, 1988.
Qalat al-shams li-l-atfal (The Sun Told the Children, children's literature). Damascus: Arab Writers' Union, 1992.
al-Nafidha (The Window, children's literature). Damascus: Arab Writers' Union, 1994.

al-Muji, Sahar (?–), Egyptian short-story writer and novelist. She has a B.A. and an M.A. in English literature from Cairo University. She is an assistant instructor of English at Cairo University and an announcer for Radio Cairo. She is a member of the Women and Memory Forum. Her stories have been published in Egyptian and Arabic magazines and periodicals, and she was awarded a prize for her novel, *Dariya*, from the Girls' Clubs in Sharjah in 1998.
Sayyidat al-manam (The Dream Woman, short stories). Cairo: Dar Sharqiyat, 1998.
Dariya (Dariya, novel). Cairo: Dar al-Misriya al-Lubnaniya, 1999.

Mukhtar, Amal (?–), Tunisian novelist. She is a journalist and writes essays, short stories, and novels.
Nakhb al-hayah (A Toast to Life, novel). Beirut: Dar al-Adab, 1993.

al-Mu'la, Khulud (?–), Emirati poet born in the Emirates.
Huna dayya't al-zaman (Here I Lost Time, poetry). Cairo: Dar 'Arabiya Printing and Publishing, 1997.
Wahdak (You Alone, poetry). Cairo: al-Dar al-Misriya al-Lubnaniya, 1999.

Mu'mina, Salwa Mahmasani (1908–1957), Lebanese pioneer and short-story writer born in Beirut. She received her primary education at a girls' school run by the al-Maqasid Islamic Charitable Association. She studied Arabic literature with Julia Tu'ma and Salma Sa'igh, and she continued her education at the St. Joseph School. She taught Arabic at a school run by the al-Maqasid Islamic Charitable Association for thirteen years. She published her literary articles in the Arabic press in journals such as the Egyptian *al-Mar'a al-jadida*. She was the vice president of the Women of Lebanon Association.
Ma'a al-hayah (With Life, short stories). Beirut: Dar al-'Ilm li-l-Malayin, 1956.

Murad, Majida 'Attar (?–?),Lebanese novelist born in Beirut. She received her primary and secondary education at the al-Ahliya School in Beirut and a B.A. in education from the Beirut College for Girls (later the American Lebanese University). She taught Arabic literature and was editor in chief for the Beirut magazine, *al-Hasna'*. She also worked in Lebanese radio.
Murahiqa (An Adolescent, novel). Beirut: Dar al-Rawa'i', 1966.
Fi-l-bad' kan al-hubb (In the Beginning Was Love, novel). Beirut: Dar al-Afaq al-Jadida, 1978.

al-Murr, Fatin (?–), Lebanese short-story writer.
Bayn intizarayn (Between Two Waitings, short stories). Beirut: Dar al-Jadid, 1999.

Muruwwa, Dunya (?–), Lebanese dramatist born in Sidon in the south. She received her primary education at the American Girls' College and a B.A. in political science from the Beirut College for Women and the American University of Beirut in 1951. She continued her higher education in journalism at the University of Michigan, Ann Arbor, in the U.S. in 1954. She wrote for the journals, *al-Mar'a* and *al-Kulliya*, before returning to Beirut in 1954. She was editor in chief of the *Daily Star*, published by Dar al-Hayat, and she taught at the Beirut University College in 1964 and at the Faculty of Media at the Lebanese University from 1968 to 1976. She also headed the Association of Women of Mount 'Amil for the Development of the South. Her works include *Kamil Muruwwa kama 'ariftuh* (Kamil Muruwwa as I Knew Him, 1967).
al-Zawja al-ghaniya (The Rich Wife, play). Beirut: Dar al-Kitab al-Jadid, 1967.

Musa, Nabawiya (1886–1951), Egyptian writer, journalist, activist, and a pioneer in education in Egypt born in a village near al-Zaqaziq. Like most girls of her class, she began her education at home with the help of her brother. She was later a student at the al-Saniya Primary School. In 1906 she received a teaching certificate and in 1907 she became the first Egyptian woman to receive a high school diploma. She began working as soon as she earned her teaching certificate. She was appointed a teacher in the 'Abbas Primary School, girls' section, in Cairo. She was the first female teacher of Arabic. Before her, the teaching of this subject was limited to shaykhs from al-Azhar and graduates of the Academy of Sciences. She was also the first female inspector in the Ministry of Education. She was involved in several conflicts with senior Ministry of Education officials because of her criticisms of the curriculum and the methods used in girls' schools. In 1926, she was dismissed from her job. She established the network of al-Ashraf girls' schools in Alexandria and devoted herself to running them. Given her pioneering role in girls' education, she gave lectures at the women's section of Cairo University. She played an important role politically and socially and often wrote stinging articles for newspapers and journals. In 1922 she founded the Association for the Progress of Women and represented Egypt at the global women's conference in Rome, the first conference to be attended by a representative of the Egyptian women's movement. She established the magazine, *al-Fatah*, in 1937, which continued to appear until 1943. She harbored a deep hostility toward the Wafd Party, and in 1942, the year the Wafd came to power, she was arrested and her schools and magazine were closed. She wrote many books, including two reading textbooks for girls in 1911; *al-Mar'a wa-l-'amal* (Women and Work, 1920), a collection of poetry; and a book in which she responded to Makram 'Ubayd's *al-Kitab al-aswad* (The Black Book).

Diwan al-Sayyida Nabawiya Musa (The Poetry of Nabawiya Musa, poetry). Cairo: al-Fatah Magazine Press in al-'Abbasiya, 1938.

Tub Hutab aw al-fadila al-mudtahada (Tubhotep or the Persecuted Virtue, historical novel). Cairo: al- Muqtataf Press, 1939.

Tarikhi bi-qalami (My History by My Pen, autobiography). N.p.: n.p., n.d.

Musa, Nadiya al-Nubi (?–), Egyptian short-story writer.

Aghniya' fuqara' wa fuqara' aghniya', ahlan wa sahlan, al-imtihan (Poor Rich and Rich Poor, Hello, The Test, short stories). Cairo: Dar al-Hira', 1987.

al-Mazluma, Mukhtar wa Karima, Salim wa Rabiha (The Downtrodden, Mukhtar and Karima, Salim and Rabiha, short stories). Cairo: Dar al-Hira', 1988.

Qisas qasira wa asatir (Short Stories and Legends, short stories). Cairo: Dar al-Hira', 1988.

Musadafa, Suhayr (1961–), Egyptian poet born in Cairo. She has a Ph.D. in economics and works in the General Egyptian Book Organization. She has translated children's books.

Hujum wadi' (A Mild Attack, poetry). Cairo: General Egyptian Book Organization, 1997.

Fatah tujarrib hatfaha (A Woman Rehearses Her Death, poetry). Cairo: al-Dar al-Misriya, 1999.

Musalima, In'am (1938–), Syrian novelist and short-story writer born in the province of Dar'a, where she went to school. She received a medical degree from Damascus University in 1960 and continued her studies at the University of London. She worked as a surgeon and dentist in the Syrian countryside for several years. She began publishing in Syrian newspapers and magazines in the early 1960s. She won the Fiction Prize from the United Arab Republic in 1958.

al-Hubb wa-l-wahl (Love and Mud, novel). Damascus: Dar al-Thaqafa, 1963.

al-Kahf (The Cave, short stories). Damascus: Dar al-Ajyal, 1973.

al-Musawi, Hashimiya Ja'far 'Ali (1972–), Omani poet born in al-Batina-al-Khabura. She received a B.A. in education, Arabic language department, from Sultan Qabus University. She has taken part in many poetry readings and won several prizes, including the Rashid ibn Hamid Prize for Culture and Sciences. She won third place for that prize in 1987 in a Gulf-wide competition.

Ilayk anta (To You, poetry). Beirut: Dar Lamis, 1993.

al-Musawi, Sajida (1950–), Iraqi poet born in Baghdad. She graduated from the College of Liberal Arts in 1975. In 1982 she was the editor in chief of *al-Mar'a* magazine. She is a member of the Central Council of the General Union of Iraqi Women and a member of the Central Council for the Iraqi Writers' and Authors' Union.

Tiflat al-nakhl (Child of the Palm, poetry). Baghdad: Dar al-Hurriya Printing, 1979.

Hawa al-nakhil (The Palm's Desire, poetry). Baghdad: Ministry of Culture and Information and Dar al-Rashid, 1983.

al-Tal' (Pollen, poetry). Baghdad: Dar al-Shu'un al-Thaqafiya al-'Amma, 1986.

'Ind nab' al-qamar (At the Moon's Spring, poetry). Baghdad: Dar al-Shu'un al-Thaqafiya al-'Amma, 1987.

Diwan al-Babiliyat (The Babel Poems, poetry). Baghdad: Dar al-Shu'un al-Thaqafiya al-'Amma, 1989.

Qamar fawq jisr al-Mu'allaq (A Moon over the Mu'allaq Bridge, poetry). Amman: Aram for Studies, Publishing, and Distribution, 1993.

Shahqat (Gasps, poetry). Baghdad: Dar al-Shu'un al-Thaqafiya al-'Amma, 1996.

al-Muslimani, Zabya Khamis (1958–), Emirati poet and short-story writer born in the emirate of Dubai. She studied political science, philosophy, and literature at Indiana University in Bloomington (1975–1980) and later studied in London (1982–1989). She works at the Arab League. She also has worked in social planning, journalism, and television. She has published several works of non-fiction and translations, among them *al-Shi'riya al-Urubiya wa diktaturiyat al-ruh* (European Poetics and the Dictatorship of the Spirit, 1993), *Sanam al-mar'a al-shi'ri* (Woman's Poetic Idol, 1997), *Quftan al-dhakira: qira'a fi-l-mawruth al-'Arabi* (The Caftan of Memory: Readings in the Arab Tradition, 1998), *al-Bahth 'an al-dhat 'ind al-sha'ira al-Khalijiya al-mu'asira* (The Search for the Self: Contemporary Women Poets from the Gulf), *Qadaya al-mar'a al-'Arabiya* (Arab Women's Issues), and *al-Shi'r al-jadid* (The New Poetry, translation).

Khatwa fawq al-ard (A Footstep on the Earth, poetry). Beirut: Dar al-Kalima, 1981.

al-Thuna'iya ana al-mar'a, al-ard, kull al-dulu' (The Dichotomy, I Am Woman,

Earth, Every Rib, poetry). London: Dar al-Kamil, 1982.

Sababat al-muhra al-'Umaniya (Longings of the Omani Mare, poetry). Beirut: Arab Institute for Research and Publishing, 1985.

'Uruq al-jir wa-l-hinna' (Veins of Lime and Henna, short stories). Beirut: Arab Institute for Research and Publishing, 1985.

Qasa'id hubb (Love Poems, poetry). Beirut: Arab Institute for Research and Publishing, 1985.

al-Sultan yarjum imra'a hubla bi-l-bahr (The Sultan Stones a Woman Pregnant with the Sea, poetry). London: Riyad al-Rayyis Books and Publishing, 1988.

Khulkhal al-sayyida al-'arja' (The Anklet of the Lame Woman, short stories). Cairo: Dar al-Nadim, 1990.

Jannat al-jiniralat (The Generals' Paradise, poetry). Cairo: Dar Su'ad al-Sabah, 1993.

Mawt al-'a'ila (Death of the Family, poetry). Cairo: Dar al-Nadim, 1993.

Intihar hadi' jiddan (A Very Quiet Suicide, poetry). Cairo: al-Zabya Publications, 1995.

al-Qurmuzi (Crimson, poetry). Cairo: al-Zabya Publications, 1995.

Ibtisamat makira wa qisas ukhra (Deceptive Smiles and Other Stories, short stories). Kuwait: al-Rabi'an Publishing Company, 1996.

al-Mashi fi ahlam rumantikiya (Walking in Romantic Dreams, poetry). Cairo: Dar 'Uyun Jadida, 1996.

Mustafa, Asma' (?–), Iraqi short-story writer.
Nahw al-hulm (Toward the Dream, short stories). Baghdad: Dar al-Shu'un al-Thaqafiya, 1999.

Mustafa, Ghada Ahmad Nabil (1960–), Egyptian poet born in al-Isma'iliya. She has an M.A. in modern English and American literature.

al-Mutarabbisa bi-nafsiha (Lying in Wait for Herself, poetry). Cairo: Ida'a Publishers, 1999.

M

Mustafa, Inas Muhammad Rashad (?–), Egyptian writer.
al-'Izba wa-l-watan (The Manor and the Homeland). N.p.: n.p., 1989.

Mustafa, Kawthar (?–), Egyptian poet.
Mawsim zar' al-banat (The Season for Planting Girls, colloquial poetry). Cairo: General Egyptian Book Organization, 1989.

Mustafa, Nawal (1955–), Egyptian short-story writer and journalist born in Cairo. She received a B.A. in media in 1972 and a diploma in journalism from Boston University in 1993. She heads the women's investigative desk at *al-Akhbar* and the "You Are Not Alone" section of the newspaper, which cares for the needy. She is the president of the Children of Women Prisoners Association. She was awarded a prize from the Journalists' Syndicate for her interview with Benazir Bhutto in 1990, and she received the 'Ali and Mustafa Amin Prize for a human interest story. She has worked as a foreign correspondent and has written stories and essays about the U.S., England, Switzerland, Greece, and Morocco. She published *Hayat 'ashiq al-sahafa* (The Life of a Lover of the Press) in 1997, about Mustafa Amin, one of the founders of Dar al-Akhbar. Her other non-fiction works include *Nujum wa aqlam* (Celebrities and Writers, 1995, interviews), *Nizar wa qasa'id mamnu'a* (Nizar and the Forbidden Poems, 1998, study), *Rihla ila a'maqihim* (A Journey to Their Depths, 1988, interviews), and *al-Banju qunbula infajarat fi a'maq al-shabab* (Marijuana: a Bomb Detonated in the Depths of Youth, anthology).
al-Hayah marra ukhra (Life Again, short stories). Cairo: al-Mu'assasa al-'Arabiya al-Haditha, 1992.
Hanin (Yearning, short stories). Cairo: Arab Youth Center, 1993.
Mudhakkirat durra (Memoirs of a Second Wife, short stories). Cairo: al-Raya Center, 1994.
Raqsat al-hubb (The Dance of Love, short stories). Cairo: al-Dar al-Misriya al-Lubnaniya, 1995.
'Ashiqat khalf al-aswar (Lovers Behind Walls, short stories). Cairo: Akhbar al-Yawm Foundation, 1996.
Raqsat al-hubb al-sakhina wa qisas ukhra (The Hot Dance of Love and Other Stories, short stories). Cairo: al-Dar al-Misriya al-Lubnaniya, and Giza: 'Arabiya Press, 1996.
al-'Asafir la yamlikuha ahad (The Sparrows Belong to No One, short stories). Cairo: Akhbar al-Yawm, 1999.

Mustafa, Thuraya (?–), Egyptian poet.
Milyun risala (A Million Letters, colloquial poetry). Cairo: Qasid Khayr Press, 1970.
'Ayni 'alayk ya balad (I Feel for You, My Country, poetry). Cairo: General Egyptian Book Organization, 1993.

Mustazraf, Malika (1969–), Moroccan novelist born in Casablanca. She was unable to finish university or to work because of health problems.
Jirah al-ruh wa-l-jasad (Wounds of the Spirit and Body, novel). al-Qunaytira: Accent Press, 1999.

al-Mutawakkil, Ibtisam Husayn (1970–), Yemeni poet born in Sana'a. She received a B.A. in Arabic. She is an assistant instructor at Sana'a University and is preparing her M.A. She is a member of the Authors of Yemen Union. She has taken part in many literary activities in Yemen and in the wider Arab world. She began to publish while in university, and her work has appeared in many Yemeni papers.
Shadha al-jamr (The Scent of Embers, poetry). Sana'a: General Book Organization, 1998.

Mutawalli, Suhayr (?–), Egyptian poet born in the province of Kafr al-Shaykh.
Awwal hudud al-dhakira (At the Boundaries of Memory, poetry). Cairo: al-Fursan Publishing and Distribution, 1994.

Muzaffar, Mayy (1940–), Iraqi poet and short-story writer born in Baghdad. She has a B.A. in English literature from Baghdad University. She has translated several books from English into Arabic, including poetry and books on painting and art. Her essays and research in both Arabic and English have contributed to the general understanding of the plastic arts and poetry. She published a biography of intellectual Nasir al-Din al-Asad as *Safar fi-l-mada* (Traveling in the Distance). She has worked as a researcher at the Royal Academy for Research on Islamic Civilization (Al al-Bayt) in Amman. She currently lives in Bahrain with her husband, artist Rafi' al-Nasiri.

Khatawat fi layl al-ghajar (Steps on the Night of the Gypsies, short stories). Baghdad: al-Iman Press, 1970.

al-Baja' (The Swan, short stories). Baghdad: Dar al-Shu'un al-Thaqafiya al-'Amma, 1979.

Ta'ir al-nar (Bird of Fire, poetry). Baghdad: Tuwayni Press, 1985.

Ghazala fi-l-rih (Gazelle on the Wind, poetry). Baghdad: Dar al-Shu'un al-Thaqafiya al-'Amma, 1988.

Nusus fi hajar karim (Texts on a Precious Stone, short stories). Beirut: Arab Institute for Research and Publishing, 1993.

Layliyat (Night Things, poetry). Amman: Dar al-Shuruq Publishing and Distribution, 1994.

al-Na"as, Mardiya (1949–), Libyan novelist and short-story writer born in Darna. She has been a teacher and an editor at *al-Fajr*, *al-Raqib*, *al-Zaman*, and *al-Mar'a* magazine.

Shay' min al-dif' (A Little Bit of Warmth, novel). Libya: Dar Maktabat al-Fikr, 1972.

Ghazala (Gazelle, short stories). Libya: General Publishing and Distribution, 1976.

al-Mazruf al-azraq (The Blue Envelope, novel). Tripoli, Libya: al-Kitab wa-l-Tawzi' Publications, 1982.

Rijal wa nisa' (Men and Women, short stories). Tripoli, Libya: al-Dar al-Jamahiriya Publishing and Distribution, 1993.

Nabrawi, Sayza (1897–1985), Egyptian journalist and a pioneer of the women's movement in Egypt born in Qasr al-Minshawi in Cairo. She was adopted by her relative, 'Adila Nabrawi, and traveled with her to Paris where she attended French schools. Upon her return to Cairo, she enrolled in Les Dames de Sion School in Alexandria. She refused to live with her biological parents and chose to live with her maternal grandmother. Huda Sha'rawi, a friend of her adopted mother, took her under her wing. Nabrawi participated in many international women's conferences. When she returned from the women's conference in Rome, she and Huda Sha'rawi publicly removed their face veils. She published the newspaper, *L'Egyptienne*, the organ of the Egyptian Women's Union, from 1925 to 1940 and wrote several articles on various social issues.

Nafi', Nur (1932–), Egyptian poet born in Cairo. She did not complete secondary school.

La'allak tarda (Perhaps You Will Be Satisfied, poetry). N.p.: n.p., 1980.

Faris al-hubb wa-l-harb (Knight of Love and War, poetic drama). N.p.: n.p., 1985.

al-Na'ib, Fatina (Saduf al-'Amiriya or Suduf al-'Ubaydiya) (1917–1993), Iraqi poet born in Baghdad. She graduated from the Primary Teachers' Institute in 1937 and continued her studies in English at the College of Queen 'Aliya in Baghdad. She taught secondary school and worked in educational management. She was fluent in English and French. Much of her poetry was broadcast on Arab radio stations and many of her poems were published in the local press. She is the sister of short-story writer Mahira al-Naqshbandi.

Lahib al-ruh (The Spirit's Blaze, poetry). Baghdad: al-Ma'arif Press, 1955.

Ranin al-quyud (The Clang of the Fetters, poetry). Baghdad: n.p., 1962.

Rasis al-hubb (Love's Patina, poetry). Baghdad: Ministry of Information, 1977.

Na'im, 'Awatif (1950–), Iraqi actress, writer, director, and theater critic. She is a graduate of the College of Fine Arts (with a degree in acting). She also earned a B.A. in film direction. She has written many works for the stage, television, and radio and has taken part in directing many of them in the Arab world and Europe. She won the Best Acting Award at the second Cairo International Festival for Experimental Theater. She was honored at the Carthage International Film Festival and received a world prize from the Mediterranean Festival.

Unzur wajh al-ma' (Look at the Water's Surface, play). *al-Hayah al-thaqafiya*. Tunis: 1993.

Yas'alunak (They Ask You, play). *al-Masrah*. Cairo: 1993.

al-Muharrij (The Clown, play). In *Arba' masrahiyat 'Iraqiya* (Four Iraqi Plays). Cairo: Dar 'Ishtar, 1998.

al-Na'imi, Huda (?–), Qatari short-story writer.

al-Makhala (The Kohl Jar, short stories). Cairo: Amun Press, 1997.

al-Na'imi, Salwa (?–), Syrian poet.

Kitab al-asrar (The Book of Secrets, poetry). Cairo: privately published, distributed by Dar al-Thaqafa al-Jadida, 1994.

Ghiwayat mawti (The Seduction of My Death, poetry). Cairo: Dar Sharqiyat, 1996.

Najib, Malika (1959–), Moroccan short-story writer born in Erfoud. She has a B.A. in Arabic literature and a law degree. Since 1976 she has worked at the Ministry of Civil Service and Administrative Re-

form. She was active in the theater in the 1970s. She is interested in children's issues, women's issues, issues of the disabled, and housing issues. She is a founder of the Moroccan Women's Union and was elected the secretary of the League of Social Service Associations in Morocco.

al-Hulm al-akhdar (The Green Dream, short stories). Rabat: Firdaws Press, 1997.

Najib, Victoria (?–), Egyptian novelist.

Nawafidh maftuha (Open Windows, novel). Cairo: Dar al-Udaba', 1962.

al-Nakhi, Shaykha Mubarak (1952–), Emirati short-story writer born in Sharjah. She has a B.A. in the humanities and a degree in education. She is the principal of a girls' school and the head of the Emirati Women Authors' League in the Girls' Clubs. She is also a member of the Emirati Writers' and Authors' Union.

al-Rahil (The Departure, short stories). Sharjah: Emirati Writers' and Authors' Union Publications, 1992.

al-Naluti, 'Arusiya (1956–), Tunisian short-story writer and children's writer born on the island of Djerba. She has a degree in Arab civilization and literature and a proficiency certificate in research. After graduating from college, she worked as a high-school teacher. She is currently the head of the Authority to Foster Literature and Art at the Ministry of Culture. She produces the television program '*Uyun al-adab* (Choice Literary Selections) and has made various contributions to the press and radio. She is a member of the Tunisian Writers' Union and was elected to its directorate for the 1992–1994 session. Several of her plays have been staged. She has written screenplays and a fifteen-episode television drama. Her *Maratij* was translated into Spanish by Rosario Montoro Murillo as *Cerrojos* in 1996. Stories from her collection, *al-Bu'd al-khamis*, have been translated as part of an anthology of women's voices from Tunisia, and *Maratij* and *Tamass* have been translated into Dutch. She received the Medal of Cultural Achievement in 1992 from the Tunisian Ministry of Culture, the Zubayda Bashir Women's Literature Award in 1995, and the Best Novel Award in 1995 from the Tunisian Ministry of Culture. She has published a work of non-fiction titled *Tamaththulat al-jasad fi-l-riwaya al-Tunisiya al-mu'asira* (Portrayals of the Body in the Contemporary Tunisian Novel).

al-Bu'd al-khamis (The Fifth Dimension, short stories). Tunis: al-Dar al-'Arabiya Books, 1975.

Juha (Juha, children's literature). Tunis: al-Dar al-'Arabiya Books, 1975.

Busaybis (Little Kitten, three children's literature). Tunis: Tunisian Distribution Company, 1982.

Maratij (Bolts, novel). Tunis: Dar Saras Publishers, 1985.

Jazirat al-tin wa-l-zaytun (Island of Figs and Olives, children's literature). Tunis: Amnesty International Publications, 1994.

Tamass (Contact, novel). Tunis: Dar al-Janub Publishers, 1995.

Nana, Hamidah (Na'na', Hamida) (1946–), Syrian novelist and journalist born in the province of Idlib. She lives in Paris. She received a Ph.D. after writing a dissertation on the rights of women in the Qur'an. She works as a journalist for the Arab and international press and has published several political works: *al-Subh al-dami fi 'Adan* (Bloody Morning in Aden, 1988), *Hiwarat ma'a mufakirri al-gharb* (Conversations with Western Thinkers, 1989), and *Tunis al-'aql zaman al-'asifa* (Tunisia of Reason in the Time of the Storm, 1997).

Anashid imra'a la ta'rif al-farah (Hymns of Joyless Woman, poetry). Damascus: Dar al-Ajyal, 1971.

al-Watan fi-l-'aynayn (*The Homeland*, novel). Beirut: Dar al-Adab, 1979.

Mann yajru' 'ala-l-shawq (Who Dares to Desire, novel). Beirut: Dar al-Adab, 1989.

al-Naqib, Aydan (?–), Iraqi poet.

A'tasir al-hajar (I Squeeze the Stone, poetry). Kirkuk: al-Jumhuriya Press, 1969.

al-Naqqash, Farida (1940–), Egyptian short-story writer and journalist born in al-Daqahliya. She received a B.A. in English literature from Cairo University in 1962. She is a journalist and editor in chief at *Adab wa naqd*. She has published several critical and literary studies on women's issues. She translated the play, *The Road*, by Nigerian writer Wole Soyinka, published as part of the world theater series in Kuwait in 1976 and in the publications of the Ghad Experimental Theater Troupe in 1995. Selections from her autobiography, *al-Sijn . . . al-watan* have been translated into English.

al-Sijn . . . al-watan (Prison . . . Homeland, autobiography). Beirut: Dar al-Nadim, 1981.

al-Sijn dam'atan wa warda (Prison is Two Tears and a Flower, autobiography). Cairo: Dar al-Mustaqbal al-'Arabi, 1986.

Yawmiyat al-mudun al-maftuha (Diary of the Open Cities, poetry). Cairo: Dar al-Thaqafa al-Jadida, 1987.

Yawmiyat al-hubb wa-l-ghadab (Diary of Love and Anger, short stories). Cairo: Dar Sharqiyat, 1994.

al-Nashawati, Khadija al-Jarrah (Umm 'Isam) (1923–2000), Syrian short-story writer and novelist born in Damascus. She grew up in a conservative environment and received only a preparatory education. She published her first works in Syrian newspapers and journals starting in the 1950s under the name Umm 'Isam. She also published in the Cairo-based *al-Ahram* and *al-Akhbar* in the 1960s.

Dhakir ya tura (I Wonder, Does He Remember, short stories). Damascus: Dar al-Thaqafa, 1960.

Ilayk (To You, short stories). Damascus: Dar al-Ajyal, 1970.

Arsifat al-sa'm (Sidewalks of Tedium, novel, with Hiyam Nuwaylati). Damascus: n.p., 1973.

'Indama yaghdu al-matar thaljan (When the Rain Turns to Ice, short stories). Damascus: Dar al-Thaqafa, 1980.

Nashif, Hala Bitar (1932–), Palestinian short-story writer born in Ramle. She has a B.A. and an M.A. in Arabic language and literature from the American University of Beirut. She taught Arabic to non-native speakers at the Jordanian University from 1985 to 1997.

Urid huwwiya (I Want an Identity, short stories). Beirut: Arab Institute for Research and Publishing, 1993.

al-Ruju' (The Return, novella). Amman: Arab Institute for Research and Publishing, 1996.

Lam a'ud utqin fann al-hikaya wa qisas ukhra (I'm No Longer Good at Storytelling and Other Stories, short stories). Beirut: Arab Institute for Research and Publishing, 1999.

Nasif, Malak Hifni (Bahithat al-Badiya) (1886–1918), Early Egyptian writer, speaker, and pioneer of feminist thought in Egypt who devoted her attention to social and cultural issues relevant to women. She was the first woman to receive a primary school certificate from a public school, al-Saniya School, in 1900. In 1903 she made the highest marks on the first graduation test for women teachers. In 1910 she presented the Egyptian parliament with a list of ten demands to improve women's status. In 1911 she gave a public lecture at the offices of *al-Jarida* magazine to revive the medieval tradition of Arab women speakers. She wrote for *al-Jarida*, edited by Ahmad Lutfi al-Sayyid, and wrote a regular weekly column, "Nisa'iyat." She later published the articles in book form in *Nisa'iyat* (Women's Things, 1910), with an introduction by Ahmad Lutfi al-Sayyid. The book contains encomiums from public figures who were asked to comment on the text. After her marriage, she lived in

Fayyum. She published her articles under the name "Bahithat al-Badiya" (Seeker in the Desert). She died at a young age in the global influenza pandemic. All of her articles were published posthumously in 1925 in a two-volume collection, also titled *Nisa'iyat*.

al-Nasir, Su'ad (Umm Salma) (1959–), Moroccan poet, novelist, and short-story writer born in Tetouan. She has a graduate degree in humanities and is in the process of preparing her state Ph.D. She is a research professor at the College of Liberal Arts and Humanities in Tetouan. She is the vice-president of the Literary Development Association and a member of several other social and cultural associations. She has taken part in cultural and literary seminars and forums and has made contributions to the plastic arts. Her works have been published in several Moroccan periodicals. Her non-fiction works include *al-Rihla al-Tatwaniya ila-l-diyar al-Faransiya li-l-Shaykh Muhammad ibn 'Abd Allah al-Saffar* (al-Shaykh Muhammad ibn 'Abd Allah al-Saffar's Tetouan Journey to France, 1995, critical edition and analysis) and *Bawh al-unutha* (Confession of Femininity, 1998, study). She is also known as Umm Salma.

Lu'bat al-laniha'iya (The Game of Infinity, poetry). Tetouan: al-Amal Press, 1985.

Fusul min maw'id al-jamr (Seasons From the Time of Embers, poetry). Tetouan: al-Amal Press, 1986.

Iqa'at fi qalb al-zaman (Rhythms in the Heart of Time, short stories). Casablanca: al-Najah Modern Press, 1994.

al-Nasir, Umayma Rashrash (196?–), Jordanian short-story writer born in Amman. She received a B.A. in Arabic literature from the Jordanian University in 1986 and a degree in philosophy from the same institution in 1992. She has written a manuscript titled *al-Ghina' ba'idan* (The Distant Singing).

Arju alla yata'akhkhar al-radd (R.S.V.P., short stories). Amman: Ministry of Culture, 1996.

Al Nasiri, Buthaina (al-Nasiri, Buthayna) (1947–), Iraqi short-story writer born in Baghdad. She has a B.A. in English literature from Baghdad University. She is a translator and publisher (Dar 'Ishtar). She resides in Cairo. She has written several essays, collected in *'Ala hudud al-watan* (On the Borders of the Homeland), published in 1995. She received the Cultural Arts Prize at the first Arab Women's Book Fair, held in Cairo in 1995, for her collection, *Watan akhar*. Her stories have been translated into English, German, Spanish, and Norwegian.

Hidwat hisan (Horseshoe, short stories). Baghdad: Ministry of Information, 1974.

Mawt ilah al-bahr (Death of the Sea God, short stories). Cairo: Dar al-Thaqafa al-Jadida, 1977.

Fata al-sardin al-mu'allab (Boy of the Canned Sardines, short stories). Baghdad: Dar al-Kharif, 1990.

Watan akhar (Another Homeland, short stories). Cairo: Dar Sina Publishers, 1994.

al-Tariq ila Baghdad (The Road to Baghdad, short stories). Cairo: Dar 'Ishtar, 1999.

Nasr Allah, Fahmiya (?–), Lebanese poet.

'Asimat al-ard Bayrut (Beirut: The Capital of the Earth, poetry). Beirut: Dar Ghandur Printers and Publishers, 1979.

Ajyal al-riyah wa 'asimat al-harb (Generations of the Wind and the Capital of War, poetry). Beirut: Dar al-Nahar Publishers, 1982.

Nasrallah, Emily Abi Rashid (Nasr Allah, Emily Abi Rashid) (1931–), Lebanese journalist and novelist born in al-Kufayr in southern Lebanon. She studied at the Beirut College for Girls and later the American University of Beirut, where she received a B.A. in literature in 1958. She has worked in teaching and journalism since 1962. She has taken part in several cultural seminars and conferences in the Arab world and abroad, and her books have been translated into several languages.

She published *Nisa' ra'idat min al-sharq wa-l-gharb* (Pioneering Women from the East and West) in 1986 and has published several articles for the journal, *Sawt al-mar'a*. She worked as an editor at *al-Sayyad* (1955–1970) and later at *Fayruz*. Awards include the Fayruz Magazine Prize (1983), the Sa'id 'Aql Prize and the Friends of the Book Prize for *Tuyur Aylul*, the Gibran Kahlil Gibran Prize awarded by the League of Arabic Heritage in Australia (1991), and an honorable mention from the International Board on Books for Young People (IBBY) for the children's novel, *Mudhakkirat qitta*.

Tuyur Aylul (The Birds of September, novel). Beirut: Dar al-Ahliya, 1962.

Shajarat al-difla (The Oleander Tree, novel). Beirut: al-Najwa Press, 1968.

Jazirat al-wahm (The Island of Illusion, short stories). Beirut: Bayt al-Hikma, 1973.

al-Rahina (The Hostage, novel). Beirut: Nawfal Foundation, 1974.

al-Yanbu' (The Spring, short stories). Beirut: Nawfal Foundation, 1978.

Tilka-l-dhikrayat (Those Memories, novel). Beirut: Nawfal Foundation, 1980.

al-Iqla' 'aks al-zaman (*Flight Against Time*, novel). Beirut: Nawfal Foundation, 1981.

al-Mar'a fi 17 qissa (Women in 17 Stories, short stories). Beirut: Nawfal Foundation, 1984.

al-Tahuna al-da'i'a (The Lost Mill, short stories). Beirut: Nawfal Foundation, 1984.

Mudhakkirat qitta (A Cat's Diary, children's literature). N.p.: n.p., 1988.

Khubzuna al-yawmi (Our Daily Bread, short stories). n.p., 1990.

al-Jamr al-ghafi (The Sleeping Ember, novel). Beirut: Nawfal Foundation, 1995.

Mahattat al-rahil (Stations on a Journey, short stories). Beirut: Nawfal Foundation, 1996.

al-Bahira (Dazzling, novel). Beirut: Nawfal Foundation, n.d.

Nassar, Nadiya (1934–1994), Syrian poet born in Kafrun (Safita). She has published in the Lebanese and Syrian press. She was a representative of the Beirut-based Dar al-Fann wa-l-Adab.

Wajd ta'arra (An Exposed Passion, poetry). Beirut: Dar Ghandur, 1968.

Zahrat al-rih (Flower of the Wind, poetry). Beirut: Dar Ghandur, 1975.

Zaman al-'ishq (Time of Love, poetry). Damascus: n.p., 1983.

Anashid Anada (Hymns of Anada, poetry), Damascus: n.p., n.d.

Nawasir, Nadiya (?–), Algerian poet.

Rahiba fi dayriha al-hazin (A Nun in Her Melancholy Monastery, poetry). Qasantina: al-Ba'th Press, 1981.

al-Nawawi, Fatin 'Ali Ahmad (1951–), Egyptian poet and artist. She received an M.A. in electrical engineering from Cairo University in 1995 and a degree from the Criticism Institute at the Academy of Arts in 1990. She is a free-lance computer engineer. She has had several art exhibitions in Egypt. She is a member of the Association of Art Lovers, the Authenticity Association, and the Artists of al-Ghuri Association.

Bardiyat al-ash'ar (Papyri of Poems, poetry). Cairo: Apollo, 1992.

Ahlam al-tami wa-l-fakhkhar (Dreams of Mud and Clay, poetry). Cairo: Dar Misr Press, 1994.

Sifr al-dhuhul (Book of Astonishment, poetry). Cairo: Akhbar al-Yawm Foundation, 1995.

Ra'isa (A Woman President, novel). Cairo: Apollo, 1997.

Nawfal, Hind (1875–1957), Pioneering Lebanese journalist, who emigrated to Egypt and established *al-Fatah* magazine in Alexandria in 1889, in which she defended women's rights. The magazine stopped appearing in 1894. She was educated in Alexandria, where she lived with her parents, writer Maryam Nahhas and journalist Nasim Nawfal.

Nawfal, Maryam Nahhas (1856–1888), Pioneering Lebanese writer born in Beirut. She was educated at the Syrian Anglican School and lived in Egypt after her marriage. She published in *al-Muqtataf.*

Ma'rad al-hasna' fi tarajim al-nisa' min al-amwat wa-l-ahya' (An Excellent Exposition on the Biographies of Famous Women Past and Present, biography). Alexandria: Misr Newspaper Press, 1879.

al-Nawwaf, Sara (1965–), Emirati short-story writer born in Dubai. She has a B.A. in education and psychology. She is the head of the art therapy unit for the city of Dubai (libraries department).

Takh takh (Bang Bang, short stories). Dubai: privately published, 1996.

Nazir, Ruqayya (?–), Saudi poet.

Khafaya qalb (Secrets of a Heart, poetry). Jeddah: Dar al-Bilad Press, 1985.

Shams lan taghib (A Sun That Will Not Set, poetry). Jeddah: Dar al-'Ilm, 1987.

al-Rih wa-l-bahr wa-l-ramad (Wind, Sea, and Ashes, poetry). Jeddah: Dar al-'Ilm, 1989.

al-Rahil (The Departure, poetry). N.p.: Dar Mazin Printing and Publishing, 1995.

Nazzal, Khulud Muhammad (1969–), Palestinian poet.

Tafasil al-hulm al-qadim (Details of the Ancient Dream, poetry). Jerusalem: Palestinian Writers' Union Publications, 1998.

Nazzal, Rana (1969–), Palestinian writer. She has a B.A. and an M.A. in Arabic literature. She has written an unpublished study titled "Qasidat al-nathr wa Unsi al-Hajj" (The Prose Poem and Unsi al-Hajj).

Fima kan (Since It Was, poetry). Beirut: Arab Institute for Research and Publishing, 1998.

N

Ni'ma, Raja' (?–), Lebanese short-story writer and novelist born in Tyre. She received a B.A. in archaeology and history from the Lebanese University in 1968 and a Ph.D. in psychoanalysis from the Sorbonne. She also received a diploma in the sociology of literature. She has worked in development and adult education and has published several studies in literary criticism, including *al-Mar'a fi adab Yusuf Idris* (Women in the Works of Yusuf Idris) and *Sira' al-maqhur ma'a al-sulta: al-tahlil al-nafsi li-adab al-Tayyib Salih* (The Conflict between the Downtrodden and the Authorities: A Psychological Analysis of the Works of al-Tayyib Salih, 1968). She has published children's stories in *al-'Arabi al-saghir*.

Taraf al-khayt (End of the Thread, novel). Beirut: Dar al-Afaq al-Jadida, 1973.
al-Sura fi-l-hulm (The Image in the Dream, short stories). Beirut: Dar al-Afaq al-Jadida, 1979.
Kanat al-mudun mulawwana (The Cities Were Colored, short stories). Cairo: Dar al-Hilal, 1990.
Maryam al-nur (Maryam of Light, novel). Beirut: Dar al-Adab, 1995.

Nizar, Mayada (?–), Iraqi short-story writer.
Hikayat hubb 'Iraqiya (An Iraqi Love Story, short stories). Baghdad: Salma Press, 1986.

Nu'ayna', Salwa (1949–), Egyptian poet born in Alexandria. She received a B.A. in Arabic from Alexandria University in 1975. She is a member of the Agency for the Arts, Humanities, and Social Sciences in Alexandria.
al-Asda' (Echoes, poetry). N.p.: n.p., n.d.

al-Nujum, Manal (1972–), Palestinian poet born in Jerusalem. She has a B.A. in Arabic and Islamic law from the Jordanian University.
Wujuh wa maraya (Faces and Mirrors, poetry). Jerusalem: Palestinian Writers' Union Publications, 1998.

Nu'man, Jumana (1940–), Syrian short-story writer born in Batgharamu. She lives in Damascus. She received a B.A. in philosophy from Damascus University and works in Syrian television in the children's programming department. She has written for *al-Tali'i* and *Usama*.
Sayd al-dhi'b hayyan (Hunting a Wolf Alive, short story). Damascus: al-Tala'i' Organization, n.d.
Subbar (Cactus, children's literature). Lebanon: Dar al-Nawras, n.d.
al-Bahr yuqarrir al-hijra (The Sea Decides to Emigrate, children's literature). Damascus: Arab Writers' Union, n.d.

Numani, Huda (al-Nu'mani, Huda) (1930–), Syrian poet born in Damascus. She received a law degree from Damascus University and later studied humanities and Islamic art at the American University in Cairo. She began to publish in the late 1960s.
Ilayk (To You, poetry). Beirut: Dar al-Nahar Publishers, 1970.
Anamili lam (My Fingers Did Not, poetry). Beirut: Dar al-Kutub, 1971.
Qasidat hubb (A Love Poem, poetry). Beirut: Dar al-Nahar Publishers, 1975.
Adhkur kunt nuqta kunt da'ira (I Was a Point, I Was a Circle, poetry). Beirut: Dar al-Nahar Publishers, 1978.
Ha' tatadahraj 'ala-l-thalj (H. Rolls in the Snow, poetry). Beirut: Dar al-Nahar Publishers, 1982.
Ru'ya 'ala 'arsh (A Vision on a Throne, poetry). Beirut: Arab Institute for Research and Publishing, 1989.
Khatabani qal: Huda ana al-haqq (He Spoke to Me Saying: Huda, I Am the Truth, poetry). N.p.: Huda al-Nu'mani Publishers, 1990.

al-Nunu, Asma' Muhammad Hashim (1928–2000), Yemeni short-story writer born in Sana'a in the generation prior to the revolution. She received some informal education. She is interested in collecting Sana'a folkoric songs and proverbs and has published a book of Yemeni tales and

a book of songs from Sana'a, *al-Aghani al-Sana'aiya* (Songs of Sana'a, songs), Sana'a: al-Ufuq, 1995.
Qissat hayah (A Life Story, autobiography). N.p.: n.p., n.d.

Nur al-Din, 'Afaf (?–), Egyptian poet.
Sharkh fi mira'at al-hubb (A Crack in Love's Mirror, poetry). Cairo: Akhbar al-Yawm Foundation, 1975.

Nuri, Huriya Hashim (Fatat Baghdad) (?–), Iraqi short-story writer. She is also known as Fatat Baghdad.
Dima' wa dumu' (Blood and Tears, short stories in two volumes). Baghdad: al-Hilal Press, 1950 and 1951. Vol. 1 contains "Ba'i'at al-dam" (Peddler of Blood), "Ba'i'at al-atfal" (Peddler of Children), and "Laylat al-hayah" (Night of Life). Vol. 2 contains "Barid al-qadar" (Fate's Mailman) and "Khalisa al-bari'a" (Khalisa the Innocent).

al-Nusur, Basma (1960–), Jordanian short-story writer born in al-Zarqa'. She lives in Jordan. She completed her primary and secondary education in Amman and received a law degree from the Beirut Arab University in 1986. She is an attorney and writes for the press. With Huzama Habayib, she was co-recipient of the Jerusalem Festival for Youth Literature Award in 1993.
Nahw al-wara' (Backwards, short stories). Beirut: Arab Institute for Research and Publishing, 1990.
I'tiyad al-ashya' (Habit, short stories). Amman: Dar al-Shuruq, 1993.
Qabl al-awan bi-kathir (Long Before, short stories). Amman: Dar al-Shuruq, 1999.

Nuwayhid, Nadiya al-Jardi (1929–), Pioneering Lebanese short-story writer born in al-Shuwayfat. After receiving her high school diploma, she immigrated to Brazil and lived there from 1947 to 1957. She established the Women's Agency in the Druze Charitable Association and

published several articles of criticism in newspapers and journals. She wrote a book of biographies of Lebanese women entitled *Nisa' min biladi* (Women from My Country, 1986) and published a book about Simón Bolivar in 1993. She received the Medal of Knowledge in 1986 and the National Cedar Medal (rank of officer) in 1992. She also received a medal of distinction from the president of Venezuela in 1995 for her book on Simón Bolivar.
Wisam al-jurh (Medal of Injury, short stories). Beirut: Nawfal Foundation, 1994.

Nuwaylati, Hiyam (1932–1977), Syrian poet and novelist born in Damascus. She has a B.A. in philosophy from Damascus University. She published articles in the Syrian press and produced a work of nonfiction, *al-Ghazali: 'aqidatuhu wa hayatuh* (al-Ghazali: His Faith and His Life).
Fi-l-layl (At Night, novel). Damascus: Dar al-Sarkha, 1959.
Arsifat al-sa'm (Sidewalks of Tedium, novel, with Umm 'Isam [Khadija al-Jarah al-Nashawati]). Damascus: National Security Press, 1973.
al-Harb (Escape, poetry). Damascus: Khalid al-Tarabishi Press, 1973.
al-Qadiya (The Cause, poetry). Damascus: Khalid al-Tarabishi Press, 1973.
Tishrin (October, poetry). Damascus: n.p., 1973.
Kayf tammahi al-ab'ad (How Distances Are Erased, poetry). Damascus: n.p., 1974.
Madinat al-salam (City of Peace, poetry). Damascus: n.p., 1974.
Washm 'ala-l-hawa' (Love Tattoo, poetry). Beirut: al-Ahliya Publishing and Distribution, 1974.
Zawabi' al-ashwaq (Cyclones of Passion, poetry). Damascus: n.p., 1974.
al-Ma'bar al-khatar (The Dangerous Crossing, poetry). Beirut: al-Ahliya Publishing and Distribution, 1975.
Ya Sham (O Damascus, poetry). Damascus: n.p., 1977.

Prince, Muna (1970–), Egyptian novelist and short-story writer born in Cairo. She has a Ph.D. in English literature. She is an assistant professor at Suez Canal University.
Thalath haqa'ib li-l-safar (Three Suitcases, novel). Cairo: Maktabat Madbuli, 1998.

al-Qaba'ili, Lutfiya (1948–), Libyan short-story writer. She graduated with a degree in geography from al-Fatih University and works in the media. She was the editor of *al-Bayt* magazine for several years.
Amani mu'allaba (Canned Hopes, short stories). Tripoli, Libya: al-Dar al-Jamahiriya, 1977.

Qabbani, Ghaliya (?–), Syrian short-story writer raised in Kuwait. She has worked as a journalist since 1979.
Haluna wa hal hadha-l-'abd (Our Condition and the Condition of This Slave, short stories). Damascus: Dar al-Yanabi', 1993.

Qabbani, Widad (1944–), Syrian short-story writer born in Damascus. She works as a journalist and is a member of the Arab Writers' Union.
Ilayk ya waladi (To You, My Son, short stories). Damascus: al-Thaqafa Magazine Publishers, 1991.
al-Sawt al-ba'id (The Distant Sound, short stories). Damascus: al-'Ilm Press, n.d

Qabil, Thuraya Muhammad (1943–), Saudi poet born in Jeddah. She has a high-school diploma. She was the chief editor of *Zina* magazine from 1986 to 1987 and has been an editor for *al-Bilad* and *'Ukaz* newspapers. She was the first Saudi woman to publish a collection of poetry in the Hijaz.
al-Awzan al-bakiya (The Weeping Rhythms, poetry). Beirut: Dar al-Kutub, 1963.

Qablan, Hiyam Mustafa (1956–), Palestinian poet and short-story writer born in the village of 'Isfiya, near Mt. al-Karmel, in the part of Palestine occupied in 1948. She received her primary education in the village school and attended high school at the Franciscan Sisters' School in Nazareth. She studied history and education at Haifa University. She is an Arabic teacher in the town of Daliyat al-Karmel, where she lives, and she has a regular column, "'Ala ajnihat al-rish" (On the Wings of a Feather), in *al-Sinnara*. Some of her poems have been translated into Hebrew.
Amal 'ala al-durub (Hopes on the Roads, poetry). Haifa: al-'Ataqi Press, 1975.
Hamasat sarikha (Booming Whispers, poetry). Shafa 'Amr: Dar al-Mashriq, 1981.
Wujuh wa safar (Faces and a Journey, poetry). Shafa 'Amr: Dar al-Mashriq, 1991.
Bayn asabi' al-bahr (Between the Sea's Fingers). Shafa 'Amr: Dar al-Mashriq, 1996.
Tifl kharij min mi'tafih (A Child Out of His Coat, short stories). Daliyat al-Karmel: Asiya, 1998.

al-Qadi, Lilian (1960–), Lebanese novelist and short-story writer born in Bayt Mari. She received a B.A. in Arabic literature from the Lebanese University. She writes music and composes anthems and songs. She teaches high school at the Sisters of Bésançon School.
al-Liqa' al-jarih (The Painful Meeting, short story). Beirut: Dar al-Thaqafa, 1993.
Imra'a fawq al-qadar (A Woman above Fate, novel). Beirut: Dar al-Mufid, 1995.

al-Qadi, Nidal (?–), Iraqi short-story writer.
Makan ma'luf ladaya (A Familiar Place of My Own, short stories). Baghdad: Dar al-Shu'un al-Thaqafiya, 1999.

Qahwaji, Munira (1947–), Palestinian short-story writer born in Tiberias. She lives in Irbid, Jordan. She received her education in Irbid and al-Zarqa'.

She studied at the Beirut Arab University. She teaches for schools run by U.N.R.W.A. and owns the Dar Tabariya publishing house.

Atfal al-Quds (The Children of Jerusalem, children's literature). Amman: Dar al-Jahiz, 1984.

Lan arhal (I Will Not Leave, children's literature). Irbid: Irbid Modern Press, 1984.

al-Shaykh Nu'man ya'kul al-subbar fi Bab al-'Umud (Shaykh Nu'man Eats the Cactus at Bab al-'Umud, short stories). Amman: Dar al-Karmel, 1986.

al-Rajul alladhi ba' ra'sah (The Man Who Sold His Head, children's literature). Amman: Dar al-Karmel, 1987.

Nafidhatan 'ala-l-watan (Two Windows on the Homeland, novel). Irbid: Dar Tabariya, 1989.

Rihlat al-hubb wa-l-mawt (Journey of Love and Death, novel). Irbid: Kan'an Press, 1997.

Sanabil li-huqul Filistin (Grain Spikes of the Fields of Palestine). N.p.: n.p., n.d.

Qal'aji, Insaf (1946–), Jordanian short-story writer of Syrian origin. She was born in Haifa. She studied Arabic at the Jordanian University, from which she graduated in 1969. She received an M.A. from the School of Oriental and African Studies at the University of London.

Li-l-huzn baqaya farah (Sorrow Has Remnants of Joy, short stories). Amman: Dar Saba wa 'Aksha, 1987.

Ra'sh al-madina (The City's Tremor, short stories). Amman: Dar al-Karmel, 1990.

al-Nisr fi-l-layla al-akhira (The Eagle on the Last Night, short stories). Beirut: Arab Institute for Research and Publishing, 1999.

Qal'aji, Najwa (?–), Lebanese poet and short-story writer.

Raqiq al-qarn al-'ishrin (Twentieth-century Slave, short stories). Beirut: Arab Institute for Research and Publishing, 1979.

Anwar maliha (Salty Lights, poetry). Beirut: Dar al-'Awda, 1981.

Qasa'id li-Bayrut al-bayda' (Poems to the White Beirut, poetry). Beirut: Dar al-Kitab al-'Arabi, 1994.

Mazamir al-wujud (Psalms of Existence, poetry). Beirut: Dar al-Hamra', 1995.

al-Qalamawi, Suhayr (1911–1987), Pioneering Egyptian writer born in Cairo. She received a B.A. in Arabic language and literature from Cairo University in 1933 and an M.A. and Ph.D. from the same department in 1937 and 1941, respectively. She was one of the first female university students. She studied with Taha Hussein and was the first woman to receive a Ph.D. from the Egyptian University. She was also the first woman to occupy a professorship, in the Arabic department in 1956. She was the head of the Arabic language and literature department at the Research Institute and was the president of the General Egyptian Book Organization at the Ministry of Culture from 1967 to 1971. She was a boardmember of the Writers' Union and a member of the Story Club, the Literary Association, and the Supreme Council for Culture. She was the head of the Committee for Children's Culture, a member of the Supreme Council for Arts, Humanities, and Social Sciences, and an officer of the arts and child committees. She was also the secretary of the women's organization in the Arab Socialist Union in 1975 and occupied the same position in the National Democratic Party from 1977 to 1984. She was an M.P. for al-Ma'adi and Helwan from 1979 to 1984. She was interested in women's issues and took part in many international conferences on the topic. She was awarded a prize from the Language Academy in 1941, the State Encouragement Prize in 1955, and the Medal of Appreciation in 1977. In 1978 she received the Medal of Achievement. Her non-fiction and academic works include *Adab al-Khawarij fi-l-'asr al-Umawi* (Kharijite Literature in the

Umayyad Period, 1945), *Fann al-adab* (The Art of Literature, 1953–1973), *Muhadarat fi-l-naqd al-adabi* (Lectures in Literary Criticism, 1955), *al-Muhaka fi-l-adab* (Mimesis in Literature, 1955), *al-'Alam bayn daffatay kitab* (The World between the Covers of a Book, 1958), *Thumma gharabat al-shams* (Then the Sun Set, 1965), *Dhikra Taha Husayn* (Remembering Taha Hussein, 1974), and *al-Riwaya al-Amrikiya al-haditha* (The Modern American Novel).

Ahadith jaddati (My Grandmother's Stories, short stories). Cairo: Committee for Composition, Translation, and Publishing Press, 1935.

Alf layla wa layla (The Thousand and One Nights, short stories). Cairo: Dar al-Ma'arif, 1943.

al-Shayatin talhu (Devils at Play, short stories). Cairo: Dar al-Qalam, 1964.

al-Qalla, Fathiya (1942–), Palestinian short-story writer and novelist born in Safad. Her family left for Damascus in 1948, and she completed primary and preparatory school in Damascus. She married and moved with her husband to Doha, Qatar. She completed high school and earned a B.A. in Arabic literature from the Beirut Arab University. She lives in Doha.

Kan yushbihuni (He Resembled Me, novel). Beirut: Arab Institute for Research and Publishing, 1997.

al-Intizar (Waiting, short stories). Doha: privately published at al-Dawha Press, 1998.

Li-l-hubb wajh akhar (Love Has Another Face, short stories). Doha: privately published at al-Dawha Press, 1999.

al-Qallini, Rawhiya (1915–1980), Egyptian poet and literary pioneer born in Disuq. Her father was a shaykh with an appreciation for education who sent her to primary school in Tanta and secondary school in Alexandria. She enrolled in Cairo University, from which she obtained a B.A. in Arabic in 1942. After graduation she traveled to Iraq to work in education and became the director of the Mosul Girls' School. She returned to Cairo in 1944 to work in a primary and later a secondary school. She established the Union of Women University Students in Egypt. The last public position she held was director of the General Department of Sabbaticals and Cultural Centers, which awards sabbatical grants to writers and artists in Egypt.

Ibtihalat qalb (A Heart's Supplications, poetry). Cairo: Supreme Council for Islamic Affairs, 1959.

Hamsat al-ruh (Whisper of the Soul, poetry). Cairo: Dar al-Ma'rifa, 1960.

Angham halima (Dreaming Melodies, poetry). Cairo: al-Dar al-Misriya Composition and Translation, 1964.

'Abir qalb (A Heart's Fragrance, poetry). Cairo: Dar al-Kitab al-'Arabi Printing and Publishing, 1968.

Laka anta (For You, poetry). Cairo: al-Dar al-Misriya Composition and Translation, 1970.

Hanini ila (My Longing for . . . , poetry). Cairo: General Egyptian Book Organization, 1975.

'Itr al-iman (Faith's Perfume, poetry). Cairo: Supreme Council to Foster Arts, Humanities, and Social Sciences, 1976.

Rahiq al-dhikrayat (The Nectar of Memories, poetry). Cairo: General Egyptian Book Organization, 1980.

al-Qalyubi, Zinat (?–), Egyptian poet.
Alf layla (A Thousand Nights, poetry). Cairo: n.p., 1992.

Qanawati, Da'd (1944–), Syrian poet born in Hums. She received a B.A. in English literature from the College of Liberal Arts at Damascus University and taught at al-Ba'th University in Hams.

Huzmat al-daw' (A Bundle of Light, poetry). Damascus: Ministry of Culture, 1986.

Qandil, Fatima Hasan (1958–), Egyptian poet born in Suez. She received a B.A. in Arabic from Ain Shams University in 1992. She is an editor at *al-Fusul*, a literary journal, and an assistant instructor at the College of Liberal Arts at Helwan University. She has published poetry and critical studies in Arab journals and periodicals, and some of her poems have been translated into English and French. She published the critical study, *al-Tanass fi shi'r al-sab'inat* (Intertexuality in the Poetry of the 1970s), in 1999. Her play, *al-Layla al-thaniya ba'd al-alf* (The Night After the One Thousand and One Nights), a poetic drama in Egyptian dialect, was staged at the Youth Theater (formerly al-Ghurfa) in the 1991–1992 season.

'Ashan ni'dar ni'ish (So We Can Live, colloquial poetry). Cairo: n.p., 1984.

Samt qutna mubtalla (The Silence of a Wet Cottonball, poetry). Cairo: Dar Sharqiyat, 1995.

Hazr al-tajawwul (Curfew, colloquial poetry). Cairo: n.p., n.d.

Qari, Latifa 'Abd al-Rahim (?–), Saudi poet born in al-Ta'if. She received a B.A. in organic chemistry from King 'Abd al-'Aziz University in Jeddah.

Lu'lu'at al-masa' al-sa'b (Pearl of the Difficult Evening, poetry). N.p.: n.p., 1998.

al-Qasabji, Diya' (1939–), Syrian short-story writer and novelist born in Aleppo. She was educated in Aleppo's schools and studied at the Faculty of Law at Damascus University. She has worked as a teacher and writes for Arab newspapers and magazines. She is also an artist. She is a member of the Story and Novel Association and the Arab Writers' Union.

al-'Alam bayn qawsayn (The World in Parentheses, short stories). Damascus: Dar al-Ajyal, 1973.

al-Qadima min sahat al-zill (Coming from Places of Shade, short stories). Aleppo: al-Maktaba al-'Arabiya, 1979.

Antum ya man uhibbukum (You Whom I Love, short stories). Beirut: Dar al-Afaq al-Jadida, 1981.

Jasad yahdun al-hubb wa yabta'id (A Body Embraces Love and Departs, short stories). Damascus: al-Katib al-'Arabi Press, 1981.

Imra'a fi da'irat al-khawf (A Woman in the Circle of Fear, novel). Tripoli, Libya: General Facility for Publication and Distribution, 1985.

Thuluj dafi'a (Warm Snows, short stories). Damascus: Arab Writers' Union, 1992.

Iha'at (Insinuations, short stories). Damascus: Dar Ishbiliya Research, 1995.

Qasim, Zaynab (?–), Iraqi short-story writer.

Sa'at idafiya (Overtime, short stories). Baghdad: Dar al-Shu'un al-Thaqafiya, 1999.

al-Qasimi, Maysun Saqr (1959–), Emirati poet. She studied political science at Cairo University. In 1989 she began working at the Cultural Complex in Abu Dhabi as the head of the culture department. She became the head of the arts department and later the head of the arts and publishing department. She is an artist as well as a poet.

Hakadha usammi al-ashya' (That's How I Call Things, poetry). Cairo: privately published, 1982.

Kharbashat 'ala jidar al-ta'awidh wa-l-dhikrayat/al-mar'a mashduha bi-l-huruf wa-l-lawn (Scratches on the Wall of Spells and Memories/The Woman Is Perplexed by Letters and Color, poetry). N.p.: privately published, 1990.

al-Wuquf 'ala khara'ib al-rumanisya (Standing at the Ruins of Romance, poetry). N.p.: privately published, 1991.

al-Bayt (The House, poetry). N.p.: privately published, 1992.

Jarayan madat al-jasad (Flow of the Body's Material, poetry). N.p.: privately published, 1992.

al-Rayhuqan (Saffron, poetry). N.p.: privately published, 1992.

al-Sard 'ala hay'atih (Proper Narrative, poetry). N.p.: privately published, 1993.

Makan akhar (Another Place, poetry). N.p.: privately published, 1994.

al-Akhar fi 'atmatih (The Other in His Gloom, poetry). N.p.: privately published, 1995.

al-Qassab, Mi'ad (?–), Iraqi poet.
Hawa' al-'alam (The World's Air, poetry). Najaf: n.p., 1968.

Qatqut, Sa'ida Muhammad (1942–), Egyptian short-story writer born in Rosetta.
Basmat amal (A Smile of Hope, short stories). Cairo: n.p., 1976.
Farasha hawl al-nur (A Moth Around the Light, short stories). N.p.: n.p., 1981.
Ibtisama fi bahr al-dumu' (A Smile in the Sea of Tears, short stories). N.p.: n.p., 1984.
Umm Mu'adh fi-l-sijn (Umm Mu'adh in Prison, novel). N.p.: n.p., 1988.

Qa'war, Nuha Za'rub (1936–), Palestinian poet and playwright born in Nazareth. She completed high school at the city's Baptist school and continued her education through correspondence courses. She studied theology and languages.
Hutaf al-kibriya' (Cry of Hubris, poetry). Nazareth: Venus Press, 1995.
Shajarat al-majd (Tree of Glory, poetic drama). Nazareth: Venus Press, 1995.
Wahaj al-yara' (The Firefly's Glow, poetry). Nazareth: Venus·Press, 1995.

al-Qazwini, Khawla (?–), Kuwaiti novelist. Her non-fiction works include *Rasa'il min hayatina* (Letters from Our Life, 1988).
Mutallaqa min waqi' al-hayah (Divorced from Reality, novel). Beirut: Dar Ahl al-Bayt, 1986.
'Indama yufakkir al-rajul (When Men Think, novel). Beirut: Dar al-Safwa, 1993.
Jirahat al-zaman al-radi' (Injuries of the Wicked Time, novel). Beirut: Dar al-Safwa, 1993.
Sayyidat wa anisat (Married Women and Single Women, novel). Beirut: Dar al-Safwa, 1994.

Mudhakkirat mughtariba (Memoirs of an Exile, novel). Beirut: Dar al-Safwa, 1995.
al-Bayt al-dafi' (The Warm House, novel). Beirut: Dar al-Safwa, 1996.

Qindil, Taghrid (1967–), Jordanian short-story writer born in Irbid. She has a B.A. in English literature. She was awarded the League of Jordanian Writers' Prize for Young Writers in 1985–1986 and the *al-Dustur* Cultural Supplement Prize in 1987.
Armalat al-farah (Widow of Joy, short stories). Amman: n.p., 1995.
Ghada al-bahr (Ghada of the Sea, short stories). Beirut: Arab Institute for Research and Publishing, 1997.

al-Qiyadi, Sharifa (1947–), Libyan short-story writer and novelist born in Tripoli. She received an M.A. in humanities from al-Fatih University for her thesis, *Rihlat al-qalam al-nisa'i al-Libi* (Journey of Libyan Women's Writing), in 1981.
Hadir al-shifah al-raqiqa (Roaring of the Delicate Lips, short stories). Tripoli, Libya: al-Dar al-Jamahiriya, 1983.
Ka'ay imra'a ukhra (Like Any Other Woman, short stories). Tripoli, Libya: al-Dar al-Jamahiriya, 1984.
Hadhihi ana (This Is Me, novel). Libya: Dar al-Hikma, 1997.
Mi'at qissa qasira (One Hundred Short Stories, short stories). Libya: Dar Alfa, 1997.
Ba'd al-hams (Some Whispers, short stories). Libya: Dar Alfa, 1999.

al-Qubasi, Amira Mansur (1948–2001), Lebanese poet born in al-Qasiba in southern Lebanon. She was self-educated and had a natural talent for poetry. She was a member of the Bayt al-Mar'a al-Janubi Association.
Wa sayabqa al-janub (And the South Will Endure, poetry). Beirut: Dar al-Khulud, 1985.
Mawakib al-nur (Processions of Light, poetry). Beirut: Dar al-Khulud, 1999.

Q

al-Qurayni, Janna (1955–), Kuwaiti poet. She received a B.A. in philosophy from Kuwait University in 1980. She works in the office of the secretary-general of the National Council for Culture, Arts, and Humanities.

Min hada'iq al-lahab (From the Gardens of the Blaze, poetry). Kuwait: al-Rabi'an Publishing, 1988.

al-Faji'a (The Misfortune, poetry). Kuwait: Dar al-Kutub, n.d.

Qurman, Su'ad (?–), Palestinian poet born in the village of Ibtin, near Haifa.

Hanin al-hazar (Yearning of the Nightingale, poetry). N.p.: Office of Arab Culture: 1995.

Qurra'a, Saniya (?–), Egyptian novelist. She has published several works of nonfiction, including *al-Bahth 'an al-sa'ada* (The Search for Happiness, 1943), *Sitt al-Mulk al-Fatimiya* (The Fatimid Sitt al-Mulk, 1946), *Nisa' Muhammad* (Muhammad's Women, 1957), *Masajid wa duwal* (Mosques and Countries, 1958), *'Arus al-zuhd Rabi'a al-'Adawiya* (Bride of Asceticism: Rabi'a al-'Adawiya, 1960), *al-Risalat al-kubra* (The Great Messages, 1966), *Tarikh al-Azhar fi alf 'am* (One Thousand Years of the History of al-Azhar, 1968), *Muslimat khalidat* (Immortal Muslim Women, 1972), and *Hikayat Islamiya* (Islamic Stories, 1984).

Udhkuruni (Remember Me, novel). Cairo: al-Sharq al-Islamiya Press, 1940.

Nifirtiti (Nefertiti, novel). Cairo: Kusta Thomas Press, 1945.

al-Iskandar al-akbar (Alexander the Great, novel). Cairo: Maktab al-Sahafa al-Dawli, 1958.

Min wahi al-sama' (Heavenly Inspiration, novel). Cairo: Maktab al-Sahafa al-Dawli, 1958.

Umm al-mamluk (The Mamluk's Mother, novel). Cairo: Maktab al-Sahafa al-Dawli, 1959.

Dhat al-nitaqayn: Asma' Bint Abi Bakr (She of Two Domains: Asma' Bint Abi Bakr, play). Cairo: Maktab al-Sahafa al-Dawli, 1981.

Qurtas, Widad al-Maqdisi (1909–1979), Lebanese pioneer in education born in Beirut. She received her primary education at Ra's Beirut School and the al-Ahliya School for Girls. She continued her education at the Beirut College for Girls and received a B.A. in humanities from the American University of Beirut in 1930. She taught in Baghdad in 1930 and 1931, and she earned an M.A. in humanities from the University of Michigan in 1933. She headed the al-Ahliya School for Women in Beirut for forty years and contributed to the founding and management of several educational institutions. She was a founding member of the Lebanese Academy (1940–1974), a founding member of the National Council for Secondary Education (1960–1974), and a boardmember of trustees at the Institute for Palestinian Studies (1962–1974). She also sat on the board of trustees for the Friends of Jerusalem Association (1960–1972). She received the Lebanese Gold Medal of Achievement in 1960 and the National Cedar Medal (rank of knight) in 1970.

Dhikrayat 1917–1977 (Memories 1917–1977, memoir). Beirut: Arab Research Institute, 1982.

Dunya ahbabtuha (A World I Loved, memoir). Beirut: al-Ahliya Foundation for Printing and Publishing, n.d.

Rabi', Mawahib Sidqi (?–), Egyptian short-story writer and novelist.

Du'a' umm wa qisas ukhra (A Mother's Prayer and Other Stories, short stories). Alexandria: Dar Luran Printing and Publishing, 1964.

Innahu al-qadar (It's Fate, short stories). Alexandria: Dar Nashr al-Thaqafa, 1965.

al-Zujaja al-farigha (The Empty Bottle, novel). Cairo: al-Dar al-Qawmiya Printing and Publishing, 1966.

Rabi', Najat Shawir (?–), Egyptian poet.

Ana ruh sha'ira (I Am a Poet's Spirit, poetry). Cairo: Supreme Council to Foster the Arts, 1984.

al-Rabi'i, Ma'ida (?–), Iraqi novelist and short-story writer. She has a Ph.D. in English language and literature. She has taught at the College of Education in Baghdad since the 1980s.

Jannat al-hubb (Love's Paradise, short stories). Najaf: al-Gharri Modern Press, 1968.

al-Hubb wa-l-ghufran (Love and Forgiveness, novel). Najaf: al-Qada' Press, 1971.

Radwan, Nuha (1968–), Egyptian short-story writer. She studied economics at the American University in Cairo. She has written several stories about women, child laborers, and Palestinian children. She has published in *Sabah al-khayr*.

al-Quyud al-haririya (The Silken Bonds, short stories). N.p.: n.p., n.d.

Ahla min al-safar (Sweeter Than Travel, short stories). N.p.: n.p., n.d.

Rafi', I'tidal (1937–), Syrian short-story writer born in Mt. Lebanon. She received a B.A. in history. She worked at *al-Ba'th* newspaper, for which she wrote a column, "Talk of the Morning" (1982–1990). She then wrote a column, "Horizons," for *Tishrin* in 1991. She also wrote for *Sawt al-Kuwayt* (1990–1991) and *al-Azmina al-'Arabiya* (1989–1991). She published a collection of essays entitled *Bayrut kull al-mudun Shahrazad kull al-nisa'* (Beirut Is All Cities, Sheherazade Is All Women). She is a member of the Story and Novel Association.

Madinat al-Iskandar (Alexander's City, short stories). Damascus: Ministry of Culture, 1980.

Imra'a min burj al-haml (An Aries Woman, short stories). Damascus: Ministry of Culture, 1986.

al-Sifr (The Zero, short stories). Damascus: Dar Ibla, 1988.

Yawm harabat Zaynab (The Day Zaynab Fled, short stories). Damascus: Ministry of Culture, 1996.

Rahil al-baja' (The Swan's Departure, short stories). Damascus: Ministry of Culture, 1998.

al-Raf'i, Salwa (1942–), Egyptian novelist. She received a B.A. from the Institute of Dramatic Arts in 1967 and a B.A. from the Film Institute, screenwriting department, in 1989. She is a member of the National Theater Agency in the Ministry of Culture, the Filmmakers' Syndicate, the Actors' Syndicate, and the Organization for African and Asian Solidarity. Her novel, *Rasasa fi-l-'aql*, has been translated into French. She has written several films, including "Ittihad al-nisa'" (Union of Women), "Nisf shaqqa" (screened as "al-Shaqqa min haqq al-zawja" or The Woman Has a Right to the Apartment), and "al-Atfal fi-l-manfa" (Children in Exile), as well as several television screenplays.

Jasus raghm anfih (An Unwilling Spy, novel). Cairo: Dar al-Hurriya Publishers, 1982.

Karitha taht al-tashtib (A Catastophe in the Making, novel). Cairo: Dar al-Hurriya Publishers, 1986.

Rasasa fi-l-'aql (A Bullet to the Mind, novel). Cairo: General Egyptian Book Organization, 1988.

Sharkh fi jidar al-'aql (A Crack in the Wall of Reason, novel). Cairo: General Egyptian Book Organization, 1990.

D. 'Ismat wa (Dr. 'Ismat and . . . , novel). Cairo: General Egyptian Book Organization, 1994.

Rafiqat al-Tabi'a (see: Fahmi, Zaynab)

Rahbani, Rima (?–), Lebanese poet.

Faj'a (Suddenly, colloquial poetry). Beirut: Dar al-Nahar Publishers, 1996.

al-Rahbani, Salwa (?–), Lebanese novelist.

Wajhi al-akhar (My Other Face, novel). Beirut: Dar al-Fikr al-Lubnani, 1992.

al-Rahbi Mayya, (1954–), Syrian short-story writer and novelist born in Rome. She has a Ph.D. in medicine. She writes literary and medical articles for Syrian newspapers and magazines. She published a medical work, *al-Da' al-sukkari* (Diabetes), in 1986.

Imra'a mutaharrira li-l-'ard (A Liberated Woman for Display, short stories). Damascus: Dar al-Ahali, 1995.
Furat (Furat, novel). Damascus: Dar al-Ahali, 1998.

Rahhal, Ghusun (?–), Palestinian novelist.
Muzayik (Mosaic, novel). Amman: Dar al-Shuruq, 1999.

Rahmat Allah, Zahra (1954–), Yemeni short-story writer born in Aden, where she lives. She has a B.A. in English literature from Aden University. She has been an editor for the Saba' News Agency and the head of the women's magazine published by the Women of Yemen Union. She has published many short stories in Yemeni newspapers and magazines.
Bidaya ukhra (Another Beginning, short stories). Sana'a: Dar al-Hikma, 1994.

al-Ra'i, Luris (1959–) , Lebanese short-story writer born in Tyre. She received a B.A. in sociology and development from the Lebanese University and worked in the Ministry of Social Affairs. She now works as a coordinator at the Center for Field Studies. She has published several articles in the Lebanese press.
al-Mahatta (The Station, short stories). Beirut: Dar al-Jadid, 1995.

Rajab, Muna Muhammad (1953–), Egyptian short-story writer and journalist born in Cairo. She has a B.A. in economics and political science from Cairo University. She is a journalist for *al-Ahram*. She is a member of the Egyptian Writers' Union, the Egyptian Women Writers' Association, the Journalists' Syndicate, and the Huda Sha'rawi Association. She is a founding member and the general secretary of the Authors' Club and a member of the writers' section of the Supreme Council for Culture. Her works have been translated into English and German. She won first prize in cultural news coverage in a competition sponsored by the Journalists' Syndicate in 1987.

She translated the autobiography of Farah Diba from French as *Hayati fi alf yawm wa yawm: sirat hayat Farah Diba* (My Life in a Thousand and One Days: The Life Story of Farah Diba, 1979).
Lu'bat al-aqni'a (The Game of Masks, short stories). Cairo: Dar al-Shuruq, 1984.
'Indama tathur al-nisa' (When Women Rise Up, short stories). Cairo: Dar al-Shuruq, 1991.
Wujuh bila rutush (Faces without Makeup, short stories). Cairo: Dar Gharib Publishing and Printing, 1997.

Rajih, Yasmin 'Abd Allah (1953–), Yemeni poet born in Aden. She received a degree in Arabic from the Higher College of Education. She is a member of the Yemeni Writers' and Authors' Union and has been honored for her literary activities on World Women's Day. Her first piece of literature was the poem, "Sa'at thaljiya" (Icy Hours, 1973). *Al-Hikma* magazine has published three of her poems, including "Hadhayan imra'a tusafir 'ishqan" (The Raving of a Woman Who Travels for Love), "Khatamt 'ala-l-hubb bi-dami" (I Sealed Love with My Blood), and "Raqsa 'ala-l-majamir" (A Dance on the Hot Coals).
Qayd wa in'itaq (Restraint and Release, poetry). Aden: Dar al-Hamdani, n.d.

Ramadan, 'Azza Ahmad Anwar (1968–), Egyptian short-story writer. She has a B.A. in philosophy and a degree in theater. She is a cultural official at the Tal'at Harb Library.
al-Bint allati ahabbat baytan min al-rimal (The Girl Who Loved a House of Sand, children's literature). Cairo: General Authority for Culture Palaces, 1997.
al-'Asafir la tuhalliq ba'idan (The Sparrows Do Not Fly Far, short stories). Cairo: General Authority for Culture Palaces, 1998.
al-Waqt yamurr (Time Passes, children's literature). Cairo: General Authority for Culture Palaces, 1999.

Ramadan, Somaya (Ramada, Sumaya) (1951–), Egyptian short-story writer. She received a B.A. from Cairo University in 1972 and a Ph.D. in Irish literature from Trinity College, Dublin University, in 1982. She is active in the field of women's rights. She joined the Arab Women's Solidarity Group and took part in the international conference it organized in 1984. She was a member of the Egyptian Organization for Human Rights, the Women's Committee, and the Arab Organization for Human Rights. She was the director of the teacher training center at the Misr Languages School from 1990 to 1992. Since 1992, she has worked as a lecturer and translator at the Arts Academy.

Khashab wa nuhas (Wood and Brass, short stories). Cairo: Dar Sharqiyat, 1995.

Manazil al-qamar (Phases of the Moon, short stories). Cairo: Supreme Council for Culture, 1999.

Rashad, Izis Muhammad (?–), Egyptian novelist.

al-Sindbad al-'Arabi fi-l-Jaza'ir (The Arab Sindbad in Algeria, novel). Cairo: Sijill al-'Arab Foundation, 1965.

al-Rashid, 'A'isha (?–), Kuwaiti short-story writer.

9 qisas qasira (Nine Short Stories, short stories). Kuwait: n.p., n.d.

Rashid, Bahija Mahmud Sidqi (192?–), Pioneering Egyptian writer probably born in the 1920s. She is a graduate of the American College for Girls in Cairo. Since the 1940s she has worked in social services and has taken part in many international and Arab women's conferences. She studied pottery, music composition, and song. She was a founding member of the Egyptian Association for Music Lovers in 1942. She also collected and published songs by her husband, Hasan Rashid. She received an honorable mention at the annual International Competition for Folk Arts at the University of Chicago in 1966 for her book, *Aghani wa al'ab sha'biya*

Misriya li-l-atfal (Egyptian Folksongs and Games for Children). She is interested in Egyptian folklore and has transcribed Egyptian folk songs and translated them into English. She has also collected *taqtuq* songs and other forms of popular song from the Nile Valley.

Aghani al-atfal (Children's Songs, poetry). Cairo: Dar al-Ma'arif, 1953.

Aghani al-shabab (Songs of Youth, poetry). Cairo: Dar al-Ma'arif, 1953.

Rashid, Fawziya Muhammad (1954–), Bahraini short-story writer and novelist born in al-Mahraq. She received her high-school degree. She has worked in Dubai at the U.N. office under the Ministry of Housing. Since 1984 she has written for the Sharjah-based *al-Khalij*.

Maraya al-zill wa-l-farah (Mirrors of Shadow and Joy, short stories). Beirut: Dar al-Farabi, 1983.

Kayf sar al-akhdar hajaran (How the Green Became a Stone, short stories). Damascus: Arab Writers' Union, 1988.

Tahawwulat al-faris al-gharib fi-l-bilad al-'Ariba (Transformations of the Knight, a Stranger in Arab Lands, novel). Beirut: Arab Institute for Research and Publishing, 1990.

al-Hisar (The Siege, novel). Cairo: Sina Publishers, 1993.

Ghaba fi-l-'ara' (Forest in the Open Land, short stories). Cairo: Sina Publishers, 1994.

Imra'a wa rajul (A Man and a Woman, short stories). Damascus: Dar al-Mada, 1995.

al-Rashid, Huda 'Abd al-Muhsin (?–), Saudi writer born in al-Qasim. She resides in London. She is an announcer for the Arabic division of the B.B.C.

Nisa' 'abr al-athir (Women over the Ether, short stories). Jeddah: al-Madina Printing and Publishing, 1973.

'Abath (Folly, novel). Cairo: Rose al-Yusuf Foundation, 1977.

Ghadan sayakun al-khamis (Tomorrow Is Thursday, novel). Cairo: Rose al-Yusuf Foundation, 1977.

Talaq (Divorce, play). Cairo: Rose al-Yusuf Foundation, 1992.

Rashid, Khadija Ahmad (?–), Jordanian poet. She works for the Jordanian armed forces in the military culture section and lectures at the Military College.
al-Khulud (Immortality, poetry). Amman: n.p., 1974.
Thulathi al-khulud (The Trio of Immortality, poetry). Amman: Armed Forces Press, 1979.
Jamal al-khulud (The Beauty of Immortality, poetry). Amman: Military Press Office, 1981.
Darb al-khulud (The Path of Immortality, poetry). Amman: n.p., 1986.
Wajadt fik al-khulud (I Found Immortality in You, poetry). Amman: Military Press Office, 1992.
Mawakib al-khulud (Processions of Immortality, poetry). Amman: n.p., 1994.
Nabadat al-khulud (Heartbeats of Immortality, poetry). Amman: Jordanian Armed Forces Press, n.d.

Rashid, Nutayla (Mama Lubna) (1934–), Egyptian journalist and short-story writer. She received a B.A. in philosophy and sociology from Cairo University in 1957. She was the director of *Samir* (1959), the chief editor of children's books at Dar al-Hilal (1966), and the chief editor of *Samir* (1970). She was a member of the Supreme Council for Culture (1970, children's culture committee). She has translated many children's books into Arabic. She received the State Encouragement Prize in children's literature and the Medal of Arts and Sciences in 1980.
Abu Qir wa Abu Sir (Abu Qir and Abu Sir, children's literature). Cairo: Dar al-Hilal, n.d.
Hikayat kifah did al-isti'mar (A Story of Struggle against Colonialism, children's literature). Cairo: Dar al-Hilal, n.d.
Mu'askar al-jazira al-khadra' (Camp of the Green Island, children's literature). Cairo: Dar al-Hilal, n.d.

Tahya al-hayah (Long Live Life, children's literature). Cairo: Dar al-Hilal, n.d.
Yawmiyat 'a'ilat Yasir (Yasir's Family Diary, children's litetature). Cairo: Dar al-Hilal, n.d.

Rashid, Rawiya (?–), Egyptian novelist.
Hawas al-bahr (Folly of the Sea, novel). Cairo: Amadu Publishers, 1992.
Samt al-rih (Silence of the Wind, novel). Cairo: Dar al-I'timad, 1995.

Rashu, Mary (1942–), Syrian novelist and short-story writer born in Latakia. She received only a high-school education. She published her first works in Syrian newspapers and magazines. She is a member of the Story and Novel Association of the Arab Writers' Union. She was awarded a prize from the Friends of Literature and the Novel in Syria in 1991 for her work, *Harwala fawq saqi' Tulidu*.
Wajh wa ughniya (A Face and a Song, short stories). Damascus: Dar Qaws Quzah, 1989.
Qawanin rahn al-qana'at (Rules Bound by Convictions, short stories). Damascus: Arab Writers' Union, 1991.
Harwala fawq saqi' Tulidu (Clamor above the Toledo Frost, novel). Damascus: Dar al-Hisad, 1993.
'Ind al-tilal bayn al-zuhur (At the Hills Among the Flowers, novel). Latakia: Dar al-Hiwar, 1995.
al-Hubb fi sa'at ghadab (Love in a Moment of Anger, novel). Damascus: Dar al-Ahali, 1998.
Tulidu thaniya (A Second Toledo, novel). Damascus: Palmyra Distribution, 1998.
Kalimat fi sahifa muhmala (Words on a Neglected Page, short stories). N.p.: n.p., n.d.

al-Rawda, Maha (?–), Kuwaiti poet.
Diwan al-sha'ira Maha al-Rawda (The Poetry of Maha al-Rawda, colloquial poetry). Kuwait: n.p., 1982.

al-Rawi, Fatima (?–), Moroccan novelist born in Casablanca, where she resides. She stopped publishing many years ago.
Ghadan tatabaddal al-ard (Tomorrow the Earth Will Change, novel). Casablanca: Ambirijima, 1967.

al-Rawi, Sharqiya (1942–), Iraqi poet and short-story writer born in Mosul. She was an active member of many charitable associations in Iraq and took part in drawing up the first anti-illiteracy campaign in the country. She has attended many conferences, including the fifth conference of Arab writers in Baghdad in 1965 and the seventh conference of Arab writers in 1969.
Li-l-sha'b qadiya (The People Have a Cause, poetry). Baghdad: Dar al-Basri, 1970.
'Aynak 'allamatani (Your Eyes Taught Me, short stories). Kuwait: Dar al-Siyasa, 1972.
Anta dir' wa sayf (You Are a Shield and a Sword, poetry and articles). Cairo: Dar al-Hamami Press, 1974.

Rayhan, Rabi'a (1951–), Moroccan short-story writer born in Asifi, Morocco. She is a high-school teacher. She is a member of the Moroccan Writers' Union and was elected to the union's central committee for the 1993–1996 session. She publishes her stories in the Moroccan press. She was awarded the Sharjah Girls' Clubs Prize for Women's Literature in 1998 for her collection, *Matar al-masa'*.
Zilal al-khuljan (Shadows and Gulfs, short stories). Marrakech: Tanmal Printing and Publishing, 1994.
Masharif al-tih (Outskirts of the Wilderness, short stories). al-Muhammadiya: Fudala Press, 1996.
Matar al-masa' (Evening Rain, short stories). Cairo: Girls' Clubs of Sharjah and al-Dar al-Misriya al-Lubnaniya, 1998.
Sharkh al-kalam (The Crack of Speech, short stories). Damascus: Syrian Ministry of Culture, 1999.

al-Rayhani, Lauren (1912–1996), Lebanese short-story writer born in al-Shuwayfat. She was educated at the American University of Beirut. She wrote poetry in English and published poems in *al-Kulliya* magazine in 1937. She headed several associations, including the Young Christian Women's Association in 1965, the Village Revival Association, and the Women of Lebanon Union. She taught English and math in Baghdad and Beirut, and in 1954 she published the magazine, *Dunya al-ahdath*.
Lughat al-suwar (The Language of Pictures, children's literature). Beirut: Dar al-Rayhani, 1957.
'Arus 'ala zahr fil (A Bride on an Elephant's Back, children's literature). Beirut: Dar al-Rayhani, 1955–1963.
Fa'ra tunqidh asadan (A Mouse Saves a Lion, children's literature). N.p.: n.p., 1955–1963.
Ghayma dahika (Laughing Cloud, children's literature). Beirut: Dar al-Rayhani, 1955–1963.
Iram madinat al-dhahab (Iram: The City of Gold, children's literature). Beirut: Dunya al-Ahdath series, 1963–1970.
Bunayy (My Son, children's literature). Beirut: Dar al-Rayhani, 1963–1970.
Jazirat al-nasr (The Eagle's Island, children's literature). Beirut: Dunya al-Ahdath series, 1963–1970.
Samir wa malikat al-bihar (Samir and the Queen of the Seas, children's literature). Beirut: Dunya al-Ahdath series, 1963–1970.
al-'Usfura wa-l-ustura (The Sparrow and the Legend, children's literature). Beirut: Dunya al-Ahdath series, 1963–1970.
Qasr al-ghuyum wa asatir ukhra (The Palace of the Clouds and Other Legends, children's literature). Beirut: Dar al-Rayhani, 1968.
Nadira wa-l-amir Majid (Nadira and Prince Majid, children's literature). N.p.: n.p., n.d.

al-Rayhani, Mayy (1945–), Lebanese poet born in Beirut. She received an M.A. in political science from the American University of Beirut. She lives in Washington. She works in human and economic development and on strengthening women's role in development. Her poetry is characterized by its defiant tone.

Hafr 'ala-l-ayyam (Etching on the Days, poetry). Beirut: Dar al-Rayhani, 1969.

Ismi siwaya (My Name: Someone Else, poetry). Beirut: Dar al-Rayhani, 1974.

Yaliff khasr al-ard (Revolving Around the Earth's Waist, poetry). Beirut: Dar al-Rayhani, 1992.

al-Rayis, Hayat (1954–), Tunisian short-story writer born in Tunis. She has a B.A. in philosophy. She is a member of the Women Short Story Writers' Club.

Layt . . . Hind (Would That . . . Hind, short stories). Tunis: Samid, 1991.

al-Razim, 'A'isha (1952–), Palestinian writer born in the al-Nuway'ma refugee camp in Jericho. She lives in Amman. She went to school in Jericho and Amman. She received a B.A. in Arabic literature from the Beirut Arab University in 1987. She then earned a degree in nursing. She worked as a nurse and in children's education. She has published in newspapers and magazines and has a collection of critical essays entitled *Hiwariyat Samih al-Qasim* (The Dialogic of Samih al-Qasim, 1990).

al-Asir (The Prisoner, short stories). Amman: Dar al-Karmel, 1985.

Marthat al-nusur (The Eagles' Dirge, poetry and prose). Amman: Gharabili Company, 1985.

Junud al-Aqsa (Soldiers of al-Aqsa, poetry). Amman: Gharabili Company, 1986.

'Urs al-shahid (The Martyr's Wedding, poetry). Amman: Dar al-Karmel, 1987.

al-Qalb al-khadda' (The Deceptive Heart, poetry). Amman: Dar al-Quds Publishing and Distribution, 1987.

Hasan al-Filistini wa thawrat al-hijara (Hasan the Palestinian and the Revolution of Stones, poetry). Amman: Dar Ibn Rashid, 1988.

Ila Filistin (To Palestine, short stories). Amman: Dar al-Khawaja Publishing and Distribution, 1991.

'Amman zahra wa naghm (Amman: A Flower and a Melody, poetry). N.p.: n.p., n.d.

Bisan ya Kan'an (Bisan or Kan'an, children's literature). N.p.: n.p., n.d.

Madrasat 'asafir al-watan (The School of the Homeland's Sparrows, children's literature). N.p.: n.p., n.d.

Rida, Amjad Mahmud (?–), Saudi short-story writer born in Jeddah. She received a B.A. in media studies from Cairo University in 1980. In 1991 she was the editorial director of the women's section at *'Ukaz* newspaper.

Hikayat qalb (Stories of a Heart, short stories). N.p.: n.p., 1992.

Rida, Fatima (1903–1978), Lebanese poet born in al-Nabatiya in the south.

Mawawil ta'ir al-khuzam (Wails of the Lavender Bird, poetry). Beirut: n.p., n.d.

Rida, Jalila (1920–2001), Egyptian poet and novelist born in Alexandria. She attended the French Sisters of the Good Shepherd School in Cairo and married before completing her education. She began to compose songs and then wrote Romantic poetry. She was close to Ibrahim al-Naji. She was a member of the poetry committee at the Supreme Council for Arts and Humanities and a member of the Writers' Union. She was awarded the State Encouragement Prize in 1983 for her collection of poetry, *al-'Awda ila-l-mahara*, and the Medal of Arts and Sciences in 1983.

al-Lahn al-baki (The Weeping Melody, poetry). Cairo: Dar Misr Press, 1954.

al-Lahn al-tha'ir (The Furious Melody, poetry). Cairo: al-Misriya Printing and Publishing, 1955.

al-Ajniha al-bayda' (White Wings, poetry). Cairo: al-'Arabiya Printing and Publishing, 1959.

Ana wa-l-layl (The Night and I, poetry). Cairo: al-Nashir al-'Arabi Press, 1961.

Khadsh fi-l-jarra (A Scratch in the Jar, poetic play). Cairo: al-Dar al-Bayda' Printing, Journalism, and Publishing, 1969.

Diwan salah ila-l-kalima (A Prayer to the Word, poetry). Cairo: General Egyptian Book Organization, 1975.

Taht shajarat al-jummayz (Under the Sycomore Tree, novel). Cairo: Supreme Council for Culture, 1975.

al-'Awda ila-l-mahara (Return to the Shell, poetry). Cairo: Maktabat Misr, 1981.

Rida, Nadiya Baydun (?–), Lebanese poet.
Sanabil al-'ata' (Gifts of Grain, poetry). Beirut: n.p., 1971.

Rifaat, Alifa (Rif'at, Alifa) (Fatima Rif'at) (1930–1995), Egyptian novelist and short-story writer born in the village of al-Zahra' in the al-Zaqaziq district. She studied at the Cultural Center for Women's Culture in Hilmiyat al-Zaytun in 1948. She was raised in a conservative environment that did not allow her to write. After her marriage, her husband refused to be married to a public woman so she published under pseudonyms ('Ayda Bint Banha, Alifa, and Fatima Rif'at). Her husband discovered this in 1960 and made her choose between writing and her marriage; she stopped writing. Thirteen years later, her husband allowed her to return to writing on condition that she publish all her works in *al-Thaqafa* magazine. When the editor of *al-Thaqafa* refused to print the story, "'Alami al-majhul," Rifaat published it in *al-Hilal* periodicals in 1974, where it was met with great success. The story was translated into several languages, including English, Dutch, Swedish, and German. A collection of her short stories has been translated into English as *Distant View of a Minaret and Other Stories*.

Hawwa' ta'ud bi-Adam (Eve Returns with Adam, short stories). Cairo: al-Thaqafa al-Usbu'iya Magazine, 1975.

Man yakun al-rajul? (Who Is the Man?, short stories). Cairo: National Center for Arts and Humanities, 1981.

Salat al-hubb (Love's Prayer, short stories). Cairo: Supreme Council for Culture, 1982.

Fi layl al-shita' al-tawil (On the Night of the Long Winter, short stories). Cairo: al-'Asima Press, 1985.

Kad li al-hawa (Love Was Almost Mine, short stories). Cairo: Maktab al-Nil Academic Services, 1990.

Jawharat fir'awn (Pharaoh's Gem, novel). Cairo: Dar al-Hilal, 1991.

al-Rifa'i, Huda 'Abd Allah Hasan (?–), Saudi poet born in Mecca. She received a B.A. in education with a major in Arabic from the College of Education for Girls in Riyadh in 1976 and an M.A. in education from Umm al-Qura University in Mecca in 1992. She has been an Arabic counselor in the Office of Educational Counseling in al-Dammam since 1992.

'Ala shurfat al-azhar (On the Balcony of Flowers, poetry). Cairo: n.p., 1982.

al-Rifa'i, Iqbal (1938–), Syrian poet born in Dayr 'Atiya in the province of Damascus. She was the director of the Center for Rural Development in the Ministry of Social Affairs and Labor and a member of the Poetry Association.

'Indama raka' al-ward (When the Flower Knelt Down, poetry). Beirut: n.p., 1980.

al-Rifa'i, Tal'at (1922–), Syrian poet born in Hums. She received a law degree in 1947 and a Ph.D. in law and economics from the University of Paris in 1955. She works in the secretariat of the Arab League in Cairo.

Mahrajan al-sharq (Festival of the East, poetry). Tripoli, Libya: Maktabat al-Fikr, 1970.

Fatah min al-Quds (A Young Woman from Jerusalem, poetry). Beirut: Dar al-Fikr, 1971.

Tha'ira (A Rebel, poetry). Beirut: Dar al-Fikr, 1971.
Hasna' qahirati (My Beautiful Cairo, poetry). Cairo: n.p., 1990.

al-Rifay'a, Jawahir (1969–), Jordanian short-story writer born in Bi'r Haddad in al-Shawbak, Jordan. She lives in Amman. She was educated in the schools of the Ma'an province and attended the Jordanian University, where she graduated from the Arabic department. She currently works at the Royal Academy for Research on Islamic Civilization. Her stories have been translated into English, Kurdish, and Korean. She was awarded the Su'ad al-Sabah Prize for Fiction in 1996).
al-Ghajar wa-l-sabiya (The Gypsy and the Young Girl, short stories). Amman: Dar al-Azmina Publishers, 1993.
Akthar mimma ahtamil (More Than I Can Bear, short stories). Beirut: Arab Institute for Research and Publishing, 1996.

Rim Husam (see: al-'Asimi, Malika)

Riyad, Evelyne (?–), Egyptian short-story writer. She received a B.A. in English from Cairo University in 1955 and an M.A. in dramatic writing. She was the deputy editor for *Akhir sa'a* and worked for Dar al-Hilal's *al-Musawwar*. Her works have been translated into other languages and she has adapted some of her stories for television.
al-Rajul wa-l-mar'a fi laqatat (Snapshots of Men and Women, short stories). Cairo: n.p., 1987.

Rizq, Shafiqa Iskandar (?–?), Lebanese playwright. She produced her play at the al-Bursa Stage in Zahla in 1925.
al-Ba'isa aw Qayin (The Wretched Woman, or Cain, play). N.p.: n.p., 1925.

Rose al-Yusuf (see: al-Yusuf, Fatima)

Rumaya, 'Atifa (?–), Iraqi poet.
Saqiyat al-khulud (Barmaid of Immortality, poetry). Baghdad: 'Ishtar Press, 1986.

al-Rumayli, Amina al-Waslati (1958–), Tunisian short-story writer born in Salyana. She currently resides in Susa. She graduated from the Higher Teachers' Academy in Tunis in 1982 and received a proficiency certificate in research from the University of Tunis I in 1990. She is a professor of Arabic at the Secondary Institute.
Sakhr al-maraya (Stone of Mirrors, short stories). Tunis: Dar al-Ithaf Publishers, 1998.
Yawmiyat tilmidh . . . hazin (Diaries of a Melancholy Pupil, short stories). Tunis: Dar Sahar Publishers, 1998.

Rushdi, Fatima (1908–1996), Egyptian pioneer and film and stage actress. She began her artistic life in Alexandria at the age of twelve when she sang some of Sayyid Darwish's songs. She went to Cairo with her mother where she met 'Aziz 'Id, who spotted her talent and later married her. In 1923, she joined Yusuf Wahbi's theater troupe, Ramsis.
Fatima Rushdi bayn al-hubb wa-l-fann (Fatima Rushdi between Love and Art, autobiography). Cairo: Sa'di and Shindi Press, 1970.
Kifahi fi-l-masrah wa-l-sinima (My Struggle in the Theater and Cinema, autobiography). Cairo: Dar al-Ma'arif, 1971.

Rushdi, Thuraya (?–), Egyptian novelist.
al-Bunya khatafaha al-jinn (The Building Was Abducted by Genies, novel). Cairo: General Egyptian Book Organization, 1988.

Rushdi, Zaynab (1936–1998), Egyptian short-story writer born in Cairo. She received a B.A. in business from Ain Shams University in 1972. She worked as a television censor and as a screenwriter. She was a member of the Egyptian Women Writers' Association, the Filmmakers'

Syndicate, and the Writers' Union. She wrote many television dramas.

Yahduth ahyanan (It Happens Sometimes, short stories). Cairo: Dar al-Sha'b Foundation, 1975.

Arfud an akun rajulan (I Refuse to Be a Man, short stories). Cairo: Supreme Council for Culture, 1980.

Taghyir al-jild (Shedding the Skin, short stories). Cairo: General Egyptian Book Organization, n.d.

Rustum, Duriya (?–), Pioneering Egyptian short-story writer and journalist. She studied at the College of Liberal Arts and graduated with a B.A. in Arabic from Cairo University. While still a student, she translated several literary works into Arabic. She also studied journalism at the Sorbonne and Oxford through correspondence. She has worked in media departments in several ministries.

Thalath sadiqat (Three Friends, novel). Cairo: Dar al-Qahira Press, 1958.

'Asr al-salam (The Age of Peace, novel). Cairo: Anglo Egyptian Bookstore, 1964.

Ghadan hayah jadida (Tomorrow Is a New Life, novel). Cairo: Anglo Egyptian Bookstore, 1964.

al-Nazzara al-tibbiya (The Glasses, novel). Cairo: Anglo Egyptian Bookstore, 1964.

al-Ha'ira (The Confused Woman, short stories). Cairo: Anglo Egyptian Bookstore, 1965.

Radd al-jamil (Returning the Favor, novel). Cairo: Anglo Egyptian Bookstore, 1965.

Sayyidat al-mata'ib (Woman of Woes, novel). Cairo: Anglo Egyptian Bookstore, 1965.

Qissat raqsat al-thu'ban (The Story of the Snake's Dance, novel). Cairo: Anglo Egyptian Bookstore, 1967.

Ikhtafa al-shaytan (Satan Disappeared, novel). Cairo: Anglo Egyptian Bookstore, 1970.

al-Mudarrib al-akbar wa dahh wa bahh (The Big Coach, novel). Cairo: Anglo Egyptian Bookstore, 1971.

Mamnu' mamnu' (Forbidden Forbidden, novel). Cairo: Anglo Egyptian Bookstore, 1972.

al-Ba'd yufaddilunaha 'ariya (Some Prefer Her Naked). Cairo: Dar al-Sha'b, 1973.

Fi-l-zill (In the Shade, novel). Cairo: Dar al-Sha'b, 1973.

S

Sa'ada, Mayy Hanna (1916–), Pioneering Lebanese poet born in Amyun in the district of al-Kura. She received a B.A. in medicine from the American University of Beirut in 1942. She works as a doctor in al-Jumayzat.

Awraq al-'umr (Papers of a Lifetime, poetry). Beirut: Fikr Foundation, 1982.

Last wahdi (I Am Not Alone, poetry). Beirut: n.p., 1997.

Sa'b, 'Afifa Fandi (1900–1986), Pioneering Lebanese journalist born in al-Shuwayfat. She was educated at the English School in Beirut and at the National al-Shuwayfat School. She published the monthly women's literary magazine, *al-Khidr* (1919–1927), and, with her sister, established the al-Sarat School in 'Aliya in 1925. She published in *al-Muqtataf* and *Sawt al-mar'a*. She also contributed to the book, *al-Waqi' al-Durzi wa hatmiyat al-tatawwur* (The Druze Reality and the Inevitability of Development, 1962).

Dawhat al-dhikra (The Great Tree of Memory, memoir). Al-Shuwayfat: n.p., n.d. (Sa'b wrote the introduction).

Saba, Miray (?–), Lebanese poet and novelist. She lives in Australia and works at the news division of the Australian Lebanese Arab Foundation for Broadcasting as a presenter for a program on Arab community issues. She is editor in chief for *al-Farasha*, issued in Australia, and was editor in chief for the Australian *al-Bayraq* from 1993 to 1995. She selected and translated the poems in *Antulujiya al-shi'r al-Ustrali al-hadith* (An Anthology of Modern Australian Poetry) and won a prize in a short-story competition. She published *Qisas muhajira* (Immigrants' stories) and has been published in the Arabic and Australian press.

al-'Afaf al-jarih (Wounded Chastity, novel). Beirut: privately published, 1984.

Raqsat al-ghubar (The Dance of Dust, poetry). Beirut: Mukhtarat, 1995.

al-Sabah, Hidaya Sultan al-Salim (?–), Kuwaiti short-story writer. She had a degree in women's education. She was a member of the Kuwaiti Journalists' Association and the Kuwaiti Teachers' Association. She became the first Kuwaiti woman to own and edit a magazine, *al-Majalis*, a Beirut-based magazine she bought in 1970. Al-Salim began to write for the press from as early as 1961. She was assassinated in 2001. She published several historical and literary studies, including *Awraq min dafatir musafira fi-l-Khalij* (Pages from the Notebooks of a Traveler in the Gulf, 1968), *Ahmad al-Jabir ra'id al-nahda al-haditha fi-l-Kuwayt* (Ahmad al-Jabir: Pioneer of the Modern Renaissance in Kuwait, 1980), and *Nisa' fi-l-Qur'an al-Karim* (Women in the Qur'an).

Kharif bila matar (An Autumn Without Rain, short stories). Kuwait: al-Risala Press, 1973.

al-Sabah, Su'ad Muhammad (1941–), Kuwaiti poet. She received a B.A. in political science and economics from Cairo University in 1973 and a Ph.D. from the University of Surrey in England. She is a member of the Arab Thought Forum and the founder of Dar Su'ad al-Sabah Publishers in Kuwait and Cairo. Her non-fiction works include *al-Suq al-nafti al-jadid: al-Sa'udiya tastaridd zamam al-mubadara* (The New Petroleum Market: Saudi Arabia Retakes the Initiative, 1986), *al-Ubik bayn tajarib al-madi wa malamih al-mustaqbal* (OPEC Between Past Experience and Future Scenarios, 1986), and *Saqr al-Khalij 'Abd Allah al-Mubarak al-Sabah* (Falcon of the Gulf: 'Abd Allah al-Mubarak al-Sabah, 1995).

Lahazat min 'umri (Moments from My Life, poetry). Beirut: Dar al-Yawm Publishers, 1964.

Umniya (A Wish, poetry). Cairo: Dar al-Ma'arif, 1971.

Ilayk ya waladi (To You My Son, poetry). Cairo: Dar al-Ma'arif Press, 1982.

Fatafit imra'a (Fragments of a Woman, poetry). Baghdad: Asfar Publications, 1986.

Fi-l-bad' kanat al-untha (In the Beginning Was Woman, poetry). London: Riyad al-Rayyis Books and Publishing, 1988.

Hiwar al-ward wa-l-banadiq (Conversation of the Flower and the Rifles, poetry). London: Riyad al-Rayyis Books and Publishing, 1990.

Akhir al-suyuf (The Last Sword, poetry). Kuwait: Dar Su'ad al-Sabah, 1992.

Qasa'id hubb (Love Poems, poetry). Kuwait: Dar Su'ad al-Sabah, 1992.

Imra'a bila sawahil (A Woman Without Shores, poetry). Kuwait: Dar Su'ad al-Sabah, 1994.

Khudhni ila hudud al-shams (Take Me to the Borders of the Sun, poetry). Kuwait: Dar Su'ad al-Sabah, 1997.

al-Qasida untha wa-l-untha al-qasida (The Poem Is Woman and Woman Is the Poem, elegiac poems). Kuwait: Dar Su'ad al-Sabah, 1999.

Wamdat bakira (Early Gleams). N.p.: Kuwait, 1961.

Sabbagh, Najla (?–?), Lebanese writer.

Rihla bayn al-Wilayat al-Muttahida wa Suriya wa Lubnan (A Journey to the United States, Syria, and Lebanon, travel literature). Beirut: al-Adabiya Press, 1911.

al-Sabbagh, Zinat (1935–), Egyptian poet and playwright born in Cairo. She graduated from the English department at Cairo University in 1959 and worked as an English teacher in Egypt, Kuwait, and Saudi Arabia. She began to work with the Akhbar al-Yawm News Group in 1969.

Thalath masrahiyat ijtima'iya siyasiya (Three Sociopolitical Plays, plays). Cairo: Dar al-Nashr al-'Arabi, 1984.

Jarati Hatshibsut (My Neighbor Hatshepsut, short stories). Cairo: General Egyptian Book Organization, 1987.
Baqaya hubb (Remnants of Love, poetry). Cairo: Dar al-Nashr al-'Arabi, n.d.

Sabir, Khayriya (1946–), Egyptian poet. She has a law degree and works as an attorney.
Kimiya' al-hubb (The Chemistry of Love, poetry). Cairo: n.p., 1993.
Sahil al-masafa (Whinny of the Distance, poetry). Cairo: n.p., 1994.

Sabira (see: al-'Izzi, Khadija Mahmud)

al-Sabunji, Nisrin Muhammad (1937–), Iraqi poet born in al-Sulaymaniya. She received a Ph.D. in linguistics (Kurdish) from Kirov University in the Soviet Union in 1965. She was a professor in the College of Education at Baghdad University. She attended a conference on Near East studies in the U.S. in 1978. She started publishing in 1957 with the poem, "al-Lahn al-akhir" (The Final Melody). She has published a book on linguistics, *al-Al'ab al-sha'biya* (Folk Games).
Ana fi jurhik al-nazf (I Am the Bleeding in Your Wound, poetry). N.p.: n.p., 1986.

Sa'd al-Din, Sumaya (1952–), Egyptian poet born in Cairo. She received her B.A. from the College of Communications at Ain Shams University, an M.A. from the Advanced Studies Institute for Childhood at Ain Shams University, and a Ph.D. in philosophy from the same institution. She is the assistant deputy editor of *al-Akhbar* newspaper.
Qarar imra'a (A Woman's Decision, poetry). Cairo: Dar al-'Alam al-'Arabi Press, 1994.

al-Sa'dawi, Nawal (1931–), Egyptian author and physician born in Kafr Tahla. She received a B.A. in medicine from the College of Medicine at Ain Shams University in 1955. She received an M.A.

from Columbia University in New York in 1966, as well as a Ph.D.. She has written several works on psychology and the humanities. She has a special interest in women's issues, and most of her works address these issues and women's relationship to men and society. She was employed as a doctor at the Ministry of Health from 1955 to 1972. She was also the director of the health education department at the ministry from 1966 to 1972. She has been a consultant for UNIFEM in Addis Ababa and Beirut and a visiting professor at Duke University. She received an honorary doctorate from York University in 1994 and from the University of Illinois in 1996. She has received many prizes and awards, most important an award from the Supreme Council for the Arts and Humanities in 1974, the Medal of Achievement from Libya in 1989, and the Gibran Literature Prize, as well as an award from the Arab League in Australia. She takes part in many social and cultural activities. She is a founding member of the Arab Organization for Human Rights, the founder and head of the Arab Women's Solidarity Group, the chief editor of *Nun*, a magazine she publishes, the founder and deputy head of the African Women's League for Research and Development, and the founder of the Egyptian Women Writers' League. She is also the general secretary of the Medical League in Cairo. Her works have been translated into English, French, German, Spanish, Persian, Indonesian, Turkish, Dutch, and other languages.
Ta'allamt al-hubb (I Learned Love, short stories). Cairo: n.p., 1957.
Lahzat sidq (Moment of Truth, short stories). Cairo: n.p., 1959.
Mudhakkirat tabiba (*Memoirs of a Woman Doctor*, novel). Cairo: General Egyptian Book Organization, 1960.
Imra'atan fi imra'a (*Two Women in One*, novel). Beirut: Dar al-Adab, 1971.
al-Khayt wa-l-jidar (The Thread and the Wall, short stories). Cairo: n.p., 1972.

S

Imra'a 'ind nuqtat al-sifr (*Woman at Point Zero*, novel). Beirut: Dar al-Adab, 1973.

al-Khayt wa 'ayn al-hayah (*The Well of Life and The Thread*, two novellas). Beirut: Dar al-Adab, 1976.

Mawt al-rajul al-wahid 'ala-l-ard (*God Dies by the Nile*, novel). Beirut: Dar al-Adab, 1976.

al-Ughniya al-da'ira (*The Circling Song*, novel). Beirut: Dar al-Adab, 1976.

Kanat hiya al-ad'af (*She Was the Weaker*, short stories). Beirut: Dar al-Adab, 1977.

Ithna 'ashar imra'a fi zinzana wahida (*Twelve Women in One Cell*, play). Cairo: n.p., 1984.

Mudhakkirat fi sijn al-nisa' (*Memoirs from the Women's Prison*, memoir). Cairo: Dar al-Mustaqbal al-'Arabi, 1984.

Izis (*Isis*, play). Cairo: n.p., 1985.

Hanan qalil (*A Little Sympathy*, short stories). Beirut: Dar al-Adab, 1986 (second printing).

Rihlati hawl al-'alam (*My Travels Around the World*, travel literature). Cairo: Dar al-Hilal, 1986.

al-Gha'ib (*Searching*, novel). Beirut: Dar al-Adab, 1987 (second printing).

Suqut al-imam (*The Fall of the Imam*, novel). Cairo: Dar al-Mustaqbal al-'Arabi, 1987.

Mawt ma'ali al-wazir sabiqan (*Death of an Ex-minister*, short stories). Beirut: Dar al-Adab, 1988 (third printing).

Mudhakkirat tifla ismuha Su'ad (Memoirs of a Child Named Su'ad, novel). Cairo: Dar Tadamun al-Mar'a al-'Arabiya, 1990.

Jannat wa Iblis (*The Innocence of the Devil*, novel). Beirut: Dar al-Adab, 1992.

al-Hubb fi zaman al-naft (*Love in the Kingdom of Oil*, novel). Cairo: Maktabat Madbuli, 1994.

al-Saddani, Nuriya al-Salih (1946–), Kuwaiti short-story writer. She studied television direction in Cairo in 1965 and has worked at Kuwait television and radio. She helped found the Kuwaiti Women's Union (1974–1977). Her non-fiction works include *al-Haraka al-nisa'iya al-'Arabiya fi-l-qarn al-'ishrin* (The Arab Women's Movement in the Twentieth Century, 1983), *Tarikh al-mar'a al-'Umaniya* (The History of Omani Women), and *Tarikh al-mar'a al-Kuwaytiya* (The History of Kuwaiti Women).

al-Hirman (Deprivation, story). Kuwait: n.p., 1972.

Wahat al-'ubur (Oasis of Crossing, story). Kuwait: al-Saddani Foundation, 1972.

Sa'di, Nura (1956–), Algerian poet and short-story writer born in Valma. She attended the Teachers' Institute in Algeria. She is a professor of Arabic literature and an editor of *al-Jaza'iriya* magazine. She was a program researcher at Algerian radio in 1977.

Jazirat al-hulm (The Dream Island, poetry). Qasantina: Dar al-Ba'th, 1983.

Aqbiyat al-madina al-hariba (Cellars of the Fleeing City, short stories). Algeria: al-Wataniya Book Foundation, 1989.

'Ubur al-mamarrat al-sa'ba (Crossing the Difficult Passages, novel). N.p.: n.p., n.d.

Sadiq, Su'ad (?–), Egyptian writer.

Rasa'il Su'ad al-gharamiya: ajmal wa ajra' rasa'il al-hubb (Su'ad's Love Letters: The Boldest, Most Beautiful Love Letters, letters). Cairo: al-Dar al-Haditha li-l-Qari' al-'Arabi, 1995.

Sadiq, Zaynab (1935–), Egyptian journalist and short-story writer born in Cairo. She received a B.A. in journalism from Cairo University in 1958. She writes on social affairs and is a journalist for *Sabah al-khayr*. Her stories have been translated into German, Italian, Bulgarian, and English. She received the Media Shield from the College of Communications at Cairo University in 1998. Her non-fiction works include *al-Hubb wa-l-zawaj* (Love and Marriage, 1986) and *Idarat al-'awatif* (Management of Emotions, 1998).

Yawm ba'd yawm (Day After Day, novel). Cairo: Dar al-Hilal, 1969.

'Indama yaqtarib al-hubb (When Love Draws Nigh, short stories). Cairo: Rose al-Yusuf Foundation, 1971.

La tasriq al-ahlam (Don't Steal the Dreams, novel). Cairo: Rose al-Yusuf Foundation, 1978.

Hadha-l-naw' min al-nisa' (That Type of Woman, short stories). Cairo: Dar Gharib, 1981.

Anqidhni min ahlami (Save Me from My Dreams, short stories). Cairo: Dar Gharib, 1983.

Anta shams hayati (You Are the Sun of My Life, short stories). N.p.: Dar al-Ma'arif, 1987.

Da' minha fi-l-ziham (She Lost It in the Crowd, short stories). Cairo: General Egyptian Book Organization, 1987.

Umniyat fi daw' al-qamar (Wishes in the Moonlight, short stories). Alexandria: al-Mustaqbal Publishers and Printers, 1987.

Yawmiyat imra'a mutallaqa (Diaries of a Divorcée, novel). Cairo-Alexandria: al-Mustaqbal Publishers and Printers, 1994.

Nasim al-saba (The East Wind, short stories). Cairo: General Authority for Culture Palaces, 1997.

Akhir layali al-shita' (The Last Night of Winter, novel). Cairo: Dar Qiba', 1998.

Hikayat Zaynab Sadiq (Tales of Zaynab Sadiq, tales). Cairo: General Egyptian Book Organization, Family Library Series, 1999.

al-Sadr, Amina Haydar (Bint al-Huda) (1937–1980), Iraqi novelist and short-story writer born in al-Kazimiya. She lived there until the age of eleven, when she moved to al-Nafaj. She was instructed at home by her brothers, Ayatollah Isma'il al-Sadr and Muhammad Baqir al-Sadr. Since religious institutions of higher education in Najaf did not admit women, she completed her education in Islamic studies and modern sciences through private tutors. She wrote novels, short stories, and poetry and published her complete works of fiction in three volumes.

Sira' (Conflict, short stories). Najaf: al-Adab Press, 1964.

al-Fadila tantasir (Virtue Triumphs, novel). Baghdad: Ufsit al-Mina' Press, 1969.

Imra'atan wa rajul (Two Women and a Man, short stories). Baghdad: Dar al-Anwar Publications, 1977.

al-Khala al-da'i'a (The Lost Aunt, novel). N.p.: Ufsit al-Mina' Press, 1978.

Liqa' fi-l-mustashfa (A Meeting in the Hospital, novel). Baghdad: al-Andalus Press, 1979.

al-Majmu'a al-qisasiya al-kamila (The Complete Works of Fiction, three vols.). Beirut: Dar al-Ta'aruf Publications, n.d. Vol. 1 contains *al-Fadila tantasir*, *Laytani kunt a'lam* (I Wish I Had Known), and *Imra'atan wa rajul*. Vol. 2 contains *Sira' ma'a waqi' al-hayah* (Conflict with the Facts of Life), *Liqa' fi-l-mustashfa*, and *al-Khala al-da'i'a*. Vol. 3 contains *al-Bahitha 'an al-haqiqa* (Searching for the Truth), *Kalima wa da'wa* (A Word and an Invitation), *Dhikrayat 'ala tilal Makka* (Memories on the Hills of Mecca), *Butulat al-mar'a al-Muslima* (The Heroism of the Muslim Woman), and *al-Mar'a ma'a al-nabi* (Women with the Prophet).

Saduf al-'Amiriya (see: al-Na'ib, Fatina)

al-Sa'dun, Nasira (1946–), Iraqi novelist born in al-Hayy in the province of Wasit. She received a B.A. in economics and political science from Baghdad University in 1966. She was the director of the economic office at the Arab Union for Food Industries. She is the president of the Women's Cultural Forum and a member of the Authors' Union.

Law damat al-afya' (If Shadows Endured, novel). Baghdad: Babel Press, 1986.

Dhakirat al-madarat (Memory of the Orbits, novel). Baghdad: Bayt Sin Books, 1989.

Safadi, Dalal Khalil (?–?), Lebanese short-story writer. She published a book in English on Arabic songs and proverbs, and she published translations from English in *al-'Urfan* magazine in Sidon in 1932.

Hawadith wa 'ibar (Incidents and Lessons, story). Najaf: al-Ra'i Press, 1937.

Arba'un qissa haqiqiya waqi'iya (Forty Real Life Stories, short stories). Canada: al-Amrikiya Press, 1965.

Safi, Salwa (1935–), Lebanese short-story writer born in al-'Ibadiya. She received her high school diploma from al-Sarat College in 'Aliya and published several stories in *al-Hasna'*, *Samar*, and *al-Sayyad*.

Hadiqat al-sukhur (Rock Garden, short stories). Beirut: Dar al-Nahar Publishers, 1969.

al-Sahili, Shafiqa (1955–), Tunisian short-story writer born in Tunis. She received her primary education at a convent school and her secondary education at the Nahj Marseilles Institute for Girls. She received a B.A. in 1975. She initially worked as a secretary and later at the Ministry of Culture, the National Library, and for radio and television. She is a member of the Tunisian Writers' Union. She has published in Tunisian literary papers and journals.

Imra'a ta'tarif (A Woman Confesses, short stories). Tunis: privately published, 1984.

al-Sahrawi, Fatima (?–), Egyptian poet.

al-'Umr fi 'aynayk (Life in Your Eyes, poetry). Giza: Center Line Press, 1988.

al-Rasm bi-l-lawn al-a'maq (Painting with the Darker Color, short stories). Cairo: al-Ahram Press, 1990.

al-Sa'id, Amina (1910–1995), Egyptian writer born in Asyut. She was educated at the Shubra Secondary School and received a B.A. in English from Fu'ad I University in 1934. She was the first female student to enroll in the English department. She started working in journalism in 1934 and became the first woman to head the Dar al-Hilal institution in 1976. She was also editor in chief of *Hawwa'* magazine. She was well known for the column, "Ask Me," which she began editing in 1945 and continued to edit for fifty years. She was interested in women's issues and involved in many activities. She was the president of the Egyptian Women Writers' Association and a member of the Writers' Association. She was awarded the Medal of Achievement, the Medal of the Republic, and Medal of Arts and Sciences. She translated several books and published several collections of essays as books, as well as children's books she wrote with Sayyid Qutb and Yusuf Murad.

Awraq al-kharif (Autumn Leaves, short stories). Cairo: Dar al-Ma'arif, 1943.

al-Jamiha (The Defiant Woman, novel). Cairo: Dar al-Ma'arif, 1950.

Wujuh fi-l-zalam (Faces in the Dark, novel). Cairo: Dar al-Hilal, 1963.

al-Hadaf al-kabir wa qisas ukhra (The Big Goal and Other Stories, short stories). Cairo: al-'Arabiya Printing and Publishing, 1985.

Sa'id, Fifi (?–), Egyptian playwright.

al-Rijala fi khatar (The Men Are in Danger, play). Cairo: Akhbar al-Yawm Press, 1972.

Sa'id, Hadiya (1947–), Lebanese short-story writer and screenwriter. She received a liberal arts B.A. from the Beirut Arab University in 1969. She has worked for several Arabic newspapers in Lebanon, Iraq, and Morocco. She currently lives in London.

Hurufuna al-jamila (Our Beautiful Letters, children's literature). Baghdad: Ministry of Culture, 1975.

Hikayat al-sa'at al-jamila (A Story of the Lovely Hours, screenplay). Baghdad: General Film Organization, 1976.

Tahqiq 'an Umm Hamid (An Exposé about Umm Hamid, screenplay). Baghdad:

General Organization for Radio and Television, 1979.

Urjuhat al-mina' (The Port's Swing, short stories). Beirut: Arab Institute for Research and Publishing, 1981.

Ya layl (O Night, short stories). Beirut: Dar al-Sadaqa, 1987.

Nisa' kharij al-nass (Women Outside the Text, short stories). Rabat: Babel Publications, 1989.

Rahil (Departure, short stories). Rabat: African Arab Publishers, 1989.

Bustan aswad (Black Garden, novel). Beirut: Arab Institute for Research and Publishing, 1996.

Sa'id, Hala Ahmad (?–), Egyptian poet.
'Aynak ayyami (Your Eyes Are My Days, poetry). Cairo: Egyptian Association to Foster Talent, 1995.

Sa'id, Salwa (1945–), Palestinian poet born in Jenin in the West Bank. She has a B.A. in psychology from the University of California. She has worked in education and journalism.

Agharid li-l-hubb wa-l-manfa (Warblings for Love and Exile, poetry). Amman: Dar al-Shuruq, 1985.

Sarkhat 'ala jidar al-samt (Screams on the Wall of Silence, poetry). Amman: Shuqayr wa 'Uksha Printing and Publishing, 1987.

Ishti'alat imra'a Kan'aniya (Flames of a Canaanite Woman, poetry). Amman: Dar al-Karmel, 1988.

Nawaris bila ajniha (Wingless Gulls, poetry). Beirut: Arab Institute for Research and Publishing, 1992.

Ad'uk li-hadha-l-ihtiraq (I Invite You to This Burning, poetry). Amman: Dar al-Karmel, 1995.

Li-l-habib alladhi fi rida'i (To the Beloved in My Cloak, poetry). Beirut: Arab Institute for Research and Publishing, 1999.

al-Sa'id, Sana' (?–), Palestinian poet born in Nazareth in the part of Palestine occupied in 1948.

Lan aqul wada'an (I Will Not Say Goodbye, poetry). Nazareth: n.p., 1986.

Lana nuqush 'ala janahay farasha (We Have Inscriptions on the Butterfly's Wings, poetry). Nazareth: al-Jamahir Media Center, 1988.

al-Sa'idi, 'Ayda (?–), Lebanese short-story writer. She received a B.A. in media studies in 1983 and an M.A. in education in 1997.

Asabi' Maryam (Maryam's Fingers, short stories). Beirut: al-'Alamiya Books, 1999.

al-Sa'idi, Nuriya (?–), Iraqi novelist and short-story writer.

Fi zinzanat al-hayah (In Life's Cell, short stories). Baghdad: al-'Abayiji Press, 1978.

al-Hams al-samit (The Silent Whisper, novel). Baghdad: al-'Abayiji Press, 1978.

al-Sa'igh, Rihab Husayn (?–), Iraqi poet.
Qasa'id la tuhzin (Poems That Do Not Sadden, poetry). Mosul: n.p., 1998.

al-Sa'igh, Salma (1889–1953), Lebanese writer and pioneer born in Beirut. She was educated at the Zahrat al-Ihsan convent school and was a student of the author, Ibrahim al-Mundhir. She taught in schools run by the al-Maqasid Islamic Charitable Association and at the secular French School. She worked in translation and founded the Women's Awakening Association, the Zahrat al-Ihsan, and the Women's Union. She was fluent in both Arabic and French. She immigrated to Brazil and lived there from 1939 to 1947. She joined the Andalusian League. Her most important writings were articles, speeches, and lectures published in the press. She published a memoir, *Suwar wa dhikrayat*, in 1946 and another book on Pierre Loti, who lived in the East and wrote stories about his attachment to the land and peoples of the East. Her most famous work is *al-Nasamat* (Breezes), published in 1923, which is a collection of her essays compiled by Jurji Niqula Baz. The book is marked by the style of the Mahjar (exile) school of writers. Critic Rose Ghurayyib considers Sa'igh a pioneer of poetic prose. Sa'igh was awarded the Lebanese Gold Medal of Achievement, but refused to accept it.

Mudhakkirat sharqiya (Memoirs of an Eastern Woman, memoir). n.p., n.d.

Suwar wa dhikrayat (Images and Memories, memoir). São Paolo: Dar al-'Arabiya for Printing and Publishing, 1946.

Sakakini, Widad (1913–1991), Pioneering Lebanese-Syrian novelist, short-story writer, and critic born in Sidon. She was educated at the al-Maqasid Islamic College and taught at the Higher Institute for Girls before devoting herself to writing. She had several critical debates, the most prominent being with Tawfiq al-Hakim. She published her many essays and critical studies in *al-Khatarat* (Thoughts, 1943), *Ummahat al-mu'minin* (Mothers of the Faithful, 1945), *Insaf al-mar'a* (Justice for Women, 1950), *al-'Ashiqa al-mutasawwifa Rabi'a al-'Adawiya* (The Sufi Lover Rabi'a al-'Adawiya, 1955), *Sawad fi bayad* (Black on White, 1956), *Nisa' shahirat min al-sharq wa-l-gharb* (Famous Women from the East and West, with Tamadir Tawfiq, 1959), *Nuqat 'ala-l-huruf* (Dots on Letters, 1960), *Qasim Amin* (Qasim Amin, 1965), *Zawjat al-rasul wa akhawat al-shuhada'* (The Prophet's Wives and Martyrs' Sisters, 1968), *'Umar Fakhuri* ('Umar Fakhuri, 1970), *Shawk fi-l-hasid* (Thorn in the Harvest, 1981), and *Sutur tatajawab* (Lines in Harmony, 1987).

Maraya al-nas (People's Mirrors, short stories). Cairo: Lajnat al-Nashr li-l-Jami'iyin, Maktabat Misr, 1945.

Bayn al-Nil wa-l-nakhil (Between the Nile and the Palm Tree, short stories). Cairo: Dar al-Fikr al-'Arabi, 1947.

al-Hubb al-muharram (Forbidden Love, novel). Cairo: Dar al-Fikr al-'Arabi, 1947.

Arwa bint al-khutub (Arwa, Daughter of Woe, novel). Cairo: Dar al-Fikr al-'Arabi, 1949.

al-Sitar al-marfu' (The Raised Curtain, short stories). Cairo: Akhbar al-Yawm Foundation, 1955.

Nufus tatakallam (Souls Speak, short stories). Cairo: Akhbar al-Yawm Foundation, 1962.

Aqwa min al-sinin (Stronger Than the Years, short stories). Damascus: Union of Arab Writers, 1978.

al-Sakhawi, 'Ayda Ibrahim (1959–), Egyptian poet born in Kafr al-Shaykh.

Harfayn izaz (Two Glass Letters, colloquial poetry). Central Delta: General Authority for Culture Palaces, 1998.

Salah, Huda (193?–), Palestinian short-story writer born in Nablus. She attended the Quaker College in Ramallah and received a high-school diploma in London.

Dam'atan (Two Tears, short stories). Amman: Dar al-Sharq Press, n.d. (Most likely written in the 1950s.)

Salahian, Lucy (?–), Syrian short-story writer and poet born in Aleppo. She sponsors a literary salon for Syrian and Armenian writers who write in Arabic and Armenian.

al-Qulub al-ha'ira (Confused Hearts, short stories). Aleppo: n.p., n.d.

Salaliha, Hadiya (1968–), Palestinian novelist born in Bayt Jann in the part of Palestine occupied in 1948. She received her early education in the village and earned a B.A. from Haifa University.

Ajras al-rahil (Bells of the Departure, novel). Shafa 'Amr: Dar al-Mashriq Printing, Translation, and Publishing, 1989.

Salama, Fawziya (?–), Egyptian short-story writer and journalist.

Shari' Wahdan (Wahdan Street, short stories). Cairo: Akhbar al-Yawm Foundation, 1991.

Salama, Hind (?–), Lebanese novelist and poet. She published a work of non-fiction, *al-Nisa'iyat wa-l-khamriyat fi-l-Tawrah* (Women and Wine in the Torah), in 1950. She has written sentimental literature and prose poems.

Alhan da'i'a (Lost Melodies, novel). Beirut: al-Istiqlal Press, 1950.

Amwaj (Waves, poetry). Beirut: al-Ma'arif Press, 1952.

al-Hijab al-mahtuk (The Torn Veil, poetry). Beirut: Dar al-Thaqafa Publishers, 1962.

Fi ma'badi (In My Temple, poetry). Beirut: n.p., 1964.

al-Duma al-hayya (The Living Dolls, novel). Beirut: Commerical Office for Printing and Publishing, 1968.

Samra' al-shati' (Brown Girl of the Shore, novel). Beirut: Ma'tuq Brothers, 1973.

Lam' (Gleam, poetry). Sidon: al-Maktaba al-'Asriya, n.d.

Salama, Maryam (1965–), Libyan poet and short-story writer born in Tripoli. She graduated from the English department of al-Fatih University. She works as a translator at the department of historical documents and studies for the Old City Project in Tripoli. Her literary works have been published in Libyan and Arab magazines and newspapers.

Ahlam tifla sajina (Dreams of an Imprisoned Child, poetry). Libya: Dar al-Firjani, 1992.

La shay' siwa al-hulm (Nothing But the Dream, poetry). Libya: Dar al-Firjani, 1992.

Salama, Salma al-Shaykh (1959–), Sudanese short-story writer born in 'Atbara. She lives in Cairo. She received a B.A. from the Higher Institute for Music and Theater in 1987. She works in radio. She is the head of the culture desk at the international paper, *al-Ittihadi*, in which she has a regular column entitled "Area of Love of the Nation." She has published many short stories and some studies in periodicals and newspapers.

Atfal al-samgh (Children of Glue, short stories). Cairo: General Egyptian Book Organization, 1993.

Matar 'ala jasad al-rahil (Rain on the Body of the Departed, short stories). Cairo: al-Ittihad Printing and Publishing, 1998.

Ibn al-nakhil (Son of the Palm, short stories). Cairo: n.p., 1999.

Salama, Salwa (1883–1945), Pioneering Syrian short-story writer. She immigrated to Brazil in 1914 and established *al-Karma*, an Arab women's magazine, in São Paolo, which she continued to publish for thirty years. She collected her lectures and published them as *Jarrat al-mann* (Jar of Manna) and *Hadiqat khutab* (Garden of Lectures, 1928). She also published *Tarikh al-Barazil* (The History of Brazil) in 1946.

Amam al-mawqid (In Front of the Fireplace, short stories). São Paolo: Dar al-'Arabiya Printing and Publishing, 1941.

Salem, Ibtihal (Salim, Ibtihal) (1949–), Egyptian short-story writer born in Giza. She received a B.A. in psychology from Ain Shams University in 1974. She worked as an executive director at al-Samir Theater, run by the General Authority for Culture Palaces, and as a translator for cultural programs for Egyptian radio. She is a member of the Association of Egyptian Women Writers. Several of her stories have been translated into English, German, and French.

al-Nawras (The Seagull, short stories). Cairo: General Egyptian Book Organization, 1989.

Dunya saghira (Small World, short stories). Cairo: General Egyptian Book Organization, 1992.

Nakhb iktimal al-qamar (A Toast to the Full Moon, short stories). Cairo: General Authority for Culture Palaces, n.d.

Saliba, Rula (?–), Lebanese poet born in the northern town of Bataghrin. She received a B.A. in Arabic language and literature from the Lebanese University. She worked as the coordinator for Arabic literature of the al-Matn Public Secondary School for Girls, of which she is now director. She has published essays of criticism in *al-Diyar*.

Wa lakin al-bahr (But the Sea, poetry). Beirut: Dar al-Nahar Publishers, 1993.

Salih, Arwa (1951–1997), Egyptian writer. She received a B.A. in English from Cairo University in 1974. She was an active member of the student movement and later in political life. She worked in translation and journalism.

al-Mubtasarun: dafatir wahida min jil al-haraka al-tullabiya (The Premature Ones: Papers of a Member of the Student Movement, autobiography). Cairo: Dar al-Nahr for Publishing and Distribution, 1996.

Saratan al-ruh (Cancer of the Spirit, poetry). Cairo: Dar al-Nahr for Publishing and Distribution, 1998.

Salih, Layla Muhammad (?–), Kuwaiti short-story writer. She has a B.A. in Arabic from the Beirut Arab University. She works for the Ministry of Information and is a cultural and literary program researcher for Kuwaiti radio. She has been interested in documenting women's literature in the Gulf, and her contributions to the field include *Adab al-mar'a fi-l-Jazira al-'Arabiya wa-l-Khalij al-'Arabi* (Women's Literature in the Arabian Peninsula and Gulf, two vols., 1983 and 1987), *Adab al-mar'a fi-l-Kuwayt* (Women's Literature in Kuwait, 1986), and *Udaba' wa adabiyat al-Kuwayt* (The Authors and Literature of Kuwait, 1996).

Jirah fi-l-'uyun (Wounds in the Eyes, short stories). Kuwait: al-Yaqza Press, 1986.

Liqa' fi mawsim al-wurud (A Meeting in the Season of Flowers, short stories). Kuwait: Dar Su'ad al-Sabah, 1994.

al-Salih, Nidal (?–), Syrian novelist.

Hajar al-mawta (Stone of the Dead, novel). N.p.: n.p., 1991.

Salih, Salima (1942–), Iraqi short-story writer born in Mosul. She has worked in journalism.

Fi rakb al-hayah (In Life's Cavalcade, short stories). Mosul: al-Jumhuriya Press, 1961.

Li-annak insan (Because You Are a Human Being, short stories). Baghdad: Telegraph Press, 1963.

al-Tahawwulat (Transformations, short stories). Damascus: Arab Writers' Union, 1975.

Zahrat al-anbiya': yaqzat al-dhakira (Flower of the Prophets: Memory Awakened, autobiographical fragments). Damascus: Dar al-Mada, 1994.

Shajarat al-maghfira (The Tree of Forgiveness, short stories). Damascus: Dar al-Mada, 1996.

Salih, Samiya Khidr (?–), Egyptian short-story writer born in Cairo. She received an M.A. from Ain Shams University in 1983 and a Ph.D. in 1986. She is a professor at the College of Education at Ain Shams University. She has published several works on unemployment and women's political participation.

'Abr nafidha fi Baris (Through a Window in Paris, short stories). Cairo: n.p., 1981.

Lahazat 'umr hariba (Fleeting Moments of a Life, short stories). Cairo: n.p., 1987.

al-'Azf 'ala awtar al-zaman (Playing the Strings of Time, short stories). Cairo: Anglo Egyptian Bookstore, 1995.

Salih, Saniya (1935–1986), Syrian poet born in Misyaf (Hama). She studied English literature at Damascus University and worked as a civil servant. She was a member of the Poetry Association.

al-Zaman al-dayyiq (Narrow Time, poetry). Sidon: al-Maktaba al-'Asriya, 1964.

Jisr al-i'dam (Execution Bridge, poetry). Beirut: Dar al-Ajyal, 1969.

Qasa'id (Poems, poetry). Beirut: Dar al-'Awda, 1980.

al-Ghubar (Dust, short stories). Beirut: Fikr Foundation for Research and Publication, 1982.

Dhakar al-ward (The Male Rose, poetry). London: Riyad al-Rayyis Books and Publishing, 1988.

Salim, Fatima (1942–), Tunisian short-story writer born in Tunis. She received her early education in Tunis. She earned a pedagogical certificate from the Teachers' School in 1961 and graduated from the College of Islamic Law and the Fundamentals of Religion in 1974. She has taught in Tunisia and the Gulf. She was the editorial supervisor at *al-Mar'a*, the organ of the Feminist Union. She is a member of the Story Club and the Tunisian Writers' Union. She has taken part in many conferences and seminars on women and literature in Tunisia and abroad.

Nida' al-mustaqbal (Call of the Future, short stories). Tunis: Dar al-Kutub al-Sharqiya, 1972.

Tajdif fi-l-Nil (Rowing on the Nile, short stories). Tunis: Dar al-Kutub al-Sharqiya, 1974.

Nisa' wa aqlam (Women and Pens, short stories). Tunis: Tunisian Employment Union Press, 1995.

Salim, Ghada (?–), Iraqi short-story writer.

al-Hawiya (The Abyss, short stories). Baghdad: 'Ishtar Press, 1987.

al-Salim, Latifa (1951–), Saudi short-story writer born in Mecca. She received a B.A. in English from the College of Education for Girls run by the General Office for Girls' Education. She has been an administrative counselor for the college since 1986. She is a member of the al-Wafa' Women's Charitable Association in Riyadh.

al-Zahf al-abyad (The White March, short stories). Riyadh: Saudi Story Club, 1982.

Salim, Layla Saya (1933–), Syrian short-story writer born in Latakia. She received a degree in philosophy and worked as an instructor in teaching academies. She received a B.A. in pedagogy from Aleppo University. She writes children's stories and is a member of the Story and Novel Association.

al-Qitt al-kaslan (The Lazy Cat, children's literature). Beirut: Dar al-Fata al-'Arabi, 1975.

al-Sulhufah al-hakima (The Wise Turtle, children's literature). Beirut: Dar al-Fata al-'Arabi, 1975.

Najm li-Samir (A Star for Samir, children's literature). Damascus: Arab Writers' Union, 1977.

Awraq min al-ard al-muhtalla (Papers from the Occupied Land, children's literature). Damascus: Tala'i' al-Ba'th Publications, 1978.

al-Bilad al-jamila (The Beautiful Countries, children's literature). Damascus: Ministry of Culture Publications, 1978.

al-Farah (The Wedding, children's literature). Damascus: Arab Writers' Union, 1979.

Rihlat himar yud'a Ghandur (The Journey of a Donkey Named Ghandur, children's literature). Damascus: Ministry of Culture Publications, 1981.

Hikayat al-muluk wa-l-ru'ah (Stories of Kings and Subjects, children's literature). Damascus: Arab Writers' Union, 1985.

Mudhakkirat tayyar (Memoirs of a Pilot, children's literature). Damascus: Arab Writers' Union, 1985.

Salma sayyidat al-ghaba al-saghira (Salma: Mistress of the Little Forest, children's literature). Damascus: Ministry of Culture Publications, 1987.

Intaliq ya bisat al-rih (Spread Out, Flying Carpet, children's literature). Damascus: Tala'i' al-Ba'th Publications, n.d.

Salima (see: Abu Rashid, Salma)

Sallum, Alice (?–), Lebanese poet.

Sammamt an ahwak ya sayyidi (I'm Determined to Love You, Sir, poetry). Beirut: Dar al-Afaq al-Jadida, 1983.

La li-l-harb na'm li-l-hubb (No to War, Yes to Love, poetry). Beirut: Arab Institute for Research and Publishing, 1985.

Arhal ma'a al-zaman (I Go with Time, poetry). Beirut: Arab Institute for Research and Publishing, 1987.

Untha taht al-raml (A Woman under the Sand, poetry). Beirut: Dar al-Afaq al-Jadida, 1990.

Najmat sa'd (Lucky Star, poetry). Beirut: Dar al-Afaq al-Jadida, 1993.

Sallum, 'Aziza (1967–), Iraqi poet born in al-Khalidiya in the province of al-Anbar. She completed her primary and preparatory education and graduated from a teachers' institute. She was appointed a teacher.

'Udhran anni istabaht al-haqiqa (Sorry That I Seized the Truth, poetry). Baghdad: n.p., 1984.

Salman, Nur (1937–), Lebanese novelist, poet, and short-story writer born in Beirut. She received a B.A. in Arabic literature from the Beirut College for Girls (later the American Lebanese University), an M.A. in comparative literature from the American University of Beirut, and a state doctorate in Arabic literature from St. Joseph University in Beirut. She is a professor of Arabic literature at the Lebanese University. She has written several works in comparative literature and literary criticism, including: *al-Shi'r al-sufi* (Sufi Poetry, 1980), *al-Adab al-Jaza'iri fi rihab al-rafd wa-l-tahrir* (Algerian Literature in the Broad Expanses of Rejection and Liberation, 1981), *al-Lughat al-Samiya wa-l-lugha al-'Arabiya* (Semitic Languages and Arabic, 1981), *Madkhal ila dirasat al-shi'r al-ramzi fi-l-adab al-hadith* (Introduction to the Study of Symbolic Poetry in Modern Literature, 1981), and *Adwa' 'ala-l-tasawwuf al-Islami* (Illuminating Sufism, 1982). She is a boardmember of the National Conservatory and a member of the Lebanese Child Care Association and the Lebanese Women's Council.

Fadahikat (And She Laughed, novel). Beirut: Dar al-Nashr li-l-Jami'iyin, 1960.

Yabqa al-bahr wa-l-sama' (The Sea and Sky Remain, short stories). Sidon: al-Maktaba al-'Asriya, 1966.

Ila rajul lam ya'ti (To a Man Who Did Not Come, poetry). Beirut: Al-'Alamiya Books, 1986.

al-'Ayn al-hamra' (The Red Eye, short stories). Beirut: Riyad al-Rayyis Books and Publishing, 1991.

Li-fajr yashuqq al-hajar (Toward a Rock-splitting Dawn, poetry). Beirut: privately published with al-Nahhal Foundation for Printing and Advertising, 1994.

Lan utfi' al-wajd (I Will Not Snuff Out Love, poetry). Beirut: al-Nahhal Foundation, 1997.

Salman, Suhayla Dawud (1937–), Iraqi novelist and short-story writer born in Baghdad. She received a B.A. in Arabic language and literature from Baghdad University in 1957. She worked for the Ministry of Housing and later the Ministry of Culture and Information. She was the director of the Music and Ballet School from 1976 to 1980, after which she was appointed a language specialist at Dar al-Ma'mun for Translation and Publishing. She has lived in and traveled to various countries in the Arab world, Europe, and Africa. She began writing in the early 1960s, publishing short stories in magazines and newspapers based in Beirut.

Intifadat qalb (Uprising of the Heart, short stories). Sidon-Beirut: Dar al-Maktaba al-'Asriya Publications, 1966.

Wa faj'a abda' bi-l-surakh (And Suddenly I Start to Scream, short stories). Beirut: Dar al-Maktaba al-'Asriya Publications, 1976.

Kan ismuh Dari (His Name Was Dari, short stories). Baghdad: Dar al-Shu'un al-Thaqafiya Publications and the Ministry of Culture and Information, 1978.

al-Liqa' (The Meeting, short stories). Baghdad: Dar al-Shu'un al-Thaqafiya Publications and the Ministry of Culture and Information, 1988.

al-Qahr (Subjugation, novel). Amman: Dar al-Sabah Journalism and Publishing, 1994.

al-Tariq al-sari' (The Fast Road, six short stories and a novel). Amman: Dar al-Sabah Journalism and Publishing, 1994.

al-Samadi, Ibtisam (1956–), Syrian poet born in the province of Dar'a. She lives in Damascus. She received a B.A. in English literature and a diploma in educational rehabilitation. She teaches at Damascus University and runs a literary salon, the Tuesday Salon.

Safira fawq al-'ada (Ambassador-at-Large, poetry). Damascus: Dar al-Yanabi', 1990.

Hiya wa ana wa shu'un ukhra (She and I and Other Things, poetry). Damascus: Dar al-Yanabi', 1995.

Samara, Munya (195?–), Palestinian poet. She works in journalism and translation.

Kitab al-nahr wa-l-bahr wa ma baynahuma (The Book of the River and the Sea and What Lies Between, poetry). London: Riyad al-Rayyis Books and Publishing, 1992.

Samara, Nuha (1944–1992), Palestinian writer born in Tulkarm. She moved to Lebanon with her family in 1948. She worked in journalism, editing the cultural and women's issues columns at *al-Muharrir* and *al-Nahar* from the mid-1960s to the mid-1970s. With the beginning of the Lebanese civil war, she moved to London and then settled in Cyprus, where she worked at *al-Shahid* magazine for eight years. A collection of her articles was published posthumously as *al-Mar'a al-'Arabiya: nazra mutafa'ila* (Arab Women: An Optimistic View) in 1993.

Fi madinat al-mustanqa' (In the City of the Swamp, novel). Beirut: Dar al-Afaq al-Jadida, 1973.

al-Tawilat 'ashat akthar min Amin (The Tables Lived Longer Than Amin, short stories). Beirut: Zuhayr Ba'labakki Publications, 1981.

Samir, Wisal (1940–), Syrian novelist and poet born in Damascus. She has a B.A. in Oriental languages (Hebrew) from Cairo University and a degree in Eastern literatures. She worked as a lecturer at the Liberal Arts College at Damascus University and taught at the Political Science College and the Institute for Scientific Preparation. She is the head of the Hebrew section of Syrian radio. She is a member of the Story and Novel Association and a founder of the Journalists' Union in Syria.

Laysat jarimati (It's Not My Crime, short stories). Damascus: n.p., 1993.

Zayna (Zayna, novel). Damascus: al-Ahali Press and Publishing, 1990.

'Ariyan ya'tik sawti (Naked My Voice Comes to You, poetry). Damascus: Dar al-Ahali, 1996.

La adri sirr mahabbati (I Don't Know the Secret of My Love, poetry). Damascus: al-Thaqafa Magazine, 1997.

Hin ghadiba al-qamar (When the Moon Grew Angry, short stories). Damascus: Arab Writers' Union, 1998.

Samira Bint al-Jazira al-'Arabiya (see: Khashuqji, Samira Muhammad)

al-Samirra'i, Lahib 'Abd al-Khaliq (1956–), Iraqi poet born in Baghdad. She received a degree in tourism from the College of Management and Economics at al-Mustansiriya University in 1980. She has worked in the media and as an editor for *al-Jumhuriya*. She has attended the Marbad Poetry Festival, the Jarash Poetry Festival (1989), and the National Palestinian Council in Algeria (1991).

Inkisarat li-tufulat ghusn (Ruptures in a Bough's Childhood, poetry). Baghdad: 'Ishtar Press, 1987.

Watan wa khubz wa jasad (Country, Bread, and Body, poetry). N.p.: n.p., 1993.

al-Samman, Dima (196?–), Palestinian novelist born in Jerusalem. She graduated from Birzeit University in 1987. She is a member of the administrative organization of the Palestinian Writers' and Authors' Union.

al-Asabi' al-khafiya (Hidden Fingers, novel). Jerusalem: Dar al-Katib, 1992.

al-Dil' al-mafqud (The Lost Rib, novel). Beirut: Palestinian Writers' Union and Dar al-'Awda, 1992.

al-Qafila (The Caravan, novel). Kafr Qar': Dar al-Huda, 1993.

Janah daqat bihi al-sama' (A Wing Too Big for the Sky, novel). Umm al-Fahm: Ibda' Foundation, 1995.

Samman, Ghada (al-Samman, Ghada) (1942–), Syrian novelist and short-story writer born in Damascus. She lives between Beirut and Paris. She received a B.A. in English from Damascus University and an M.A. from the American University of Beirut. She worked as a lecturer in the Liberal Arts College at Damascus University and as a journalist and preparer of radio programs. She is a member of the Story and Novel Association. She established a publishing house, Ghada al-Samman Publications, in 1977. She has collected and published her press writings in a series of books entitled *al-A'mal ghayr al-kamila* (The Incomplete Works). These include *al-Qabila tastajwib al-qatila* (The Tribe Questions the Murdered Woman) and *al-Bahr yuhakim samaka* (The Sea Prosecutes a Fish).

'Aynak qadari (Your Eyes Are My Fate, short stories). Beirut: Dar al-Adab, 1962.

La bahr fi Bayrut (There's No Sea in Beirut, short stories). Beirut: Dar al-Adab, 1963.

Rahil al-marafi' al-qadima (Departure of the Ancient Ports, short stories). Beirut: Dar al-Adab, 1973.

Bayrut 75 (*Beirut 75*, novel). Beirut: Dar al-Adab, 1975.

Kawabis Bayrut (*Beirut Nightmares*, novel). Beirut: Dar al-Adab, 1976.

A'lant 'alayk al-hubb (I Declared Love on You, texts). Beirut: Ghada al-Samman Publications, 1978.

I'tiqal lahza hariba (The Arrest of a Fleeting Moment, texts). Beirut: Ghada al-Samman Publications, 1979.

al-Hubb min al-warid ila-l-warid (Love from Vein to Vein, texts). Beirut: Ghada al-Samman Publications, 1981.

Laylat al-milyar (*The Night of the First Billion*, novel). Beirut: Ghada al-Samman Publications, 1986.

Ashhad 'aks al-rih (I Witness Against the Wind, texts). Beirut: Ghada al-Samman Publications, 1987.

al-Qamar al-murabba' (*The Square Moon*, short stories). Beirut: Ghada al-Samman Publications, 1994.

'Ashiqa fi mahbara (A Lover in an Inkwell, poetry). Beirut: Ghada al-Samman Publications, 1995.

al-Riwaya al-mustahila: fusayfisa' Dimashqiya (The Impossible Novel: A Damascus Mosaic, novel). Beirut: Ghada al-Samman Publications, 1997.

Sanjab, Najah (?–), Lebanese poet and critic born in Tannurin. She received a degree from the Holy Spirit University and a B.A. in education from the Lebanese University. She taught Arabic literature and philosophy at several high schools and worked as an editor for the theological journal, *Bilbiya*, published by Dayr al-Ma'unat in Jubayl. She is the secretary of the Cultural Forum in Jubayl. She translated a book on Greek religious civilization into Arabic.

Atin bila ajniha (Coming Without Wings, poetry). al-Bawar: Dakkash Press, 1989.

Li-ta'ti al-'asifa (Let the Storm Come, poetry). 'Amshit: 'Amshit Press, 1996.

al-Saqqaf, Khayriya Ibrahim (1951–), Saudi short-story writer born in Mecca. She received a B.A. in English from King Sa'ud University in 1974, an M.A. in teaching methodologies and curricula from the U.S. in 1976, and a Ph.D. in Arabic language and literature. She is an assistant professor in the curricula department at King Sa'ud University. She was the dean of the Center of University

Studies for Girls and has also been the editorial director of *al-Riyad*. She is the recipient of several awards, among them the Shield of Women's Leadership in Education in the kingdom in 1980, the Silver Jubilee Shield of King Sa'ud University in 1982, and the Silver Jubilee Shield of *al-Riyad* newspaper, awarded by the founders of the paper in 1990. Her stories have been translated into English and other languages. Her non-fiction works include *Manahij wa turuq dirasa wa tadris al-adab fi-l-jami'at al-Sa'udiya* (Methods for Studying and Teaching Literature at Saudi Universities, 1998) and *Ma'zaq fi-l-mu'adala* (A Dilemma in the Equation, a collection of essays).

An tubhir nahw al-ab'ad (To Sail toward the Distances, short stories). Riyadh: Dar al-'Ulum Publishers, 1982.

al-Saqqat, Thuraya (1935–1992), Moroccan poet born in Fez. She was a teacher in Casablanca. She was a member of the Moroccan Writers' Union and the women's department in the Socialist Union Party. She used this position to defend women's issues and raise awareness of their importance. She wrote poetry and children's stories.

Manadil wa qudban (Kerchiefs and Bars, prison letters). Casablanca: Dar al-Nashr al-Maghribiya, 1988.

Ughniyat kharij al-zaman (Songs Outside Time, poetry). Casablanca: 'Uyun al-Maqalat Publications, 1990.

al-Labu'a al-bayda wa qisas ukhra (The White Lioness and Other Stories, children's literature). Casablanca: Dar al-Atfal Publications, 1988.

Sarhan, Hala (?–), Egyptian writer. She has a B.A. in English from Cairo University, an M.A. from Louisville University, and a Ph.D. in theater from George Washington University. She was the deputy editor of the Cairo-based *Kull al-nas* and the editor in chief of *Sayyidati sadati* magazine. Her non-fiction works include *al-Madam marfu'a mu'aqqatan min al-khidma* (The Mrs. Is Temporarily Out of Order, a collection of essays) and *Qalat Shahrazad: aktub lakum min al-haramlik* (Sheherazade Said: I Write to You from the Harem, 1990). *Amrika khabt lazq: mudhakkirat taliba ba'tha* (America Head On: Memoirs of a Foreign Student, memoir). Cairo: Dar al-Shuruq, 1995.

Sari al-Din, Rajiya (?–), Lebanese poet.
Sada al-samt (The Echo of Silence, poetry). Beirut: Arab Center for Research and Documentation, 1999.

Sa'ud, In'am (?–), Kuwaiti short-story writer.
Saqatat muzlima (Dark Slip-ups, short stories). Kuwait: al-Rabi'an Publishing, 1998.

Saudi, Fathieh (Sa'udi, Fathiya) (1949–) (see also: Bibliography of Works in French), Jordanian writer and physician born in Amman. She studied medicine in France and graduated from the College of Medicine at the University of Paris in 1977. She moved to Lebanon, where she documented the siege of Beirut by Israeli forces in 1982. She lives in Amman, where, in addition to her work as a pediatrician, she writes, translates, and publishes. Her non-fiction works include *Sihhat al-atfal: dalil al-ummahat* (Children's Health: A Guide for Mothers, Amman, Dar al-Mada, 1977). She has translated two books on children's health.

Ayyam al-jamr: hisar Bayrut 1982 (Days of Embers: The 1982 Siege of Beirut, memoirs). Amman: Dar al-Mada, 1990; first published in French as *L'Oubli rebelle*. Paris: Harmattan Publishers, 1985.

al-Sa'udi, Muna (1949–), Jordanian poet and artist born in Amman. She graduated from the College of Arts in Paris in 1967. She has worked in photography, painting, and sculpture, and has painted and designed many book covers. She published *Shahadat al-atfal fi zaman*

S

al-harb (Testimonies of Children in a Time of War, drawings of children from refugee camps). (Beirut: Mawaqif Publications, 1970.)

Ru'ya ula (A First Vision, poetry and illustrations). Beirut: Mawaqif Publications, 1972.

Muhit al-hulm (Dream Ocean, poetry and illustrations). Amman: Dar al-Mada Publishers, 1992.

al-Sa'udi, Naziha (?–), Algerian short-story writer.

al-Hubb fi zaman al-harib (Love in the Time of the Fugitive, short stories). Qasantina: Dar al-Ba'th, 1983.

Sawalha, Julia (1905?–), Jordanian novelist born in Ma'daba. She was educated in Amman and Jerusalem. She ran the first seamstress shop in Ma'daba in 1925.

Salwa (Salwa, novel). Amman: al-Tawfiq Press, 1976.

al-Nashmi (A Man of Courage, novel). Amman: Association of Cooperative Presses, 1978.

Hal tarji'in (Are You Coming Back, novel). Amman: al-Safadi Press, 1979.

al-Haqq al-da'i' (The Lost Right, novel). Amman: Shahin Press, 1984.

Nar wa ramad (Fire and Ash, novel). Amman: Shahin Press, 1984.

al-Yatima (The Orphan, novel). Amman: Shahin Press, 1985.

Sawaya, Labiba Mikha'il (1876–1916), Pioneering Lebanese poet and novelist born in Tripoli. She graduated from the Higher American School for Girls in 1892 and later taught there for five years. She moved to Syria where she taught in schools and served as the principal of a national school in Hums, where she died. She composed poetry and wrote articles for *al- Mabahith al-Tarabulusiya*, and wrote for *al-Mawrid al-safi* and *Lisan al-ittihad*. She also translated novels and stories.

Hasna' Salunik (The Beauty of Salonica, novel). Damascus: Orthodox Patriarch Press, 1909.

al-Sawi, Amina (1922–1988), Egyptian writer. She was educated at the Acting and Theater Institute and wrote radio dramas. She adapted for radio great dramatic works, such as Naguib Mahfouz's *Zuqaq Midaqq* (Midaq Alley), and received a prize for theatrical adaptation. She gained renown as a pioneer in Islamic dramatic works. She received the State Medal of Appreciation in the Creative Arts in 1978. She published several works of non-fiction, including *al-Tafsir al-drami li-l-qisas al-Qur'ani* (A Dramatic Interpretation of Qur'anic Stories), *Bidayat al-bidaya: qissat Adam wa Hawwa'* (The Beginning of the Beginning: The Story of Adam and Eve), *al-Bidaya: qissat Nuh 'alayhi al-salam* (The Beginning: The Story of Noah), *al-Bidaya: qissat Hud 'alayhi al-salam* (The Beginning: The Story of Hud), *al-Bidaya: qissat Salih 'alayhi al-salam* (The Beginning: The Story of Salih), and *al-Bidaya: qissat Ibrahim 'alayhi al-salam* (The Beginning: The Story of Abraham).

al-Azhar al-sharif manarat al-Islam (The Venerable al-Azhar: The Beacon of Islam, religious novel). Cairo: Maktabat Misr, 1984.

Huwwa hubbi wa qad nadhart lahu qalbi (He Is My Love and I Dedicated My Heart to Him, play). Cairo: Maktabat Misr, 1984.

al-Mu'jiza al-kubra wa imra'at al-'Aziz (The Great Miracle and the Wife of 'Aziz, play). Cairo: Maktabat Misr, 1984.

La ilaha illa Allah (No God But God, screenplay). Cairo: Maktabat Misr, 1985.

al-Sawi, Sabrine (?–), Egyptian poet.

Ughniyat min al-qalb (Songs from the Heart, poetry). al-Daqahliya: n.p., 1991.

al-Sayd, Na'ima (1945–), Tunisian short-story writer born in al-Qayrawan. She received her primary and secondary education in al-Qayrawan. She graduated from the High Institute for Theater in Tunis. She is a high-school theater teacher in Tunis. From 1973 to 1986 she worked for the office of the minister of national education and at the Tunisian Writers' Union, where she ran the magazine, *al-Fikr*. She has written short stories, poetry, and reflections. In 1983 she was awarded the Tunisian Cultural Medal and the Gold Medal from Kuwait.

Ri'shat hulm (Tremor of a Dream, texts). Tunis: Tunisian Distribution Company, 1982.

al-Zahf (The March, short stories). Kuwait: Dar al-Rabi'an, 1982.

al-'Ushb al-ma' (Grass, Water, texts). Tunis: al-Dar al-'Arabiya Books, 1986.

al-Saydawi, Asmahan Budayr (1944–), A Lebanese poet born in Beirut, she lives in Paris. She received a B.A. in painting and fine arts in 1974 and a Ph.D. in social sciences from the Sorbonne in Paris in 1985. She taught at the Teachers' School in Lebanon and was the director of the Arab Beirut College in Paris. She owns the publishing house, Dar al-Mutanabbi, based in Paris. She has published several political works, including *al-Dalala al-fikriya li-harakat al-ikhwan al-Muslimin fi Misr* (The Intellectual Significance of the Muslim Brothers in Egypt) and *Fi-l-bad' kanat al-untha* (In the Beginning Was Woman). She founded and headed the Arab Women's Union in France.

Ma zal 'aliqan (Still Suspended, poetry). Beirut: privately published, 1986.

al-Mahara (The Oyster, poetry). Beirut: Dar al-Mutanabbi, 1987.

Taqasim 'ala-l-jurh (Recitals on the Wound, poetry). Beirut: privately published, 1989.

Saydawi, Bilqis Abu Khudud (1935–), Lebanese poet born in al-Nabatiya. She received her primary education at the Anglican School and the Ahliya Girls' School in Beirut. She earned a B.A. in Arabic literature from the International Institute in Cairo.

Hamsat min Saba' (Whispers from Sheba, poetry). Beirut: Nasr Allah Press, 1980.

Dumu' tughanni (Singing Tears, poetry). Lebanon: al-Nur Press and Jean Abu Dahir, 1997.

Baqa' wa zawal (Permanence and Evanescence, poetry). Beirut: al-Ashraf Printing and Publishing, 1998.

Rimi fi-l-ghaba (Rimi in the Forest, poetic drama). Beirut: al-Ashraf Printing and Publishing, 1998.

Sayf al-Nasr, 'Aliya (1948–), Egyptian short-story writer. She has a B.A. in journalism. She works at the women's desk and the reportage desk at *al-Ahram*.

al-Sayr dakhil al-murabba'at (Walking in Squares, short stories). Cairo: n.p., 1983.

al-Nisa' yaghsilna awraq al-shajar (Women Wash the Leaves, short stories). Cairo: Dar Su'ad al-Sabah, 1993.

al-Sayf, Qumasha (1953–), Saudi short-story writer born in al-Qaysuma. She received a B.A. in Arabic from King Sa'ud University. She is a counselor in the Office of Educational Counseling of the Higher Office for Girls' Education in Hafr al-Batin. She was an editor for *al-Riyad*.

Muhadatha barriya shamal sharq al-watan (A Wild Discussion Northeast of the Homeland, short stories). Riyadh: Story Club, 1992.

Sayf, Salma Matar (1968–), Emirati short-story writer. She received a B.A. in education and works at the Curriculum and Books Authority in Dubai.

'Ushba (A Blade of Grass, short stories). Beirut: Dar al-Kalima Publishers, 1988.

Hajar (Hajar, short stories). Sharjah: Emirati Writers' and Authors' Union Publications, 1991.

Sayigh, Mayy (1940–), Palestinian poet born in Gaza. She lives in Jordan. She received her early education in Gaza. She earned a B.A. in philosophy from Cairo University. She has worked for Fatah since 1968 and is a member of the movement's Central Council. She has been a member of the P.L.O.'s National Council since 1973. She also has been a member of the permanent bureau of the World Democratic Women's Union since 1975. She was the secretary-general of the Palestinian Women's General Union from 1971 to 1986 and has represented Palestinian women at many international and Arab conferences and seminars.

Iklil al-shawk (The Thorn Wreath, poetry). Beirut: Dar al-Tali'a, 1969.

Qasa'id manqusha 'ala masallat al-Ashrafiya (Poems Inscribed on the al-Ashrafiya Obelisk, poetry anthology). Amman: Fatah Publications, 1972.

Qasa'id hubb li-ism mutarad (Love Poems for a Fugitive Name, poetry). Beirut: Dar al-'Awda, 1974.

'An al-dumu' wa-l-farah al-ati (On Tears and the Coming Joy, poetry). Baghdad: Ministry of Information, 1975.

al-Hisar (The Siege, memoir about the Israeli invasion of Lebanon in 1982 and the siege of Beirut). Beirut: Arab Institute for Research and Publishing, 1988.

al-Sayih, Layla (1936–), Palestinian writer born in Haifa. She finished primary school in Haifa and then left with her family in 1948. She completed her university education in Beirut in 1972. She has lived in Kuwait and has been a journalist.

Qisasi ana (My Stories, short stories). Beirut: Arab Institute for Research and Publishing, 1972.

Dafatir al-matar (Notebooks of Rain, poetry). Beirut: Arab Institute for Research and Publishing, 1979.

al-Judhur allati la tarhal (Roots That Do Not Depart). Damascus: Dar al-Jalil, 1984.

Tuqus al-bara'a (Rituals of Innocence, poetry). Beirut: Arab Institute for Research and Publishing, 1989.

'Awdat al-banafsaja (Return of the Violet, short stories). Beirut: Arab Institute for Research and Publishing, 1990.

al-Sayyid, 'Afaf (1963–), Egyptian journalist and short-story writer born in Suez. She has a B.A. in philosophy and a degree in Islamic studies. She is an editor at *al-Nida'* magazine, published by the al-Nida' Foundation. Her stories have been translated into English and Dutch. She is a member of the Writers' Union and the Cairo Atelier.

Qadr min al-'ishq (A Bit of Passion, short story). Cairo: General Egyptian Book Organization, 1994.

Sa'adat al-saghira (The Little One's Joys, short story). Cairo: Dar al-Ahmadi, 1995.

Brufat (Rehearsals, story). Cairo: General Authority for Culture Palaces, 1998.

Saradib (Cellars, novel). Cairo: Center for Arab Civilization, 1998.

al-Siqan al-rafi'a li-l-kidhb (The Lie's Slender Legs, novel). Cairo: Dar Qiba', 1998.

al-Sayyid, Fatima (?–), Egyptian poet. She has published the non-fiction work, *Mudhakkirat sahafiya fi ghurfat al-i'dam* (Memoirs of a Female Journalist in the Execution Chamber, 1986).

Ahlam al-sinin (Dreams of the Years, poetry). Cairo: General Egyptian Book Organization, 1990.

Asda' al-'ishq (Echoes of Passion, poetry). Cairo: League of Modern Literature, 1990.

al-Sayyid, Manal Muhammad (1971–), Egyptian short-story writer and artist. She has a B.A. in fine arts. She works as an activities specialist in public relations at Helwan University.

Alladhi fawq (The One Upstairs, short stories). Cairo: General Authority for Culture Palaces, 1995.

al-Sayyid, Najwa (1956–), Egyptian poet and children's writer born in Alexandria. She is a member of the Writers' Union, the Arts and Humanities Organization, and the League of World Peace.

Shahrazad (Sheherazade, colloquial poetry). Cairo: General Egyptian Book Organization, 1988.

'Arayis al-shi'r (Brides of Poetry, poetry). Alexandria: General Authority for Culture Palaces, 1993.

Dafayir al-shams (The Sun's Plaits, colloquial poetry). Alexandria: General Authority for Culture Palaces, 1996.

Madrasat al-ghaba (School of the Forest, children's poetry). Alexandria: General Authority for Culture Palaces, 1996.

al-Sayyid, Rashida Muhammad (?–), Egyptian poet.

Li-kull 'ashiq watan (Every Lover Has a Homeland, poetry). Cairo: n.p., 1992.

al-Sayyid, Sharifa (1959–), Egyptian poet born in Cairo. She completed her education at the College of Sciences in Cairo University in 1981 and received an M.A. in 1985. She was a teacher of Arabic before turning to journalism. She is a researcher at the Egyptian Library. She received a prize from the Supreme Council of Culture in 1995.

Malamihi (My Features, poetry). Cairo: Dar Andalusiya, 1991.

al-Mamarrat la tahtawi 'abiriha (The Corridors Do Not Contain Their Crossers, poetry). Cairo: Dar Gharib Printing, Publishing, and Distribution, 1995.

Farashat al-samt (Butterflies of Silence, poetry). Cairo: Supreme Council for Culture, 1997.

Sahil al-'ishq (The Whinny of Passion, poetry). Cairo: Dar al-Qiba', 1998.

Sha'ban, Nadiya Zafir (1941–), Lebanese novelist born in Tripoli. She received a state doctorate from the Open University in Madrid. She teaches Spanish at the al-Hariri Lycée in Beirut and Arabic at the French Laic Mission in Beirut. She has translated poetry from Spain and Latin America into Arabic.

Rasa'il Qadesh (Letters of Qadesh). N.p.: n.p., 1975.

Rihlat al-tifla (The Child's Journey, novel). Beirut: Dar al-Wahda, 1991.

Sha'ban, Najwa (1959–), Egyptian novelist and short-story writer. She received a B.A. in journalism from the College of Communications at Cairo University. She is a journalist at the Middle East News Agency. She received a prize from the Girls' Clubs of Sharjah for her novel, *al-Ghurr*, in 1999. She is a member of the Cairo Atelier, *al-Nida'* magazine's editorial staff, and the Historical and Geographical Association.

Jada'il al-tih (Braids of the Wilderness, poetry). Cairo: General Egyptian Book Organization, 1994.

al-Ghurr (The Immigrant Bird, novel). Cairo: al-Dar al-Misriya al-Lubnaniya, 1998.

al-Shabib, Ruqaya Hammud (1957–), Saudi short-story writer born in Ha'il. She received a B.A. in social sciences, with a focus on history, from the Imam Muhammad Bin Sa'ud Islamic University in Riyadh in 1980. She has worked in the literacy division of the General Office for Girls' Education in Riyadh since 1987.

Hulm (Dream, short stories). Riyadh: Culture and Arts Association, 1984.

al-Maw'id al-mu'ajjal (The Postponed Appointment, short stories). N.p.: n.p., 1986.

al-Huzn al-ramadi (Gray Melancholy, short stories). Riyadh: Culture and Arts Association, 1987.

Ahlam qasira (Short Dreams, short stories). N.p.: n.p., 1993.

al-Shabibi, Wadi'a Ja'far (1927–), Iraqi poet born in Baghdad. She grew up in a home dedicated to knowledge and literature. She completed her primary and secondary education and enrolled in the Queen 'Aliya Institute in the Arabic department, from which she obtained a B.A. with honors in 1948. She was appointed an Arabic teacher until she devoted herself to writing full time. She published a work of non-fiction, *Umm Kulthum fi afaq al-shi'r wa-l-fann* (Umm Kulthum on the Horizons of Poetry and Art) in 1985.

Khawatir mulawwana (Tinted Reflections, poetry). N.p.: n.p., 1988.

al-Sha'bini, Yaqut (?–), Egyptian poet.

al-Kalima fann (The Word Is Art, poetry). Cairo: Dar Ma'mun Press, 1976.

Kalam lahu waznuh (Weighty Words, poetry). Cairo: Dar Ma'mun Press, 1978.

Ahla kalam (The Loveliest Words, poetry). Cairo: Dar Ma'mun Press, 1981.

Kalamuna baladi (Our Words Are in the Vernacular, poetry). Cairo: Dar Ma'mun Press, 1987.

al-Kalam al-mufid (Helpful Talk, poetry). Cairo: Dar al-Ta'lif Press, 1991.

Ramadan karim: 30 yawm ful (Ramadan Is Generous: Thirty Days of Beans, colloquial poetry). Cairo: n.p., 1992.

al-Shaburi, Zaynab (?–), Egyptian poet.

Kull al-hubb (All of Love, poetry). Alexandria: Authors of the People Association, 1994.

Shafi', Majida (?–), Egyptian poet.

Kalam al-layl (Night Talk, poetry). Alexandria: Qaytbay Printing and Publishing, 1994.

al-Shafi'i, Ghada (1977–), Palestinian poet born in Acre in the part of Palestine occupied in 1948. She is a student at the Hebrew University.

al-Mashhad yukhabbi' sahilan (The Scene Conceals a Whinny, poetry). Ramallah: Palestinian Cultural Center, and Beirut: Arab Institute for Research and Publishing, 1999.

al-Shafi'i, Layla (1960–), Moroccan writer born in Rabat who currently resides in Madrid. She received a B.A. in sociology from Muhammad V University in Rabat and is currently preparing a state Ph.D. in international and Mediter-

ranean relations at the Open University in Madrid. She is a member of the Moroccan Writers' Union and was elected to the union's central bureau for the 1993–1996 session. She is a member of several women's and human rights associations. Her articles and essays have been published in several Moroccan newspapers, including *al-'Ilm*, *al-Mawja*, and *al-Mithaq al-watani*, as well as in the London-based *al-Quds* and *Afaq*, the journal of the Moroccan Writers' Union.

al-Wahm wa-l-ramad (The Illusion and Ashes, fictional texts). Rabat: al-Mawja Publications, 1994.

al-Shafi'i, Muna (1946–), Kuwaiti short-story writer. She has a B.A. in history from Alexandria University. She is an editor at *al-Watan* newspaper. She is a member of the Authors' League in Kuwait and the Kuwaiti Journalists' Association. She was the director of the Girls' College at Kuwait University.

al-Nakhla wa ra'ihat al-hayl (The Palm and the Scent of Cardamom, short stories). Kuwait: Dar Su'ad al-Sabah, 1992.

al-Bad' marratayn (Starting Twice, short stories). Kuwait: distributed by al-Rabi'an Publishing, 1994.

Drama al-hawass (Drama of the Senses, short stories). Kuwait: distributed by al-Rabi'an Publishing, 1995.

Shahhud, Juliet 'Ad (?–), Lebanese poet and novelist. She received a B.A. in French language and literature. She moved to Sweden, where she learned Swedish and worked at the newspaper, *Le reveil*. She has published several poems in Swedish and wrote of the tragedy of the Lebanon war in her novels.

Safar fi-l-dhat (A Journey into the Self, novel). N.p.: privately published, 1995.

Ufuq la yartasim (Unattainable Horizon, novel). N.p.: privately published, 1995.

Shahin, Hanna Khuri (1910–1985), Lebanese pioneer and playwright born in Suq al-Gharb. She was a member of several associations in Beirut, including the Lebanese Women's Union and the Young Christian Women's Association. She staged her play in Bishmazin in the district of al-Kura in 1930.

Jaza' al-fadila (Virtue's Reward, play). Beirut: al-Amrikiya Press, 1930.

Shahin, Siham 'Aytur (?–), Palestinian poet born in Haifa. She studied in Lebanon and lives in Syria.

al-Ibhar fi-l-mawasim al-sa'ba (The Sailing in the Difficult Seasons, poetry). Beirut: Occupied Palestine Publications, n.d.

Shahwan, Najla' Muhammad (1960–), Palestinian poet born in Jerusalem. She went to school in Jerusalem. She studied English and education at the Open University of Jerusalem from 1992 to 1994. She is currently studying English literature in London. She has published two studies of children's literature and has translated several children's stories.

Fi Hamasat rabi' al-'ishrin (On Whispers on the Twentieth Spring, poetry) Jerusalem: al-Difa' Press, 1985.

Watani nadhart li-'aynayk 'umri (My Homeland, I Pledged My Life to Your Eyes, poetry). Jerusalem: Palestinian Writers' Union, 1989.

Filistin ya taw'am al-ruh (Palestine, O Twin Spirit, poetry). Jerusalem: Masudi Press, 1990.

Hiwar al-banafsaj (The Violet's Conversation, poetry). Jerusalem: Dar al-Katib, 1992.

'Abiq al-yasamin (Fragrance of Jasmine, poetry). Jerusalem: n.p., 1995.

Shakir, 'Azza Fu'ad (?–), Saudi poet and novelist born in Mecca. She has a B.A. in philosophy and psychology from the International University in Rome. She has been an announcer on Saudi radio since its establishment and is a member of the Women's Charitable Association in Riyadh.

Ashri'at al-layl (The Night's Sails, poetry). Riyadh: Dar al-'Ulum, 1977.

Ilayk wahdak (To You Alone, novel). Cairo: Dar al-Watan al-'Arabi, 1989.

al-Sha'lan, Jamila 'Uthman Hamad (?–), Saudi short-story writer born in Riyadh. She received a B.A. in geography from King Sa'ud University in 1987 and is a primary-school teacher.

Zawja wahida la takfi (One Wife Is Not Enough, short stories). Riyadh: n.p., 1994.

al-Shalaq, Maqbula (1921–1986), Syrian short-story writer born in Damascus. She was the first Syrian woman to obtain a law degree from Damascus University, in 1944. She was a teacher and a member of the Story and Novel Association.

Qisas min baladi (Stories from My Country, short stories). Damascus: al-'Umumiya Press, 1978.

'Urs al-'asafir (The Sparrows' Wedding, children's literature). Damascus: Arab Writers' Union, 1979.

Mughamarat dajaja (The Adventures of a Hen, children's literature). Damascus: Dar al-Fikr, 1981.

Ughniyat al-qalb (A Heart's Songs, poetry). Damascus: al-'Umumiya Press, 1982.

Sayyidat al-thimar (The Fruit Lady, children's literature). Damascus: Ministry of Culture, 1985.

Shalash, Su'ad (1946–), Egyptian novelist born in the province of al-Buhayra.

La taqul li wada'an (Don't Say Goodbye, novel). Cairo: General Egyptian Book Organization, 1990.

Tarannuh 'itruha (Her Perfume's Swaying, short stories). Cairo: General Egyptian Book Organization, 1994.

al-Shami, Amal Muhammad 'Ali (Bint al-Yaman) (1956–2001), Yemeni poet and short-story writer born in Sana'a. Before her death, she had withdrawn from social and cultural activities after having made many pioneering contributions in several cultural fields. She wrote poetry, short stories, screenplays for television and radio,

children's stories, songs, and essays. She published under the pen names Bint al-Yaman, Bint al-Sharq, Amal Kamal, and Amal al-Shami. She is one of the first women short-story writers in northern Yemen. Her stories have been published by Arab and Yemeni journals, including the story, "al-Mutakabbirun" (The Arrogant Ones), published in *Mu'in* in 1977. She also published the poem, "Ahfu li-l-luqyak" (I Fly to Meet You), in *Bilqis* magazine in 1966. *Al-Thawra* published many of her articles, including the story of Indira Gandhi in 1977, and many of her short stories were aired on the Arabic channel of London radio between 1980 and 1985. She wrote several works that remain unpublished, such as the collection, *Hubbi al-'aziz* (My Dear Love), written in 1993. She published a collection of children's songs titled *Ya Rabb tawwil 'umr man habb al-'amal* (May Those Who Love Work Live Long). She was known as a feminist activist. In the 1970s she wore a dark red cloak with no face covering instead of the traditional black cloak with the face covering in the streets of Yemen as a challenge to prevailing thought in Yemeni society. In 1974 she won second place in a competition sponsored by *Sawt al-sharq* for the symbolic story. During a time of social unrest, she burned her library. She published a collection of poetry that has since disappeared. It was referred to in a critical article published in the official *al-Thawra* newspaper.
Bara'a (Innocence, poetry). N.p.: n.p., n.d.

al-Shamlan, Sharifa Ibrahim (1948–), Saudi short-story writer born in al-Zubayr. She received a B.A. in journalism from Baghdad University in 1968. She has been the director of the Social Supervision Office in the Eastern Province since 1985.
Muntaha al-hudu' (The Utmost Calm, short stories). Riyadh: Culture and Arts Association, 1989.
Maqati' min al-hayah (Passages from Life, short stories). al-Dammam: Culture and Arts Association, 1992.

Shammas, Fadiya (?–), Syrian novelist born in Aleppo.
al-Hubb al-muharram (Forbidden Love, novel). Damascus: Dar al-Manhal, 1996.
Rasha wa-l-duktur (Rasha and the Doctor, novel). Damascus: Dar al-Manhal, 1997.
Qarya kharij al-zaman (A Village Outside Time, novel). Stockholm: Dar Afanta, 1998.
Imra'a bayn ashwak al-hayah (A Woman Between Life's Thorns, novel). Beirut: Dar Amwaj, 1999.

Sharaf al-Din, Fawziya (1939–), Egyptian novelist and short-story writer born in Zifta. She studied at the Higher Institute for Education and taught in Kuwait. She is a screenwriter and a member of the Writers' Union, the Small Screen Association, and the Association of Egyptian Women Filmmakers.
Laytah 'araf al-haqiqa (I Wish He Knew the Truth, novel). Cairo: Dar al-Fikr al-Hadith Printing and Publishing, 1965.
al-Rajul dhu al-wajhayn (The Man with Two Faces, novel). Kuwait: n.p., 1967.
Qusur min rimal (Sandcastles, novel). Kuwait: n.p., 1977.

Sha'rawi, Huda (1879–1947), A pioneer Egyptian activist. She was born in Minya, Upper Egypt, and was taught to read and write at home. Later, she learned Turkish and French. At the age of 13, she was married to 'Ali Sha'rawi, who was to become one of the leaders of the 1919 revolution. Sha'rawi led the first women's demonstration against British occupation in 1919 and she was the first Egyptian woman to take off the face veil. In 1923 Sha'rawi, Sayza Nabrawi, and Nabawiya Musa founded the Egyptian Women's Union. In 1925 she began publishing articles in *L'Egyptienne* and in 1938 she organized the First Arab Women's Congress in Support of Palestine. In 1944 she was elected vice-chair of the newly founded Arab Women's Union, a position she held until her death.

Mudhakkirat Huda Sha'rawi, ra'idat al-mar'a al-'Arabiya al-haditha. (Harem Years: The Memoirs of an Egyptian Feminist, 1879–1924, memoir). Cairo: Dar al-Hilal, 1981.

Sharbati, Ihsan (?–), Syrian short-story writer born in Damascus. She studied law at Damascus University.

Baqaya al-hubb wa-l-ramad (The Remnants of Love and Ashes, short stories). Damascus: Dar al-Manhal for Research and Translation, 1988.

al-Sharbati, Samira (1943–), Palestinian poet born in Hebron. She received her early education in Hebron and later studied at the Beirut Arab University. After graduating, she worked in education. She has written several novels and poems that have not been published.

Qasa'id bahth 'an rafiq musafir (Poems Searching for a Fellow Traveler, play). Jerusalem: Abu 'Arafa Agency, 1976.

Kalimat li-l-zaman al-ati (Words for the Coming Era, poetry). Jerusalem: Abu 'Arafa Agency, 1977.

Adunis al-rafid li-l-ghurba (Adonis, Who Rejects Exile, play). Beirut: Palestinian Writers' Union, n.d.

al-Sharif, 'Ayda (1937–1997), Egyptian writer. She received a law degree from Cairo University and is a graduate of the Institute for Dramatic Arts.

Shahidat rub' qarn (Witness to a Quarter Century). Cairo: General Egyptian Book Organization, 1995.

al-Insan wa-l-ta'ir (The Man and the Bird). Cairo: General Egyptian Book Organization, n.d.

al-Sharini, Rashida (?–), Tunisian short-story writer born in Bardu, where she lives. She works in education. In 1997, she was awarded the Zubayda Bashir Prize for Literature for her collection, *al-Hayah 'ala haffat al-dunya*.

al-Hayah 'ala haffat al-dunya (Life on the Edge of the World, short stories). Susa: Dar al-Ma'arif Printing and Publishing, 1988.

al-Sharqawi, Nafisa (Umm Ahmad) (?–), Sudanese short-story writer. Her stories have been published in Sudanese periodicals. Her first published story was "'Indama bakat 'uyun al-Bahr al-Ahmar" (When the Red Sea Cried) and her most recently published was "al-Rahil" (The Departure).

al-Shartuni, 'Afifa (1886–?), Pioneering Lebanese journalist born in Beirut. She was educated at the Sisters of Nazareth School and later at the al-Taqaddum School in Beirut. She studied the fundamentals of Arabic with her father, Sa'id al-Khuri al-Shartuni. She immigrated to Brazil and published in several newspapers and journals, including *al-Muqtataf*, *al-Muqtabas*, and *al-Rawda*. She and her sister, Anisa, published a collection of essays, *Nafhat al-wardatayn* (Scents of the Two Roses, 1909).

Shata, Amal Muhammad Ahmad (?–), Saudi novelist. She received a B.A. in medicine and surgery from Cairo University and a degree in internal medicine from the same institution in 1975. She works at King 'Abd al-'Aziz University in Jeddah.

Ghadan ansa (Tomorrow I Will Forget, novel). Jeddah: Tuhama Foundation for Publishing, 1980.

Lawla 'ash qalbi (If My Heart Had Not Lived, novel). Jeddah: al-Madina Printing and Publishing, 1989.

Adam ya sayyidi (Adam, Sir, novel). Medina: al-Madina Printing and Publishing, n.d.

Shatila, Muna (1957–), Lebanese novelist and short-story writer born in Beirut. She received a teaching certificate in social sciences at the Lebanese University and devoted herself to writing full-time.

Iqa'at 'ala dhanb Maykal (Rhythms on Michael's Misdeed, short stories). Beirut: Maryam Publications, 1990.
al-Kha'ibun (The Failures, novel). Beirut: Dar al-Kitabat, 1995.

al-Shaybani, Khayra (1950–), Tunisian short-story writer born in Safaqis. She was educated in Safaqis and Tunis. She graduated from high school in 1967 and received a B.A. in philosophy from the College of Humanities in Tunis in 1971. She has taught high school and worked as a correspondent for Arab newspapers, magazines, and radio. She worked in the Ministry of Cultural Affairs, where she supervised the publication of *al-Hayah al-thaqafiya* magazine. She is a member of the Tunisian Writers' Union and she writes journalistic articles, critical essays, and short stories.
al-Khayt al-abyad (The White Thread, short stories). Tunis: Dar al-Riyah al-Arba'a, 1986.

al-Shaybani, Kulthum (?–), Emirati poet born in the Emirates. She received a B.A. in sciences with a specialization in geology from Emirates University in 1988. She is a member of the Women Authors' League, a founding member of Friends of the Environment, and a member of the Sciences and Hydrotechnology Association.
Taranim al-khuzama (Hymns of the Lavender, poetry). Sharjah: Women Authors' League, 1992.

Shaybub, Idvik Juraydini (1922–), Lebanese poet and journalist born in al-Shuwayfat. She obtained an M.A. in Arabic literature from the American University of Beirut and studied in Iraq from 1933 to 1940. She was the editor of *Sawt al-mar'a* from 1951 to 1958 and *Dunya al-mar'a* from 1960 to 1966. She presented several radio programs, among them "Ma'a al-usra" (With the Family) and "Dunya al-bayt" (World of the House), and taught for a short time at the Lebanese Women's Association's kindergarten. Her non-fiction works include *al-Tabib al-saghir* (The

Little Doctor, 1963), *al-Hiraf al-sha'biya al-Lubnaniya* (Lebanese Folk Crafts, 1964), and *Rasa'il hubb Antwan Sa'ada* (The Love Letters of Antoine Sa'ada). She was a member of the International Women's Council. She was awarded a prize from Friends of the Book for *al-Tabib al-saghir* in 1963. She also received the Lebanese Medal of Valor and Honor, the Lebanese Cedar Medal (1968), the President's Prize for her literary works (1974), and the Cedar Medal (rank of officer) (1985).
Bawh (Confession, poetry). Beirut: Dar al-Ahad, 1954.
Shawq (Desire, poetry). Beirut: Dar al-Ahad, 1962.
al-'Anbar raqam 12 (Ward 12, short stories). Beirut: Nawfal Foundation, 1979.

Shaykh al-'Arab, Thuraya Muhyi al-Din (?–), Iraqi novelist.
Last dumya ya ummi (I'm Not a Doll, Mother, novel). Baghdad: al-Hurriya Press, 1981.

al-Shaykh, Hanan (1945–), Lebanese novelist and short-story writer born in Beirut to parents from the south. She studied in Lebanese schools and later at the American Girls' College in Cairo (1964–1966). She was an editor at *al-Hasna'* and *al-Nahar* (1967). She moved between various Arab Gulf countries from 1977 to 1985, settling in London in 1982. Her works have been translated into English, French, and Dutch, and she has written two plays in English, *Dark Afternoon Tea* and *Paper Husband*, both staged in London.
Intihar rajul mayyit (Suicide of a Dead Man, novel). Beirut: Dar al-Nahar Publishers, 1970.
Faras al-shaytan (The Devil's Coach Horse, novel). Beirut: Dar al-Nahar Publishers, 1975.
Hikayat Zahra (The Story of Zahra, novel). Beirut: privately published, 1980.
Wardat al-sahra' (Desert Flower, short stories). Beirut: al-Dar al-Jami'iya, 1982.
Misk al-ghazal (Women of Sand and Myrrh, novel). Beirut: Dar al-Adab, 1986.

Barid Bayrut (*Beirut Blues*, novel). Cairo: Dar al-Hilal, 1992.

Aknus al-shams 'an al-sutuh (*I Sweep the Sun off Rooftops*, short stories). Beirut: Dar al-Adab, 1994.

al-Shaykh, Hiyam 'Afifi (?–), Egyptian writer.

Hams nabadat imra'a (Whisper of a Woman's Heartbeats). Cairo: Egyptian Association to Foster Talent, 1995.

Thawrat al-qalb (Rebellion of the Heart). Cairo: Egyptian Association to Foster Talent, 1995.

Shibli, Asiya (?–), Palestinian short-story writer and novelist born in the village of al-Shibli, located at the foot of Mt. al-Tur in the part of Palestine occupied in 1948. She received her primary and secondary education at the Sisters of St. Joseph School in Nazareth. She works in the local press.

Khuyut al-fajr (The Threads of Dawn, short stories). Shafa 'Amr: Dar al-Mashriq, 1989.

al-Jazzar (al-Jazzar, novel). N.p.: privately published, 1990.

Safinat Nuh (Noah's Ark, novel). N.p.: privately published, 1994.

Mawsim al-hijra ila-l-janub (Season of Migration to the South, novel). N.p.: privately published, 1995.

al-Shirbini, Hikmat Mahmud (1939–), Egyptian poet born in the village of al-'Aziziya in Minya al-Qamh. She helped found Middle East Radio. She is the director of the variety section and the deputy head of the radio station.

al-Qamar wa-l-banadiq (The Moon and Rifles, poetry). Cairo: Dar al-Ma'arif, 1970.

al-Shirbini, Layla (1936–1998), Egyptian novelist and short-story writer born in al-Daqahliya. She earned a B.A. in pure mathematics from Cairo University and an M.A. in mathematical statistics from the University of Paris. She was a researcher at the Institute of Statistics at Cairo University and a professor of mathematical statistics at Benin University in West Africa. She had a special interest in quantitative linguistics. Her non-fiction works include *Intrubiyat al-iqa' fi-l-'Arabiya* (The Entropy of Rhythm in Arabic, 1992) and *al-Tawzi' al-ihsa'i li-tul al-jumla 'ind Yusuf Idris* (Statistical Distribution of Sentence Length in the Works of Yusuf Idris, 1995).

al-Karaz (Cherries, short stories). Cairo: General Egyptian Book Organization, 1994.

al-Akhar (The Other, short stories). Cairo: General Authority for Culture Palaces, 1995.

Tranzit (Transit, novel). Cairo: Dar al-Hadara al-'Arabiya, 1997.

Shlabi, Fawziya (1955–), Libyan poet and novelist born in Tripoli. She is the secretary of the Popular Committee for Culture, Media, and Mobilization. Her non-fiction works include *Fi-l-thaqafa wa-l-harb* (On Culture and War, 1984), *Qira'at munawi'a* (Resistant Readings, 1984), and *Qira'at 'aqila jiddan* (Very Reasonable Readings, 1985).

Fi-l-qasida al-taliya uhibbuk bi-su'uba (In the Following Poem I Love You With Difficulty, poetry). Tripoli, Libya: General Publishing and Distribution Facility, 1984.

Bi-l-banafsaj anta muttaham (You Are Accused of Violet, poetry). Tripoli, Libya: General Publishing and Distribution Facility, 1985.

Fawdawiyan kunt wa shadid al-waqaha (An Anarchist You Were, and Very Impudent, poetry). Tripoli, Libya: General Publishing and Distribution Facility, 1985.

Rajul li-riwaya wahida (A Man for One Novel, novel). Tripoli, Libya: General Publishing and Distribution Facility, 1985.

Sura tibq al-asl li-l-fadiha (Replica of the Scandal, texts). Tripoli, Libya: General Publishing and Distribution Facility, 1985.

'Arabiyan kan al-Mutanabbi (Mutanabbi Was an Arab, poetry). N.p.: n.p., n.d.

S

Shu'ayb, 'Aliya (1964–), Kuwaiti short-story writer and poet. She received a B.A. in philosophy from Kuwait University in 1985, an M.A. from Birmingham University in Britain in 1991, and a Ph.D. from the same institution in 1994. She teaches in the philosophy department at Kuwait University. She is a member of the Plastic Arts Association, the Authors' League, and the Graduates' Association in Kuwait.

Imra'a tatazawwaj al-bahr (A Woman Marries the Sea, short stories). Kuwait: n.p., 1989.

Bila wajh (Faceless, short stories). London: n.p., 1992.

'Anakib tarthi jarhan (Spiders Mourn a Wound, poetry). Kuwait: 'Aliya Publications, 1994.

al-Dhakhira fiya usrukhi fi fami (The Ammunition Is in Me, Scream in My Mouth, poetry). Kuwait: n.p., 1995.

Nahj al-warda (The Rose's Way, poetry). Damascus: Dar al-Mada for Culture and Publishing, 1997.

Shuman, Nadiya (?–), Syrian novelist.

Khuta kutibat 'alayna (Fated Steps, novel). Damascus: Dar al-Hisad, 1997.

Shuquray, 'Aziza Ahzziya 'Umar (?–), Moroccan poet.

Sahra' hinna' za'faran (Desert, Henna, Saffron, poetry). Casablanca: al-Najah Modern Press, 1993.

Bawh Tantan (Tintin's Confession, poetry). Casablanca: al-Fanak Publications, 1998.

Shurayh, Munira (1955–), Palestinian playwright who lives in Amman. She attended school in Aleppo. She works in children's education. Her play, *Yazan*, was awarded a prize from the Association of Jordanian Libraries in 1985.

'Uruba (Arabism, children's literature). al-Zarqa': al-Haramayn Modern Press, 1985.

Yazan (Yazan, children's literature). Amman: Dar al-Karmel, 1987.

Lahzat intibah (A Moment of Attention, play). Amman: Dar al-Karmel, 1989.

Sidqi, Jadhibiya (1927–), Egyptian writer born in Cairo. She graduated from the American College for Girls and hosted a literary salon in her home from 1953 to 1960. She was a visiting professor at Western Illinois University in 1961. She is a member of the Journalists' Syndicate and the Authors' Association. She received first prize from the Language Academy in 1954 for her first book, *Mamlakat Allah*. She has published several social and literary studies, including *Lamahat min al-masrah al-'alami* (A Look at World Theater, 1970), *al-Dunya wa ana* (The World and I, 1972), *Jadhibiya Sidqi 'ala bab Allah* (Jadhibiya Sidqi at God's Door, 1973), and *Bawwabat al-Mutawalli* (al-Mutawalli Gate, 1975).

Rabib al-tuyur (The Birds' Foster Son, children's stories). Cairo: al-Sayyid Yusuf Mahmud Zaki, 1951.

Mamlakat Allah (God's Kingdom, short stories). Cairo: al-Sayyid Yusuf Mahmud Zaki, 1954.

Innahu al-hubb (It's Love, short stories). Cairo: Dar al-Kitab al-'Arabi, 1955.

Sukkan al-'imara (Residents of the Building, play). N.p.: n.p., 1955.

Murjan wa ibn 'ammih Habbahan (Murjan and His Cousin Habbahan, children's literature). Cairo: Maktabat al-Sharq, 1957.

Nur al-buyut (The Light of Homes, play). Cairo: Maktabat al-Sharq, 1957.

Sattar ya layl (Night the Protector, short stories). Cairo: Rose al-Yusuf Foundation, 1957.

Ta'ali (Come, war stories). Cairo: Maktabat al-Sharq, 1957.

Wa baka qalbi (And My Heart Wept, short stories). Cairo: Rose al-Yusuf Foundation, 1957.

Zabiba wa-l-hajja Umm Habiba (Zabiba and Hajja Umm Habiba, children's literature). Cairo: Maktabat al-Sharq, 1957.

al-Bint min Bahri (The Girl from Bahri,

short stories). Cairo: Arab Foundation for Printing and Publishing, 1958.

Bayn al-adghal (Amid the Jungles, children's literature). Cairo: Maktabat al-'Ahd al-Jadid in Fajjala, 1959.

Shay' haram (A Forbidden Something, short stories). Cairo: Rose al-Yusuf Foundation, 1959.

Layla bayda' (A White Night, short stories). Cairo: Rose al-Yusuf Foundation, 1960.

Amrika wa ana (America and I, travel literature). Cairo: Maktabat al-Nahda al-Misriya, 1963.

Fi bilad al-dima' al-harra (In the Hotblooded Lands, travel literature). Cairo: Rose al-Yusuf Foundation, 1964.

Anta qasin (You Are Cruel, short stories). Cairo: al-Dar al-Misriya for Composition and Translation, 1966.

Layta al-shabab (Oh My Youth, play). Cairo: al-Dar al-Qawmiya, 1966.

Ummuna al-ard (Mother Earth, novel). Cairo: al-Dar al-Qawmiya Printing and Publishing, 1966.

Dabib al-naml (Creeping of the Ant, short stories). Cairo: Rose al-Yusuf Foundation, 1968.

Shafatah (His Lips, short stories). Cairo: Akhbar al-Yawm Foundation, 1980.

al-Sindi, Fawziya (1957–), Bahraini poet born in Manama. She received a B.A. in business and economics from Cairo University in 1977. She is an economic researcher in the banking sector and a member of the Family of Writers and Authors in Bahrain.

Istifaqat (Awakenings, poetry). Bahrain: al-Sharqiya Press, 1984.

Hal ara ma hawli . . . hal asif ma hadath (Do I See What Is Around Me . . . Do I Describe What Happened, poetry). Bahrain: al-Sharqiya Press, 1986.

Hanjarat al-gha'ib (The Missing Person's Throat, poetry). Bahrain: Family of Writers and Authors in Bahrain, 1990.

Akhir al-mahabb (The Last of the Wind, poetry). Beirut: Dar al-Kunuz al-Ahliya, 1998.

Maladh al-ruh (The Soul's Refuge, poetry). Beirut: Dar al-Kunuz al-Ahliya, 1999.

al-Sinini, Umm al-'Izz (1972–), Egyptian short-story writer born in Marsa Matruh.

Tilka (This, short stories). Western Delta: General Authority for Culture Palaces, 1999.

Subh, 'Alawiya (1954–), Lebanese writer born in Beirut. She received her primary education at public schools in Beirut and her secondary education at the public Raml al-Zarif School. She received a B.A. in Arabic literature and language from the College of Education at the Lebanese University in 1978 and a B.A. in English literature from the College of Liberal Arts at the Lebanese University. She worked at the newspaper, *al-Nida'*, in 1979 and at *al-Nahar* from 1981 to 1986. She was editor in chief of *al-Hasna'* from 1984 to 1993. She founded the journal, *Snob al-hasna'* in 1994 and was its editor. She has published several literary pieces in the Lebanese and Arab press, and she has been a literary and art critic for *al-Nahar*, *al-Nida'*, *al-Tariq*, and *al-Safir*. She is a member of the Lebanese Writers' Union. For twelve years she taught in public high schools in Beirut.

Nawm al-ayyam (The Sleep of Days, texts). Beirut: Arab Research Institute, 1986.

al-Sudayri, Sultana (?–), Saudi poet and short-story writer born in al-Qarabat. She lives in Riyadh. She writes poetry in both classical and colloquial Arabic and is considered a pioneering Saudi poet in this regard. She is a member of the al-Nahda Charitable Association in Riyadh. She has written for many local and Gulf papers since 1975 and has become quite popular, particular among women and especially for her colloquial poetry. She also writes essays and has published the non-fiction work, *Bayn al-'aql wa-l-qalb* (Between the Mind and the Heart, 1996).

'Abir al-sahra' (Fragrance of the Desert, poetry). Beirut: al-Ahliya Foundation for Printing and Publishing, 1956.

'Aynay fadak (For You I Would Give My Eyes, poetry). Beirut: Dar al-Kitab al-Jadid, 1964.

Suwar min al-mujtama' (Portraits from Society, short stories). Beirut: Dar al-Afaq al-Jadida, 1975.

Qahr (Subjugation, poetry). Kuwait: Maktabat Umm al-Qura, 1984.

Sahaba bila matar (A Cloud Without Rain, poetry). Kuwait: Maktabat Umm al-Qura, 1984.

'Ala masharif al-qalb (On the Outskirts of the Heart, poetry). Riyadh: al-Farazdaq Press, 1995.

al-Hisan wa-l-hawajiz (The Horse and the Roadblocks, colloquial poetry). Riyadh: al-Farazdaq Press, 1995.

Suduf al-'Ubaydiya (see: al-Na'ib, Fatina)

al-Sufi, Habiba (1953–), Moroccan poet born in Marrakech. She received a B.A. in Arabic literature and a teaching certificate in Arabic language and literature. She is an Arabic teacher. She currently works in the research and survey department at the Marrakech Academy. She takes part in literary and cultural salons and publishes her poetry in magazines and newspapers.

Fawq al-waraq (On Paper, poetry). Marrakech: Tanmal Press, 1996.

Dam'at al-jil al-hazin (The Sad Generation's Tear, poetry). Marrakech: Dar Walili, 1997.

Maraya ta'kis imra'a (Mirrors Reflecting a Woman, poetry). Marrakech: Dar Walili, 1998.

Sulafa al-'Amiri (see: al-'Uf, Mu'mina)

Sulayha, Sana' (1955–), Egyptian short-story writer. She received a B.A. in journalism from Cairo University and an M.A. from the American University in Cairo. In 1982 and 1983 she studied drama, media, and feminist criticism at Illinois University. She is a cultural editor at *al-Ahram*. She has translated many works into Arabic, including the play, *Virginia*, by Edna O'Brien (translated as *Firjiniya*); *The Swiss Family Robinson*, by Johann Wyss; a collection of short stories (published as *Duwwamat al-qahr*, 1990); and *Ummi qalat la*, by Charlotte Kinley (published as part of the Experimental Theater Festival in 1997). She has also translated several articles on women's theater that were published in *al-Masrah* magazine.

Atfal al-samgh (Children of Glue, short stories). Cairo: General Egyptian Book Organization, 1993.

'Ala 'atabat al-hayah (On the Threshold of Life, short stories). Cairo: General Egyptian Book Organization, 1995.

Arajuzat (Puppets). Cairo: General Egyptian Book Organization, 1999).

Sulayman, Sahar (?–), Syrian short-story writer of the 1990s generation.

Harq al-layl (Passing Time, short stories). Damascus: n.p., 1997.

Sultan, 'Azza al-Sayyid Hasan (1974–), Egyptian author of children's stories born in Alexandria. She is an information specialist at the Ministry of Education.

Rihlat al-hamama al-'ajiba (The Dove's Strange Journey, children's literature). Cairo: General Authority for Culture Palaces, 1998.

al-Hayawanat al-mariha (The Merry Animals, children's literature). Cairo: Dar al-'Arabi Publishers, 1999.

Imra'a talid rajulan yushbihuk (A Woman Gives Birth to a Man Who Resembles You, short stories). Cairo: General Authority for Culture Palaces, 1999.

Sultan, Maha (1957–), Lebanese poet born in Tripoli. She received a B.A. in art and archaeology from the Lebanese University and worked at *al-Hasna'* from 1978 to 1984. She has published articles of criticism in *al-Nahar* and *al-Safir* (1982–1986), and she worked as an announcer on Lebanese television from 1984 to 1987. She also worked with the French Television Production Company, preparing programs on Arab poets living in Paris.

Tasabih al-miyah (The Water's Songs of Praise, poetry). Beirut: Dar al-Hamra', 1992.

Wardat al-mataha (Rose of the Labyrinth, poetry). Beirut: Dar al-Jadid, 1997.

al-Suruji, Saliha 'Abd Allah (?–), Saudi short-story writer born in Medina. She received a B.A. in education with a speciality in history from King 'Abd al-'Aziz University in Medina in 1995. She is a school principal in the Riyadh area. She is a member of the Charitable Association for Social Services and the Tiba Women's Charitable Association in Medina.

Kana hulman (It Was a Dream, short stories). al-Ta'if: Literary Club, 1995.

Surur, Malak Fahmi (?–), Egyptian novelist.

Sabiha (Fresh Young Woman, novel). Cairo: Dar al-Fikr al-'Arabi, 1948.

Sururi, Nadira (1940–), Palestinian poet born in Nablus. She studied sociology at the American University of Beirut, from which she graduated in 1961. She received an M.A. in sociology in 1972 and a Ph.D. in 1974.

Makhad imra'a (A Woman's Labor Pains, poetry). Amman: al-Jam'iya al-Malakiya Publications, 1976.

al-Susu, Nahla (1950–), Syrian short-story writer born in Hums. She received a B.A. in Arabic literature and works as an announcer for Radio Damascus. She has produced dozens of radio serials and two television screenplays: *al-Ziyara* (The Visit) and *Hulm* (A Dream). She published her first stories in Syrian newspapers and journals. She is a member of the Story and Novel Association.

Sitt zaharat bayda' (Six White Flowers, children's literature). Damascus: Ministry of Culture, 1989.

Siwar Daliya (Daliya's Bracelet, short stories). Damascus: Arab Writers' Union, 1992.

Tuqus mawt wahmi (Rituals of an Imagined Death, short stories). Damascus: Arab Writers' Union, 1995.

al-Suwaylim, Fawziya (?–), Kuwaiti short-story writer.

Tumuhat khadima (Aspirations of a Servant, short stories). Kuwait: al-Rabi'an Publishing, 1995.

al-Tabi'i, 'Aliya' Bint al-Munsif (1961–), Tunisian novelist. She graduated from the Higher Teachers' Institute in 1983 and received a proficiency certificate in research from the College of Humanities in Tunis in 1984. She works in journalism and television and is a critic and translator. She has made cultural contributions in Tunisia and abroad. She has published in Arabic and French in Tunisian periodicals such as *IBLA* and in *Le Monde* and the Paris-based *Qantara*. She received the Grand Literature Prize from the Tunisian Ministry of Culture in 1991.

Zahrat al-subbar (Cactus Flower, novel). Tunis: Dar al-Janub Publishers, 1991.

al-Tabyaniya, Natila (1949–), Tunisian short-story writer and novelist born in Tunis. She helps produce radio programs for literature lovers. She writes short stories and novels and has an interest in painting.

al-Mawt wa-l-ba'th wa-l-hadith (Death, Resurrection, and Discourse, short stories). Tunis: al-Dar al-Tunisiya Publishers, 1990.

Tariq al-nisyan (The Road of Forgetting, novel). Tunis: al-Dar al-'Arabiya Books, 1993.

Taha, Jumana (1941–), Syrian short-story writer born in the province of Jabla. She lives in Damascus. She received a B.A. in literature from Damascus University and works as a librarian at the Arab Broadcasting Union. She has published a work of comparative history entitled *al-Jamal fi-l-amthal* (The Beauty in Proverbs).

Sindbad fi rihla mu'ajjala (Sindbad on a Postponed Trip, short stories). Damascus: Dar al-Ahali, 1994.

'Indama tatakallam al-abwab (When the Doors Speak, short stories). Damascus: Arab Writers' Union, 1998.

al-Tahawy, Miral (al-Tahawi, Miral) (1968–), Egyptian short-story writer and novelist. She has a B.A. in Arabic and an M.A. in Arabic literature. She is an assistant instructor at the College of Arab Studies at Cairo University in the comparative literature department. Her non-fiction works include *al-Tamarrud wa-l-ightirab: dirasa fi-l-nass al-qisasi 'ind Ghada al-Samman* (Rebellion and Alienation: A Study of Ghada al-Samman's Short Stories).

Rim al-barari al-mustahila (Antelope of the Impossible Wilderness, short stories). Cairo: General Egyptian Book Organization, 1993.

al-Khiba' (*The Tent*, novel). Cairo: Dar Sharqiyat, 1996.

al-Badhinjana al-zarqa' (*Blue Aubergine*, novel). Cairo: Dar Sharqiyat, 1998.

Ta'ima, Nevine (?–), Egyptian poet.

Sirr al-dunya wa qasa'id ukhra (Secret of the World and Other Stories, poetry). N.p.: n.p., 1993.

Tal'at, Munira (?–), Egyptian novelist.

al-Ba'isa (The Wretched Woman, play). Alexandria: al-Mustaqbal Press, 1930.

al-Ghafla (Carelessness, novel). Cairo: al-Taqaddum Press, 1932.

al-Maghfira (Forgiveness, novel). Cairo: al-Taqaddum Press, 1932.

Taht rayat Faysal (Under Faysal's Banner, poetry). Cairo: al-Matba'a al-Haditha, 1934.

Qissa sinima'iya (A Film Story, play). al-Minya: al-Nil Press, 1937.

Talib, 'Aliya (1957–), Iraqi short-story writer born in Baghdad. She studied at the School of Business at the Beirut Arab University. She works in journalism and is responsible for the cultural desk at *al-Jumhuriya* newspaper in Baghdad. She is also a press liaison for the Bayt al-Hikma Library. Her short-story collection, *Ba'idan dakhil hudud*, won a medal of appreciation in Iraq.

al-Mamarrat (Corridors, short stories). Baghdad: Dar al-Shu'un al-Thaqafiya, 1998.

Ba'idan dakhil al-hudud (Deep Inside the Borders, short stories). Baghdad: Dar al-Shu'un al-Thaqafiya, 1999.

Talib, Duna (1963–), Iraqi short-story writer and novelist born in Basra. She resides in Denmark. She has a B.A. in horticulture and palm-tree agriculture from Basra University and a teaching certificate in Denmark. She is a translator and consultant at the Royal Library of Copenhagen, working on a project to translate and publish the works of Hans Christian Andersen.

Harbnama (The Book of War, short stories). Damascus: Dar al-Mada, 1988.

Talib, Nuha (?–), Iraqi short-story writer.

al-Akharun (Others, short stories). Baghdad: Dar al-Shu'un al-Thaqafiya, 1996.

al-Tall, Suhayr (1952–), Jordanian short-story writer and journalist born in Irbid. She completed primary school in Damascus and preparatory and secondary school in Irbid. She went to university in Beirut, from which she received a graduate degree in philosophy. She has been a journalist since 1975. She has published many investigative stories and critical essays on fiction and the plastic arts. She is a member of the Journalists' Syndicate and of many women's groups and national and syndicate committees in Jordan. She has published several non-fiction works, including *Muqaddimat hawl qadiyat al-mar'a wa-l-haraka al-nisawiya fi-l-Urdun* (Introductions to the Women's Cause and the

Feminist Movement in Jordan, Beirut, 1985) and *Madinat al-ward wa-l-hajar* (City of Roses and Stone, Amman, 1997).

al-'Id ya'ti sirran (The Holiday Comes in Secret, short stories). Amman: Dar al-Ufuq al-Jadid, 1982.

al-Mashnaqa (The Gallows, short stories). Amman: privately published, 1987.

Tannus, Asma' (1946–), Palestinian poet born in al-Makar in the part of Palestine occupied in 1948. She completed her primary education in the town school and continued her secondary education at Kafr al-Yasif School. She is a graduate of the Arab Teachers' Institute in Haifa. She works in education.

Karm al-Masih (Christ's Vineyard, poetry). Acre: Abu Rahmun Press, 1992.

Bustan al-aghani (Garden of Song, poetry). Acre: Abu Rahmun Press, 1993.

Lisan al-qalb wa-l-ruh (The Tongue of Heart and Spirit, poetry). Acre: Abu Rahmun Press, 1995.

al-Shita' hubb wa amal (Winter Is Love and Hope, poetry). Acre: Abu Rahmun Press, 1995.

al-Tabi'a lahn wa naghm (Nature Is a Melody and a Tune, poetry). Acre: Abu Rahmun Press, 1995.

Taqi al-Din, Nawal (1942–), Syrian short-story writer, novelist, and journalist born in Damascus. She received a B.A. in philosophy and psychology from Damascus University.

Shams khalf al-dabab (Sun Behind the Fog, novel). Damascus: Arab Writers' Union, 1986.

Fajr al-hubb (Love's Dawn, novel). Damascus: Dar al-Jumhuriya Press, 1995.

Tarabiya, Andree (1940?–), Lebanese poet and short-story writer born in Sawfar. She attended the public girls' secondary school in Beirut and obtained a B.A. in Arabic literature from the American University of Beirut, as well as a B.A. in journalism and media from Cairo University. She worked in journalism and published

in the Lebanese *al-Nahar* and *al-Diyar*, as well as in the Cairo newspaper, *al-Ahram*. She was editor in chief of the journals, *al-Hasna'*, *Fayruz*, and *al-Sharqiya*. She has taught Arabic language and media training at university level and worked as a media consultant for several ministries. She works at Lebanese radio. She has published a book of social criticism, *Masamir* (Nails, 1975), and an academic study, *al-Qanun wa-l-mar'a* (The Law and Women, 1975).

Zam'ana fi waha (Thirsty in the Oasis, novel). Beirut: Maktabat al-Ma'arif, 1961.

Taranim zawja (A Wife's Hymns, poetry). Beirut: Maktabat al-Ma'arif, 1972.

Tarzi, Falak (1912–1987), Syrian literary pioneer. She published her articles in Egyptian journals, particularly *al-Risala*, as well as in the Lebanese *al-Adib*. She wrote and lectured on literature and nationalism. She was fluent in French and was influenced by French literature, and she had personal relationships with many of France's greatest thinkers, including Jean-Paul Sartre. She translated many works and several plays from French into Arabic. She wrote a collection of articles, *Ara'i wa masha'iri* (My Opinions and Emotions), published in 1939 with an introduction by Khalil Mardam. She also published *Salah al-Din al-Tarazi wa-l-qadiya al-Filistiniya* (Salah al-Din al-Tarazi and the Palestinian Cause) in 1982.

Tawfiq, Huda Hasan (1972–), Egyptian short-story writer born in Bani Suwayf. She teaches English.

Kull al-ahzan mukhti'a (All Sorrows Are Incorrect, short stories). Northern Upper Egypt: General Authority for Culture Palaces, 1998.

al-Tawfiq, Maryam (?–), Moroccan writer.

Dhikrayati min al-Ittihad al-Sufiyati (My Memories From the Soviet Union, memoir). Rabat: Dar al-Aman, 1999.

Tawfiq, Munira (1893–1965), Pioneering Egyptian poet born in Port Said. Her family encouraged her to read and memorize poetry. She married in 1911. When only four years later her husband was killed in a painful accident, she wrote poetry eulogizing him. Her poetry was closer to a social and political document, and dominated by melancholy. She was awarded the Gold Medal of Literary Excellence in the poetry festival of 1942. She was an active member of the Young Muslim Women's Association in Alexandria, which published her collection of poetry, *Anwar Munira*, on the fortieth anniversary of her death. She had collected and arranged her poems in a book but she died before its publication.

Anwar Munira (Munira's Lights, poetry). Alexandria: Young Muslim Women's Association, 1965.

Tawfiq, Sahar (1951–), Egyptian short-story writer. She received a B.A. in Arabic, with a speciality in literature and criticism, from al-Azhar University in 1974. She has translated several works of literature to and from English. A translated English collection of her short stories, *Points of the Compass*, translated by Marilyn Booth, received the University of Arkansas Press Arabic Translation Award. She teaches Arabic in Cairo schools.

An tanhadir al-shams (For the Sun to Sink, short stories). Cairo: General Egyptian Book Organization, 1985.

Taymur, 'A'isha (al-Taymuriya, 'A'isha) (1840–1902), Egyptian poet who played a pioneering role in women's writing. She was educated at home and was well versed in Persian, Turkish, Arabic, and jurisprudence. Her father brought tutors to the house to instruct her in Persian, Arabic, and prosody until she had mastered them. Her tutor, Stayta al-Tablawiya, taught her poetry, while Fatima al-Azhari instructed her in grammar. She worked as a translator for the royal court and accompanied the Queen Mother when she received members of the Persian royal family. She produced three collections of poetry in three languages: Arabic, Turkish, and Persian. Her daughter died at age eighteen, which drove 'A'isha into a life of complete seclusion for seven years, during which she burned her Persian poetry. She has one extant collection of poetry in Persian, *Ashkufa*.

Hilyat al-tiraz (Decorative Embroidery, poetry). Cairo: al-Sharafiya Press, 1884.

Nata'ij al-ahwal fi-l-aqwal wa-l-af'al (The Consequences of Circumstances in Words and Deeds). Cairo: al-Sharafiya Press, 1887.

Mir'at al-ta'ammul fi-l-umur (The Mirror of Contemplation, epistle). Cairo: al-Mahrusa Press, 1892.

al-Taytun, Fatima Ahmad (1962–), Bahraini poet. She is an Arabic teacher at the primary level for the Ministry of Education and a member of the Family of Writers and Authors.

Arsum qalbi (I Draw My Heart, poetry). Bahrain: al-Sharqiya Press, 1991.

al-Awqat al-mahjura (The Desolate Times, poetry). Manama: n.p., 1994.

Tuqus al-'ishq (The Rituals of Love, poetry). N.p.: n.p., 1996.

al-Tayyib, Fatima (1955–), Yemeni poet born in the village of Dhu'ab in the province of Ta'iz. She currently resides in Sana'a. She has written many *muwashshah* poems that are currently being prepared for publication.

Itlalat Bint al-Tayyib (Bint al-Tayyib's View, poetry). N.p.: n.p., n.d.

Telmissany, May (al-Tilmisani, Mayy) (1965–), Egyptian short-story writer and novelist born in Cairo. She received a B.A. in French literature from Ain Shams University in 1987 and an M.A. in French literature from Cairo University in 1994. She teaches at Cairo University. She has translated many books about film and theater from English to Arabic. She published a work of non-fiction, *Fu'ad al-Tuhami wa zahrat al-mustahil* (Fu'ad al-Tuhami and the Flower of the Impossible), in 1995.

Naht mutakarrir (Recurrent Carvings, short stories). Cairo: Dar Sharqiyat, 1995.

Dunyazad (*Dunyazad*, novel). Cairo: Dar Sharqiyat, 1997.

Tergeman, Siham (Turjuman, Siham) (1932–), Syrian short-story writer born in Damascus. She received a B.A. in philosophy from Damascus University in 1955. She started working in journalism in 1956 and works in the counseling department. She presented a cultural program on Damascus radio that gained her renown in literary circles. She has published a collection of articles entitled *Jabal al-shaykh fi bayti* (Mount Hermon in My House, 1982). She also published *Dimashq fi matla' al-qarn al-'ishrin* (Damascus at the Turn of the Twentieth Century) and *Ya mal al-Sham: dirasa fulkluriya 'an Dimashq*, a personal account of a Syrian woman's youth spent in the Old City of Damascus. Parts of this are translated as *Daughter of Damascus*, 1994.

Ya mal al-Sham: dirasa fulkluriya 'an Dimashq (O Wealth of Damascus: A Study of Damascus memoirs, 1969).

Ah ya ana (Poor Me, short stories). Damascus: Dar Tlas for Research, Translation, and Publishing, 1986.

Thabit, Fatima (?–), Egyptian poet.

Qasa'id majruha (Dubious Poems, poetry). Cairo: Egyptian Association to Foster Talent, 1993.

Thabit, Katiya (?–), Egyptian novelist.

Wa la 'aza' li-l-sayyidat (And No Solace for Women, novel). Cairo: Dar al-Hilal, 1979.

Rihla ghariba fi 'alam al-hubb (A Strange Journey in the World of Love, novel). Cairo: al-Dar al-Fanniya Press, 1982.

Thabit, Munira (M.T.) (1902–1967), Egyptian journalist and political activist born and raised in Alexandria. She learned

English, Italian, and Arabic and moved to Cairo to work in journalism in 1925. She published the French-language *Le Poire* newspaper, a political and literary weekly. She then put out the Arabic-language *al-Amal*. She published a series of articles in *al-Ahram* entitled "Khawatir tha'ira" (Reflections of a Revolutionary), all signed "M.T." Her non-fiction works include *Qadiyat Filistin: ra'i al-mar'a al-Misriya fi-l-kitab al-abyad al-Injlizi* (The Cause of Palestine: Egyptian Women's Opinion on Britain's White Paper, 1939).

Thawra fi-l-burj al-'aji: mudhakkirati fi 'ishrin 'aman 'an ma'rakat huquq al-mar'a al-siyasiya (A Revolution in the Ivory Tower: My Memoirs of Twenty Years of Struggle for Women's Political Rights, memoir). Cairo: Dar al-Ma'arif, 1946.

Thamir, Najiya (Bint al-Waha) (1926–1988), Tunisian short-story writer born in Damascus to a father of Turkish origin. She received her primary education in Ba'labakk, Lebanon, and her secondary and university education in Damascus. She settled in Tunis after her marriage and worked in Tunisian radio as a producer of literary and social programs. She wrote essays, short stories, radio plays, and novels. She was a member of the Story Club, the Tunisian Writers' Union, and the New Pen Association. Her non-fiction works include a collection of articles, *al-Mar'a wa-l-hayah* (Women and Life, 1956), and *Asma' Bint Asad ibn al-Furat* (Asma' Bint Asad ibn al-Furat, 1978). She was also known as Bint al-Waha.

'Adalat al-sama' (Heaven's Justice, short stories). Tunis: Dar al-Kutub al-Sharqiya, 1956.

Aradna al-hayah (We Wanted Life, short stories). Tunis: Dar al-Kutub al-Sharqiya, 1956.

Samar wa 'ibar (Conversation and Lessons, short stories). Tunis: Dar al-Kutub al-Sharqiya, 1972.

Hikayat jaddati (My Grandmother's Tales,

children's literature). Tunis: Tunisian Distribution Company, 1973.

al-Taja'id (Wrinkles, short stories). Tunis: al-Dar al-'Arabiya Books, 1978.

al-Tibi, Lina (1963–), Syrian poet born in Damascus. She use to live in London but now lives in Cairo. She was on the editorial board of the London-based *al-Katiba* magazine.

Shams fi khizana (A Sun in the Vault, poetry). London: privately published, 1991.

Sura shakhsiya (A Personal Portrait, poetry). London: Dar al-Sura, 1994.

Huna ta'ish (Here She Lives, poetry). Beirut: Arab Institute for Research and Publishing, 1996.

al-Tilmisani (see: al-Balghithi, Asiya al-Hashimi)

Tubi, Asma (1905–1983), Palestinian writer born in Nazareth, where she remained until completing primary school. She was concerned with women's issues and was an active member of the Women's Union in Acre from 1929 to 1948. In the late period of the British Mandate she was the president of the Arab Women's Union in Acre, a leader of the Orthodox Young Women's Association, and a prominent member of the Young Christian Women's Association. When she was forced to leave Palestine in 1948, she left behind a book manuscript at the printer titled *al-Mar'a al-'Arabiya fi Filistin* (The Arab Palestinian Woman). She appeared on several Palestinian radio programs, including "Huna al-Quds" (Jerusalem Here) and "al-Sharq al-Adna" (The Near East) in Jaffa. She also appeared on Lebanese radio in Beirut in 1948. That year, she assumed the editorship of the women's page of *Filistin* newspaper. She was also the editor of the women's page of *Kull shay'* and *al-Ahad* magazines. She wrote drama, poetry, and fiction and published several works in English. She received the Lebanese Constantine the Great Award in 1973 and was posthumously awarded the Jerusalem Medal for Culture and Arts in December 1990.

Masra' qaysar Rusiya wa 'a'ilatih (The Death of the Czar and His Family, play). Acre: n.p., 1925.

al-Fatah wa kayf uriduha (The Young Woman and How I Want Her, essays). Acre: n.p., 1943.

Sabr wa faraj (Patience and Relief, play). Acre: n.p., 1943.

'Ala madhbah al-tadhiya (On the Sacrificial Altar, poetry, two vols.). Acre: n.p., 1946.

Ahadith min al-qalb (Stories from the Heart, short stories). Beirut: Qalfat Press, 1955.

'Abir wa Majd (Fragrance and Glory, essays). Beirut: Qalfar Press, 1966.

Jibal al-murjan (The Coral Mountain). N.p.: n.p., 1972.

Hubbi al-kabir (My Big Love, poetry). Beirut: Dar al-'Awda, 1972.

Nafahat 'itr (Wafts of Perfume, essays). Beirut: Nawfal Foundation, 1975.

Nisa' wa asrar (Women and Secrets, play). N.p.: n.p., n.d.

Shahidat al-ikhlas (The Martyr of Faithfulness, play). N.p.: n.p., n.d.

Wahida bi-wahida wa-l-qimar (One to One and the Wager, one-act play). N.p.: n.p., n.d.

Tulib, Bahiya (1966–), Egyptian poet. She received a B.A. in Arabic in 1989 and a degree from the Higher Institute for Folk Arts in 1996. She is a researcher working on an atlas of Egyptian folklore for the General Authority for Culture Palaces.

I'tirafat 'ashiqa qarawiya (Confessions of a Village Lover, poetry). Cairo: General Egyptian Book Organization, 1993.

al-'Ishq tamima janubiya (Love is a Southern Talisman, poetry). Cairo: General Authority for Culture Palaces, 1995.

Tuqan, Fadwa (1917–2003), Palestinian poet born in Nablus, where she attended primary school. She was forced to leave school, so her brother, Ibrahim Tuqan, a prominent Palestinian poet, instructed her. Tuqan became one of the most well-known Arab poets of the twentieth century. She was awarded several prizes, most important the al-Babtin Poetry Prize in 1994 in Kuwait; an award from the World Festival of Women Writers in Palermo, Italy, in 1992; the Jerusalem Medal from the P.L.O. in 1990; and the 'Arar Prize for Poetry from the League of Jordanian Writers in Amman in 1983. Her poetry has been translated into English and Persian, including *Selected Poems of Fadwa Tuqan*, translated by Ibrahim Dawood, Irbid: Yarmouk University, 1994.

Akhi Ibrahim (My Brother Ibrahim). Jaffa: al-Maktaba al-'Asriya, 1946.

Wahdi ma'a al-ayyam (Alone With the Days, poetry). Cairo: Lajnat al-Nashr li-l-Jami'iyin, 1952.

Wajadtuha (I Found Her, poetry). Beirut: Dar al-Adab, 1957.

A'tina hubban (Give Us Love, poetry). Beirut: Dar al-Adab, 1960.

Amam al-bab al-mughlaq (Before the Closed Door, poetry). Beirut: Dar al-Adab, 1967.

al-Layl wa-l-fursan (The Night and the Horsemen, poetry). Beirut: Dar al-Adab, 1969.

'Ala qimmat al-dunya wahidan (Alone on Top of the World, poetry). Beirut: Dar al-Adab, 1973.

Qasa'id siyasiya (Political Poems, poetry). Acre: Dar al-Aswar, 1980.

Rihla sa'ba rihla jabaliya (*A Mountainous Journey*, autobiography). Acre: Dar al-Aswar, 1985. Reprinted as *Rihla jabaliya rihla sa'ba* (Mountainous Journey, Hard Journey). Amman: Dar al-Shuruq, 1985, and Cairo: Dar al-Thaqafa al-Jadida, 1989.

Diwan Fadwa Tuqan (The Poetry of Fadwa Tuqan, poetry). Beirut: Dar al-'Awda, 1988 (includes the poetry collections *Wajadtuha*, *A'tina hubban*, and *Amam al-bab al-mughlaq*).

Tammuz wa al-shay' al-akhar (July and the Other Thing, poetry). Amman: Dar al-Shuruq, 1989.

al-Rihla al-as'ab (The Harder Journey, autobiography). Amman: Dar al-Shuruq, 1993.

al-A'mal al-shi'riya al-kamila (The Complete Works of Poetry, poetry). Beirut: Arab Institute for Research and Publishing, 1993 (includes *Wahdi ma'a al-ayyam*, *Wajadtuha*, *Qasa'id min rawasib wahdi ma'a al-ayyam* [Selected Poems from *Wahdi ma'a al-ayyam*], *A'tina hubban*, *Amam al-bab al-mughlaq*, *Qasa'id ila J.H.* [Poems to J.H.], *al-Layl wa-l-fursan*, *'Ala qimmat al-dunya wahidan*, and *Tammuz wa-l-shay' al-akhar*).

al-Turki, Rashida (?–), Tunisian short-story writer.

'Asr al-hanin (The Age of Longing, short stories). Beirut: Dar al-Adab, 1990.

'Ubayd, Malak Hajj (1946–), Syrian short-story writer and novelist born in Jabla. She is a teacher in Kuwait and a member of the Story and Novel Association in Damascus. She published her first stories in Syrian newspapers and magazines.

al-Khuruj min da'irat al-intizar (Escape from the Circle of Waiting, novel). Damascus: Arab Writers' Union, 1983.

Qal al-bahr (The Sea Said, short stories). Damascus: Arab Writers' Union, 1986.

al-Ghuraba' (The Strangers, short stories). Latakia: Dar al-Hiwar, 1992.

Hikayat al-layl wa-l-nahar (Stories of the Night and Day, short stories). Damascus: Arab Writers' Union, 1994.

al-'Ubaydi, Nihal Hasan (1948–), Iraqi poet born in Ba'quba in the province of Diyala. She spent her childhood in Baghdad and grew up and studied in Basra. She graduated from Basra University with a degree in Arabic in 1970 after which she worked as a teacher. She was interested in the resistance literature of occupied Palestine and wrote an academic study on the topic. She also wrote a study in comparative religion. She was a volunteer war correspondent during the Iran-Iraq War.

Shay' akhar li-l-hubb (Something Else for Love, poetry). Basra: Haddad Press, 1975.

al-'Udwan, Amina (195?–), Jordanian poet born in Amman, where she still resides. She studied at Ain Shams University in Cairo (1967–1971). She was the editor in chief of *al-Funun* magazine and *Sawt al-jil*, as well as the editorial secretary for *Afkar*. She has written critical articles on contemporary Arabic literature and has published the non-fiction work, *Maqalat fi-l-riwaya al-'Arabiya al-mu'asira* (Essays on the Contemporary Arabic Novel, Amman, 1982).

Watan bila aswar (Country Without Walls, poetry). Beirut: Arab Institute for Research and Publishing, 1982.
Amam al-hajiz (Facing the Checkpoint, poetry). Amman: Dar al-Ufuq al-Jadid, 1983.
Ghuraf al-ta'mid al-ma'daniya (Metal Baptismals, poetry). Amman: Dar al-Ufuq al-Jadid, 1985.
al-A'mal al-shi'riya 1982–1988 (Poetic Works 1982–1988, poetry). Beirut: Arab Institute for Research and Publishing, 1989.
Qasa'id 'an al-intifada (Intifada Poems, poetry). Amman: Dar al-Karmel, 1991.
Ahkam al-i'dam (Death Sentences, poetry). Amman: Dar al-Yanabi', 1992.
Akhi Mustafa (My Brother Mustafa, poetry). Amman: Dar al-Karmel, 1993.
al-A'mal al-shi'riya 1988–1993 (Poetic Works 1988–1993, poetry). Beirut: Arab Institute for Research and Publishing, 1994 (includes *Qasa'id 'an al-intifada*, *Ahkam al-i'dam*, and *Akhi Mustafa*).

al-'Udwani, Najat (1958–), Tunisian poet born in Qabis who currently resides in Tunis. She graduated from the English department of the Bourguiba Institute of Modern Languages in 1982. She has been a journalist and worked for the Palestinian News Agency. Her works have been published in Tunisian newspapers and magazines. She has taken part in many poetry festivals and fairs in Tunisia and abroad. She is a member of the Tunisian Writers' Union and the Story Club.

Fi kull jarh zanbaqa (A Lily in Every Wound, poetry). Tunis: n.p., 1982.
Judhur li-sama'i (Roots of My Sky, poetry). Beirut: Dar al-'Awda, 1986.
Hadil ruh min fuladh yatahaddal (The Flowing Coo of a Spirit of Steel, poetry). Tunis: Nuqush 'Arabiya, 1994.

al-'Uf, Mu'mina (Sulafa al-'Amiri) (?–), Syrian novelist and poet born in Damascus. She received a B.A. in Arabic from Damascus University and a Ph.D. in Islamic philosophy from St. Joseph University in Beirut in 1987. She worked at *al-Manar* newspaper, published by her father, Bashir al-'Uf, in Damascus. Since 1975 she has worked in the Center for the Study of the Contemporary Arab World at St. Joseph University in Beirut. She used a pseudonym, Sulafa al-'Amiri, to publish her literary works from 1963 to 1978.

Shira' bila marsa (A Sail Without a Port, poetry). Beirut: al-Muttahida, 1973.
Tarnima li-l-harb wa-l-bara'a (A Hymn to War and Innocence, poetry). N.p.: n.p., 1981.
Madd bila jazr (Flow Without Ebb, novel). Damascus: al-Manar Publications, 1992.

al-Uhaydab, Layla Ibrahim (?–), Saudi short-story writer born in al-Ahsa'. She resides in Riyadh. She has taught high school since 1980.

al-Bahth 'an yawm sabi' (The Search for a Seventh Day, short stories). Cairo: al-Amin Press, n.d.

al-'Ukayli, Rashida (?–), Iraqi poet.
al-Bishara (Glad Tidings, poetry). Basra: Maysalun Press, 1970.
Fakihat al-zaman al-ati (Fruit of the Coming Age, poetry). Baghdad: Wa'i al-'Ummal Press, 1987.

'Ulaywa, Suhayr (?–) , Egyptian poet.
Saturaddad yawman ash'ari (My Poetry Will Be Repeated One Day, poetry). Cairo: n.p., 1985.
Arfud an (I Refuse to, poetry). Cairo: General Egyptian Book Organization, 1989.
Wa la'allak yawman tafhamuha (Perhaps One Day You Will Understand Her, poetry). Cairo: League of Modern Literature, 1989.
Wa lan ubali (And I Will Not Care, poetry). Cairo: General Egyptian Book Organization, 1991.

'Ulaywa, Suzanne (?–), Egyptian poet.
'Usfur al-maqha (Sparrow of the Café, poetry). Cairo: n.p., 1994.

'Umar, Malakat al-Fadil (?–), Sudanese novelist and short-story writer born in al-Shallal on the White Nile. She received a B.A. from the College of Education at Khartoum University, with a specialty in English and psychology. She has published several short stories in various periodicals. Her poem, "Zaman nasr" (Time of Victory), received first prize in a television competition.
al-Judran al-qasiya (The Cruel Walls, novel). Cairo: privately published, 1999.

'Umar, Najwa (?–), Egyptian poet.
Wa sha'ira (And a Poet, poetry). Cairo: General Egyptian Book Organization, 1994.

'Umar, Zahra (1938–2000), Jordanian novelist born in Amman to Circassian parents who emigrated from the Caucasus to Jordan in the early part of the century. She did not complete her education because of her early marriage. She lost her husband when she was twenty-seven years old and assumed the responsibility of raising her four children. She worked as a secretary and published several short stories, although they were never collected in book form. For years she worked on an epic, multi-volume novel about the history of the Circassian migration to Jordan.
al-Khuruj min Susruqa: riwayat al-shatat al-Sharkasi (Out of Sosriqwe: a Novel of the Circassian Diaspora, novel). Amman: Dar al-Azmina, 1992.
Susruqa khalf al-dabab (Sosriqwe Behind the Fog). Amman: Dar al-Azmina, 2001.

al-'Umda, Amal (?–), Egyptian short-story writer born in Luxor. She received a B.A. in business from Ain Shams University in 1973. She has worked at Youth and Sport Radio, Middle East Radio, and Public Radio. She has released a collection of interviews entitled *'Uqdati* (My Complex).
al-Bawh ba'd al-samt (Confession after Silence, short stories). Cairo: General Egyptian Book Organization, 1993.

Umm Ahmad (see: al-Sharqawi, Nafisa)

Umm 'Isam (see: al-Nashawati, Khadija al-Jarrah)

Umm Nizar (see: al-Mala'ika, Salma)

Umm Salma (see: al-Nasir, Su'ad)
Umm Siham (see: Bilal, 'Ammariya)

al-'Umri, 'Atifa (?–), Egyptian novelist.
Hadrat sahib al-dawla (Mr. President, novel). Cairo: General Egyptian Book Organization, n.d.

'Urabi, Kulthum Malik (1936–), Palestinian poet born in the Galilee. She went to school in Haifa. She moved after the *nakba* to Lebanon, where she attended university.
Musharrada (Homeless, poetry). Beirut: al-Maktab al-Tijari, 1963.
Ajras al-samt (The Bells of Silence, poetry). Beirut: Dar al-Nashr li-l-Jami'iyin, 1965.
al-Nabalm ja'al qamh al-Quds murran (Napalm Has Made Jerusalem Wheat Bitter, poetry). Beirut: al-Maktaba al-'Asriya, 1968.

Nahr al-samt al-hadi' yakhdarr (The River of Quiet Silence Turns Green, poetry). Beirut: n.p., 1968.

al-Daw' wa-l-turab (The Light and the Dust, poetry). Beirut: Dar al-Afaq al-Jadida, 1977.

'Uyun (Eyes, poetry). N.p.: al-Jami'iya Foundation for Research and Publishing, 1980.

Ma' li-zama' al-shams (Water for the Thirsty Sun, poetry). N.p.: n.p., n.d.

al-'Uraymi, Su'ad (?–), Emirati short-story writer born in the Emirates. She works at the Ministry of Education and is a member of the Emirati Writers' and Authors' Union.

Tuful (The Tender Ones, short stories). Sharjah: Emirati Writers' and Authors' Union, 1990.

Haql Ghamran (Ghamran's Field, short stories). Sharjah: Emirati Writers' and Authors' Union, 1997.

al-'Urayyid, Thuraya Ibrahim (1946–), Saudi poet born in Bahrain. She received a B.A. in education from the American University of Beirut in 1966, an M.A. in educational administration from the same university in 1969, and a Ph.D. in educational planning and administration from North Carolina University in 1976. She works in the planning department at Aramco and writes for several local and Arab papers. Her poems have been translated into English.

'Ubur al-qifar furada (Crossing the Wastelands One by One, poetry). al-Ta'if: Literary Club, 1993.

Ayna ittijah al-shajar? (Which Direction Are the Trees?, poetry). al-Dammam: al-Turki Press, 1995.

Imra'a dun ism (A Nameless Woman, poetry). N.p.: n.p., 1998.

'Uruq, Shawqiya (1957–), Palestinian poet and short-story writer born in Nazareth in the part of Palestine occupied in 1948. She went to school in her hometown and studied for one year at Haifa University. She

lives in al-Tira and is a high-school librarian.

Imra'a bila ayyam (A Woman Without Days, short stories). Nazareth: Maktab al-Mujtama' Journalism and Publishing, 1979.

Khatawat fawq al-ard al-'ariya (Footsteps on the Naked Earth, short stories). Shafa 'Amr: Dar al-Mashriq, 1980.

al-Nabd fi jawf mahara (Pulse in a Clam's Belly, reflections). N.p.: n.p., 1980.

Dhakirat al-matar (The Rain's Memory, poetry). Acre: Dar al-Aswar, 1986.

Shams hudurik ustura (The Glow of Your Presence Is a Legend, poetry). Nazareth: Office of Arab Culture, 1993.

Ismuk tahlilat zumurrud (Your Name is an Emerald's Rejoicing, poetry). Nazareth: Office of Arab Culture, 1995.

al-'Ushbi, Fatima (1959–), Yemeni poet born in Bayt 'Ushbi in the province of al-Muhit. She works at the Yemen Center for Studies and Research. Since the 1980s al-'Ushbi has been writing poetry in both classical Arabic and Yemeni colloquial Arabic. She has published two poetry collections, the first in collaboration with another woman poet.

Wahaj al-fajr (The Glow of Dawn). N.p.: n.p., 1991.

Innaha Fatima (She Is Fatima, 2000). Baghdad: Maktabat Mada.

'Ussayran, Layla (1934–2007), Lebanese novelist born in Sidon. She received a B.A. in political science from the American University of Beirut in 1954. She worked for the Lebanese publisher, Dar al-Sayyad, and was a correspondent for the Cairo-based *Rose al-Yusuf*. She received the National Cedar Medal (knight's rank) in 1996.

Lan namut ghadan (We Will Not Die Tomorrow, novel). Beirut: Dar al-Tali'a, 1962.

al-Hiwar al-akhras (The Mute Conversation, novel). Beirut: Dar al-Tali'a, 1963.

al-Madina al-farigha (The Empty City, novel). Beirut: Dar wa Maktabat al-Hayat, 1966.

'Asafir al-fajr (Dawn Sparrows, novel). Beirut: Dar al-Tali‘a, 1968.

Khatt al-af‘a (The Trace of the Snake, novel). Beirut: Dar al-Fatah, 1972.

Qal‘at al-usta (The Craftsman's Fortress, novel). Beirut: Dar al-Nahar Publishers, 1979.

Jisr al-hajar (The Stone Bridge, novel). Beirut: al-Matbu‘at Distribution and Publication, 1986.

al-Istiraha (The Respite, novel). Beirut: al-Matbu‘at Distribution and Publication, 1988.

Shara'it mulawwana min hayati (Colored Ribbons from My Life, autobiography). London: Riyad al-Rayyis Books and Publishing, 1994.

Ta'ir min al-qamar (A Bird from the Moon, novel). Beirut: Dar al-Nahar Publishers, 1996.

al-‘Utaybi, Fatima Faysal (1966–), Saudi short-story writer born in al-Dammam. She received a liberal arts B.A. from the College of Education for Girls, run by the General Office for Girls' Education in al-Qasim, in 1988. She has been a primary-school teacher since 1989.

Ihtifal bi-anni imra'a (A Celebration Because I'm a Woman, short stories). Jeddah: Maktabat Tuhama, 1991.

Dif' yadayha (The Warmth of Her Hands, short stories). Riyadh: n.p., 1995.

‘Uthman, I‘tidal (1942–), Egyptian short-story writer born in Tukh in the province of al-Qalyubiya. She received a B.A. in English from Cairo University in 1963 and an M.A. in Arabic literature from the American University in Cairo in 1979. She was a supervisor of publications at the General Egyptian Book Organization and editor in chief of the journal, *al-Fusul*. She is currently the editor of *Sutur*. Several of her stories have been translated into other languages, and she has published studies on the novel and the short story in Egypt and in the Arab world. She published a work of non-fiction, *Ida'at al-nass: qira'at al-shi‘r*

al-‘Arabi al-hadith (Illuminating the Text: Reading Modern Arabic Poetry), in 1988.

Yunus al-bahr (Jonah of the Sea, short stories). Cairo: General Egyptian Book Organization, 1987.

Washm al-shams (The Sun's Tattoo, short stories). Cairo: General Egyptian Book Organization, 1992.

al-‘Uthman, Layla (1945–), Kuwaiti novelist and short-story writer born in Kuwait. She graduated from high school. She is a member of the Authors' League in Kuwait, the Writers' Union, the Journalists' Association, Amnesty International (Kuwaiti branch), and the Kuwaiti Association for the Defense of War Victims. Her stories have been translated into English, Russian, and Serbo-Croatian.

Hamasat (Whispers, poetry). Kuwait: Ministry of Information, 1972.

Imra'a fi ina' (Woman in a Jar, short stories). Kuwait: Dhat al-Salasil Publications, 1976.

al-Rahil (The Departure, short stories). Beirut: Dar al-Adab, 1979.

Fi-l-layl ta'ti al-‘uyun (At Night the Eyes Come, short stories). Beirut: Dar al-Adab, 1980.

al-Hubb lahu suwar (Love Has Images, short stories). Kuwait: al-Watan Press, 1982.

al-Mar'a wa-l-qitta (The Woman and the Cat, novel). Beirut: Arab Institute for Research and Publishing, 1985.

Wa Sumaya takhruj min al-bahr (And Sumaya Emerges from the Sea, novel). Cairo: Dar al-Shuruq, 1986.

Fathiya takhtar mawtaha (Fathiya Chooses Her Death, short stories). Cairo: Dar al-Shuruq, 1987.

La yasluh al-hubb wa qisas ukhra (Love Is No Good and Other Stories, short stories). Beirut: Arab Institute for Research and Publishing, 1987.

Halat hubb majnuna (A Crazy Case of Love, short stories). Cairo: General Egyptian Book Organization, 1989.

55 hikayat hubb (Fifty-five Tales of Love, tales). Kuwait: al-Rabi‘an, 1992.

al-Hawajiz al-sawda' (The Black Barricades, short stories). Kuwait: al-Qabas Press, 1994.

Zahra tadkhul al-hayy (Zahra Comes to the Neighborhood, short stories). Beirut: Dar al-Adab, 1995.

Yahduth kull layla (It Happens Every Night, short stories). Beirut: Arab Institute for Research and Publishing, 1998.

'Uthman, Rawda al-Hajj Muhammad (1969–), Sudanese poet born in Kassala. She received a B.A. in Arabic from al-Nilayn University in 1992 and completed her M.A. exams at the Islamic Umm Durman University. She was a director of programming at Kassala radio from 1994 to 1996 and an announcer and program writer in 1996. She has taken part in many local and Arab cultural and literary conferences, seminars, and salons. She has been awarded several literary prizes, including the Kassala Women's Literature Prize in 1994 and an award at the first Women's Art Festival in 1997.

Hatafti la (I Shouted No, poetry). Khartoum: n.p., n.d.

'Uwayti, Nadira (1949–), Libyan short-story writer and novelist born in Damascus. She has a law degree from the Beirut Arab University. She has worked as an editor for the literary page of the Libyan *al-Bayt* magazine.

al-Mar'a allati istantaqat al-tabi'a (The Woman Who Questioned Nature, novel). Tripoli, Libya: al-Dar al-Jamahiriya, 1983.

Hajiz al-huzn (Barrier of Sorrow, short stories). Tripoli, Libya: al-Dar al-Jamahiriya, 1988.

I'tirafat ukhra (Other Confessions, short stories). N.p.: Maktabat Tarabulus, 1994.

Wahba, Farida (?–?), Lebanese novelist.

Ya'qub wa ibnatuh Maryam (Ya'qub and His Daughter, Maryam, novel). Beirut: al-Salimiya Press, 1873.

Wahba, Tahiya Ahmad (1967–), Egyptian poet born in 'Ayn Shams.

Dawayir (Circles, poetry). Cairo: General Authority for Culture Palaces, 1997.

Wahbi, Nazima (?–), Iraqi poet.

Anashid wa aghani al-silm wa-l-hurriya (Hymns and Songs of Peace and Freedom, poetry). Baghdad: al-Rabita Press, 1954.

Wajdi, Wafa' (1945–), Egyptian poet born in Port Said. She received her B.A. from the Higher Institute of Theater Arts in 1970. She worked as a supervisor of children's theater at the Center for Children's Culture in Cairo. She is a founder of the Children's Theater. She was the assistant director to Zaki Tulaymat on *Mawwal min Misr* (A *Mawwal* from Egypt). She was an art researcher at the al-Hakim Theater and al-Tali'a Theater, and she has written many poetry programs for Egyptian radio. She is a member of the Writers' Union. She received the State Encouragement Prize in poetry in 1987.

Madha ta'ni al-ghurba (What Does Exile Mean, poetry). Cairo: Dar al-Katib al-'Arabi Printing and Publishing, 1967.

al-Ru'ya min fawq al-jurh (The View from the Wound, poetry). N.p.: Arab Research Foundation, 1973.

al-Hubb fi zamanina (Love in Our Time, poetry). Cairo: General Egyptian Book Organization, 1980.

Bisan wa-l-abwab al-sab'a (Bisan and the Seven Doors, poetic drama). Cairo: General Egyptian Book Organization, 1984.

al-Harth fi-l-bahr (Tilling the Sea, poetry). Cairo: Maktabat Madbuli, 1985.

Rasa'il hamima ila Allah (Intimate Letters to God, poetry). Cairo: General Egyptian Book Organization, 1986.

Mirath al-zaman al-marir (Legacy of the Bitter Age, poetry). Cairo: General Egyptian Book Organization, 1990.

al-Shajara al-su'ud ila-l-shams (The Tree, Rising to the Sun, poetic drama).

Cairo: General Egyptian Book Organization, 1993.

Wannisi, Zuhur (1936–), Algerian short-story writer and novelist born in Constantine, Algeria. She currently resides in Algiers. She received a B.A. in humanities and philosophy and continued her graduate studies in sociology. She works in teaching and the media. She has served as a member of parliament. She was a member of the Algerian government for five years starting in 1982 and was the first woman to serve in this capacity. She is a member of the National Council of the Algerian Writers' Union and the academic council of the Center for Studies and Research in the National Movement and the November First Revolution. She has published her works in the following Algerian papers: *al-Thaqafa, al-Asala, al-Mujahid, al-Sha'b, al-Jaysh,* and *al-Salam,* as well as periodicals such as *al-Hurriya,* the Syrian *al-Thawra, al-Sha'b, al-Tadamun, al-Jil, Hawwa', Le Monde Diplomatique,* and *al-Ightirab al-adabi.* Some of her stories were adapted for television in 1984. She received the Medal of Resistance in the Algerian national revolution, the National Merit Award, and the Medal of Appreciation in Media and Culture. She was the first Algerian woman to write fiction in Arabic.

al-Rasif al-na'im (The Sleeping Sidewalk, short stories). Cairo: Dar al-Kitab al-'Arabi Printing and Publishing, 1967.

'Ala-l-shati' al-akhar (On the Other Shore, short stories). Algiers: al-Wataniya Publishing and Distribution, 1974.

Min yawmiyat mudarrisa (From the Diary of a Woman Teacher, novel). Algiers: al-Wataniya Publishing and Distribution, 1979.

al-Zilal al-mumtadda (Extended Shadows, short stories). Algiers: al-Wataniya Book Foundation, 1985.

Lunja wa-l-ghul (Lunja and the Ghoul, short stories). Syria: Arab Writers' Union Publications, 1993.

'Aja'iz al-qamar (Old Men of the Moon, short stories). Algiers: Dahlab Publications, 1995.

al-Wardi, Samira (?–), Iraqi playwright. *Thalath qisas li-'unwan wahid* (Three Stories in One, three-act play). Baghdad: Runiyu Press, 1973.

Warraq, Ruqaya (?–), Sudanese poet. Her poems have been published in Sudanese newspapers and magazines. Her earliest published poem was "Qasa'id saghira" (Little Poems) and the latest was "Manahat al-saqi'" (The Frost's Lamentation).

al-Wilayati, Su'ad (?–), Kuwaiti short-story writer and novelist.

Wa Kuwaytah (Oh My Kuwait, novel). Kuwait: n.p., 1992.

al-Gharib (The Stranger, short stories). N.p.: n.p., n.d.

Urid umman (I Want a Mother, short stories). N.p.: n.p., n.d.

Wa inqasha' al-dabab (And the Fog Lifted, novel). Kuwait: Maktabat al-Manar, n.d.

al-Yafi, Layla (?–), Syrian novelist and poet born in Damascus. She was educated in Damascus. She received an award in 1960 from the Ministry of Culture of the United Arab Republic for her first novel, *Thuluj taht al-shams.* She also writes prose poetry.

Thuluj taht al-shams (Snows under the Sun, novel). Cairo: Dar al-Fikr al-'Arabi, 1960.

al-Waha (The Oasis, novel). Damascus: Arab Writers' Union, 1982.

Hamasat al-qalb (Whispers of the Heart, poetry). N.p.: n.p., n.d.

Yakan, Habiba Sha'ban (1915–), Pioneering Lebanese playwright born in Tripoli. She received her primary education at the Anglican School in Tripoli and earned a B.A. from the American University of Beirut. She established the Association of Young Muslim Women in

1947 and was the secretary of the Arab Women's Union. She has written several works on social affairs and literature, including *'Ashar sanawat li-dhikra al-'Arab fi Gharnata* (Ten Years of the Arabs' Memory in Granada).

al-Batala aw safha min tarikh al-Andalus al-akhir (The Heroine, or a Page from the Last Days of Andalusia, play). Sidon: al-'Urfan Press, 1936.

Yamnak, Khadija Ja'far (?–), Iraqi poet.
Diwan muhriq al-qulub fi-l-marathi al-Husayniya (A Heart-Rending Collection of Elegies for Hussein, folk poetry). Najaf: Maktabat al-Warraq, 1973.

Yamut, Hanan (?–), Lebanese poet.
al-Farah al-ma'jur (Leased Joy, poetry). Beirut: Iqra' Publications, 1980.
Waja' al-marakib (Pain of the Ships, poetry). Beirut: Dar al-Afaq al-Jadida, 1982.

Yanni, Mary 'Ata Allah (1895–1967), Lebanese poet of Greek extraction born in Beirut. She was educated at the Zahrat al-Ihsan convent school and studied Arabic with writer Ibrahim al-Mundhir. She published in various newspapers, including *al-Nafa'is, al-Ahwal, al-Watan,* and *Hums.* She issued the hand-written magazine, *Minirfa,* from September 4, 1916, to March 1917. The magazine, a social, literary women's journal, later appeared in printed form and lasted until 1932. She also published in *al-Fatah, al-Fajr, al-Mar'a al-jadida, al-Khidr, al-Ma'arif, al-Hasna', Lisan al-hal, al-Bayraq, al-Haqiqa, al-Nasir,* and *al-Sha'b.* She worked at the Association of Lebanese Women and immigrated to Chile with her husband in 1926. There, she translated Isma'il Falus' history of Chile, published in *al-'Usba* magazine in Brazil.
Ahlami wa amali (My Dreams and Hopes, poetry). N.p.: al-Fajr, 1921.

Ya'qub, Lucy (1935–), Egyptian writer. She was educated at Egyptian and American institutions. She worked in the public relations department of the Iron and Steel Company and was the general director of the Sinai Manganese Company. She is now a full-time writer. She has published several literary studies and has translated many books from English into Arabic. She is a boardmember of the Egyptian Cultural Club and a founding member of the Egyptian Women Writers' Association. She received the Sash of Excellence in battle literature from the Supreme Council for Arts and Humanities for her short-story collection, *'Adhra' Sina'.* Her non-fiction works include *Hazzuk min al-Hind* (Your Fortune Comes from India, 1979), *Nahnu la nazra' al-shukuk wa lakkin nahsiduh* (We Do Not Sow Thorns, But We Reap Them, 1979, a study of Yusuf al-Siba'i), *al-Tufula wa-l-mustaqbal al-sa'id* (Childhood and a Happy Future, 1979), *'Usfur min al-sharq: Tawfiq al-Hakim fi hiwar hawl afkarih* (A Sparrow from the East: Tawfiq al-Hakim in a Conversation about His Ideas, 1987), *Inhirafat al-shabab: asbabuha wa 'ilajuha* (The Depravities of Youth: Their Cause and Treatment, 1989), *al-Quwa al-khafiya bayn al-ghaybiyat wa-l-mu'taqadat* (Hidden Forces between the Unseen and Beliefs, 1989), *al-Sa'ada* (Happiness, 1989), *al-Usra al-Taymuriya wa-l-adab al-'Arabi* (The Taymur Family and Arabic Literature, 1993), *Anis Mansur mufakkiran wa faylasufan* (Anis Mansur: Thinker and Philosopher, 1994), *Fikr wa fann wa dhikrayat* (Thought, Art, and Memories, 1995), *al-Malamih al-khafiya: Jubran wa Mayy* (Concealed Features: Gibran and Mayy, 1995), and *Ihsan 'Abd al-Quddus wa-l-hubb* (Ihsan 'Abd al-Quddus and Love, 1996).
'Uyun zalima (Oppressive Eyes, novel). Cairo: Dar al-'Alam al-'Arabi Press, 1970.
Ahdanuh zilal (His Embraces Are Shadows, poetry). Cairo: al-Fanniya Modern Press, 1972.
'Adhra' Sina' (The Virgin of Sinai, short stories). Cairo: Anglo Egyptian Bookstore, 1978.

Mudhakkirat imra'a 'amila (Memoirs of a Working Woman, novel). N.p.: n.p., 1979.

Sina' wa farhat al-liqa' (Sinai and the Joy of Meeting, poetry). Cairo: Anglo Egyptian Bookstore, 1979.

Amjad yawm fi-l-tarikh (The Most Glorious Day in History, novel). Cairo: General Egyptian Book Organization, 1988.

Awtar al-shajan (Chords of Grief, novel). Cairo: General Egyptian Book Organization, 1988.

Yarid, Nazik Saba (1928–), Palestinian novelist and researcher born in Jerusalem. She earned a B.A. in philosophy from Fu'ad I University (now Cairo University) and a Ph.D. in Arabic literature from the American University of Beirut. She has published many critical studies on classical and modern Arabic poetry. She taught at the Anglican College in Beirut and since 1978 has taught Arabic literature at the American Lebanese University. She was decorated as a knight in l'Ordre des Palmes Académiques in 1980. She is a member of the Ba'labakk International Festivals Committee, the Alliance of Women Researchers, and the Alliance to Defend Women from Violence. In conjunction with Nuha Bayumi, she published a bibliographical work entitled *al-Katibat al-Lubnaniyat bayn 'amay 1850–1950* (Lebanese Women Writers 1850–1950, 2000). In 1999, she was awarded the Best Juvenile Fiction Award by the Lebanese Writers' Association.

Nuqtat al-da'ira (The Circle's Point, novel). Beirut: Dar al-Fikr al-Lubnani, 1983.

al-Sada al-makhnuq (The Stifled Echo, novel). Beirut: Nawfal Foundation, 1986.

Kan al-ams ghadan (Yesterday Was Tomorrow, novel). Beirut: Nawfal Foundation, 1988.

Taqasim 'ala watar da'i' (Improvisations on a Missing String, novel). Beirut: Nawfal Foundation, 1992.

Bayrut hal na'rafuha (Do We Know Beirut, children's literature). Beirut: n.p., 1994.

Fi zill al-qal'a (In the Shadow of the Citadel, young adult literature, Beirut: Dar al-Kitab al-'Alami, 1996.

al-Dhakira al-mulghah (The Canceled Memory, novel). Beirut: Nawfal Foundation, 1998.

al-Yatim, Mayy (1963–), Jordanian short-story writer of Syrian origin born in Kuwait. She graduated from the School of Medicine at Damascus University. She has published short stories and poems in several periodicals. She moves between Damascus and Amman.

Mulsaqat 'ala abwab Dimashq (Flyers on the Gates of Damascus, short stories). Amman: Ministry of Culture Publications, 1990.

al-Yaziji, Warda Nasif (1838–1924), Lebanese poet born in Kafr Shima, the daughter of Nasif al-Yaziji. She studied in the American Mission School for Girls in Beirut and went to Alexandria, Egypt, in 1899. She maintained correspondence with several women writers and poets, such as 'A'isha al-Taymuriya and Mayy Ziyada. She published articles in *al-Firdaws*, *Fatat al-sharq*, *al-Diya'* (owned by her brother Ibrahim al-Yaziji), and *Lisan al-hal*. She addressed the Europeanization of Arab women and their need to develop their sense of national identity.

Hadiqat al-ward (Rose Garden, poetry). Beirut: St. Georgius Press, 1867.

Younes, Iman Humaydan (Yunus, Iman Hamidan) (1956–), Lebanese novelist born in 'Ayn 'Anub. She received her primary education at the Anglican School and received a B.A. in social science and anthropology at the American University of Beirut in 1980. She taught English and children's literature from 1984 to 1989. Since 1989 she has worked in journalism and in research at al-Masar Publishing and Research.

Ba' mithl bayt . . . mithl Bayrut (*B as in Beirut*, novel). Beirut: al-Masar Publishing and Research, 1997.

Yunus, Basima Muhammad (1964–), Emirati novelist and short-story writer born in al-Mazra'a in the U.A.E. She received a B.A. in English from Emirates University in 1986, a degree in computer programming and science in 1988, and a law degree from the Beirut Arab University in 1993. She is a boardmember of the Emirati Writers' and Authors' Union and a member of the Emirati Women Writers' League, the Arab Writers' and Authors' Union, and the Lawyers' Association. She is an English teacher and legal translator in the Emirates. She also works as a journalist. She has received several awards and is the owner of the Hajir Production Company. She received the Su'ad al-Sabah Prize for Literature for Arab Youth for her collection, *Hajir*, in 1992.
'Adhab (Torture, short stories). N.p.: privately published at Dubai Press, 1986.
Tariq ila-l-hayah (The Road to Life, short stories). N.p.: privately published, 1989.
Ightiyal untha (The Assassination of a Female, short stories). N.p.: privately published at Dubai Press, 1990.
Mala'ika wa shayatin (Angels and Devils, novel). Dubai: privately published, 1990.
Hajir (High Noon, short stories). N.p.: privately published at Dubai Press, 1993.

al-Yunus, Nahla Shihab Ahmad (?–), Iraqi poet.
Tartilat li-ibnat al-rih (Recitations for the Daughter of the Wind, poetry). Jordan: n.p., 1998.

Yusra, Zahra (1974–), Egyptian poet born in Cairo. She received a B.A. in Arabic from Cairo University in 1996.
Zujaj yatakassar (Breaking Glass, poetry). Cairo: al-Kitaba al-Ukhra, 1996.

al-Yusuf, Fatima (Rose al-Yusuf) (1898–1957), Pioneering Lebanese journalist known as "Rose al-Yusuf." She was born in Tripoli, where she received her primary education. She moved to Alexandria, Egypt, at the age of ten and lived there under the care of stage actor Iskandar Farah. She then met stage director 'Aziz 'Id and worked in the George Abyad troupe and later with the Ramsis troupe, founded by Yusuf Wahbi. She retired from the stage and worked in journalism from 1925. She published several bold articles, including "Qadiyat al-rajul wa-l-mar'a" (The Cause of Men and Women), "Hawl ma li-Allah wa ma li-qaysar" (On What Is God's and What Is Caesar's), "La hayah ma'a al-malik" (No Life with the King), "Ya umm al-Misriyin" (O Mother of Egyptians), and "Khitab ila-l-Nahhas: kam 'adad al-mufsidin" (A Letter to al-Nahhas: How Many Destroyers). She founded Rose al-Yusuf Publishers in 1925 and produced the magazines, *Rose al-Yusuf* and *Sabah al-khayr*.
Dhikrayat (Memories, autobiography). Cairo: Rose al-Yusuf Foundation, 1953.

Yusuf, Fatima 'Abd al-Maqsud (?–), Egyptian poet.
'Aynak ma'awi (Your Eyes Are Havens, poetry). Cairo: al-Istiqlal Press, 1973.
al-Shahid (The Martyr, poetry). Cairo: al-Hadara al-'Arabiya Press, 1974.

Yusuf, Fawziya Jirjis (?–), Egyptian novelist.
Ayyam min nar (Days of Fire, novel). Cairo: al-'Arabiya Modern Press, 1972.

Yusuf, Iman Ahmad (?–), Egyptian poet born in Alexandria.
'Arayis al-shi'r (Brides of Poetry, poetry). Alexandria: General Authority for Culture Palaces, 1992.
Masha'ir (Feelings, colloquial poetry). Alexandria: Agency for Arts, Humanities, and Social Sciences, 1995.
Tanhidat sabiya (A Young Girl's Sigh, poetry). Cairo: General Egyptian Book Organization, 1995.

Washwashat al-bahr (Whispers of the Sea, poetry). Alexandria: Agency for Arts, Humanities, and Social Sciences, 1995.

Lahn al-hanin (The Melody of Longing, poetry). Alexandria: Manarat al-Iskandariya Publishers, 1997.

Ya farah sahibni (Joy, Keep Me Company, poetry). Alexandria: Dar al-Wafa', 1998.

Yusuf, Yusriya 'Abd al-Majid Ahmad (?–), Egyptian short-story writer born in Kafr Shukr. She is a computer specialist at the Ministry of Education.

Tarh al-burtuqal (Orange Produce, short stories). Cairo: General Authority for Culture Palaces, 1997.

'Anaqid al-karm (Grape Bunches, short stories). Cairo: General Authority for Culture Palaces, 1999.

al-Zahawi, Amal (1946–), Iraqi poet born in Baghdad. She received her primary and secondary education in al-A'zamiya and graduated from Baghdad University in 1963. She received a teaching certificate in psychology in 1967. She has worked in journalism in Iraq and Syria and was a founder of *Alif ba'* magazine in the late 1960s.

al-Fida'i wa-l-wahsh (The Freedom Fighter and the Monster, poetry). Beirut: Dar al-'Awda, 1969.

al-Tariqun bihar al-mawt (Passengers on the Seas of Death, poetry). Beirut: Dar al-'Awda, 1971.

Da'ira fi-l-daw' . . . da'ira fi-l-zulma (A Circle in the Light . . . A Circle in the Dark, poetry). Baghdad: Ministry of Information, 1975.

Ikhwat Yusuf (Joseph's Brothers, poetry). Baghdad: Ministry of Culture and Information, 1979.

Tada'iyat (Consequences, poetry). Baghdad: Amal al-Zahawi Publications, 1982.

Yaqul Qass ibn Sa'ida (Qass ibn Sa'ida Says, poetry). Baghdad: Tammuz Press, 1987.

al-Zahiri, Khawla (?–), Omani short-story writer. She received a B.A. in education from Emirates University in 1991. She won third prize in the short-story competition sponsored by the Girls' Clubs in Sharjah in 1998. She also contributed to a short-story anthology, *Aswatuhunna* (Their Voices, Beirut, Dar al-Farabi, 1998), of writers from the Gulf. Her stories have been published in the cultural press in Oman and the U.A.E.

Saba' (Sheba, short stories). Cairo: Girls' Clubs of Sharjah and al-Dar al-Misriya al-Lubnaniya, 1998.

al-Zahra (see: 'Abd al-Shahid, Olivia 'Uwayda)

al-Zahra al-Bayda' (see: Jasim, Hayat)

Zahran, Najwa (?–), Egyptian poet.

Baghanni lik (I Sing for You, poetry). Alexandria: n.p., 1994.

Zahran, Yasmin (1933–), Palestinian novelist. She studied at Columbia University, the University of London, and the Sorbonne and received a Ph.D. in archaeology. She has worked in education and for U.N.E.S.C.O. She lives in Paris. She published a novel in English, *A Beggar at Damascus Gate.*

al-Lahn al-awwal (min ayyam Filistin) (The First Melody from the Days of Palestine, novel). Amman: Dar al-Karmel, 1991.

A Beggar at Damascus Gate. Sausalito, California: Post-Apollo Press, 1995.

Harat al-Bayadir (al-Bayadir Alley, novel). Ramallah: Palestinian Ministry of Culture, 1999.

Zaka, Huda Fu'ad (1939–), Lebanese playwright born in al-Shuwayfat. She received her secondary education at the Charles Sa'd School in al-Shuwayfat. She received a B.A. from the Beirut College for Girls in 1958 and an M.A. in Arabic literature from the American University of Beirut in 1962. She helped found the Lebanese Center for International Theater in 1966. She staged her first play, *al-Masir al-tawil*, at the al-Jib Theater in Cairo in 1967. It was directed by Egyptian Karam Mutawi'. The Modern Theater Troupe in Beirut staged her second play, *al-Mawsim*, in 1969. It was directed by Berge Vazilian. Her play, *Mudhakkirat majnun*, adapted from Nikolai Gogol's *Diary of a Madman*, was directed in 1971 by Ya'qub al-Shadrawi.

al-Masir al-tawil (The Long Road, play). Beirut: al-Maktaba al-'Asriya, 1965.

al-Mawsim (The Season, play). Beirut: n.p., 1969.

al-Shay' (The Thing, play). Beirut: al-Maktaba al-'Asriya, n.d.

al-Zamili, Su'ad 'Ali (?–), Iraqi novelist.

Khafaya al-qadar (Mysteries of Fate, novel). Najaf: al-Gharri Modern Press, 1970.

Zangana, Haifa (Zankana, Hayfa') (1950–), Iraqi novelist and short-story writer born in Baghdad to a Kurdish father and an Arab mother. She graduated from the College of Pharmacy in 1974. Her literary and art works have been published in Arabic and English periodicals. She showed her work in eight group exhibitions (1977–1991) and had solo exhibitions in Iceland in 1982 and in London in 1988. She prepared and published the book, *Halabja* (Halabja), in Arabic and English in 1989. She has lived in London since 1976.

Fi arwiqat al-dhakira (*Through the Vast Halls of Memory*, novel). London: Dar al-Hikma, 1995.

Bayt al-naml (The Ant Hill, short stories). London: Dar al-Hikma, 1996.

Ab'ad mimma nara (Further Than We Can See, short stories). London: Dar al-Hikma, 1997.

Zaqtan, Zahira (195?–), Palestinian novelist and researcher born in the 'Aqbat Jabr refugee camp. After completing her preparatory education, she studied psychology and then took up the study of the Palestinian heritage. She now works as a researcher in that field. She is the officer of the folk heritage committee in the League of Jordanian Writers. She has organized dozens of exhibitions of Palestinian embroidery work.

Awraq ghazala (Papers of a Gazelle, short stories). Amman: Dar al-Karmel, 1987.

al-Mawa'id (Appointments, novel). Amman: n.p., n.d.

al-Zar'uni, Asma' 'Ali (1961–), Emirati poet and short-story writer born in Sharjah. She has a B.A. in education and is a librarian. She is the vice president of the Emirati Writers' and Authors' Union. She writes for *al-Ittihad* and *al-Khalij* newspapers and *al-Sada* magazine.

Ahmad wa-l-samaka (Ahmad and the Fish, children's literature). N.p.: privately published, 1992.

al-'Usfura wa-l-watan (The Sparrow and the Homeland, children's literature). N.p.: privately published, 1992.

Ghabat al-sa'ada (The Forest of Happiness, children's literature). N.p.: privately published, 1995.

Hams al-shawati' (Whisper of the Shores, short stories). N.p.: privately published, 1995.

Hadha al-masa' lana (This Night Is Ours, poetry). N.p.: privately published, 1996.

al-Zawi, Naziha (?–), Algerian short-story writer.

al-Tufula wa-l-hulm (Childhood and Dreams, short stories). Algeria: al-Wataniya Book Foundation, 1985.

al-Zawqari, Shafiqa Ahmad (1942–), Yemeni short-story writer born in Aden. She currently resides in the U.A.E. She was the first woman to publish a short-story collection in southern Yemen. She received first prize in the Youth Competition of 1968 for her story, "Armalat shahid" (A Martyr's Widow). She is a school principal.

Nabadat qalb (Heartbeats, short stories). Beirut: n.p., 1970.

Hirman dalla ukhra (Another Unfulfilled Desire, short stories). Beirut: n.p., 1977.

al-Zaybaq, Yumna (?–), Syrian novelist who lives in Riyadh.
Wujuh fi zaman al-harb (Faces in the Time of War, novel). Damascus: n.p., 1993.

Zayd, Nura 'Ali (?–), Egyptian poet.
Uriduk kafani (I Want You As My Shroud, poetry). Cairo: Midu Printing and Publishing, 1989.

Zaydan, Amina (1966–), Egyptian short-story writer born in Suez. She has a B.A. in business and works as an accountant at the Ministry of Finance. She won the Book Fair Prize in 1995 for her collection of stories, *Hadath sirran*.
Hadath sirran (It Happened in Secret, short stories). Cairo: Supreme Council for Culture, 1995.

Zaydan, Ruqaya (1958?–), Palestinian poet born in the village of Yamma in the Triangle in the part of Palestine occupied in 1948. She completed her primary and secondary education and then enrolled in the Teachers' Academy, where she specialized in Arabic. She teaches Arabic in her village.
'Indama turkha al-sudul (When the Curtains Drape, poetry). West Baqa: al-Di'aya wa-l-Nashr Press, 1986.
Dakhalt hada'iq ummati (I Entered My Nation's Gardens, poetry). Shafa 'Amr: Dar al-Mashriq, 1986.
Qira'a fi sifar al-'adala (A Reading in the Book of Justice, poetry). Yamma: Dar al-Mashriq, 1991.
Hafif fawq al-adim (A Rustle on the Surface, poetry). Jerusalem: Office of Arab Culture, 1995.

Zayid, Safa' 'Abd al-Mun'im (1960–), Egyptian short-story writer born in Cairo. She works as a teacher.
Hikayat al-layl (The Night's Tale, short stories). Cairo: General Authority for Culture Palaces, 1993.

Tilka-l-Qahira tughrini bi-siqani al-rafi'a (This Cairo Seduces Me with My Slender Legs, short stories). Cairo: General Authority for Culture Palaces, 1994.
Ashya' saghira wa alifa (Little Familiar Things, short stories). Cairo: General Authority for Culture Palaces, 1996.

Zayn al-'Abidin, Halima (1954–), Moroccan writer born in Marrakech. She received a B.A. in Arabic language and literature from Muhammad V University in 1981. She works as a high-school teacher. She is a member of human rights and women's associations and is on the faculty at the Academy of Secondary School Education in Rabat. She has contributed to a play and has published the non-fiction work, *Qira'a wa iqra' al-nusus al-sardiya* (Reading and Teaching Narrative Texts).
Hajis al-'awda (The Anxiety of Return, novel). Rabat: al-Mawja Publications, 1999.

al-Zayn, Amira (?–), Lebanese poet. She teaches Arabic literature at Georgetown University in Washington, D.C., and is a member of the editorial board for the English-language journal, *Jusur*.
Kitab al-nakhil (Book of the Palm Trees, poetry). Beirut: Arab Institute for Research and Publishing, 1974.
Badu al-jahim (Hell's Nomads, poetry). Beirut: Arab Institute for Research and Publishing, 1992.

al-Zayn, Huda (?–), Syrian poet born in Tartus. She received a law degree from Damascus University. She worked at *Tishrin* newspaper in 1973 and published *Talal*, a children's magazine. She works in Paris at the Syrian Arab News Agency.
Bidayat al-asfar (Beginning of the Journeys, poetry). Damascus: Arab Writers' Union, 1980.
al-Ibhar fi zaman al-rahil (Sailing in the Time of Departure, poetry). Damascus: Arab Writers' Union, 1990.

Yawmiyat imra'a 'Arabiya fi Baris (Diary of an Arab Woman in Paris, memoir). N.p.: al-'Ayn Advertising, Distribution, and Publishing, 1991.

al-Zayyat, 'Inayat (?–1967), Egyptian novelist.
al-Hubb wa-l-samt (Love and Silence, novel). Cairo: Dar al-Kitab al-'Arabi Printing and Publishing, 1967.

al-Zayyat, Latifa (1923–1996), Egyptian writer and political activist born in Damietta. She received a B.A. in English literature from Cairo University in 1946 and a Ph.D. from the same institution in 1957. She was a professor of English literature and criticism at the Girls' College at Ain Shams University from 1952 until her death. She was the director of the Arts Academy and a member of the Supreme Council for Arts and Humanities. She published many works on politics, literary criticism, and creation in the novel, the short story, autobiography, and drama. She also published several translations and studies in English. She was a leader of the National Committee of Students and Workers in the 1940s. Her political activity led to her arrest on more than one occasion. She was the president of the Committee to Defend National Culture from 1979 until her death. She was arrested in 1981 as part of a state campaign against intellectuals and writers. She was a member of the Council for World Peace and an honorary member of the General Union of Palestinian Writers and Journalists. She was awarded the State Medal of Appreciation in humanities in 1996, only a few months before her death. She translated Maynard Solomon's *Marxism and Art* (New York: Vintage Books, 1973) as *Hawl al-fann: ru'ya Marksiya*, published 1994. Her works of non-fiction include *Najib Mahfuz: al-sura wa-l-mithal* (Naguib Mahfouz: Image and Parable, 1989), *Suwar al-mar'a fi-l-qisas wa-l-riwayat al-'Arabiya* (Images of Women in Arabic Short Stories and Novels, 1989,

critical study), *Adwa'* (Lights, 1995, essays on literary criticism), and *Furd Maduks Furd wa-l-hadatha* (Ford Madox Ford and Modernity, 1996).
al-Bab al-maftuh (*The Open Door*, novel). Cairo: Anglo Library, 1960.
al-Shaykhukha wa qisas ukhra (Old Age and Other Stories, short stories). Cairo: Dar al-Mustaqbal al-'Arabi, 1986.
Hamlat taftish: awraq shakhsiya (*The Search: Personal Papers*, memoir). Cairo: Dar al-Hilal, 1992.
Bi' wa shira' (Buying and Selling, play). Cairo: General Egyptian Book Organization, 1994.
Sahib al-bayt (*The Owner of the House*, novel). Cairo: Dar al-Hilal, 1994.
al-Rajul alladhi 'arafa tuhmatah (The Man Who Knew His Charge, short stories). Cairo: Dar Sharqiyat, 1995.

Zirawi, Zuhra (1938–), Moroccan short-story writer born in Casablanca. She completed her second year of university and currently works in high-school theater. She has published her works in newspapers and periodicals.
Alladhi kan (He Who Was, short stories). Casablanca: al-Najah Modern Press, 1994.
Nisf yawm yakfi (Half a Day Is Enough, short stories). Casablanca: al-Najah Modern Press, 1996.

Ziyada, Mayy (1886–1941) Pioneering Lebanese writer born in Nazareth, Palestine, to a Lebanese father, Ilyas Zukhur Ziyada, a teacher in Nazareth, and a Palestinian mother of Syrian origin. She received her primary education in Nazareth and at the age of thirteen entered the Sisters of the Visitation Boarding School in 'Ayntura in Lebanon (1898–1903). She transferred to the Sisters of Lazarus Convent School in Beirut for a year. In 1907 she moved with her family to Egypt, where her father worked as a journalist for *al-Mahrusa* newspaper, which he came to own and direct in 1909. Mayy Ziyada taught French to the girls of prominent families in Cairo, wrote poetry, and studied English and German. She published *Fleurs de rêve* (1911) under a pseudonym (Isis Copia). The work includes poems, prose texts, and fragments of a memoir written during her stay in Lebanon. After reading the works of pioneering authors like Labiba Hashim, the articles of Bahithat al-Badiya, and the works of the leaders of the women's movement in Egypt, such as Huda Sha'rawi, she decided to perfect her Arabic. Ahmad Lutfi al-Sayyid advised her to read the Qur'an and guided her through the texts of the Arabic literary tradition. She took part in a ceremony to honor poet Khalil Mutran at the Egyptian University in 1913, where she read a speech on behalf of Gibran Kahlil Gibran and commented on it. From that point on, she became the mistress of the pulpit in the Arab world. She began to receive contemporary writers in her father's home every Tuesday evening. Her salon gained renown, attracting intellectuals, writers, and poets, and lasted from 1912 to 1932. She published her articles in *al-Mahrusa*, *al-Zuhur*, *al-Hilal*, *al-Muqtataf*, *al-Ahram*, and *al-Siyasa al-usbu'iya*. She excelled in public speaking and lecturing and enrolled in the Egyptian University for three years during the First World War. Her contemporaries dubbed her "the Writer of Genius," "Mistress of the Arab Pen," and "Author of the Age." She and Gibran Kahlil Gibran carried on a correspondence from 1912 to 1931 but they never met in person. After her father's death in 1929, Gibran's death in 1931, and her mother's death in 1932, she became withdrawn and suffered a breakdown. In 1936 she returned to Lebanon, where it was rumored that she had gone mad and was committed to the Hospital for Mental and Nervous Disorders by her relatives. She staged a hunger strike to protest this injustice. An old friend, Marun Ghanim, waged a campaign in the press to save her, and she was moved to the American University Hospital in 1938. She left three weeks later and returned to Egypt, where she died in 1941. She used several pseudonyms, including Khalid Ralant, Sindbad, and 'A'ida, but used her real name in many works. She published her critical essays in four books: *Sawanih fatah* (A Young Woman's Thoughts, 1922), *Zulumat wa ashi''a* (Darknesses and Rays, 1923), *Bayn al-jazr wa-l-madd* (Between the Ebb and Flow, 1924), and *al-Saha'if* (The Papers, 1924). Her collected speeches are found in the first volume of *Kalimat wa isharat* (Words and References), published in 1922. The second volume was published posthumously and includes speeches, lectures, and articles published from 1922 to 1940. Her biographical works include *Bahithat al-Badiya* (Bahithat al-Badiya, 1920), *'A'isha Taymur* ('A'isha Taymur, 1926), and *Warda al-Yaziji* (Warda al-Yaziji, 1926). She was the first to write a book on equality, natural disparities, and political systems, titled *al-Musawah* (Equality, 1923). She translated three novels: Friedrich Max Müller's *Deutsche Liebe* (Ibtisamat wa dumu', 1912); *Le Retour du flot (Ruju' al-mawja)* by Contessa Henriette Consuelo di Puliga; and Arthur Conan Doyle's *The Refugees* (*al-Hubb fi-l-'adhab*, 1911), about French immigration to America.

"al-Hubb fi-l-madrasa" (Love at School, short story). *al-Hilal*. Cairo: 1934.

"Nashid al-sharq" (Hymn of the East, poem). *al-Muqtataf*. Cairo: 1934.

"al-Sirr al-muwazza'" (The Open Secret, short story). *al-Risala*. Cairo: 1935.

Zouein, Sabah Kharrat (Zuwayn, Sabah Kharrat) (?–) (see also: Bibliography of Works in French)

'Ala rasif shati' 'arin (poetry). Harisa: Antun Shamali Press, 1983.

Kama law anna khalalan aw fi khalal al-makan (As if an Imperfection, or On the Imperfection of Place, poetry). Harisa: Antun Shamali Press, 1988.

Ma zal al-waqt da'i'an (The Time Is Still Lost, poetry). Cologne, Germany: al-Jamal Publications, 1993.

al-Bayt al-ma'il wa-l-waqt wa-l-judran (The Inclined House and Time and Walls, texts). Beirut: Amwaj Publishers and Distributors, 1995.

Bad'an min aw rubbama (Starting From, or Perhaps, poetry). Beirut: Amwaj Publishers and Distributors, 1998.

Z

al-Zubaydi, Hayat (Hayat al-Nahr) (1934–), Iraqi poet and novelist born in al-Suwayra in the province of Wasit. She graduated from a convent school and al-Mansur High School in Baghdad. She enrolled in al-Mustansiriya University, from which she graduated with a degree in English in 1970. She was appointed a translator at the Ministry of Agriculture.

al-Ghad al-mushriq (The Bright Tomorrow, poetry). Baghdad: n.p., 1958.

Ughniyat li-l-thawra (Songs for the Revolution, poetry). Baghdad: n.p., 1958.

al-Shahir (Shahir, novel). Baghdad: n.p., n.d.

al-Zubayr, Nabila Muhsin 'Ali (1964–), Yemeni poet born in the village of al-Hijra, in Haraz. She currently resides in Sana'a. She began to publish under the initials M.A.Z. She received a B.A. in psychology. She participates in many cultural festivals and has been a member of the Arab Writers' Union in Jordan since 1998. She and several of her colleagues founded a literary salon that meets on the second Thursday of every month in her home. She published many social articles in an almost daily column for *al-Thawra* from 1981 to 1982. She has published prose and poetry in *al-Mithaq* and *al-Mar'a* and from 1990 to 1995 she wrote about politics for *al-Thawra* and *al-'Uruba*.

Mutawaliyat al-kidhba al-ra'i'a (Successions of the Magnificent Lie, poetry). Damascus: Dar al-Mustaqbal, 1990.

Thammat bahr yu'awiduni (There Is a Sea That Comes Over Me, poetry). Damascus: Dar al-Fikr, 1997.

Mahaya (Erasers, poetry). Sana'a: General Book Organization, 1999.

La . . . laysat ma'qula (No . . . It's Not Reasonable). Forthcoming.

Zuhayr, Su'ad (1925–2000), Egyptian novelist and journalist born in al-Rahmaniya in the Egyptian Delta. Her father was an English teacher, poet, and journalist who was fired for his participation in the 1919 revolution. Zuhayr completed her secondary education in 1938. She dropped out of university because of her family's failing financial situation after her father's death. She was imprisoned in 1948 because of her political activities. She worked at the magazine, *Rose al-Yusuf*, and many of her novels were published in serial form there, most important, *Khitab ila rajul 'asri* (Letter to a Modern Man, 1994).

I'tirafat imra'a mustarjila (Confessions of a Masculine Woman, novel). Cairo: Arab Egyptian Center, 1960.

Zunayr, Jamila (?–), Algerian short-story writer.

Da'irat al-hulm wa-l-'awatif (Circle of Dreams and Emotions, short stories). Algiers: al-Wataniya Book Foundation, 1983.

Jinniyat al-bahr (Genie of the Sea, short stories). Algiers: al-Tabyin al-Jahiziya Publications, 1988.

Sources

Primary sources

Dar al-Kutub al-Misriya (Egyptian National Library) list of holdings.
Forms for Arab women writers prepared by Nour: Foundation for Arab
  Women's Research and Studies, Cairo.
Interviews with women writers from around the Arab world.
National Council for Culture and Arts in Kuwait (a letter containing the
  names of women writers in Kuwait).

Secondary sources

'Abbas, Nasr Muhammad. *al-Bina' al-fanni fi-l-qissa al-Sa'udiya al-
  mu'asira*. Riyadh: Dar al-'Ulum Printing and Publishing, 1983.
'Abbud, Khazin. *Nisa' sha'irat min al-jahiliya ila-l-qarn al-'ishrin*. Beirut:
  Dar al-Afaq al-Jadida Publications, 2000.
'Abd Allah, Nahla. *Aswat nisa'iya fi-l-qissa al-Yamaniya*. Sana'a: al-Mufaddal
  Press, 1992.
'Abd al-Qadir, Munir Salih. *Adibat al-Sudan*. Cairo: al-I'timad Press, n.d.
'Abd al-Rahman, 'Abd al-Jabbar. *Fihrist al-matbu'at al-'Iraqiya 1856–1972*.
  Baghdad: Ministry of Culture and Information, 1979.
Achour, Christiane, ed. *Dictionnaire des oeuvres algériennes en langue
  française*. Paris: L'Harmattan, 1990.
Ahmad, Falih Hamad. *Sha'irat al-khalij al-'Arabi*. Basra: Center for Arabian
  Gulf Studies, 1985.
Al Tu'ma, Salman Hadi. *Sha'irat 'Iraqiyat mu'asirat*. Damascus: n.p.,
  1995.
al-'Alwaji, 'Abd al-Hamid. *al-Nitaj al-nisawi fi-l-'Iraq khilal 1923–1974*.
  Baghdad: Ministry of Information, 1975.

al-A'raj, Wasini, ed. *Diwan al-hadatha: bi-sadad antulujiyat al-shi'r al-jadid fi-l-Jaza'ir*. Algiers: Algerian Writers' Union Publications, n.d.

Barrière, Loïc. *Des nouvelles du Maroc*. Casablanca: Ed. EDDIF, 1997.

Bibliyughrafiya mawdu'iya 'an al-mar'a al-'Iraqiya. Baghdad: General Union of Iraqi Women, 1978.

al-Bibliyughrafiya al-wataniya al-'Iraqiya. Baghdad: National Library, n.d.

"Bibliyughrafiyat al-masrah al-Sa'udi," *Qawafil* vol. 3, no. 6 (1996).

Bulus, Habib. *Antulujiyat al-qissa al-'Arabiya fi Isra'il 1948–1998*. Sakhnin: Academic College and al-Jalil Center, 1999.

Campbell, Robert. *A'lam al-adab al-'Arabi al-mu'asir: siyar wa sira dhatiya*. Beirut: St. Joseph University, 1996.

Daghir, Yusuf As'ad. *Masadir al-dirasat al-adabiya*, vol. 1. Beirut: Lebanese University Publications, 1972.

———. *Masadir al-dirasat al-adabiya*, vol. 2. Beirut: Ahl al-Qalam Association Publications, 1956.

Dawud, Sabiha al-Shaykh. *Awwal tariq ila-l-nahda al-nisawiya fi-l-'Iraq*. Baghdad: al-Rabita Press, 1958.

Déjeux, Jean. *Dictionnaire des auteurs maghrébins de langue française*. Paris: Ed. Karthala, 1984.

———. *La littérature féminine de langue française au Maghreb*. N.p.: Ed. Karthala, 1994.

Dughan, Ahmad. *Fi-l-adab al-Jaza'iri al-hadith*. Damascus: Arab Writers' Union Publications, 1996.

al-Fahmawi, Kamal Mustafa al-Shaykh Ahmad. *Adab al-mar'a al-Filisti al-hadith 1914–1979*. Ph.D. dissertation, al-Azhar University, 1979.

Farraj, 'Afif. *al-Hurriya fi adab al-mar'a*. Beirut: Arab Research Foundation, 1985.

al-Faysal, Samar Rawhi. *Mu'jam al-riwa'iyin al-'Arab*. Tripoli: Jarus Bars, 1995.

———. *Mu'jam al-qassat wa-l-riwa'iyat al-'Arabiyat*. Tripoli: Jarus Bars, 1996.

Fontaine, Jean. *Ecrivaines tunisiennes*. Tunis: Gai Savoir, 1994.

Futuh, 'Isa. *Adibat 'Arabiyat: siyar wa dirasat*. Damascus: Cultural Club Publications, 1984.

Gaasch, James. *Anthologie de la nouvelle maghrébine*. Casablanca: Ed. EDDIF, 1996.

Ghurayyib, Ruz. *Nasamat wa a'asir fi-l-shi'r al-nisa'i al-'Arabi al-mu'asir*. Beirut: Arab Institute for Research and Publishing, 1980.

Guide de littérature mauritanienne. Paris: L'Harmattan, 1992.

al-Habashi, 'Abd Allah Muhammad. *Mu'jam al-nisa' al-Yamaniyat*. Sana'a: Dar al-Hikma al-Yamaniya, 1988.

al-Haqil, 'Abd al-Karim Hamad Ibrahim. *Min adab al-mar'a al-Sa'udiya al-mu'asira*. Riyadh: al-Matabi' al-Namudhajiya al-Fanniya, AH 1413 (1992–1993).

Ibn Mansur, 'Abd al-Wahhab. *A'lam al-Maghrib al-'Arabi*, four vols. Rabat: Royal Press, 1979 and 1986.

Ibn Salim, 'Umar, ed. *Ittihad al-kuttab al-Tunisiyin: al-qanun al-asasi wa tarajim al-a'da'*. Tunis: National Foundation for Translation, Editing, and Research, 1989.

———. *Ittihad al-kuttab al-Tunisiyin: mukhtarat qisasiya li-kuttab Tunisiyin*. Tunis: al-Dar al-'Arabiya Books, 1990.

al-Iryani, Ramziya. *Ra'idat Yamaniyat*. Sana'a: Ministry of Social Affairs and Labor, 1990.

'Isa, Rashid. *Mu'adalat al-qissa al-nisa'iya al-Sa'udiya*. Riyadh: al-Nakhil Publications, 1994.

'Isma'il, Isma'il Fahd. *al-Qissa al-'Arabiya fi-l-Kuwayt*. Damascus: Dar al-Mada, 1996.

'Izzat, Adib. *Mu'jam kuttab Suriya*. Damascus: Dar al-Wathba, n.d.

al-Jabburi, Jamil. *Dalil matbu'at wizarat al-i'lam 1968–1974*, two vols. Baghdad: Ministry of Culture and Information, 1995 and 1996.

al-Jabiri, Muhammad Salih. *Diwan al-shi'r al-Tunisi al-hadith: tarajim wa mukhtarat*. Tunis: Tunisian Distribution Company, 1976.

al-Jundi, Adham. *A'lam al-adab al-'Arabi al-mu'asir*. Beirut: University Publishers, 1964–1985.

al-Jundi, Anwar. *Adab al-mar'a al-'Arabiya*. Egypt: al-Risala Press, n.d.

Kahhala, 'Umar Rida. *Mu'jam al-mu'allifin: a'lam al-nisa'*. Damascus: n.p., 1959.

al-Kitabat al-nisa'iya al-Tunisiya (bibliyughrafiya 1994). Prepared by the Centre de Recherches de Documentation et d'Information sur la Femme in conjunction with the Tahir al-Haddad Cultural Club. Tunis: CREDIF Publications, 1995.

al-Kitabat al-nisa'iya al-Tunisiya (bibliyughrafiya 1995). Prepared by the Centre de Recherches de Documentation et d'Information sur la Femme in conjunction with the Tahir al-Haddad Cultural Club. Tunis: CREDIF Publications, 1996.

al-Kitabat al-nisa'iya al-Tunisiya (bibliyughrafiya 1998). Prepared by the Centre de Recherches de Documentation et d'Information sur la Femme in conjunction with the Tahir al-Haddad Cultural Club. Tunis: CREDIF Publications, 1999.

Littératures francophones du monde arabe: anthologie. Paris: Nathan/Almadariss, 1994.

Malak, Suhayla 'Abd al-Husayn. al-Malih, Sa'di. "Bibliyughrafiyat al-adab al-'Iraqi fi-l-manfa," *al-Badil* 11 (May 1988): 44–66.

Mardam-Bey, Farouk, ed. *Ecrivains arabes d'hier et d'aujourd'hui*. Paris: Institut du Monde Arabe, Sindbad, Actes Sud, 1996.

Ma'rufi, 'Abd al-Wahid. *Dalil al-shu'ara' al-Maghariba*. Marrakech: Tansift Press, 1991.

al-Matba'i, Hamid. *Mawsu'at a'lam al-'Iraq fi-l-qarn al-'ishrin*, two vols. Baghdad: Ministry of Culture and Information, 1995 and 1996.

al-Misri, Marwan and Muhammad 'Allani. *al-Katibat al-Suriyat 1893–1978*. Damascus: al-Ahali Printing and Publishing, 1988.

Misriyat ra'idat wa mubdi'at. Cairo: General Egyptian Book Organization, 1995.

Muhammad, Fathiya. *Balaghat al-nisa' fi-l-qarn al-'ishrin*. N.p.: al-Maktaba al-Misriya, 1928.

Mu'jam Asbar li-l-nisa' al-Sa'udiyat. Riyadh: Asbar Research and Media, 1997.

Mu'jam al-Babtin li-l-shu'ara' al-mu'asirin, six vols. Prepared by the 'Abd al-'Aziz al-Babtin Foundation. Kuwait: al-Qabas Press, 1995.

Mu'jam al-kuttab wa-l-mu'allifin fi-l-mamlaka al-'Arabiya al-Sa'udiya. Riyadh: al-Da'ira li-l-I'lam al-Mahduda, 1993.

Nuwayhid, Nadiya al-Jardi. *Nisa' min biladi*. Beirut: Arab Foundation for Research and Publishing, 1986.

al-Qadi, Iman. *al-Riwaya al-nisawiya fi bilad al-Sham 1950–1985*. Damascus: al-Ahali Printing, Publishing, and Distribution, 1992.

Qasimi, Muhammad. *Bibliyughrafiyat al-qissa al-Maghribiya*. Wajda: Dar al-Nashr al-Jusur, 1999.

Qasimi, Muhammad and Ahmad Sayhal. *Bibliyughrafiyat al-shi'r al-'Arabi al-hadith fi-l-Maghrib*. Wajda: Faculty of Humanities in Wajda Publications, 1996.

Qazanji, Fu'ad Yusuf. *al-Nitaj al-fikri al-'Iraqi li-'am 1975*. Baghdad: Ministry of Information, 1977.

———. *al-Nitaj al-fikri al-'Iraqi li-'am 1977*. Baghdad: Ministry of Information, 1981.

Sadiq, Habib, ed. *al-Dalil, ma'rad janub Lubnan, kitab wa shaziya*. Beirut: Cultural Council for Southern Lebanon, 1981.

Sa'id, Khalida. *al-Haraka al-masrahiya fi Lubnan 1960–1975*. Beirut: Arab Theater Committee, Ba'labakk International Festivals, 1998.

al-Sakkut, Hamdi. *al-Riwaya al-'Arabiya al-haditha: bibliyughrafiya wa madkhal naqdi (1865–1995)*, five vols. Cairo: Supreme Council for Culture, 1998.

Salih, Layla. *Adab al-mar'a fi-l-jazira wa-l-khalij al-'Arabi*. Kuwait: al-Yaqza Press, 1983.

———. *Udaba' wa adibat al-Kuwayt*. Kuwait: Authors' League and al-Faysal Press, 1996.

Shahin, Ahmed 'Umar. *Mawsu'at kuttab Filistin fi-l-qarn al-'ishrin*. Damascus: P.L.O.'s Cultural Department, 1992.

Shihab, Usama Yusuf Muhammad. *Adab al-mar'a fi Filistin wa-l-Urdun*. Ph.D. dissertation, Ain Shams University, 1991.

Tabana, Badawi. *Adab al-mar'a al-'Iraqiya fi-l-qarn al-'ishrin*. Beirut: Dar al-Thaqafa, 1974.

'Ussayran, Haniya and Fatima Sharaf al-Din, eds. *al-Adab al-nisa'i al-Lubnani al-mu'asir: dirasat, siyar, bibliyughrafiya*. Beirut: Center for Women's Studies in the Arab World, American Lebanese University, 1997.

Wahba, Muhammad Badawi. *Adibat mu'asirat*. N.p.: n.p., n.d.

al-Wazzani, Hasan, ed. *Dalil al-kuttab al-Maghariba*. Rabat: Moroccan Writers' Union Publications, 1993.

Yarid, Nazik Saba and Nuha Bayyumi. *al-Katibat al-Lubnaniyat: bibliyughrafiya 1850–1950*. Beirut: Dar al-Saqi, 2000.

al-Yusuf, Khalid. *al-Rasid: bibliyughrafiya*. Riyadh: al-Farazdaq Commercial Press, 1989.

———. "al-Ibda' al-nisa'i fi-l-shi'r wa-l-qissa al-qasira wa-l-riwaya bi-l-mamlaka al-'Arabiya al-Sa'udiya," *Qawafil* vol. 8, no. 4 (1995).

———. *Dalil al-kuttab wa-l-katibat*. Riyadh: Bahr al-'Ulum Press, 1995.

Zaydan, Juzif. *Masadir al-adab al-nisa'i al-'Arabi al-hadith (1800–1996)*. Beirut: Arab Institute for Research and Publishing, 1999.

Zein, Ramy. *Dictionnaire de la littérature libanaise de langue française*. Paris: L'Harmattan, 1998.

Periodicals

14 Uktubir. Aden (1979–1985).

Adhru' al-wahat al-mushmisa, supplement published by the Saudi Story Club, Saudi Arab Cultural Association. Riyadh, nos. 1 (1979), 2 (1989), 3 (1994), and 4 (1997).

al-Anba'. Khartoum, no. 328 (1998).

Annales de l'Afrique du Nord. Paris: Centre National de la Recherche Scientifique Publications, 1970–1996.

al-'Asima. Khartoum (1965).

Bayadir, supplement issued by the Abha Literary Club, no. 2 (1988).

al-Bayan. Khartoum, no. 46 (1999).

Bilqis. Sana'a, no. 17 (1996).

Hawa'. Cairo, nos. 1–5 (1969).

al-Hayat. Khartoum, no. 47 (1968).

al-Hikma. Sana'a, nos. 62 (1977), 160 (1989), and 206/07 (1997).

Huna Umm Durman. Khartoum, nos. 11 (1947), 46 (1958), and 49 (1963).

Ibla, Journal of the Arabic Literature Institute. Tunis (1975–1997).

al-Idha'a wa-l-tilivisyun wa-l-masrah. Sudan (September 22, 1977).

al-Inqadh al-watani. Khartoum (1996).

al-Ittihadi. Cairo, nos. 326 (1996), 355 (1997), 356 (1997), and 367 (1997).

al-Jami'a. Khartoum (1981).

al-Katib. Khartoum, no. 210 (1981).

al-Khartum. Cairo (1980).

al-Kitab al-Maghribi. Rabat (1983–1986).

Majallat rabitat al-qalam. Sudan, no. 2 (1963).

al-Mar'a. Sana'a (1998).

al-Mar'a al-jadida. Sudan, nos. 8 (1975) and 10 (1976).

al-Mithaq. Yemen (1997).

Mu'in. Sana'a (1979).

Mulhaq al-jumhuriya al-thaqafiya. Sudan (1998).

al-Ra'i al-'Amm. Khartoum.

al-Ra'i al-'Amm. al-Makla, Yemen, no. 25 (1963).

Sawt al-mar'a. Khartoum, nos. 102 (1967) and 108 (1968).

al-Shabab wa-l-riyada. Khartoum, nos. 417 and 419 (1981).

al-Sharara. Hadramawt (1975 and 1979).

al-Shari' al-siyasi. No. 346 (1998).

al-Shuri. Yemen (1998).

Shu'un adabiya, journal of the Emirati Writers and Authors Union, vol. 8 (1994).

al-Sinama wa-l-mujtama'. Sudan (1980).

al-Thaqafa al-Sudaniya. Nos. 6 (1978) and 27 (1995).

al-Thawra. Sana'a, nos. 1783 (1973), 476 (1980), and 3013 (1997).

al-Tufula. Sana'a, nos. 1 and 2 (1993).

al-Wihda. Yemen (1998).

al-Wihdawi. Yemen (1998).

Websites

Arab Writers' Union for biographies of Arab writers in Syria and the Arab world: www.awu-dam.com/dalil. Last accessed January 2001.